MANAGERIAL ECONOMICS

MANAGERIAL ECONOMICS

By

DR. SHIVANI KAPOOR
Principal of Dayanand Academy of Management Studies,
Kanpur, Uttar Pradesh

PROF. O. P. SHUKLA
Principal of thePrestigious National Defence Academy
Khadakwasla, Pune
Maharashtra

UNIVERSITY SCIENCE PRESS
(An Imprint of Laxmi Publications Pvt. Ltd.)
An ISO 9001:2008 Company

BENGALURU • CHENNAI • COCHIN • GUWAHATI • HYDERABAD
JALANDHAR • KOLKATA • LUCKNOW • MUMBAI • RANCHI • NEW DELHI
BOSTON (USA) • ACCRA (GHANA) • NAIROBI (KENYA)

MANAGERIAL ECONOMICS

Printed and bound in India
Typeset at Monu Printographics, Delhi
First Edition: 2015
ISBN 978-93-83828-37-1

Branches

	Branch	Telephone	
✆	Bengaluru	080-26 75 69 30	
✆	Chennai	044-24 34 47 26,	24 35 95 07
✆	Cochin	0484-237 70 04,	405 13 03
✆	Guwahati	0361-254 36 69,	251 38 81
✆	Hyderabad	040-27 55 53 83,	27 55 53 93
✆	Jalandhar	0181-222 12 72	
✆	Kolkata	033-22 27 43 84	
✆	Lucknow	0522-220 99 16	
✆	Mumbai	022-24 91 54 15,	24 92 78 69
✆	Ranchi	0651-220 44 64	

PUBLISHED IN INDIA BY

UNIVERSITY SCIENCE PRESS
(An Imprint of Laxmi Publications Pvt. Ltd.)
An ISO 9001:2008 Company
113, GOLDEN HOUSE, DARYAGANJ,
NEW DELHI - 110002, INDIA
Telephone : 91-11-4353 2500, 4353 2501
Fax : 91-11-2325 2572, 4353 2528
www.laxmipublications.com info@laxmipublications.com

C—
Printed at : Repro Knowledgecast Limited, Thane

CONTENTS

PREFACE

Managerial Economics is the economics of today. Modern management demands it. In the last quarter of the century we have witnessed an evergrowing report between economic theorists and managerial economists, based on realization of their mutual interdependence. That, in fact, is the spirit behind writing this book.

Managerial economics is concerned with discussion making at the managerial level. The book presents the alternative theories of firm behaviour, decision making problems and different approaches to arrive at the most appropriate answers to such problems. This is accomplished through a brief and logical discussion on the various relevant concepts and techniques and through hypothetical examples, to illustrate the decision-making process. At the end of each chapter, small caselets are incorporated for students to work on in order to ascertain their understanding of the material presented in the corresponding chapter. The approach adopted is a good mix of verbal language, geometry and algebra. While the emphasis is on theory and normative answers numerous practical examples are cited and integrated in the material presented in the text.

Managerial economics draws heavily from micro-economics, econometrics and operations research. Accordingly, the book borrows the relevant concepts from all these disciplines and also some from macro-economics. The approach of the text is to first pose problems relating to the decision making process and then seek answers. The book does not give the detailed exposition of micro-economics or of any other disciplines, rather it accords a synthesis of all the relevant aspects of the related subjects to arrive for decision-making problems faced by the firms.

The book is written primarily for students pursuing post-graduate courses in management. It should also be useful to those who are doing M. Com and CA. Since many instructors of economics emphasize applications the book could serve as good reference book for those students who are doing MA in Economics as well.

Attempt has also been made to illustrate the solutions to such business problems as optimization of output-mix, input-combination, profit-maximization and choice of investment projects. In writing this book, I have drawn heavily from scholarly writings on economics.

I must acknowledge the patience of my family during the inevitable trial while I was busy in writing the book. Last but not the least, I express my sense of gratitude to my publishers M/s Laxmi Publications for their interest, encouragement and co-operation, and for bringing out the book in such an elegant form.

—Authors

FOREWORD

"To appreciate the charms of quantum physics, sophisticated mathematical techniques must first be mastered, but no sense the aesthetic structure of economic analysis requires only a feeling for wonderment that such mental constructs really do have a life-and-death significance for billions of men all over the world. Of course, mere beauty is not enough. One studies economics for the light is sheds; any pleasure along the way is an incidental bonus."

Interestingly, managers in all organizations, while running their business, wittingly or unwittingly, contend with economic issue and problems and take logical decisions that are shaped by one's sense of economics. Indeed, the working of organizations is inextricably linked with economics and it would be useful for scholars and professors in economics, such as the authors, to disseminate knowledge of the subject as simplify and comprehensively as possible. A basic knowledge of economics is essential for managers to be able to run their business intelligently. This helps in the analysis of the several economic problems that managers' daily encounter and leads to decisions that are in the organization's best interest.

'Managerial Economics' by Dr. Shivani Kapoor and Dr O. P. Shukla aims at making economics simple to understand. It will not only help the students in having conceptual clarity with respect to various topics, but will also aid the teachers in making their presentations and lectures more absorbing. The book gives a good conceptual overview of the entire range of topics which would be of interest to existing and prospective managers. The layout of the book is well-planned with each chapter clearly defining its objective and then smoothly taking the reader through the nuances of the topic. The language used is simple, almost conversational in nature, and avoids jargon and 'tyranny of words'.

I congratulate the authors of their splendid overview of economics and I am certain that it will prove useful to all those who want to improve their understanding of the subject and bring it to bear while strategizing their business and in dealing with issues and problems. It has been a pleasure writing their foreword.

KD GAUR
Ex Director and Consultant
ICSSR

Unit 1

SCOPE OF MANAGERIAL ECONOMICS

1.1 INTRODUCTION

For most purposes economics can be divided into two broad categories, microeconomics and macroeconomics. Macroeconomics as the name suggests is the study of the overall economy and its aggregates such as Gross National Product, Inflation, Unemployment, Exports, Imports, and Taxation Policy, etc.

Macroeconomics addresses questions about changes in investment, government spending, employment, prices, and exchange rate of the rupee and so on. Importantly, only aggregate levels of these variables are considered in the study of macroeconomics. But hidden in the aggregate data are changes in output of a number of individual firms, the consumption decision of consumers like you, and the changes in the prices of particular goods and services. Although macroeconomic issues are important and occupy the time of media and command the attention of the newspapers, micro aspects of the economy are also important and often are of more direct application to the day to day problems facing a manager. Microeconomics deals with individual actors in the economy such as firms and individuals. Managerial economics can be thought of as applied microeconomics and its focus is on the interaction of firms and individuals in markets.

When you read a newspaper or switch on a television, you hear economic terminology used with increasing regularity. For a manager, some of these economic terms are of direct relevance and, therefore, it is essential to not only understand them but also apply them in relevant situations. For example, GDP growth rate could impact the product a manager is marketing, change in money supply by the RBI could impact inflation and affect the demand for your product, fiscal deficit could affect interest rates and, therefore, investment spending by a manager, etc. The focus of managerial economics is on how the firm reacts to changes in the economic environment in which it operates and how it predicts these changes and devises the best possible strategies to achieve the objectives that underlie its existence.

The economy is the institutional structure through which individuals and firms in a society coordinate their desires. Economics is the study of how human beings in a society go about achieving their wants and desires. It is also defined as the study of allocation of scarce resources to satisfy individual wants or desires. The latter is perhaps the best way to broadly define the study of economics in general. The emphasis is on allocation of scarce resources across competing ends. You should recognize that human wants are unlimited and, therefore, choice is necessary.

Choices necessarily involve trade-offs. For example, if you wish to acquire an MBA degree, you must take time-off to devote to study. Your time has many uses and when you devote more time to study you are allocating it to a particular use in order to achieve your goal. Economics would be a most uninteresting subject if resources were unlimited and no trade-offs was involved in decision-making. There are many general insights economists have gained into how the economy functions. Economic theory ties together economists' terminology and knowledge about economic institutions. An economic institution is a physical or mental structure that significantly influences economic decisions. Corporations, Governments, markets are all economic institutions. Similarly cultural norms are the standards people use when they determine whether a particular activity or behaviour is acceptable. For example, Hindus avoid meat and fish on Tuesdays. This has an economic dimension as it has a direct impact on the sale of these items on Tuesdays. Further, economic policy is the action usually taken by the government, to influence economic events. And finally, economic reasoning helps in thinking like an economist. Economists analyze questions and issues on the basis of trade-offs, *i.e.,* they compare the cost and the benefits of every issue and make decisions based on those costs and benefits.

The market is perhaps the single most important and complex institution in our economy. A market is not necessarily a physical location, but a description of any state that involves exchange. The exchange could be instantaneous or it could be over time, *i.e.,* exchange which is agreed today but where the transaction takes place, say after 3 months. You will learn in this course the myriad functions that markets perform, most significantly bringing buyers and sellers together. Markets could be competitive or monopolistic, with a large number of firms or a small number of firms, with free entry and exit or government licensing restricting entry of firms and so on. The major point is that firms operate in different types of markets and use the well-established principles of managerial economics to improve profitability. Managerial economics draws on economic analysis for such concepts as cost, demand, profit and competition. It attempts to bridge the gap between the purely analytical problems that intrigue many economic theorists and the day-to-day decisions that managers must face. It offers powerful tools and approaches for managerial policy-making. It will be relevant to present here several examples illustrating the problems that managerial economics can help to address. These also explain how managerial economics is an integral part of business. Demand, supply, cost, production, market, competition, price, etc. are important concepts in real business decisions.

1.2 APPROPRIATE DEFINITIONS

Managerial economics can be defined as the study of how to direct scarce resources in the way that most efficiently achieves a managerial goal.

According to McNair and Merriam, "Managerial economics is the use of economic modes of thought to analyze business situations." According to Prof. Evan J Douglas, 'Managerial economics' is concerned with the application of economic principles and methodologies to the decision-making process within the firm or organization under the conditions of uncertainty." Spencer and Siegel man define it as "The integration of economic theory with business practices for the purpose of facilitating decision-making and forward planning by management." According to Hailstones and Rothwel, "Managerial economics is the application of economic theory and analysis to practice of business firms and other institutions." A common thread runs through all these descriptions of managerial economics which is using a framework of analysis to arrive at informed decisions to maximize the firm's objectives, often in an environment of uncertainty. It is important to recognize that decisions taken while employing a framework of analysis are likely to be more successful than decisions that are knee jerk or gut feel decisions.

It is a very broad discipline in the sense that it describes useful methods for directing everything from the resources of a household to maximize household welfare to the resources of the firm to maximize profits. To understand the nature of decisions that confronts managers of firms, imagine that you are the manager of a company that makes computers. You must make a host of decisions to succeed as a manager. Should you purchase components such as disk drive and chips from the other manufacturers or produce them within your firm? Should you specialize in making of one type of computers or produce several types? How many computers should you produce and at what price should you sell them? How many employees should you hire, and how should you compensate them? How can you ensure that employee work hard? And produce quality products? How can the actions of the rival computer firms affect your decisions?

The key to making sound decisions is to know what information is needed to make an informed decision and then to collect and process the data. If you work for a large firm, your legal department can provide data about the legal ramifications of alternative decisions; your accounting department can provide tax advise and basic cost data; your marketing department can provide you with the data on the characteristics of the market for your product; and your firm's financial analysts can provide summary data for alternative methods of obtaining financial capital. Ultimately, however, the manager must integrate all of this information, process it, and arrive at a decision.

1.3 FUNDAMENTAL NATURE OF MANAGERIAL ECONOMICS

A close relationship between management and economics has led to the development of managerial economics. Management is the guidance, leadership and control of the efforts of a group of people towards some common objectives. While this description does inform about the purpose or function of management, it tells us little about the nature of the management process. Koontz and O'Donnell define management as the creation and maintenance of an internal environment in an enterprise where individuals, working together in groups, can perform efficiently and effectively towards the attainment of group goals. Thus, management is:

Coordination

An activity or an ongoing process

A purposive process

An art of getting things done by other people.

On the other hand, economics as stated above is engaged in analyzing and providing answers to manifestations of the most fundamental problem of scarcity. Scarcity of resources results from two fundamental facts of life:

Human wants are virtually unlimited and insatiable, and

Economic resources to satisfy these human demands are limited.

Thus, we cannot have everything we want; we must make choices broadly in regard to the following:

What to produce?

How to produce? and

For whom to produce?

These three choice problems have become the three central issues of an economy as shown in Fig. 1.1. Economics has developed several concepts and analytical tools to deal with the question of allocation of scarce resources among competing ends. The non-trivial problem that needs to be addressed is how an economy through its various institutions solves or answers the three crucial questions posed above. There are three ways by which this can be achieved. One entirely by the market mechanism, two, entirely by the government or finally, and more reasonably, by a combination of the first two approaches. Realistically all economies employ the last option, but the relative roles of the market and government vary across countries. For example, in India the market has started playing a more important role in the economy while the government has begun to withdraw form certain activities. Thus, the market mechanism is gaining importance. A similar change is happening all over the world, including in China. But there are economies such as Myanmar and Cuba where the government still plays an overwhelming part in solving the resource allocation problem. Essentially, the market is supposed to guide resources to their most efficient use. For example, if the salaries earned by MBA degree holders continue to rise, there will be more and more students wanting to earn the degree and more and more institutes wanting to provide such degrees to take advantage of this opportunity. The government may not force this to happen, it will happen on its own through the market mechanism. The government, if anything, could provide a regulatory function to ensure quality and consumer protection. According to the central deduction of economic theory, under certain conditions, markets allocate resources efficiently. 'Efficiency' has a special meaning in this context. The theory says that markets will produce an outcome such that, given the economy's scarce resources, it is impossible to make anybody better-off without making somebody else worse-off.

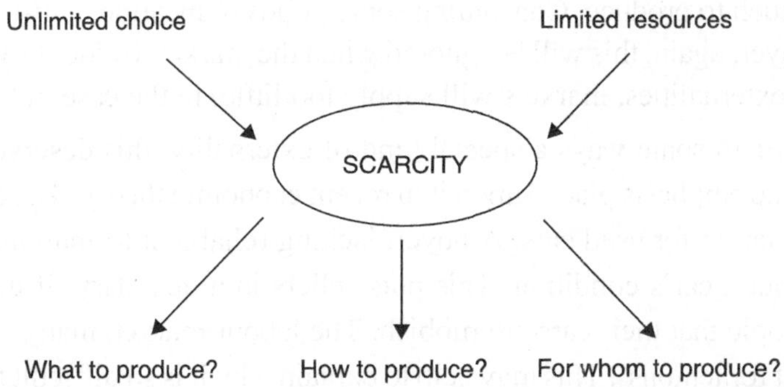

Fig. 1.1. Problem of choice.

In rich countries, markets are too familiar to attract attention. Yet, a certain awe is appropriate. Let us take an incident where Soviet planners visited a vegetable market in London during the early days of perestroika, they were impressed to find no queues, shortages, or mountains of spoiled and unwanted vegetables. They took their hosts aside and said: "We understand, you have to say it's all done by supply and demand. But can't you tell us what's really going on? Where are your planners and what are their methods?"

The essence of the market mechanism is indeed captured by the supply and demand diagram. At the place where the curves intersect, a price is set such that demand equals supply. There, and only there, the benefit from consuming one more unit exactly matches the cost of producing it. If output were less, the benefit from consuming more would exceed the cost of producing it. If output were higher, the cost of producing the extra units would exceed the extra benefits. So the point where supply equals demand is "efficient".

However, the conditions for market efficiency are extremely demanding—far too demanding ever to be met in the real world. The theory requires "perfect competition": there must be many buyers and sellers; goods from competing suppliers must be indistinguishable; buyers and sellers must be fully informed; and markets must be complete—that is, there must be markets not just for bread here and now, but for bread in any state of the world. (What is the price today for a loaf to be delivered in Timbuktu on the second Tuesday in December 2014 if it rains?) In other words, market failure is pervasive.

It comes in four main varieties:

(*a*) **Monopoly:** By reducing his sales, a monopolist can drive up the price of his good his sales will fall but his profits will rise. Consumption and production are less than the efficient amount, causing a deadweight loss in welfare.

(*b*) **Public Goods:** Some goods cannot be supplied by markets. If you refuse to pay for a new coat, the seller will refuse to supply you. If you refuse to pay for national defense, the "good" cannot easily be withheld. You might be tempted to let others pay. The same reasoning applies to other "non-excludable" goods such as law and order, clean air, and so on. Since private sellers cannot expect to recover the costs of producing such goods, they will fail to supply them.

(*c*) **Externalities:** Making some goods causes pollution: the cost is borne by people with no say in deciding how much to produce. Consuming some goods (education, anti-lock brakes) spreads benefits beyond the buyer, again, this will be ignored when the market decides how much to produce. In the case of "good" externalities, markets will supply too little; in the case of "bads" too much.

(*d*) **Information:** In some ways a special kind of externality, this deserves to be mentioned separately because of the emphasis placed upon it in recent economic theory. To see why information matters, consider the market for used cars. A buyer, lacking reliable information, may see the price as providing clues about a car's condition. This puts sellers in a quandary: if they cut prices, they may only convince people that their cars are rubbish. The labour market, many economists believe, is another such 'market for lemons'. This may help to explain why it is so difficult for the unemployed to price themselves into work. When markets fail, there is a case for intervention. But two questions need to be answered first. How much does market failure matter in practice? And can governments put the failure right? Markets often correct their own failures. In other cases, an apparent failure does nobody any harm. In general, market failure matters less in practice than is often supposed. Monopoly, for instance, may seem to preclude an efficient market. This is wrong. The mere fact of monopoly does not establish that any economic harm is being done. If a monopoly is protected from would be competitors by high barriers to entry, it can raise its prices and earn excessive profits. If that happens, the monopoly is undeniably harmful. But if barriers to entry are low, lack of actual (as opposed to potential) competitors does not prove that the monopoly is damaging: the threat of competition may be enough to make it behave as though it were a competitive firm. Many economists would accept that Microsoft, for instance, is a near-monopolist in some parts of the personal-computer software business yet would argue that the firm is doing no harm to consumers because its markets remain highly contestable. Because of that persistent threat of competition, the company prices its products keenly. In this and in other ways it behaves as though it were a smaller firm in a competitive market.

Even on economic grounds (never mind other considerations), there is no tidy answer to the question of where the boundary between state, *i.e.*, governments and market should lie. Markets do fail because of monopoly, public goods, externalities, lack of information and for other reasons. But, more than critics allow, markets find ways to mitigate the harm and that is a task at which governments have often been strikingly unsuccessful. All in all, a strong presumption in favour of markets seems wise. This is not because classical economic theory says so, but because experience seems to agree. And as stated above, the real world seems to be moving in the direction of placing more reliance on markets than on governments.

1.4 SCOPE OF MANAGERIAL ECONOMICS

From the point of view of a firm, managerial economics, may be defined as economics applied to "problems of choice" or alternatives and allocation of scarce resources by the firms. Thus managerial economics is the study of allocation of resources available to a firm or a unit of management among the activities of that unit. Managerial economics is concerned with the application of economic concepts and analysis to the problem of formulating rational managerial decisions. There are four groups of problem in both decisions-making and forward planning.

Resource Allocation

Scarce resources have to be used with utmost efficiency to get optimal results. These include production programming and problem of transportation, etc. How does resource allocation take place within a firm? Naturally, a manager decides how to allocate resources to their respective uses within the firm, while as stated above, the resource allocation decision outside the firm is primarily done through the market. Thus, one important insight you can draw about the firm is that within it resources are guided by the manager in a manner that achieves the objectives of the firm.

Inventory and Queuing Problem

Inventory problems involve decisions about holding of optimal levels of stocks of raw materials and finished goods over a period. These decisions are taken by considering demand and supply conditions. Queuing problems involve decisions about installation of additional machines or hiring of extra labour in order to balance the business lost by not undertaking these activities.

Pricing Problem

Fixing prices for the products of the firm is an important decision-making process. Pricing problems involve decisions regarding various methods of prices to be adopted.

Investment Problem

Forward planning involves investment problems. These are problems of allocating scarce resources over time. For example, investing in new plants, how much to invest, sources of funds, etc.

1.5 STUDY OF MANAGERIAL ECONOMICS

Study of managerial economics essentially involves the analysis of certain major aspects like:

(*a*) Demand Analysis, Estimation and Forecasting

A business firm is an economic organization, which is engaged in transforming productive resources into goods that are to be sold in the market. A major part of managerial decisions depend upon accurate estimates of demand. A forecast of sales in future aids the management in preparing production schedules and employing resources. It will help the management to strengthen its market position and profit base. It includes demand determinants, demand forecasting, etc.

(*b*) Cost and Production Analysis

Cost estimates are very important while taking decisions. The different factors that cause variations in the cost should be considered while planning. The chief topics included under cost and production analysis are cost concepts and classifications, cost output relationship, economies and diseconomies of scale, production functions and cost control.

(*c*) Pricing Decisions, Policies and Practices

Pricing is very important area of managerial economics. In fact price is the genesis of the revenue of a firm and as such the success of the firm largely depends upon the correctness of the price decisions taken by the firm. The important aspects dealt with under this area are: Price determination in various market forms, Pricing methods, Differential pricing, Product-line pricing and Price forecasting.

(*d*) Profit Management

Business firms are generally organized for the purpose of making profits and in the long run, profits provides the chief measure of success. In this connection, an important point worth considering is the element of uncertainty existing about profits because of variations in costs and revenues which in turn are caused by factors both internal and external to the firm. If knowledge about the future is perfect, profit analysis would have been a very easy task. However, in the world of uncertainty, expectations are not always realized so that profit planning and measurement constitute the difficult area of managerial economics. The main topics dealt with are: cost of capital, Rate of return and selection of projects, important aspects covered under this area are: Nature and Measurement of Profit, Profit Policies and techniques of Profit Planning like Break-even Analysis.

(*e*) Capital Management

Of the various types and classes of business problems, the most complex and troublesome for the business manager are likely to be those relating to the firm's capital investments. Relatively large sums are involved, and the problems are so complex that their disposal not only requires considerable time and labour but is a matter for top level decision. Briefly capital management implies planning and control of capital expenditure.

Conclusion

Demand analysis and forecasting help a manager at the earliest stage for choosing the product and planning output levels. A study of demand elasticity goes a long way in helping the firm to fix prices for its products. The theory of cost also forms an essential part of this subject. Estimation is necessary for making output variations with fixed plants or for the purpose of new investments in the same line of production or in a different venture. The firm works for profits and optimal or near maximum profits depend upon accurate price decisions. Theories regarding price determination under various market conditions enable the firm to solve the price fixation problems. Control of costs, proper pricing policies, break-even analysis, alternative profit policies are some of the important techniques in profit planning for the firm which has to work under conditions of uncertainty. Thus managerial economics tries to find out which course is likely to be the best for the firm under a given set of conditions.

1.6 MANAGERIAL ECONOMICS AND OTHER DISCIPLINES

Managerial economics is linked with various other fields of study like:

(*a*) Microeconomic Theory

As stated in the introduction, the roots of managerial economics spring from microeconomic theory. Price theory, demand concepts and theories of market structure are few elements of microeconomics used by managerial economists. It has an applied bias as it applies economic theories in order to solve real world problems of enterprises.

(*b*) Macroeconomic Theory

This field has little relevance for managerial economics but at least one part of it is incorporated in managerial economics, *i.e.*, national income forecasting. The latter could be an important aid to business condition analysis, which in turn could be a valuable input for forecasting the demand for specific product groups.

(*c*) Operations Research

This field is used in managerial economics to find out the best of all possibilities. Linear programming is a great aid in decision-making in business and industry as it can help in solving problems like determination of facilities on machine scheduling, distribution of commodities and optimum product mix, etc.

(*d*) Theory of Decision-Making

Decision theory has been developed to deal with problems of choice or decision-making under uncertainty, where the applicability of figures required for the utility calculus are not available. Economic theory is based on assumptions of a single goal whereas decision theory breaks new grounds by recognizing multiplicity of goals and persuasiveness of uncertainty in the real world of management.

(*e*) Statistics

Statistics helps in empirical testing of theory. With its help, better decisions relating to demand and cost functions, production, sales or distribution are taken. Managerial economics is heavily dependent on statistical methods.

(*f*) Mathematics

Mathematics is yet another tool-subject closely related to managerial economics. This is because managerial economics is metrical in character estimating various economic relationship, predicting relevant economic quantities and using them in decision-making and forward planning. A knowledge of geometry, trigonometry and algebra is not only essential but certain mathematical tools and concepts such as logarithms and exponentials, vectors, determinants and matrix algebra and above all calculus differentials are the hand-maids.

(*g*) Management Theory and Accounting

Maximization of profit has been regarded as a central concept in the theory of the firm in microeconomics. In recent years, organization theorists have talked about "satisfying" instead of "maximizing" as an objective of the enterprise. Accounting data and statements constitute the language of business. In fact the link is so close that "managerial accounting" has developed as a separate and specialized field in itself.

1.7 ECONOMIC ANALYSIS

Economic activity is the constant effort to match ends to means because of scarcity of resources. The optimal economic activity is to maximize the attainment of ends, the means and their scarcities or to minimize the use of resources, given the ends and their priorities. Decision-making by management is truly economic in nature because it involves choices among a set of alternatives—alternative courses of action. The optimal decision-making is an act of optimal economic choice, considering objectives and constraints. This justifies an evaluation of managerial decisions through concepts, precepts, tools and techniques of economic analysis of the following types:

(*a*) Micro- and Macro-analysis

In micro-analysis the problem of choice is focused on single individual entities like a consumer, a producer, a market, etc. Macro-analysis deals with the problem in totality like national income, general price level, etc.

(*b*) Partial and General Equilibrium Analysis

To attain the state of stable equilibrium, the economic problem may be analyzed part by part—one at a time—assuming "other things remaining the same." This is partial equilibrium analysis. In general equilibrium analysis the assumption of "given" or "other things remaining equal" may be relaxed and interdependence or interactions among variables may be allowed.

(*c*) Static, Comparative Static and Dynamic Analysis

This is in reference to time dimension. A problem may be analyzed—allowing no change at a point of time (static)—allowing once for all change at a point of time (comparative static)—allowing successive changes over a period of time (dynamic).

(*d*) Positive and Normative Analysis

In positive economic analysis, the problem is analyzed in objective terms based on principles and theories. In normative economic analysis, the problem is analyzed based on value judgment (norms).

In simple terms, positive analysis is 'what it is' and normative analysis is 'what it should be.' For example, CEOs in private Indian enterprises earn 15 times as much as the lowest paid employee is a positive statement, a description of what is. A normative statement would be that CEOs should be paid 4–5 times the lowest paid employee.

1.8 BASIC CHARACTERISTICS: DECISION-MAKING

Managerial economics serves as 'a link between traditional economics and the decision-making sciences' for business decision-making. The best way to get acquainted with managerial economics and decision-making is to come face to face with real world decision problems.

Tata's Vision 2000

Presently there are about 87 firms in the Tata empire. Of them, about 16 recorded losses in 1995–96. The Tata's companies that are in the limelight are TISCO, TELCO, ACC, Tata Exports and Tata Chemicals.

Contribution of bottom companies—In terms of turn-over: 35% of total of group.
20 companies—In terms of net profit: 0.2% of total sales of group.
—In terms of assets and net worth <1% of total sales of group.

The question is—Do such non-performers warrant an existence or will the group be better off if it could hive off the divisions, or else amalgamate them with other existing units?

On the three basics—Last two companies are way below the group providing 4.2% return on shareholders; 1.9% returns on capital employed.

Keeping these figures in mind, Tatas planned refocusing exercises like

- Divestment-mergers
- Amalgamations-takeovers.
- To create a learner and suggestive group with an estimated turnover of ₹ 1,10,000 crores by 2000.
- From being production-led to being consumer and market-led; being up in top three in every segment.

Tata's "Vision 2000" is a group. Why not give someone else a chance to run your business more efficiently if you cannot do so? It makes better economic as well as business sense. But then, the ball is in the court of Tata's. The what and how to do is their prerogative.

The basic characteristics of managerial economics can now be enumerated as follows:

- It is concerned with "decision-making of an economic nature."
- It is "microeconomic" in character. This is because the unit of study is a firm. Managerial economics does not deal with entire economy as a unit of study.
- It largely uses that body of economic concepts and principles, which is known as "theory of the firm" or "economics of firm." In addition it also seeks to apply profit theory which forms part of distribution theories in economics.

- It is "goal oriented and prescriptive."
- Managerial economics is both "conceptual and metrical." It includes theory with measurement.
- Managerial economics belong to normative economics rather than positive economics.
- Macroeconomics is also useful to managerial economics since it provides an intelligent understanding of the environment in which business must operate. This understanding enables a business executive to adjust in the best possible manner with external forces over which he has no control but which plays a crucial role in the well being of his concern. The important topics are: business cycles, national income accounting and economic policies of the government like those relating to taxation, foreign trade anti-monopoly measures, labour relations, etc.

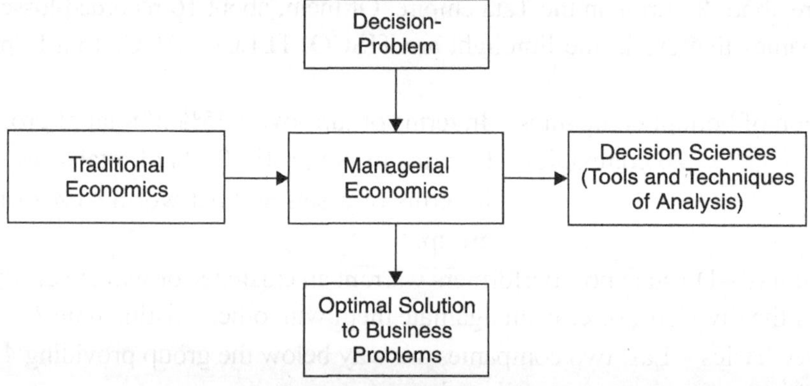

Fig. 1.2. Significance of managerial economics.

Managerial economics should be thought of as applied microeconomics, which focuses on the behaviour of the individual actors on the economic stage; firms and individuals.

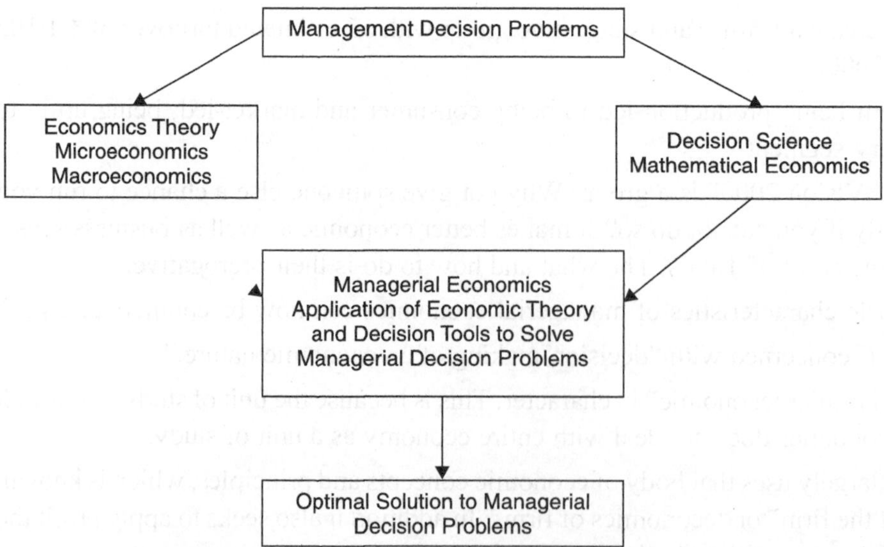

Fig. 1.3. Significance of managerial economics in decision-making.

A decision is simply a selection from two or more courses of action. The essence of economic decision is the solution to the economic problem. Once one of the available alternative actions is chosen, the economic problem is solved. The act of choice signifying solution of an economic problem is economic decision-making. A manager has to take several decisions in the management of business. Decision-making is a process and decision is the product of that process. Managerial economics is an evolutionary science; it is a journey with continuing understanding and application of economic knowledge—theories, models, concepts and categories in dealing with the emerging business/managerial situations and problems in a dynamic economy. It serves as a link between traditional economics and the decision-making sciences for business decision-making.

Managerial economics accomplishes several objectives. First, it presents those aspects of traditional economics which are relevant for business decision-making in real life. For this purpose it calls from economic theory the concepts, principles and techniques of analysis which have a bearing on the decision-making process. These are, therefore, adapted or modified with a view to enable the manager to take better decisions. Thus, managerial economics accomplishes the objectives of building a suitable kit from traditional economics.

Secondly, it also incorporates useful ideas from other disciplines such as psychology, sociology, etc. if they are found relevant for decision-making. In fact managerial economics take the aid of other academic disciplines having a bearing upon the business decisions of managers in view of various explicit and implicit constraints subject to which resource allocation is to be optimized.

Thirdly, managerial economics help in reaching a variety of business decisions in a complicated environment. A few examples are:

What products and services should be produced?

What inputs and production techniques should be used?

How much output should be produced and at what prices should it be sold?

What are the best sizes and locations of new plants?

When equipment should be replaced?

Fourthly, managerial economics makes a manager more competent model builder. Thus, he can capture the essential relationship which characterizes a situation while leaving out the cluttering details and peripheral relationships.

Fifthly, at the level of the firm where for various functional areas, functional specialists or functional department exists, *e.g.* finance, marketing personnel, production, etc. managerial economics serve as integrating agent by coordinating the different areas and bringing to bear on the decisions of each department or specialist the implication pertaining to other functional areas. It thus enables business decision-making not in water tight compartments but in an integrated perspective, the significance of which lies in the fact that the functional departments or specialists often enjoy considerable autonomy and achieve conflicting goals.

Finally, managerial economics take cognizance of the interaction between the firm and society and accomplishes the key role of business as an agent in the attainment of social and economic welfare. It has been realized that business apart from its obligations to shareholders, has certain social obligations/constraints subject to which business decisions are to be taken. In doing so, it serves as an instrument in further economic welfare of the society through socially oriented business.

To conclude, the usefulness of managerial economics lies in borrowing and adopting the tool kit from economic theory, incorporating relevant ideas from other disciplines to achieve better business decisions, serving as a catalytic agent in the course of decision-making by different functional departments/specialists at the firm level and finally accomplishing a social purpose through orienting business decisions towards social obligations.

1.9 ROLE OF A MANAGERIAL ECONOMIST IN BUSINESS

Making decisions and processing information are the two primary tasks of managers. While we separate these two tasks for analytical purposes, in reality they are practically inseparable. That is in order to make intelligent decisions, managers must be able to obtain process and use information. The purpose of the economic theory is to help managers know what information should be obtained and how to process and use the information. Managerial economist has, therefore, gained an increasing importance in business in recent times. He can be very useful for successful management.

The task of organizing and processing information and the basic theory can take two general forms.

- Task of making special decisions by managers and
- General task of managers is to use readily available information to make a decision or carry out a course of action that furthers the goals of the organization.

Specific Decisions

There are several specific decisions that managers have to take, *e.g.*, whether or not to close down a branch of a firm that has recently been unprofitable; whether or not a store stay open more hours a day; or whether to pay for computing services rather than install an in house computer. After conducting a survey it has been found that managerial economist perform the following functions:

- Production scheduling
- Demand forecasting
- Market research
- Economic analysis of the industry
- Investment appraisal
- Security management analysis
- Advice on foreign exchange management
- Advice on trade
- Pricing and the related decisions
- Analyzing and forecasting environmental factors

General Tasks

Economic theory helps decision makers know what information is necessary to make intelligent decisions to find the correct solutions to a problem and to learn how to process and use that information. After obtaining the information or as much information as is economically feasible to obtain, the manager must analyze this information and use it in correspondence with the theoretical and statistical tools available to make the best decision possible under the prevailing circumstances. We find that business is influenced by two sets of decision factors:

(*a*) External factors (*b*) Internal factors

Business is influenced not only by what decisions are taken within the firm but also by the general business environment. The role of the managerial economist is to understand these external factors and to suggest policies which the firm should follow to make the best use of these external and internal factors.

External Factors

- The **most important** external factor is the **general economic** condition of the economy, such as level and rate of growth of national income, regional income distribution, influence of international factors on the domestic economy, the business cycle, etc. The managerial economist must obtain and process information with regards to these changes, advise the management regarding their likely effects on the operations of the firm and suggest possible ways to further the organization's goals.
- **Prospects of demand for the product:** Is there a change occurring in the purchasing power of the public in general or in some particular regions? Is the change in purchasing power a result of changes in population and migration or is it due to changes in real income of the people as a result of price level changes? Are fashions, taste and preferences undergoing any changes and thus affecting the demand for the product? A managerial economist tries to find out their answers and advises the firm accordingly.
- **Input cost:** The managerial economist also tries to find out if there is anything which is influencing the **input cost** of the firm. For example, what about the cost of labour in different regions and for different operations? What about the credit conditions in the market? Is there going to be some changes in the government credit policy? How different inputs can be combined to minimize the cost of production? And so on....
- **The market conditions** of raw material and finished product is also a subject of study by the managerial economist. He has to understand the nature of the market from which the firm is buying its raw material and of the market where it is selling its output. This understanding helps the managerial economist to recommend a pricing policy for successful management of the firm.
- Managerial economist can also help in the expansion of the **firm's share in the market.** He is to find out the opportunities and the policies which help in the expansion of the firm's

share in local and internal markets. This he can do by understanding the nature and trend of demand.

- Managerial economics has to keep in touch with the government's economic policies and the central bank's monetary policies, annual budgets of the government, etc.

Internal Factors

The role of managerial economist in internal management is as important as his contribution towards the management of external factors. He helps in deciding about the production, sales and inventory schedules of the firm. He not only provides information regarding their present level but also forecasts their future trend.

Perhaps a managerial economist is used best to provide the pricing and profit policies. As the present day firms are often multi-product firms, a successful managerial economist tries to find for the firm the most profitable output mix and the best price for its various outputs, given the market conditions.

The firm also needs the help of managerial economist for its investment decisions. For this, he needs to forecast the return on the investment and the cost that the firm incurs by taking up the investment.

Thus, we find that managerial economist has a very significant role to play. He not only helps in the internal management but also analyses the external factors and also advises the firm regarding their likely effects.

In short, the first role of a manager is to recognize a problem or to see a possible way to further the goal of the organization and then to obtain and process information in order to make a decision or to reach a solution. His second task is to use readily available information to make a decision or carry out a course of action that furthers the goals of organization. Successful managers know how to pick out the useful information from the vast amount of information they receive. In all these roles of a manager, the knowledge of managerial economics is extremely helpful.

Though at one point of time or other, managerial economist has to take each one of the specific decisions mentioned above, the decisions most commonly undertaken are the analysis of competing firms, sales forecasting and market research. This is done in order to keep the firm in a competitive position vis-â-vis other firms in the market. In addition the managerial economist also undertakes the job of economic intelligence, which involves obtaining and processing information regarding the likely effects of changes in government policies, tax rate structure, exchange and tariff rates, etc. Though the managerial economists in general perform the above mentioned functions, the degree to which they participate in overall management and the extent to which they pursue these functions vary from firm to firm.

1.10 RESPONSIBILITY OF A MANAGERIAL ECONOMIST

As mentioned above managerial economist has a role to play. Let us now find out what are his responsibilities towards his job?

The most important obligation of a managerial economist is that his objectives coincide with that of the business. Since in most of the cases the firms try to maximize profits on their invested capital, the managerial economist should also help in achieving this goal. So long as he maintains the conviction and helps in enhancing the ability of the firm to maximize profits he will be a successful managerial economist.

The other most important responsibility of a managerial economist is to make forecasts as accurate as possible. We know that every decision, a management takes normally has implications beyond the present, while; future is rather uncertain. It is, therefore, necessary and obligatory for a managerial economist to make future forecast in such a manner that the risks involved in the uncertainties of future are minimized for the firm. He will have to make these forecasts on the basis of data on the market conditions, the general economic environment, the government policies, etc. For forecasting, he uses the techniques of probability. A managerial economist is supposed to forecast the trends and shifts in the activities of importance to the firm be it sales, profits, demand, cost, etc. Once such a forecast along with its possible implications for the firms is available, the management can follow a more orderly course of business planning. If a managerial economist can keep on providing successful forecasts at the required time, he is bound to be a successful executive. Here a couple of important points need be mentioned.

First, if the managerial economist finds that due to some sudden and unaccounted factors, the presented forecast has undergone a change, it is his duty to work out the new forecast and present it at the earliest possible time. By drawing timely and prompt attention to changes in forecasts he serves well both the management and his own interest.

Secondly, a managerial economist's caliber is generally judged by his ability to obtain necessary information quickly by personal contacts rather than by lengthy research from either the readily available sources or obscure reference sources. Though thorough familiarity with reference sources and material is essential, yet it is even more important that he knows from where to get the additional information quickly. He must, therefore, personally know those individuals who are specialists in the area of his concern. For this he needs to join professional associations and take active interest in them.

Finally, the contribution of a managerial economist will be adequate only when he is a member of full status in the business team. He must be ready to take up challenging tasks. Whenever some special assignments come to him, he should be ready to undertake them with full seriousness. It is for the managerial economist himself that he makes his services indispensable and most sought after, both with the help of his ability, training and experience as well as his capacity to win continuing support for himself and his professional ideas. For the latter, a necessary condition is that he can put even the most sophisticated ideas in the easiest form in common language and in a convincing manner.

In short, there is a growing realization that they can significantly contribute to the working and growth of firms. However, a lot depend upon managerial economists themselves as to how they project themselves.

Self-Assessment Questions

1. Discuss the nature and scope of managerial economics.
2. "Managerial economics is the integration of economic theory with business practice for the purpose of facilitating decision-making and forward planning by manager." Explain and comment.
3. Define scarcity and opportunity cost. What role do these two concepts play in the making of management decisions?
4. Managerial economics is often said to help the business student integrate the knowledge gained in other courses. How is this integration accomplished?
5. Compare and contrast microeconomics with macroeconomics. Although managerial economics is based primarily on microeconomics, explain why it is also important for managers to understand macroeconomics?
6. Justify that managerial economics is economics applied in decision-making.
7. What is the role of managerial economics in preparing managers?
8. How is managerial economics related to different disciplines?

Unit 2

The Firm: Stakeholders

2.1 INTRODUCTION

The firm is an organization that produces a good or service for sale and it plays a central role in theory and practice of Managerial Economics. In contrast to non-profit institutions like the 'Ford Foundation', most firms attempt to make a profit. There are thousands of firms in India producing large amount of goods and services; the rest are produced by the government and non-profit institutions. It is obvious that a lot of activities of the Indian economy revolve around firms. One of the crucial determinants of a firm's behaviour is the state of technology. Technology imposes a limit on how much a firm can produce. It is the sum total of society's pool of knowledge concerning the industrial and agricultural arts. Production is any activity that transforms inputs into output and is applicable not only to the production of goods like steel and automobiles, but also to production of services like banking and insurance. The firm changes hired inputs into saleable output. An input is defined as anything that the firm uses in its production process. Most firms require a wide array of inputs. For example, some of the inputs used by major steel firms like SAIL or TISCO are iron ore, coal, oxygen, skilled labour of various types, the services of blast furnaces, electric furnaces, and rolling mills as well as the services of the people managing the companies. To give another example, the inputs in production and sale of "chaat" by a street vendor are all the ingredients that go into making of the "chaat", *i.e.,* the stove, the "carrier", and the services of the vendor.

The inputs or the factors of production are divisible into two broad categories—human resources and capital resources. Labour resource and entrepreneurial resource are the two human resource inputs while land, man-made capital, forests, rivers, etc., are the capital resources. Thus the four major factors of production (FOP) are land, man-made capital, labour, and entrepreneur (organization) while the remuneration they get is rent, interest (capital rental), wage, and profit, respectively. The function of the firm, thus, is to purchase resources or inputs of labour services, capital and raw materials in order to convert them into goods and services for sale. There is a circular flow of economic activity between individuals and firms as they are highly interdependent. Labour has no value in the market unless there is a firm willing to pay for it. In the same way, firms cannot rationalize production unless some consumer is willing to buy their products. However, there is some incentive for each. Firms earn profits in turn satisfying the consumption demand of individuals and resource owners get wage, rent and interest payment.

In the process of supplying the goods and services that consumers demand, firms provide employment to workers and also pay taxes that government uses to provide service (education, defense) that firms could not provide at all or efficiently. Essentially a firm exists because the total cost of production of output is lower than if the firm did not exist. There are several reasons for lower costs. Firstly, long term contract with labour saves the transaction costs because no new contract has to be negotiated every time a labour is to be hired or given new assignment. Secondly, there are government regulations like price-control and sales taxes also saved by having the transaction within the firm. Recall that sales tax is levied for transaction between firms and not within firms. When transactions take place within a firm they may be cheaper and hence such savings decrease the total cost of production of an output. In other words, the existence of firms could be explained by the fact that it saves transaction costs. However, the size of the firm has to be limited because as the firms grow larger, a point is reached where the cost of internal transaction becomes equal to or greater than the cost of transaction between firms. When such a stage is reached, it puts a limit to the size of the firm. Further, the cost of supplying additional services like legal, medical etc. within the firm exceeds the cost of purchasing these services from other firms; as such services may be required occasionally.

Let us consider the size of different kinds of firms around us and try to understand the reasons for such differences. Why are service firms generally smaller than capital-intensive firms like SAIL, Maruti Udyog, and ONGC etc? What is the reason that a number of firms are choosing the BPO route? A part of the explanation must lie in the fact that it is cheaper to outsource than to absorb that activity within the firm. Consider a firm that needs to occasionally use legal service.

Under what conditions will it choose to hire a full-time lawyer and take her on its rolls and under what conditions will the firm outsource the legal activity or hire legal services on a case-by-case basis. Naturally, the answer depends upon the frequency of use for legal services. The transaction cost framework demonstrates that the firm will contract out if the cost of such an arrangement is lower and will prefer in-house legal staff when the opposite is true.

Firms are classified into different categories as follows:

(*a*) Private sector firms.

(*b*) Public sector firms.

(*c*) Joint sector firms.

(*d*) Non-profit firms.

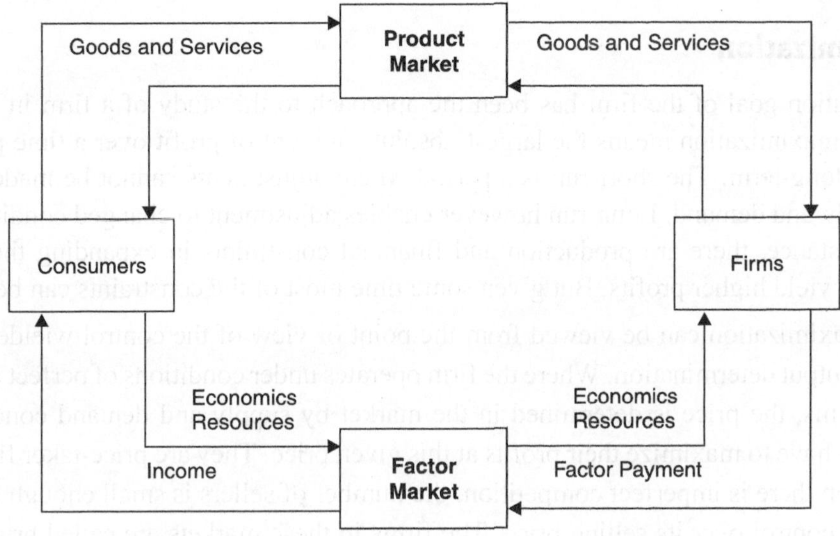

Fig. 2.1. Interrelation between consumers and firms.

Firms can also be classified on the basis of number of owners as:

(*a*) Proprietorship.

(*b*) Partnership.

(*c*) Corporations.

Some firms mentioned below are different from above. They may provide service to a group of clients for example, patients or to a group of its members only:

(*i*) Universities.

(*ii*) Public Libraries.

(*iii*) Hospitals.

(*iv*) Museums.

(*v*) Churches.

(*vi*) Voluntary Organizations.

(*vii*) Cooperatives.

(*viii*) Unions.

(*ix*) Professional Societies, etc.

The concept of a firm plays a central role in the theory and practice of managerial economics. It is, therefore, valuable to discuss the objectives of a firm.

2.2 OBJECTIVES OF THE FIRM

Profit Maximization

Profit maximization goal of the firm has been the approach to the study of a firm in equilibrium analysis. Profit maximization means the largest absolute amount of profit over a time period, both short-term and long-term. The short-run is a period where adjustments cannot be made quickly in matters of supply and demand. Long-run however enables adjustment to changed conditions. In the short-run *for* instance, there are production and financial constraints in expanding the firm even though it would yield higher profits. But given some time most of the constraints can be overcome.

Profit maximization can be viewed from the point of view of the control wielded by a firm over price and output determination. Where the firm operates under conditions of perfect competition from several firms, the price is determined in the market by supply and demand conditions. The individual firms have to maximize their profits at this given price. They are price-taker firms. On the other hand, when there is imperfect competition, the number of sellers is small enough so that each seller has some control over its selling price. The firms in these markets are called price searchers because they must constantly search out the price that will maximize profits. The price-searcher firm is a broad term encompassing the market structures of monopoly, oligopoly and to some extent monopolistic competition.

Though profit maximization can be viewed from many different perspectives, the marginal approach helps to formulate a rule which is applicable for both price takers and price searchers. Profit can be defined as the difference between total revenue (TR) and total cost (TC).

$$\text{Profit} = \text{TR} - \text{TC}$$

The output which yields the maximum profits is the ideal to be achieved. Fig. 2.2 below illustrates this simple profit maximization rule.

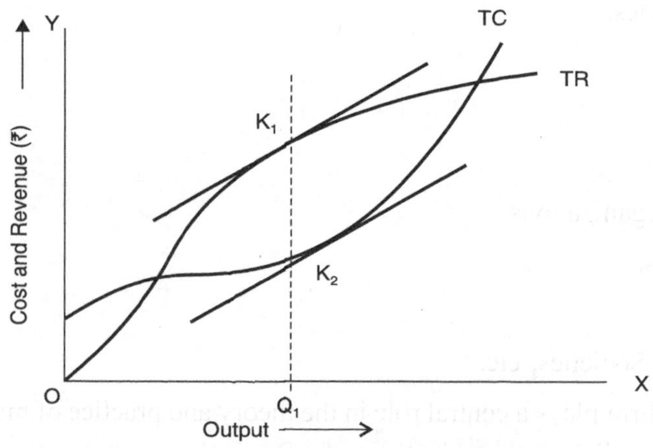

Fig. 2.2. Profit maximization of a firm (total cost and total revenue).

TC and TR represent total cost and total revenue curves respectively.

The gap between the two curves is maximum ($K_1 - K_2$) at OQ_1 output. Here the slopes of the two curves show by "tangents" are also equal *i.e.,* marginal revenue is equal to marginal cost. Therefore, OQ_1 is the profit maximizing output.

As the firm increases its production it results in additional cost. The generalized decision making rule for propitiation can be stated as follows:

"As long as marginal revenue exceeds marginal cost, the firm should expand its output. The firm should produce that level of output which equates marginal revenue with marginal cost".

Marginal revenue is the change in revenue which comes, from selling an additional unit. Marginal cost is the change in cost which results from producing an additional unit. The profit maximization rule in simple terms means the firm should continue production as long as the incremental cost of production is less than the increase in revenue. Profit maximization by equating marginal cost with marginal revenue is illustrated in Fig. 2.3.

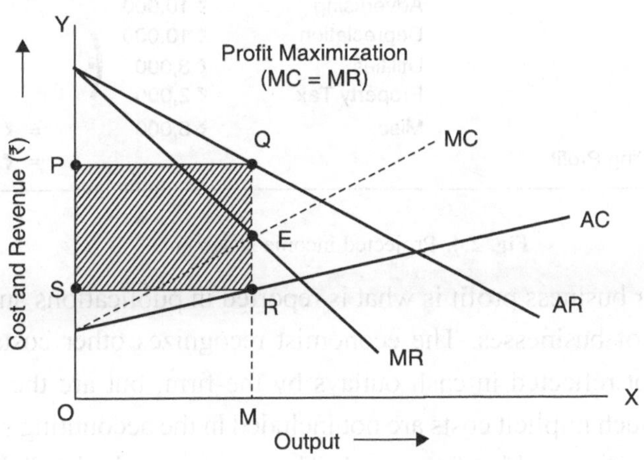

Fig. 2.3. Profit maximization in a firm: (MC = MR Rule).

Fig. 2.3 above shows the profit maximization rule applied to a firm. AC and AR are the average cost and average revenue curves respectively. MC is the marginal cost and MR is the marginal revenue. As the firm expands its output from O, there is a fall in marginal revenue and a rise in marginal cost. So long as marginal revenue is higher than marginal cost, the additional output gives profit. When the output reaches OM, marginal revenue equals marginal cost at E and gets a profit of PQRS (the shaded area). Beyond OM output, the MC curve is higher than MR curve indicating losses. The maximum profit is shown by the shaded rectangular area. Thus profits are maximum when MR = MC. (A detailed discussion of profit maximization in the short-run and long-run for the price taker firm under perfect competition and price searcher firm under imperfect competition is given in the chapter on price determination under different market structures).

There are some reasons why a firm should adopt the profit maximization goal. Firstly, in the case of owner managed firms it is only natural that they should get the adequate and maximum returns. Maximizing profits is, therefore, a rational behaviour of the firm. Secondly, profit maximization is an aspect of the survival of the firm. When there are many firms as under perfect competition, he can survive only if the firm makes profits. Under monopoly there are no rivals but he would naturally wish to pursue maximization for his efforts.

The traditional objective of the firm has been profit maximization. It is still regarded as the most common and theoretically the most plausible objective of business firms. We define profits as revenues less costs. But the definition of cost is quite different for the economist than for an accountant. Consider an independent businessperson who has an MBA degree and is considering investing ₹1 lakh in a retail store that she would manage. There are no other employees. The projected income statement for the year as prepared by an accountant is as shown below:

Sales:			₹ 90,000
Less: Cost of Goods sold		₹ 40,000	
Gross Profit:			₹ 50,000
Less:	Advertising	₹ 10,000	
	Depreciation	₹ 10,000	
	Utilities	₹ 3,000	
	Property Tax	₹ 2,000	
	Misc.	₹ 5,000	= ₹ 30,000
Net Accounting Profit			= ₹ 20,000

Fig. 2.4. Projected income statement.

This accounting or business profit is what is reported in publications and in the quarterly and annual financial reports of businesses. The economist recognizes other costs, defined as implicit costs. These costs are not reflected in cash outlays by the firm, but are the costs associated with foregone opportunities. Such implicit costs are not included in the accounting statements but must be included in any rational decision-making framework. There are two major implicit costs in this example. First, the owner has invested ₹ 1 lakh in the business. Suppose the best alternative use for the money is a bank account paying a 10 per cent interest rate. This risk less investment would return ₹ 10,000 annually. Thus, ₹ 10,000 should be considered as the implicit or opportunity cost of having ₹ 1 lakh invested in the retail store.

Let us consider the second implicit cost, which includes the manager's time and talent. The annual wage return on an MBA degree may be taken as ₹ 35,000 per year. This is the implicit cost of managing this business rather than working for someone else. Thus, the income statement should be amended in the following way in order to determine the economic profit:

Looking at this broader perspective, the business is projected to lose ₹ 25,000 in the first year. ₹ 20,000 accounting profit disappears when all relevant costs are included. Another way of looking at the problem is to assume that ₹ 1 lakh had to be borrowed at, say, 10 per cent interest and an MBA graduate hired at ₹ 35,000 per year to run the store. In this case, the implicit costs become explicit and the accounting made explicit. Obviously, with the financial information reported in this way, an entirely different decision might be made on whether to start this business or not.

Sales:			₹ 90,000
Less: Cost of Goods sold		₹ 40,000	
Gross Profit:			₹ 50,000
Less Explicit Cost:			
	Advertising	₹ 10,000	
	Depreciation	₹ 10,000	
	Utilities	₹ 3,000	
	Property Tax	₹ 2,000	
	Misc.	₹ 5,000	= ₹ 30,000
Accounting Profit		₹ 20,000	
Less:Implicit Costs:			
	Return on ₹ 1 lakh of capital	₹ 10,000	
	Foeign wages	₹ 35,000	= ₹ 45,000
Net "Economic Profit"			= ₹ 25,000

Fig. 2.5. Income statement for determining economic profit.

Thus, we can say that economic profit equals the revenue of the firm minus its explicit costs and implicit costs. To arrive at the cost incurred by a firm, a value must be put to all the inputs used by the firm. Money outlays are only a part of the costs. As stated above, economists also define opportunity cost. Since the resources are limited, and have alternative uses, you must sacrifice the production of a good or service in order to commit the resource to its present use. For example, if by being the owner manager of your firm, you sacrifice a job that offers you ₹ 2,00,000 per annum, then two lakhs is your opportunity cost of managing the firm. Similarly, if he was not playing cricket, Sachin Tendulkar, could have earned a living (perhaps, not such a good one!) by being a cricket commentator. Sachin's opportunity cost of playing cricket is the amount he could have earned being a television commentator. The assignment of monetary values to physical inputs is easy in some cases and difficult in others. All economic costing is governed by the principle of opportunity cost. If the firm maximizes profits, it must evaluate its costs according to the opportunity cost principle. Assigning costs is straightforward when the firm buys an input on a competitive market. Suppose the firm spends ₹ 20,000 on buying electricity. For its factory, it has sacrificed claims to whatever else ₹ 20,000 can buy and thus the purchase price is a reasonable measure of the opportunity cost of using that electricity. The situation is the same for hired factors of production.

However, a cost must be assigned to factors of production that the firm neither purchases, nor hires because it already owns them. The cost of using these inputs is implicit costs and has to be imputed. Implicit costs arise because the alternative (opportunity) cost doctrine must be applied to be firm. The profit calculated after including implicit as well as explicit costs in total cost is called economic profit. Profit plays two primary roles in the free-market system. First, it acts as a signal to producers to increase or decrease the rate of output, or to enter or leave an industry. Second, profit is a reward for entrepreneurial activity, including risk taking and innovation. In a competitive industry, economic profits tend to be transitory. The achievement of high profits by a firm usually results in other firms increasing their output of that product, thus reducing price and profit. Firms that have monopoly power may be able to earn above normal profits over a longer period; such profit does not play a socially useful role in the economy. Although, profit maximization is a dominant objective of the firm, other important objectives of the firm, other than profit maximization that we will discuss in this unit are:

1. Maximization of sales revenue.
2. Maximization of firm's growth rate.
3. Maximization of manager's own utility or satisfaction.
4. Making a satisfactory rate of profit.
5. Long-run survival of the firm.
6. Entry-prevention and risk avoidance.

2.3 PROFIT AS BUSINESS OBJECTIVE

Meaning of Profit

Profit means different things to different people. The word "Profit" has different meaning for businessmen, accountants, tax collectors, workers and economists and it is often used in a loose polemical sense that buries its real significance. In a general sense, "profit" is regarded as income accruing to the equity holders, in the same sense as wages accrue to the labour rent accrues to the owners of rentable assets; and interest accrues to the money lenders. To, a layman, profit means all income that flows to the investors. To an accountant, 'profit' means the excess of revenue over all paid out costs including both manufacturing and overhead expenses. It is more or less the same net profit. For all practical purposes, profit or business income means profit in accountancy sense plus non-allowable expenses. Economic concept of profit is of pure profit and is called economic profit or just profit. Pure profit is a return over and above opportunity cost *i.e.,* the income which a businessman might expect from the second best alternative use of his resources.

Economic Versus Accounting Profits

When most people hear the word profit, they think of accounting profits. Accounting profits are the difference between the total amount of money taken in from sales (total revenue, or price times quantity sold) minus the dollar cost of producing goods or services. Accounting profits are what show up on the firm's income statement, and are typically reported to the manager by the firm's accounting department.

A more general way to define profits is in terms of what the economist refers to as economic profits. Economic profits are the difference between total revenue and total opportunity cost of producing the firms goods or services. The opportunity cost of using a resource includes both the explicit cost of the resource and the implicit cost of giving up the next best alternative use of the resource. The opportunity cost of producing a good or service generally is higher than accounting cost because it includes both the dollar value of the cost and any implicit costs.

Implicit costs are very hard to measure and therefore are often overlooked by managers. Effective managers, however continually seek data from other sources to identify and quantify implicit costs. Managers of large firms can use sources within the company, including the firm's finance, marketing, and/or legal departments to obtain data about the implicit costs of decisions. In other instances managers must collect data on their own. For example, what does it cost to you to read this book? The price you paid to the bookstore for this book is explicit (or accounting) cost, while the implicit cost is the value of what you are giving up by reading the book. You could be studying some other subjects or watching TV and each of these alternatives have some value to you. The "best" of these alternatives is the implicit cost of reading this book: you are giving up this alternative to read the book. Similarly, the opportunity cost of going to school is much higher than the cost of tuitions and books; it also includes the amount of money you would earn had you decided to work rather than go to school.

In the business world, the opportunity cost of opening a restaurant is the next best alternative use of the resources used to establish the restaurant—say, opening a hair styling saloon. Again these resources include not only the explicit financial resources needed to open the business but any implicit cost as well.

Accounting profit = TR – (W+R+I+M)

where W = Wages and salaries

R = Rent

I = Interest

M = Cost of materials

If an entrepreneur uses his capital in his business, he forgoes interest which he might earn by purchasing debentures of other companies or depositing his money with joint stock companies for a period. Furthermore if an entrepreneur uses his labour in his own company he foregoes his income which he might earn by working as a manager in another firm. Similarly, by using productive assets in his own business, he sacrifices his market rent. The foregone incomes—interest, salary, and rent are called opportunity cost or transfer costs. Accounting profit does not take into account the opportunity cost.

It may be noted that the economic or pure profit makes provisions also for (*a*) insurable risk, (*b*) depreciation, and (*c*) necessary payment to shareholders to prevent them from withdrawing their capital. Pure profit may thus be defined as 'a residual left after all contractual costs have been met, including the transfer costs of management, insurable risks, depreciation and payments to shareholders sufficient to maintain investment at its current level. Thus, Pure profit = Total revenue – (explicit costs + implicit costs).

Pure profit so defined may not be necessarily positive for a single firm in a single year—it may be even negative, since it may not be possible to decide beforehand the best way of using the resources. Besides, in economics, pure profit is considered to be a short-term phenomenon—it does not exist in the long-run especially under perfectly competitive conditions.

2.4 THE PROFIT MAXIMIZATION PRINCIPLE

The profit maximization principle has been criticized on several grounds.

1. Divorce of Ownership from Control

The rise of corporate firm of organization has resulted in a separation of ownership and control. Ownership is vested with the shareholders and control is wielded by the managers. It has not been empirically proved that shareholders are more concerned with profitability than anything else. Profitability is not the only criterion by which shareholders appraise the performance of a company.

2. Difficulties in Pursuing Profit Maximization

The business environment is considerably more complex than what the neoclassical theorists thought of, when they propounded the profit maximization theory of the firm. 'The modern firm faces lot of uncertainties. As a result, short run profit maximizing behaviour is subordinated to the more important objective of long-run equilibrium of the firm. For example, the firm's objective to pursue 'good-will' in the long-run may clash with short-run profit objective. The structure of competition may be such that the firm may be concerned about market share and diversification of the enterprise rather than profit-maximization in the short-run.

3. Problems in the Measurement of Profit

There are some problems about the measurement of a profit as a measure of firm's efficiency. Profit may be the result of imperfections in the market and profits may be the reward of monopolistic exploitation. Worse still, profit measurement process itself is dubious. For instance, many business firms often present the business accounts in such a way as to show good profits on a particular day by the clever manipulation of the value of its assets.

4. Social Responsibility of the Firm

The firm is now-a-days not just an economic entity concerned with production or sales alone. The firm owes a. responsibility to offer good, well-paid jobs for employees, to provide efficient services to customers. In short the firm has a social responsibility beyond profit maximization.

5. Deliberate Limitation of Profits

Firms may deliberately show lesser profits in the short-run in order to discourage labourers from asking for higher wages or to" discourage entry of new firms. Limited profits may be shown to prevent the government from taking over the business.

6. A Version for Business Expansion

Profit maximization requires business expansion and it means additional risk and responsibility. Businessmen may be satisfied with the present level of profits and may not expand.

Conclusion

There is no doubt that in a competitive world, the main measure of business efficiency is the profit made by a firm. In a very dynamic society, profitability is essential for the survival of the business. Several firms have disappeared due to inability to make profits. However, society's attitude towards profits is less indulgent. Many feel that profit is socially unacceptable and excess profits are even immoral. But this disenchantment of Western societies regarding the profit objective of the firm is in sharp contrast to the changing attitude of the communist countries which have come to accept that incentives provided by the profit motive have some role to play in the allocation of resources.

2.5 SATISFACTORY LEVEL OF PROFITS

Herbert A. Simon has presented the concept of satisfactory level of profits to be the major goal of firms as opposed to maximization of profits. In his view an entrepreneur "must expect the firm's goals to be not maximizing profits, but attaining a certain level or rate of profit, holding a certain share of the market or a certain level of sales. Firms would try to "satisfy" rather than maximize with reference to profits. However, this goal has been criticized for two reasons:

1. It is often difficult if not impossible to distinguish between satisfactory level of profits and maximum profits. Firms may be satisfied only when they earn the maximum profits. In that case, the implications of both the theories become the same;
2. Firms which have a satisfactory level of profits may be left behind by the profit maximizing firm in their struggle for survival. This results in all firms getting involved in a mad race for maximum profits.

2.6 VALUE MAXIMIZATION

Most firms have sidelined short-term profit as their objective. Firms are often found to sacrifice their short-term profit for increasing the future long-term profit. Thus, the theory states that the objective of a firm is to maximize wealth or value of the firm. For example, firms undertake research and development expenditure, expenditure on new capital equipment or major marketing programmers which require expenditure initially but are meant to generate future profits. The objective of the firm is thus to maximize the present or discounted value of all future profits and can be stated as:

$$PV(\pi) = \frac{\pi_1}{(1+r)^1} + \frac{\pi_2}{(1+r)^2} + \ldots\ldots + \frac{\pi_u}{(1+r)^2}$$

$$= \sum_{t=1}^{n} \frac{\pi_t}{(1+r)^t}$$

where, PV = Present value of all expected future profits of the firm.

$p, \ldots, p_n$ = Expected profit in 1, 2, ..., n years

r = Appropriate discount rate

t = Time period 1, ..., n.

Assumed profit is equal to total revenue (TR) minus total cost (TC), then the value of the firm can also be stated as:

$$\text{Value of the firm} = \sum_{t=1}^{n} \frac{TR_t - TC_t}{(1+r)^t}$$

Thus maximizing the discounted value of all future profits is equivalent to maximizing the value of the firm.

A careful inspection of the equation suggests how a firm's managers and workers can influence its value. For example, in a company, the marketing managers and sales representatives work hard to increase its total revenues, while its production managers and manufacturing engineers strive to reduce its total costs. At the same time, its financial managers play a major role in obtaining capital, and hence influence the equation, while its research and development personnel invent and reduce its total costs. All of these diverse groups affect the company's value, defined here as the present value of all expected future profits of the firm.

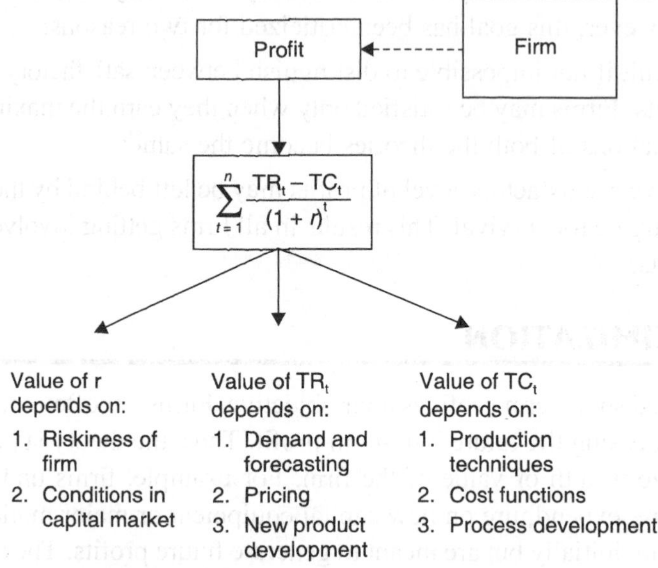

Fig. 2.6. Present value of all expected future profits.

2.7 ALTERNATIVE OBJECTIVES OF FIRMS

Economists who do not accept profit maximization as the sole objective of the firm has suggested alternative goals. These may be classified into two types:

1. Explanations where something other than profit is maximized.
   These are known as optimizing models;
2. Explanation where non-maximizing behaviour is described.
   (Non-optimizing models). Sales Revenue maximization
   Approach given by Prof. J. Baumol belongs to the first category.

Sales Maximization

Economists have also examined other objectives of firms. We shall discuss some of them here. According to Baumol, most managers will try to maximize sales revenue. There are many reasons for this. For example, the salary and other earnings of managers are more closely related to sales revenue than to profits. Banks and financers look at sales revenue while financing the corporation. The sales revenue trend is a readily available indicator of performance of the firm.

Growth in sales increases the competitive strength of the firm. However, in the long-run, sales maximization and profit maximization may converge into one objective. Another economist Robin

Marris assumes that owners and managers have different utility functions to maximize. The manager's utility function (U_m) and Owner' utility functions (U_o) are:

$U_m = f$(Salary, job, power, prestige, status)

$U_o = f$(Output, capital, profit, share)

By maximizing the variables, managers maximize both their own utility function and that of the owners. Most of the variables of both managers and owners are correlated with a single variable, namely, the size of the firm. Maximization of these variables depends on the growth rate of the firm. Thus, Marris argues that managers will attempt to maximize growth rate of firms. However, this objective does not completely discard the profit maximization objective. According to Oliver Williamson, managers seek to maximize their own utility function subject to a minimum level of profit. The utility function which managers seek to maximize include both quantifiable variables like salary and slack earnings and non-quantifiable variables like power, status, security of job, etc. The model developed by Cyert-March focuses on satisfying behavior of managers. The firm has to deal with an uncertain business world and managers have to satisfy a variety of groups—staff, shareholders, customers, suppliers, authorities, etc. All these groups often have conflicting interests in the firm. In order to reconcile between the conflicting interests and goals, managers form an aspiration level of the firm combining the following objectives—production, sales and market share, inventory and profit. The aspiration levels are modified and revised on the basis of achievements and changing business environment. As is true with most economic models, the application will depend upon the situation and one cannot say that a particular model is better than the other. In general, one can assert that the profit maximizing assumption seems to be a reasonable approximation of the real world, although in certain cases there might be a deviation from this objective.

Firms prefer maximization of sales revenue for various reasons:

1. Financial institutions evaluate the success and strength of the firm in terms of rate of growth of its sales revenue.
2. Empirical evidence shows that the stock earnings and salaries of top management are correlated more closely with sales than with profits.
3. Increasing sales revenue over a period of time gives prestige to the top management, but profits are enjoyed only by the shareholders.
4. Growing sales means higher salaries and better terms. Hence sales revenue maximization results in a healthy personal policy.
5. It is seen that managers prefer a 'steady performance with satisfactory profits' than spectacular profit maximization. Because it is difficult for managers to present spectacular profits year after year. They will be criticized if spectacular profits decline. Hence, they may prefer a safe and steady performance with satisfactory profits but good sales.
6. Large and increasing sales help the firm to obtain a bigger market share which gives it a greater competitive power.

Baumol's sales maximization model is based on the following assumptions:

(*i*) Sales maximization goal is subject to a minimum profit. Prof. Baumol does not give a clear definition of minimum profit. It may be defined as "the funds to pay some satisfactory rate of dividends, to reinvest for growth and ensure financial safety.

(*ii*) Advertisement is a major instrument of 'sales maximization *i.e.,* advertisement will shift the demand curve to the right.

(*iii*) Advertisement costs are independent of production costs.

(*iv*) Price of the product is assumed to be constant.

Sales maximization objective is explained in the following figure:

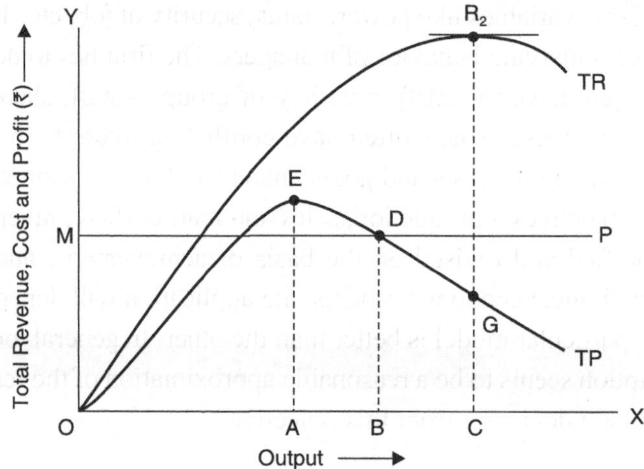

Fig. 2.7. Sales maximization.

Total Revenue, cost and profits are measured on Y axis and output on X axis. TR is the total revenue curve and TC is the total cost curve. TP shows the total profit curve which rises up to E and then starts declining. MP denotes Minimum Profit Line. If the firm's objective is to maximize profits it will produce OA output because at this level it gets the maximum profit EA. But the firm wants to achieve sales maximization. This can be done up to the point where its marginal revenue becomes zero. This is R_2 on the total revenue curve. Hence OC is the sales maximization output which is larger than the profit maximization output of OA. But the total profits are only GC which is less than EA, the maximum profits possible. But the firm operates with a constraint that it must make a minimum profit of OM. The total profits earned by the firm are equal to minimum profit goal at D. Hence sales maximization firm will produce OB output.

Baumls explanation has more implications than the traditional profit maximization principle. His theory is more consistent with observed behaviour. In the traditional theory changes in fixed costs do not influence output or prices except for fixing the break-even point. But according to Baumol a firm which experiences any increase in fixed costs will try to reduce them or pass them on to the consumer in the form of higher prices, through large sales. This theory also establishes that businessmen may consider non-price competition through sales maximization to be the more advantageous alternative.

However, Baumol's theory does not explain how the firms maximize their sales volume within a profit constraint. Further it explains business behaviour, without elaborating the mechanisms by which they try to find new alternative.

2.8 ECONOMIC OBJECTIVES

Besides maximization of profits and sales, a firm may have certain other economic goals.

1. Maximum Growth Rate

This is a dynamic objective for a firm which is consistent with profit constraint *i.e.,* a firm can attain maximum rate of growth with optimal net profits. While tracing the growth process of a firm, Kenneth E. Bounding has traced the various stages in the life cycle of a firm. In the early stage, the main aim of a firm is to establish itself in new markets for which it may introduce new products. In the second stage, when it is well established it may focus its attention on the goal of improving internal efficiency to achieve high growth rates. Bounding points out that at a later stage "as the industry approaches maturity, the near-term potential becomes dimmed partly through saturation of demand and partly because of the very high costs of further market penetration at the expense of competition. At this point, major emphasis at the expense of competition is placed on long-term growth and flexibility". Finally in the long-run, the firm may face adverse conditions such as a falling demand for its products or rising prices for its inputs. As a result, if it incurs losses, it may continue for a short while but will eventually go out of business because the resources can find more profitable employment elsewhere.

2. Desire for Liquidity

Prof. Joel Dean considers the liquidity criterion to be more important than that of profit maximization. This refers to the desire of a firm to keep adequate amount of cash so that it can avoid a liquidity crisis. This is referred to as 'Banker Mentality' *i.e.,* the fear of financial crisis and the fear of bankruptcy are very powerful factors in influencing the firm to keep adequate cash.

2.9 NON-ECONOMIC OBJECTIVES

1. Survival

Peter F. Ducker says that survival is the main goal of any firm. This is a long-term goal. Of course profitability is required for survival. But it need not be maximum profits but reasonable profits. It can survive only if it wins the goodwill of the people by producing goods and services of good quality. A good name earned would help the firm to enjoy a bigger share of the market and this will enable it in its aspirations of survival, over a long period. This may be considered as a conservative objective by some economists. Prof. K. Rothschild and Pellner supported this objective.

2. Building up Public Confidence for the Product

This is a secondary objective to the goal of survival. The primary aim of some firms may be to build up the customer confidence for its product and services. It may also adopt vigorous advertising techniques.

3. Welfare

The business firm has to keep welfare of different groups of people as its objective. First and foremost, the welfare of the workers has to be considered. They should be provided good working conditions, fair wages and other benefits to increase their involvement in the firm. Labour welfare goal is very important as it can improve labour efficiency and productivity.

Such labour welfare schemes may include subsidized canteen, medical care, schools and housing for the workers. The business firm depends upon the patronage of the society for its survival. Hence it owes some moral responsibility towards social welfare for which it may undertake charitable works like construction of hospitals, schools, etc.

4. Sound Business Practices

A firm may give more importance to business ethics. This will make it adopt only sound business practices like providing price lists, replacement or refund for defective products, which again will go a long way in building up the goodwill for the company.

5. Progressive Management

Progressive management is very essential for dynamic growth of the firm. Hence, as a part of this goal, the firm may implement suitable policies like worker's participation in management, workers training programmes etc.

An analysis of the different goals of the firm shows that the firms keep several goals before them, of which profit maximization may be the more important one. The short-run goals may be different from long-term objectives. Different firms prefer different objectives at different points of time. They may continue different economic and non-economic objectives within a framework of social responsibilities.

2.10 SOCIAL RESPONSIBILITIES OF A BUSINESS FIRM

The concept of social responsibility of a business firm is of recent origin. Traditional economic theory considered the business firm as an economic entity operating with the sole criterion of profit maximization. But profits have to be earned through sales which requires good public image. To the extent the business profits emerge from the society in which it operates, the firm owes a responsibility to the society. Kenneth Andrews defines social responsibility as "the intelligent and objective concern for the welfare of society that restrains individual and corporate behaviour from ultimately destructive activities no matter how immediately profitable." In short it must result in positive contribution to human betterment. This is also known as the philanthropic theory of the firm whereby it is expected to make efforts to share its profits with the society.

Business firms are expected to have social responsibility for three reasons. Firstly, business firms are able to operate only because of the support it enjoys from the society. Therefore, they are expected to be worthy of confidence reposed by the society. Secondly, a business corporation cannot operate in a vacuum. It cannot stand alone by disrupting the stability of the society. The firms must help in the attainment of certain social goals like sponsoring hospitals and technical institutes in the interest of its long-term survival and lasting growth. Thirdly, if the business firms show a greater social responsibility, the need for governmental controls and regulations will be minimal. Thus greater the social responsibility shown by a firm, greater will be the autonomy and economic freedom it would be permitted to enjoy. Prof. Milton Friedman does not give much credit to the concept of social responsibility but Prof. Paul Samuelson advocates a spirit of social responsibility as an inherent feature of a modern business firm. Operating in an anti-social way can be subjected to social regulation.

Social responsibility of the firms may be viewed from the point of its impact on constituent elements of the social environment in which it operates viz., the employees, the consumers, the owners and the society.

As far as the employees are concerned they should be provided with a congenial work atmosphere and fair wages. It should keep a part of its profits for workers' training programmes and education. The firm should allocate funds generously for workers' welfare programmes like maintenance of crèches for working mothers, operation of canteens, provision of recreational facilities, etc. The culmination of social responsibility towards employees takes the shape of allowing them an opportunity to participate in management. Workers' participation in management can be called an internal aspect of social responsibility. Any attempt on the part of the firm to extend social responsibility to its employees will result in an increase in workers' efficiency and productivity and it is therefore in the interest of the firm to discharge this duty.

The firm owes a social responsibility to the consumers on whose patronage its very existence depends. Thus the firms should provide goods and services of the proper and standard quality. Any lapse on its part in this respect must be corrected by replacement of the article or refunding of money as far as possible. This alone will win over the confidence of the consumers. Similarly price policy should be fair enough to give normal profits. Any prosperity the firm enjoys should be" shared with the consumers either through lowering of prices or provision of incentives and discounts. Discharge of this social responsibility is an external function which will increase its goodwill and help in sales promotion and further profits.

The firm owes a social responsibility to the owners who have been enterprising enough to invest their savings to carry on the business activity. Hence the firm should be managed well to give a fair return on capital to the owners. Only then they would have the incentive for future investment and expansion policies of the firm. While this will naturally occur in sole proprietorship or partnership, it may be overlooked in a joint stock firm where shareholders interests may not be taken into account. Firms should share their prosperity with shareholders by giving them good dividends. Similarly as reserves increase, they should be automatically given bonus shares and rights equity. This will also help to generate more capital for the firm. Thus discharge of social responsibility to the shareholders ultimately turns out to be to the advantage of the firm itself.

Finally the firm is responsible to the society at large. The firm is expected to take anti-pollution measures. It can undertake financial sponsorship for the maintenance of parks, entertainment centre, hospitals, schools, etc. Firms are even found to sponsor by providing funds for research activities in science, industry and medicine which may not be possible by individuals on account of financial constraints. Though such external activities do not directly benefit the firm, it results in better public relations and hence is good for its long-term survival policy.

In the discharge of such social responsibility function, the firm will have to deal with three types of problems. The first set of problems is those social problems which are not created by the firm. They may be like poverty, drug abuse, urban disintegration, etc., yet the firm can try to solve them in any small way it can, for instance, new firms can decide to set up their new units in undeveloped regions instead of setting up in already congested areas like Mumbai. Free medical camps to poor sections may be financially sponsored. The second set of problems are those which are caused by the routine business operations like control of pollution, safety measures in the industrial unit, production of safe goods, etc. The Bhopal gas tragedy is the result of gross negligence of a firm to undertake proper safety measures in maintenance. Similarly cigarette companies are required to give a statutory warning about the hazards of smoking on the covering on the packet. These are all aspects of social responsibility for problems for which the firm is responsible. The third set of problems is connected with regular economic activities within the firm; they may vary from providing equal employment opportunity to promotion, consideration for occupational health or improving the quality of life and work for its employees.

In India the Sachar Committee Report recognized that social responsibility of business must be given a serious consideration. It pointed out a few instances where private companies have shown a sense of social responsibility in problems of rural development and environmental protection or provision of basic amenities, etc. Several firms have now taken up the practice of adopting small villages in their area to provide basic amenities in health, education and housing for the poor in a phased manner. The Committee insisted that private business should give proper information to the shareholders, consumers and workers. Secrecy in corporate operations should be avoided. The Committee recommended that private enterprise in India must have public accountability as in the case of public enterprises.

The concept of social responsibility of firms is very important for poor, developing countries like India, where social problems are rampant. Yet social responsibility alone cannot be the over-riding concern above economic criteria.

Milton Friedman feels that advocacy of social responsibility by firms is the green signal to pure socialism. Businessmen should discharge their duty of managing their business responsibilities and they cannot be expected to be trained for shouldering social responsibilities. Nevertheless the concept of social responsibility has emerged to be the pre-dominant non-economic objective to be pursued by firms along with other economic objectives of profit maximization.

2.11 GOALS OF REAL WORLD FIRMS

By now we know that firms that maximize profits are not just concerned about short-run profits, but are more concerned with long-term profits. They may not take full advantage of a potential monopolistic situation, for example, many stores have liberal return policies; many firms spend millions on improving their reputation and want to be known as 'good' citizens. The decision maker's income is often a cost of the firm. Most real-world production takes place in large corporations with 8–9 levels of management, thousands of stockholders and boards of directors. Self-interested decision makers have little incentive to hold down their pay. If their pay is not held down, a firm's profit will be lower. Most firms manage to put some pressure on managers to make at least a pre-designated level of profit. In the modern corporation, the owners or stakeholders (*i.e.,* the principals) hire managers (*i.e.,* agents) to conduct the day-to-day operations of the firm. These managers are paid a salary to represent the interest of the owners, ostensibly, to maximize the value of the firm. A board of directors is elected by the owners to meet regularly with the managers to oversee their activity and to try to ensure that the managers are, in fact, acting in the best interest of the owners. Because of the difficulty of monitoring the managers on a continual basis, it is possible that goals other than profit maximization may be pursued.

In addition to those mentioned earlier, the managers may seek to enhance their positions by spending corporate funds on fancy offices, excessive and expensive travel, club memberships, and so forth. In recent years, many corporations have taken action to align the interests of owners with the interests of the managers by tying a large share of managerial compensation to the financial performance of the firm. For example, the manager may be given a basic salary plus potentially large bonuses for meeting such goals as attaining a specified return on capital, growth in earnings, and/or increase in the price of the firm's stock. With regard to the latter, the use of stock options awarded to top managers is a most effective way to ensure that managers act in the interest of the shareholders. Typically, the arrangement provides that the manager is to receive an option to buy a specified number of shares of common stock at the current market price for a specified number of years. The only way the executives can benefit from such an arrangement is if the price of stock rises during the specified term. The option is exercised by buying the shares at the specified price, and the gain equals the increase in share price multiplied by the number of shares purchased. Sometimes the agreement specifies that the stock must be held for several years following purchase. Essentially, this option arrangement makes the manager a *de facto* owner, even if the option has not been exercised. In almost every case of a report of unusually high executive compensation, the largest part of that compensation is associated with gains from stock option. Emergence of oligopoly, a market structure characterized by the existence of a few large firms, mergers and amalgamations have made the structure of industries concentrated so that few large (dominant) firms account for a major portion of an industry's output. This shifts the pressure on each firm to maximise profit independently and leads to joint profit maximizations through cartels and collusions. Profit maximization may not be the only inevitable objective.

India's Global Companies and their Objectives: One of the most significant business and economic trends of the late twentieth century is the rise of 'global' or 'stateless' corporation. The trends toward global companies are unmistakable and are accelerating. The sharpest weapon that a corporation can develop to survive and thrive, in the globalized market place is competitiveness. Its cornerstone as articulated by strategy guru Michael Porter is its ability to create more value on a sustainable basis for the customer than its rivals can.

For the first time, many Indian corporations such as Reliance Industries, Ranbaxy, Sundaram Fasteners, Arvind Mills and Bajaj Auto among others are competing on the world stage. Whatever product or service a company offers, it must meet the customers wants in the most satisfactory manner. This should be the aim of the company. The competitiveness of Reliance in the global marketplace comes from both quality and scale. The challenge is to remain at the top. That challenge is linked with productivity. Ranbaxy's greatest strength lies in the fact that it is strongly backward integrated. It helps them manage cost across the entire value chain making them extremely cost competitive. Cost leadership is a function of scale and technology. By upgrading technology, Ranbaxy could continue to be a cost leader. A company has to continuously upgrade itself on several parameters: production efficiency, product development, quality management and marketing skills. Sundaram has programmes to address all these parameters. This competitiveness—defined by Michael Porter as the sustained ability to generate more value for customers than the cost of creating that value—is what will keep India's companies alive in the bitter battle for survival that they are waging even on their home turf with rivals pouring in from all corners of the globe.

2.12 FIRM'S CONSTRAINTS

Decision-making by firms takes place under several restrictions or constraints, such as:

Resource Constraints: Many inputs may be available in a limited or fixed quantity *e.g.,* skilled workers, imported raw material, etc.

Legal Constraints: Both individuals and firms have to obey the laws of the State as well as local laws. Environmental laws, employment laws, disposal of wastes are some examples.

Moral Constraints: These imply to actions that are not illegal but are sufficiently consistent with generally accepted standards of behaviour.

Contractual Constraints: These bind the firm because of some prior agreement such as a long-term lease on a building or a contract with a labour union that represents the firm's employees. Decision-making under these constraints with optimal results is a fundamental part of managerial economics.

2.13 BASIC FACTORS OF DECISION-MAKING

Managerial economics is a discipline, oriented towards business decision-making with full realization that knowledge of future is uncertain. Management must nevertheless make decisions daily; and they must formulate plans for the future. Experience has shown that the following five fundamental concepts viz. the incremental concept, the concept of time perspective, the discounting concept, and the opportunity cost concept and the equimarginal principle help to take correct decisions.

The Incremental Concept

Incremental reasoning involves estimating the impact of decision alternatives. The two basic concepts in the incremental analysis are: Incremental Cost (IC), and Incremental Revenue (IR). Incremental costs are the added costs of a change in the level or nature of activity.

Incremental cost is defined as the change in total cost as a result of change in the level of output, investment etc. They can refer to any kind of change: adding a new product, changing distribution channels, adding new machinery. Incremental costs are not the same as marginal costs. It simply measures the difference between the old and the new total costs. Marginal cost refers to the cost of an added unit of output. It is the per unit cost of the added units. Incremental costs are more flexible than the marginal costs because incremental costs refer to any kind of change while marginal costs are calculated for unit changes in output. Incremental cost appears to be more relevant in decision-making at the firm level. The incremental costs can be computed by employing the formula:

$$IC = C_2 – C_1 = \Delta C$$

where IC stands for incremental costs

C_2 indicates new total costs

C_1 indicates old total costs.

Similarly marginal costs may be computed by using the following formula:

$$MC = C_2 - C_1/Q_2 - Q_1 = \Delta C/\Delta Q = dC/dQ$$

where MC shows marginal cost

C_2 implies new total costs

C_1 denotes old total costs

Q_2 indicates new total output

And Q_1 represents old total output

Most business decisions require cost estimates that are essentially incremental in nature. Incremental cost though familiarly short-run are not necessarily variable. In many short-run problems, the most important incremental cost is the foregone opportunity of using strictly limited facilities in their present work rather than shifting them to a new activity.

Incremental revenue is defined as the change in total revenue resulting from a change in the level of output, prices etc. The formula for incremental revenue is

$$IR = R_2 - R_1 = \Delta R$$

where IR stands for incremental revenue

R_2 indicates new total revenue and

R_1 denotes old total revenue

"Δ"- delta means change in

Incremental revenue concept is akin to the marginal revenue concept of the economic theory. But there exists some difference between the incremental revenue and the marginal revenue. Marginal revenue means the addition made to the total revenue per unit of output change. It is derived by employing the following formula :

$$MR = R_2 - R_1/Q_2 - Q_1 = \Delta R/\Delta Q = dR/dQ$$

where MR shows marginal revenue

R_2 represents new total revenue

R_1 measures old total revenue

Q_2 stands for new quality of output sold

Q_1 indicates old quantity of output sold.

d or Δ indicate change in

R-Revenue

Q-Output

A manager always determines the worth of a decision on the basis of the criterion that IR>IC.

A decision is profitable if:

It increases revenue more than it increases cost

It reduces some costs more than it increases others

It increases some resources more than it decreases others

It decreases costs more than it decreases revenues.

To illustrate the above points, let us take a case where a firm gets an order that can get it additional revenue of ₹ 2,000. The normal cost of production of this order is:

Labour	: ₹ 600
Materials	: ₹ 800
Overheads	: ₹ 720
Selling and administration expenses	: ₹ 280
Full cost	: ₹ 2,400

Comparing the additional revenue with the above cost suggests that the order is unprofitable. But, if some existing facilities and underutilized capacity of the firm were utilized, it would add much less to cost than ₹ 2,400. For example, let us assume that the addition to cost due to this new order is, say, the following:

Labour	: ₹ 400
Materials	: ₹ 800
Overheads	: ₹ 200
Total incremental cost	: ₹ 1,400

In the above case the firm would earn a net profit of ₹ 2000 – ₹ 1400 = ₹ 600, while at first it appeared that the firm would make a loss of ₹ 400 by accepting the order.

The worth of such a decision can be judged on the basis of the following theorem:

Theorem: A course of action should be pursued up to the point where its incremental benefits equal its increment costs. According to the theorem, the firm represented in Table 2.1 will produce only seven units of output as its Marginal Revenue (MR) = Marginal Cost (MC) at that level of output. As can be calculated from the table, the MC of the 8th unit is more than its MR. Hence the firm gets negative profit from the 8th unit and thus is advised not to produce it.

The acceptance or rejection of an order by a firm for its product depends on whether the resultant costs are greater or less than the resultant revenue. If these principles are not followed, the equilibrium position would be disturbed. But the problem with the concept of marginalize is that the independent variable may be subject to "bulk changes" instead of "unit changes". For example, a builder may not change one labourer at a time, but many of them together. Similarly, the output may change because of a change in process, pattern or a combination of factors, which may not always be measured in unit terms. In such cases, the concept of marginalize is changed to instrumentalism. Or, in other words, instrumentalism is more general, whereas marginalize is more specific. All marginal concepts are incremental concepts, but all incremental concepts need not be marginal concepts.

Table 2.1. Profits derived from units of output.

Units of Output 1	*Total Revenue* 2	*Total Cost* 3	*Total Profit* 4	*Average Profit* 5	*Marginal Profit* 6
1	20	15	5	5.0	—
2	40	29	11	5.5	6
3	60	42	18	6.0	7
4	80	52	28	7.0	10
5	100	65	35	7.0	7
6	120	81	39	6.5	4
7	140	101	39	5.6	0
8	160	125	35	4.4	–4

Though incremental reasoning of managerial economics is closely related to the marginal reasoning of economic theory, yet there are differences between these two, both of which demand attention. Firstly, managerial costs and revenues are always defined in terms of unit changes in output whereas incremental costs and revenues are not necessarily restricted to unit changes. The marginal analysis enables one to have a microscopic examination of such unit by unit changes. But the decision-maker may not be interested in such a microscopic analysis of the situation.

Secondly, incremental concepts are more flexible than marginal concepts. Marginal costs and marginal revenues are restricted to the effects of unit changes in output.

2.14 THE EQUI-MARGINAL PRINCIPLE

According to this principle, different courses of action should be pursued up to the point where all the courses provide equal marginal benefit per unit of cost. It states that a rational decision-maker would allocate or hire his resources in such a way that the ratio of marginal returns and marginal costs of various uses of a given resource or of various resources in a given use is the same. For example, a consumer seeking maximum utility (satisfaction) from his consumption basket, will allocate his consumption budget on goods and services such that

$$MU_1/MC = MU_2 / MC_2 = \ldots\ldots.= MU_n / MC_n,$$

where MU_1 = Marginal utility from good one,

MC_1 = Marginal cost of good one and so on.

Similarly, a producer seeking maximum profit would use the technique of production (Input-mix.) Which would ensure?

$$MRP_1/MC_1 = MRP_2/MC_2 = \ldots\ldots\ldots\ldots = MRP_n / MC_n$$

where MRP_1= Marginal revenue product of input one (*e.g.*, Labour),

MC_1= Marginal cost of input one and so on.

It is easy to see that if the above equation was not satisfied, the decision makers could add to his utility/profit by reshuffling his resources/input *e.g.*, if $MU_1/MC_1 > MU_2/MC_2$ the consumer would add to his utility by buying more of good one and less of good two. Table 2.2 summarizes this principle for different sellers.

Example: A multi-commodity consumer wishes to purchase successive units of A, B and C. Each unit costs the same and the consumer is determined to have a combination including all the three items. His budget constraint is such that he cannot buy more than six units in all. Again, he is subject to diminishing marginal utility *i.e.*, as he has more of an item, he wants to consume less of it. Table 2.3 shows the optimization example:

Table 2.2. The equi-marginal principle.

Unit	Equi-marginal Principle
Multi-market seller	$MR_1 = MR_2 = MR_3 = \ldots\ldots MR_n$
Multi-plant monopolist	$MC_1 = MC_2 = MC_3 = \ldots\ldots MC_n$
Multi-factor employer	$MP_1 = MP_2 = MP_3 = \ldots\ldots MP_n$
Multi-product firm	$Mp_1 = Mp_2 = Mp_3 = \ldots\ldots Mp_n$
Multi-commodity consumer	$MU_1 = MU_2 = MU_3 = \ldots\ldots MU$

MR = Marginal revenue, MC = Marginal cost, MP = Marginal product,
Mp = Marginal profit ; MU = Marginal utilities

Table 2.3. Marginal utilities.

Units	*Item A*	*Item B*	*Item C*
1	10	9	8
2	9	8	7
3	8	7	6
4	7	6	5
5	6	5	4
6	5	4	3

The utility maximizing consumer will end up with a purchase of 3A + 2B + 1C because that combination satisfies equi-marginalism:

$$MUa = MUb = MUc = 8$$

In the real world, often the equi-marginalism concept has to be replaced by equi-incrementalism.

This is because, changes in the real world are discrete or lumpy and therefore the concept of marginal change may not always apply. Instead, changes will be incremental in nature, but the decision rule or optimizing principle will remain the same.

2.15 THE DISCOUNTING PRINCIPLE

This principle has its genesis in valuing the money received at different points of time.

Many transactions involve making or receiving cash payments at various future dates. A person who takes a house loan trades a promise to make monthly payments for say, fifteen or twenty years for a large amount of cash now to pay for a home. This case and other similar cases relate to the time value of money. The time value of money refers to the fact that a rupee to be received in the future is not worth a rupee today. Therefore, it is necessary to have techniques for measuring the value today (*i.e.,* the present value) of rupees to be received or paid at different points in the future. This section outlines the approach to analyzing problems that involve payment and/or receipt of money at one or more points in time.

One may ask how much money today would be equivalent to ₹ 100 a year from now if the rate of interest is 5%. This involves determining the present value of ₹ 100 to be received after one year. Applying the formula:

$$PV_1 = \frac{100}{1.05}$$

We obtain ₹ 95.24,

₹ 95.24 will accumulate to an amount exactly equal to ₹ 100 in one year at the interest rate of 5 per cent. Looked at another way, you will be willing to pay maximum of ₹ 95.24 for the benefit of receiving ₹ 100 one year from now if the prevailing interest rate is 5 per cent. The same analysis can be extended to any number of periods. A sum of ₹ 100 two years from now is worth:

$$PV_2 = \frac{100}{1.05^2}$$

In general, the present value of a sum to be received at any future date can be found by the following formula:

$$PV = \frac{R_n}{(1+i)^n}$$

PV = present value, R_n = amount to be received in future, i = rate of interest, n = number of years lapsing between the receipt of R.

If the receipts are made available over a number of years, the formula becomes

$$PV = \frac{R_1}{1+i} + \frac{R_2}{(1+i)^2} + \frac{R_3}{(1+i)^3} + \ldots + \frac{R_n}{(1+i)^n}$$

$$PV = \sum_{K=1}^{n} \frac{R_k}{(1+i)^k}$$

In the above formula if $R_1 = R_2 = R_3$ etc., it becomes an 'annuity'. An annuity has been defined as a series of periodic equal payments. Although the term is often thought of in terms of a retirement pension, there are many other examples of annuities. The repayment schedule for a home loan is an annuity. A father's agreement to send his son ₹ 1000 each month while he is in college is another example. Usually, the number of periods is specified, but not always. Sometimes retirement benefits are paid monthly as long as a person is alive. In other case, the annuity is paid forever and is called 'perpetuity.'

It must be emphasized that the strict definition of an annuity implies equal payments. A contract to make 20 annual payments, which increase each year by, say, 10 per cent, would not be an annuity. As some financial arrangements provide for payments with periodic increase, care must be taken not to apply an annuity formula if the flow of payments is not a true annuity.

The present value of an annuity can be thought of as the sum of the present values of each of several amounts. Consider an annuity of three ₹ 100 payments at the end of each of the next three years at 10 per cent interest. The present value of each payment is:

$$PV_1 = 100\frac{1}{1.10}$$

$$PV_2 = 100\frac{1}{(1.10)^2}$$

$$PV_3 = 100\frac{1}{(1.10)^3}$$

and the sum of these would be

$$PV = 100\frac{1}{1.10} + 100\frac{1}{(1.10)^2} + 100\frac{1}{(1.10)^3}$$

Or

$$PV = 100\left[\frac{1}{1.10} + \frac{1}{(1.10)^2} + \frac{1}{(1.10)^3}\right]$$

The present value of this annuity is:

$$PV = 100\ (0.9091 + 0.8264 + 0.7513) = 100\ (2.4868) = 248.68$$

Although this approach works, it clearly would be cumbersome for annuities of more than a few periods. For example, consider using this method to find the present value of a monthly payment for 40 years if the monthly interest rate is 1 per cent. That would require evaluating the present value of each of 480 amounts! In general, the formula for the present value of an annuity of A rupees per period for n periods and a discount rate of i is:

$$PV = A\frac{1}{(1+i)} + A\frac{1}{(1+i)^2} + \ldots\ldots + A\frac{1}{(1+i)^n}$$

The process of reducing future values to their present values is often referred to as discounting. In this context, the interest rate used in present value problem is sometimes referred to as a discount rate. This concept is highly useful in managerial economics in making investment decisions.

2.16 THE OPPORTUNITY COST PRINCIPLE

Fundamental to the managerial economics is the concept of opportunity cost. It is the cost of displaced alternatives. By the opportunity cost of a decision is meant the sacrifice of alternatives required by the decision. The opportunity cost of anything is the return that can be had from the next best alternative use. A farmer who is producing wheat can also produce sugar cane with the same factors. Therefore, the opportunity cost of a quintal of wheat is the amount of the output of sugar cane given up. The opportunity costs are the 'costs of sacrificed alternatives.'

Whenever the manager takes a decision he chooses one course of action, sacrificing the other alternative courses. We can therefore evaluate the one, which is chosen in terms of the other (next best) alternative that is sacrificed. A machine can produce either X or Y. The opportunity cost of producing a given quantity of X is the quantity of Y which it would have produced.

The opportunity cost of holding ₹1000 as cash in hand for one year is the 10% rate of interest, which would have been earned had it been invested in the form of fixed deposits in the bank.

All decisions which involve choice must involve opportunity cost calculation. The opportunity cost may be either real or monetary, either implicit or explicit, either non-quantifiable or quantifiable.

Opportunity costs' relevance is not limited to individual decisions. Opportunity costs are also relevant to government's decisions, which affect everyone in society. A common example is the guns-versus-butter debate. The resources that a society has are limited; therefore its decisions to use those resources to have more guns (more weapons) means that it must have less butter (fewer consumer goods). Thus when society decides to spend 100 crores on developing a defense system, the opportunity cost of that decision is 100 crores not spent on fighting drugs, helping the homeless, or paying off some of the national debt. For the country as a whole, the production possibility reflects opportunity costs. Fig. 2.8 shows the Production Possibility Curve (PPC) reflecting the different combinations of goods, which an economy can produce, given its state of technology and total resources. It illustrates the menu of choices open to the economy. Let us take the example that the economy can produce only two goods, butter and guns. The economy can produce only guns, only butter or a combination of the two, illustrating the trade-offs or choice inherent in such a decision. The opportunity cost of choosing guns over butter increases as the production of guns is increased.

The reason is that some resources are relatively better suited to producing guns. The quantity of butter, which has to be sacrificed to produce an additional unit of guns, is called the opportunity cost of guns (in terms of butter). Due to the increasing opportunity cost of guns, the PPC curve will be concave to the origin. Increasing opportunity cost of guns means that to produce each additional unit of guns, more and more units of butter have to be sacrificed. The basis for increasing opportunity costs are the following assumptions:

(*i*) Some factors of production are more efficient in the production of butter and some more efficient in the production of guns. This property of factors is called specificity. Thus specificity of factors of production causes increasing opportunity costs.

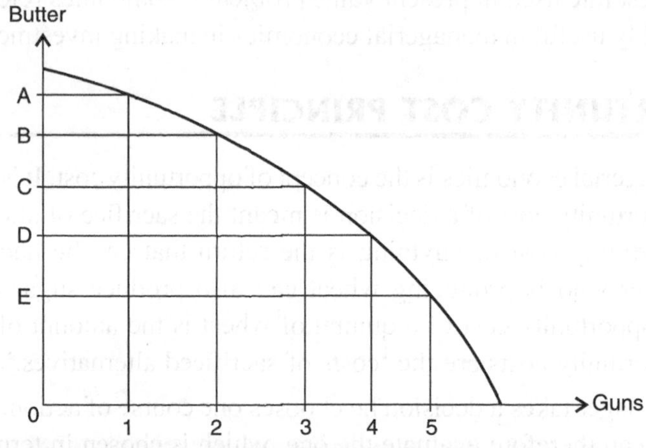

Fig. 2.8. The production possibility curve.

(*ii*) The production of the goods requires more of one factor than the other. For example, the production of guns may require more capital than that of butter. Hence, as more and more of capital is used in the manufacture of guns, the opportunity cost of guns is likely to increase.

Let us assume that an economy is at point A where it uses all its resources in the production of butter. Starting from A, the production of 1 unit of guns requires that AC units of butter be given up. The production of a second unit of guns requires that additional CD units of butter be given up. A third requires that DE be given up, and so on. Since DE > CD > AC, and so on, it means that for every additional unit of guns more and more units of butter will have to be sacrificed, or in other words, the opportunity cost keeps on increasing.

The opportunity cost of the first few units of guns would initially be low and those resources, which are more efficient in the production of guns move from, butter production to gun production. As more and more units of guns are produced, however, it becomes necessary to move into gun production, even for those factors, which are more efficient in the production of butter. As this happens, the opportunity cost of guns gets larger and larger. Thus, due to increasing opportunity costs the PPC is concave.

If the PPC curve were to be a straight line, the opportunity cost of guns would always be constant. This would mean equal and not increasing amounts of butter would have to be forgone to produce an additional unit of guns. The assumption of constant opportunity costs is very unrealistic. It implies that all the factors of production are equally efficient either in the production of butter or in the production of guns.

For many of the choices society makes opportunity costs tend to increase as we choose more and more of an item. Such a phenomenon about choice is so common that it has acquired a name: the principle of increasing marginal opportunity cost. This principle states that in order to get more of something, one must give up ever-increasing quantities of something else. In other words, initially the opportunity costs of an activity are low, but they increase the more we concentrate on that activity.

The concept of opportunity cost has a wide application in managerial economics. It is also applied in price determination, consumption and public expenditure.

The concept of opportunity cost is subject to the following criticism:

- In many cases, a specific factor has no opportunity cost. For instance, a barren land has no attractive alternatives.
- Immobility of factors of production makes this concept a limited scope.
- The foregone alternatives cannot be quantatively measured. For example, a landlord does not know how much of rent he will be getting by cultivation of wheat instead of cotton. This concept is based on perfect competition which is not true in reality.

2.17 THE INVISIBLE HAND

Adam Smith, the father of modern economics believed that there existed an "invisible hand" which ruled over the economic system. According to him the economic system, left to itself, is self-regulating. The basic driving force in such a system is trying to enhance its own economic well-being. But the actions of each unit, acting according to its own self-interest, are also in the interests of the economy as a whole.

Producers are led by the profit motive to produce those goods and services which the consumers want. They try to do this at the minimum possible cost in order to maximize their profits. Moreover, if there is competition among a number of producers, they will each try to keep the price of their product low in order to attract the consumers. The goods produced are made available in the market by traders. They also act in their own self-interest. However, in a self-regulating economy, there is rarely any shortage of goods and services.

Decisions to save and invest are also taken by the individual economic units. For example, households save some of their income and deposit part of it in the banks, or invest it in shares and debentures and so on. The producers borrow from the banking system and also issue shares and debentures to finance their investments. In turn, they reinvest a part of their profits.

All the economic functions have been carried out by individuals acting in isolation. There is no government or centralized authority to determine who should produce what and in what quantity, and where it should be made available. Yet in a self-regulating economy there is seldom a shortage of goods and services. Practically everything you want to buy is available in the market. Thus according to Adam Smith, the economic system is guided by the "invisible hand". In a more technical way we can say that the basic economic problems in a society are solved by the operation of market forces.

Self-Assessment Questions

1. Write notes in about 200 words on the following:
   (*a*) The incremental concept.
   (*b*) Opportunity cost.
   (*c*) Scope of managerial economics.
   (*d*) The invisible hand.
2. 'Managerial economics serves as a link between traditional economics and decision sciences for business decision-making.' Elucidate.
3. Calculate, using the best estimates you can make:
   (*a*) Your opportunity cost of attending college.
   (*b*) Your opportunity cost of taking this course.
   (*c*) Your opportunity cost of attending yesterday's lecture of your course.
4. The following is the hypothetical production possibility table of India:

Resources Devoted to Clothing	*Output of Clothing*	*Output of Food*
100%	20	0
80%	16	5
60%	12	9
40%	8	12
20%	4	14
0%	0	15

   (*a*) Draw India's production possibility curve.
   (*b*) What is happening to marginal opportunity costs as output of food increases?
   (*c*) If the country gets better at the production of food, what will happen to the production possibility curve?

(*d*) If the country gets equally better at producing food and producing clothing, what will happen to the production possibility curve?

5. Use the following interest rates for government bonds for the risk-free discount rate and answer the following:

Time of Maturity (years)	*Interest Rate (%)*
1	5.75
2	6.00
3	6.25
4	6.50
5	6.75

(*i*) Calculate the PV of a ₹ 1 lakh payment to be received at the end of 1 year, 2 years, 3 years, 4 years and 5 years.

(*ii*) What is the present value of a firm with a 5 years life span that earns the following stream of expected profit at the year-end?

Years	*Expected Profit (in Crores)*
1	10
2	20
3	50
4	25
5	50

6. Value maximization has become the major objective of a modern firm. Comment.

7. (*a*) "Among the various objectives of a modern firm, profit animation is the most important" Comment.

....

....

....

....

(*b*) Outline the circular flow of economic activity between individuals and firms.

....

....

....

....

(*c*) (*i*) .... profit is a cost of doing business and is the amount by which .... exceeds .... profit.

(*ii*) When a firm earns just a normal rate of return, ... equals total economic cost and .... profit is zero.

(*d*) A firm collects ₹ 1.75 lakhs in revenue and spends ₹ 80 thousands on raw materials in a year. The owners of the firm have provided ₹ 5 lakhs of their own money to the firm instead of investing the money and earning a high rate of interest.

(*i*) The firm earns economic profit of .... The firms normal profit is ....

(*ii*) The firm's accounting profit is ....

(*iii*) If the firm's costs stay the same but its revenue falls to ...., only a normal profit is earned.

Unit **3**

BASIC TECHNIQUES

3.1 INTRODUCTION

The manager needs various techniques to assist him in making decisions that will ultimately maximize the value of the firm. These techniques and tools are quantitative in nature. The introduction of some commonly used tools used in managerial decision-making becomes imperative.

In this unit, we are going to discuss some basic techniques which would be helpful in understanding the concept of managerial economics, in turn helping us to apply these techniques as and when required.

3.2 OPPORTUNITY SET

A set is a collection of distinct or well defined objects like (5, 6, 7) or (a, b, c). For example, listing of all residents of Delhi or all animals in a zoo is difficult. Thus a set is also formed by developing a criterion for membership. For example, the set of all positive numbers between 1 and 10 or set of all points lying on the line $x + y = 4$. In managerial economics the need is to define an opportunity set of a decision maker, *i.e.,* the set of alternative actions which are feasible. For example, the opportunity set of a consumer is the set of all combinations of goods which the consumer can buy with his given income. Given the consumer's budget and prices of all goods, the opportunity set is well defined, and we can find out whether the consumers can buy that combination of goods. If a person consumes only two goods (x, y), whose prices are ₹ 5 and ₹ 4 per unit, and his income is ₹ 100, then the opportunity set is as shown in Fig. 3.1.

If the consumer spends all his income on X, he can buy 20 units of X with no Y.

(B), or if he spends all on good Y, then he buys 25 units of Y and no X (A). All other alternatives of spending ₹ 100 will lie on the line AB. Hence the area OAB constitutes the consumer's opportunity set.

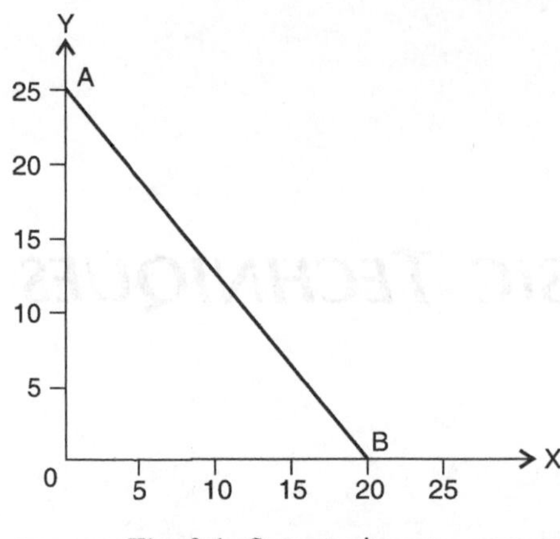

Fig. 3.1. Opportunity set.

3.3 VARIABLES AND CONSTANTS

Variables are a measure which change and can take a set of possible values within a given problem. A constant or parameter is a quantity which does not change in a given problem. For example, consider Y = *a* + *b*X; here, *a* and *b* are constants and X and Y are variables. X is the **independent variable** or **exogenous variable** while Y is the **dependent** or **endogenous variable.** The values of X will be given from outside the system, while values of Y will be determined from within the system (by the equation). X can assume different values and this will cause Y to assume different values also.

We can show the relationship between two variables Q and P by a function, such that for every value of P there is only one value of Q. In this case the function is Q = Q(P). These are the basic building blocks of economic models. The function Q = Q(P) is a demand function and its graph with price on one and quantity on the other axis will give a demand curve. P is the argument of the function or the independent variable and Q is the dependent variable. It indicates the cause-effect relationship between variables. (P is the cause variable, while Q is the effect variable). A function can be represented by means of a table or graph.

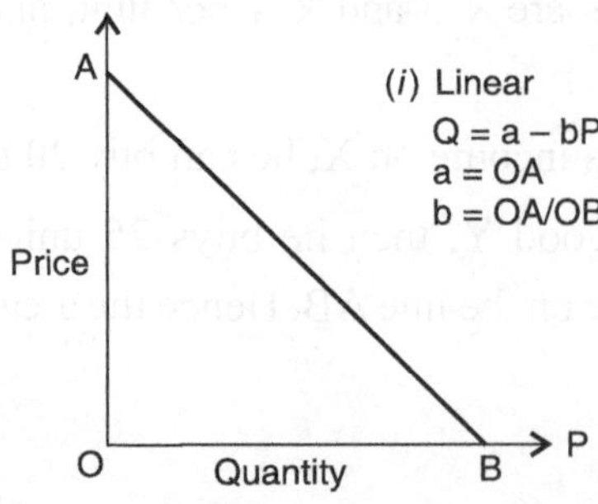

Fig. 3.2. Price vs. quantity (Linear).

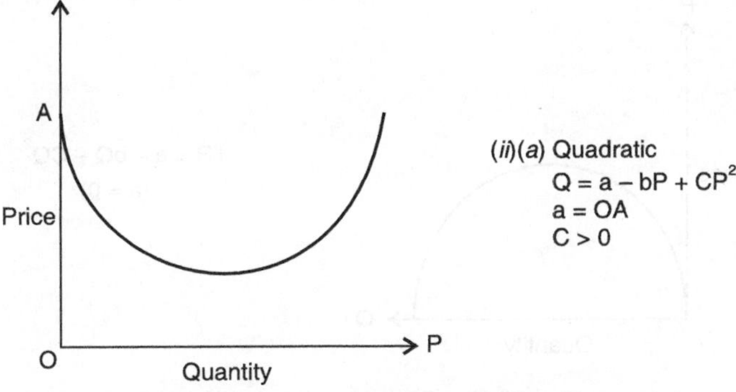

Fig. 3.3. Price vs. quantity (Quadratic).

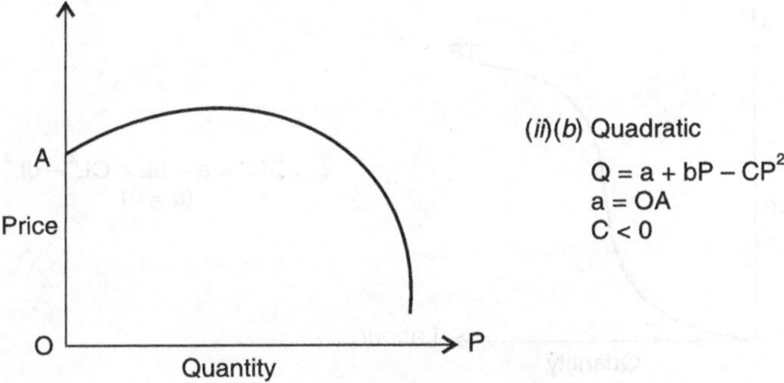

Fig. 3.4. Price vs. quantity ($C < 0$).

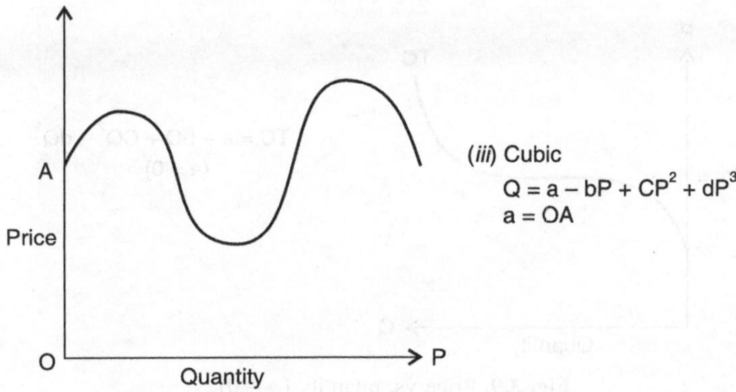

Fig. 3.5. Price vs. quantity (Cubic).

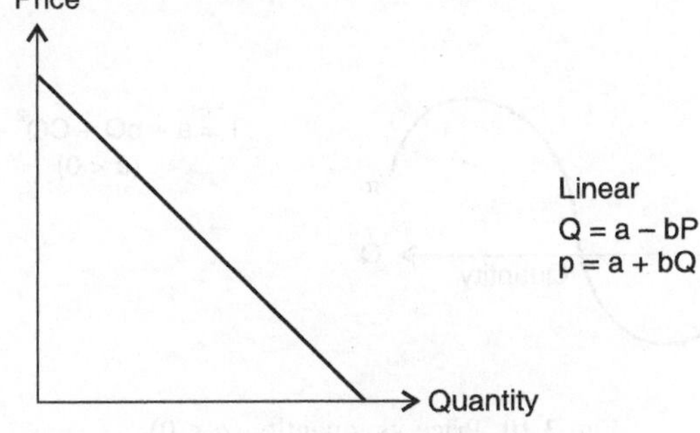

Fig. 3.6. Price vs. quantity ($P = a + bQ$).

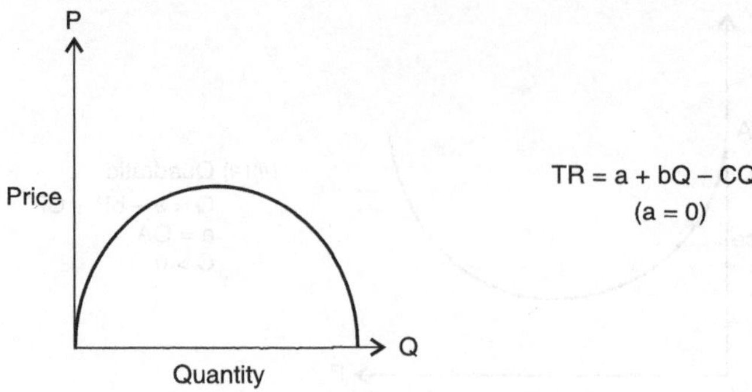

Fig. 3.7. Total revenue (Quadratic).

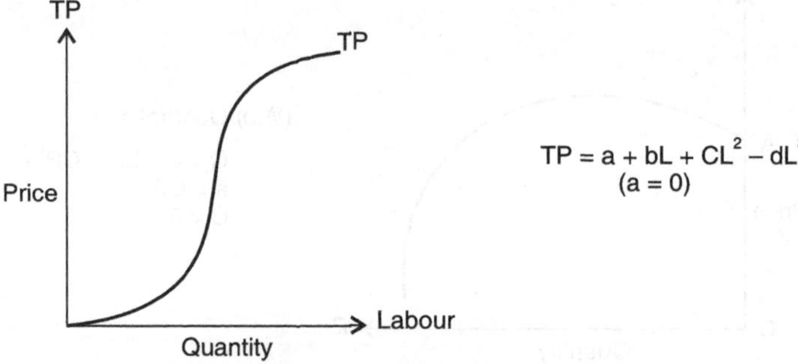

Fig. 3.8. Production (short-run) (Cubic).

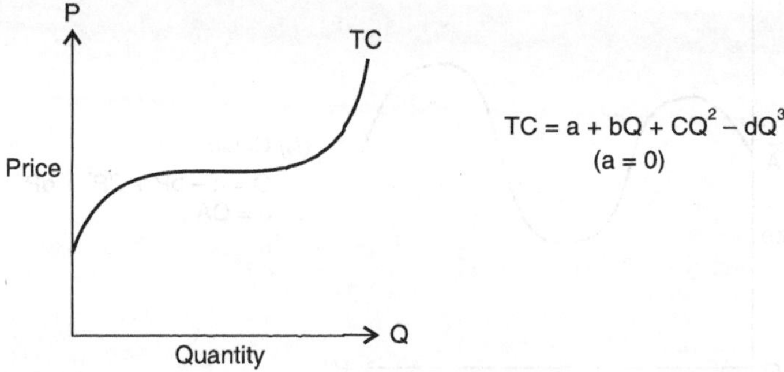

Fig. 3.9. Price vs. quantity ($a = 0$).

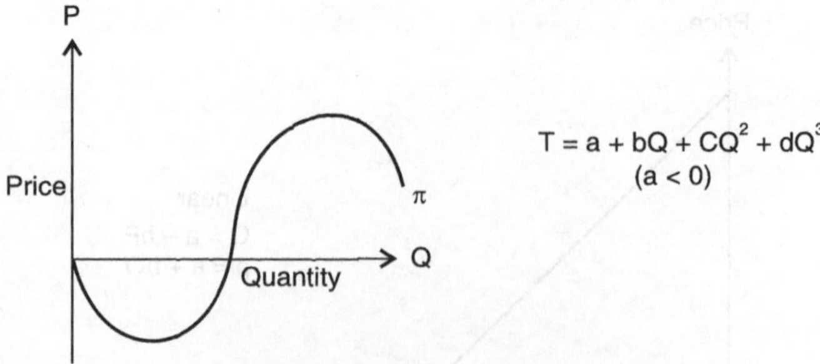

Fig. 3.10. Price vs. quantity ($a < 0$).

3.4 DERIVATIVES

The "slope" in mathematical use is the concept of 'marginalize' in economic use. Thus, if Y=Y(*x*), *dy*/*dx* stands for change in Y as a result of one unit change in X, *i.e.*, marginal *y* of *x*. This slope or marginal function has enormous use in managerial economics.

Thus, $\frac{dS}{dA}$ = Marginal sales of advertisement, when S = S(A)

$\frac{dR}{dQ}$ = Marginal revenue of output, when R = R(Q)

$\frac{dC}{dQ}$ = Marginal cost of output, when C = C(Q)

In case of 'averages' Average demand

$\frac{S}{A}$ = Average sales

$\frac{R}{Q}$ = Average revenue

$\frac{C}{Q}$ = Average costs

When marginal concept is divided by corresponding average concept, we get the measure of economic concept of elasticity.

$$\frac{dQ}{dP} * \frac{P}{Q} = \text{Price elasticity of demand}$$

$$\frac{dC}{dQ} * \frac{Q}{C} = \text{Output elasticity of cost}$$

$$\frac{dS}{dA} * \frac{A}{S} = \text{Advertisement elasticity of sales revenue}$$

Thus, such elasticity measures the proportion of change, *e.g.*, if the percentage change in demand is greater than the percentage change in price, then

$$\left[\frac{dQ}{dP} * \frac{P}{Q}\right] > 1 \text{ is elastic demand}$$

$$\left[\frac{dQ}{dP} * \frac{P}{Q}\right] < 1 \text{ is inelastic demand}$$

$$\left[\frac{dQ}{dP} * \frac{P}{Q}\right] = 1 \text{ is unitary elastic demand and so on}$$

Elasticity is discussed in detail in Block 2.

The standard rules of differentiation in calculus are given in the Appendix.

3.5 PARTIAL DERIVATIVES

In managerial economics, usually a function of several independent variables is encountered instead of a single variable case shown above. For example, a consumer's demand for a product depends on the price of the product, price of other related goods, income, tastes, etc. When price changes, the effect on quantity demanded of the goods can be analyzed only when all other variables are kept constant. The functional relationship that is obtained between the quantity demanded of a product and its own price is called a Partial Function (a function of one variable when all other variables are kept constant). The derivative of the partial functions are known as partial derivatives of the original function and is shown as df/dx_1 or $f_1(x)$ or $f'(x)$. The conventional symbol used in maths for the partial derivative is delta, δ. Partial derivatives are functions of all variables entering into the original function $f(x)$.

Examples:

(*i*) If $\quad Y = f(x_1 ; x_2)\, x_1^2\, x_2^2$

Then $\quad \dfrac{\delta y}{\delta x_1} = 2x_1x_2^2$

and $\quad \dfrac{\delta y}{\delta x_2} = x_1^2 2x_2 = 2x_2x_1^2$

(*ii*) If $\quad Y = \sqrt{x_1x_2} = (x_1x_2)^{1/2} = x_1^{1/2}\, x_2^{1/2}$

$$= x_1^{1/2}\, x_2^{1/2}$$

Then $\quad \dfrac{\delta y}{\delta x_1} = \dfrac{1}{2}x_1^{-1/2}\, x_2^{1/2} = \dfrac{1x_2^{1/2}}{2x_1^{1/2}} = \dfrac{1}{2}\sqrt{\dfrac{x_2}{x_1}}$

and $\quad \dfrac{\delta y}{\delta x_2} = \dfrac{1}{2}x_1^{1/2}x_2^{-1/2} = \dfrac{1}{2}\dfrac{x_1^{1/2}}{x_2^{1/2}} = \dfrac{1}{2}\sqrt{\dfrac{x_1}{x_2}}$

(*iii*) If $\quad Z = 4x^2 + 3xy + 5y^2$

Then $\quad \dfrac{\delta Z}{\delta y} = 8x + 3y$

Then $\quad \dfrac{\delta Z}{\delta y} = 3x + 10y$

Remember the derivative of a constant is 0, *i.e.*, $\delta z/\delta x$ of $5y^2$ is 0. Thus, in the above equation while calculating dz/dy we hold x constant and hence $\delta z/\delta x$ of $4x^2$ is 0. This gives $\delta z/\delta x$ to be $8x + 3y$; and $\delta z/\delta x$ to be $3 + 10y$.

$$\frac{\delta f}{\delta x}, \frac{\delta f}{\delta y}, \frac{\delta y}{\delta x}, \frac{\delta f}{\delta x_2}, \text{ are called first order partial derivatives.}$$

The second order partial derivatives indicate that the function has been differentiated partially twice with respect to a given variable, all other variables being held constant. These are shown in case of function $Z = f(x, y)$ by

$\frac{\delta^2 f}{\delta x^2}$ or f_{xx} and $\frac{\delta^2 f}{\delta y^2}$. Thus $\frac{\delta^2 f}{\delta x^2}$ shows the rate of change of first order partial derivatives fx with respect to x with y held constant.

Similarly $\frac{\delta^2 f}{\delta y^2}$ is the second order partial derivative of the function with respect to y with x held constant.

3.6 OPTIMIZATION CONCEPT

Optimization is the act of choosing the best alternative out of the available ones. It describes how decisions or choices among alternatives are taken or should be made. All such optimization problems have three elements:

(*a*) Decision Variables

These are variables whose optimal values have to be determined. For example, a production manager wants to know at what level to set output in order to achieve maximum profit or maximum sales revenue. Here output is the decision or choice variable. Similarly labour, machine, time and raw materials are choice variables if a works manager wants to know what amount of these are to be used so as to produce a given output level at minimum cost. The quantity of any choice variable must be measurable (20 kg, 5 labourers, 10 hours, etc.).

(*b*) The Objective Function

It is a mathematical relationship between the choice variables and some variables whose values are to be maximized or minimized. For example, the objective function could relate profit to level of output or cost to amount of labour, machine, time, raw materials, etc. in the above example.

(c) The Feasible Set

The available set of alternatives is called a feasible set. A solution to an optimization problem is that set of values of the choice variables which is in the feasible set and which yields maximum or minimum of the objective function over the feasible set.

Unconstrained Optimization Technique

For unconstrained optimization problem involving single independent variable, we need to satisfy some "conditions". In economics, the necessary (first order) condition is called the equilibrium condition and sufficient (second order) condition is called the stability condition (continuation of state of equilibrium). There may be equilibrium but it may not be stable. Thus first order condition does not guarantee second order condition. This is summarized in Table 3.1.

Table 3.1. First order condition does not guarantee second order condition.

Order	*Conditions*	*Optimization*	*Unconstrained*
First order	Necessary Conditions	Maximization $\frac{\delta y}{\delta x} = 0$	Maximization $\frac{\delta Y}{\delta X} = 0$
Second order	Sufficient conditions	$\frac{\delta^2 y}{\delta x^2} < 0$	$\frac{\delta^2 y}{\delta x^2} > 0$
	Y = *y*(*x*) (assumed)		

Some economic uses of these conditions are discussed below. Given a firm's demand function, P = 45 – 0.5 Q and the average cost function, AC = Q^2 – 8Q + 57 + 2/Q, we have to find the level of output Q which

(*a*) Maximizes total revenue

(*b*) Maximizes profits.

Solution:

(*a*) Since demand function is P = 45 – 0.5Q the total revenue function will be,

$$TR = PQ = (45 - 0.5Q); Q = 45 - 0.5Q^2$$

To maximize TR, we find the derivative and set it to 0 (the first order or necessary condition)

$$\text{Now, } \frac{dR}{dQ} = 45 - 2(0.5)\,Q$$

$$= 45 - Q = 0$$

$$Q = 45$$

The second order condition (sufficient condition) needs $\frac{d^2R}{dQ^2}$ to be negative

Since $\frac{dR}{dQ} = 45 - Q$

$$= \frac{d^2R}{dQ^2} = -1$$

which is negative, hence total revenue is maximized when output is 45 units.

(*b*) From profit function

$$p = TR - TC$$

$$TC = (AC) \times Q$$

$$= (Q^2 - 8Q + 57 + 2/Q); Q = Q^3 - 8Q^2 - 57Q + 2$$

$$TR = (45 - 0.5 Q)Q$$

$$= 45 Q - 0.5 Q^2$$

After substituting TR and TC, we get

$$p = 45Q - 0.5Q^2 - Q^3 + 8Q^2 - 57Q - 2$$

$$dp/dQ = 45 - Q - 3Q^2 + 16Q - 57$$

$$= -3Q^2 + 15Q - 12$$

Now set $\frac{d\pi}{dQ} = 0 - 3Q^2 + 15Q - 12 = 0$

Dividing by – 3

$$Q^2 - 5Q + 4 = 0$$

$$(Q - 4)(Q - 1) = 0$$

$$\Rightarrow \quad Q = 4 \text{ or } 1$$

Constrained Optimization Technique

There are many situations where the objective function has to be maximized or minimized subject to certain constraints present in the problem. Thus a consumer may be maximizing utility subject to the income constraint. The techniques used to analyze such problems are based on that used for unconstrained problems. The constrained problem is converted into an unconstrained one with the help of Lagrange Multiplier Technique and then the latter is solved. In this technique, the objective function and constraint is combined in one expression (Lag range expression) such that the constrained maximization or minimization problems are reduced to unconstrained ones. For example,

Maximize Y = – x^2 + 8x + 20

Subject to x 7 2

(Function of single independent variable)

The objective function (function to be optimized) is Y= – x^2 + 8x + 20, plotted on graph:

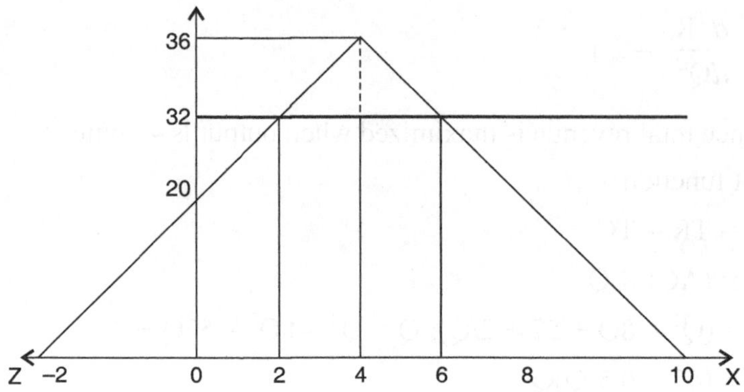

Fig. 3.11. The objective function.

The objective function $y = -x^2 + 8x + 20$ can be written as $y = -(x-4)^2 + 36$

Now $-(x-4)^2$ has an unconstrained maximum value of zero at $x = 4$. However, our objective function is $-(x-4)^2 + 36$, and hence will have an unconstrained maximum of 36 (at $x = 4$). This is so for the first derivative test.

The second derivative test $\dfrac{d^2y}{dx^2}$ gives – 2 since $\dfrac{dy}{dx}$ – 2x + 8 $\dfrac{dy}{dx} = -2x + 8$ $\dfrac{d^2y}{dx^2} = -2$

Thus both tests give $x = 4$ as the value of the variable. This is the value at which the objective function attains unconstrained maximum. However, the problem has a constraint $x = 2$. Thus, we have to consider the function only up to value of $x = 2$ (graph) starting from $x = -2$. The maximum value of the function is then 32 which occurs when $x = 2$. Thus the constrained maximum of the function $y = -(x-4)^2 + 36$ with constraint $x = 2$ would occur at $x = 2$ and not $x = 4$.

The Lagrange expression for constrained maximization is formed as follows:

$$Y = -(x-4)^2 + 36 \text{ with constraint } x = 2 \text{ or } x - 2 = 0.$$

Combining, we get the Lagrange expression L = [– $(x-4)^2$ + 36] + l (x – 2). Adding objective function and product of l (Lagrange Multiplier) and the constraint function $x - 2 = 0$. Now L is a function of x and we find:

$\dfrac{\delta L}{\delta x}$ and $\dfrac{\delta L}{\delta \lambda}$ set them to 0

$$\frac{\delta L}{\delta \lambda} = -2(x-4) + \lambda = 0$$

$$\frac{\delta L}{\delta x} = (x-2) = 0$$

The last equation gives $x = 2$. Hence the constrained maximum occurs at $x = 2$. In this problem $1 = 2(x-4) = 2(2-4) = -4$ when applying Lagrange technique to solve economic decision problem, 1 will have an economic significance. For example, in consumer's utility maximizing problem (where quantities of commodities are choice problems), 1 will be the marginal utility of money income. In producer's cost minimization profit, 1 will be the marginal cost of production. In complex problems, as many 1's as many there are constraints have to be used.

The problem with two independent variables can also be solved with Lagrangian technique. To find out whether the optimized value is maximum or minimum however, requires second derivative test as well as use of some more determinants not to be discussed here.

Activity 1

(*a*) Draw graph of the following functions:

(*i*) Q = 10 – 0.4 P

(*ii*) $Q = 15 - 2P + 4P^2$

(*iii*) C = 100 + 0.8 Y.

(*b*) A firm's fixed costs are ₹ 6000 regardless of output (they do not change when output changes), variable cost is ₹ 5 per unit of output (variable cost is dependent on output). Total cost = fixed costs + variable costs. The selling price of the goods is ₹ 100 per unit. Let Q be the output. State the

(*i*) Firms fixed cost function

(*ii*) Variable cost function

(*iii*) Total cost function

(*iv*) Total revenue function.

(*c*) Maximize $Z = 10xy - 2y^2$

Subject to $x + y = 12$

(*d*) Maximize $R = 737 - 8Q^2 + 14A + QA - 4a^2 + 20Q$

Subject to 2Q + A = 2.

Answers:

(*c*) $x = 7, y = 5, 1 = -50$

(*d*) Q = 0.52, A = 0.96, 1 = – 6.36.

3.7 REGRESSION ANALYSIS

A manager must often determine the total cost of producing various levels of output. The relation between total cost (C) and quantity (Q) is,

$$C = a + bQ + cQ^2 + dQ^3$$

where *a*, *b*, *c* and *d* are parameters of the equation. Parameters are coefficients in an equation that determine the exact mathematical relation among the variables in the equation. If the numerical values of parameters are determined, the manager knows the quantitative relation between output and total cost. If the value of parameters of cost equation are calculated to be $a = 1262$, $b = 1$, $c = -0.03$ and $d = 0.005$, the equation becomes,

$$C = 1262 + 1Q - 0.03Q^2 + 0.005Q^3$$

This equation can be used to compute the total cost of producing various levels of output. If, for example, the manager wishes to produce 30 units of output, the total cost can be calculated as

$$C = 1262 + 30 - 0.03(30)^2 + 0.005(30)^3 = ₹\ 1400.$$

Thus, in order for the cost function to be useful for decision making, the manager must know the numerical value of the parameter. The values of the parameters are often obtained by using a technique called regression analysis. It determines the mathematical relation between a dependent variable and one or more explanatory variables.

Dependent variable: The variable whose variation is to be explained.

Explanatory variables: The variables that are thought to cause the dependent variable to take on different values.

In the simple regression model, the dependent variable Y is related to only one explanatory variable X, and the relation between X and Y is linear:

$$Y = a + bX$$

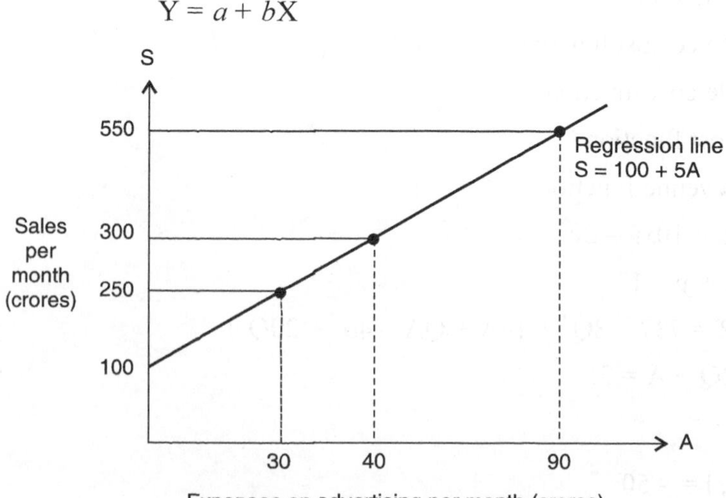

Fig. 3.12. Sales vs. expenses on advertising.

This is the equation for a straight line, with X plotted along the horizontal axis and Y along the vertical axis. The parameter *a* is called the intercept parameter because it gives the value of Y at the point where the regression line crosses the Y-axis. (X is equal to zero at this point). The parameter *b* is called the slope parameter because it gives the slope of the regression line. The slope of a line measures the rate of change in Y as X changes (DY/DX); it is therefore the change in Y per unit change in X.

Intercept parameter: The parameter that gives the value of Y at the point where the regression line crosses the Y-axis.

Slope parameter: The slope of the regression line, $b = |Y/|X$, or the change in Y associated with a one-unit change in X. Y and X are linearly related in a regression model. The effect of change in X on the value of Y is constant. A one-unit change in X causes Y to change by a constant *b* units.

The figure shows the true relation between sales and advertising expenditures. If a firm chooses to spend nothing on A, its sales are expected to be 100 crores per month. If the firm spends 30 crores on A then it can expect sales of 250 crores (=100 + 5 × 30). |S/|A = 5, *i.e.,* for every 1 unit increase on advertising, the firm can expect a 5 unit increase in sales. Regression involves identifying and calculating specific relationships between the independent variables and the dependent variable. It involves a number of stages which are described in another section.

Activity 2

(*a*) The slope parameter is .... and the intercept parameter is .... in the equation $R = a + bW$.

(*b*) In Fig. 3.12, what will be the monthly sales of the firm, if the advertising expenditure is increased from 30 crores to 40 crores per month?

....

....

....

....

3.8 SPECIFYING THE REGRESSION EQUATION

The first thing that the organization carrying out the regression analysis needs to do is to determine the range of variables which may affect demand for the product concerned. For example, the own price of a good might reasonably be expected to be a determinant of demand for most products, as would any advertising being done by the firm. The question of whether there is any substitute or complementary goods which need to be taken into account could then be raised. In the case of, an expensive consumer durable good, the cost and availability of credit might be a consideration. Any special 'other' factors affecting demand could then be identified and so on. This choice of variables has to be made before it is possible to progress to the next stage.

Data Collection

Once the relevant variables have been identified, quantitative data needs, to be assembled for each of them. This will be easier for some of the variables than for others. In dealing with an established product, for example, the firm might reasonably be expected to have access to a range of information regarding the variables which it controls such as own price and advertising. What may be more difficult to obtain, however, is information about competitors' products. On this front, price data can be obtained through observing retail prices, as this information by definition is in the public domain and cannot be hidden. This requires continued market observation, perhaps over a long period of time. Likewise, information about product design changes can be obtained by buying the competitors' product(s), but this may be expensive if there are many in the market. Confidential, commercially sensitive information such as actual advertising expenditure by competitors and their proposed new products present much more difficult problems in terms of access and may have to be left out of the process altogether.

Data on levels of disposable income, population variables, interest rates and credit availability are easier to obtain, for example from government statistics, but other variables are more problematic. How can things like expectations and tastes be measured for instance? In these cases the available data, perhaps resulting from market surveys, may be qualitative rather than quantitative. Some means of conversion need to be found if they are to be included in the regression analysis at all. These are the things which the decision maker needs to keep in mind while collecting and selecting data on the relevant variables. Once the first two steps have been completed, the next stage is to specify the likely form of the regression equation. There are two main forms which are used in practice—the linear demand function and the non-linear or power function. Both treat the demand for the product as the dependent variable, while the independent variables are those which have previously been identified as having an effect on demand. If, for example, the firm had decided that the only variables affecting demand for a particular product with its own price and advertising levels then the linear demand function would be written as:

$$Q = a + bP + cA$$

Alternatively, under these conditions the exponential (power) function would be written as:

$$Q = aPbAc$$

In each case, the term represents the intercept of the line drawn from the equation with the vertical axis. The b and c terms represent the regression coefficients with respect to own price and advertising respectively. These show the impact of each of these variables on product demand. Once they have been estimated it is possible to predict the level of demand for any set of values of the independent variables simply by substituting them into the equation.

The exponential form of the equation has the advantage that it can be rewritten to give direct estimates of the respective elasticity of demand for the independent variables. This is done by taking the log-linear form of the equation which in this case would be:

$$\log Q = \log a + b \log P + c \log A$$

Where b and c are the own price and advertising elasticity of demand respectively. This is a much easier approach than calculating elasticity through use of the linear form which involves using the equation: ED = b to calculate the elasticity in each case. In this case values of P and Q need to be obtained from the data set. Usually average values are substituted in the above equation to estimate elasticity. This idea will be explored in greater detail in Block 2. Which of the two forms of equation is chosen depends upon the expected relationship between the variables being included. In practice, however, the actual relationship between them may not be known in advance. In this case, the decision maker may experiment with both forms of equation in order to find the one which most closely fits the data.

Activity 3

(*a*) What are the things which the decision maker needs to keep in mind while collecting and selecting data on the relevant variables?

....

....

....

....

(*b*) Show that estimated coefficients using a log-linear technique are estimates of elasticity with respect to the relevant variable.

....

....

....

....

3.9 ESTIMATING THE REGRESSION EQUATION

Consider a firm with a fixed capital stock that has been rented under a long-term lease for ₹ 100 per production period. The other input in the firm's production process is labour, which can be increased or decreased quickly depending on the firm's needs. In this case, the cost of the capital input (₹100) is fixed and the cost of labour is variable. The manager of the firm wants to know the relationship between output and cost, that is, the firm's total cost function. This would allow the manager to predict the cost of any specified rate of output for the next production period. Specifically, the manager is interested in estimating the coefficients a and b of the function

$$Y = a + bX$$

where the dependent variable Y is total cost and the independent variable X is total output. If this function is plotted on a graph, the parameter a would be the vertical intercept (*i.e.*, the point where the function intersects the vertical axis) and b would be the slope of the function. Recall that the slope of a total function is the marginal function. As $Y = a + bX$ is the total cost function, the slope, b, is marginal cost or the change in total cost per unit change in output. Assume that data on cost and output have been collected for each of seven production periods and are reported in Table 3.2. Note that there is a cost of ₹ 100 associated with an output rate of zero. This represents the fixed cost of the capital input, which must be paid regardless of the rate of output. These data are shown as points in Fig. 3.13. They suggest a definite upward trend, but they do not trace out a straight line. The problem is to determine the line that best represents the overall relationship between Y and X. One approach would simply be to "eyeball" a line through these data in a way that the data points were about equally spaced on both sides of the line. The coefficient *a* would be found by extending that line to the vertical axis and reading the Y-coordinate at that point. The slope, *b*, would be found by taking any two points on the line, $\{X_1, Y_1\}$ and $\{X_2, Y_2\}$ and using the slope formula.

$$b = \frac{Y_2 - Y_1}{X_2 - X_1}$$

Although this approach could be used, the method is quite imprecise and can be employed only when there is just one independent variable. What if production cost depends on both the rate of output and the size of the plant? To plot the data for these three variables (total cost, output, and plant size) would require a three dimensional diagram; it would be nearly impossible to eyeball the relationship in this case. The addition of another independent variable, say average skill levels of the employees, would place the data set in the fourth dimension, where any graphic approach is hopeless.

Table 3.2. Total cost vs. total output.

Total Cost (Y_i) ₹	*Total Output* (X_i)
100	0
150	5
160	8
240	10
280	15
370	23
410	25

There is a better way. Statisticians have demonstrated that the best estimate of the coefficients of a linear function is to fit the line through the data points so that the sum of squared vertical distances from each point to the line is minimized. This technique is called ordinary least-squares regression (OLS) estimation and a number of statistical packages, including excel. Based on the output and cost data in Table 3.3, the least-squares regression equation will be shown to be $\hat{Y} = 87.08 + 12.21X$.

This equation is plotted in Fig. 3.13. Note that the data points fall about equally on both sides of the line. Consider an output rate of 5. As shown in Fig. 3.13, the actual cost associated with this output level is 150. The value predicted by the regression equation, referred to as $\hat{Y}$, is 148.13. That is, $\hat{Y} = 87.08 + 12.21(5) = 148.13$. The deviation of the actual Y value from the predicted value (*i.e.*, the vertical distance of the point from the line), $\hat{Y}\ i - \hat{Y}$ is referred to as the residual or the prediction error.

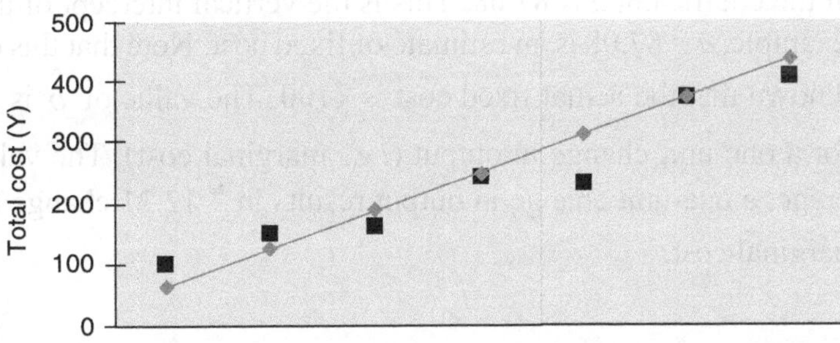

Fig. 3.13. The least-squares regression equation.

There are many values that might be selected as estimators of *a* and *b*, but only one of those sets defines a line that minimizes the sum of squared deviations [*i.e.*, that minimizes $q(Y_i - Y_i)^2$]. The equations for computing the least-squares estimators and $\hat{b}$ are

$$\hat{a} = Y - \hat{b}\,x\_$$

where Y and $- \hat{b}\,x\_$ are the means of the Y and X variables. Using the basic cost and output data from the example, the necessary calculations are shown in Table 3.3. Substituting the appropriate values into the following equations, the estimates $\hat{a}$ of $\hat{b}$ and are computed to be,

$$\hat{b} = \frac{\Sigma(X_i - \overline{X})(Y_i - \overline{Y})}{\Sigma(X_i - \overline{X})^2} = 12.21$$

Table 3.3. Basic cost and output data.

Cost (Y_i)	*Output* (X_i)	$Y_i -$	$X_i -$	$(X_i -)^2$	$(X_i -)(Y_i -)$
100	0	– 137.14	– 12.29	151.04	1,685.45
150	5	– 87.14	– 7.29	53.14	635.25
160	8	– 77.14	– 4.29	18.40	330.93
240	10	– 002.86	– 2.29	5.24	– 6.55
230	15	– 7.14	2.71	7.34	– 19.35
370	23	132.86	10.71	114.70	1,422.93
410	25	172.86	12.71	161.54	2,197.05
$\hat{Y} = 237.14$	$X\_ = 12.29$			$\Sigma(X_i - \overline{X})^2 = 511.40$	$\Sigma(X_i - \overline{X})(Y_i - \overline{Y}) = 6{,}245.71$

Thus the estimated equation for the total cost function is

$$\hat{Y} = 87.08 + 12.21X$$

The estimate of the coefficient a is 87.08. This is the vertical intercept of the regression line. In the context of this example, $\hat{a} = 87.08$ is an estimate of fixed cost. Note that this estimate is subject to error because it is known that the actual fixed cost is ₹100. The value of $\hat{b}$ is an estimate of the change in total cost for a one-unit change in output (*i.e.,* marginal cost). The value of $\hat{b}$, ₹ 12.21, means that, on an average, a one-unit change in output results in ₹ 12.21 change in total cost. Thus $\hat{b}$ is an estimate of marginal cost.

Activity 4

Suppose, for example, that the estimation process had given the following figures for the coefficients:

log QD = log 200 – 1.5 log P + 2.4 log A, where QD is quantity demanded, P is own price and A is advertising expenditure. What can we deduce from the estimated equation?

....

....

....

....

....

3.10 DECISION UNDER RISK

The focus of this section is decision-making under risk. The objective will be to develop guidelines for making rational decisions given the decision makers attitudes towards risk. Attitudes towards risk may be of three types: (*a*) A risk-seeker is one who prefers risk, given a choice between more or less risky investments, with identical expected money returns; he will select the riskier investment. (*b*) A risk averter is one who faced with the same situation will select the less risky investment. (*c*) A risk-neutral person is one who faced with the same situation will be in different to the choice. For him any investment is equally preferable to the other. It is difficult to slot people in one of these categories. You would perhaps have observed both risk averse and risk seeking behaviour in the real world. The analysis of risk is based largely on the concepts of probability and probability distribution that are commonly encountered in elementary statistics. First the terms strategy, states of nature and outcomes need to be defined. A strategy is one of the many alternative plans or courses of action that could be implemented in order to achieve managerial goals. A manager might be considering three strategies to increase profits—build a more modern plant which may produce at low cost, implement a new marketing programme to increase sales or change the design of product to decrease cost and increase sales.

A state of nature is a condition that may exist in the future and that will have a significant effect on the success of a strategy. For example, the manager may not be aware of the economic conditions in the future. The possible states of nature may be normal, recession or boom. The outcome results in either gain or loss based on a particular combination of strategy and state of nature. The decision maker has no control over the states of nature that will prevail in future but the future states of nature will certainly affect the outcome of any strategy that he or she may adopt. The particular decision made will depend, therefore, on the decision maker's knowledge or estimation of how a particular future state of nature will affect the outcome of each particular strategy. Given a set of outcomes, X_i, and the probability of each occurring, P_i, three statistics relating to probability distributions can be used, the expected value or mean is a measure of expected return. This is represented by:

$$\mu = \sum_{i=1}^{n} P_i(X_i)$$

where P_i is the probability and X_i is the outcome.

The standard deviation is a measure of risk. This is represented by

$$\sigma = \sqrt{\sum_{i=1}^{n} P_i(X_i - \mu)^2}$$

These statistics have a direct application in measuring the expected return and risk associated with any business decision for which a set of outcomes and their probabilities have been determined. The expected value, standard deviation, and the coefficient will be referred to as risk-return evaluation statistics. Having defined risk and reviewed some of the related terminology, the task now is to develop quantitative measures of return and risk and to show how they are applied in decision-making. We know that individuals have different preferences concerning risk taking. It is also important that such preferences be identified and their effect on decisions evaluated. Rational decision-making requires that the expected return be determined and the risk be measured, and that there be information about the manager's preference for risk. The expected value, the standard deviation, and the coefficient of variation will be referred to as risk-return evaluation statistics.

Let us take an example where two investments, I and II, are being considered. Both investments require an initial cash outlay of ₹100 and have a life of five years. The return on each depends on the rate of inflation over the five-year period. Of course, the inflation rate is not known with certainty, but supposes that the collective judgement of economists is that the probability of no inflation is 0.20, the probability of moderate inflation is 0.50, and the probability of rapid inflation is 0.30. The outcomes are defined as the present value of net profits for the next five years. These outcomes for each state of nature (*i.e.*, rate of inflation) for each investment are shown in Table 3.4. Analysis of these investments can be made by calculating and comparing the three evaluation statistics for each alternative. The expected value μ is an estimate of the expected return for the investment. Because risk has been defined in terms of the variability in outcomes, the standard deviations is a measure of risk associated with the investment. The larger the *m* the greater is the risk. Risk per rupee of expected return is measured by the coefficient of variation (*y*). The evaluation statistics for each investment alternative are computed as follows:

$$\mu_{\text{I}} = \sum_{i=1}^{n} P_i X_i = 0.2(100) + 0.5(200) + 0.3(400) = 240$$

$$\sigma_I = \sqrt{\sum_{i=1}^{n} P_i(X_i - \mu)^2}$$

$$= \sqrt{0.2(100-240)^2 + 0.5(200-240)^2 + 0.3(400-240)^2} = 111.36$$

$$v_I = \frac{\sigma_I}{\mu_I} = \frac{111.36}{240} = 0.46$$

$$\mu_{II} = 0.2(150) + 0.5(200) + 0.3(250) = 205$$

$$\sigma_{II} = \sqrt{0.2(150-205)^2 + 0.5(200-205)^2 + 0.3(250-205)^2} = 0.35$$

$$v_{II} = \frac{35.00}{205} = 0.17$$

The expected return for investment I of ₹ 240 is higher than for II (₹ 205), but I is a riskier investment because $\sigma_I = 111.36$ is greater than $\sigma_{II} = 0.35$. Also, risk per dollar of expected returns for I ($v_I = 0.46$) is higher than' for ($v_{II} = 0.17$). Which is the better investment? The choice is not clear. It depends on the investor's attitude about taking risks. A young entrepreneur may well prefer I, whereas an older worker investing in a retirement account where risk ought to be minimized might prefer II. Generally higher returns are associated with higher risk.

Table 3.4. Outcomes for rate of inflation.

State of Nature	*Probability (P_i)*		*Outcome (X_i)*
		Investment I	
No inflation	0.20		100
Moderate inflation	0.50		200
Rapid inflation	0.30		400
		Investment II	
No inflation	0.20		150
Moderate inflation	0.50		200
Rapid inflation	0.30		250

Decision Tree

Some strategic decisions are based on a sequence of decisions, states of nature and possibly even strategic decisions. Alternative strategies can be evaluated then, by using a decision tree, which traces sequences of strategies and states of nature to arrive at a set of outcomes. The probability of each outcome is found by multiplying the probabilities on each branch leading to that outcome.

A decision tree shows two or more branches at each point where a decision or event (state of nature) leads to the various outcomes. The decision tree approach can be directly applied to managerial decision-making. A firm entering a new market may decide to build a small or large plant (managerial decisions). This has no probabilities. But there may be stochastic elements (an outcome determined by chance) associated with each decision *e.g.,* reaction of a major competitor and the economic condition. The competitor may react by starting a national, regional, or a new advertising programme. The probability of each occurrence will depend on the size of the plant.

The possible economic conditions and then probabilities may be recession, normal or boom. Here also the probability will depend on the size of the plant. The probability of each combination is found by multiplying the probability along each of the branches leading to the outcome. For example, if the manager decides to build a large plant there is a 70 per cent chance that the competitor will respond with a national advertisement. We are given that there is a 30 per cent chance of a boom. The probability associated with the outcome of 80 is therefore 0.21 (= 0.7 * 0.3).

Decision trees are particularly useful if sequential decision-making is involved. In a game of chess, white has the first move. White has several options at this stage. To keep the problem tractable, let us assume that there are four possible moves for white : (*i*) move the king's pawn two squares; (*ii*) move the queen's pawn two squares; (*iii*) move the king's knight to king bishop three; and (*iv*) move the queen's knight to queen bishop three. In chess notation, the four moves are—(*i*) e_4; (*ii*) d_4; (*iii*) Nf_3; and (*iv*) Nc_3. Once white has made the first move, black has several different moves at its disposal. To keep the problem tractable, let us follow the decision tree only when white has moved e_4. Even then, black has several moves at its disposal. Let us assume that it has only four options — (*i*) move the king's pawn two squares (e_5); (*ii*) move the queen's pawn two squares (d_5); (*iii*) move the queen's bishop's pawn two squares (c_5); and (*iv*) move the king's pawn one square (e_6). Once white has moved e_4 on the first move and black has moved e_5 on the first move, white has several moves at its disposal. One of them is, move the king's knight to bishop three (Nf_3). And so the game goes on.

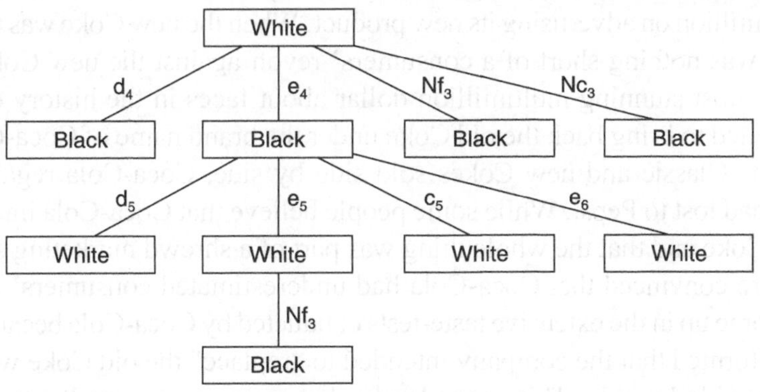

Fig. 3.14. Decision tree.

Each vertex or node indicates a decision to be taken by one of the players, the number within the rectangle indicating whose turn it is to move. There need not actually be two players; one of the players can be regarded as nature or chance. The main advantage of using a decision tree is that it helps one to isolate each chain and follow it through to the very end.

3.11 UNCERTAINITY ANALYSIS AND DECISION-MAKING

Certainty appears to be a theoretical and impractical state, as here the investor has perfect knowledge of the investment environment such that he is definite about the size, regularity and periodicity of flow of returns. Such situations may exist in the short-run (*e.g.* fixed deposit in a nationalized bank). However, long-run or long-range investments are not predictable as they are influenced by many kinds of changes taking place with time: political, economic, market and technology etc. Risk is more common in the real world. A situation with more than one possible outcome to a decision such that the probability of each of these outcomes can be measured is a risk situation. For example, tossing of a coin (*i.e.*, 50–50) or investing in a stock. The greater the number and range of outcomes, the greater is the risk associated with the decision or action. Uncertainty is a situation where there is more than one possible outcome to a decision but the probability of each specific outcome occurring is not known or even meaningful. This may be due to insufficient information or instability in the nature of variables. In extremes cases of uncertainty, the outcomes may not be clear. Decision-making under uncertainty is necessarily subjective.

The Risk Faced by Coca-Cola in Changing its Secret Formula

On April 23, 1985, the Coca-Cola Company announced that it was changing its 99-year-old recipe for Coke. Coke is the leading soft drink in the world; the company took an unusual risk in tempering its highly successful product. The Coca-Cola Company felt that changing its recipe was a necessary strategy to ward off the challenge from Pepsi-Cola, which had been chipping away at Coke's market over the years. The new Coke, with its sweeter less fizzy taste, was clearly aimed at reversing Pepsi's market gains. Coca-Cola spent over $ 4 million to develop its new Coke and conducted taste tests on more than 1,90,000 consumers over a three-year period. These seemed to indicate that consumers preferred the new Coke by 61 per cent *i.e.*, 39 per cent over the old Coca Cola—Cola then spent over $ 10 million on advertising its new product. When the new Coke was finally introduced in May 1985, there was nothing short of a consumers' revolt against the new Coke and in what is certainly one of the most stunning multimillion dollar about faces in the history of marketing, the company felt compelled to bring back the old Coke under the brand name of Coca-Cola Classic. The irony is that with the Classic and new Cokes sold side by side, Coca-Cola regained some of the market share that it had lost to Pepsi. While some people believe that Coca-Cola intended all along to reintroduce the old Coke and that the whole thing was part of a shrewd marketing strategy, yet most marketing experts are convinced that Coca-Cola had underestimated consumers' loyalty to the old Coke. This did not come up in the extensive taste-tests conducted by Coca-Cola because the consumers tested were never informed that the company intended to "replace" the old Coke with the new Cola, rather than sell them side by side. This case clearly shows that even a well conceived strategy is risky and can lead to results estimated to have a small probability of occurrence. Indeed, the failure rate for new products in the United States is a stunning 80 per cent.

3.12 ROLE OF MANAGERIAL ECONOMIST

In general, managerial economics can be used by the goal-oriented manager in two ways. First, given an existing economic environment, the principles of managerial economics provide a framework for evaluating whether resources are being allocated efficiently within a firm. For example, economics can help the manager if profit could be increased by reallocating labour from a marketing activity to the production line. Second, these principles help the manager to respond to various economic signals. For example, given an increase in the price of output or the development of a new lower-cost production technology, the appropriate managerial response would be to increase output. Alternatively, an increase in the price of one input, say labour, may be a signal to substitute other inputs, such as capital, for labour in the production process. Thus, the working knowledge of the principles of managerial economics can increase the value of both the firm and the manager.

Self-Assessment Questions

1. Find the present value of ₹ 10, 000 due in one year if the discount rate is 5 per cent, 8 per cent, 10 per cent, 15 per cent, 20 per cent and 25 per cent.
2. Apply the decision-making model to your decision to attend college at MBA level.
3. Discuss with examples how managerial economics is an integral part of business activity.
4. Suppose a seller has two markets to serve. The demand schedules in them are given in the table. Suppose that he has 1400 units to sell and maximize profits thereby. What prices will he set in the two markets? Apply equi-incrementalism principle to get your answer. Could you have applied equi-marginalism?

Market A		*Market B*	
Price	*Quantity*	*Price*	*Quantity*
50	400	60	600
40	600	50	800
30	900	40	1100
20	1000	34	1400

[**Hint:** First get total revenue in each market by multiplying price with quantity]

5. A firm is producing two products x and y, and has the following profit function $p = 64x - 2x^{22} + 4xy - 4y^2 + 32y - 14$. Find the profit maximizing levels of output for each of the two products.

(**Ans.** $x = 40, y = 24, p = 1650$)

6. Maximize $Z = 10xy - 2y^2$

Subject to $x + y = 12$

7. What are central or basic problems of an economy?
8. Which problems of an economy constitute the subject matter of microeconomics?

Unit **4**
THEORY OF PROFITS

4.1 INTRODUCTION

After having discussed the determination of rent of land, wages of labour and interest on capital, we now pass on to the study of profits which are said to be the reward for enterprise, the fourth factor of production. No doubt profits are associated with an entrepreneur and his functions but the economists from time to time have expressed diverse and conflicting views about the nature, origin and role of profits. Till today, there is no complete agreement among economists about the true nature and origin of profits. As a matter of fact, there has been perhaps no topic in the whole economic theory which has been in such a confused and tangled state as the theory of profits.

A part of the confusion in the theory of profits is due to the lack of agreement among economists about the true or proper function of an entrepreneur. Some have held the view that the function of an entrepreneur is to organize and co-ordinate the other factors of production. According to them, an entrepreneur earns profits for performing this function. According this view, an enterprise special type of labour and profits offers a special form of wages. Some others have described an entrepreneur as performing joint and inseparable functions of *responsibility* (*i.e.,* ultimate risk bearing) and control (*i.e.,* ultimate decision making). An entrepreneur earns profits because he takes a risk of incurring losses when his price and output policies prove to be incorrect in view of the future business movements. Schumpeter has assigned to an entrepreneur the role of an innovator and profits as a reward for introducing innovations. Lastly, F. H. Knight has emphasized the uncertainty in the economy as a factor which gives rise to profits and bearing uncertainty is the task of the entrepreneur.

Besides, some economists have described profits as *non-functional income.* Thus, J. M. Keynes expressed the view that profits resulted from the favourable movements of the general price level. Ms. Joan Robinson, Prof. Chamberlin and Mr. Kalecki have associated profits with the imperfect competition and monopoly. According to them, the greater the degree of imperfection or, in other words, the greater the degree of monopoly power, the greater the profits made by the entrepreneur. Thus profit has been associated with uncertainity by F.H. Knight, by Schumpeter with innovations, by Hawley with risk-bearing, and by Mrs. Robinson, Prof. Chamberlin and Mr. Kalecki with the degree of monopoly power. As a matter of fact, profits arise from all these sources. Therefore, no single explanation or theory of profits is adequate; each omits some crucial points and fails to bring out some important economic phenomena having a relation with profits. Prof. B. S. Keirstead, therefore, expresses the view that profits originate from monopoly, successful innovation and a correct estimate of an uncertain future. He thus says, "Profits may come to exist as a result of monopoly, as a reward for innovation, as a reward for the correct estimate of uncertain factors, either particular to the industry or in general to the whole economy."!

It is worth mentioning that profits are *residual income* left after the payment of the contractual rewards to other factors of production. An entrepreneur while engaging other factors of production enters into contract with them. He thus pays wages to the workers, rent on the land employed, and interest on the loans taken at the rate already fixed by contracts. In fact, an entrepreneur makes payments to these factors much in advance of the realization of the values of the output produced after sale of the product. What is left after paying the contractual rewards of other factors employed is the profit of an entrepreneur. Thus, profits are *non-contractual income* and therefore they may be positive or negative, whereas the contractual income of other factors such as wages, rent and interest are always positive and never negative. It should be further noted that *pure profits* of an entrepreneur are found by subtracting from the gross residual income the *imputed values of rent and interest* on the self-owned land and capital employed by an entrepreneur and also the *imputed wages* for his work of routine management.

4.2 PROFIT AS A DYNAMIC SURPLUS

A popular conception of profits is that they arise in a dynamic economy, that is, in an economy where changes are taking place. In a static economy where nothing changes there can be no profits. It was J.B. Clark who first propounded that profits are a dynamic surplus. He argued that in a stationary state where no changes in conditions of demand and supply are occurring, the prices paid to the factors on the basis of their marginal productivity would increase the value of production and no profits would accrue to the entrepreneur. Profits result when selling prices of the goods exceed their cost of production. Now, in a competitive long-run equilibrium price equals average cost of production (including normal profits which are in fact wages for routine supervision and management) and therefore no pure profits are made. Now, if no changes either in the conditions of demand or in the conditions of supply occur, competitive equilibrium will persist and therefore no profits will be earned by the entrepreneur. On the contrary, if due to the changes in either demand or supply, price exceeds cost of production profits will emerge. If due to these changes, price falls below the cost of production, negative profits, that is losses will accrue to the entrepreneur. It is evident that change disturbs the equilibrium and thereby gives rise to profits. In other words, profits arise due to disequilibrium caused by the changes in demand and supply conditions. Prof. Stigler rightly says. "Firms in a competitive industry may receive profits because of a state of disequilibrium these profits can arise even if all entrepreneurs are identical for disequilibrium can characterize a whole industry. If prices are higher, or costs lower than were anticipated, entrepreneurs will receive a return in excess of the alternative product of their resources. If prices were lower or costs higher than were anticipated, entrepreneurs will receive less than the alternative product of their resources *i.e.,* negative profits. Positive profits may persist for a long time if firms outside the industry are slow to enter the industry and negative profits can persist as long as specialized equipment yields more when used in the industry than when used elsewhere, say as scrap."

It should be noted that these disequilibrium profits arise from *unanticipated* change in demand or cost conditions. If the changes could have been foreseen in advance, then suitable adjustments could have been made according to the anticipated changes so that forces of competition would have driven profits to zero.

Now the question is what changes occur in the economy and give rise to profits. J. B. Clark mentioned five changes that occur in a dynamic economy and which give rise to profits. These five changes are; changes in the quantity and quality of human wants, changes in methods or techniques of production, changes in the amount of capital and changes in the forms of business organization. These changes are constantly taking place and bring about the divergence between price and cost and thereby give rise to profits, positive or negative. If the demand for a commodity increases due to the increase in population or increase in the incomes of the people or due to the increase in consumer's preference for the commodity, the price of the commodity will rise, and if cost remains the same, profits would accrue to the entrepreneurs producing the commodity. On the other hand, cost of production may go down as a result of the adoption of a new technique of production, or as a result of cheap raw material, and if price remains constant or does not fall to the same extent, then profits would emerge.

Apart from the five changes mentioned by Clark, there are other changes also which occur in the economy. All the changes which take place and as a result of which profits arise in a dynamic economy may be classified into two types: (1) *innovations* and (2) *exogenous changes.* Innovations represent changes which are introduced by individual entrepreneurs themselves. The entrepreneur earns large profits from introducing innovations such as a new product, a new and cheaper method of production, a new method of marketing the product, a new way of advertisement. These changes may either reduce cost or increase the demand for the product and thereby bring profits into existence. Those entrepreneurs who introduce successful innovations earn large profits. But as the innovation gets known to other entrepreneurs or they adopt similar other innovations, profits which arose because of a particular innovation tend to disappear. But new innovations are being continuously introduced by the entrepreneurs and profits continue to arise out of them.

Exogenous changes refer to those changes which are external to the firms or industries in an economy. These changes affect all firms in an industry or sometimes all the industries in the economy.

Examples of exogenous changes are breaking out of wars, occurrence of periods of inflation and rising prices and sometimes business depression and falling prices, changes in the monetary and fiscal policies of government affecting favourably or unfavourably, changes in the technology of production, changes in tastes and preferences of the consumers, changes in income and spending habits of the people, changes in the availability of substitute products, alteration in the legislative and legal environment affecting the industries, and changes in preferences between income and leisure. All these changes affect either the cost or demand of the products and give rise to profits, positive or negative as the case may be. For instance, during war when prices of goods mount up, and costs lag behind, the entrepreneurs make a lot of profits. Similarly, when inflation occurs due to the increased demand for goods caused by the rising incomes, increasing population and expansion in the money supply, huge profits accrue to the firms. On the contrary, when period of depression comes due to the fall in effective aggregate demand, firms suffer huge losses and some may go into liquidation. During periods of depression all prices, rents, wages, and interest tend to fall but because of the non-contractual nature, profits fall sharply and even become negative.

Here the views of Prof. F. H. Knight about dynamic changes giving rise to profits are worth mentioning. According to him, "Dynamic changes give rise to a peculiar form of income only in so far as the changes and their consequences are unpredictable in character. It cannot, then, be the change which is the cause of profits, since if the law of change is known, as in fact is largely the case, no profits can arise. The connection between change and profits is uncertain and always indirect. Change may cause a situation out of which profit will be made, if it brings about ignorance of the future. It is not dynamic change, nor any change as such which causes profits, but divergence of actual conditions from those which have been expected and on the basis of which business arrangements have been made. For satisfactory explanation of profit we seem to be thrown back from the dynamic theory to the *uncertainty* of the future."

As far as unpredictable, unforeseen changes and uncertainty about the future giving rise to profits are concerned, there can be no disagreement with Prof. Knight. But with his assertion that dynamic changes as such are not the cause of profits, one can differ. Against Knight's view it may be pointed out that if there is no change there will be no uncertainty about the future and therefore no profits. Thus the factor of change is fundamental in bringing profits into existence. Professors Stonier and Hague rightly maintain "in an economy where nothing changes, there can be no profits. There is no uncertainty about the future, so there are no risks and no profits."

4.3 INNOVATIONS AND PROFITS: SCHUMPETER'S THEORY OF PROFITS

Successful innovations as important dynamic changes and as source of profit have been, in brief, explained above. But since innovation has been signed out as a very important factor responsible for the occurrence of profits to the entrepreneurs it requires to be dealt with separately. It has been held by Joseph Schumpeter that the main function of an entrepreneur is to introduce innovations in the economy and profits are reward for performing this function. Now, what is innovation? Innovation, as used by Schumpeter, has a very wide connotation. Any *new* measure or policy adopted by an entrepreneur to reduce his cost of production or to increase the demand for his product is an innovation. Thus, innovations can be divided into two categories.

First type of innovations is those which reduce cost of production, or in other words, which change the production functions. In this first type of innovations are included the introduction of a new machinery, new and cheaper technique or process of production, exploitation of a new source of raw material and better method of organizing the firm, etc. Second type of innovations are those which increase the demand for the product, or in other words, which change the demand or utility function. In this category are included the introduction of a new product, a new variety or design of the product, a new and superior method of advertisement, discovery of new markets etc. If an innovation proves successful, that is, if it achieves its aim of either reducing the cost of production or enhancing the demand for the product, it will give rise to profit. Profits emerge because due to successful innovation either cost falls below the prevailing price of the product or the entrepreneur is able to sell more and at a better price than before. It should be noted that profits accrue not to him who conceives innovation nor to him who finances it but to him who introduces it. Further, whenever any new innovation is contemplated to be introduced, it always calls for a new combination of factors or reallocation of resources.

It is worth mentioning that profits caused by a particular innovation are only temporary. An innovation ceases to be new or novel, when others also come to know of it and adopt it. When an entrepreneur introduces a new innovation, he is first in a monopoly position, for the new innovation is confined to him only. He therefore makes large profits. When after some time others also adopt it in order to get a share, profits will disappear. If the law allows and the entrepreneur is able to get his new innovation *e.g.*, new product patented, then he will continue to earn profits.

But in a competitive economy and without patent laws, the existing competitors or the new firms will soon adopt any successful innovation and profits would be eliminated. But in a competitive and progressive economy the entrepreneurs always continue to introduce new innovations and thus profits continue emerging out of them. Thus, Prof. Stigler says, "unless one can construct a permanent monopoly, such profits as are realized by successful innovation are essentially transitional and will be eliminated by the attempts of other firms to share them. But these profits may exist for a considerable time because of the ignorance of other firms of their existence or because of the time required for the entry of new firms. More important, the successful innovator can continuously seek new disequilibrium profits since the horizon of conceivable innovations is unlimited.

We have seen that innovations are an important source of profits. Obtaining profits is a necessary incentive for the entrepreneurs to conceive and introduce innovations, which help the economic development of the country. Since innovations, if successful, yield profits and profit is also the motive to introduce innovations, profits are both the cause and effect of innovations.

4.4 RISK, UNCERTAINTY AND PROFITS: KNIGHT'S THEORY OF PROFITS

An important theory associates profit with risk and uncertainty. According to F. H. Knight, profit is a reward for bearing uncertainty. Even before Knight, F. B. Hawley and A. C. Pious had pointed out that entrepreneurs earned profits because they had to bear the risks of undertaking production. But Knight has greatly developed the theory of profits based on uncertainty. He has distinguished between risk and uncertainty on the one hand and predictable and unpredictable changes on the other. According to him, dynamic changes give rise to profits in so far as changes and their consequences are unpredictable in character. Only those changes whose occurrence cannot be known beforehand give rise to profit.

As we have noted earlier, if there were no changes or if the changes were foreseen and predictable, there would have been no uncertainty about the future and no profits. Profits arise because of the uncertainty of future. If the future conditions could be completely known in the present, then competition would certainly adjust things to the ideal state where all prices would equal costs and profits would not emerge. Thus, it is our ignorance about the future and uncertainty of it that give rise to profits. In other words: it is the divergence of actual conditions from those which have been expected and on the basis of which business arrangements have been made that give rise to uncertainty and profits. Prof. A. K. Dass Gupta rightly maintains "uncertainty is thus a permanent feature of the economic system. It is one of the limitations of human ingenuity that it cannot unearth the contents of the future. Trained instincts of businessmen coupled with statistical information may go a long way, but in so far as the course of nature (both physical and human) is anything but rhythmical the future would always remain more or less of a mystery." He further writes "so long as entrepreneurs start operations with imperfect knowledge about the state of the market and so long as the anticipated marginal product of the hired factors deviates from their actual product, so long a surplus would persist."

We thus see that entrepreneurs have to undertake the work of production under conditions of uncertainty. In advance they have to make estimates of the future conditions regarding demand for the product and other factors which affect price and costs. In view of their estimates and anticipations, they make a contract with the suppliers of factors of production in advance at fixed rates of remuneration. They realize the value of the output produced by the hired factors after it has been produced and sold in the market. But a good deal of time is spent in the process of producing and selling the product. It follows, therefore, that a good time gap elapses between the contracts made by the entrepreneur with the factors of production at fixed rates and the realization of sale proceeds from the output made by them. As mentioned before, these contracts are based upon anticipation about the future conditions. But between the time of contracts and the sale of the output many changes may take place, which may upset anticipations for good or for worse and thereby give rise to the profits, positive and negative. Now, if the conditions prevailing at the time of the sale of output could be known or predicted when the entrepreneurs enter into contractual relationships with the factors of production about their rates of remuneration, there would have been no uncertainty and, therefore, no profits. Thus *uncertainty, that is, ignorance about the future conditions of demand and supply, is the curve of profits*. It should be noted that positive profits accrue to those entrepreneurs who make correct estimates of the future or whose anticipation proves to be correct. Those whose anticipation proves to be incorrect will have to suffer losses.

We thus see that profit is a residual and non-contractual income which accrues to the entrepreneurs because of the fact of uncertainty. An entrepreneur hires others for work of production. It is, therefore, an entrepreneur who bears uncertainty and earns profits as a reward for that. Weston who has been a prominent exponent and supporter of uncertainty theory of profits explains the emergence of profits in the following way: "Under uncertainty total product may not be equal to total costs (explicit and implicit) *because plans are not fulfilled*. How this occurs is briefly indicated. Two classes of owners of productive services are distinguished. First, those with rates of compensation fixed in advance of the determination of the results of operations, are called *hired factors* and receive contractual returns. Second, those with rates of compensation dependent upon the results of operation are referred to as *unwired factors* who receive non-contractual or residual returns. Whatever the basis upon which contractual relationships have been entered, actual results will not have been accurately foreseen because of uncertainty. Hence, *whatever the basis upon which contractual commitments have been made events actually do not turn out that way*. This is the significance of economic profit. *It is not possible to plan in advance exactly what the total product or total costs will be.*"

Now, the question is what changes cause uncertainty. As has been explained earlier, there are *two types of changes* which take place and are responsible for conditions of uncertainty. First type of changes refers to the innovations (for example, introduction of a new product or a new and cheaper method of production etc.) which are introduced by the entrepreneurs themselves. These innovations not only create uncertainty for the rivals or competitors who are affected by them but they also involve uncertainty for the entrepreneur who introduces them, for one cannot be certain whether a particular innovation will be definitely successful. The second type of changes which cause uncertainty are those which are external to the firms and industries. These changes are: changes in tastes and fashions of the people, changes in Government policies and laws especially taxation, wage and labour polices and laws, movements of prices as a result of inflation and depression, changes in the incomes of the people, changes in production technology etc. All these changes cause uncertainty and bring profits, positive or negative, into existence.

We have seen above that entrepreneurs work under conditions of uncertainty and that they bear uncertainty and earn profits as a reward for that. Here a distinction drawn by F. H. Knight between *insurable risk* and *non-insurable risk* is worth mentioning. Because of the changes that are continuously occurring in the economy, an entrepreneur has to face many risks. But all risks do not cause uncertainty and give rise to profits. It is only *non-insurable risks* that involve uncertainty and the entrepreneur earns profits for bearing these non-insurable risks. This raises the question as to what kind of risks are insurable and what are non-insurable risks. The entrepreneur faces risks like fire, theft, accident etc. which may cause him huge losses. But these risks of fire, theft, accident etc. can be insured against on the payment of a fixed premium. Insurance premium is included in the cost of production. Thus, no uncertainty arises due to insurable risks as far as individual entrepreneurs are concerned and therefore, they cannot give rise to profits.

Only those risks can be insured the probability of whose occurrence can be calculated. Thus, an insurance company knows by its calculation on the basis of past statistics that how much percentage of the factories will catch fire in a year. On the basis of this information, it will fix the rate of premium and is able to insure the factories against this risk. But there are risks which cannot be insured and therefore, they have to be borne by entrepreneurs. These non-insurable risks relate to the outcomes of the price-output decisions to be taken by the entrepreneurs. Whether it will pay him to increase output, reduce output and what will be the outcome in terms of profits or losses as a result of his particular output decision. Again, whether it will pay him to lower the price or to raise it and when he takes a particular price decision whether he would make profits or losses. Similarly, he has to face risks as a result of his decisions regarding mode of advertisement and outlay to be made on it, product variation etc. For taking all these decisions he has to guess about demand and 'cost conditions and there is always the risk of suffering losses—as a result of these decisions. No insurance company can insure the entrepreneurs against commercial losses which may emerge out of decisions regarding price, output, product variation and also against the losses which may fall upon the entrepreneurs due to the structural, cyclical and other exogenous changes which take place in the economy. It is, therefore, clear that *it is non-insurable risks that involve uncertainty and give rise to profits.* To quote Knight "It is uncertainty, distinguished from insurable risk that effectively gives rise to the entrepreneurial form of organization and to the much condemned 'profit' as an income for Knight's theory rightly emphasized that uncertainty in a dynamic business environment gives rise to profits. The bearing of uncertainty is an important function to be performed by the entrepreneurial class in a society. This makes the profits as functional income that is earned for performing the function of bearing uncertainty. But all profits are not functional nor do they arise due to uncertainty. As we have studied in the theories of monopoly, monopolistic competition, oligopoly in product markets and monophony in factor markets, that a significant amount of profits arises due to the monopoly power enjoyed by the producers. Knight's theory ignores the fact of monopoly power giving rise to profits. Prof. Kalecki whose theory of profits we will discuss below propounded that monopoly power was an important source of profits in modern free-market economies. It is also worth mentioning that monopoly profits can arise even in a stationary economy where no changes are taking place.

Further, in our view that while the profits may emerge as a result of dynamic changes, innovations and uncertainty but the *appropriation* of profits by the recipients is *institutionally* determined. The *separate* theories must be developed to explain the origin of profits and *sharing out* of profits. For instance, Weintraub points out that "the entrepreneur's function is directed and executed with an eye towards profit making; *the sharing of profits is an entirely separate issue.*" Likewise, R.A. Gordan states: "It is important to bear in mind that accounting for the *origin* and *existence* of an income does not in itself explain its allocation to particular persons or classes. The way in which a given income accrues to various individuals will depend largely on how those individuals fit into the *institutional setting* which prevails. Thus, though 'pure profits' may be explainable in terms of change, uncertainty and friction (essentially a non-functional explanation), the fact that these gains go to particular persons is related not to exercise of entrepreneurial function, but rather to the *nature and distribution of ownership rights.*"

4.5 MONOPOLY AND PROFITS

We have explained above that profits can originate from dynamic changes, innovations, and from making a correct estimate of future under conditions of uncertainty. But monopoly is another source of profits. Monopolistic position gives rise to profits both in static and dynamic conditions. Monopolist commands a control over the price of a product and therefore, manages to make profits by virtue of his monopoly power. It *raises* price by restricting his level of output and thereby makes profits. Monopoly is a matter of degree only. Monopoly power is exercised not only by a pure monopolist who produces a product which has no close substitutes but also to a somewhat lesser extent by the producers working under monopolistic competition and oligopoly. We have seen in our chapter on product pricing under imperfect competition that the element of monopoly is present in various categories of imperfect competition, namely, pure monopoly, monopolistic competition and oligopoly. It is due to this element of monopoly in these categories of imperfect competition that demand curve slopes downward in them. Thus, monopoly power is associated with downward sloping demand curve.

We have seen in our chapters on pricing and output under pure monopoly, monopolistic competition and oligopoly that due to monopoly power and the resultant downward–sloping demand curve, a firm's equilibrium, that is, equality between marginal revenue and marginal cost, is reached at a price which is higher than marginal cost of production. Further, the price so determined is often higher than average cost of production which yields positive profits to the firm enjoying monopoly power to a greater or smaller degree. Owing to the strong barriers for the entry of new firms, the firms working under pure monopoly and oligopoly continue to make supernormal profits even in the long-run. Even under monopolistic competition with a large number of firms, due to product differentiation, entry into the industry is not fully free, as was later realized by Chamberlin himself. Product differentiation gives a firm a certain degree of monopoly power in setting his own price and no new firms can produce exactly the same product as that of any existing firm under monopolistic competition. With only restricted entry of firms under monopolistic competition, demand curve does not fall, even in the long-run, to the tangency position with the average cost curve so that the entrepreneurs working under monopolistic competition also continue to enjoy positive profits by virtue of their monopoly power. Commenting on monopoly as a source of profits, Professor Pen writes, "The real monopolist—the one and only supplier in a branch of industry is rare, but in many cases a breath of monopoly pervades competition. One brand is not the same as another—economists call that product differentiation, and as a result an element of monopoly power creeps into the market that yields an extra profit for the supplier. He can fix his own price, which is impossible under perfect competition, and perhaps he extends his volume of production a little less than he would otherwise have done. In some cases this limitation of production is an obvious danger; contrived scarcity leads to profit for a small group and to harm for the public."

As we have discussed in a previous chapter, A. P. Lerner has provided a quantitative measure of the degree of monopoly present in any market situation. Lerner's quantitative measure of the degree of monopoly is based on the fact that whenever monopoly power is present and as a result demand curve is downward-sloping, price set by the producer will deviate from marginal cost. Further, this measure of degree of monopoly power is based upon an ideal market situation of perfect competition, in which monopoly element is completely absent and inequilibrium price is equal to marginal cost. According to Lerner, if p stands for price and m for marginal cost, the difference $p - m$ measures the deviation from perfect competition ideal, or in other words, the extent of monopoly power present in any real market situation. The difference, $p - m$, expressed as a fraction of price, p, that is, $p–m$.

p is Lerner's measure of degree of monopoly. Now, it has been asserted by many exponents of monopoly theory of profits, especially M. Kalecki that the greater the degree of monopoly the greater the size of profits earned by the entrepreneur or firm. According to M. Kalecki, the degree of monopoly as given by Lerner's measure, $p - m$, is the most important factor determining the volume of profits; indeed, according to him, it is the only determinant of the level of profits.

It should be noted that the degree of monopoly power of a firm, or in other words, its power to set price above marginal cost of production depends upon the elasticity of the demand curve facing him. The smaller the elasticity of demand for a product, the greater the degree of monopoly power. But the elasticity of demand for a firm's product depends on the extent to which the product is different from others; the greater the extent to which its product is differentiated, the less the elasticity and consequently the greater the degree of monopoly.

The second factor on which the monopoly power of a firm depends is its share in the market or in the total output of the industry. The greater its share in the industrial output or markets for the product, the greater the extent of monopoly power wielded by a producer. This is because the greater its share in the market or total output of the market, the greater will be his freedom and independence in setting the price. Now, with the monopoly power gained by the extent of distinctiveness of his product and his share in the total output or market, the producer succeeds in setting price above cost of production and thereby earns supernormal profits for himself.

It is often pointed out that monopoly power possessed by a producer is no guarantee of positive profits, if demand for the product is inadequate and cost of production is high. In case of unfavourable demand-cost situations, producers working under pure monopoly, monopolistic competition and oligopoly enjoying varying degrees of monopoly power can make losses. In fact, in earlier chapters we too have shown that producers under pure monopoly and monopolistic competition respectively make losses in the short-run inspite of the monopoly power possessed by them. When the demand conditions for the product produced by them are not favourable. Thus, according to Professor Bober, "he skates on thin ice who identifies profits with monopoly and monopoly with profits."

No doubt there is a good deal of possibility of losses being earned in the short-run by firms under monopolistic competition (when there is a large number of firms), but the possibility of losses in case of pure monopoly and oligopoly should not be exaggerated. Pure monopoly and oligopoly generally go together with big business which is organized on corporate basis. Big corporate firms working under pure monopoly and oligopoly and enjoying a lot of monopoly power do not take the consumer's demand as given but seek to *manipulate,* and *create* demand and have enough resources to do so. Through product variation, advertisements and other sales promotion devices, big corporate firms having a good deal of monopoly power, *succeed in shifting the demand curve for their product.* Thus, through the devices of persuasive advertisement, product variation and other sales promotion activities the big firms with greater monopoly power see to it that the demand curve for their product remains above cost of production yielding them a good deal of profits.

Further, firms with varying degrees of monopoly power not only exploit the consumers by setting a higher price and thereby earn profits but often they are also *monopolist or oligopsonist in various factor markets.* With their monopolistic power they also exploit the factors, especially labour and pay them less than their marginal revenue products. By exploiting the hired factor, they increase their share of profits.

Monopoly power of a firm manifests itself in its ability to raise price of the product. But if a firm sets a higher price and thereby earns excessive profits, it will attract other firms into the industry and will reduce the monopoly power of the existing firms and eliminate excessive profits. Therefore, authors such as F. Machlup, F. H. Hahn and Jean Marchal have emphasized that in order that the monopoly power be enduring and lasting and therefore firms continue to enjoy monopoly profits, there must be *strong barriers to the entry of firms*. Thus, monopoly power and the profits accruing because of that ultimately depend on the restrictions on the entry of firms. Control over the supply of an essential raw material, legal restrictions in certain cases such as patent rights, the existence of goodwill enjoyed by the existing firms, reputation of brands and trade names of the products of existing firms, economies of large-scale production and difficulty of organizing production on a large-scale are some of the important factors that put restrictions on the entry of firms and make possible the earning of the monopoly profits by the existing firms enjoying a high degree of monopoly power.

Critical Evaluation of Monopoly Theory of Profits

It is certainly true that monopoly is a good source of profits. Theories of imperfect competition and monopolistic competition by Joan Robinson and Chamberlin involving downward sloping demand curve with its implication of price-setting power made a significant contribution not only to price theory as such but also to the profit theory. But Kalecki's assertion that monopoly is the *only source or determinant* of profits is not right. Dynamic changes, innovations by the entrepreneurs themselves, uncertainty are also important causes of profits and in any adequate explanation of profits these things can hardly be neglected. Further, there is no contradiction between uncertainity and monopoly theories of profits. As has been asserted by F. H. Hahn, market imperfections in monopolistic competition and oligopoly increase uncertainty and this uncertainty makes the entry of firms more difficult. Thus, the theory which attributes profits to monopoly power only supplements the uncertainty theory of profits rather than replaces it. Kalecki's concept of the degree of monopoly $(p–m)/p$ and profits resting on it has been criticized. For instance, measure of the degree of monopoly $(p – m)$ is zero under perfect competition, since price (P) is equal to marginal cost (m) under it. It implies that under perfect competition with zero degree of monopoly the share of profits (*i.e.*, capital) will be zero and the share of labour will be 100% which is obviously unrealistic and ridiculous. To quote Pen, "unfortunately upon closer examination the Kaleckian theory proves disappointing. We have an example of this when we examine what happens under perfect competition, *i.e.,* a neo-classical world. Then the formula produces odd results: the degree of the monopoly is zero, and the share of labour is 100%. But nevertheless capital remains scarce and productive—it is improbable that it would receive no remuneration. Now, of course, it may be argued that Kalecki's theory was not designed for such a world but all the same it ought to be able to embrace this borderline case as well."

It should be noted that much of the criticisms against monopoly theory of profits is against Kalecki's measure of degree of monopoly and its association with profits. That monopoly is an important cause and source of profits cannot be denied. Kalecki particularly used macro degree of monopoly and explained with it the distributive shares of profits and wages in national income. We will discuss Kalecki's macro-theory of distribution based on the Lerner's concept of degree of monopoly in the next chapter.

Self-Assessment Questions

1. A true theory of profits may reconcile the risk theory and dynamic theory of profits. Comment.
2. Discuss the role played by the following in the determination of profits:
   (*a*) Risk and uncertainty (*b*) Dynamic changes
   (*c*) Innovation (*d*) Monopoly.
3. Critically examine the dynamic theory of profits.
4. Critically examine the view that profit is the reward for the entrepreneur for bearing non-insurable risks and uncertainty.
5. Uncertainty and not risk froms the basis of a valid theory of profits.

Unit **5** # THEORY OF PRODUCTION: CONTENT AND IMPORTANCE

5.1 INTRODUCTION

Having discussed the demand side of the price theory, we now proceed to discuss the supply side. Supply side relates to the production of goods and services. Production of goods depends on the cost of production, which in turn depends on the prices of inputs or the factors of production. Cost of production is determined by the physical relationship between inputs and outputs. In the theory of production, we largely discuss the relation between inputs and output.

Production in economics is generally understood as the transformation of inputs into outputs. The inputs are what a firm buys (*i.e.,* productive resources) and outputs (*i.e.,* goods and services produced) what it sells. Apart from physical changes of the matter, production also includes services like buying and selling, transporting and financing. But in economic analysis we restrict the use of the term 'production' to the production of goods only, because in the production of goods we can precisely specify the inputs and also identify the quantity and quality of outputs.

Fig. 5.1. Production means transformation of inputs into output.

In the theory of production, we study the factors of production and their organization. We also study the laws of production, *i.e.,* the generalizations governing the relations between the outputs and inputs. We shall also study the theories of population, which govern the supply of an important factor of production, viz., labour. We shall also study the 'production function, *i.e.,* the relation between the output and inputs of a firm. The analysis of production function leads us to the quantity in which the various factors of production are combined, *i.e.*, whether they are combined in fixed proportion or in variable proportions. When all the factors are varied, we have the laws of return to scale. We also see how a firm hits at the most economical or optimum combination of factors so that the unit costs are the lowest.

The theory of production occupies a very important place in economic analysis and it has a great relevance to the study of various economic problems. The theory of production plays an important role in the theory of relative prices. Specifically, (*a*) it helps in the analysis of relations between costs and volume of output; it tells us how a manufacturer combines various inputs in order to produce a given output in an economically efficient manner, *i.e.*, at the minimum cost. (*b*) The theory of production also provides a base for the theory of the demand of firms for reproductive resources. Thus, we find that the theory of production has a great relevance to the theory of firm. Firm seeks to produce that level of output at which its profits are maximum. For this purpose, it will have to consider the marginal and average cost of production besides considering the demand conditions, *i.e.*, average and marginal revenues.

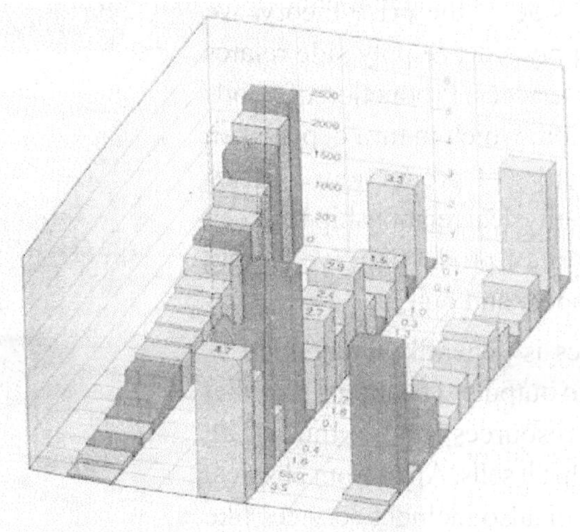

Fig. 5.2. Production refers to creation of utility.

The theory of production also explains the forces which determine the marginal productivity of factors and so the prices that have to be paid for the factors of production. The relative prices of the factors form the subject-matter of the theory of distribution. In this way, the theory of production has a great relevance to the theory of distribution in its microform, *i.e.*, the relative shares of the various factors of production. It has also a great relevance to the macro theory of distribution, *i.e.*, the aggregate distributive shares of the various factors of production, *e.g.*, aggregative share of wages and profits in the national income. The aggregative shares are influenced by the elasticity of substitution between factors of production which is also an important concept in the theory of production.

We shall first study the various factors of production in this chapter and then in the next chapter the forms of entrepreneurial organization. Then in the subsequent chapters, we shall study the population theories, the scale of production, the production possibility curve and production function, the laws of returns, the isoquants or equal product curves, cost and cost curves and supply. This will complete the study of the theory of production.

Meaning of Production

Production is sometimes defined as the creation of utility or the creation of wants - satisfying goods' and services. It is said that just as man cannot destroy matter, he also cannot create matter. "If consuming means extracting utilities from," says Fraser, "producing means putting utility into." But this is not a scientifically correct definition to produce a thing, which has utility, but not value is not production in the economic sense. One may spread the cult of Yoga and promote the physical and spiritual well being of one's friends—a thing of great utility but unless one makes it one's profession, his activities will not come under production.

Production, therefore, should be defined, not as creation of utility, but creation (or addition) of value. Utilities are created in three forms: (*i*) form utility, (*ii*) time utility, and (*iii*) place utility.

Production essentially means transformation of one set of goods into another. A good may be transformed by being physically changed (from utility); or being transported to the place of use (place utility) or being kept in store till required time (time utility). Pure exchange is also an act of transformation.

5.2 FACTORS OF PRODUCTION

Productive resources required to produce a given product are called factors of production. These productive resources may be raw materials or services of the various categories of workers or of capitalism supplying capital or of entrepreneurs assembling the factors and organizing the work of production. They are now generally called 'inputs'. Fraser defined "factor of production as a group or class of original productive resources." The term "factor" is used for a class of productive elements, the individual members of which are known as "units" of the factor. Modern economists prefer to talk in terms of anonymous productive services rather than the classical factors of production.

The factors of production have been traditionally classified as land, labour, capital and organization (or enterprise). Now, we shall briefly deal with them one by one. These factors are complementary in the sense that their co-operation or combination is essential in the production process.

The typical situation in production is that a group of complementary factors is required between which there is some degree of substitutability. Between labour and capital, the relation is both of substitution and complementarily.

Specificity

A factor is said to be specific when it can be used for one purpose only and for none other, *e.g.*, spare part of a particular machine.

Versatility

A factor is said to be versatile when it can be put to every and any use.

These are, however, two extremes. No factor is completely specific or versatile. That is, a factor can be put to several uses but not all uses. A factor of low versatility is called a specialized factor. The specific or specialized nature of the factors of production play an important role in the disposition of productive resources.

Fig. 5.3. Irrigated land and building.

5.3 LAND

Meaning and Importance of Land

The term 'land' has been given a special meaning in economics. It does not mean soil as in the ordinary speech, but it is used in a much wider sense. In the words of Marshall, land means "the materials and the forces which nature gives freely for man's aid, in land and water, in air and light and heat." Land stands for all natural resources which yield an income or which have exchange value. It represents those natural resources, which are useful and scarce, actually or potentially.

Peculiarities of Land

In contrast to the other factors of production, land presents certain well-marked peculiarities:

(*i*) Land is nature's gift to man.

(*ii*) Land is fixed in quantity. It is said that land has no supply price. That is, price of land prevailing in the market cannot affect its supply; the price may be high or low, its supply remains the same.

(*iii*) Land is permanent. There are inherent properties of the land which Ricardo called 'original and indestructible.'

(*iv*) Land lacks mobility in the geographical sense.

(*v*) Finally, land provides infinite variation of degrees of fertility and situation so that no two pieces of land are exactly alike. This peculiarity explains the concept of margin of cultivation.

These are a few peculiarities of land and they have a bearing on economic rent.

5.4 LABOUR

Meaning of Labour

In the ordinary speech, the term 'labour' means a mass of unskilled labour. But in Economics it is used in a wider sense. Any work, whether manual, or mental, which is undertaken for a monetary consideration, is called: 'labour' in Economics. Any work done for the sake of pleasure or love does not fall under labour in the economic sense. In Marshall's words, "Any exertion of mind or body undergone partly or wholly with a view to some good other than the pleasure derived directly from the work is called labour."

Fig. 5.4. The division of labour.

Peculiarities of Labour

Labour is manifestly different from the other factors of production. It is a living thing, and that makes all the difference. Labour is not only a means of production but also an end of production. There are certain characteristics, which distinguish labour from the rest of the factors of production:

(*i*) Labour is inseparable from the labourer himself.

(*ii*) Labourer has to sell his labour in person.

(*iii*) Labour does not last. It is perishable: As Erich Roll remarks, "He has no reserve price." The labourer has, therefore, to accept the wage offered to him.

(*iv*) Labour has a very weak bargaining power.

(*v*) Changes in the price of labour react rather curiously on its supply. In the case of ordinary commodities, supply is directly proportionate to price, *i.e.,* the higher the price the greater the supply, and vice versa. But, in the case of labour, a fall in price *i.e.,* wage below a certain point may increase the supply. For instance, some members of the family, who were not working before, may start working to supplement the family income.

(*vi*) There can be no rapid adjustment of the supply of labour to demand for it, because supply cannot be increased quickly, nor can it be reduced.

These peculiarities of labour have an intimate bearing on the determination of wages.

That labour should be treated differently from a commodity is a social rather than an economic question.

Factors Determining Efficiency of Labour

The following are some of the main factors, which affect labour efficiency:

(*i*) **Racial Qualities:** Labour efficiency largely depends on heredity and the racial stock to which a worker belongs.

(*ii*) **Climatic Factors:** A cool bracing climate is conducive to hard work, whereas the tropical climate is not suitable.

(*iii*) **Education:** Efficiency also depends on education, both general and technical.

(*iv*) **Personal Qualities:** A worker's efficiency also depends upon his personal qualities, *e.g.,* physique, mental alertness, intelligence, resourcefulness and initiative etc.

(*v*) **Industrial Organization and Equipment:** The level of organization and the nature of equipment supplied to the workers, too, determine their efficiency.

(*vi*) **Factory Environments:** Cramped and ill-ventilated factories, situated in crowded and non-sanitary surroundings, are not conductive to efficiency.

(*vii*) **Working Hours:** Long hours impair labour efficiency.

(*viii*) **Fair and Prompt Payment:** A well-paid worker is generally contented and puts his heart into the job.

(*ix*) **Organization:** An organized effort is always more effective.

(*x*) **Social and Political Factors:** Social security schemes guaranteeing freedom from want and fear, and which remove the dread of unemployment that always hangs over their head like Damocles' sword, are bound to invest labour with dignity and respect and add to their efficiency.

5.5 DIVISION OF LABOUR

Meaning and Types

Division of labour is an important characteristic of modern production. In fact, there is hardly any producing unit of a respectable size, which does not organize production on the basis of division of labour. Division of labour is associated with efficiency of production. "The division of labour is not a quaint practice of eighteenth century pin factories; it is a fundamental principle of economic organization." (Benjamin Franklin).

When making of an article is split up into several processes and each process is entrusted to a separate set of workers, it is called division of labour.

The division of labour is of the following main types:

Simple Division of Labour: This means division of society into major occupations, *e.g.,* carpenters, blacksmiths, weavers, etc. It may also be called functional division of labour.

Complex Division of Labour: In this case, no group of workers makes a complete article. Instead, the making of an article is split up into a number of processes and sub-processes and each process or sub process is carried out by a separate group of people. This is proper division of labour.

Fig. 5.5. Increasing productivity skills.

Territorial Division of Labour: This form of division of labour refers to certain localities, cities or towns specializing in the production of some commodity. This is also called localization of industries.

Advantages

Several advantages are claimed for the system of division of labour. Adam Smith's contribution to this part of the economic theory is still regarded as classic. Division of labour has proved beneficial in the following ways:

Increase in Productivity: Adam Smith takes the example of a pin-making industry to illustrate the immense increase in productivity. He describes pin-making as divided into 18 distinct operations. Ten men can make 48,000 pins in a day; one worker may, therefore, be considered to have made 4,800 pins in a day. In the absence of division of labour and machinery, one man could scarcely have made one pin in a day, and certainly not twenty.

Increase in Dexterity and Skill: Practice makes a man perfect. After repetitive performance of the same task, a worker becomes an expert.

Inventions are Facilitated: In division of labour, the movement becomes mechanical and the worker can freely think while at the job. New ideas often occur leading to inventions.

Introduction of Machinery Facilitated: When a man is doing the same job over and over again, he will be able to think of some mechanical procedure to relieve himself. A machine is, therefore, bound to take over this simple movement sooner or later.

Saving in Time: Under the system of division of labour, a worker has only to do one process or a part of a process. Less time is, therefore, needed to learn a specialized trade.

Saving in Tools and Implements: When a worker has to perform a part job only, *e.g.*, making the legs of a chair, he need not be supplied with a complete set of tools. One set of tools can serve many workers at the same time.

Diversity of Employment: Division of labour increases the number and variety of jobs. Employment is thus diversified.

Large-scale Production: Division of labour involves production on a large-scale. The community reaps all the economies of large-scale production. Production improves not only in quantity but also in quality since goods are made by specialists.

Right Man in the Right Place: Under division of labour, workers are so distributed among the various jobs that each worker occupies the right place. There are no round pegs in square holes.

Disadvantages

We have seen that division of labour enhances the productive capacity of the community. But as Chapman puts it, "Productiveness of a method of production is not the sole test of its value—to get many commodities is not the only end in life." We have rather to see how man, for whom production is meant, has been affected by the division of labour. Considered in this light, division of labour has not proved to be an unmixed blessing.

The following may be mentioned as some of the disadvantages of division of labour:

Monotony: Under division of labour, a worker has to do the same job over and over again. The work becomes monotonous. It is drudgery, pure and simple. The work ceases to be interesting.

Retards Human Development: A person's development, physical and mental, is greatly affected by the job he is engaged in. Under division of labour, a worker has to repeat the same movement over and over again. His muscles and mind move in the same direction. Repetitive movement cramps a person's mind and narrows his outlook. Monotony is soul-killing.

Industry De-humanized: Under division of labour, many people combine to produce an article. "Everybody's business is nobody's business." The worker loses all sense of responsibility and pride in his work. The industry is thus de-humanized.

Loss of Skill: The master craftsman loses his skill. He knows, for instance, only either spinning or weaving, making the legs of the chair or its seat. He does not know how to make the whole chair.

Risk of Unemployment: Knowing only a part of the job, the worker is in danger of becoming unemployable. If he happens to lose his present job, he may not be able to get similar job elsewhere. He thus becomes unemployable.

Disrupts Family Life: Division of labour facilitates employment of women and children. The influx of women into the factory disrupts domestic life and the employment of children involves the deterioration of valuable human resources of the nation. It is a great national loss.

Division of Labour and Evils of the Factory System: Division of labour is associated with the factory system which has given rise to evils like water pollution and air pollution, the countryside is contaminated with foul smell; over-crowding endangers morals; and non-sanitary surroundings spread disease. Man becomes a slave of machine and of the factory owner.

Conclusion

Division of labour has, however, come to stay. Shortening of the working day thus increasing leisure, diffusion of education and rising of remuneration are some of the measures that can be adopted to counteract the bad effects of division of labour on a worker's life and personality.

Division of Labour is Limited by the Extent of the Market

This is so obvious. If, for instance, a shoemaker is able to dispose one pair of shoes in six months, it will look foolish for him to employ half a dozen persons on the making of soles, half a dozen on the making of uppers, and another six persons in joining them. There must be adequate demand for his product before he can adopt such methods. Division of labour implies large-scale production, and it is meaningless to produce more in the absence of a sufficient market for goods. The limiting factor for the introduction and extension of labour is, therefore, the existence of a wide market.

But no individual entrepreneur looks at the matter like this. He no doubt considers the market while fixing the size of his plant. But when he has done that, the extent of the division of labour will depend on the nature of the machinery installed and the number and the variety of the people employed. It will depend also on an entrepreneur's own organizing ability. But the extent of the market is not so much in his mind.

Market also Depends on Division of Labour: Under division of labour, production is done on a large-scale, which means cheaper production. When goods are cheap, more people will buy them. Thus, the boundaries of the market are extended by division of labour.

Hence, division of labour and the market are interdependent. But it is more true to say that division of labour is limited by the extent of the market than that the extent of the market depends on division of labour.

5.6 TERRITORIAL DIVISION OF LABOUR

Localization of Industries

Territorial division of labour is also called localization of industries. By localization we mean the establishment of an industry in a certain place or a region. A certain town or a territory specializes in a certain place or a region in a certain industry. Indian jute industry is centered in Bengal, iron and steel industry in Bihar, sugar industry in U.P. and Bihar, cotton mill industry in Mumbai, and so on. For instances of localization in State towns, we may mention hosiery industry of Ludhiana (Punjab), bangles in Firozabad (U.P.), silk manufactures in Hazaribagh (Bihar), etc.

Causes of Localization

The chief factors that govern localization are as follows:

Nearness to Raw Materials: To have raw materials near at hand is a great advantage. Transport costs will be considerably reduced. Production will be more economical. It is not surprising that most of the industries have been started in the region where abundant supplies of the necessary raw materials are available, *e.g.* "jute mills in Bengal, sugar mills in U.P. and iron and steel industry in Bihar and Orissa.

Nearness to Sources of Power: Another attraction for the industries is the availability of power resources. If coalmines are near, several industries will soon crop up, *e.g.*, iron and steel works and several other industries in the coal regions.

Indian cotton mill industry in North India and in Bengal has been located by a desire to be near the markets.

Availability and ability of Labour: If trained labour is available, it is regarded as a great facility. That is why new industrialists flock to old established industrial centres. If somebody wants to start a hosiery industry, he will find it to his advantage to start it at Ludhiana (Punjab) because there is ample trained labour available there besides several other external economies.

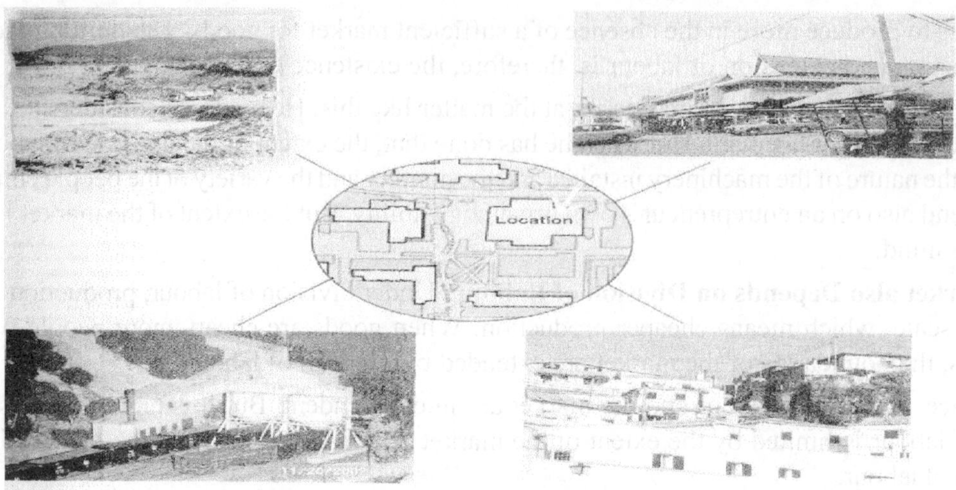

Fig. 5.6. A good location mean's proximity to the market.

Availability of Capital: Finance is the very breath of industry. Where there are banks and other financiers ready to assist industry, it is a great attraction. Cities like Mumbai and Kolkata are the centres of industry, because they enjoy better credit facilities.

Political Factor: Sometimes, the political factor is responsible for the establishment of an industry. Some of the old princely States in India, like Hyderabad, offered special concessions, incentives and facilities to industrialists to attract them and to induce them to set up industries in their states.

Religious Factor: In some cases, religious causes, making for larger number of people, give rise to some industries. It is generally seen that places of pilgrimage specialize in the manufacture and sale of articles generally purchased by pilgrims.

Momentum of an Early Start: In some cases, it is not possible to point to any particular cause of the localization of industry except the momentum of an early start: the industry just happened to be started there first. The example of the pioneer industrialists is followed by others in the place. In this way, the industry becomes established in that place.

Causes of Further Concentration

After an industry has got going in a certain place, it then has a tendency to stick to and further gravitate to that place. If any new entrepreneur wants to enter this industry, he, too, will go to that place to start his business rather than start it elsewhere. Several reasons account for this tendency. Trained labour is readily available there. Plant and accessories and raw materials can be conveniently had. Financing agencies are also established in that place. Several supplementary and subsidiary industries are established in course of time, and they are a valuable aid to the main industry. Technical journals are published which are found useful by the industrialists. Associations of entrepreneurs are formed to safeguard and promote common interests. Means of communication and transportation become specialized and adapted to the needs of the industry. All these factors considerably assist the entrepreneurs. In a new place, they will find even easy and ordinary problems difficult.

Above all, there is what is called industrial inertia. Once established in a place, the industry does not like to move out. It is human nature that one is prepared to put up with known difficulties rather than face unknown ones.

Consequences of Localization

Localization, however, is not an unmixed blessing. All the factors mentioned above as the causes of persistence of an industry, are the several advantages afforded by the place in which it has become localized, viz., availability of labour, capital, raw materials, etc., and the benefit of specialized transport, subsidiary industries, technical journals, associations, etc. Besides, there are ample opportunities for exchange of ideas: quality can be improved, costs lowered and common problems thoroughly thrashed out and successfully solved. Labour of that category is sure to find employment in that place. Localization, however, is not an unmixed blessing. Dependence of a place on one industry is dangerous. If the industry happens to be in a depressed state, all the people depending on the main as well as subsidiary industries will suffer. It is like placing all the eggs in one basket. Further, there is little scope for the employment of any other type of labour. The specialized labour loses mobility and may not find alternative openings.

Remedy

The obvious remedy is to start supplementary and subsidiary and other allied industries. The establishment of such industries goes a long way in mitigating the difficulties arising out of the localization of industries and removing the evils.

Decentralization of Industry

Several developments have taken place in modern times, which have displaced old industries from their native soil and planted them in other lands. The development in the means of transportation is one such factor. This development is really a double-edged weapon. On the one hand, it has helped the localized industries to keep to their original home. If the supply of raw materials, on the basis of which they originally developed, has been exhausted, the materials can be brought there. If the market, originally wide enough, is no longer adequate, distant markets can be tapped through improved transport. But, on the other hand, improvement in transport has also helped the transfer of heavy plants to distance countries, which are better markets, *e.g.,* Swedish match factories were started in India. Labour and technicians can also move out.

Further, the rise of rents, congestion, high land prices and higher municipal taxation in the industrial centres have driven out the old established industries, *e.g.,* cotton mills were shifted from Mumbai to Ahmedabad, Sholapur and other places.

Finally, the advent of electricity, which can be carried to a long distance, has enabled the industries to start at more convenient places. They need no longer cling to the source of power, say coal mines, and suffer from other handicaps.

Conclusion

Owing to the causes stated above, several of the factors, which were responsible for localization, have ceased to operate and industries have been decentralized.

5.7 CAPITAL

Meaning

Capital refers to that part of a man's wealth which is used in producing further wealth or which yields an income. But capital is not a primary or original factor of production. It is a 'produced means of production'. The term 'capital' is generally used for capital goods, *e.g.,* plant and machinery, tools and accessories, stocks of raw materials, goods in process, and fuel. The raw materials are used up in a single act of consumption. Moreover, money spent on them is fully recovered when goods made with them are sold in the market. But plant and machinery is a permanent investment.

Fig. 5.7. Machines are capital goods used for production.

Is land capital? Land is not regarded as capital because (*a*) land is a free gift of nature but capital is man-made or is a 'produced' agent of production; (*b*) capital is perishable, whereas land is indestructible and permanent; (*c*) capital is mobile but land has no mobility; (*d*) the amount of capital can be increased but the quantity of land is fixed and limited; and (*e*) income from capital is uniform whereas rent of land varies.

Importance of Capital

Capital plays a vital role in the modern productive system. Production without capital is hard for us even to imagine. Nature cannot furnish goods and materials to man unless he has the tools and machines for mining, farming, fishing, etc.

Because of its strategic role in raising productivity, capital occupies a central position in the process of economic development. In fact, capital formation is the very core of economic development.

Another important economic role of capital formation is the creation of employment opportunities in the country. Capital formation creates employment at two stages. First, when the capital is produced, some workers have to be employed to make capital goods like machinery, factories, dams, irrigation works, etc. Secondly, more men have to be employed when capital has to be used for producing further goods.

5.8 CAPITAL FORMATION

Importance of Capital Formation

Capital accumulation is the very core of economic development. It may be a predominantly private enterprise system like the American, or a communist economy like the Soviet Union economic development cannot take place without capital accumulation. No economic development is possible without the construction of irrigation works, the production of agricultural tools and implements, land reclamation, building of dams, bridges and factories with machines installed in them, roads, railways, and airports, ships and harbors—all the "produced means of further production" associated with high levels of productivity. It seems unquestionable that the insufficiency of capital accumulation is the most serious limiting factor in underdeveloped countries. In the view of many economists, capital formation occupies the central and strategic position in the process of economic development.

Meaning of Capital Formation

Capital formation means the increase in the stock of real capital in a country. In other words, capital formation involves making of more capital goods such as machines, tools, factories, transport equipment, materials, electricity, etc., which are all used for further production of goods. For making additions to the stock of capital, saving and investments are essential. Professor Nurkse has, therefore, defined capital formation as follows:

"The meaning of 'capital formation' is that society does not apply the whole of its current productive activity to the needs and desires of immediate consumption, but directs part of it to the making of capital goods: tools and instruments, machines, and transport facilities, plant and equipment —all the various forms of real capital that can so greatly increase the efficiency of productive effort. The essence of the process, then, is the diversion of a part of society's currently available resources for the purpose of increasing the stock of capital goods so as to make possible an expansion of consumable output in the future."

It is thus evident that in order to accumulate capital goods some current consumption has to be sacrificed. The greater the extent that people are willing to abstain from present consumption, the greater the extent that society will devote resources to new capital formation.

From the above, it is clear that saving is essential for capital formation. But in a monetary economy, savings may not directly and automatically result in the production of capital goods. Savings must be invested in order to have capital goods. In a modern economy, where savings and investment are done mainly by two different classes of people, there must be certain means or mechanism whereby savings of the people are obtained and mobilized in order to give them to the businessmen or entrepreneurs to invest in capital goods. Therefore, in a modern free-enterprise economy the process of capital formation consists of the following three stages:

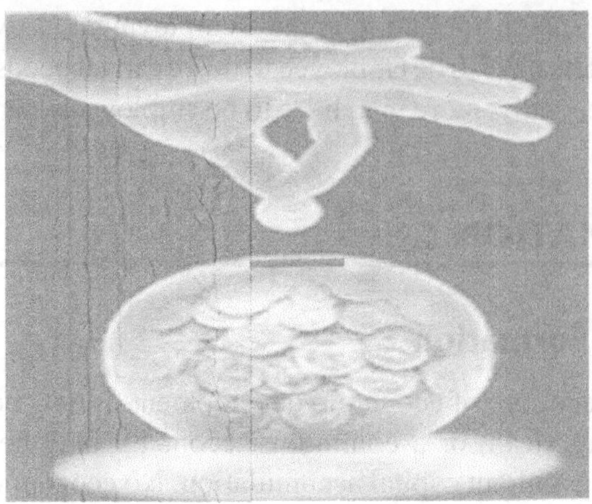

Fig. 5.8. Savings depends on power and willingness to save.

***(i)* Creation of Savings:** Savings are done by individuals or households. They save by not spending all their income on consumer goods. When individuals or households save, they release resources from the production of consumer goods. Workers, natural resources, materials, etc., thus released are made available for the production of capital goods.

The level of savings in a country depends upon the power to save and the will to save. The power to save or saving capacity of an economy mainly depends upon the average level of income and the distribution of national income. The higher the level of income, the greater will be the amount of savings. The countries having higher levels of income are able to save more. That is why the rate of savings in the U.S.A. and Western European countries is much higher than that in under-developed and poor countries like India, Further, the greater the inequalities of income, the greater will be the amount of savings in the economy.

Apart from the power to save, the total amount of savings also depends upon the will to save. Various personal, family, and national considerations induce the people to save. People save in order to provide for themselves in old age and unforeseen emergencies. Some people desire to save a large sum to start a business or to expand the existing business. Moreover, people want to make provision for education, marriage, and a good start in business for their children.

Further, it may be noted that savings may be either voluntary or forced. Voluntary savings are those, which people do of their own free will. As explained above, voluntary savings depend upon the power to save and the will of the people to save. On the other hand, taxes by the Government represent forced savings.

Furthermore, savings may be done not only by households but also by business enterprises and government. Business enterprises save when they do not distribute the whole of their profits but retain a part of them in the form of undistributed profits. They then use these undistributed profits for investment in real capital.

The third source of savings is government. The government savings constitute the money collected as taxes and the profits of public undertakings. The greater the amount of taxes collected and profits made, the greater will be the government savings. The savings so made can be used by the government for building up new capital goods like factories, machines, roads, etc., or it can lend them to private enterprise to invest in capital goods.

***(ii)* Mobilization of Savings:** The next step in the process of capital formation is that the savings of the households must be mobilized and transferred to businessmen or entrepreneurs who require them for investment. In the capital market, funds are supplied by the individual investors (who may buy securities or shares issued by companies), banks, investment trusts, insurance companies, finance corporations, government, etc. If the rate of capital formation is to be stepped up, the development of capital market is very necessary. A well-developed capital market will ensure that the savings of the society will be mobilized and transferred to the entrepreneurs or businessmen who require them.

***(iii)* Investment of Savings in Real Capital:** For savings to result in capital formation, they must be invested. In order that the investment of savings should take place, there must be a good number of honest and dynamic entrepreneurs in the country who are able to take risks and bear uncertainty of production.

Given that a country has got a good number of entrepreneurs, investment will be made by them only if there is sufficient inducement to invest. Inducement to invest depends on the marginal efficiency of capital *i.e.,* the prospective rate of profit on the one hand and the rate of interest on the other.

But of the two determinants of inducement to invest—the marginal efficiency of capital and the rate of interest, it is the former, which is of greater importance. Marginal efficiency of capital depends upon the cost or supply price of capital as well as the expectations of profits. Fluctuations in investment are mainly due to the changes in expectations regarding profits. But it is the size of the market, which determines the scope for profitable investment. Thus, the primary factor which determines the level of investment or capital formation in an economy is the size of the market for goods.

Foreign Capital

Capital formation in a country can also take place with the help of foreign capital, *i.e.,* foreign savings.

Foreign capital can take the form of (*a*) direct private investment by foreigners, (*b*) loans or grants by foreign governments, (*c*) Loans by international agencies like the World Bank.

There are very few countries, which have successfully marched on the road to economic development without making use of foreign capital in one form or the other. India is receiving a good amount of foreign capital from abroad for investment and capital formation under the Five-Year Plans.

In recent days foreign capital is playing a vital role in the economic development of less developed countries. After the GATT agreement as well as the establishment of WTO (World Trade Organization) on 1st January 1995, there is an enormous increase of foreign capital from developed countries to developing countries.

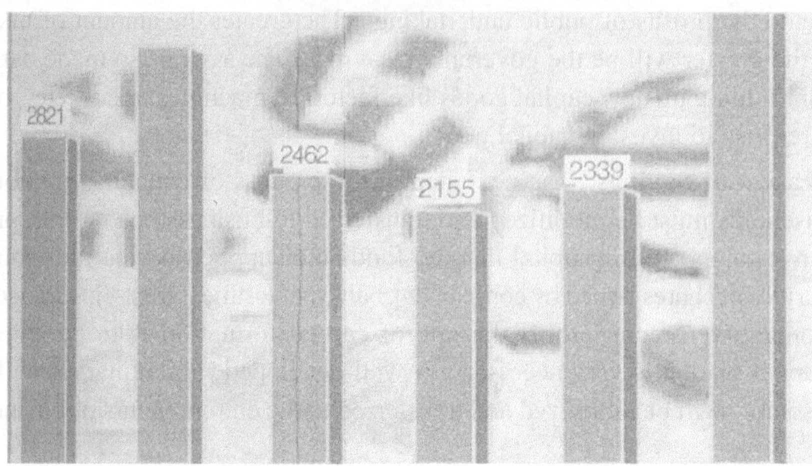

Fig. 5.9. Net inflow of foreign capital.

Foreign capital is divided into two categories; viz.

(*a*) Foreign Direct Investments, (FDI) and,

(*b*) Foreign Institutional Investments (FIIs).

(***a***) **Foreign Direct Investment:** (FDI) This is a very important aspect of foreign capital. The FDI means the foreigners are allowed investment either in collaboration with public and government (including both state and central) or directly starting of factories, mills, departmental stores, chain stores, and infrastructure and so on. The FDI plays a vital role in the economic development of a country. Due to FDI the employment and economic growth of an economy increases. This further with multiplier effects accelerates the economic growth and also cumulative economic process take place. For developing countries this is a very good opportunity. There is a direct relation between FDI and economic development.

(***b***) **Foreign Institutional Investments (FIIs):** In this category of foreign capital the foreigners either directly or through their institutions invest in the portfolio investment of an economy. This may help the economy or may harm the economy. Generally the investment in stock exchange is of speculative nature. Due to the liberalization and globalization policy the world-over the FIIs are increasing their investment in developing countries. It has accelerated the tempo of speculation in almost all the markets of the world.

Along with the FIIs there is another kind of investment in India, that is the NRI (Non Resident Indian) deposits or investments. If it is in government bonds, than it may not be a non-speculative, otherwise it may be of FIIs type of investment.

Deficit Financing: Deficit financing, *i.e.,* newly created money, is another source of capital formation in a developing economy. Owing to very low standard of living of the people, the extent to which voluntary savings can be mobilized is very much limited. Also, taxation beyond limit is quite unpleasant and therefore politically inexpedient. Deficit financing is, therefore, the method on which the government can fall back to obtain funds.

However, the danger inherent in this source of development finance is that it may lead to inflationary pressure in the economy, although a certain measure of deficit financing can be had without creating much pressure.

There is specially a good case for using deficit financing to utilize the existing and under-employed labour in schemes which yield quick returns so that the inflationary potential of deficit financing may be neutralized by an increase in the supply of output in the short-run.

Disguised Unemployment: Another source of capital formation is to mobilize the saving potential that exists in the form of disguised unemployment. Surplus agricultural workers can be transferred from the agricultural sector to the non - agricultural sector without diminishing agricultural output. The objective is to mobilize these unproductive workers and employ them on various capital-creating projects, such as roads, canals, building of schools, health centres and funds for flood control in which they do not require much more capital to work with.

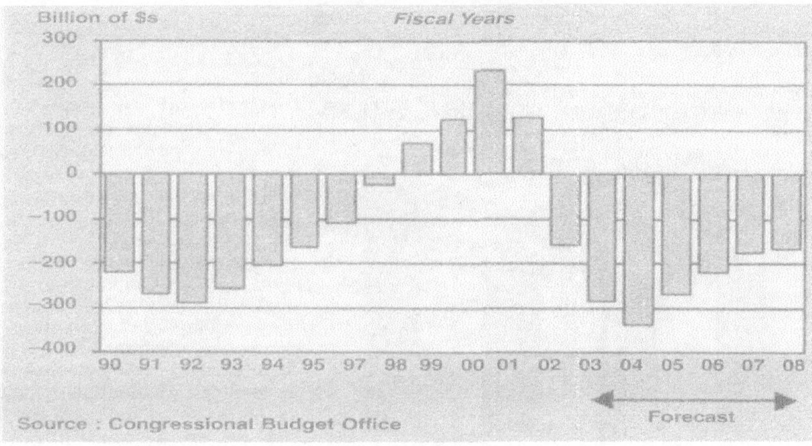

Fig. 5.10. Big budget deficits.

5.9 ENTERPRISE

The fourth factor of production is enterprise, which is supplied by the entrepreneur.

Entrepreneur's Role

The role that the entrepreneur plays consists in co-ordinating and correlating the other factors of production. He starts the work, organizes and supervises it. He undertakes to remunerate all the factors of production: to pay rent to the landlord, interest on the borrowed capital, and wages to labour, and pays them in advance of the sale of goods. The residue, if any, is his. Nothing may be left after he has made the necessary payments. In that case, his venture will have been miscarried. But it is also possible that he may be lucky enough to make a handsome profit. Whatever may be the outcome, he must be prepared to accept it. He thus takes the final responsibility of the business.

If he has anticipated the consumers' wishes right and interpreted them correctly, he is amply rewarded. Organizing and risk-taking, or 'uncertainty is bearing', as it is sometimes called, are the two chief functions of the modern entrepreneur.

The entrepreneur is the innovator. Innovation by the entrepreneur implies a variety of things. It may mean the introduction of a new method of production or an improvement in the old method. It may consist of the introduction of a new commodity like the transistor radio sets or a new make of an old product, *e.g.,* yet another brand of toothpaste. Innovation may refer to the discovery of new materials; fresh sources of old materials, or new uses for materials or final goods. It also includes the opening up of new markets. Innovation may also take the form of new techniques in the way of administration, finance, marketing, or human relations inside the business and public relations outside, *i.e.,* with suppliers of material and customers of products. It is involved, finally, when new forms of business organizations are instituted, such as chain stores, the merger of several establishments, or a monopolistic combination among producers.

It will be easily understood that uncertainty is inherent in the making of the decisions like those enumerated earlier and also in any innovations that may be adopted. The all–embracing function that the entrepreneur performs is, therefore, that of bearing uncertainty.

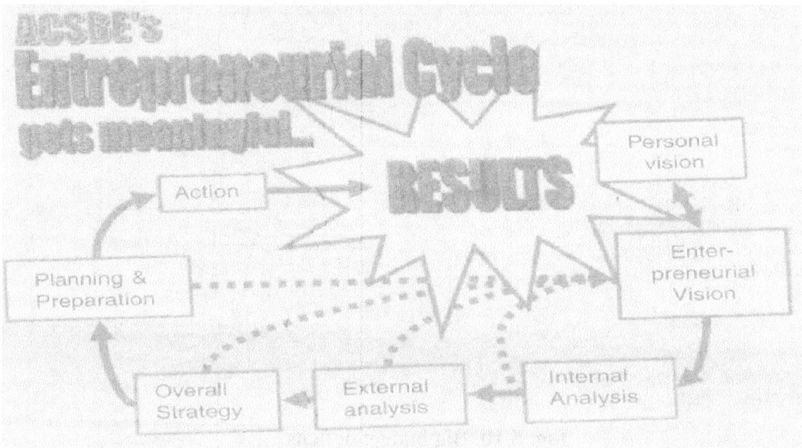

Fig. 5.11. Entrepreneurship.

Schumpeter's Concept of Entrepreneur

J.A. Schumpeter, a German economist, has put more emphasis on the role of an entrepreneur. According to him, and entrepreneur can "change the direction of an economy", in the Japanese economy during the Meiji Era after 1868 the 'Zaibtsu' (Five main Entrepreneurs) played a vital role in its economic development.

According to Schumpeter the entrepreneur is one who combines the factor of production and carries out the production process. He is not just an investor but also one who can be a manager. An entrepreneur is dynamic and possesses initiative and foresight. He is a risk-taker and an innovator. He introduces the five types of innovations:

1. Introduction of a new product
2. Introduction of a new machine
3. Discovery of a new source of supply of raw-materials.
4. Opening up of a new market, and
5. Introduction of scientific methods of organization

As a leader an entrepreneur possesses the following motives, whose main aim is not only to earn profit, but also a:

1. Desire to establish private commercial kingdom.
2. Will to conquer and prove superiority over others.
3. Joy of creation and getting things done.

Schumpeter said, an entrepreneur does not belong to a particular class, "Because being an entrepreneur is not a profession and as a rule not a lasting condition, entrepreneurs do not form a social class in the technical sense like the class of landowners or capitalists or workers."

Summing Up

An entrepreneur's functions may be summarized thus:

(*i*) Initiating a business enterprise by mobilizing and harnessing the necessary productive resources.

(*ii*) Taking the final responsibility of the business enterprise—risk-taking and uncertainty bearing.

(*iii*) An entrepreneur's role as an innovator.

In the words of Professor Harvey Eisenstein, an entrepreneur's role is to "search and discover economic opportunities, evaluate economic opportunities, the financial resources necessary for the enterprise, make time-binding arrangements, take ultimate responsibility for management, be the ultimate uncertainty and/or risk-bearer, provide and be responsible for the motivational system within the firm, search and discover new economic information, translate new information into new markets, techniques and goods and provide leadership for the work groups."

Who is an Entrepreneur in a Joint Stock Company?

The main parties involved in a joint stock company are the shareholders, directors and the management. The shareholders have risked their money but they do not exercise any control over the business except in a very small corporation. There is thus a divorce between the two functions of an entrepreneur, viz., ownership (risk-taking) and control. The shareholders elect the directors who exercise control over the business on behalf of the shareholders. The directors are also usually the biggest shareholders. Thus, they can be considered the entrepreneurs, for they generally initiate the enterprise, mobilize resources and risk their capital, although they do not bear the entire risk. The management runs no risk nor do they exercise the ultimate control. Thus, in a corporation the entrepreneurial functions are shared between the shareholders, the directors and top executives.

Why is There Low Capital Formation in Underdeveloped Countries?

Lack of real capital is so characteristic a feature of all under-developed economies that they are often called "capital poor economies." Low rate of capital formation in under-developed countries is due to the following reasons:

(*i*) **Low Level of Domestic Savings:** In under-developed countries, the level of savings is very low. The main reason is that their level of national income or per capita income is very low. Under-developed countries are, in fact, caught up invicious circle of poverty: Low income–small savings–low investment–less productivity, ending in low income. Apart from the low level of absolute income, their low relative level of real income also reduces their capacity to save. This tendency of the people of under-developed countries to copy the higher levels of consumption prevailing in the advanced countries has been called "international demonstration effect" by Nurkse. The people, who get large incomes, general use much of their income for conspicuous consumption, investment in land and real estate, speculative transaction, inventory accumulation and hoarding of gold and jewellery rather than using it for productive investment.

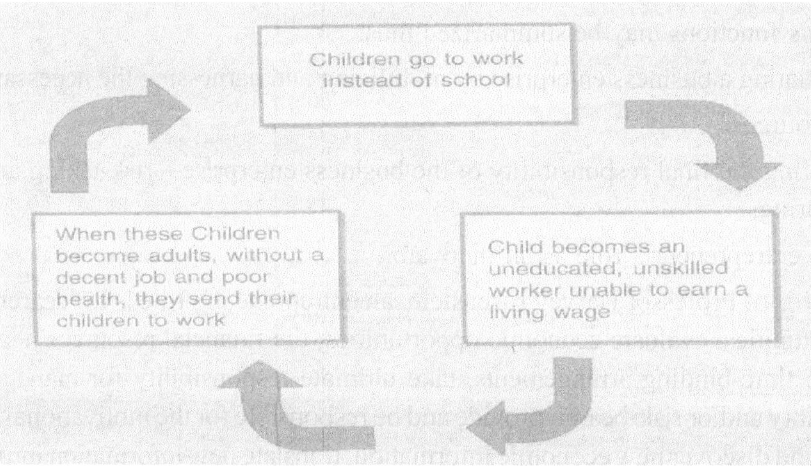

Fig. 5.12. Cycle of poverty and illiteracy.

(*ii*) **Lack of Entrepreneurship:** Another reason is the lack of good entrepreneurs who can invest the savings and carry out innovations. They are not daring enough to bear large risks involved in making capital goods.

(*iii*) **Weak Inducement to Invest:** A vicious circle also operates on the demand side of capital formation. "The inducement to invest may be low because of the small buying power of the people, which is due to their small real income, which again is due to low productivity. The low level of productivity, however, is a result of the small amount of capital used in production, which in its turn may be caused at least partly by the small inducement to invest". According to Nurkse.

Conclusion

Thus, under-developed economies are caught up in the vicious circle of poverty on both the supply and the demand sides of capital formation. Once the vicious circle is broken and the country starts developing, the growth becomes cumulative and then these "vicious circles" become beneficent.

Self-Assessment Questions

1. Indicate the criticism to which the traditional classification of the factors is subjected.
2. What are the peculiarities of traditional factors of production?
3. Distinguish between productive and unproductive labour. What are the factors which determine the efficiency of labour?
4. What is meant by division of labour? Briefly discuss its advantages and disadvantages.
5. "Division of labour is limited by the extent of the market." Discuss.
6. Discuss the causes of localization of industries and its advantages and disadvantages.
7. What are the advantages of decentralization of industries?
8. Discuss the role of the following in capital formation: (*a*) savings; (*b*) investments; (*c*) capital market and finance mechanism; and (*d*) foreign capital.
9. Account for the low rate of capital formation in under-developed countries. How far can disguised unemployment be regarded as a potential source of capital?

   Or

   Suggest measures to step up capital formation in under-developed countries with special reference to India.
10. Explain the role of machinery in large-scale production and state the economic and social consequences of mechanization.
11. "The introduction of machinery may create short-run unemployment while creating general long-term employment". Discuss.
12. Examine the role and functions of an entrepreneur in a capitalist economy.
13. Explain the concept of foreign direct investment and foreign institutional investment.
14. Discuss the main features of Schumpeter's importance to entrepreneurs and innovations.

Unit **6** **FORMS OF ENTREPRENEURIAL ORGANIZATION**

6.1 INTRODUCTION

Organization of business in modern times assumes several forms, *e.g.,* sole proprietorship, individual entrepreneur or one-man business, partnership, joint-stock companies, industrial combination, co-operative enterprises and state enterprises.

6.2 INDIVIDUAL ENTREPRENEUR

The organizer of the 'one-man' concern invests his own capital and may also borrow some. He rents a shop and hires the service of an assistant, if necessary. He himself makes purchases and personally attends to the sales. He is his own manager. He initiates, organizes, directs all economic activity and takes the entire risks. Thus, the sole proprietor combines in his person the functions of capital, enterprise and even labour in many cases.

Advantages

This form of business organization offers several advantages:

(*i*) The combination of financial interest and the sole responsibility for running the business is conductive to efficiency.

(*ii*) All transactions and operations are, through prudent management, performed in the most economical manner; and wastage of all kinds is eliminated.

(*iii*) It is possible to pay personal attention to all customers satisfy them at minimum cost.

(*iv*) This form of business is also the easiest to start and the easiest to wind up.

Limitations

But there are limitations also which the individual entrepreneur suffers:

(*i*) The capital at the command of the sole proprietor is generally meager.

(*ii*) Also, one man feels very much handicapped in looking after the many sides of his business.

(*iii*) No first-rate business can be built up in this way.

(*iv*) It cannot enjoy the economies of large-scale production.

6.3 PARTNERSHIP

Limitations of the one-man business give rise to another form of business organization, *viz.*, partnership. Two, three or more people combine, contribute capital, and agree to share profits and bear losses in agreed proportions.

Advantages

This form of organization offers several advantages over the one-man business:

(*i*) It commands larger resources.

(*ii*) It is possible to establish wider personal contacts.

(*iii*) Business can be run on a larger-scale enjoying the various economies of 'scale'.

(*iv*) The union of ownership and management fasters efficient and economical working.

(*v*) Partnership responds promptly to changes in business conditions and is very highly adaptable. There is no red-tapism.

(*vi*) The existence of unlimited liability curbs the speculative tendencies of the partners, and prevents the launching of rash and risky enterprises.

Disadvantages

If the partners work in close and cordial co-operation, the business is bound to go up. But, this is a very big if.

(*i*) In actual practice, partners behave in a selfish manner, doing the minimum and trying to get the maximum out of the business.

(*ii*) According to the law, partnership must be dissolved in the event of a partner's retirement, death, bankruptcy or lunacy. There is thus no continuity of existence.

(*iii*) But the greatest handicap is the unlimited liability. The unlimited liability makes the policy of the firm non-enterprising.

(*iv*) Further, the partnership resources are too limited to enable the concern to do big business.

On the whole, this form of organization cannot meet the requirements of modern trade and industry.

6.4 JOINT-STOCK COMPANY

The joint-stock company is undoubtedly the most important type of business organization today. It seeks to rectify the disabilities and the handicaps of the partnership arising out of small financial resources and limited business talent.

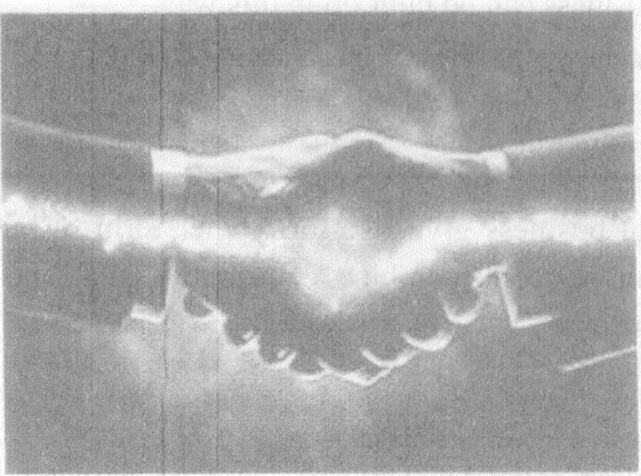

Fig. 6.1. Joint stock company.

Merits

There are several advantages which can be claimed for this form of organization:

(*i*) The company business is generally a large-scale business. Therefore, it enjoys all the economies of large-scale production, internal and external, *e.g.*, economies arising from the use of specialized labour and machinery, economy of space, of buying and selling, publicity, research or experiments, etc.

(*ii*) Besides these, there are several advantages peculiar to the organization itself. Shares are of small denomination, and they suit all pockets and temperaments ranging from the cautious to the speculative. Hence, large capital can be raised.

(*iii*) The fact that liability is limited and shares are transferable induces many people to subscribe to the share capital. Thus, small and scattered amounts of capital are mobilized and turned into productive channels. The habit of thrift is strengthened.

(*iv*) The limitation of liability enables new risks to be taken and many new fields of business to be opened out. The actual loss, if any, is widely distributed. The limited liability principle encourages the prospective investor to invest freely. He need not be afraid of losing all he has. This also helps in raising large capital.

(*v*) From the point of view of the individual investor, too, it has great advantages. Not only is his liability limited, but he is also enabled to spread out his investment. He need not place all his eggs in one basket. Further, he is not wedded to one company for good. Whenever he wishes to leave, he can sell his shares.

(*vi*) Unlike the partnership, the company is a legal person apart from the shareholders or directors. It can sue and be sued upon. It thus enjoys a perpetual existence. Further, it is on account of it's ever–lasting existence that the investors can be persuaded to invest money even though for years there may be no prospect of profit.

(*vii*) Separation of functions has been effected between the capitalist and the entrepreneur. This specialization has enhanced productive efficiency, because formerly the capitalist often lacked business ability, while the entrepreneur often lacked capital. This principle, therefore, is the secret of economic progress of the nations.

(*viii*) The management is democratic, efficient and economical. The directors are elected by the shareholders. They are supposed to be persons with wider vision, outstanding administrative ability and business acumen. Their expert advice and guidance are available to the company at a very moderate cost.

Demerits

But there is the other side too:

(*i*) The management is democratic only in theory. The directors are practically self-appointed, and they remain there as long as they choose. For practical purposes, the shareholders have little voice.

(*ii*) Some of the directors may be unscrupulous and exploit the unwary investor. They may use inside knowledge for their own benefit. For instance, they may falsely inform that the company is going to fail and when the value of shares goes down, they purchase them.

Fig. 6.2. Consumer store.

(*iii*) Fraudulent publicity deceives the public. Rosy pictures given in the prospectus are sometimes misleading.

(*iv*) The directors are often lawyers or doctors and have no business experience or knowledge. Their only qualification is the share qualification. Such directors may not prove competent.

(*v*) Business is de-personalized. The owners of business, *i.e.,* the shareholders, are concerned only with profit. The welfare of the employees is utterly neglected. The paid managers express their helplessness. This loss of human touch is a great loss. The business becomes purely a mercenary affair.

(*vi*) The liability being limited and the shares being transferable, the shareholders take no interest in the company. Few of them attend the shareholders' meetings. Their apathy throws all the powers in the hands of a few directors. Thus, the company loses its democratic character.

(*vii*) Sometimes the directors launch rash enterprises, because it is easy to play ducks and drakes with other people's money.

(*viii*) The organization is too unwieldy. It cannot take quick decisions. It is only suited to a business which can be reduced to set rules, which are both fool-proof and knave-proof. This form of organization is not fit for pioneering work, or where changing conditions require constant changes in policy of production, or where customers are won with difficulty and lost at the slightest pretext.

Conclusion

Inspite of these short comings, it must be said that, in the absence of the joint-stock principal, industrial development and efficient exploitation of the natural resources of a country would not have been possible. It has proved to be a powerful and an efficient engine of economic growth.

6.5 CO-OPERATIVE ENTERPRISE

Producers' Co-operation

As distinguished from the ordinary 'capitalist' enterprise, there is the co-operative enterprise. The workers are painfully aware of the fact that the entrepreneur takes away the lion's share of profits. Being convinced that they could themselves run the industry without the aid of the entrepreneur, the workers decide to take up the entrepreneurial work. They contribute some capital themselves and borrow the rest; they elect their own foremen and managers and employ some staff. After paying all expenses, interest on capital, salaries and wages, the profits are divided among themselves. This type of co-operation is called the Productive Co-operation or Producers' Co-operation.

Producers' Co-operation has been generally a failure. The reasons are not far to seek. With the disappearance of the entrepreneur profits also disappear. It is his initiative, power of direction and organizing ability which produce profits. The workers are not in a mood to pay well to their managers. The elected foremen are not able to enforce discipline over their own people. Everybody's business is nobody's business. It's not surprising that there are no profits.

Consumers' Co-operation

There is another type of co-operation which has a long record of success. It is Consumers' Co-operation. The arrangement is that the consumers of a locality contribute capital in small shares and start a store of their own. The co-operative store buys goods from wholesalers like other dealers, and sells these goods to their members at the ordinary market rates. Profits are distributed among the members in proportion to their purchases or, what is more common, in proportion to the share capital. Generally, share capital is equally contributed and profits are, therefore, also equally divided among members.

These co-operative stores have been a splendid satisfied success and some of them count thousands among their members. In several cases, they have not satisfied themselves with merely retailing of consumers' goods but have added their own manufacturing organizations. They are run on ordinary capitalist lines, employing high-grade managers working under the control of able committees.

The co-operative movement has proved specially suitable for agricultural and allied occupations. It was successfully applied first in Germany and Denmark, and it has now spread to almost every country. In India, Co-operative Departments are functioning in every state. Mostly these are agricultural credit societies, but non-credit and non-agricultural societies are also being established. Special attention is being paid to the establishment of co-operative farms and service co-operatives under the Five-Year Plans.

6.6 STATE ENTERPRISE

In every country, there are public undertakings run by Central or State Governments or local bodies. Postal and telegraph arrangements are generally under the Central Government; and public utility services like water supply, gas, electric supply or tram or bus services are managed by municipal corporations.

The organization of state enterprise is on the same lines as private enterprise with the usual paraphernalia of general manager, foremen, works manager, accountants, treasurer, departmental heads, and so on. The work is done generally in the same manner as in a joint-stock company.

But there is a fundamental difference. All the employees are government servants with a fixed tenure and the prospect of getting a pension on retirement. The capital is provided from the state coffers, which comes ultimately from the tax-payers. The profits, if any, too, go to the state.

Fig. 6.3. Bharat-heavy electronics Ltd.

Merits

A state enterprise has certain advantages of its own. The credit of the government stands higher than that of any private individual or company. The state has, therefore, a special facility in raising capital and on favourable terms.

In under-developed countries like India, the state has a special role to play in creating an infrastructure of overhead capital like the development of means of transport and communications. These enterprises require large amounts of capital and are generally not sufficiently productive (in the narrow sense of the term) to yield enough profits to attract private capital. Yet they are crucial for the future development of the country. Hence, government has to step in to establish these enterprises. From this point of view, public enterprise assumes a greater importance in under-developed countries than in the developed countries.

Moreover, a modern state is called upon to reduce inequalities in income and wealth. The traditional weapons of fiscal policy and progressive taxation, however, have serious limitations in being used as an instrument of bringing about greater equality. Therefore, there are many people who advocate the state operation of enterprises, the state appropriating to itself the profits of such undertakings.

Further, government is in a position to command the best talent. Government service attracts first-class brains. There is a certain glamour about government service. Thus, from the point of view of the human factor, too, the state enterprise is favourably placed.

The state enterprise is generally a monopoly. It has all the advantages of monopoly. The custom is assured. Expenditure on publicity is unnecessary. Better service at less cost is the usual rule in a government undertaking.

Demerits

Economists generally agree that governmental machinery, in the matter of running a business, compares very unfavourably with private management. The government manager's tenure is fixed. He gets a fixed annual increment, and will get promotion according to seniority. He can not, therefore, be expected to show the same degree of initiative or hard work as the manager of a private company. The latter may receive notice to quit any fine morning, if the management is convinced that he is not doing his best.

A government employee will not be much interested in lowering costs or improving the methods, because he himself will gain nothing thereby. The state employee, who has no ambition to rise, can flout the senior officers. At the most, he will be transferred or his increment stopped if it comes to the worst. He does not consider himself the servant of any particular person, but the servant of the impersonal state and that makes all the difference.

In a government-managed enterprise, routine replaces responsibility. There is the tyranny of the desk or red-tape. There are exasperating delays. A paper has to pass through very many hands, none making any material alteration or improvement. Frequent transfers, nepotism and entry into service by the back door, merit being not necessarily the test of promotion, are some of the drawbacks in a government enterprise.

If there are losses nobody seems to bother. There is no counterpart of the shareholders whom the directors have to face every year. The tax-payers are dumb. If there is loss, nobody really feels that it is his loss, their representatives in the legislature will no doubt raise a hue and cry, yet the government usually has a comfortable majority, and the government caravan continues to move on.

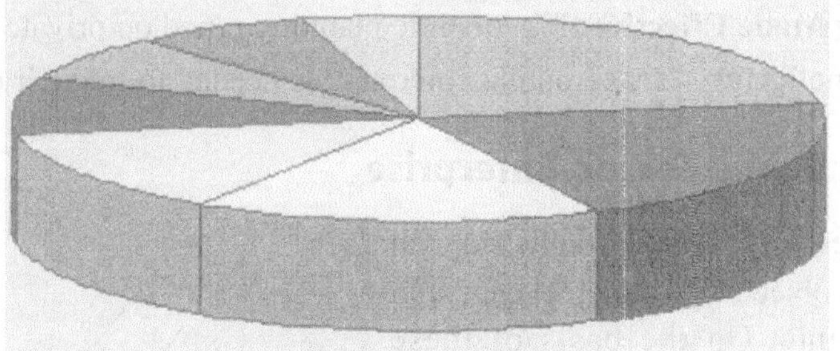

Fig. 6.4. Investment in various areas.

Forms of Organization of Public Enterprises

Public enterprises may be organized as (*a*) Departmental *i.e.*, run by a Government department *e.g.*, Railways and Posts and Telegraph in India, (*b*) Corporation *e.g.*, Life Insurance Corporation of India created by a special act of Parliament, (*c*) Limited liability Company registered under the Companies Act.

Role of Public Enterprise in Under-developed Countries

In under-developed countries, public enterprises are badly needed to initiate and accelerate the developmental process. They can promote economic development in the following ways:

(*i*) **By Creating Social and Economic Overheads:** Only state can provide educational facilities and technical training, medical aid and public health measures and develop irrigation and means of transport—all which is indispensable for economic growth.

(*ii*) **By Building Basic Heavy Industries:** It is beyond private enterprise to develop basic heavy industries like iron and steel, heavy electrical and heavy engineering industries. But these are essential for providing a base for industrial development.

(*iii*) **By Optimum Allocation of Resources:** Private enterprise is notorious for misallocation of the country's resources, lured by profit motive. Public enterprise, which is guided by social gain rather than private profit, is needed to correct this tendency and help in bringing about an optimum allocation of resources.

(*iv*) **Ensuring Balanced Regional Growth:** State, as a guardian of people's welfare, takes special pains to develop backward regions. For this purpose, industrial units are deliberately located in backward areas. In this way, regional balanced development is brought about.

(*v*) **Utilizing Surplus Labour for Capital Formation:** The public enterprises favourably located can drain out from the rural areas surplus labour in the form of disguised unemployment and use it more productively. This will promote economic development.

(*vi*) **Creating Surplus:** The profits of public enterprises are a good source of finance for economic development.

(*vii*) **Planning Made Effective:** If economic planning relied on private enterprise, it would be very ineffective. Hence public enterprise is needed to make it effective.

Pricing Policy of Public Sector Enterprise

Public sector enterprises (PSEs) were established with an economic and social objective to be achieved within a particular time-frame. On the basis of these objectives the following price policy was introduced.

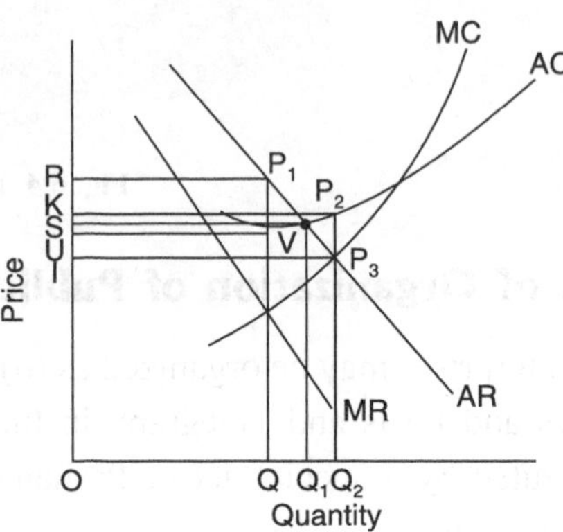

Fig. 6.5. Price vs. quantity.

In the diagram QP_1 is the price per unit. Hence,

$$ORP_1Q - OUVQ = RP_1VU.$$

$$T_R - T_C = (\pi)$$

Hence, the government is able to make abnormal profit.

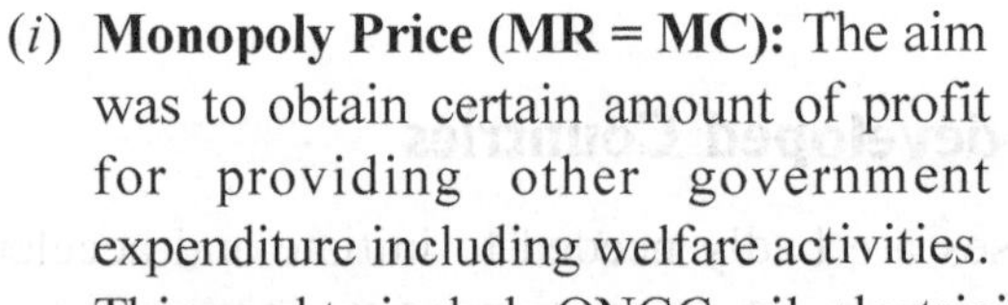

(*i*) **Monopoly Price (MR = MC):** The aim was to obtain certain amount of profit for providing other government expenditure including welfare activities. This used to include ONGC, oil, electricity etc.

(*ii*) **No Profit no Losses Basis (AR = AC):** In this the aim of the government was to provide the services without earning profit but to recover the cost of providing these services. In other words no loss no profit.

In this case 'P_2Q_1' price is charged. Hence

$$OSP_2Q_1 - OSP_2Q_1 = \text{Zero}$$

$$T_R - T_C = 0 \ (\pi = 0).$$

(*iii*) **Marginal Cost Pricing:** In this case the government is charging only the marginal cost. In other words AR = MC. The government is charging only the amount of additional cost incurred to manufacture the additional unit.

$$T_R - T_C = \pi$$

$$OIP_3Q_2 - OKJP_3Q_2 = IKJP_3$$

The amount of money $IKJP_3$ is the subsidy provided by the government.

Disinvestment Policy of Pubic Sector Enterprises

Immediately after independence the government put more emphasis on the socialistic pattern of the society. Those days the economy was picking up and required inducement. The Keynesian concept of welfare state was applied in different countries of the world. The role of public sector enterprises was to (*i*) bring about basic and key industries, (*ii*) accelerate the role of economic growth, (*iii*) achieve balanced regional development, (*iv*) develop infrastructure, (*v*) mobilize capital formation, (*vi*) reduce the concentration of economic power etc.

Up to 1970, the public sector enterprises started making good progress and contributed a lot to different economic variables. Later due to certain amount of inefficiency, political interference, problem of finance, poor and non-cordial industrial relations, these units started incurring heavy losses.

On the other hand due to the signing of GATT agreement and the new industrial policy of 1991, the government initiated a process of disinvestment in public sector units. Though the privatization and disinvestment policy was started in 1984, the objectives of the government completely changed. The government aimed at:

- Concentrating on other areas of human development.
- The amount of money received by means of disinvestment would be invested on the priority sector, which would help in the economic development process.
- To reduce the burden on budget which was due to the losses of public sector enterprise.
- Modernization of existing profit-making public sector units.
- Other social security measures of displaced workers.

Though the policy is good in light of the competitive nature of the economy due to globalization and liberalization, but the disinvestment policy has raised many questions. How the government will make best use of these resources, so that the money should not be misused? On the other hand the government must see that the employees of these units are not put to hardship. Proper policy may give benefits; otherwise private sector as well as foreign sector may take undue advantage and exploit the economy.

Self-Assessment Questions

1. Discuss the different forms of business organization.
2. What are the merits and demerits of joint-stock companies?
3. Explain, pricing policy of public-undertakings. Discuss the role of public enterprises in under-developed countries.

Unit 7

POPULATION THEORIES

7.1 INTRODUCTION

An economy supports population, but population too, in a sense, supports the economy. It is the aim of an economy to supply people's wants for goods and services, but the people too make an important contribution to the productive capacity of an economy. A study of population trends, therefore, is of great importance in the study of economic theory.

There are two well-known theories of population: The Malthusian Theory and Optimum Theory. We shall now briefly discuss them here.

Fig. 7.1. Malthus.

7.2 MALTHUSIAN THEORY

The most well-known theory is the Malthusian theory of population. Thomas Robert Malthus wrote his "Essay on the Principle of Population" in 1798 and modified some of his conclusions in the next edition in 1803. The rapidly increasing population of England, encouraged by a misguided poor law, distressed him very deeply. He feared that England was heading for a disaster, and he considered it his solemn duty to warn his countrymen. He developed "the strange contrast between excessive care in breeding animals and carelessness in breeding men".

His theory is very simple. To use his own words: "By nature human food increases in a slow arithmetical ratio; man himself increases in a quick geometrical ratio unless want and vice stop him. The increase in numbers is necessarily limited by the means of subsistence. Population invariably increases when the means of subsistence increase, unless prevented by powerful and obvious checks."

Malthus based his reasoning on the biological fact that every living organism tends to multiply to an unimaginable extent. A single pair of thrushes would multiply into 19,500,000 within the life of the first pair and 20 years later to 1,200,000,000,000,000,000,000, and if they stood shoulder to shoulder about one in every 150,000 would be able to find space on the whole surface of the globe. According to Huxley's estimate, the descendants of a single greenfly, if all survived and multiplied, would, at the end of one summer, weigh down the population of China! Human beings are supposed to double every 25 years and a couple can increase to the size of the present population in 1,750 years!

Such is the prolific nature of every species including man. The power of procreation is inherent, and must find expression. Cotillion says, "Men multiply like mice in a barn." Production of food, on the other hand, is subject to the law of diminishing returns. On the basis of these two premises, Malthus concluded that population tended to outstrip the food supply. If preventive checks, like avoidance of marriage, are not exercised, then positive checks, like war, famine and disease, will operate.

The theory propounded by Malthus can be reduced to the following four propositions:

(*i*) Food is necessary to the life of man and, therefore, exercises a strong check on population. In other words, population is necessarily limited by the means of subsistence (*i.e.,* food).

(*ii*) Human population increases faster than food production. Whereas population increases in geometric progression, the food production increases in arithmetic progression.

(*iii*) Population always increases when the means of subsistence increase unless prevented by some powerful and obvious checks.

(*iv*) There are two types of checks which can keep population on a level with the means of subsistence. They are the preventive and positive checks.

The first proposition is that the population of a country is limited by the means of subsistence. In other words, the size of population is determined by the availability of food. The greater the food production, the greater the size of population which can be sustained. The check of deaths caused by want of food and poverty would limit the maximum possible population.

The second proposition states that the growth of population will outrun the increase in food production. Malthus thought that man's sexual urge to bear offspring knows no bounds. He seemed to think that there is no limit to the fertility of man. Man multiplies at an enormous rate. But the power of land to produce food is limited. Malthus thought that the law of diminishing returns operated in the field of agriculture and that the operation of this law put a limit on increase in the supply of food.

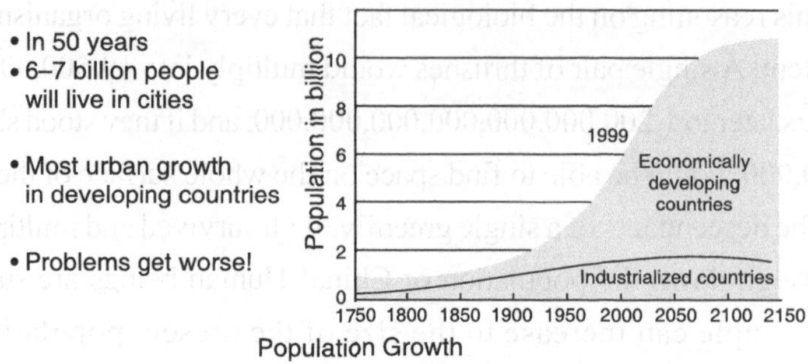

Fig. 7.2. World population growth 1750–2150.

Malthus asserted that the population of a country tends to double every twenty-five years (as it was actually happening in the American Colonies and the UK at that time), but the food supply could be increased much less rapidly. In fact, Malthus observed that the population tended to increase at a geometric rate (2, 4, 8, 16, 32, 64, etc.), but the food supply tended to increase at an arithmetic rate (2, 4, 6, 8, 10, 12). Thus at the end of two hundred years "population would be to the means of subsistence as 259 to 9; in three centuries as 4,096 to 13 and in two thousand years the difference would be incalculable." Therefore, Malthus asserted that the population would ultimately outstrip the food supply. For this reason, Malthus said that people were doomed for-ever to live at a bare subsistence level. When food supply runs short, people must starve and be plunged into misery.

According to the third proposition, as the food supply in a country increases, the people will produce more children and would have larger families. This would increase the demand for food and the availability of food per person will again diminish. Therefore, according to Malthus, the standard of living of the people cannot rise permanently, unless they exercised restraints and limited the size of the family.

Malthus pointed out that there were two possible checks which limited the growth of population: (1) Preventive Checks, and (2) Positive Checks.

Preventive Checks

Preventive checks exercise their influence on the growth of population by bringing down the birth rate. They are applied by man himself. They arise from man's wisdom and foresight. He sees the distress which frequently visits those who have large families. He may think that with a large number of children the standard of living of the family may be lowered. He may think that if he has to support a large family, he will have to face greater difficulties and work harder than otherwise would be the case. He may not be able to give adequate education to his children if there are many of them. Further, he may expose his children to poverty or charity by his inability to provide for them. These considerations may force man to limit his family. Late marriage and self-restraint during married life are the examples of preventive checks applied by man to limit the size of his family.

Fig. 7.3. Food supply for a growing population is a major concern.

The positive checks to population are many and include every cause, whether arising from vice or misery, which in any degree contributes to shorten the natural duration of human life. Unhealthy occupations, hard labour, exposure to inclement of weather, extreme poverty, bad nursing of children, epidemics, wars and famines are some of the examples of positive checks. They all shorten human life and increase the death rate.

Malthus recommended the use of preventive checks if mankind was to escape from the impending misery. If preventive checks were not effectively used, positive checks like diseases, wars and famines would come into operation. As a result, the population would be reduced to the level which can be sustained by the available quantity of food supply.

In the first edition of his book, Malthus laid a great stress on the role of positive checks in keeping the population under control. The following remarks made by him in the first edition of his book show the way in which his mind was working.

"Famine seems to be the last resort, the most dreadful resource of nature. The power of population is so superior to the power of the earth to provide subsistence that premature death must in some shape or the other visit the human race."

In later editions of his book, Malthus softened the harshness of his theory and gave preventive checks a little more importance. Thus, he held out some hope for the human race through the operation of preventive checks reducing the birth rate. But he still remained firm in his pessimistic view. He had little faith in self-restraint and late marriages, since he was of the opinion that sexual urge among people was very strong. Moreover, in these later editions, Malthus also dropped the expressions of geometric and arithmetic progressions but still maintained that the increase in population would exceed the growth in food supply and if unchecked by the use of preventive checks, excessive population would lead to the operation of positive checks to take away the surplus population. It is mainly due to this gloomy doctrine of Malthus that economics was dubbed as a dismal science by eminent writers like Carlyle.

Criticism of Malthusian Theory

The Malthusian theory of population was the subject of a keen controversy. The following are some of the grounds on which it has been criticized.

In the first place, it is pointed out that Malthus's pessimistic conclusions have not been borne out by the history of Western European countries. The gloomy forecast made by Malthus about the miserable conditions of future generations of mankind has not proved true of the Western world. Whereas population has failed to grow as rapidly as predicted by Malthus, production has increased tremendously because of the rapid advances in technology. As a result, living standards of the people have risen instead of falling as was predicted by Malthus.

Secondly, the Malthusian theory of population is based on the law of diminishing returns as applied to agriculture. It is on the basis of this law that Malthus asserted that food production could not keep pace with population growth. By making rapid advances in technology and larger application of capital, advanced countries have been able to increase their production greatly. In fact, in most of the advanced countries, the rate of increase of food production has been much greater than the rate of population growth.

Thus, inventions and improvements in the methods of production have belied the gloomy forecast of Malthus by holding the law of diminishing returns in check almost indefinitely.

Thirdly, Malthus considered food production alone and not the production of wealth in all its forms. He compared the population growth with the increase in food production alone. Malthus held that since land was limited in quantity, food production could not increase faster than population. But, he should have taken into account all types of production in considering the question of the optimum size of the population. England did feel the shortage of land and food. If England had been forced to support its population entirely from her own soil, there can be little doubt that England would have experienced, series of famines by which its growth of population would have been checked.

But England did not experience any such disaster. It is because England industrialized itself by developing its natural resources other than land like coal and iron, and by accumulating man-made capital equipment like factories, tools, machinery, mines, ships and railways. This enabled it to produce plenty of industrial and manufactured goods which it then exported in exchange for food-stuffs from foreign countries. There is thus no food problem in Great Britain.

Thus, Malthus made a mistake in taking agricultural land and food production alone into account while discussing the population question. He should have considered all types of production instead.

Fourthly, Malthus says that the increase in the means of subsistence or of food supplies will cause population to grow so fast that ultimately means of subsistence or food supply will be in level with population and everyone would get only bare minimum subsistence. In other words, according to Malthus, living standards of the people cannot rise in the long-run above the level of minimum subsistence. But, as already pointed out, living standards of the people in the Western world have risen greatly and stand much above the minimum subsistence. There is no evidence of birth rate rising with the increases in the standard of living. Instead, there is ample evidence that birth rates fall as prosperity grows.

In the Western countries, the attitude towards children changed as they prospered. Previously, much attention was not paid to children. But, now parents feel a duty to do as much as they can for each child and, therefore, they decide not to have more children than they can attend to. People now care more for higher standard of living than rearing more children. The extensive use of contraceptives in the Western world has brought down the birth rate there. This change in the attitude towards children and the wider use of contraceptives in the Western world has proved the Malthusian doctrine to be false.

Fifthly, Malthus gave no proof of his assertion that population increased exactly in an arithmetic progression. It has been rightly pointed out that population and food supply does not change in accordance with these mathematical series. Growth of population and food supply cannot be expected to show the precision or accuracy of such series. However, Malthus, in later editions of his book, did not insist on these mathematical terms and only held that there was an inherent tendency in population to outrun the means of subsistence. We have seen that even this is far from being the truth.

The civilized world has kept the population in check. It is, however, to be regretted that population has been increasing at the wrong end. The poor people, who can ill-afford to bring up and educate children, are multiplying, whereas the rich, who can rear quality children, are applying breaks on the increase of the size of their families.

Is Malthusian Theory Valid Today?

We must, however, add that though the gloomy forecasts of Malthus have not turned out to be true due to several factors which have made their appearance only in recent times, yet the essentials of the theory have not been demolished. He said that unless preventive checks were exercised, positive checks would operate. This is true even today.

The Malthusian theory fully applies to countries like India. India is, at present, in that unenviable position which Malthus feared. We have the highest birth-rate and the highest death rate in the world. Poverty, ever-recurring epidemics, famine, communal quarrels are the order of the day. We are deficient in food supply. Our standard of living is incredibly low. Who can say that Malthus was not a true prophet, if not for his country, at any rate for countries like India and China?

7.3 MODERN THEORY OF POPULATION: THE OPTIMUM THEORY

Modern economists have rejected the Malthusian theory of maximum population which, if exceeded, will spell misery in the country. Instead of the maximum population, the modern economists have substituted the idea of the optimum population.

By optimum population is meant the ideal number of the population that a country should have, considering its resources. The optimum means the best and the most desirable size of a country's population. It is the right number. When a country's population is neither too big nor small, but just that much which the country ought to have, it is called the optimum population. Given a certain amount of resources, state of technical knowledge and a certain stock of capital, there will be a definite size of the population at which the real income of goods and services per capita will be the highest. This optimum size. The optimum number can, therefore, be defined as the one at which per capita income is the highest.

Under-population and its Disadvantages

If the population of a country is below the optimum, *i.e.,* below what it ought to be, then the country is said to be under-populated. The number of the people is insufficient to take the fullest possible advantage of the natural and capital resources of the country. This is what happens in a new country. The resources are vast. Much can be produced, but there are not enough men to carry on the work of production efficiently.

Apart from the insufficiency of the working force, the second disadvantage arises from the difficulty of specialization owing to fewness of numbers. By specialization workers acquire job dexterity and increased efficiency in the use of specialized equipment. The community will not be able to reap the economies of large-scale production. Production would thus suffer.

Under such conditions, an increase in population will be followed by an increase in the per capita income. But this increase cannot go on indefinitely. When the shortage of man power has been made up, the per capita income will reach the maximum, and we shall say that the optimum has been reached.

Over-population and its Dangers

If however, the population still goes on increasing and the optimum is exceeded, then we shall have a state of over-population. There will be too many people in the country. The country's resources will not be sufficient to provide gainful employment to all. They will be thinly spread over the teeming millions. The average productivity will diminish. Per capita income will diminish; standard of living will fall; war famine and disease will be constant companions of such a people. These are the symptoms of over-population. Capital formation will be hampered and economic development will be slowed down. The dangers of over-population, however, can be avoided by increasing the supply of capital. There is a race between productivity and population. If productivity wins the race, the danger is averted.

Optimum Level

Let us suppose that natural resources, stock of capital equipment and state of technology remain fixed in a country. Now assume that population which was initially very small relative to these other resources begins to increase. With the increase in population, labour force of the country will also increase. As more and more labour is combined with the fixed amounts of these other resources, output per capita or real income per head will rise. Why? This is because the increase in the quantity of labour will make possible greater degree of specialization and more efficient use of natural and capital resources of the country. With a very small population or labour force, there was a limited scope for specialization, for each worker was required to do all sorts of jobs.

But as population and, therefore, the quantity of labour increases, specialization becomes possible. Each man then need not do all the jobs or make all parts of a good. Everybody can concentrate on the job for which he is the best suited. Division of labour among the different workers, which is made possible by the increase in population, greatly increases the efficiency and productivity of labour.

An increase in population will also permit a fuller utilization of the natural resources and capital equipment. If the quantity of labour is small relative to the natural resources, then even the actually available resources remain under-utilized. Many actually available resources, which can be utilized for producing goods, would not be utilized for lack of labour. Moreover, even the capital equipment will not be fully and effectively utilized if there is a shortage of labour. Technology requires that capital equipment be of a certain minimum size, whether output is relatively small or large. Capital equipment would not be fully utilized if only a small number of workers are available to work with it. In other words, production will be relatively inefficient if the capital equipment is grossly undermanned. If the population increases and more labourers become available to be combined with the given stock of the natural resources and capital equipment, output per capita will rise.

There is another related factor due to which production greatly increases as population expands at initial stages. When population of a country is small, market for the products of industry will also be small. With this limited market for goods, producers will be forced to produce on a small-scale and thus would be unable to take advantage of the economies of large-scale production. As population increases, the market for goods expands and large-scale production becomes possible which adds greatly to the productivity of the economy.

For all these reasons, output per capita will rise for a time as population increases. As the population continuous to increase, a point will finally be reached when capital and natural resources are fully utilized and, therefore, output per capita is the highest. The level of population at which per capita output or real income is the maximum is called the optimum population. If population still goes on increasing, that is, crosses the optimum point, output per capita will start declining. The country would then become over-populated.

Beyond the Optimum Level

Why does the output per capita fall when the optimum point is exceeded? This is because there are now more men in the economy than needed by it. A given amount of capital and natural resources have to be shared out among a large number of workers with the result that each of them has a smaller amount of equipment, materials and natural resources to work with. For this reason the average productivity declines. It is very likely that many people may not get employment and, therefore, add nothing to production. Thus, there is likely to be unemployment of labour. It so happens that when people do not get employment outside agriculture, they cling to agriculture. The pressure of population on land increases. But the additional men, who get employment in agriculture, add nothing to total production. In other words, the marginal productivity of these extra men in agriculture is zero or nearly zero. This is what is commonly known as the phenomenon of disguised unemployment. Disguised unemployment exists in over-populated agriculture from where even if some workers are withdrawn total production does not fall.

When population exceeds the optimum level, it often happens that food problem crops up. An increase in population brings more mouths to eat. But the quantity of land being limited, it cannot meet the increased demand for food.

Low standard of living, open and disguised unemployment, prevalence of disease and food problem are all signs of over-population.

Thus, we see that both under-population and over-population have disadvantages. It is the optimum population, with the highest per capita output, which is the best for a country to aim at.

The concepts of optimum population, under-population and over-population are represented in Fig. 7.4.

In this figure, the size of the population is measured on X-axis and output per capita on Y-axis. It is evident from the figure that, in the beginning, as population increases, output per capita also increases. Output per capita goes on increasing with every increase in population till OM population is reached. At OM level of population, the output per capita MP is the highest. If population now increases beyond OM, output per capita falls. Therefore, OM is the optimum population. If the population of the country is less than OM, it will be under-populated and if the population is more than OM, it will be a case of over-population.

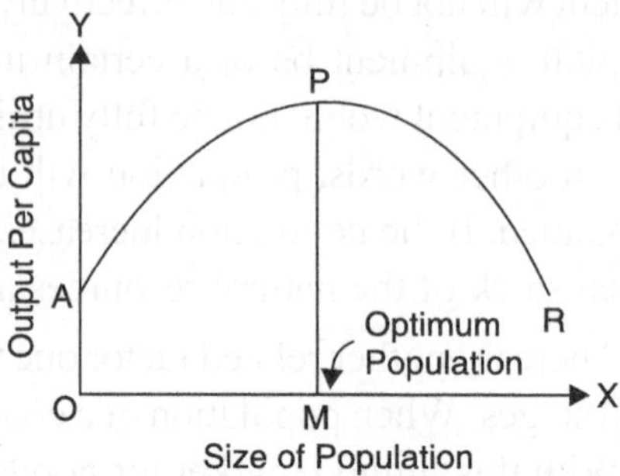

Fig. 7.4. Size of population vs. output per capita.

Optimum Population not Fixed

But it may be noted that the optimum population is not a fixed and rigid number but is moveable. As explained above, optimum population is relative to resources and technology. Given the amount of capital, natural resources and the state of technology, there is a definite size of population at which output per capita will be maximum. But the quantity of capital and natural resources and the state of technology are subjected to change. In fact, changes in them often take place. When there is any change in them, the optimum level of population will also change. For instance, when either there is an increase in the quantity of capital equipment and available natural resources or the country makes progress in technology, per capita output curve will shift upward and to the right with the result that the optimum level of population will increase.

Shifts in Optimum Population

The changes in the per capita output curve, as a result of an increase in resources or progress in technology and their effect on optimum population, are shown in Fig. 7.5. With certain given resources and technology, per capita output curve is AR and the level of optimum population is OM, at which per capita income is MP, which is the highest under the given circumstances.

When the quantity of capital and natural resources increase or technology makes an advance, the output per capita curve shifts upward and to the right and is shown as A′ R′, with per capita output curve A′ R′, optimum population is OM″ which is greater than OM, Now if the resources further increase or technology makes further advancement, the per capita output curve shifts to A″ R″, with the per capita output curve A″R″, optimum population is OM", which is greater than both OM and OM′.

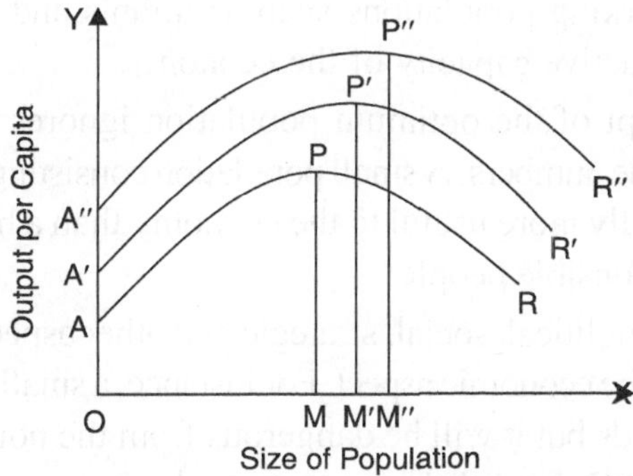

Fig. 7.5. Changes in per capita output curve.

Thus, we see that with different resources or different technology, there will be a different level of optimum population.

Dalton has given a formula with which we can judge the extent to which the actual population of a country deviates from the optimum population. The extent of the deviation is called **maladjustment.** The formula seeks to measure the degree of this maladjustment. The formula is:

$$M = \frac{A - O}{O}$$

where M stands for maladjustment, A stands for actual population and 0 for optimum population. If M is negative, the country is under-populated and if M is positive, the country is over-populated. For instance, if the actual population of a country is 60 crores and its optimum population is 40 crores, then that country is over-populated to the extent of

$$\frac{60 - 40}{40} = \frac{20}{40} = \frac{1}{2}$$

Criteria of Over-population

How to know whether a country is over-populated? Several criteria have been suggested. According to Malthus, the operation of positive checks like war, famine and disease is a sure index of a country being over-populated. Besides this, economists generally suggest several other tests of over-population.

(*i*) The concept is relative to natural resources, capital equipment and state of technical knowledge. It is assumed that they remain the same. Since these factors are subject to constant change, the optimum is a constantly shifting concept. As such we can seldom arrive at a stable optimum which may have significance in economic analysis and practice. Thus, the theory is based on wrong assumptions.

(*ii*) Also, mere size of the population is of little significance. The composition of the population, *e.g.,* age-distribution or distribution as regards workers and non-workers matter a great deal. Even if the population of a country is of the optimum size, the existence of a large number of non-working populations such as infants and the aged, is bound to affect adversely the productive capacity of the economy.

(*iii*) Besides, the concept of the optimum population ignores the quality of the people. It simply focuses on the numbers. A small population consisting of efficient and hardworking people is undoubtedly more useful to the economy than a huge population consisting of lethargic and irresponsible people.

(*iv*) The theory ignores political, social, strategic and other aspects of the population problem and considers only the economic aspect. For instance, a small population may be advocated on economic grounds but it will be dangerous from the point of view of defense. Adam Smith rightly said, "Defense is better than opulence."

(*v*) The concept of the optimum population is only of theoretical interest. Actually, it is not easy to attain the optimum size by reducing population in the case of over-population and increase in it in the case of under-population. Family planning, whether aiming at reducing population or increasing it, is a long drawn affair extending over several generations. Human beings are more influenced by culture and traditions than by rigid government regulation.

Conclusion

Thus, the concept of optimum population is more of theoretical and academic interest than of practical value.

7.4 MALTHUSIAN THEORY AND MODERN THEORY COMPARED

From the study of these theories of population, we may notice some important differences between the two:

(*i*) Malthus focused his attention on food production, whereas the optimum theory takes into consideration economic development in all its aspects.

(*ii*) Malthus seemed to be thinking of a maximum number for a country which, if exceeded, would spell misery. According to the optimum theory, there is no rigidly fixed maximum.

(*iii*) To Malthus famine, war and disease were the indices of over-population. But the optimum theory; tells us that, even in the absence of such distressing phenomena, there can be over-population, provided it can be shown that per capita income has gone down, or that with a decrease in population per capita income will go up.

(*iv*) The modern theory is optimistic, whereas the Malthusian theory is pessimistic in outlook. Malthus was haunted by the fear that population would outstrip food supply and spell misery. The modern economists do not suffer from any such apprehensions. They say that the development of a country's resources can brighten the prospects. "Malthus was obsessed by the fear of an impending economic hell; the proponents of the optimum theory are elated with the hopes of a coming paradise."

7.5 COST-BENEFIT THEORY OF POPULATION

According to this theory the additional population growth is treated in two ways (*i*) as an asset, and (*ii*) as a liability, '*a*' '*b*' and '*c*' are utility derived from additional children.

(*i*) '*a*' is the amount of utility or satisfaction from the possession of an additional child, this remains constant whether to a 'rich' person or to a poor person.

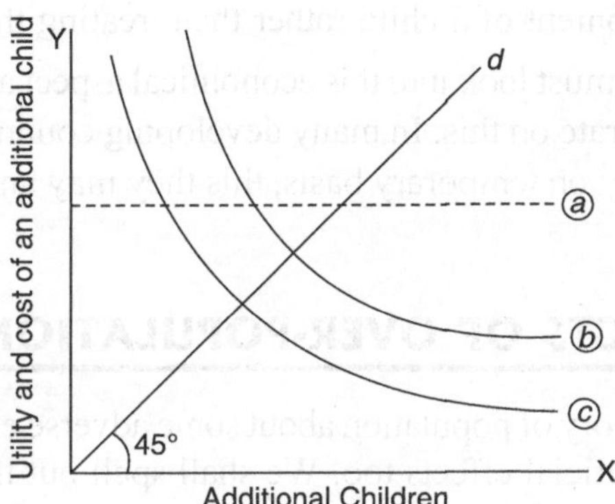

Fig. 7.6. Utility and cost of an additional child vs. additional children.

(*ii*) '*b*' is the utility of an additional child, because they treat this as a source of income to the family and;

(*iii*) '*c*' is the utility, which the family feels is the source of old age security.

(*iv*) Generally in developing countries especially in agrarian economies where the income of the family is not secured they try to have more children. They neglect the cost aspect and give importance to the utility aspect.

In urban areas, the people to a greater extent are educated, and have a nuclear family concept in which both wife and husband is employed. If such a family wants to have an additional child, then they have to look into the concept of cost to develop the child. It is one of the basic objectives of human psychology, that is, if you have a child, then he should be provided the best food, best clothing and best education. The aim is to develop the child, rather than an asset or utility aspect. Due to an additional child a family may undergo financial problems. It can be divided into two types of costs (*a*) Direct cost (*b*) Indirect cost.

(*a*) Direct cost is the amount of money incurred to look after the child (to develop the child—food, education etc.) and when a woman is on maternity leave. She may have to lose certain amount of money. In case maternity leave is not available, leave without pay has to be taken.

(*b*) Indirect cost is the amount of freedom or loss of entertainment due to an additional child in the family. A family with more number of children may not be able to go for entertainment etc.

Though the theory neglects certain socio-cultural aspects but to a greater extent economic aspects, play an important role in the population growth theory. This theory is found to be correct in developing countries specially in dual economies, where a majority of the people are living in rural areas and a smaller number in urban areas. Rural people do not have enough money to look after their families; they try to have additional children to bring in more income. In the case of landless labourer or casual workers, or even when both wife and husband is employed, the income may not be sufficient. The families may not be having any future income in the form of pension, insurance policies or other securities. Hence, they feel that additional children may help them in getting additional income as well as the old age security of the parents.

On the other hand, urban people may be employed in government, semi-government or private companies, where pensions, gratuities, insurance and other benefits are available. Due to this, they concentrate more on the development of a child rather then treating the child as an asset.

Population policy makers must look into this economical aspect and the so called 'governance' of public authority must concentrate on this. In many developing countries, the governments declare their social security measure only on temporary basis, this they may announce to obtain the votes to get elected.

7.6 ECONOMIC EFFECTS OF OVER-POPULATION

We learn from the Malthusian theory of population about some adverse effects of excessive population growth. But there are some beneficial effects too. We shall spell out these effects briefly as under:

(*i*) **Food Shortage:** Excessive population results in food shortage, because food supply does not increase in the same proportion as the increase in the mouths to be fed. This is so because production of food is subject to the law of diminishing returns whereas population grows at a galloping speed.

(*ii*) **Disease and Death:** Over-population spells misery in the form of a high incidence of diseases and high mortality rates. This is so because it is difficult to arrange for wholesome food and adequate public health measures and medical aid for a large population. It is said that "it fills our roads with cars." It pollutes air and water and spoils the countryside.

(*iii*) **Overstraining Resources:** Excessive population overstrains the available resources of all types. We have said above that the medical facilities prove inadequate. We may also add that the transport and the educational systems are subjected to severe strain as is evident from the over-crowded schools and colleges, overcrowding in trains, long queues at the bus stops, at water taps, at the fair price shops and at the cinema houses with all attendant problems of life.

(*iv*) **Increase in Dependents:** A rapidly increasing population means an ever growing number of children and the aged who constitute the non-working population. This lowers the per capita income and the level of living.

(*v*) **Stimulating Development:.** A good thing about excessive numbers is an expanding market for goods and services. This stimulates economic development. But excessive spending also generates inflationary pressures.

(*vi*) **Military Advantages:** A huge manpower is a great advantage from the military point of view.

Conclusion

Is growing population a curse or a blessing? No single and straight answer can be given. Such a general question cannot be answered by economics alone. "The joys and aches of family life are not to be measured in mere dollars and cents." On the whole, a rapidly growing population or excessive population is more of a liability than an asset.

7.7 ECONOMIC DEVELOPMENT AND POPULATION GROWTH

Theory of Demographic Transition

The Malthusian theory of population stated in effect that if people became prosperous (especially poorer sections), population would increase. In other words, an increase in the incomes of the poor would lead to an increase in their birth rates and, through the operation of positive checks, result in high death rates so that the growth of population would slow down.

But the process of economic development, which has transformed agrarian economies into urban, industrialized and market-oriented economies, has led to the emergence of a new theory, viz., the theory of demographic transition. The course of population growth since Malthus has been different from what he predicted. This course is more correctly described by this new theory. The theory of demographic transition brings out the relation between population growth and economic development.

Before economic development, an economy is characterized, among other things, by predominance of agriculture, small-scale industries using inefficient and old techniques of production, lack of mobility and division of labour, lack of adequate means of transport and communication, low levels of output and average income, a high degree of rural self-sufficiency and the existence of subsistence economy. But the outstanding feature, from the population point of view, is the prevalence of high birth rates, which are stable at a high level, and high mortality rates.

The birth rates are high owing to universal and early marriages, the influence of social beliefs and customs, religious attitudes and, above all, from economic necessity. This is so because children start working early and thus supplement the family income and because they are regarded as a sort of insurance against old age. The birth rates are also high because the death rates are high. A family must have more children to fill up the gaps caused by high death rates.

The death rates are high owing to poor diet, bad sanitary conditions, and absence of preventive and curative medical practices. High birth rates and high death rates prevalent in an under-developed economy are well in accordance with the Malthusian theory of population. In fact, high death rate is essential to prevent a population explosion which may be caused by high birth rates. The result is that population growth is not rapid, but this is achieved through suffering, disease and death. In an agrarian economy, birth rates are stable at a high level but death rates fluctuate from year to year depending on the availability of food and the prevalence of disease.

Let us now see how the situation is affected by the process of development and the social and economic changes which this development brings economic development brings about an improvement in the economic condition of the people. The level of income, employment and productivity rises bringing about a rise in the level of living. The rural self-sufficiency is broken; the market is extended and comes to dominate production. The economy becomes industrialized and urbanized; it uses more capital and capital equipment, *i.e.,* elaborate tools and machinery. There are rapid changes in the techniques of production. The means of transport and communication are extended and improved.

The striking trend in population in a developing economy is that death rates start declining. This follows an improvement in the standard of living, the availability of medical facilities and awareness of the benefits of smaller families. The food supply is more abundant and regular; there is greater security of life and property owing to improvement in the law and order situation. The medical innovations and the development of vaccines, antibiotics and insecticides and the improvement in sanitary conditions have eradicated many dangerous and fatal diseases. The public health measures have increasingly become more effective. The cumulative effect of all these developments is to reduce substantially the incidence of disease and death. There is, thus, an increasingly pervasive pattern of rapid decline in death rates in all developing economies.

However, the birth rates prove to be more intractable. They are not so readily responsive to economic improvement. They are governed more by deeply established customs and institutions.

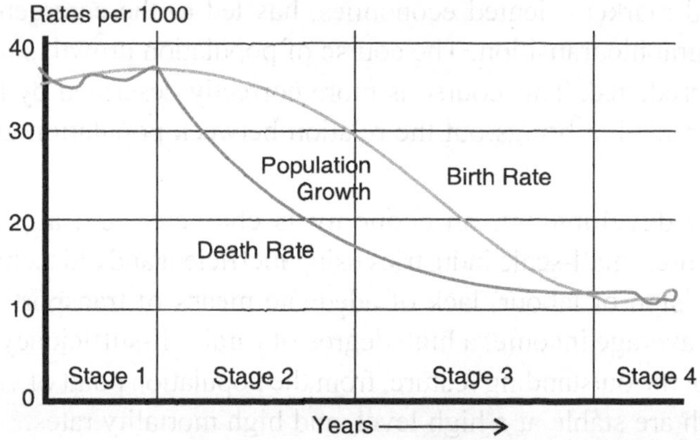

Fig. 7.7. The demographic transition.

Also, there is a general consensus in favour of reducing death but no such consensus supporting the desirability of small families. Thus, for a time, while the death rates have fallen, the birth rates continue to be high so that during the stage of incipient economic development, population growth is accelerated rather than diminished. There is rather a population explosion. There is a time lag before the reduction of birth rates follows the reduction in death rates. This is what is happening in India at present.

But when a very high stage of economic development is reached as in the West, the birth rates fall too. There is deliberate limitation of the size of the family and this is facilitated by a widespread use of efficient contraceptive devices. The changing structure of production involves a declining importance of the family as a production unit, where women come to play an increasing role outside the home and where economic mobility can better be achieved with a small family. The children are considered more of a burden than an asset. The economic advantages of a large family disappear and the fashion of having a small family first influences the higher strata of society but gradually infiltrates to the sections at the lower end of the economic scale and spreads eventually to the rural areas. Thus, the birth rates decline too and establish a parallel with the declining death rates so that the population growth slows down. Small families and low mortality become a typical pattern.

It may, however, be borne in mind that some countries like Malaysia and Shri Lanka have reduced their death rates merely through public health measures without abandoning their agrarian structure. Also, mere urbanization does not lead to reduction in fertility. In India and Egypt, for example, the differential fertility between the rural and urban sectors is practically non-existent.

Thus, substantial economic improvement may be a sufficient condition for a decline in mortality, but it is not a necessary condition. The relation between economic developments and fertility is even less certain. Small economic changes may not reduce birth rates. In many under -developed countries, social and economic changes that are now going on are not likely to reduce fertility in the next two or three decades. The theory of demographic transition does not say what conditions are essential for a fertility decline and what precisely is the period during which this decline must take place. The theory of demographic transition has been summarized as under:

"The agrarian low-income economy is characterized by high birth and death rates—the birth rates remain relatively stable, and the death rates fluctuate in response to varying fortunes. Then as the economy changes its form to a more inter-dependent and specialized market-oriented economy, the average death rate declines. It continues to decline under the impact of better organization and improving medical knowledge and care. Somewhat later the birth rate begins to fall. The two rates follow a more or less parallel downward course with decline in birth rate lagging behind. Finally, as further reductions in the death rate become harder to attain, the birth rate again approaches equality with death rate and a more gradual rate of growth is re-established, with, however, low risks of mortality and small family as the typical pattern. Mortality rates are now relatively stable from year to year and birth rates now responsive to voluntary decisions rather than to deeply imbedded customs may fluctuate from year to year."

Over-population, an Impediment to Economic Growth

It is sometimes said that a growing population helps economic development by providing an expanding market for goods. But this is an erroneous view. Actually, over-population retards economic growth. All effort at economic development under fast growing population turns out to be "writing on sand with waves of population growth washing away all that we have written." It hampers economic development in the following ways:

(*i*) **Creating Food Shortage:** Income elasticity of demand for food being high the growing population creates serious food problems as incomes increase with economic development. Valuable foreign exchange is eaten up by food imports which would have been otherwise utilized for importing capital equipment and technical know-how.

(*ii*) **Increasing Unproductive Numbers:** The greater is the increase in numbers the higher is the dependency ratio. A large number of children have to be supported without making any contribution to production.

(*iii*) **Problem of Unemployment:** An overpopulated country has to face the serious problem of unemployment and under-employment. There is disguised unemployment in rural areas and widespread unemployment in urban areas. This means that there in this way, productive resources have to be diverted to non-productive uses, *viz.,* feeding the idle persons.

(*iv*) **Reduction in Savings and Investment:** A country having a huge population to support has little capacity to save and invest. How can the country advance economically?

(*v*) **Loss of Women's Labour:** Frequent maternity disables women from work and denies their contribution to production and economic development.

Conclusion

Thus, growing population aggravates the food problem, worsens the unemployment situation, adds to the number of unproductive consumers, lowers per capita income, the level of living, labour efficiency and capital formation. In all these and many other ways, rapid rate of population growth acts as a drag on economic progress and slows down the pace of economic development.

Self-Assessment Questions

1. Explain the optimum theory of population.
2. Discuss the salient features of cost-benefit theory of population.
3. Critically examine the Malthusian theory of population. Is it applicable to your country?
4. Examine the optimum theory of population. How far is this theory an improvement on the Malthusian theory of population?
5. Explain the effects of over-population on the economy.
6. Relate population growth with economic development.

   Or

   Explain the theory of demographic transition.

Unit **8**

DEMAND ANALYSIS

8.1 INTRODUCTION

Under capitalism, price mechanism solves the central problems of the economy. Further, price of any commodity or economic service is determined by the interaction of demand and supply. It is important to understand precisely what demand and supply are, as they play an important role in the determination of price of a commodity.

The modern theory of demand rests on the structure built by Alfred Marshall (1842-1924). He taught at Cambridge University and through his book '*Principles of Economics*', influenced the thinking of the British and American economists.

8.2 DEMAND

Goods are demanded, because they have utility. These goods are demanded by everyone, who thinks that it is useful in satisfying his want. Alcohol, though actually harms a person, is demanded by one whose want it satisfies. But, every want of a consumer cannot be expressed as a demand in the economic sense of the term. Demand does not mean mere desire for a commodity. A beggar may desire to have a car, but his desire is not going to affect its market price as he is not having the necessary purchasing power to buy a car. Such a desire, which is not backed by the necessary purchasing power to fulfil it, will remain a desire and will never become the demand. To become a demand, a desire, (*i*) must be backed by the ability or the capacity to pay for the good, and (*ii*) the willingness on the part of the consumer to spend for the good. A demand is, thus, an effective desire.

Demand is always defined with reference to price and a time period. It is meaningless to specify demand without reference to price and time period. The statement that demand for apples is 2000 kg is meaningless. The price at which these apples are demanded is to be mentioned, as with the change in price, the quantity demanded may also change. Demand is also expressed with reference to time. Even at the same price, demand may change, depending upon the time period under consideration. Thus, at ₹ 10 per kg demand for apples may be different at different times during a particular period. Demand for goods may be defined as the, "quantity of a commodity that will be bought at a particular price and during a given period or point of time."

8.3 PRICE DEMAND RELATIONSHIP

Demand for a commodity during a given period of time depends on many factors including the price of the commodity. Demand schedules and demand curves are the techniques to describe the price-demand relationship. Both the demand schedules and demand curves can be for an individual or for a market as a whole.

The demand of an individual consumer for a commodity is called individual demand. An individual demand schedule is a tabular statement of prices and quantities showing how much an individual consumer will buy of a commodity at each of the given prices. It does not say anything about what the price is. It is a list of the various quantities that the individual consumer will buy at different prices. While preparing an individual demand schedule, it is assumed that other factors like prices of the related goods, income of the consumer, etc., do not change. A hypothetical demand schedule of a consumer, showing the quantities of apples demanded at different prices is shown in Table 8.1.

Table 8.1. Demand schedule for apples.

Price of Apples (per kg)	*Quantities of Apples Demanded by the Consumer (in kg)*
12	1
11	2
10	3
9	4
8	5

We can see from the table that when the price of apples is ₹ 12 per kg, only one kg of apples is demanded. When the price comes down to ₹ 8 per kg, the consumer buys 5 kg of it. Hence, we see an inverse relationship between the price and the quantity demanded. This inverse relationship between the price and quantity demanded of a commodity is known as the 'law of demand', which is explained later in the chapter.

Individual Demand Curve

The combinations of the prices and the quantities for an individual consumer is shown in the demand schedule. When plotted on a graph, it becomes the individual demand curve. This is a graphical representation of the combinations of the prices and the quantities of the commodity under consideration. While economists do use arithmetical demand schedule, the demand schedule for a commodity is more usually shown graphically by drawing the demand curve for the commodity in question.

Various market prices are measured along the vertical axis. Quantities demanded of the commodity are measured along the horizontal axis. Now, the demand schedule of the table is plotted as a series of points. The information presented in this figure is exactly the same as in the table. But, the form of presentation is different. Now, we have it in the form of a curve.

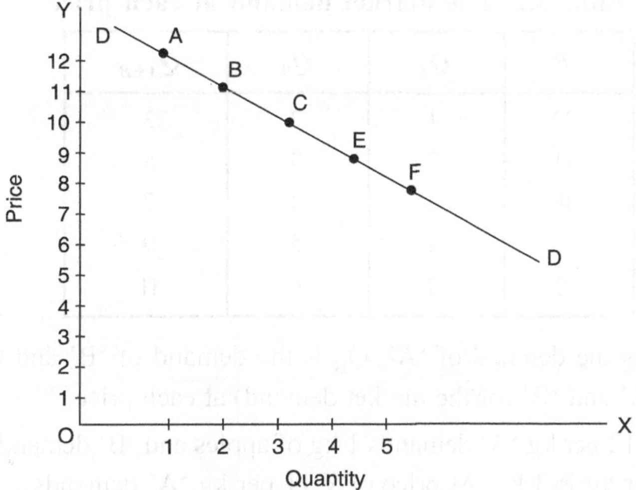

Fig. 8.1. Individual demand curve.

At point 'A' the consumer is buying 1 kg of apples, when the price of apples is ₹ 12 per kg. Point 'B' represents the purchase of 2 kg of apples at the reduced price of ₹ 11 per kg. Similarly, 'C', 'E' and 'F' represent other combinations of prices and quantities. By joining these points, we have a smooth curve DD, called the demand curve for apples. It shows the quantities of apples that the consumer would buy at each of the prices. The demand curve shows the relation between the price of the commodity and the quantity demanded. That is why, it is also called price quantity curve. Given price, corresponding quantity demanded can be read out from the curve and *vice versa.* The demand curve is downward sloping indicating that with the fall in price, quantity demanded increases. It is drawn on the assumption that other factors influencing demand, *viz.*, prices of related goods, incomes and tastes of consumers, etc. remain unchanged.

Market Demand Schedule and Market Demand Curve

So far we have considered the case of a single consumer buying goods. But, in the market, there are a large number of consumers. Market demand means the demand of all the consumers in the market for goods at a particular price. Market demand schedule shows the total demand of all the consumers in the market at various prices. It can be constructed by the summation of the individual demand schedules of all the individuals in the market. Let us take the case of two individuals in the market. The analysis can be extended to any number of buyers. The individual demand schedules of both the individual buyers, 'A' and 'B' and the market demand schedule is shown in the figure. Market demand has been found out by adding the individual demands of 'A' and 'B' at corresponding prices.

Table 8.2. The market demand at each price.

P	Q_A	Q_B	Q_{A+B}
12	1	2	3
11	2	3	5
10	3	4	7
9	4	5	9
8	5	6	11

In the table Q_A is the demand of 'A', Q_B is the demand of 'B' and Q_{A+B} represents the combined demand of 'A' and 'B' (or the market demand) at each price.

At the price of ₹ 12 per kg 'A' demands 1 kg of apples and 'B' demands 2 kg of apples. The total demand at ₹ 12 per kg is 3 kg. At price of ₹ 11 per kg 'A' demands 2 kg of apples and 'B' demands 3 kg of apples. The total demand at this price is 5 kg of apples, which is also the market demand for apples at that price on the assumption that there are only two buyers in the market. Similarly, the total demand of apples at every other price can be found out.

The same relation between price and quantity that has been shown with numbers displayed geometrically in Fig. 8.2. The market demand schedule has now been transformed into a market demand curve. The market demand curve has been found by the horizontal summation of individual demand curves of A and B. Note again that the market demand curve is downward sloping, showing the inverse relationship between price and quantity demanded. Some people who bought some of the commodity before its price fell may buy more now, because it is cheaper. Further, when price of a commodity falls, new buyers will enter the market and will further raise the demand of the commodity. This is another reason for downward slope of the market demand curve.

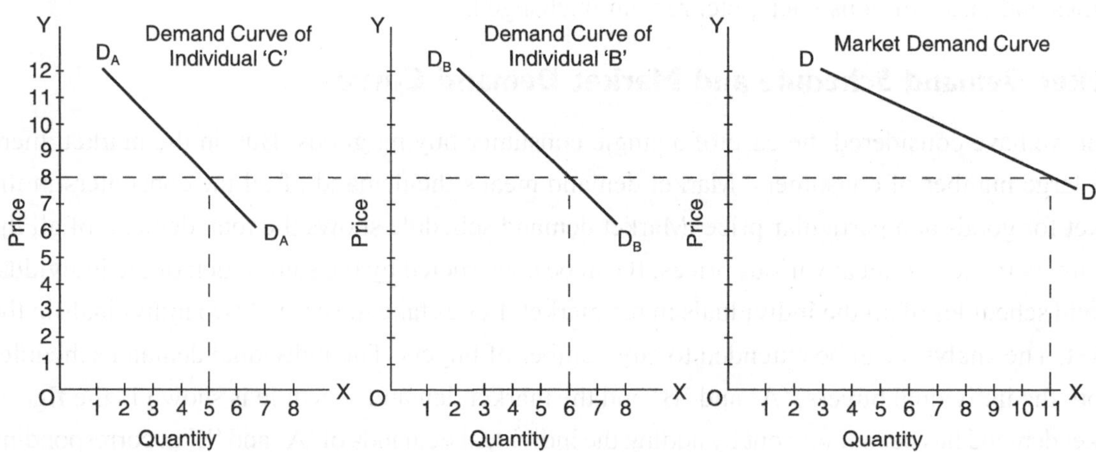

Fig. 8.2. Derivation of the market demand curve.

Demand Function

A function explains the relationship between two or more variables. If two or more variables are related *in such* a way that for each set of values of some variables (called the independent variable) there corresponds a value of some other variables (the dependent variable), then the dependent variable is called the function of the independent variable. In economics, a number of functions such as demand function, production function, cost function, etc., are discussed. Thus, the word 'function' refers to the factors on which demand, production or cost depends.

The demand function for a good is the relation between the various amounts of the commodity that might be bought and the determinants of those amounts in a given market and in a given period of time. As stated earlier, to constitute demand, desire must be backed by the necessary purchasing power to purchase the commodity. While the desire to purchase is revealed by tastes and preferences, income reveals the capability to purchase. Further, since a household spends this income to purchase a number of commodities, demand for a particular commodity depends upon its price and the prices of other commodities. Thus, the factors on which demand for a commodity depends (determinants of demand) are: (1) the price of the commodity, (2) the prices of related goods (substitutes or compliments), (3) the income of the consumers, (4) the tastes and preferences of the consumers, and (5) the expectations about the future prices of the commodity.

The demand function may be expressed symbolically as $Q = f(P, Pr, Y, T, E)$

where 'Q' stands for the quantity demanded of the commodity, 'P' for the price of the commodity, 'Pr' for prices of the related goods, 'Y' for income of the consumer, 'T' for tastes and preferences of the consumer and 'E' for the expectations about the future prices. Now, we explain, how demand for the commodity is affected by each of these determinants.

1. **Price of the Commodity:** Price of the commodity is the most important determinant of demand. Generally, it is expected that with the fall in the price, the quantity demanded of the commodity increases and with the increase in the price, the quantity demanded of the commodity decreases. Thus, there is an inverse relationship between the price of a commodity and its quantity demanded. The inverse relationship between price and quantity demanded of a commodity is commonly known as the 'law of demand'. The relation between price and quantity demanded of a commodity is also called the *price demand* or simply demand.
2. **Prices of the Related Goods:** The demand for a commodity also depends upon the prices of the goods related to it. In economics, two types of relations between goods are discussed. These are complimentarily and substitutability of goods. How the prices of the related goods affect the price of the commodity under consideration depends upon whether the related goods are complimentary or substitutes. If the two goods are used together to satisfy a given want, they are said to be *complimentary goods*, such as tea and sugar, ball pen and refill, car and petrol, etc. when two or more goods are simultaneously required to satisfy a want, their demand is called as *joint demand.* A fall in the price of a commodity raises the demand for its complimentary goods. For example, with the fall in the price of petrol, demand for car will go up. This happens because, with the fall in the price of petrol, its demand increases. Increased quantity of petrol can be used with more cars. Similar is the relation between the price of tea and demand for sugar. A fall in the price of tea causes

increase in the demand for sugar. On the other hand, those goods which can be used in place of one another are called *substitutes*. For example, tea and coffee, scooter and motor cycle, etc. Existence of alterative goods (substitutes) to satisfy a given demand divides the total demand among different goods. The larger the number of substitutes, the smaller will be demand for anyone of them. Further, the level of prices of different goods influences the demand for their substitutes. A fall in the price of goods results in the decrease in the demand for its substitutes and an increase in the price of goods results in the increase in the demand for its substitutes. With the increase in the price of coffee, demand for tea increases because people start using more of tea and less of coffee. In other words, tea is substituted for coffee. On the contrary, with the decrease in the price of coffee, demand for tea will come down. Thus, we can see a direct relation between the price of goods and demand for its substitute.

The relation between the price of one commodity and demand for another commodity is called the *cross demand*. Fig. 8.3(*a*) shows the cross demand curve that shows the relation between the price of petrol and the demand for car (complimentary goods). It has a negative slope. With the decrease in the price of petrol from OP_1 to OP_2, demand for car has gone up from OQ_1, to OQ_2 Fig. 8.3(*b*) shows the cross demand curve for tea and coffee (substitute goods). It is upward sloping, showing the direct relation between the price of coffee and demand for tea. With the increase in the price of coffee from OP_1 to OP_2, the demand for tea has gone up from OQ_1 to OQ_2 this is so because with the increase in the price of coffee people start substituting tea for coffee.

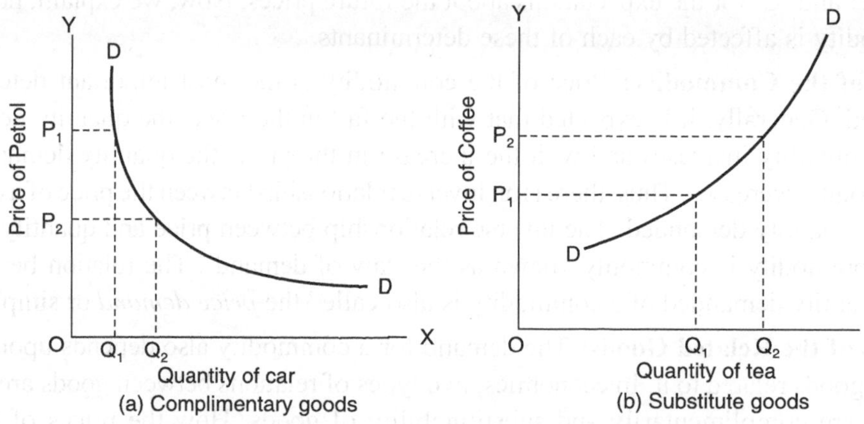

Fig. 8.3. Complimentary and substitute goods.

3. **Income of the Consumer:** The demand for goods also depends upon income of the consumer. With the increase in the income, his purchasing power increases and he is in a position to afford more goods. Consequently, their demand for goods increases. Thus, increase in income has a positive effect on the demand for goods. The relation between income and demand is called *income demand*. Generally income of the people is directly related to their demand. So, the income demand curve is upward sloping [Fig. 8.4(*a*)]. Such goods are called *normal goods* for which income effect is positive, *i.e.*, when income goes up, demand for such

goods also goes up and when income falls, demand also falls. However, for certain goods called *necessities*; demand is not related to income either way. Here, an example of salt may be given. The demand for salt does not increase with the increase in income and it does not decrease with the decrease in income. Thus, the curve showing the relation between the income of the consumer and the demand for salt is vertical. Such a curve is shown in Fig. 8.4(*b*). It is also possible that a rise in income of the consumer may lead to a fall in the quantity demanded of goods. This is the case with *inferior goods*. These goods are said to be *inferior goods*, if its demand falls with the increase in the income of the consumer. Thus, there is an inverse relationship between income and demand of inferior goods, *i.e.*, income effect is negative. Examples of inferior goods are vegetable ghee, gur, coarse grain such as bajra, etc. Fig. 8.4(*c*) illustrates the income demand curve for inferior goods.

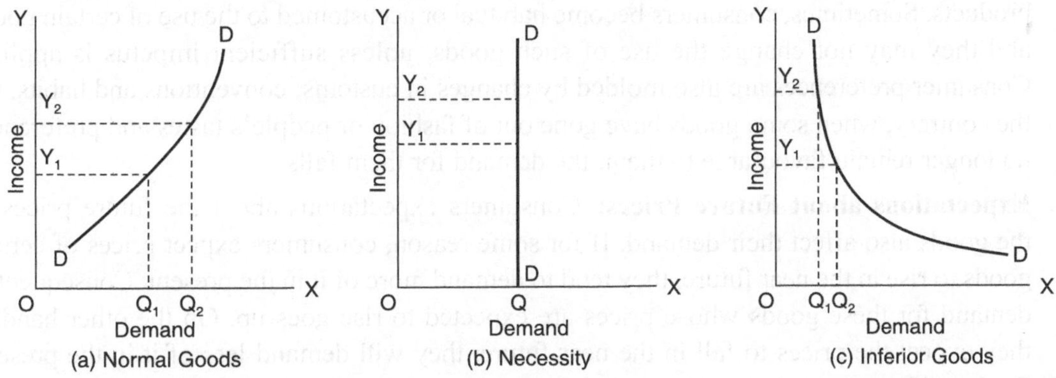

Fig. 8.4. Income vs. demand for goods.

Sometimes it may even happen that quantity demanded of a commodity increases initially. But after a certain level of income, quantity demanded remains the same or even falls.

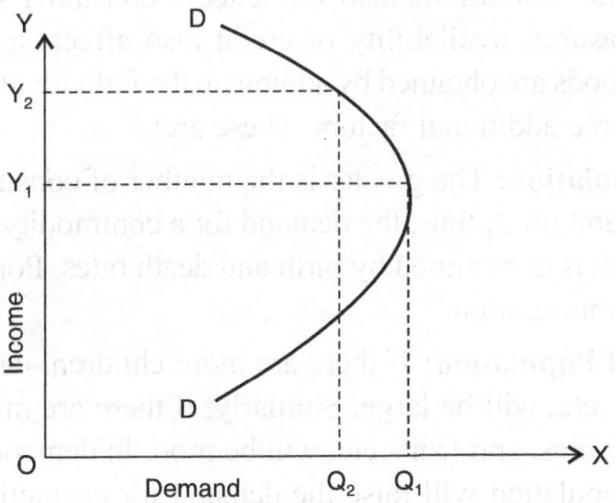

Fig. 8.5. The income demand curve.

Demand is influenced not only by changes in current income, but also by accumulated income of the preceding periods (wealth). If marginal propensity to consume by the consumer is high (*i.e.* low marginal propensity to save), a large portion of additional income earned will be used to buy goods and little will be saved and *vice versa*. Thus, change in propensity to consume (or save) brings about a change in the demand for goods.

4. **Tastes and Preferences of the Consumer:** Another important factor which affects the level of demand of a commodity in the market is the tastes and preferences of the consumer: Tastes and preferences often change, which affect the level of demand for various goods. The demand for goods are more, which is liked by consumers and for which they have a preference. Consumer's tastes and preferences may change because of a change in the fashion or as a result of the advertisement for various products. It is advertisement that to a large extent has affected the demand for Babul tooth paste. Many a times, films are responsible for the creation of fashion, which affect the demand of the various existing products. Sometimes, consumers become habitual or accustomed to the use of certain goods and they may not change the use of such goods, unless sufficient impetus is applied. Consumer preferences are also molded by changes in customs, conventions and habits. On the contrary, when some goods have gone out of fashion or people's tastes and preferences no longer remain favourable to them, the demand for them falls.
5. **Expectations about Future Prices:** Consumers expectations about the future prices of the goods also affect their demand. If for some reason, consumers expect prices of certain goods to rise in the near future, they tend to demand more of it in the present. Consequently, demand for these goods whose prices are expected to rise goes up. On the other hand, if they expect the prices to fall in the near future, they will demand less of it in the present. Further, if consumers hope that in the future they will have good income, then they will increase their purchases in the present. The present demand for goods will rise as a result.
6. **Other Factors:** Educational background, social status, marital status, age, place of residence (urban or rural) are some of the sociological factors, which affect consumer demand. Changes in climate and weather conditions also influence a consumer's demand. Advertisement, sales promotion measures, availability of credit also affects a consumer's demand. The market demand for goods are obtained by adding up the individual demands at various prices. It is influenced by three additional factors. These are:
   (*a*) **Size of the Population:** The greater is the number of consumers of goods, the greater the market demand for it, thus, the demand for a commodity is directly related with the population which is determined by birth and death rates. Population is also affected by migration and immigration.
   (*b*) **Composition of Population:** If there are more children, demand for baby food, toys, biscuits, sweets, etc. will be large. Similarly, if there are more old people, spectacles, artificial teeth, tonics, and fruits etc. will be more in demand. Predominance of young people in the population will raise the demand for cosmetics, sport goods, jeans etc. Similarly, sex composition also affects the demand for a number of commodities.
   (*c*) **Distribution of Income:** If income is equally distributed among the different sections of the society, all of them will be in a position to demand. But, there will be more demand for goods purchased by relatively poorer people, like wheat, rice, fans, etc. But,

if the income is unevenly distributed, then majority of the people will get small portion of the national income, the demand for commodity will be limited. Most of the demand in this case will come from rich people. Further, in this case, relatively greater portion of the income will be saved (by rich people).

8.4 LAW OF DEMAND

Law of demand is one of the best known and the most important laws of economic theory. It explains the general tendency of the consumers to buy more goods at a lower price and less of it at a higher price. Lower price attracts consumers to buy more. Besides, some consumers who were not buying the goods at a higher price can also afford to buy it at a lower price. Consequently, with the fall in the price of the goods, demand for it generally increases. Thus, the law of demand expresses the inverse relationship between the price and the quantity demanded of a commodity, other things being equal. In other words, when the price of goods rises, demand falls and when the price falls, demand rises, provided factors other than the price remain unchanged. The law is based on the assumption that the other determinants of demand, *viz.* income of the consumer, tastes and preferences of the consumer, prices of the related goods, future expectations, size and composition of population, distribution of income, etc. do not change during the operation of the law. If they do change, the law may fail to operate. For example, if with the fall in the price of the goods, a consumer develops disliking for it or his income declines, he may not buy more of it.

The law of demand indicates only the direction of the change of demand corresponding to a change in price. It does not say anything about the magnitude of change in the quantity demanded. For example, if price of apples comes down from ₹ 12 per kg to ₹ 10 per kg, the law tells us that demand for apples will increase. But, it does not tell the amount by which the demand for apples will increase as a result of a fall in price. There is no mathematical relationship between price and demand of a commodity.

The law of demand has been defined by various economists differently. Some of the definitions are as under:

"The greater the amount to be sold, the smaller must be the price at which it is offered in order that it may find purchasers or in other words, if other things remain the same, the amount demanded increases with a fall in price and diminishes with a rise in price." **Marshall**

"A fall in the price of a commodity causes the household to buy more of that commodity and less of the other commodities which compete with it, while rise in prices causes the household to buy less of this commodity and more of competing commodities". **Lipsey**

"When the price of the goods are raised (at the same time that all other things are held constant) less of it is demanded. Or, what is the same thing: if a greater quantity of goods are put on the market, then, other things being equal, it can be sold at a lower price." **Samuelson**

All the definitions exhibit one thing—that there exists a negative association between prices and quantities demanded. The qualifying clause 'other things remaining the same' implies the assumptions underlying this law.

The law of demand can be illustrated through a demand curve. In Fig. 8.6 price is measured along the Y-axis and quantity is measured along the X-axis. DD is the demand curve of the goods under consideration. At the price OP_1 the quantity demanded is OQ_1. If the price of the goods falls to OP_2 the quantity demanded increases to OQ_2. The demand curve is downward sloping, which is in accordance with the law of demand. It should be remembered that while drawing the demand curve, all the determinants of demand (except price of the goods in question) are assumed to remain constant. Only the relationship between price and quantity demanded of the commodity is described. The effect of a change in other determinants of demand is discussed later in this chapter.

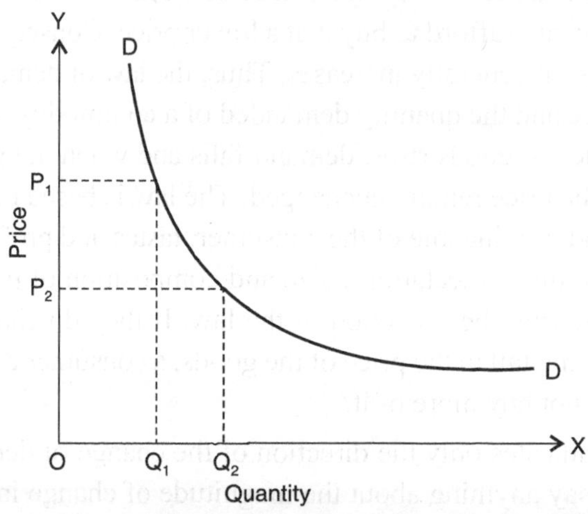

Fig. 8.6. The demand curve.

The functional relationship between demand and prices can be expressed as $Qx = f(Px)$ where Qx is demand and Px is the own price of goods 'X'.

The above expression shows that price is the cause variable and demand is effect variable.

Alternatively, price is the independent variable while demand is dependent variable. In technical terms, independent variable (here, price) is also called *exogenous variable*, while dependent variable (here, demand) is called *endogenous variable*.

When the demand curve for the goods are a straight line, the corresponding demand function will have a linear equation of the form:

$$Q x = a - b P x$$

Here, 'a' is the quantity intercept and 'b' is the slope. DQx/DPx express the rate at which quantity demanded changes, with change in the price. Negative sign in the equation shows inverse price-demand relationship. For plotting the demand curve, we normally use the inverse demand curve $P x = \alpha - \beta Q x$. here, $\alpha = a / b$ is the price intercept and $\beta = 1 / b$ is the slope of inverse demand curve and equals DPx / DQx. This inverse form of the demand curve indicates that for each given quantity demanded, the maximum price a consumer (or consumers) would be willing to pay rather than doing without that quantity. The normal form of the demand curve can also be similarly defined.

8.5 WHY DEMAND CURVE SLOPES DOWNWARD?

Law of demand states the inverse relationship between price of a commodity and its quantity demanded, other things remaining the same. The demand of a commodity is more at a lower price and less at a higher price. That is why, the demand curve slopes downward. But, a question arises as to why more quantity is demanded at a lower price and less quantity is demanded at a higher price. The factors responsible for the downward slope of the demand curve are.

1. The Law of Diminishing Marginal Utility

The law of diminishing marginal utility states that as the consumption of a commodity by a consumer increases, the satisfaction obtained by the consumer from each additional unit (*i.e.,* marginal utility) of the commodity goes on diminishing. Thus, a thirsty man gets too much satisfaction by drinking a glass of water. But, the second glass of water will not be as much satisfying to him, as the first glass of water. The satisfaction derived from the third glass will even be lesser. The price that a consumer is willing to pay for a commodity is directly related to the satisfaction that he derives from that commodity. As we have seen, the consumer gets more satisfaction from the initial units of a commodity. He is ready to pay a high price for it. Further, the satisfaction that he gets from the successive units diminishes; he will purchase additional units of the commodity only at a lower price. Thus, more quantity is bought at a lower price and less quantity is bought at a higher price.

2. Income Effect

A fall in the price of a commodity increases the purchasing power (or the real income) of the consumer. In other words, the consumer has to spend less to buy the same quantity of the commodity as before. The money so saved because of a fall in the price of the commodity can be spent by the consumer in any way he likes. He will spend a part of this money on buying some more units of the same commodity, whose price has fallen. Thus, a fall in the price of this commodity increases its demand. This is called *income effect.* Same explanation can be given for a rise in price. In this case, demand for the commodity under consideration will increase due to fall in purchasing power of the consumer.

3. Substitution Effect

This is another important reason for increase in demand as a result of a fall in the price of the commodity and *vice versa.* When the price of a commodity falls, it becomes relatively cheaper than other commodities, whose prices have not fallen. So, the consumer substitutes this commodity for other commodities, which are now relatively dearer. This is known as *substitution effect.* 'Because of this substitution effect, demand for the commodity in question rises. In most of the cases, substitution effect is stronger than the income effect. *Marshall* explained the downward slope of the demand curve with the help of substitution effect, ignoring the income effect. Later on, income effect was also considered by *Hicks* and *Allen* (under the indifference curve analysis) to explain the downward slope of the demand curve. The sum of income effect and substitution effect is called *price effect.* The demand curve slopes downward, as a fall in price of a commodity causes more of it to be demanded and *vice versa.*

4. Changes in the Number of Consumers

Many people cannot afford to buy a commodity at a high price. When the price of the commodity falls, a number of persons who could not afford it at a higher price can purchase it at the reduced price. This increases the number of consumers of the commodity. Thus, at a lower price, the quantity demanded of the commodity increases because of the increase in the number of consumers of the commodity and *vice versa.*

5. Diverse Uses of a Commodity

Many commodities can be put to several uses. A commodity having several uses in said to have a *composite demand*. For example, electricity can be used for lighting, cooking, heating, cooling and so on. At a higher price, electricity may not be used for all of these purposes, *i.e.,* the use of electricity may be restricted to lighting only. But, if price of electricity falls, people may afford to use it for other purposes also. Thus, the demand of electricity at a lower price will increase. All the factors discussed above are responsible for the downward slope of the demand curve. In other words, these factors explain the operation of the law of demand. The importance of these factors, depends upon the circumstances of the case.

Exceptions to the Law of Demand

Law of demand expressing the inverse relationship between price and quantity demanded of a commodity is generally valid in most of the situations. But, there are some situations under which there may be direct relationship between price and quantity demanded of a commodity. These are known as exceptions to the law of demand. One of the exceptions is associated with name of Torstein Veblen (1857–1929). He was a social critic and propounded the doctrine of *conspicuous consumption*. According to him, if consumers measure the desirability of the utility of a commodity solely by its price and nothing else, then they tend to buy more of the commodity at a higher price and less of it at a lower price. Thus, the relationship between price and quantity demanded of the commodity becomes direct, leading to an exception to the law of demand. Diamonds are often cited as an example. Commodities like diamond, precious stones, rare paintings, etc. have a status or prestige value (rather than intrinsic value) for the rich section of the society. In this type of situation, prestige is directly associated with the price of the good. Higher the price of the good, greater will be the status or prestige of the buyer in the society and *vice versa*. That is why, rich people buy more of it at a higher price and less of it at a lower price. Therefore, the law of demand does not apply in case of commodities which are used as status symbols. Another exception to the law of demand is associated with the name of Robert Giffen (1837–1910). Early in the nineteenth century, he observed rise in the demand for bread by low paid British workers with the increase in its price. Bread was the staple food for the British workers. When the price of bread rose, they were compelled to spend more on the same quantity of bread. With little income left with them, they could not afford to buy as much meat as before. To maintain their total intake of food, they substituted bread (still being a cheaper food) for meat even at a higher price of it. Thus, a direct relationship is established between price and quantity. After the name of Robert Giffen, these goods for which there is a direct price-demand relationship are called Giffen goods. Such basic food items (like potato, bajra, barley, gram, etc.)

consumed by poor families are some other examples of Giffen goods. In the case of Giffen goods, demand curve slopes upward and the law of demand does not operate.

The law of demand does not hold in times of emergency like flood, drought, famine or war, as households do not behave in normal way in such periods. Fear of shortage of goods in future in such periods increases their present demand, although the prices are rising. Further, an ignorant buyer may buy more of a commodity when its price in fact goes up. He may also be haunted by the phobia that higher priced commodity is better in quality and *vice versa.*

There are some other exceptions to the law of demand, which are only apparent and not real. One of these is related to the people's expectations about future prices. If people expect the price of a goods to rise in the future, they demand more of it even at a higher price. And if they expect the price to fall in the future, they demand less of it even at a lower price. Thus, more quantity of the goods are demanded at rising prices and less quantity of goods are demanded at falling prices. This seems contrary to the law of demand. But in this case the law of demand still holds. The change in demand for the goods are not due to the change in the prices, but, because of a shift in the demand curve, to the right or left as the case may be. Moreover, the law of demand assumes future expectations.

Similarly, over the course of a business cycle, it is found that during a period of prosperity larger amounts of goods are purchased at higher prices and during depression periods of a business cycle, smaller quantities are purchased at lower prices. If properly interpreted, this is also not an exception to the law of demand. This only shows that demand for many goods increases during prosperity because of increase in the income of people and not because of increase in prices of goods. Similarly, during the depression period, demand for goods decreases because of the decline in the income of the people and not because of the decrease in the prices of goods. Thus, it does not contradict law of demand.

Another apparent exception to the law of demand is found when a commodity is sold under different brand names at different prices. Almost identical 'Lux' and 'Supreme Lux' are sold at different prices. Higher priced 'Supreme Lux' is sold more than the lower priced 'Lux', even though both are almost identical. But, this is also not a real exception to the law of demand. This is so because those who buy higher priced brand think that the two brands are different. Hence, two brands should be analyzed as different commodities.

Notwithstanding these exceptions, the universal applicability of the law of demand is undoubted. Even the demand for Giffen goods have to be considered from the existence point of view. Bread is bare necessity for existence. The wage earners purchase the same or more amount of bread despite the price rise as it is cheap and people are habituated to consume it. Further, the demand for luxurious goods are considered from the social point of view and not from economic consideration.

8.6 MOVEMENT ALONG THE DEMAND CURVE

We have studied under the law of demand that other things remaining the same, if price of a commodity rises, its demand decreases and if price of the commodity falls, its demand increases. When quantity demanded of a commodity increases as a result of the fall in the price, it is called *extension* (or expansion) in demand (a movement down the demand curve) and when the quantity demanded decreases as a result of an increase in the price of the commodity, it is called contraction in demand (a movement up the demand curve). Thus, extension and contraction in demand imply change in quantity demanded due to change in the price of the commodity, other things remaining the same.

Extension in demand is shown in Fig. 8.7. At price OP_1 OQ_1, quantity of the commodity is demanded. If the price falls to OP_2, quantity demanded of the commodity increases to OQ_2. Q_1Q_2 is the extension in demand, which results from a fall in the price of the commodity from OP_1 to OP_2.

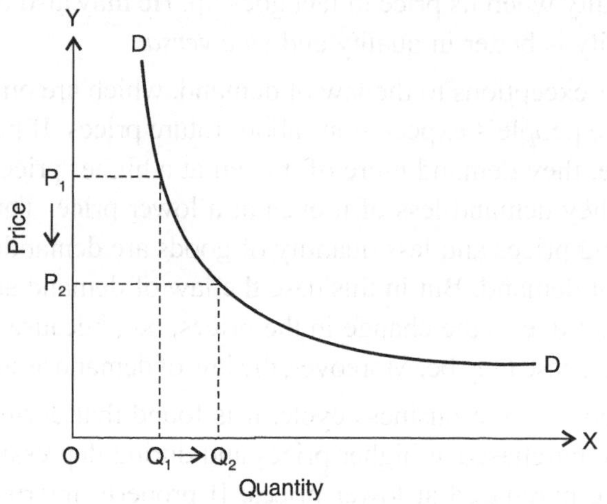

Fig. 8.7. Extension in demand.

Contraction in demand is shown in Fig. 8.8 at price OP_2. The quantity demanded of the commodity is QQ_1. When the price of the commodity rises to OP_1. The demand of the commodity falls to QQ_2, Q_1Q_2 is the contraction in demand resulting from an increase in the price from OP_2 to OP_1.

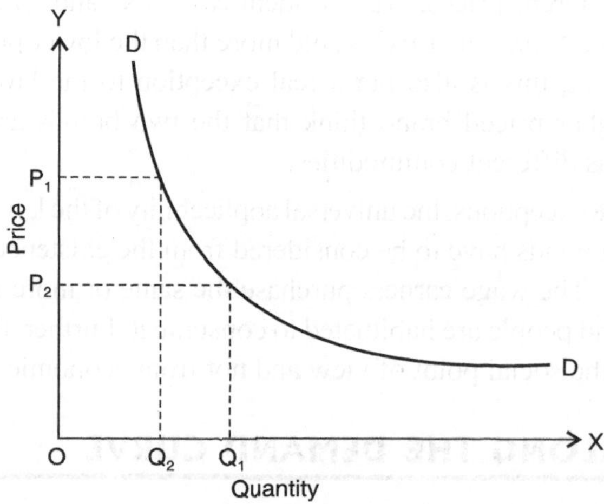

Fig. 8.8. Contraction in demand.

Both extension and contraction in demand are represented by a movement (moving down and up respectively) along the same demand curve. In these cases, there is no shift in the demand curve.

8.7 SHIFT IN THE DEMAND CURVE

The factors or determinants of demand other than price of goods are assumed to be constant for the period for which the demand curve is prepared. As long as these factors remain unchanged, the demand curve constructed on the basis of these assumptions hold good, *i.e.,* at lower prices, larger quantities will be demanded. Whenever these factors change, a new demand curve will come into existence, either at a lower level or a higher level, depending upon whether these factors have changed for the better or worse.

When demand of goods changes due to the change in the determinants of demand other than price of goods in question, it is called change (increase or decrease) in demand, as the case may be. The direction of change in quantity demanded depends on the nature of change. Increase in demand means that even at the same price more quantity is demanded (or same quantity is demanded at a higher price). This may be due to the increase in the income of the people, increase in the population, and increase in the prices of the substitutes of the good in question, a fall in the prices of complimentary goods, expectations of rise in price in future, redistribution of income toward groups who favour the commodity, favourable change in taste and preferences of the consumers for the commodity in the question. The increase in demand is shown in Fig. 8.9. DD is the initial demand curve. At price OP, OQ quantity is demanded. Due to the changes in the determinants of demand other than price, the demand curve shifts to the right. D′D′ is the new demand curve, now, at the same price OP, the quantity demanded is OQ_1'. Thus, the demand has increased from OQ to OQ_1, QQ_1 is the increase in demand.

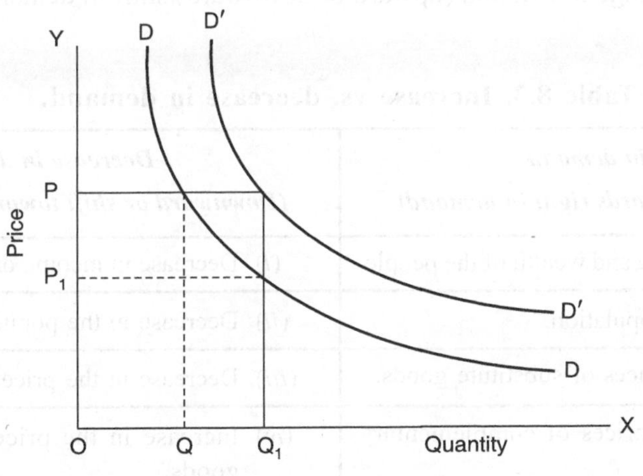

Fig. 8.9. Increase in demand.

Similarly, there is decrease in demand, when the demand curve shifts to the left. Decrease in demand means that even at the same price, small quantity is demanded or the same old amount is demanded due to the decrease in the income of the people, decrease in the population, decrease in the prices of substitute goods, increase in the prices of complementary goods, expectations of fall in price in future, redistribution of income away from groups who favour the commodity or a decline in the tastes and preferences of the consumers for the commodity. The decrease in the demand is shown in Fig. 8.10. DD is the initial demand curve. At price OP, OQ quantity is demanded. Due to the changes in the determinants of demand other than price, the demand curve shifts to the left. D′D′ is the new demand curve. Now, at the same price OP, the quantity demanded is OQ. The quantity demanded has decreased from QQ to QQ_1. QQ_1 is the decrease in demand. It can also be shown that in case of decrease in demand, same quantity may be demanded, but at a lower price. Thus, in Fig. 8.10 after a shift to the left in the demand curve, the same old quantity OQ may be demanded at a lower price OP_1.

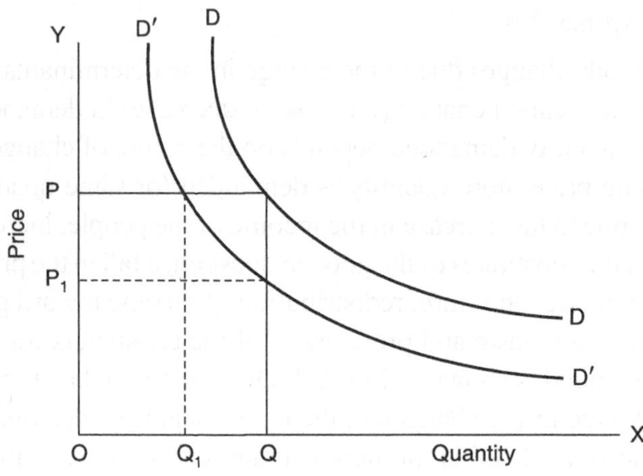

Fig. 8.10. Decrease in demand.

The causes of change in demand (upward or downward) shift in demand can be summarized as follows:

Table 8.3. Increase vs. decrease in demand.

Increase in demand ***(Upward or shift towards right in demand)***	***Decrease in demand*** ***(Downward or shift towards left in demand)***
(*i*) Increase in income and wealth of the people.	(*i*) Decrease in income or wealth of the people.
(*ii*) Increase in the population.	(*ii*) Decrease in the population.
(*iii*) Increase in the prices of substitute goods.	(*iii*) Decrease in the prices of substitute goods.
(*iv*) Decrease in the prices of complementary goods.	(*iv*) Increase in the prices of complementary goods.
(*v*) Expectations of rise in prices in future.	(*v*) Expectations of fall in prices in future.
(*vi*) Changes in tastes, preferences, fashions, customs, habits, etc., in favour of a commodity.	(*vi*) Changes in tastes, preferences, fashions, customes, habits, etc., against a commodity.

To sum up, a change in quantity demanded (extension or contraction) implies a movement along the demand curve, while a change in demand (increase or decrease) means a shift in the demand curve. Movement along a demand curve is different from the movement of the curve. A movement along a demand curve indicates that a different quantity will be demanded because the price has changed. If we move along a demand curve to the right (when the price of the commodity falls), it is a case of extension in demand. If the movement is to the left of the given point on the demand curve (when the price of the commodity rises), we get contraction of demand. On the other hand, when the demand curve moves to the right, it is called increase in demand, since at each possible price, more is demanded. Similarly, a movement of the demand curve to the left implies that there is decrease in demand. Increase or decrease (change) in demand takes place due to change in factors other than the price of the commodity in question.

8.8 PRICE ELASTICITY OF DEMAND (PED)

Ped measures the responsiveness of demand for a product following a change in its own price. The formula for calculating the co-efficient of elasticity of demand is:

Percentage change in quantity demanded divided by the percentage change in price.

Since changes in price and quantity nearly always move in opposite directions, economists usually do not bother to put in the minus sign. We are concerned with the co-efficient of elasticity of demand. Price elasticity of demand describes the effect of a given percentage change in price (P) on the percentage change in quantities(Q) that would be purchased. The simplest formula for price elasticity (E) is

$$E = \frac{\dfrac{Q_2 - Q_1}{Q_2 + Q_1}}{\dfrac{P_2 - P_1}{P_2 + P_1}}$$

where Q_1 and Q_2 are quantities that would be taken before and after a price change, and P_1 and P_2 are the corresponding prices. If E is less than 1.0, total revenue ($P \times Q$) decreases if price is decreased, and the demand is said to be inelastic; if total revenue increases price decreases (E is greater than 1.0), the demand is said to be elastic. In other words, price elasticity indicates the responsiveness of a change in quantity to change in price.

Elasticity of demand is an important concept in the determination of price policies. However, the measurement of elasticity is difficult in actual practice. The difficulty arises from the fact that elasticity is a concept relating to a given point of time, and price elasticity describes the effect of price on quantity, assuming all other determinants to be constant. Two statistical approaches attempt to estimate the nature of the demand curve: (*i*) study of time series of prices and quantities; and (*ii*) controlled experiments. However, even if a manager does not want to go to the trouble of using these methods, the concept is valuable as an aid to his judgement. The nature of demand curve, faced by a manager, obviously is important in pricing decisions. Some authorities argue that it might be best to concentrate on demand as the most important factor in pricing.

$$E_D = \frac{\text{Relative change in Quantity Demanded}}{\text{Relative Change in Price}} = \frac{\dfrac{\Delta \text{ Quantity}}{\text{Average Quantity}}}{\dfrac{\Delta \text{ Price}}{\text{Average Price}}} = \frac{\dfrac{Q_2 - Q_1}{(Q_1 + Q_2)/2}}{\dfrac{P_2 - P_1}{(P_1 + P_2)/2}}$$

Table 8.4. Demand schedule.

Price	2	3	4	5	6	7	8	9
Quantity	9	8	7	6	5	4	3	2
Total Revenue	18	24	28	30	30	28	24	1

P goes from 4 to 5 and Q from 7 to 6	*P goes from 5 to 6 and Q from 6 to 5*	*P goes from 6 to 7 and Q from 5 to 4*
$\dfrac{\frac{6-7}{(7+6)/2}}{\frac{5-4}{(4+5)/2}} = \dfrac{\frac{1}{6.5}}{\frac{1}{4.5}}$ $= \dfrac{4.5}{6.5} = .69$	$\dfrac{\frac{5-6}{(6+5)/2}}{\frac{6-5}{(5+6)/2}} = \dfrac{\frac{1}{5.5}}{\frac{1}{5.5}}$ $= \dfrac{5.5}{5.5} = 1$	$\dfrac{\frac{4-5}{(5+4)/2}}{\frac{7-6}{(6+7)/2}} = \dfrac{\frac{1}{4.5}}{\frac{1}{6.5}}$ $= \dfrac{6.5}{4.5} = 1.44$

A downward sloping demand curve yields a negative E_D. Its sign is often ignored.

Table 8.5. Interpreting elasticity of demand.

Relative change in Quantity	*Terminology*	***E_D Parameters***
None, will pay anything, numerator is zero	Perfectly Inelastic	$E_D = 0$
Small	Inelastic	$0 < E_D < 1$
Q demanded and P change same percentage	Unitary Elasticity	$E_D = 1$
Large	Elastic	$1 < E_D < \infty$
Infinitely, large, price doesn't change, denominator is zero	Perfectly Elastic	E_D is undefined, can't divide by zero.

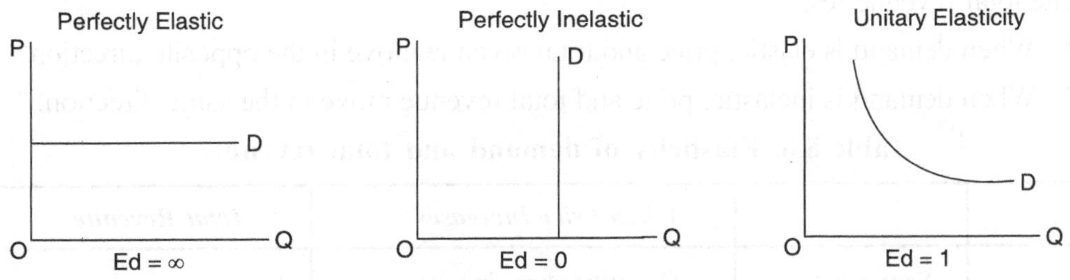

Fig. 8.11. Elasticity of demand at the extremes.

Total Revenue along a Linear Demand Curve

(*a*) Moving from left to right on the bottom graph indicates what happens to revenue as price is lowered and the quantity sold increases.

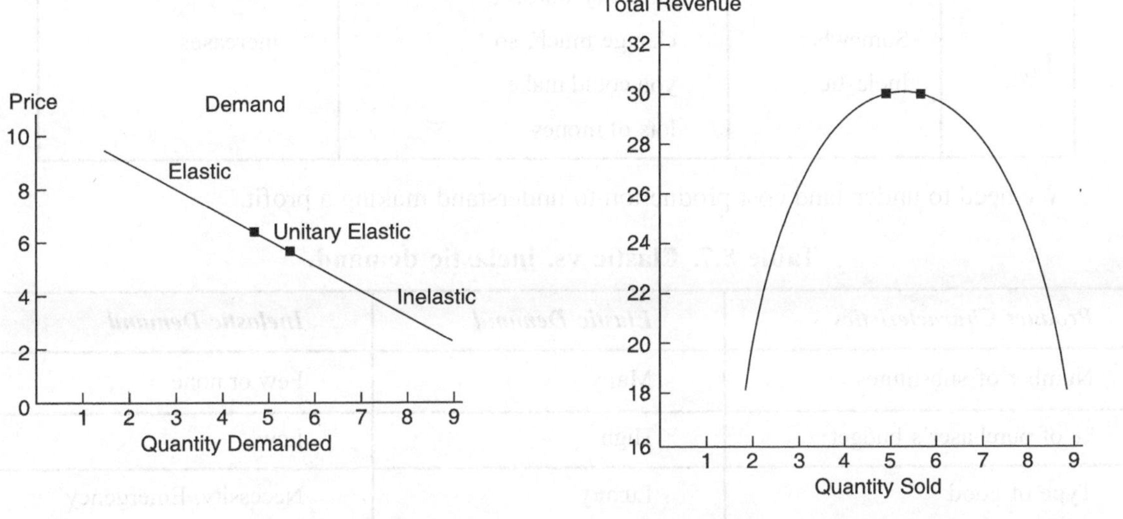

Fig. 8.12. Price vs. quantity demanded.

Fig. 8.13. Quantity sold vs. total revenue.

(*b*) At lower quantities (higher prices) demand is elastic. Quantity increases are relatively greater than price decreases and total revenue increases as more units are sold.

(*c*) This means a company facing an elastic demand can increase revenue by decreasing price. An important question to be answered concerns what happens to costs when a lower price causes more units to be sold.

(*d*) When demand becomes inelastic, quantity increases are relatively less than price decreases and total revenue falls.

(*e*) This means a company could increase total revenue by increasing price and selling fewer units. This could mean a very high profit. Important questions to be answered concern how competitors react to these higher prices, can the company produce lower quantities at reasonably low costs, exactly how much profit will the company make, and how will the government reach to these higher profits.

(*f*) The total revenue test

1. When demand is elastic, price and total revenue move in the opposite direction.
2. When demand is inelastic, price and total revenue move in the same direction.

Table 8.6. Elasticity of demand and total revenue.

		When Price Increases	*Total Revenue*
$E_D > 1$	Somewhat Elastic	Quantity changing a lot so you could lose lots of money.	decreases
$E_D = 1$	Unitary Elasticity	Quantity/Price changing by same %	no change
$E_D < 1$	Somewhat Inelastic	Quantity doesn't change much, so you could make lots of money	increases

We need to understand cost production to understand making a profit.

Table 8.7. Elastic vs. inelastic demand.

Product Characteristics	*Elastic Demand*	*Inelastic Demand*
Number of substitutes	Many	Few or none
% of purchaser's budget	High	Low
Type of good	Luxury	Necessity, Emergency
Time until purchase	No hurry	Required quickly
Examples	Steak, Vacations	Salt, Bread

Understanding Values for Price Elasticity of Demand

- If Ped = 0 then demand is said to be perfectly inelastic. This means that demand does not change at all when the price changes—the demand curve will be vertical.
- If Ped is between 0 and 1 (*i.e.,* the percentage change in demand from A to B is smaller than the percentage change in price), then demand is inelastic. Producers know that the change in demand will be proportionately smaller than the percentage change in price.
- If Ped = 1 (*i.e.,* the percentage change in demand is exactly the same as the percentage change in price), then demand is said to be elastic. A 15% rise in price

would lead to a 15% contraction in demand leaving total spending by the same at each price level.

- If Ped > 1, then demand responds more than proportionately to a change in price *i.e.,* demand is elastic. For example, a 20% increase in the price of goods might lead to a 30% drop in demand. The price elasticity of demand for this price change is 1.5.

What Determines Price Elasticity of Demand?

- **The number of close substitutes for a goods/uniqueness of the product**—the more close substitutes in the market, the more elastic is the demand for a product because consumers can more easily switch their demand if the price of one product changes relative to others in the market. The huge range of package holiday tours and destinations make this a highly competitive market in terms of pricing—many holiday makers are price sensitive.
- **The cost of switching between different products**—there may be significant transaction costs involved in switching between different goods and services. In this case, demand tends to be relatively inelastic. For example, mobile phone service providers may include penalty clauses in contracts or insists on 12-month contracts being taken out.
- **The degree of necessity or whether the goods are luxury**—goods and services deemed by consumers to be necessities tend to have an inelastic demand whereas luxuries will tend to have a more elastic demand because consumers can make do without luxuries when their budgets are stretched, *i.e.,* in an economic recession we can cut back on discretionary items of spending.
- **The % of a consumer's income allocated to spending on the goods**—goods and services that take up a high proportion of a household's income will tend to have a more elastic demand than products where large price changes makes little or no difference to someone's ability to purchase the product.
- **The time period allowed following a price change**—demand tends to be more price elastic, the longer that we allow consumers to respond to a price change by varying their purchasing decisions. In the short-run, the demand may be inelastic, because it takes time for consumers both to notice and then to respond to price fluctuations.
- **Whether the goods are subject to habitual consumption**—when this occurs, the consumer becomes much less sensitive to the price of the goods in question. Examples such as cigarettes and alcohol and other drugs come into this category.
- **Peak and off-peak demand**—demand tends to be price inelastic at peak times—a feature that suppliers can take advantage of when setting higher prices. Demand is more elastic at off-peak times, leading to lower prices for consumers. Consider for example the charges made by car rental firms during the course of a week, or the cheaper deals available at hotels at weekends and away from the high-season. Train fares are also higher on Fridays (a peak day for travelling between cities) and also at peak times during the day.

- **The breadth of definition of goods or services**—if goods are broadly defined, *i.e.,* the demand for petrol or meat, demand is often fairly, inelastic. But specific brands of petrol or beef are likely to be more elastic following a price change.

Wi-Fi Prices and Price Elasticity of Demand

From airports to hotels to conference centres to inter-city rail services to sports stadiums and libraries, more and more people are demanding wireless internet connections for personal and business use. But demand is being constrained by the limited availability of services and, in places, high user charges. However, the price of connecting to the internet through wi-fi services is set to fall as competition in the sector heats up. Nearly 90% of laptops now come with wi-fi connections as standard and many public areas are being equipped with hotspots, but users often complain about the high price of accessing the internet. At present airports and hotels can charge high prices because in many cases a wi-fi service provider has exclusively on the area. However, the supply of wi-fi services is more competitive on the high street and prices are falling rapidly as restaurants and coffee shops are using low-priced wi-fi access as a means of attracting customers. The more wi-fi providers there are in the market-place, the higher is the price elasticity of demand for wi-fi connections.

Wireless usage is growing across the UK with sales of 3G cards growing by 475%; these are mostly through business channels. In the consumer market, sales of wi-fi routers for the home have grown by 77%. Many broadband providers are now providing free wireless routers with each new broadband subscription.

Demand Curves with Different Price Elasticity of Demand

Elasticity of demand measures the responsiveness of demand to changes in price.

Where the % change in demand is greater than % change in price–demand is elastic.

Where the % change in demand is less than % change in price–demand is inelastic.

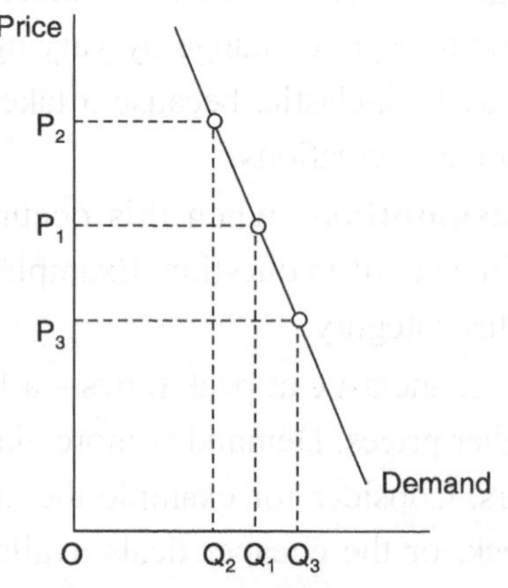

Fig. 8.14. Relatively inelastic demand.

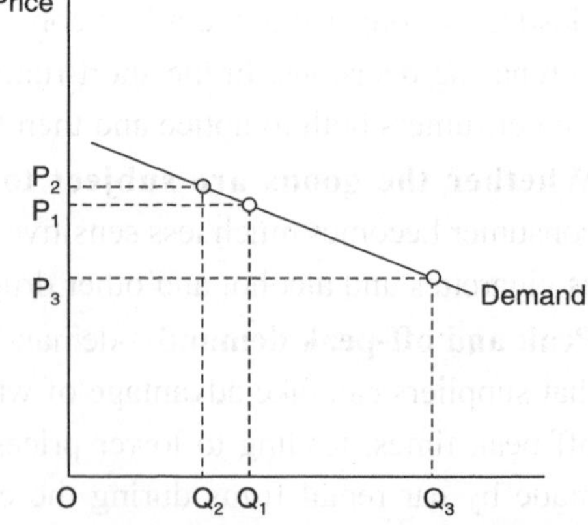

Fig. 8.15. Relatively elastic demand.

Elasticity of Demand and total Revenue for a Producer

The relationship between price elasticity of demand and a firm's total revenue is a very important one. The following figures show demand curves with different price elasticity and the effect of a change in the market price.

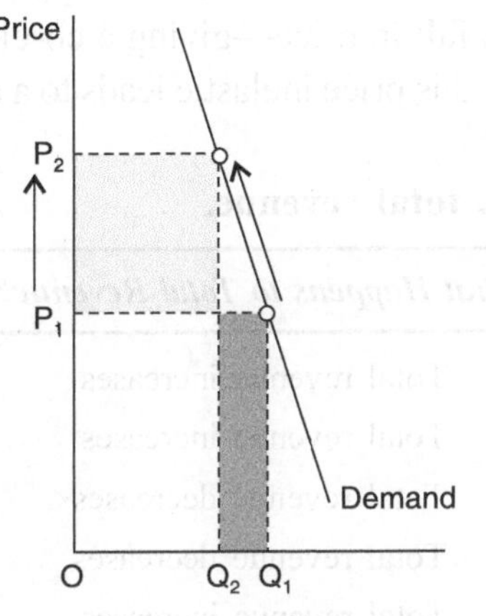

Fig. 8.16. Inelastic demand.

Fig. 8.17. Elastic demand.

When demand is inelastic—a rise in price leads to a rise in total revenue—for example, a 20% rise in price might cause demand to contract by only 5% (Ped = – 0.25)

When demand is elastic—a fall in price leads to a rise in total revenue—for example, a 10% fall in price might cause demand to expand by only 25% (Ped = + 2.5)

The following table gives a simple example of the relationships between market prices; quantity demanded and total revenue for a supplier. As price falls, the total revenue initially increases, in our example the maximum revenue occurs at a price of £12 per unit when 520 units are sold giving total revenue of £ 6240.

Table 8.8. Relationships between market-prices, quantity demanded and total revenue.

Price	*Quantity*	*Total Revenue*	*Marginal Revenue*
£ per unit	*Units*	*£s*	*£s*
20	200	4000	
18	280	5040	13
16	360	5760	9
14	440	6160	5
12	520	6240	1
10	600	6000	– 3
8	680	5440	– 7
6	760	4560	–11

Consider the price elasticity of demand of a price change from £20 per unit to £18 per unit. The % change in demand is 40% following a 10% change in price—giving an elasticity of demand of – 4 (*i.e.*, highly elastic). In this situation when demand is price elastic, a fall in price leads to higher total consumer spending/producer revenue.

Consider a price change further down the estimated demand curve—from £10 per unit to £8 per unit. The % change in demand = 13.3% following a 20% fall in price—giving a co-efficient of elasticity of – 0.665 (*i.e.*, inelastic). A fall in price when demand is price inelastic leads to a reduction in total revenue.

Table 8.9. Change in the market vs. total revenue.

Change in the Market	*What Happens to Total Revenue?*
Ped is inelastic and a firm raises its price	Total revenue increases
Ped is elastic and a firm lowers its price	Total revenue increases
Ped is elastic and a firm raises its price	Total revenue decreases
Ped is – 1.5 and the firm raises price by 4%	Total revenue decreases
Ped is – 0.4 and the firm raises price by 30%	Total revenue increases
Ped is – 0.2 and the firm lowers price by 20%	Total revenue decreases
Ped is – 4.0 and the firm lowers price by 15%	Total revenue increases

Elasticity of Demand and Indirect Taxation

Many products are subject to indirect taxation imposed by the government. Good examples include the excise duty on cigarettes (cigarette taxes in the UK are among the highest in Europe), alcohol and fuels. Here we consider the effects of indirect taxes on a producer's costs and the importance of price elasticity of demand in determining the effects of a tax on market price and quantity.

Most of the taxes are paid by producer

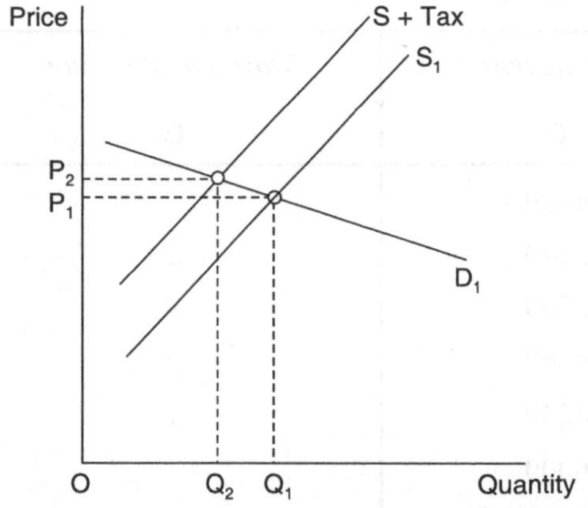

Fig. 8.18. A tax when demand is price elastic.

Most of the taxes are paid by the consumer

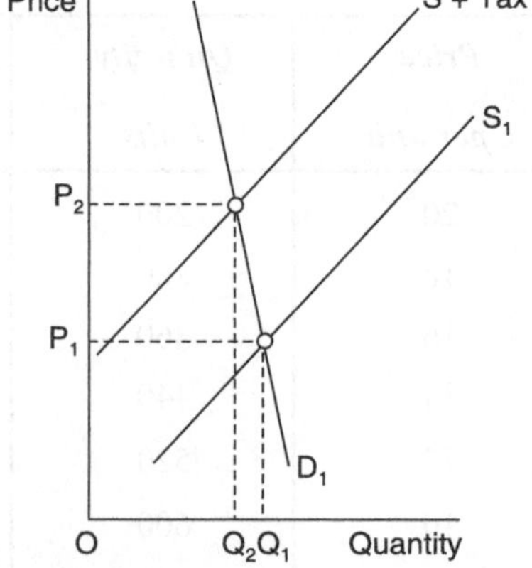

Fig. 8.19. A tax when demand is price inelastic.

A tax increases the costs of a business causing an inward shift in the supply curve. The vertical distance between the pre-tax and the post-tax supply curve shows the tax per unit. With an indirect tax, the supplier may be able to pass on some or all of this tax onto the consumer through a higher price. This is known as **shifting the burden of the tax** and the ability of businesses to do this depends on the price elasticity of demand and supply.

Consider Figs. 8.18 and 8.19 in Fig. 8.18, the demand curve is drawn as price elastic. The producer must absorb the majority of the tax itself (*i.e.,* accept a lower profit margin on each unit sold). When demand is elastic, the effect of a tax is still to raise the price—but we see a bigger fall in equilibrium quantity.

Output has fallen from Q_1 to Q_2 due to a contraction in demand. In Fig. 8.19, demand is drawn as price inelastic (*i.e.,* Ped < 1 over most of the range of this demand curve) and therefore the producer is able to pass on most of the tax to the consumer through a higher price without losing too much in the way of sales. The price rises from P_1 to P_2—but a large rise in price leads only to a small contraction in demand from Q_1 to Q_2.

The Usefulness of Price Elasticity for Producers

Firms can use price elasticity of demand (Ped) estimates to predict:

- The effect of a change in price on the total revenue and expenditure on a product.
- The likely **price volatility** in a market following unexpected changes in supply—this is important for commodity producers who may suffer big price movements from time to time.
- The effect of a **change in a government indirect tax** on price and quantity demanded and also whether the business is able to pass on some or all of the tax onto the consumer.
- Information on the price elasticity of demand can be used by a business as part of a policy of price discrimination (also known as yield management). This is where a monopoly supplier decides to charge different prices for the same product to different segments of the market *e.g.,* peak and off peak rail travel or yield management by many of our domestic and international airlines.

Income Elasticity of Demand

Income elasticity of demand is the % change in quantity demanded divided by the % change in income.

$$\varepsilon_d = \frac{\text{\% change in quantity demanded}}{\text{\% change in real income}}$$

- Income elasticity is positive for **normal (superior) goods** such as steak and vacations—more is purchased as income increases.
- Income elasticity is negative for **inferior goods** such as bread and hamburger—less is purchased as income increases.
- In times of recession, income elasticity determines loss in revenue by producing firms.

How sensitive is the demand for a product to a change in the real income of consumers? We use income elasticity of demand to measure this. The results are important since the values of income elasticity tell us something about the **nature of a product** and how it is perceived by consumers. It also affects the extent to which changes in economic growth affect the level and pattern of demand for goods and services.

Normal Goods: Normal goods have a positive income elasticity of demand so as consumers' income rises, more is demanded at each price level *i.e.,* there is an outward shift of the demand curve.

- **Normal necessities** have an income elasticity of demand of between 0 and + 1, for example, if income increases by 10% and the demand for fresh fruit increases by 4% then the income elasticity is + 0.4. Demand is rising less than proportionately to income.
- **Luxuries** have an income elasticity of demand > + 1 *i.e.,* the demand rises more than proportionately to a change in income—for example a 8% increase in income might lead to a 16% rise in the demand for restaurant meals. The income elasticity of demand in this example is + 2.0. Demand is highly sensitive to (increases or decreases in) income.

Inferior Goods: Inferior goods have a negative income elasticity of demand. Demand falls as income rises. Typically inferior goods or services tend to be products where there are **superior goods available** if the consumer has the money to be able to buy it. Examples include the demand for cigarettes, low-priced label foods in supermarkets and the demand for council-owned properties.

The income elasticity of demand is usually strongly positive for fine wines and spirits, high quality chocolates (*e.g.,* Lindt) and luxury holidays overseas, consumer durables, audio visual equipment, 3G mobile phones and designer kitchen, sports and leisure facilities (including gym membership and sports clubs).

In contrast, income elasticity of demand is lower for staple food products such as bread, vegetables and frozen foods, mass transport (bus and rail), beer and takeaway pizza. Income elasticity of demand is negative (inferior) for cigarettes and urban bus services.

Product Ranges: However, the income elasticity of demand varies within a product range. For example, the Ped for own-label foods in supermarkets is probably less for the high-value "finest" food ranges that most major supermarkets now offer. You would also expect income elasticity of demand to vary across the vast range of vehicles for sale in the car industry and also in the holiday industry.

Long-term Changes: There is a general downward trend in the income elasticity of demand for many products, particularly foodstuffs. One reason for this is that as a society becomes richer, there are changes in consumer perceptions about different goods and services together with changes in consumer tastes and preferences. What might have been considered a luxury goods several years ago might now be regarded as a necessity (with a lower income elasticity of demand).

Consider the market for foreign travel. A few decades ago, long-distance foreign travel was regarded as a luxury. Now as real price levels have come down and incomes have grown, so millions of consumers are able to fly overseas on short and longer breaks. For many an annual holiday overseas has become a necessity and not a discretionary item of spending!

How do Businesses Make use of Estimates of Income Elasticity of Demand?

Knowledge of income elasticity of demand for different products helps firms predict the effect of a business cycle on sales. All countries experience a business cycle where actually GDP moves up and down in a regular pattern causing booms and slowdowns or perhaps a recession. The business cycle means income rise and fall.

Luxury products with high income elasticity see greater sales volatility over the business cycle than necessities where demand from consumers is less sensitive to changes in the economic cycle.

Income Elasticity and the Pattern on Consumer Demand

Over time we expect to see our real incomes rise. And as we become better off, we can afford to increase our spending on different goods and services. Clearly what is happens to the relative prices of these products will play a key role in shaping our consumption decisions. But the income elasticity of demand will also affect the pattern of demand over time. For **normal luxury goods**, whose income elasticity of demand exceeds + 1, as incomes rise, the proportion of a consumer's income spend on that product will go up. For normal necessities (income elasticity of demand is positive but less than 1) and for inferior goods (where the income elasticity of demand is negative)—as income rises, the share or proportion of their budget on these products will fall.

Cross Price Elasticity of Demand

Very often, a change in the price of one product leads to a change in the demand for another, economists call this the cross-price effect and this is the focus of this chapter. Cross price elasticity (CPed) measures the responsiveness of demand for good X following a change in the price of good Y (a related goods). We are mainly concerned here with the effect that changes in relative prices within a market have on the pattern of demand. With cross price elasticity we make an important distinction between substitute products and complimentary goods and services.

Substitutes: With substitute goods such as brands of cereal or washing powder, an increase in the price of one goods will lead to an increase in demand for the rival product. Cross price elasticity for two substitutes will be positive.

Compliments: With goods that are in complimentary demand, such as the demand for DVD players and DVD videos, when there is a fall in the price of DVD players we expect to see more DVD players bought, leading to an expansion in market demand for DVD videos. The cross price elasticity of demand for two compliments is negative. The stronger the relationship between two products, the higher is the co-efficient of cross-price elasticity of demand. For example, with two close substitutes, the cross-price elasticity will be strongly positive. Likewise when there is a strong complimentary relationship between two products, the cross-price elasticity will be highly negative. Unrelated products have a zero cross elasticity.

How can Businesses Make use of the Concept of Cross Price Elasticity of Demand ?

Pricing strategies for substitutes: If a competitor reduces the price of a rival product, firms use estimates of cross-price elasticity to predict the effect on the quantity demanded and total revenue of their own product. For example, two or more airlines competing with each other on a given route will have to consider how one airline might react to its competitor's price change. Will many consumers switch? Will they have the capacity to meet an expected rise in demand? Will the other firm match a price rise? Will it follow a price fall?

Consider for example the cross-price effect that has occurred with the rapid expansion of low-cost airlines in the European airline industry. This has been a major challenge to the existing and well-established national air carriers, many of whom have made adjustments to their business model and pricing strategies to cope with the increased competition.

Pricing strategies for complimentary goods: Popcorn, soft drinks and cinema tickets have a high negative value for cross elasticity—they are strong compliments. Popcorn has a high mark up *i.e.,* popcorn costs pennies to make but sells for more than a pound. If firms have a reliable estimate for Cped they can estimate the effect, say, of a two-for-one cinema ticket offer on the demand for popcorn. The additional profit from extra popcorn sales may more than compensate for the lower cost of entry into the cinema.

Advertising and marketing: In highly competitive markets where brand names carry substantial value, many businesses spend huge amounts of money every year on persuasive advertising and marketing. There are many aims behind this, including attempting to shift out the demand curve for a product (or product range) and also build consumer loyalty to a brand. When consumers become habitual purchasers of a product, the cross-price elasticity of demand against rival products will decrease. This reduces the size of the substitution effect following a price change and makes demand less sensitive to price. The result is that firms may be able to charge a higher price, increase their total revenue and turn consumer surplus into higher profit.

For goods which are compliments, Cped will have negative sign and for goods which are substitutes, cross elasticity will have a positive sign.

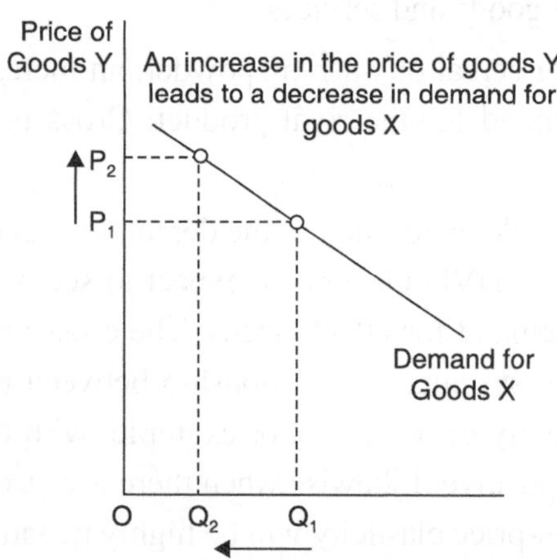

Fig. 8.20. Relationship between two close compliments.

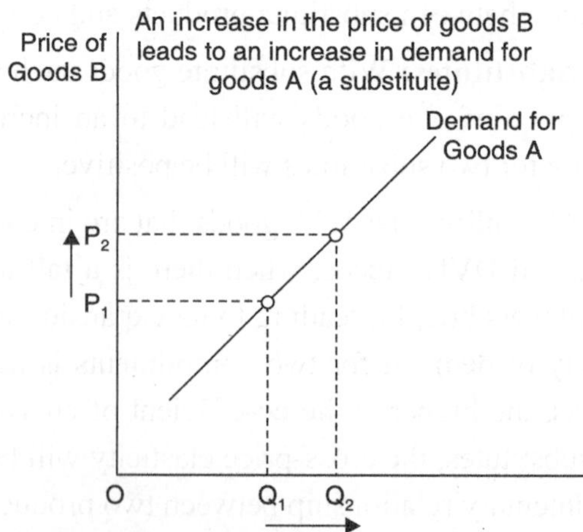

Fig. 8.21. Relationship between two substitutes.

Self-Assessment Questions

1. What do you understand by the term 'demand' in economics? Will a beggar desiring to purchase a Maruti car constitute demand? Explain.
2. Briefly point out the main determinants of demand for a commodity.
3. Individual demand schedules of Anil Batla, Sanjeev Dhingra and Vinod Nanglee are given in the following table. Prepare market demand curve geometrically.

Price	*Anil Batla*	*Sanjeev Dhingra*	*Vinod Nanglee*
1	30	60	110
2	22	40	10
3	16	30	45
4	12	24	36
5	10	20	32
6	9	18	30

4. State and explain the law of demand. State its assumptions and exceptions.
5. Give reasons for the following:
   (*a*) Why does demand for coffee rise, when price of tea increases?
   (*b*) Why does demand for car increase, when petrol becomes cheaper?
   (*c*) Why does demand for gur increase, when the price of sugar increases?
   (*d*) Give two reasons which may make a consumer buy more of a commodity even at a higher price.
6. Why does demand curve slope downward from left to right?
7. (*a*) When does a consumer buy a smaller quantity of the commodity at the same price?
   (*b*) When does a consumer buy more commodities at a particular price?
8. Distinguish between the following:
   (*i*) Demand schedule and demand curve
   (*ii*) Market demand schedule and household demand schedule
   (*iii*) Market demand curve and household demand curve
   (*iv*) Complimentary goods and substitute goods
   (*v*) Normal goods and inferior goods
   (*vi*) Income demand cross demand
   (*vii*) Income demand and substitution effect
   (*viii*) A shift of demand curve and a movement along a demand curve
   (*ix*) Extension in demand and increase in demand
   (*x*) Contraction in demand and decrease in demand.
9. Write short notes on the following:
   (*i*) Demand schedule for sugar
   (*ii*) Demand curve
   (*iii*) Giffen goods
   (*iv*) Prestige goods
   (*v*) Price effect.

Objective Type Questions

I. State whether the following statements are true or false:

(*i*) The desire and the demand of a commodity are the same.

(*ii*) The demand for cloth is 10,000 units in Rajouri Garden over one month.

(*iii*) The demand for pullovers is 5,000 units in Pitam Pura over one week, when the average price of a pullover is ₹ 300.

(*iv*) As size of population rises, the demand for commodities falls.

(*v*) The composition of population does not determine the demand for goods.

(*vi*) As income distribution becomes more equal, the demand for goods rises.

(*vii*) The demand curve always slopes downward from left to right.

(*viii*) Price effect = Income effect + Substitution effect.

(*ix*) Navpreet Kaur gave birth to a baby on March 9. The family expenditure on milk increased as a result. This is an example of extension in demand.

(*x*) Change in taste shifts the demand curve.

II. Fill in the blanks with appropriate words:

(*i*) Demand for a good is always expressed in relation to a particular ....

(*ii*) The requirement of two or more goods (like bricks and cement) at a time is an example of .... demand.

(*iii*) The demand for food is .... demand.

(*iv*) If the price of Limca goes up, the demand for Campa ....

(*v*) Demand schedule and demand curve supply the .... information.

(*vi*) Demand curve slopes .... because of the income and substitution effects.

(*vii*) If demand falls due to the rise in price of a commodity, it is called .... in demand.

(*viii*) If demand increases at the same price, it is the case of .... in demand.

(*ix*) For a given income, when price falls, there is ....

(*x*) A shift in income is known as ....

(*xi*) The amount of a commodity that consumers wish to purchase at various prices is called .... for the commodity.

(*xii*) The demand curve is a representation of the functional relation between .... and .... It differs from the demand function, because values of the other determinants of demand are assumed to be .... This assumption is frequently described by the latin term ....

(*xiii*) When an increase in the price of other good causes an increase in the demand for a commodity, the other goods are called a .... , if it causes a decrease, the other goods are called information.

(*xiv*) A movement along a demand curve implies a change in .... and therefore in the quantity ....

(*xv*) A shift in the demand curve may be caused by changes in any determinant .... function except that of the commodity.

(*xvi*) A change in the willingness of the consumer to purchase a particular product because of a change in something other than price is called a change in ....

Choose the Correct Answers

(*i*) When we draw a market demand curve, we

(*a*) Ignore tastes and incomes and all other prices.

(*b*) Assume that tastes, incomes and all other prices do not matter.

(*c*) Assume that tastes, incomes and all other prices change in the same way prices change.

(*d*) Assume that tastes, incomes and all other prices stay constant.

(*ii*) Consumer tastes and preference are

(*a*) Always treated as exogenous to the economic system.

(*b*) Always treated as endogenous to the economic system.

(*c*) So unpredictable that demand analysis is virtually impossible.

(*d*) Altered by such economic activities as advertising and demonstration effects.

(*iii*) A decrease in income can be predicted to

(*a*) Invariably cause shifts towards left in demand curves.

(*b*) Increase the quantity demanded of an inferior goods .

(*c*) Invariably cause shifts towards right in demand curves.

(*d*) Decrease the quantity demanded of an inferior goods.

(*iv*) A shift towards right in the demand curve for Corn Flakes would be predicted from

(*a*) A decrease in the number of breakfast eaters.

(*b*) A change in tastes in favour of hot cereals.

(*c*) A fall in the price of Corn Flakes.

(*d*) A rise in the price of wheat.

Unit 9

APPLICATIONS OF INDIFFERENCE CURVE ANALYSIS

9.1 INTRODUCTION

The indifference curve analysis was originally developed to study the consumer behaviour. Now, it has wide applications in explaining different economic phenomena. The indifference curve technique has also been fruitfully applied in analyzing various economic problems. The applications of the indifference curve analysis in explaining economic phenomena are discussed in this chapter. More important applications are explained in the next chapter.

9.2 DERIVATION OF DEMAND CURVE

Demand curve depicting the relationship between price and demand can be derived from the price consumption curve through indifference curve technique. The price effect and the price consumption curve are discussed below.

Price Effect and Price Consumption Curve

In consumer equilibrium, the consumer purchases such a combination of commodities on the budget line from which there is no tendency for change or rearrangement. However, if the price of only one commodity (say, 'X') changes, with everything else including consumer's income remaining unchanged, the consumer equilibrium will shift to a new budget line. The point of equilibrium corresponding to each price change will be given by the point at which the corresponding budget line touches the highest possible indifference curve. With every change in the price of commodity 'X', the budget line changes its slope, but its starting point on the Y-axis remains the same, as the price of commodity 'V' is assumed to be constant. In other words, the purchasing power of the consumer in terms of commodity 'V' remains unchanged, equal to OA. For fall in the price of commodity 'X', the budget line swings to the right and becomes flatter and flatter. On the other hand, when the price of commodity on the horizontal axis rises, the budget line will rotate about a pivot point on the Y axis clockwise (to the left). In limiting case, when the price of commodity 'X' rises to infinity, the budget line coincides with the Y-axis. In this case the consumer is forced out of buying commodity 'V' altogether and decides not to buy commodity 'X' at such a high price. Therefore, it can be said that the price consumption curve starts from that point on the axis ('X' or 'V'), whose price remains unaffected and moves to those points, where price of commodity changes.

In the figure below initial consumer equilibrium is shown at point E″ where the original budget line AB_1 touches the highest possible indifference curve IC_1. Suppose the price of commodity 'X' falls, the budget line shifts to the right from AB_1 to AB_2. The new budget line is tangent to a higher indifference curve IC_2 at point E_2. The new equilibrium of the consumer at point E_2 is to the right of point E_1 (This shows that the consumer buys more of a commodity 'X' as the price of commodity 'X' falls. He has become better off, *i.e.,* his level of satisfaction has increased as a result of the fall in the price of commodity X. When the price of commodity X further falls, the new consumer equilibrium point is point of contact (E) between the new budget line and the still higher indifference curve IC_2. When all these equilibrium points are joined together, what we get is price consumption curve. Thus, *price consumption curve* is the curve formed by connecting the various points of consumer equilibrium, depicting the most preferred combinations of the two commodities, when the price of one commodity is varied and all other things are kept constant. Price consumption curve traces out the price effect, which measures the effect of the changes in the price of one commodity (commodity 'X' in this case) on the consumer's demand of this commodity, when the price of other commodity, consumer's income and tastes as well as preferences remains unchanged. In Fig. 9.1 the movements from E_1 to E_2, and to E_3 indicate the price effect.

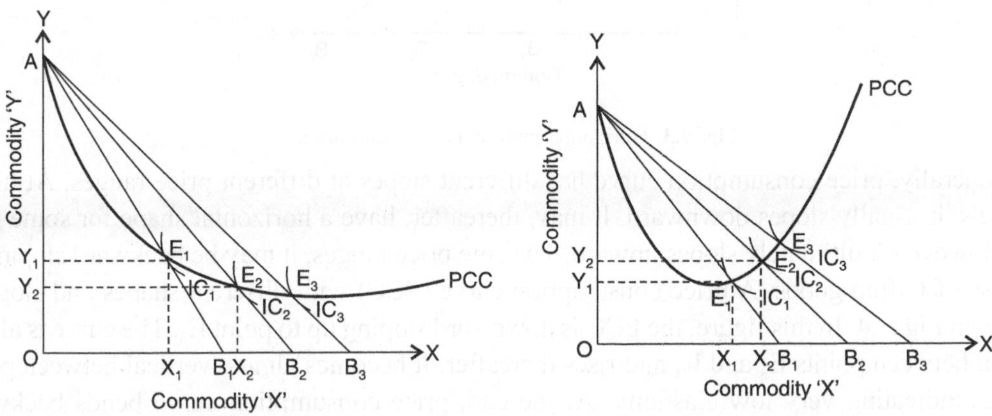

Fig. 9.1. The price effect. **Fig. 9.2.** The price consumption curve.

The shape of the price consumption curve (PCC) depends on the amount spent on commodity 'X', when its price falls. With amount spent on commodity 'X' rising, PCC will be downward sloping. When amount spent on 'X' is constant, PCC will be horizontal. Lastly, with amount spent falling, PCC will be upward sloping. These different cases are discussed below in details.

The price consumption curve (PCC) depicted in Fig. 9.2 is downward sloping. In this case, the consumer demands a larger quantity of commodity 'X' and a smaller quantity of commodity 'Y', if the price of commodity 'X' falls. When the equilibrium of the consumer shifts from point E_3 to point E_2 due to fall in the price of commodity 'X', the quantity demanded of commodity 'X' rises from OX_1 to OX_2 and the amount spent on this commodity rises from AY_1 to AY_2. Since, with fall in the price of commodity 'X' the expenditure on this commodity rises, the price elasticity of demand for commodity 'X' (by total outlay method) is greater than one. This implies that when PCC is downward sloping, the demand for commodity 'X' is elastic.

Upward sloping price consumption curve (PCC) is another possibility. In this case, as the price of commodity 'X' falls, the quantity demanded of commodities 'X' as well as 'Y' rises. Though the quantity demanded of commodity 'X' increases, when its price falls, the expenditure on this commodity falls from AY_1 to AY_2. Hence, the demand for commodity 'X' is inelastic.

Price consumption curve for a commodity can take horizontal shape also. It means that as the price of commodity 'X' falls, its quantity demanded rises proportionately, but, quantity demanded of commodity 'Y' remains the same. Fig. 9.3 illustrates horizontal price consumption curve. In this case, the expenditure on commodity 'X' remains unchanged at AY_1. Therefore, by total outlay method, the commodity has unitary elastic demand.

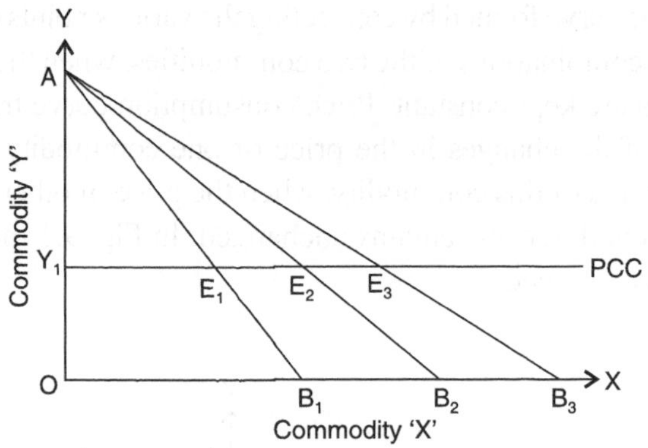

Fig. 9.3. Horizontal price consumption curve.

Generally, price consumption curve has different slopes at different price ranges. At higher price levels, it usually slopes downward. It may, thereafter, have a horizontal shape for some price ranges. However, it ultimately slopes upward. To some price ranges, it may be backward sloping, as in the case of Giffen goods. A price consumption curve (PCC) with different shapes and slopes is illustrated in Fig. 9.4. In this figure, the PCC is downward sloping up to point E_3. The curve is almost horizontal between points E_3 and E_4 and rises thereafter. It becomes almost vertical between points E_7 and E_8 indicating very low elasticity. At the end, price consumption curve bends backward, depicting direct price-demand relationship.

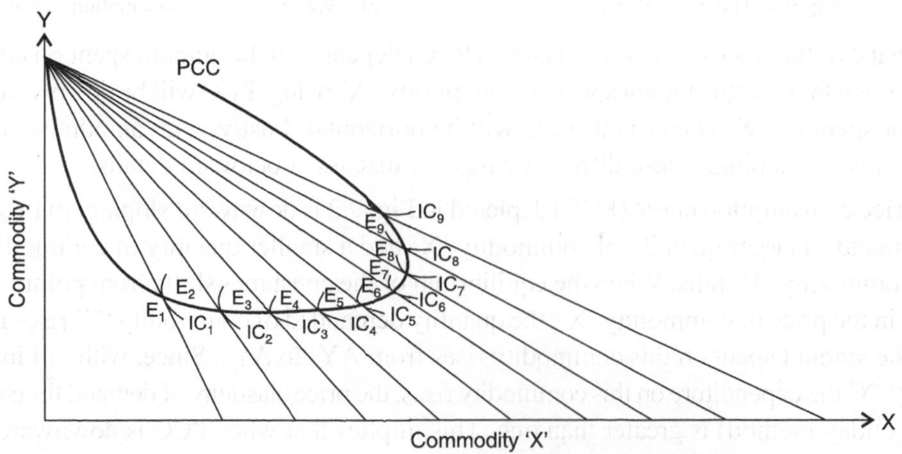

Fig. 9.4. A price consumption curve with different shapes and slopes.

Price Demand Relationship (Demand Curve)

Though price consumption curve (PCC) traces the effect of a change in the price of a commodity on its demand, yet it fails to relate the price with the quantity demanded. The diagram of PCC does not explicitly show price on either axis, whereas the demand curve clearly represents the price—demand relationship. The demand curve depicting this relationship can be derived from the price consumption curve of the indifference curve analysis.

In Fig. 9.5, the quantity of commodity 'X' is taken along the X-axis, while income of the consumer (₹ 60 in this case) is taken on the Y-axis. As the price of a commodity falls, the budget line shifts to the right in case of normal commodities. Consequently, the new equilibrium point

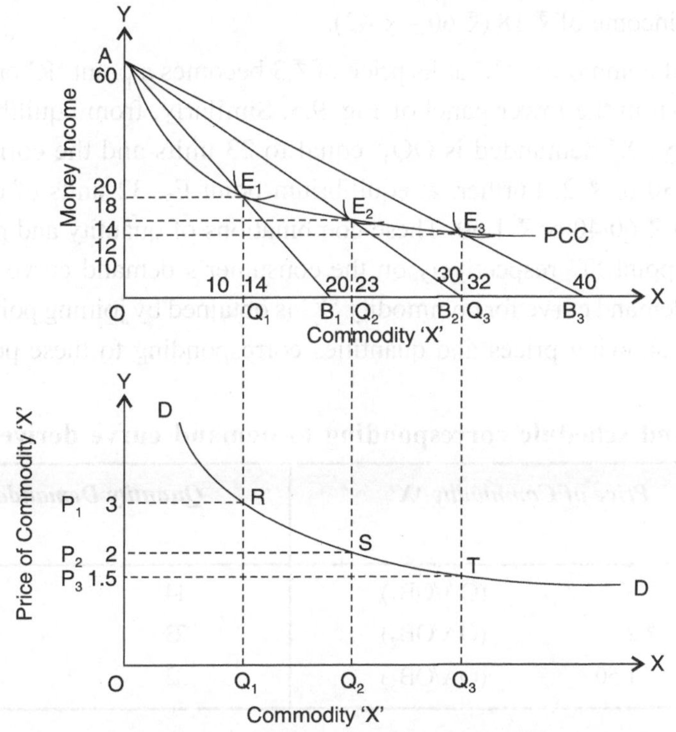

Fig. 9.5. Series of equilibrium points on budget lines.

occurs to the right of the previous equilibrium point. If the price of the commodity 'X' is allowed to fall from ₹ 3, to ₹ 2 to ₹ 1.50 and so on, we get a series of equilibrium points like E_1, E_2, E_3 on budget lines AB_1, AB_2 and AB_3, respectively in Fig. 9.5 (The consumer can purchase at the most 20, 30 and 40 units of commodity 'X' on these budget lines respectively). By joining the successive equilibrium points E_1, E_2 and E_3, we get a price consumption curve (PCC).

The demand curve in the lower panel diagram can be derived from the upper panel diagram. Since demand curve shows a relationship between price and quantity demanded of a commodity, the lower panel, like the upper panel of Fig. 9.5, still measures the quantity demanded of commodity 'X' on the horizontal axis. However, the vertical axis in the lower panel measures the price of commodity 'X'. Each point on the PCC corresponds to a particular quantity of commodity 'X'. Every point on this curve also corresponds to a particular price of this commodity, though there are no prices on the Y-axis. The price of commodity 'X' can be known from the slope of the budget line. It is, thus, clear that the PCC can provide information required to draw the demand curve, showing the quantity demanded of the commodity 'X' at various prices.

To derive demand curve from PCC, consider point of consumer equilibrium E, on budget line AB_1. The quantity demanded at this point is OQ_1. The price of commodity 'X' for this budget line is equal to money income (OA) divided by the number of units of commodity 'X' that can be bought with this money income (OB_1), OA, OB_1 or price of commodity 'X' in this case is equal to 60/20 or ₹ 3. At point E the consumer purchases 14 units of commodity 'X' by spending ₹ 42 (14 × ₹ 3) and has left with a money income of ₹ 18 (₹ 60 – ₹ 42).

Now, 14 units of commodity 'X' at its price of ₹ 3 becomes a point 'R' on the demand curve of the consumer, shown in the lower panel of Fig. 9.5. Similarly, from equilibrium point E_1' the quantity of commodity 'X' demanded is OQ_1' equal to 23 units and the corresponding price is OA/OB_2 equal to 60/30 or ₹ 2. Further, at equilibrium point E_3, 32 units of commodity 'X' are demanded at a price of ₹ 60/40 or ₹ 1.50. These combinations of quantity and price of commodity 'X' are point 'S' and point 'T' respectively on the consumer's demand curve depicted the lower panel of Fig. 9.5. The demand curve for commodity 'X' is obtained by joining points 'R', 'S' and 'T'. The demand schedule showing prices and quantities corresponding to these points is depicted in Table 9.1.

Table 9.1. Demand schedule corresponding to demand curve derived from PCC.

Price line	*Price of Commodity 'X'*		*Quantity Demanded to 'X'*	
AB_1	₹ 3	(OA/OB_1)	14	(OQ_1)
AB_2	₹ 2	(OA/OB_2)	23	(OQ_2)
AB_3	₹ 1.50	(OA/OB_3)	32	(OQ_3)

Thus, we observed that both the price consumption curve and the demand curve provide the same information, *i.e.,* how much of a commodity would be demanded by a consumer at different prices. However, the techniques of drawing the two curves are different and they assume different forms. Some of the differences between the two curves are as follows:

(*i*) The price consumption curve (PCC) is drawn with two commodities 'X' and 'Y' represented on the two axes. On one of the two axes, instead of a commodity, money income can also be taken. On the other hand, the demand curve is drawn with quantity demanded of the commodity on the X-axis and its price on the Y-axis. In the PCC, the price of the commodity is mentioned.

(*ii*) PCC tells us the size of the consumer's income and also the amount of money income left after the consumer has made the purchase of a commodity. The demand curve provides no such information, except that it is assumed to be constant.

(*iii*) PCC shows the total expenditure, when any number of units of a commodity are purchased. Price of the commodity can be calculated by dividing the total expenditure by the number of units of the commodity bought, when the entire money income is spent on it.

(*iv*) The price consumption curve clearly brings out separately the income and substitution effects of a change in the price of a commodity. The conventional demand curve does not attempt for splitting the price effect into income and substitution effects.

Deriving Demand Curve for a Giffen Good

Giffen goods are those commodities, the demand of which falls as the price of such goods falls. The demand for these goods has a positive slope, which means more is demanded when the price is higher and less is demanded when the price is lower. Derivation of demand curve for a Giffen commodity is explained below.

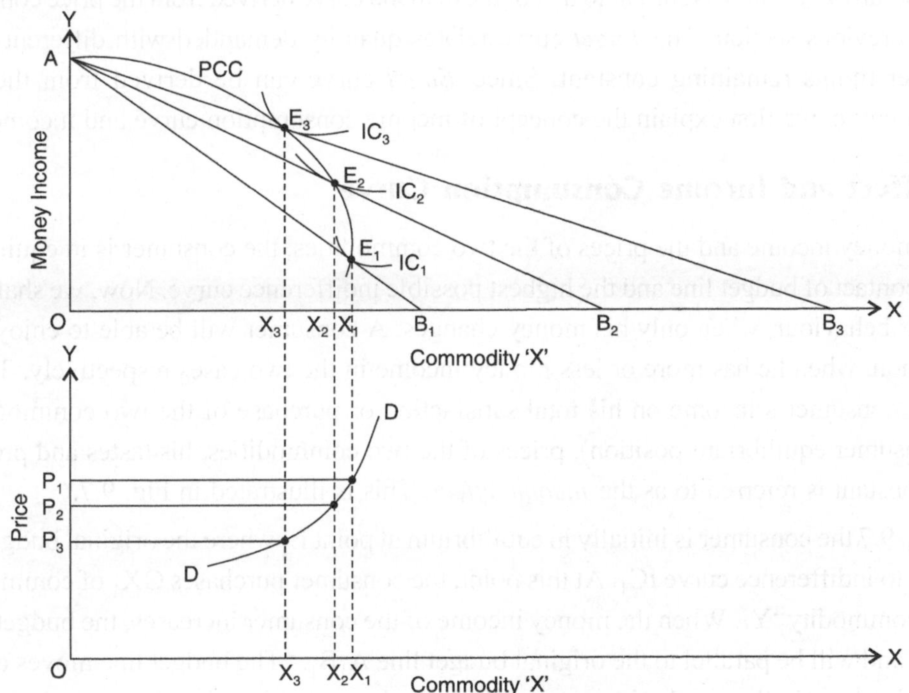

Fig. 9.6. Derivation of demand curve for a Giffen commodity.

In Fig. 9.6, commodity 'X' is assumed to be Giffen commodity. In this figure, the consumer is at equilibrium at point E_1, where the initial budget line AB_1 is tangent to the indifference curve IC_1. At this equilibrium, the consumer purchases OX_1 quantity of the commodity 'X' at price OA/OB_1. When the price of commodity 'X' falls, the new budget line AB_2 is to the right of the original budget line AB. The new equilibrium point is E_2. Since commodity 'X' is a Giffen commodity, the demand for this commodity falls to OX_2 and the new equilibrium point E_2 is to the left of the original equilibrium

E. The price of commodity 'X' in this situation is OA/OB_2 . When the price of commodity 'X' falls further, the new budget line AB_3 becomes tangent to the indifference curve IC_3 at point E_3. At this equilibrium point, the demand of the consumer for commodity 'X' falls to OX_3. The price consumption curve (PCC) for the Giffen commodity 'X' is obtained by joining the successive equilibrium points E_1, E_2 and E_3. This PCC is found to be backward bending.

With the above information from PCC, demand curve for the Giffen commodity can be drawn in the lower panel of Fig. 9.6. It may be seen that the demand curve of a Giffen commodity has a positive slope, which indicates that the quantity demanded falls (from OX to OX_2 to OX), as the price decreases (from OA/OB_1 to OA/OB_2 to OA/OB_3). In other words, the quantity demanded varies directly with the changes in price. This case is an exception to the general law of demand.

9.3 DERIVATION OF ENGEL CURVE

The concept of an *Engel* curve is similar to that of the demand curve derived from the price consumption curve in the previous section. The *Engel* curve relates quantity demanded with different levels of income, other things remaining constant. Since *Engel* curve can be derived from the income consumption curve, we first explain the concept of income consumption curve and income effect.

Income Effect and Income Consumption Curve

With given money income and the prices of the two commodities, the consumer is in equilibrium at the point of contact of budget line and the highest possible indifference curve. Now, we shall analyze the consumer behaviour, when only his money changes. A consumer will be able to enjoy more or less satisfaction, when he has more or less money income in the two cases respectively. The effect of change in consumer's income on his total satisfaction or purchase of the two commodities, (as given by consumer equilibrium position), prices of the two commodities, his tastes and preferences remaining constant is referred to as the *income effect*. This is illustrated in Fig. 9.7.

In Fig. 9.7 the consumer is initially in equilibrium at point E_1 where the original budget line $A_1 B_1$ is tangent to indifference curve IC_1. At this point, the consumer purchases OX_1 of commodity 'X' and OY_1 of commodity 'Y'. When the money income of the consumer increases, the budget line will shift upward and will be parallel to the original budget line A_1B_1. "The budget line moves out by the proportion of change in the purchasing power. With the increased income, the consumer would be able to choose a combination of the two commodities on a higher indifference curve IC_2. In Fig. 9.7, the new budget line A_2B_2 touches this indifference curve at point E_2 where the consumer consumes OX_2 of commodity 'X' and OY_2 of commodity 'Y'. It is clear from the figure that with increased money income, the consumer is able to purchase larger quantities of both the commodities. Since he is on the higher indifference curve IC_2, he will be better off than before, *i.e.,* his level of satisfaction will rise. If the money income of the consumer increases further, the budget line will have a further upward parallel shift to $A_3 B_3$. The consumer is now in equilibrium at point E_3 where the budget line

A_3 B_3 is tangent to indifference curve IC_3. Here, the consumer consumes greater quantities of both the commodities.

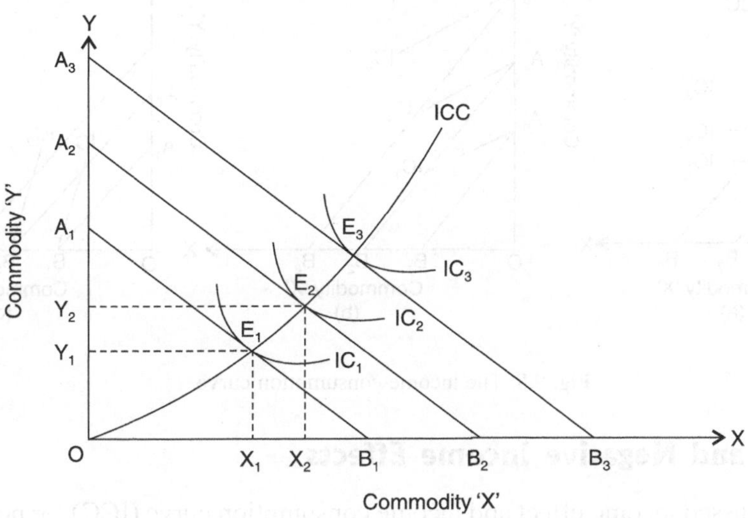

Fig. 9.7. The income effect.

The curve obtained by connecting successive consumer's equilibrium points (E_1, E_2 and E_3 in this case) at various levels of money income of the consumer, other things remaining unchanged, is known as income consumption curve. It is, thus, locus of combinations of the two commodities, when the money income is varied and prices of the commodities, tastes, preferences, etc. are held constant. The *income consumption curve* (ICC) traces out the income effect of the change in money income of the consumer. ICC invariably starts from the origin, because, if the consumer had no income, the quantities of commodities 'X' and 'Y' he could purchase must be zero. However ICC need not be a straight line curve. At every point on such a curve $Px/Py = MRSx, y$ and since $(PxPy)$ is constant for all parallel budget lines (with same slope) A_1 B_1, A_2 B_2, A_3 B_3, so $MRSx,y$ is constant throughout ICC.

In Fig. 9.7, income effect is indicated by the movements from consumer equilibrium points E_1 to E_2 to E_3. In this figure, X_1X_2 shows positive income effect for commodity 'X', while Y_1Y_2 measures positive income effect for commodity 'Y', as with rise in money income, a consumer purchases more of these commodities. Only an upward sloping income consumption curve can show rising consumption of the two commodities, as income increases.

When the two commodities are perfect complements to each other, they have to be used in fixed proportions. In such a situation, as discussed in the previous chapter indifference curves will be L-shaped and the points of consumer equilibrium will occur, where the common points of the indifference curves meet the budget line. Hence, income consumption curve will be linear (upward sloping) as shown in Fig. 9.8 (*a*). On the other hand, for perfect substitutes, the ICC will coincide with the X or Y axis, as shown in Fig. 9.8(*b*) and Fig. 9.8(*c*) respectively.

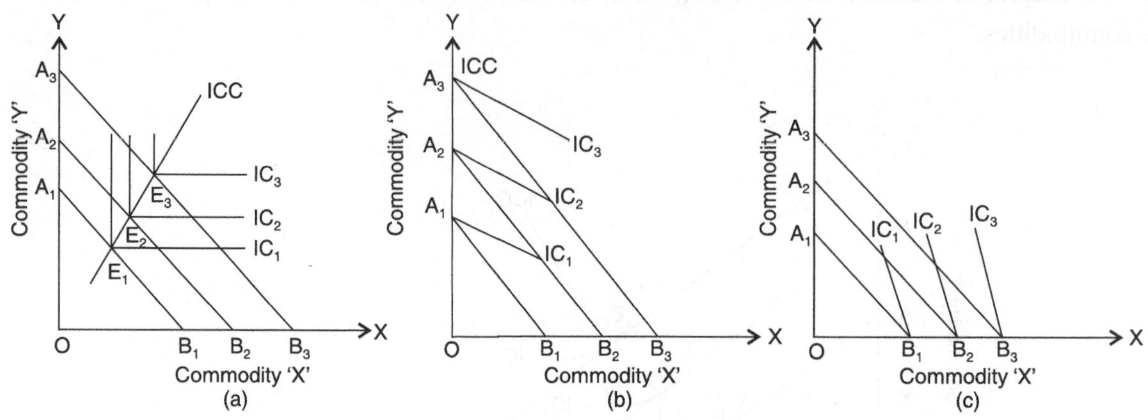

Fig. 9.8. The income consumption curve.

Positive, Zero and Negative Income Effects

So far we have discussed income effect and income consumption curve (ICC) for normal or superior commodities (luxuries or comforts). For such commodities, the income effect is positive, *i.e.*, consumers demand more of these commodities with rise in the money income and ICC is upward sloping. However, the income effect for a commodity can also be zero or negative. The income effect is zero for those commodities, which the consumer purchases in fixed quantities (*e.g.*, drugs, salt, etc.) irrespective of the level of income of the consumer. Here, an increase in income will not be followed by any increase in the quantity demanded. Zero income effect for commodity 'X' is illustrated in Fig. 9.9(*a*). In this figure, the X-axis represents the quantity of salt, whereas the Y-axis represents other commodity. The money income of the consumer rises from OA_1 to OB_1 but, the consumer continues to demand OX_1 quantity of salt. Therefore, the income effect of salt in this case is equal to zero. This means that the consumer spends the same amount of his money income on salt and the additional money income is used to purchase other commodity. ICC in case of commodities with zero income effect is vertical. Its income elasticity of demand is equal to zero, since with change in income of the consumer, the demand for commodity 'X' remains unchanged.

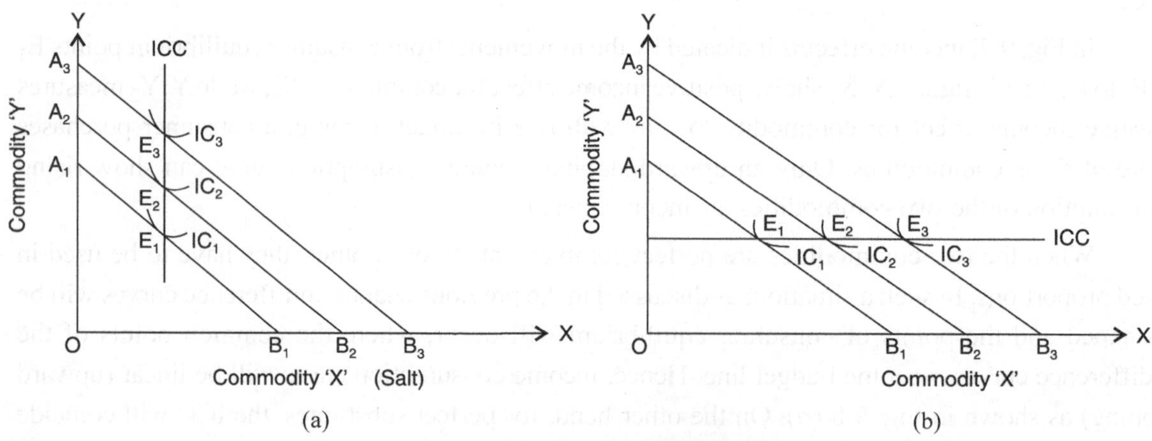

Fig. 9.9. Zero income effect.

Income consumption curve with zero income effect for commodity 'Y' will be horizontal indicating no change in the demand for this commodity in equilibrium, irrespective of any change in the income of the consumer. Income elasticity of demand for commodity 'Y' is zero.

The income effect is negative for those commodities, which are considered inferior (*e.g.*. wheat, maize, jowar, bajra, cereals, vegetable oils, cotton clothes, etc.) by the consumer. For such commodities, with the increase in income of the consumers, the consumption of the commodity falls, as the consumer starts substituting superior commodities for them. In other words, poor people cannot afford to purchase expensive superior commodities. But, when they become richer, they are in a position to shift their purchase towards more expensive superior commodities. A negative income effect is illustrated in Fig. 9.10(*a*).

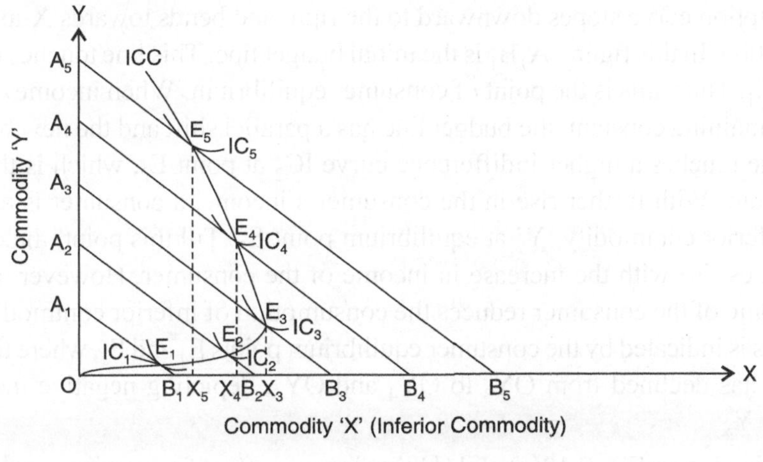

(a)

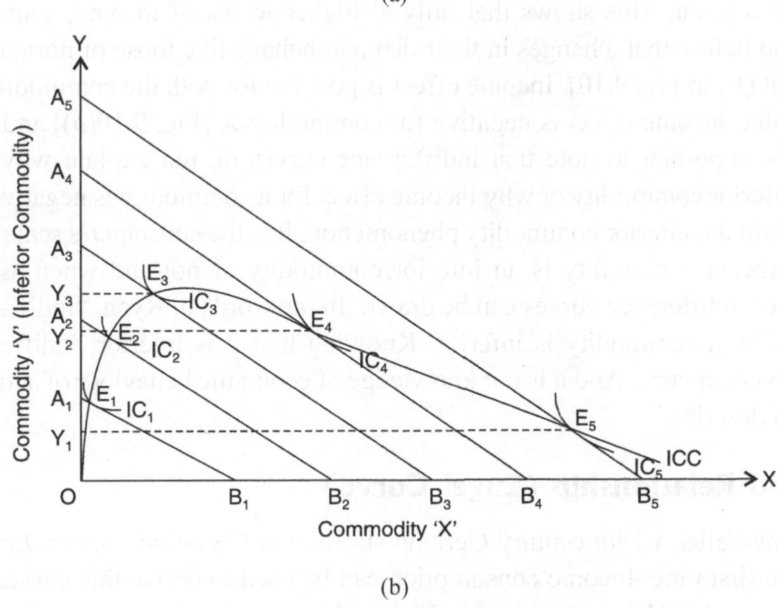

(b)

Fig. 9.10. A negative income effect.

In Fig. 9.10(*b*) with higher budget line $A_3 B_3$, $A_4 B_4$, $A_5 B_5$ the demand for inferior commodity (taken on the X-axis) declines from OX_3 to OX_4 and then to OX_5, with rise in the level of money income. This is shown by the relative positions of equilibrium points E_3, E_4 and E_2. Point E_5 lies to the left of point E_4 which lies to the left of point E_3, indicating a lower quantity of commodity 'X', despite the fact that it (E_5) is on a higher budget line and thus involves a higher income for the consumer. The consumer instead, purchases more of superior commodity (shown on the Y-axis), the income consumption curve obtained by joining the successive equilibrium points in the figure bends towards Y-axis, as increased money income of the consumer beyond point E_3 would reduce the demand for commodity 'X'. Thus, ICC slopes backward (*i.e.*. upward to the left), when commodity 'X' is an inferior commodity.

If, on the other hand, commodity shown on the Y-axis happens to be an inferior commodity, the income consumption curve slopes downward to the right and bends towards X-axis. Fig. 9.10(*b*) illustrates this situation. In this figure, A_1B_1 is the initial budget line. This line touches the indifference curve IC_1 at point E_1. Thus, this is the point of consumer equilibrium. When income of the consumer increases, prices remaining constant, the budget line has a parallel shift and the new budget line is A_2 B_2. This budget line touches a higher indifference curve IC_2 at point E_2, which is the new point of consumer equilibrium. With further rise in the consumer's income, a consumer is able to purchase OY_3 quantity of inferior commodity 'Y' at equilibrium point E_3. Till this point, the consumption of both the commodities rise with the increase in income of the consumer. However, any subsequent increase in the income of the consumer reduces the consumption of inferior commodity (commodity X_1 in this case). This is indicated by the consumer equilibrium points E_4 and E_5, where the consumption of commodity 'Y' has declined from OY_3 to OY_4 and OY_5, depicting negative income effect for inferior commodity Y.

It can be noticed from Fig. 9.10(*a*) and (*b*) that income effect for inferior commodity becomes negative only after a point. This shows that only at higher levels of income, some commodities become inferior and before that, changes in their demand behave like those of normal commodities up to a certain point (E_3 in Fig. 9.10). Income effect is positive for both the commodities up to point E_3. Beyond this point, income effect is negative for commodity X [Fig. 9.10(*a*)] and commodity Y [Fig. 9.10(*b*)]. It is important to note that indifference curves do not explain why a commodity happens to be an inferior commodity or why income effect for a commodity is negative. Indifference curves merely explain the inferior commodity phenomenon. It is the consumer's scale of preferences which tell us whether a commodity is an inferior commodity or not and when as well as why. Accordingly, a set of indifference curves can be drawn. In the words of Ryan, "Indifference analysis can never tell us why a commodity is inferior. Knowing that it is inferior, indifference analysis describes this, it never explains. And it is our knowledge of economic behaviour of actual households that tell us what to describe."

Income-Demand Relationship (Engel Curve)

Engel curve is named after a 19th century German statistician *Christian Lorenz, Ernst Engel* who developed it for the first time. Income consumption can be used to derive this curve. Derivation of *Engel* curve for commodity 'X' is illustrated in Fig. 9.11.

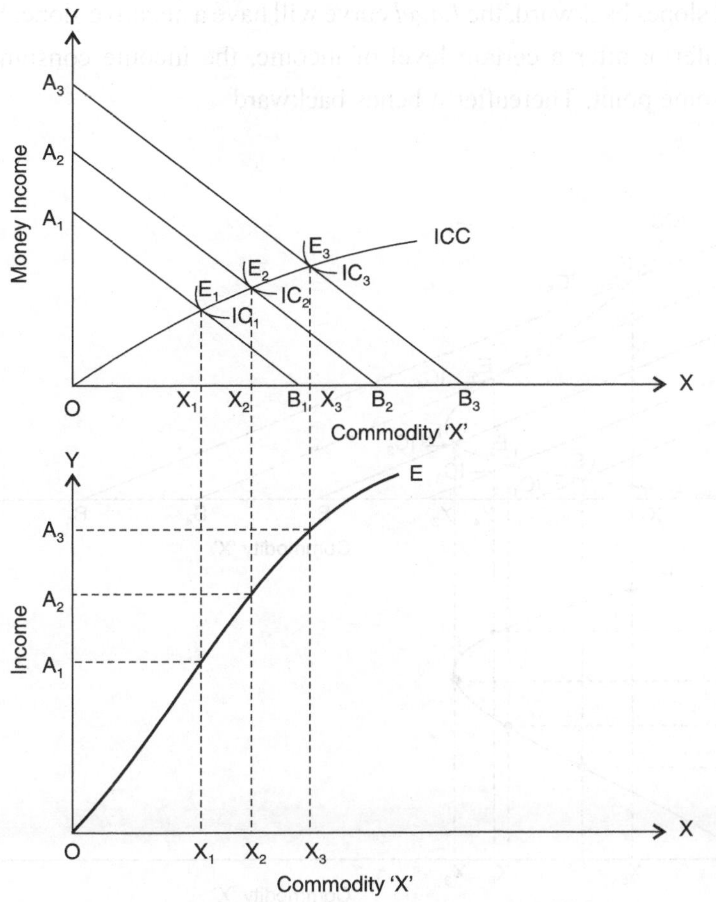

Fig. 9.11. Derivation of Engel curve for commodity X.

In the upper panel of Fig. 9.11, three parallel budget lines $A_1 B_1$, $A_2 B_2$ and $A_3 B_3$ corresponds to OA_1, OA_2 and OA_3 levels of money income respectively, prices of the commodities remaining constant. The income consumption curve (ICC) is obtained by joining the points of tangency of these budget lines with the indifference curves IC_1, IC_2 and IC_3 respectively. Each point on the ICC corresponds to a particular quantity of commodity 'X'. Each point on the ICC also corresponds to particular money incomes.

The various pairs of the income and the quantity purchased of commodity 'X' (OA_1, OX_1), (OA_2, OX_2) and (OA_3, OX_3) corresponding to three equilibrium points E_1, E_2 and E_3 are plotted in the lower panel of the Fig. 9.11 to obtain the *Engel* curve. This *Engel curve indicates the relationship between the income level and the quantity of the commodity purchased by the consumer.*

Engel Curve and Inferior Goods

The shape of *Engel* curve depends upon the shape of income consumption curve (ICC). As discussed earlier, when ICC has a positive slope the corresponding *Engel* curve will also have a positive slope.

However, when ICC slopes backward, the *Engel* curve will have a negative slope. Since commodities generally become inferior after a certain level of income, the income consumption curve has a positive slope upto some point. Thereafter it bends backward.

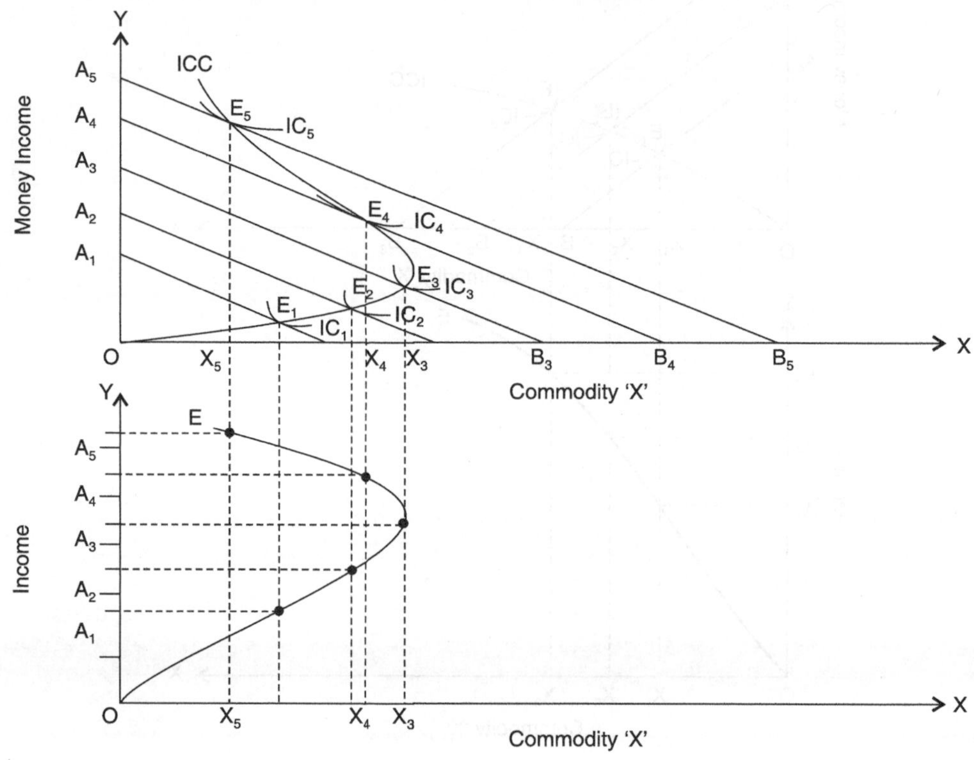

Fig. 9.12. Shape of Engel curve depends upon the shape of income consumption curve.

In Fig. 9.12 the income consumption curve is obtained by joining the points of contact of the budget lines A_1 B_1, A_2 B_2, A_3 B_3 with indifference curves IC_1, IC_2 and IC_3 respectively. As the level of income rises, the corresponding equilibrium points E_1, E_2 and E_3 represent greater and greater consumption of commodity 'X'. But, when the level of income rises further, the demand for commodity 'X' (being an inferior commodity) falls from OX_3 to OX_4 and then to OX_5. Therefore, ICC rises up to point E_3 and bends backward beyond this point. When various income levels OA_1, OA_2, OA_3, OA_4 and OA_1 are plotted against the quantities demanded corresponding to equilibrium points (E_1, E_2, E_3, E_4 and E_5 respectively) on these budget lines in the lower panel diagram of an Engel curve is formed for the inferior commodity 'X'.

This Engel curve rises upward (positive slope) initially, but bends backward beyond a point. Its shape is again similar to that of the income consumption curve.

Engel Curve and Demand Curve

A demand curve for a commodity shows how its demand changes due to changes in its price, assuming other things remain constant. On the other hand, *Engle* curve indicates how the demand for a commodity changes, when the income of a consumer changes, other things remaining unchanged. The relation between demand curve for commodity X and its *Engel* curve is illustrated in Fig. 9.13.

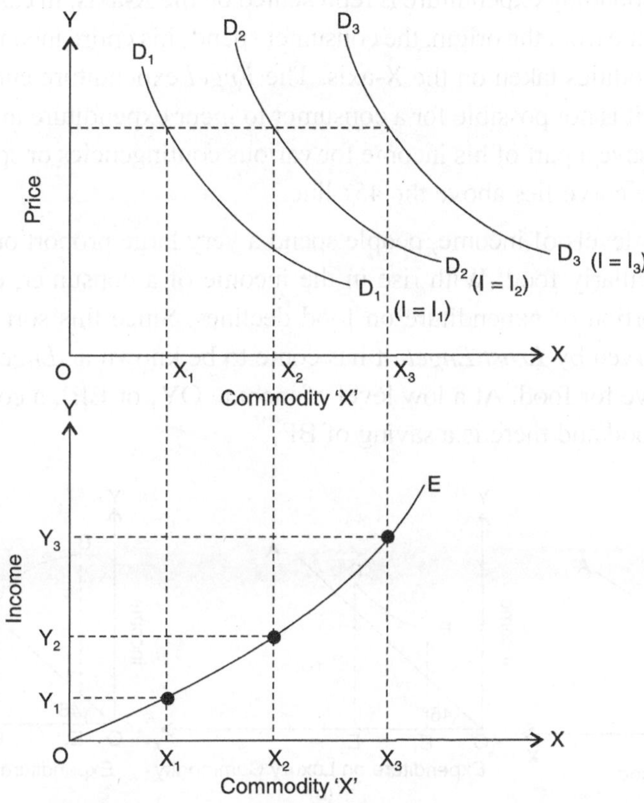

Fig. 9.13. The relation between demand curve for commodity X and its Engel curve.

The upper panel of Fig. 9.13 depicts demand curve for commodity 'X'. Price of this commodity is shown along the Y-axis and its quantity demanded is taken along the X-axis. The initial demand curve corresponds to a level of income $I = I$. When the income of the consumer rises to $I = I_2$ and then to $I = I_3$, the demand curve shifts to the right to D_2 and then to D_3. Consequent upon the rise in income of the consumer, the quantity demanded increases from OX_1 to OX_2. *Engel* curve showing the relationship between income and demand is constructed by plotting income demand points ($OY_1 = I_1$, OX_1), ($OY_2 = I_2$, OX_2) and ($OY_3 = I_3$, OX_3) in the lower panel diagram. In this figure of *Engel* curve, income is shown along the Y-axis, while quantity demanded of commodity 'X' is still shown on the X-axis.

Engel Expenditure Curve

Engel curve explains the relation between the income level and the quantity of a commodity purchased, while the *Engel* expenditure curve relates income to expenditure on the commodity purchased. Economists are often interested in conducting family expenditure surveys to determine the expenditure behaviour of the households. *Engel* expenditure curve serves as a useful device in all such studies.

An *Engel* expenditure curve is illustrated in Fig. 9.14, where the income level is shown along the Y-axis and the corresponding expenditure is represented on the X-axis. In case this curve happens to coincide with the 45° line from the origin, the consumer spends his entire income on the commodity 'X' or a group of commodities taken on the X-axis. The *Engel* expenditure curve cannot lie below this line, since normally it is not possible for a consumer to incur expenditure more than the income. As the consumer has to save a part of his income for various contingencies or speculations, thus, the actual *Engel* expenditure curve lies above the 45° line.

At extremely low levels of income, people spend a very large proportion of their income on necessities of life, particularly food. With rise in the income of a consumer, expenditure on food increases, but the proportion of expenditure on food declines. Since this sort of behaviour of the consumer was first observed by *Ernst Engel*, it has come to be known as *Engel's* law. Fig. 9.14(*a*) illustrates the *Engel* curve for food. At a low level of income OY_1 or BE_1, a consumer spends only OE_1 equal to $F_1 E_1$ on food and there is a saving of BF_1.

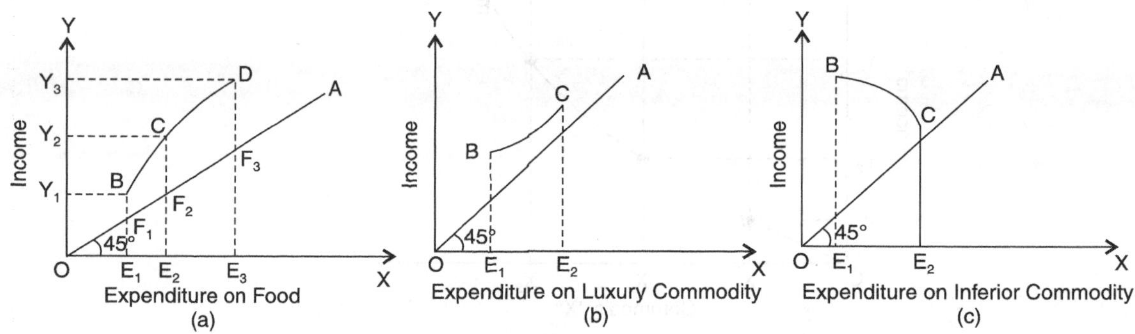

Fig. 9.14. Engel expenditure curve.

When the income level rises to OY_2 or CE_2, the expenditure of the consumer increases to OE_2 equal to $F_2 E_2$, the saving increases to CF_2. Further, when the income goes up to OY_3 or OE_3, the expenditure of the consumer on food becomes OE equal to F_3 E which is and hence there is saving of DF_3, which is still higher than CF_2. We observe that with increase in the income of the consumer, though the expenditure on food rises in absolute terms, it declines in percentage terms. As a result, the *Engel* expenditure curve diverges more and more from the 45° line, as income increases.

If an *Engel* expenditure curve is drawn for luxury commodities, we observe that the expenditure rises more than proportionately to rise in income at higher income levels (Expenditure curve for inferior commodities declines as income rises.)

9.4 SPLITTING OF PRICE EFFECT

Whenever price of a commodity falls (price of other commodity and money income remaining unchanged) or when relative price of a commodity falls, the consumer (given a constant money income) substitutes this commodity for the other one so as to maintain the original standard of living. This is referred to as *substitution effect*. Thus, the substitution effect may be defined as the change in the consumption of the two commodities (or the substitution of one commodity by the other) as a result of a change in their relative prices (given constant money income), so that the consumer is able to maintain the original standard of living by remaining on the same indifference curve.

Substitution effect implies a change in the quantity bought, when the price of the commodity changes, after 'adjusting' the income, so that the real income of the consumer remains the same as before. This adjustment of income was explained differently by Hicks and by Slutsky. Hicks assumes constancy of real purchasing power of the consumer by keeping the consumer on the same satisfaction level. Slutsky keeps real purchasing power constant in the sense that the consumer could purchase the original combination of the commodities. It will be noticed that Slutsky's substitution effect pushes the consumer to a higher indifference curve. It implies that Slutsky's substitution effect exceeds Hicksian's substitution effect.

Hicksian and *Slutsky* approaches have their own merits and demerits. Hicksian approach is useful for the analysis of consumer surplus and welfare economics. But, it is not so easy to know the compensating variation under this approach, as it requires the knowledge of indifference curve, revealing tastes and preferences of the consumer between various combinations of commodities. On the other hand, *Slutsky* approach can be easily used to establish the law of demand. Under this approach, it is easier to find out the amount of income by which income of the consumer is to be adjusted to isolate the substitution effect. It has the merit of being dependent on observable market data. However, the substitution effect isolated by this approach involves some gain in the real income, graphically shown as a movement to a higher indifference curve.

Whenever the price of a commodity changes (with the price of other commodity and money income of the consumer remaining constant), the real income of the consumer changes. As a result the consumer is able to rearrange his purchases. This implies that income effect exists as an element of price effect. Further, the consumer also intends to substitute relatively expensive commodity (whose price has remained constant) with the cheaper one (whose price has fallen). This shows that the substitution effect is also present in the price. *Hicksian* and *Slutsky* approaches for separating the price effect into substitution effect and income effect are discussed now.

Break-up of Price Effect under Hicksian Approach (Through Compensating Variation)

J.R. Hicks has defined 'original standard of living' in terms of level of satisfaction. According to him, when the relative prices of the commodities change, the money income of the consumer is altered in such a manner that his real purchasing power remains constant and he is neither better off nor worse off than before *i.e.,* he continues to remain on the same indifference curve. Let us now discuss Hicksian substitution effect in the case of price fall and price rise.

Normal Commodity Case (Price Fall): Consider two commodities, tea and coffee. Tea is shown on the X-axis and coffee on the Y-axis. The initial budget line AB is tangent to the indifference curve IC at point 'E'. At this equilibrium point, the consumer purchases OX of commodity 'X' and OY of commodity 'Y'. Suppose the price of tea declines, which will increase the purchasing power or real income of the consumer. With decline in the price of tea, the equilibrium of the consumer will shift to point 'F', where the outer new budget line AB touches a higher indifference curve IC. The movement from point 'E' to point 'F' is called the price effect. In quantity terms, the price effect is given by the expansion in the quantity demanded of tea from OX_1 to OX_2, *i.e.,* X_1 X_2, as shown in Fig. 9.15. Now, this price effect can be broken up into two parts—substitution effect and income effect. The procedure of separation is discussed as follows.

Let us assume that an income worth DB' quantity in terms of tea or CA in terms of coffee is taken away from the consumer (at the new price ratio), so that the real income of the consumer is held constant and he comes back to his original indifference curve IC. This required reduction in his money income, which is just sufficient to neutralize the income effect of the fall in price (rise in real income) is referred to as *compensating variation in income.* It is shown graphically by a parallel shift of the new budget line AB' until it becomes tangent to the original indifference curve. The purpose of the compensating variation is to allow the consumer to remain on the same level of satisfaction as before the price change and to isolate the substitution effect from the price effect. In Fig. 9.15, the compensated budget line CD is tangent to initial indifference curve IC at point 'G'. This point is to the right of the point of original tangency 'E', since budget line CD is parallel to the new budget line AB' which is less steep than the original budget line AB (the slope of indifference gets smaller towards the right). The movement from point 'E' to point 'G' reflects the *Hicksian* substitution effect of a price change. It is the response of a consumer to a change in relative price ratio, holding real income constant. As tea has become relatively cheaper, the consumer demands more of tea and less of coffee now. In quantity terms, the Hicksian substitution effect is given by the expansion in the quantity demanded of tea from OX_1 to OX_3, *i.e.,* X_1 X_3 as shown in Fig. 9.15. (The quantity purchased of commodity 'Y' gets reduced from OY_2 to OY_1). It is clear from Fig. 9.15 that the substitution effect can always be represented by a movement along an indifference curve.

In substitution effect, the consumer is on the same indifference curve. He can purchase the same quantities of commodities as before. That is why, *mathematically, the sign of substitution effect is always negative* (relative to the price of one commodity, if the price of the other commodity decreases, the quantity demanded of the latter increases and *vice versa*). It always induces the consumer to buy more of the commodity, the price of which has fallen in comparison to an other, the price of which has either increased or remained constant.

The reason is not difficult to understand. For two commodities 'X' and 'Y' if the price of commodity 'X' falls and that of commodity 'Y' remains constant, the marginal significance of commodity X in terms of commodity 'Y' increases. Thus, every rupee spent on commodity 'X' will bring more satisfaction to the consumer than commodity 'Y'. He would not mind in diverting expenditure from commodity 'Y' to commodity 'X', since the latter has become cheaper in relation to the former. Thus, quantity demanded and price move in opposite directions, even after money income is adjusted to hold real income constant. The substitution effect may however be strong or weak, depending upon the portion of income that is spent on the relevant commodity. The bigger the portion of expenditure, the stronger the effect. This is equally true for income effect (explained in the previous section) also.

To isolate the income effect from the price effect, the money taken away from the consumer is restored to him, so that he is back from equilibrium point 'G' on indifference curve IC to the equilibrium point 'F' on the higher indifference curve IC′ and budget line AB′ (parallel shift with the same relative prices). The consumer has in fact a higher purchasing power. If the commodity 'X' is a normal commodity, he will spend some of his increased 'real income' on this commodity. Change in real income will change the consumption in general and in particular of the commodity whose price has changed. The movement from point 'G' to point 'F' is only due to the increase in income and therefore measures the income effect. In quantity terms, income effect is given by the expansion of the quantity demanded of tea from OX_3 to OX_2, *i.e.*, $X_3 X_2$.

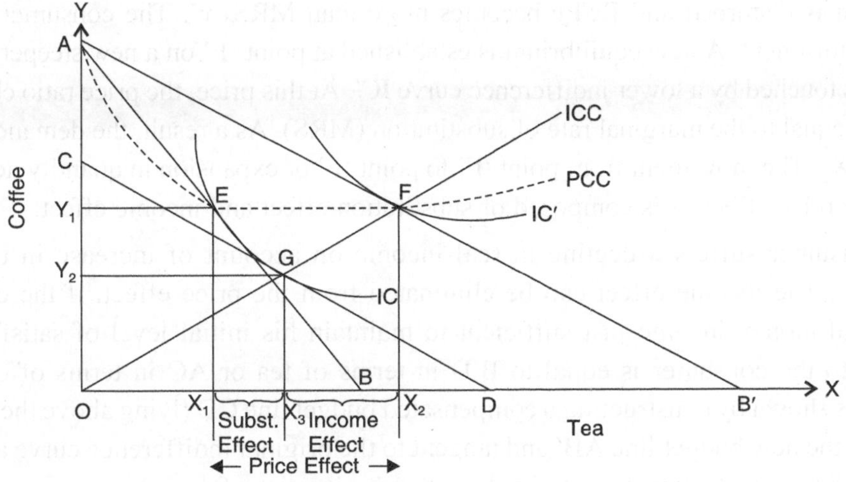

Fig. 9.15. The price effect.

Mathematically, the sign of income effect of a price change is also negative for normal commodities and it reinforces the negative substitution effect (both work in the same direction). Therefore, the total price effect (for normal goods) remains negative. Even if income effect is zero the price effect will remain negative and will be equal to substitution effect. The law of demand showing inverse price-demand relationship will hold.

We have just noticed that when the price of commodity 'X' falls, two effects—substitution effect and income effect are generated. The former makes commodity 'X' cheaper compared with another commodity and the latter increases the real income of the consumer. The total increase in quantity demanded (total price effect) is the result of the combined action of these effects. The movement of equilibrium point from 'E' to 'F' in Fig. 9.15 has occurred into two steps; first from point 'E' to point 'G' as a result of substitution effect (when compensation for the change in real income is made) and then from point 'G' to point 'F' as a result of income effect (the effect of removing the compensation). The price effect is, thus, the sum of substitution effect and income effect. The various effects on the purchase of commodity 'X' (Fig. 9.15) is as follows:

Price Effect (P.E.) = $X_1\ X_2$ (movement from point 'E' to point 'F')

Substitution Effect (S.E.) = $X_1\ X_3$ (movement from point 'E' to point 'G')

Income Effect (L.E.) = X_2X_3 (movement from point 'G' to point 'F')

Clearly,

$$X_1\ X_2 = X_1\ X_3 + X_3\ X_2$$

Price Effect = Substitution Effect + Income Effect

Normal Commodity Case (Price Rise): The procedure for splitting up of price effect is now explained, when the price of commodity 'X' (tea in our case) rises. The original budget line AB is tangent to the indifference curve IC at point 'E'. At this point, $Px\ /Py$ = MRS xy if the price of tea rises (price of commodity 'Y', *i.e.,* coffee and money income of the consumer remaining constant), this equilibrium is disturbed and Px/Py becomes more than MRS$x.v$'. The consumer undertakes consumption adjustment. A new equilibrium is established at point 'F' on a new steeper budget line AB′, where it is touched by a lower indifference curve IC′. At this price, the price ratio changes, but, again becomes equal to the marginal rate of substitution (MRS). As a result, the demand of tea falls from OX_1 to OX_2. The movement from point 'E' to point 'F' or expansion in quantity demanded $X_1\ X_2$ is called the price effect. It is composed of substitution effect and income effect.

The consumer suffers a decline in real income on account of increase in the price of commodity 'X'. The income effect can be eliminated from the price effect, if the consumer is given additional money income just sufficient to maintain his initial level of satisfaction. The compensation to the consumer is equal to B′D in terms of tea or AC in terms of coffee. This compensation is shown by constructing a compensated budget line CD (lying above the budget line AB) parallel to the new budget line AB′ and tangent to the original indifference curve at point 'G'. The income which compensates the consumer for the rise in price of tea is known as compensating variation in income.

Although the consumer is back on the original indifference curve, he purchases less of tea and more of coffee since tea has become relatively dearer. The movement from point 'E' to point 'G' measures the *Hicksian* substitution effect. In quantity terms, it is equal to $X_1\ X_3$ (a reduction in quantity demanded of tea from OX_1 to OX_3 on account of its relative expensiveness). The income effect can be known, once money given to the consumer is taken back, in which case the consumer will move back from point 'G' to equilibrium point 'F'. This movement is called income effect. In quantity terms, it is equal to $OX_3 - OX_1$.

The result can be presented as under (Fig. 9.16).

Price Effect = $X_1 X_2$

Substitution Effect = $X_2 X_3$

Income Effect = $X_3 X_2$

Since, $X_1 X_2 = X_2 X_3 + X_3 X_2$

∴ Price Effect = Substitution Effect + Income Effect

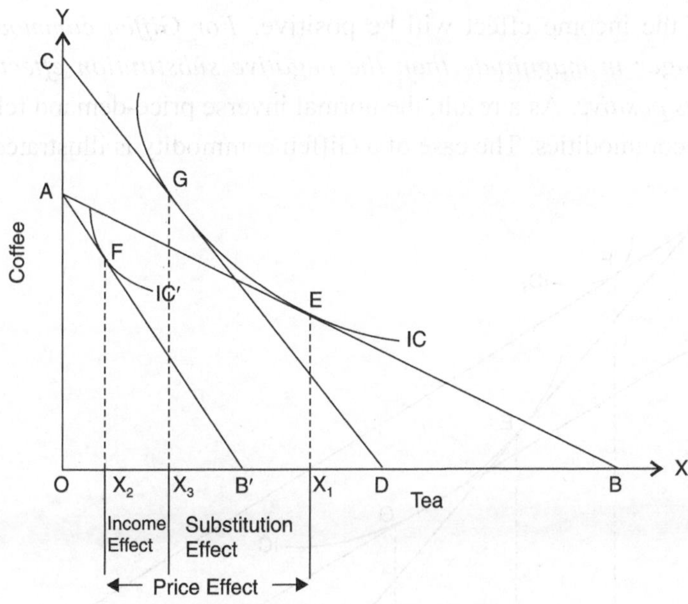

Fig. 9.16. Separation of price effect into substitution effect and income effect for a rise in the price of commodity on X-axis (Hicksian approach)

Thus, the demand curve has negative slope due to two effects, namely, substitution effect and income effect. Both of these effects extend the demand of the (normal) commodity, whose price falls and makes the demand curve slope downward.

Mathematically,

$$\text{P.E.} = \frac{\partial X}{\partial P_X}$$ (Price of other commodity P_Y and money income 'M' are constant)

$$\text{S.E.} = \frac{\partial X}{\partial P_X}$$ (Real income and hence satisfaction level held constant)

$$\text{I.E.} = \frac{\partial X}{\partial P_X}$$ (Price ratio $\frac{P_X}{P_Y}$ held constant)

Now, since P.E. = S.E. + I.E.

$$\therefore \quad \frac{\partial X}{\partial P_X}\Bigg|_{\substack{M = M_0 \\ P_Y = P_{Y0}}} = \frac{\partial X}{\partial P_X}\Bigg|_{U = U_0} + \frac{\partial X}{\partial P_X}\Bigg|_{\frac{P_X}{P_Y} = \frac{P_X}{P_Y}}$$

Giffen Commodity Case: So far we have discussed the Hicksian approach to the decomposition of price effect in case of normal commodity. If commodity happens to be a Giffen commodity, the substitution effect of the price change will continue to be negative. However, the mathematical sign of the income effect will be positive. *For Giffen commodities. the positive income effect is stronger in magnitude than the negative substitution effect. Therefore, their sum total price effect is positive.* As a result, the normal inverse price-demand relationship does not hold in case of Giffen commodities. The case of a Giffen commodity is illustrated in Fig. 9.17.

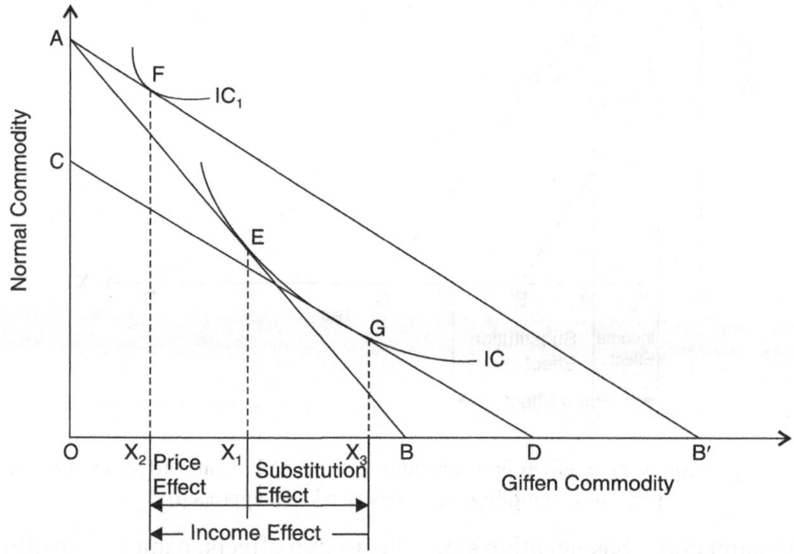

Fig. 9.17. Break-up of price effect into substitution effect and income effect in the case of Giffen commodity.

In Fig. 9.17, a Giffen commodity is shown along X-axis, while a normal commodity is taken on the Y-axis. The original equilibrium of the consumer with the given income price situation occurs at point 'E', where the original budget line touches the indifference curve IC. With a fall in the price of the Giffen commodity, the consumer shifts to point of contact 'F' between the new budget line AB' and indifference curve IC'. Consequently, the consumption of the Giffen commodity decreases from OX_1 to OX_2. Since with the fall in price of Giffen commodity, its consumption has decreased, the price effect equal to X_1 X_2 in quantity terms is positive. This price effect (the movement from point E to point F) comprises two effects. The movement from point 'E' to point 'G' in the figure is the substitution effect, which induces the consumer to buy more of the (Giffen) commodity. This effect (equal to X_1 X) is isolated from the price effect by drawing an income compensating budget line CD parallel to the new budget line AB and touching the original indifference curve IC at point 'G'.

Further, the movement from point 'G' to point 'F' is the income effect, which is equal to $X_3 X_2$ in quantity terms. Clearly, the positive income effect $X_3 X_2$ in this case is large enough to outweigh the negative substitution effect $X_1 X_3$. Therefore, the net effect of the fall in price of Giffen Commodity is the fall in the demand of this commodity. In general, it can be stated that *quantity demanded of a Giffen commodity varies directly with the price and the demand curve is upward sloping.* The law of demand is violated in the case of Giffen commodity. Following conditions are necessary for this situation termed as Giffen case or Giffen paradox:

- The commodity must be an inferior commodity having a substantial income effect with a *positive mathematical sign*. The consumption of the commodity should *fall* on account of rise in consumer's real income, when the price of the commodity *falls*.
- The income effect can be substantial, when the consumer spends a very large proportion of his income on the commodity in question. As a result, a large amount of income is released, when the price of the commodity falls.
- The substitution effect must be small so that the bigger positive income effect may outstrip the negative substitution effect making the price effect positive.

From the above discussion, it is concluded that *Giffen* commodities are those inferior commodities on which a consumer spends a major part of his total expenditure so that the positive income effect of a price change is bigger enough to overwhelm the negative substitution effect. As a result, the consumer reduces the demand of a commodity with fall in its price and *vice versa.* The negative substitution increases the quantity demanded, while the positive income effect reduces the quantity demanded by still greater amount, whenever the price of a *Giffen* commodity falls and *vice versa.*

The *Giffen* case may be theoretically conceivable, but its chance of occurrence in the real world is almost negligible. This is on account of the fact that the consumption of the households is so diversified that they spend a small proportion of their income on a single commodity. Consequently, even price induced negative income effect is too weak to swamp the substitution effect.

Inferior Commodity Case: *All Giffen commodities are inferior commodities, but all inferior commodities* are not Giffen commodities. Those inferior commodities which are not Giffen commodities too have positive mathematical sign of income effect which works in opposite direction to that of negative substitution effect. However, for such commodities, the negative substitution effect will more than offset the positive income effect, so that the total price effect will be negative. As a result the normal law of demand holds. Thus, the negative substitution effect is adequate for establishing the inverse price demand relationship in most cases.

When the price of an inferior commodity falls, the substitution effect acts to increase the quantity demanded while the income effect tends to reduce the quantity demanded. The price effect, which is the sum of the substitution effect, and income effect, depends upon the relative strength of the two effects. For inferior commodities (which are not Giffen), the positive income effect is weaker than the negative substitution effect, since a consumer spends a very small proportion of his income on a single commodity. This is illustrated in Fig. 9.18.

In Fig. 9.18, the consumer is in equilibrium at point 'E' on the original budget line AB and indifference curve IC. The fall in the price of inferior commodity (shown along the X-axis) makes the consumer to shift to point 'F', where the new budget line AB′ touches a higher indifference curve IC′. Consequently, the quantity demanded rises from OX_1 to OX_2. $X_1 X_2$ measures the price effect. The increase in real income as a result of the fall in the price of inferior commodity needs to be compensated such that the real income is held constant at the new price ratio. The required decrease in money income is called the compensating variation. Graphically, the compensating variation is depicted by constructing compensated budget line CD parallel to the new budget line AB′ and tangent to the original indifference curve IC at point 'G'. The movement from point 'E' to point 'G' is the *Hicksian* substitution effect. In quantity terms, it is equal to the increase in the quantity demanded of commodity X from OX, to OX_3' *i.e.*, $X_1 X_3$. The substitution effect is negative because the consumer demands more of this commodity on account of its relative cheapness to other commodity 'Y'. If the consumer is restored back the compensating variation that was taken away from him, the real income of the consumer rises. Since commodity 'X' is an inferior commodity, less of it (from OX_3 to OX_2) will be demanded with an increase in real income.

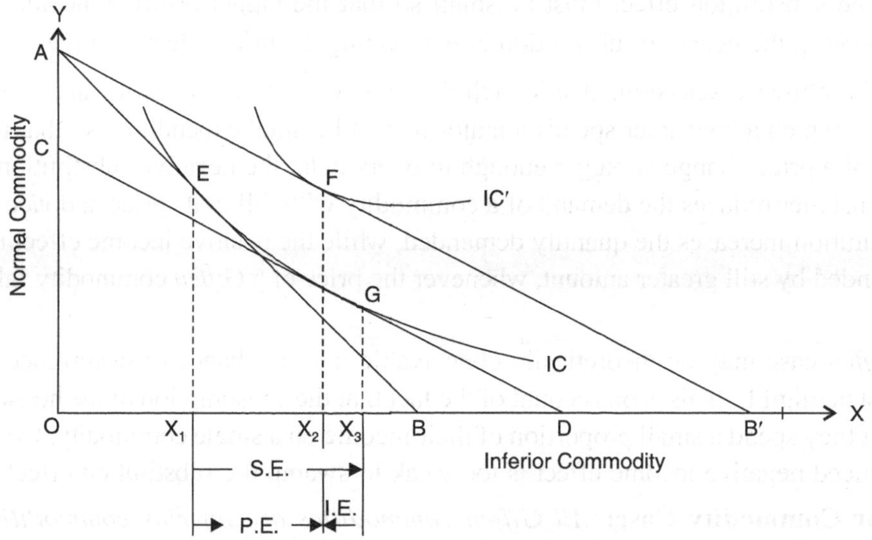

Fig. 9.18. Break-up of price effect into substitution effect and income effect in the case of inferior commodity.

The movement from point 'G' to point 'F' reflects negative income effect. In quantity terms it is equal to $X_3 X_2$. Here, substitutión effect ($X_1 X_3$) dominates over income effect ($X_3 X_2$). Hence, there is a net increase in the quantity demanded equal to $X_1 X_2$ (price effect). Thus, we conclude, the quantity demanded varies inversely with price in the case of inferior commodities.

Perfect Complements Case: As discussed in the previous chapter, for perfect complements, the indifference curves are L-shaped. The breaking up of price effect for such goods is shown in Fig. 9.19. The original equilibrium of the consumer is at point 'E', where the initial budget line AB meets the common point to L shaped indifference curve IC. At this point, OX quantity of commodity

'X' is demanded. When the price of commodity 'X' falls, the budget line shifts rightward to AB′. On this budget line, the highest possible indifference curve IC′ meets at equilibrium point 'F'. The increase in quantity demanded from OX_1 to OX_2, *i.e.,* $X_1 X_2$ depicts the price effect. As the two commodities are perfect complements to each other, the *Hicksian* substitution effect is equal to zero. This is also clear from the fact that the compensated budget line CD drawn parallel to the new budget line AB′ passes through the same point 'E' on the original budget line AB and point of original indifference curve IC. This implies that the entire increase in quantity demanded is due to the income effect. Thus, price effect of $X_1 X_2$ is equal to income effect.

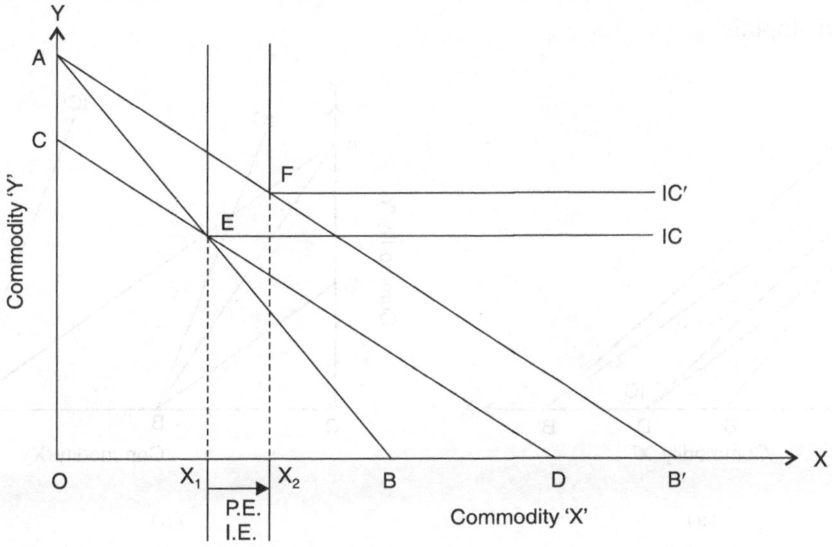

Fig. 9.19. Break-up of price effect in the case of perfect complements.

Perfect Substitutes Case: When two commodities are perfect substitutes, the indifference curves are straight lines and have constant marginal rate of substitution, which is greater than or equal to one. The decomposition of price effect in the case of such commodities for a fall in the price of commodity 'X' is represented in Fig. 9.20(*a*). In this figure, the initial equilibrium of the consumer occurs at point AB, where the initial budget line 'A' has a comer solution with the initial indifference curve IC. When the price of commodity 'X' falls, the budget line shifts to the right to AB′ and the new consumer equilibrium shifts to point B′ on the new budget line (again a common solution). The quantity demanded rises from O to DB′ as a result of a fall in the price of commodity 'X'. Thus, the price effect is equal to DB′. To isolate the substitution effect, compensated budget line CD is drawn parallel 'to the new budget line AB′ and touching the original indifference curve IC. Now, the *Hicksian* substitution effect would be a movement from point 'A' to point 'D' and the income effect would be a movement from point 'D' to point B′. Therefore, OD is the quantity of substitution effect and DB′ is the quantity of income effect. The total price effect is equal to DB′. Thus, the demand curve for the commodity 'X' is downward sloping.

Now, consider another situation (where the consumer is in equilibrium at another common point 'B' of initial budget line AB on the X-axis. At this point, he demands DB quantity of commodity 'X'. When the price of commodity 'X' falls, the equilibrium point shifts to point B′ on the new budget line AB′. The total price effect in this case is equal to BB′. When money income is decreased to hold real purchasing power constant, the compensating budget line CD so obtained is parallel to new budget line AB′ and touching original indifference curve IC. The implication is that *Hicksian* substitution effect is zero. The quantity demanded corresponding to original equilibrium and compensated budget is same at DB. Thus, the entire increase in the quantity demanded is on account of income effect. In other words, the price effect DB is equal to income effect. Further, the demand curve for commodity 'Y' is downward sloping.

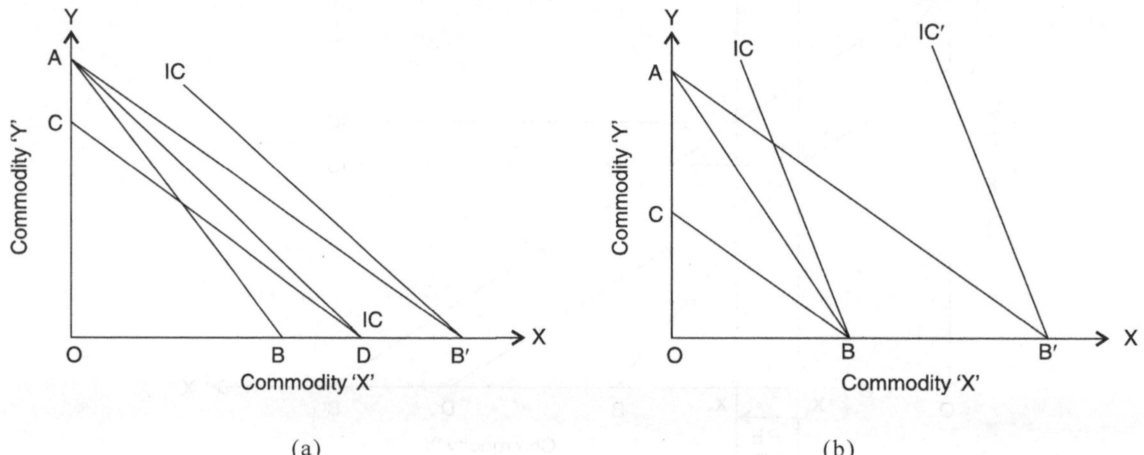

Fig. 9.20. Break-up of price effect in the case of perfect substitutes.

Equivalent Variation in Income Method

Equivalent variation is another way in which the composition of price effect can be analyzed. There is a slight difference in this method and that of compensating variation in income method. Under equivalent variation method, the consumer's income is changed (at the original equilibrium point) and he reaches a new indifference curve, relative prices remaining constant. The required change in money income is equivalent to the change in price of the commodity 'X' in terms of satisfaction. The substitution effect is shown along the subsequent indifference curve. The splitting of the price effect in this method is shown in Fig. 9.20

Commodities 'X' and 'Y' are shown along X and Y axis respectively. The initial equilibrium of the consumer is at point 'E', where the original budget line AB touches the original indifference curve IC. When the price of commodity 'X' falls the consumer is in a position to buy more of both the commodities with increased real income. Suppose, he actually buys a combination of the two commodities indicated by point 'F', where the new budget line AB′ is tangent to a higher indifference curve IC′ the movement from equilibrium point 'E' to equilibrium point 'F' shows the price effect. A fall in the price of commodity 'X' releases some amount of money, if the consumer wants to maintain the same level of satisfaction as before. Money, thus, released can be used to spend on both the commodities. In Fig. 9.21, increase in purchasing power (real income) on account of a fall in the price of commodity 'X' is CA in terms of commodity Y and DB′ in terms of commodity 'X'. In the figure, CD line is drawn parallel to AB such that it touches the indifference curve IC′ at point 'G'. The movement from point 'E' to point 'G' along income consumption curve ICC indicates the income effect of the price fall. The movement from point 'G' to 'F' on account of relative cheapness of commodity 'X' is referred to as substitution effect. In quantity terms, price effect (X_1 X_2) is equal to the sum of income effect (X_1 X_3) and substitution effect (X_3 X_2). The analysis of price effect for rise in the price can be similarly explained.

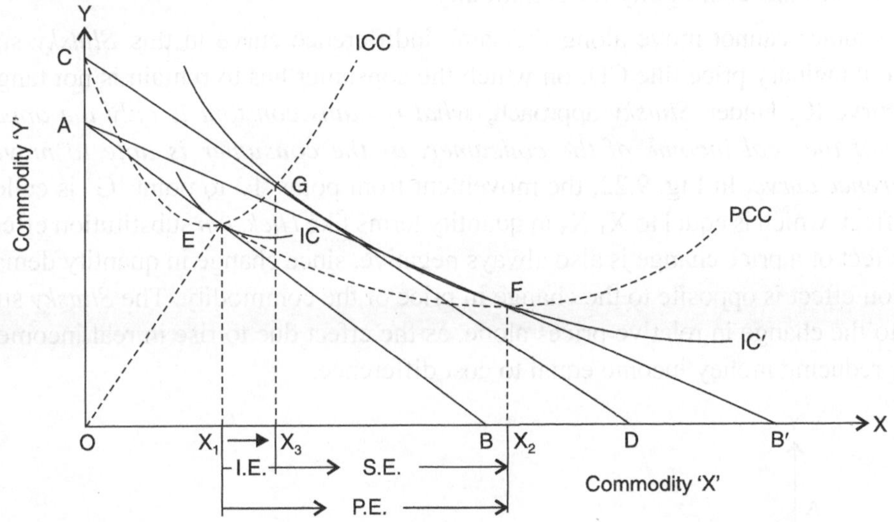

Fig. 9.21. Decomposition of price effect through equivalent variation in income.

Break-up of Price Effect under Slutsky's Approach (Through Cost Difference)

Eugen Slutsky, a Russian economist gave the indifference curve technique prior to *R.G.D. Allen* and *J.R. Hicks* in 1915. His analysis was highly mathematical and has important empirical and practical uses. It was relatively complex and was in Russian script. That is why, it did not come in the lime-light. Even *Allen* and *Hicks* admitted the fact in their analysis.

Under *Slutsky's* approach, when the price of a commodity changes, a consumer's purchasing power changes equal to the price change multiplied by the number of units of the commodity which the consumer used to buy at the original price. As a result, the income of the consumer changes by the amount equal to the change in the purchasing power. He is now able to purchase the old combination of the commodities.

The splitting of the price effect under *Slutsky's* approach is illustrated in Fig. 9.22. The initial equilibrium of the consumer is at point 'E' at the point of contact of the indifference curve IC and the initial budget line AB. Now, suppose the price of commodity 'X' falls, the new equilibrium of the consumer occurs at point 'F' on the new budget line AB′. The price effect given by the movement from point 'E' to point 'F' is equal to $X_1 X_2$ in quantity terms.

To isolate the substitution effect from the price effect, the money income of the consumer is reduced by such an amount that he is in a position to purchase the original combination of the commodities. For this purpose, an imaginary line CD is drawn parallel to new budget line AB′ and passing through original equilibrium point 'E'. In this manner, an income equal to CA in terms of commodity 'Y' or DB′ in terms of commodity 'X' has been taken away from the consumer. Now, the consumer will not choose to buy the combination of the two commodities represented by point 'E', but will opt for and settle at point 'G', where the imaginary budget line CD touches an indifference curve I_e. This is on account of the fact that commodity 'X' becomes relatively cheaper and the consumer substitutes this commodity for commodity 'Y'.

The consumer cannot move along the same indifference curve in this *Slutsky* substitution case, since the imaginary price line CD, on which the consumer has to remain is not tangent to the indifference curve IC. Under *Slutsky* approach, *what remains constant is only the apparent real income and not the real income of the consumer, as the consumer is able to move on to a higher indifference curve*. In Fig. 9.22, the movement from point 'E' to point 'G' is called *Slutsky* substitution effect, which is equal to $X_1 X_3$ in quantity terms like *Hicksian* substitution effect. *Slutsky* substitution effect of a price change is also always negative, since change in quantity demanded due to a substitution effect is opposite to the change in price of the commodity. The *Slutsky* substitution effect is due to the change in relative prices alone, as the effect due to rise in real income has been eliminated by reducing money income equal to cost difference.

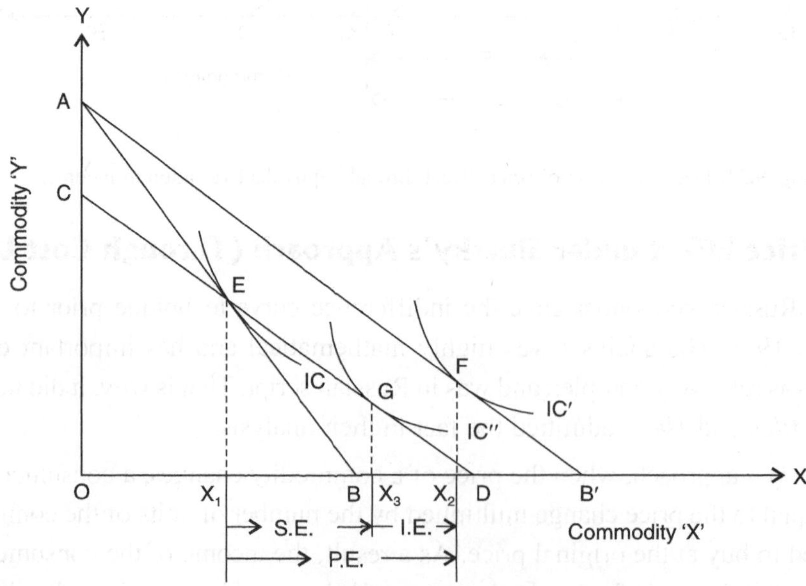

Fig. 9.22. Break-up of price effect into substitution effect and income effect (Slutsky Approach).

If now, the money income taken from the consumer is given back to him, he will move from point 'G' to point 'F' on the indifference curve IC′. The journey from point 'G' to point 'F' is income effect, which is equal to $X_3 X_2$ in quantity terms.

Now, we can say that,

$$\text{Price Effect } (X_1 X_2) = \text{Substitution Effect } (X_1 X_3) + \text{Income Effect } (X_3X_2)$$

The decomposition of price effect into substitution effect and income effect for the rise in the price of commodity 'X' under this approach can be similarly explained.

It is important to note that the direction and magnitude of the change in quantity as a result of the fall in price depends upon the direction and magnitude of income effect and substitution effect. The following points summarise the relationship between price and quantity demanded under various situations.

1. The quantity demanded of a commodity varies inversely with price, when the income effect is zero or negative, but, is weaker than the substitution effect.
2. The quantity demanded of a commodity varies directly with price, when the income effect for the commodity is negative and is more powerful than the substitution effect.

9.5 DERIVATION OF COMPENSATED DEMAND CURVE

The substitution effect of a price change under *Hicksian* approach and *Slutsky* approach has already been explained in the previous section. The compensated demand curve can be derived using these substitution effects in the same way in which demand curve and Engel demand curve were derived from price consumption curve (PCC) and income consumption curve (ICC) respectively. The derivation of compensated demand curve under the two approaches is illustrated in Fig. 9.23.

First, we consider the derivation of *Hicksian* compensated demand curve. In the upper panel of Fig. 9.23 the vertical axis shows the money income and the horizontal axis shows the quantity of commodity. The consumer is in equilibrium at point 'E', where the initial budget line is tangent to indifference curve IC. Now, suppose the price of commodity 'X' falls. The consumer's equilibrium shifts to point 'F' on the new budget line and higher indifference curve IC′. *Hicks-Allen* substitution effect is shown as a movement along the same indifference curve IC. Under *Hicksian* approach, since the consumer is just compensated for the change in his real income on account of a price change, his level of satisfaction is restored to the original level through compensating variation. We know that the consumer substitutes relatively cheaper commodity. In the figure, the consumer increases the quantity demanded of commodity 'X' from OX to OX_2, while the quantity demanded of commodity 'Y' falls from OY to OY′. The *Hicksian* substitution effect in the figure measures the effect of change in relative prices, with real income constant, since two budget lines AB and CD (with different slopes) touch the same indifference curve IC at point 'E' and 'G'. The movement from equilibrium point 'E' to equilibrium point 'G' reflects the substitution effect. It is equal to $X_1 X_2$ in quantity terms.

In the lower panel diagram, the vertical axis shows the price of commodity 'X' and the horizontal axis shows the quantity of commodity 'Y'. We record that the quantities demanded corresponding to equilibrium points 'E' and 'G' are OX and OX_3 respectively. When these quantities are plotted against their respective prices OA/OB and OA/OB′ in the lower panel of the figure, we get *Hicksian* compensated demand curve CD.

Now, we consider the derivation of *Slutsky* compensated demand curve. In upper panel of Fig. 9.23 the consumer equilibrium shifts from point E on the budget line AB to point F on the budget line AB′, when price of the commodity X falls. Again, money income of the consumer is shown along the vertical axis and the quantity demanded of commodity 'X' is shown along the horizontal axis. Indifference curves IC and IC′ touch the two budget lines at these points respectively. Now, the money income of the consumer is adjusted by taking away money, such that the consumer is able to purchase the original combination of the two commodities. For this purpose, an imaginary budget line CD is drawn parallel to new budget line AB′ and passing through original equilibrium point 'E'. We observe that the *Slutsky* approach over compensates the consumer and puts him at a point, say, 'G' on a higher indifference IC″ on the budget line CD. The journey from point 'E' to point 'G' is the substitution effect, which is equal to $X_1 X_3$ in quantity terms.

In the lower panel diagram, the vertical axis shows the price of commodity 'X' and the horizontal axis shows the quantity demanded of commodity 'X'. We observe that the quantities demanded corresponding to equilibrium points E and G are OX_1 and OX_3 respectively. When these quantities are plotted against their respective prices OA/OB and OA/OB′ in the lower panel of Fig. 9.23, we get *Slutsky* compensated demand curve (CD′).

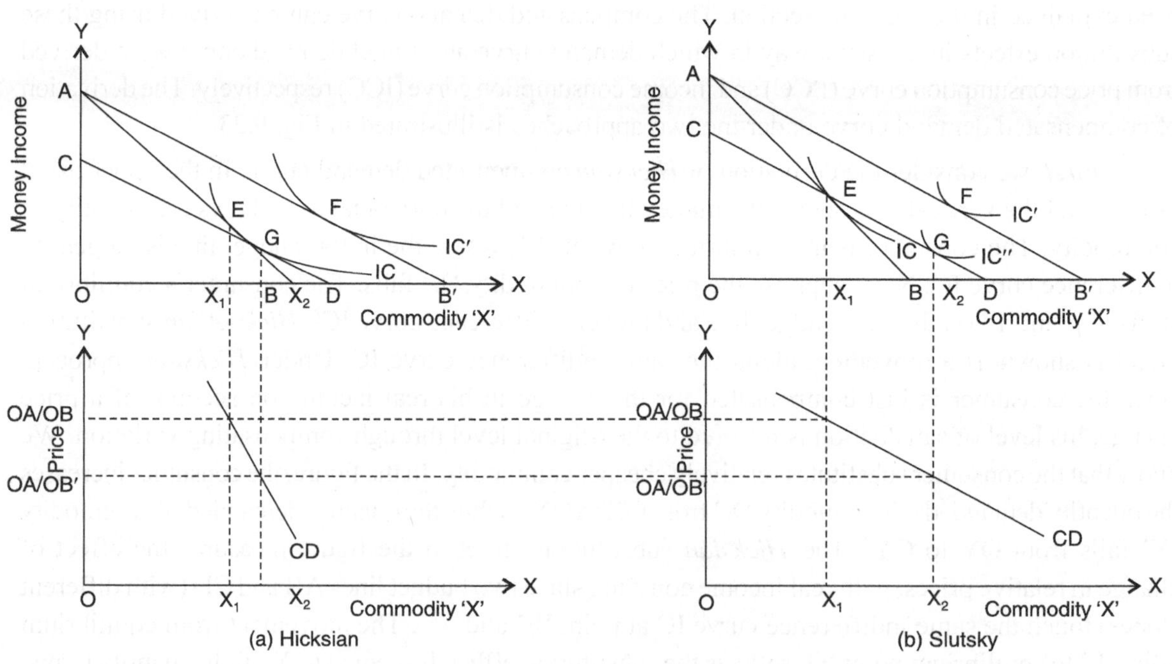

Fig. 9.23. Derivation of compensated demand curve.

It is important to note that the compensated demand curve (or constant real income demand curve) under both the approaches is downward sloping. However, the *Slutsky compensated demand curve is more elastic than the Hicksian compensated demand curve.* Further, since the sign of substitution effect is always negative, the compensated demand curve is always downward sloping, whether the commodity under consideration is a normal commodity, inferior commodity or a Giffen commodity. Thus, its shape is independent of the nature of the commodity. The conventional demand curve for a normal commodity is even more elastic than *Hicksian* as well as *Slutsky* compensated demand curve, as it includes income effect besides substitution effect of a change in the price of a commodity. For an inferior commodity, the elasticity of demand of the conventional demand curve will be less than that of the corresponding compensated demand curve. When income effect is equal to zero, the elasticity of demand of the conventional demand curve will be same as that of corresponding compensated demand curve. For a Giffen commodity, unlike compensated demand curve, the conventional demand curve is upward sloping. The elasticity of demand for such demand curve depends upon the relative strength of the substitution effect on one hand and the income effect on the other hand.

9.6 FURTHER APPLICATIONS OF INDIFFERENCE CURVE ANALYSIS

In the previous chapter, the applications of indifference curve analysis to study and explain consumer's demand and behaviour were discussed. This technique can also be fruitfully applied to analyze several other economic phenomena and in some situations to solve many economic problems. Some of the such popular applications are discussed in this chapter. The applications of the indifference curve technique in the fields of welfare economics and international trade can be discussed at length in their respective chapters.

Taxation (Direct Taxes Versus Indirect Taxes)

Taxation is the most important source of revenue for the government. The taxes are broadly divided into two categories—direct taxes and indirect taxes. Direct taxes like income tax, wealth tax and gift tax are those taxes whose initial impact and ultimate incidence fall on the same person, *i.e.,* the person on whom the tax is imposed cannot shift the burden of the tax partly or fully. These taxes have to be paid by the individuals or firms on whom these are levied. On the other hand, indirect taxes such as sales tax, excise duty and customs duty are those taxes, whose impact and incidence fall on different persons, *i.e.,* the person on whom the tax is levied can shift its buden wholly or partly to some other person. The extent of shifting depends on the elasticity of demand and elasticity of supply. Indirect taxes are levied on commodities and services which are paid by the individuals, when they buy these commodities and services. The sellers/ manufacturers of the commodities and services are, thus, able to shift the burden of tax on the consumers by raising the prices.

While raising additional revenue, the government often faces the problem of choice of levying a direct tax or an indirect tax. This requires an understanding of the welfare effects of a given amount of revenue raised through a direct tax on one hand and an indirect tax on the other hand. For this purpose, we can make use of *Hicks-Allen* indifference curve technique, as explained below.

The quantity of a commodity 'X' is measured on the X-axis, while money income is taken along the Y-axis with a given income of the consumer and the given price of commodity 'X', the initial budget line is AB. The consumer is in equilibrium at point 'E' where this budget line is tangent to indifference curve IC. This indifference curve shows the level of welfare attained in the pre-tax situation. Now, suppose that the government levies an indirect tax, say, excise duty on commodity 'X' (either at a specific rate or at an advalorem rate). This will raise the price of commodity 'X' depending on the elasticity of demand and supply. As a result, the budget line will rotate to a new position AB', which is tangent to a lower indifference curve IC′ at point 'F'. Thus, the level of a consumer's welfare falls consequent upon the imposition of a commodity tax (indirect tax). At the new consumer equilibrium point, the consumer demand OH quantity of commodity 'X' by spending IA amount of his income on it. The money income left with the consumer is equal to OI. In the absence of excise duty, the consumer could have purchased OH quantity of commodity 'X' for JA amount of money at the old price. Therefore, the excise duty paid by the consumer is equal to FK.

If instead of excise duty, the government levies an equal yield (revenue) direct tax on income then the new budget line CD passes through point 'F' and is parallel to the initial budget line AB (since prices are assumed to be unaffected). A downward shift in the budget line is on account of reduction in the individual's disposable income, when a tax is imposed on his income. The gap between the budget lines AB and CD is equal to IJ or FK. This shows that the same amount of revenue is to be raised through income tax as with the excise duty. However, with CD as the budget line, the consumer is in equilibrium at point 'G' on indifference curve IC″ which lies at a higher level than at point 'F'. This implies that when the government raises resources through direct taxes, the consumer is relatively better off as compared to the situation, when the same amounts of resources are raised through indirect taxes.

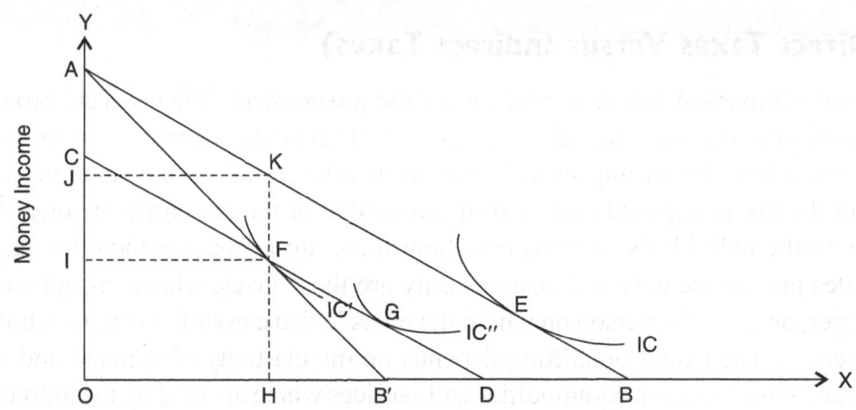

Fig. 9.24. Impact of direct and indirect taxes on consumer's welfare.

It is important to note that a tax is a compulsory payment (levy) against which the tax payer can expect no direct benefit in return (no quid pro quo). Therefore, a tax will always lower an individual's welfare. But reduction in welfare would be lesser under a direct tax system than under an indirect tax system. In Fig. 9.24, the welfare of the consumer has reduced from IC to IC″ under income tax (a direct tax), while it has reduced from IC to IC′ in the case of excise duty (an indirect tax). The reduction of welfare in the former case causes an inevitable burden on the consumer. On the other hand, the reduction in welfare in the latter case leads to excess burden. We observe that an indirect tax imposes a burden in excess of the inevitable burden.

This conclusion regarding excess burden of indirect tax as compared to with the direct tax may be true for a single individual, whose whole income is taxed at a uniform rate. Whether indirect tax reduces welfare more than direct tax depends upon other conditions also for the economy as a whole. A direct tax may not always be superior to an indirect tax or a general tax may not always be better than a specific tax. The outcome under a general equilibrium framework might become different.

This excess burden arises, as the tax on commodity 'X' distorts a consumer's choice, through a change in the relative price structure. On the contrary, a general income tax does not distort relative prices or consumer's choice. It only reduces disposable income of the consumer and hence, the attainable consumption set. It lowers welfare and imposes an inevitable burden, but no excess burden. Thus, from an individual tax payer's point of view, income tax is preferable to excise duty. The Finance Minister acting on the principle of least aggregate sacrifice should collect the given amount of revenue by introducing direct tax rather than a commodity tax.

The extent of excess burden under indirect tax depends on the elasticity of substitution or the curvature of the indifference curve. Greater is the elasticity of substitution, greater is the distortionary effect of a specific tax imposed on commodity 'X' due to substitution of the non-taxed commodity for the taxed one. Lower the elasticity; the smaller will be the excess burden of an indirect tax on account of low substitution effect. In an extreme situation, when the two commodities are perfect substitutes, the excess burden of the indirect tax will be maximum. In another extreme situation, when the two commodities are perfect complements, there will be zero tax burden.

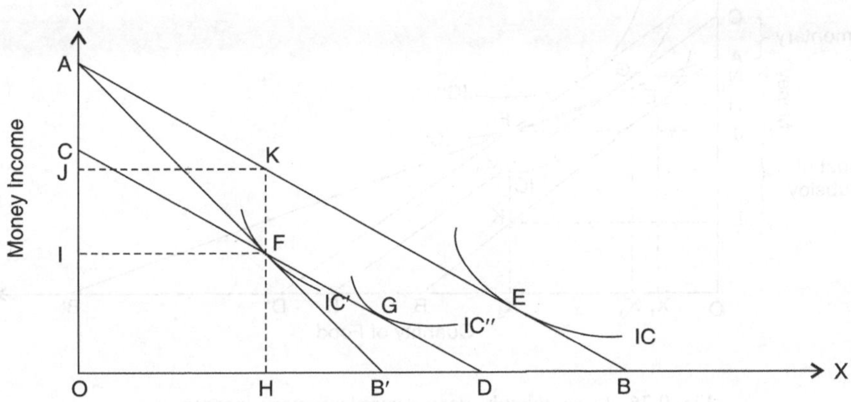

Fig. 9.25. Loss of welfare is same under direct and indirect taxes.

In Fig. 9.25, the initial equilibrium of the consumer is at point 'E' on the original budget line AB. The new equilibrium with the imposition of direct tax (which shifts the budget line downwards parallel to original budget line AB) or indirect tax (which shifts the budget line downwards to AB′) is the same, *i.e.,* point F with L-shaped indifference curves for perfect complements, it is not possible to think of equilibrium other than point F on budget line CD. The loss of welfare is, thus, the same under both the tax systems.

Alternative Government Policies

Indifference curve can also be used to evaluate the effects of alternative government policies. Modem welfare state provides different types of subsidies, particularly to the poor families and special class of people like pensioners. Subsidies may be given in kind in the form of food, medical benefits, free education, etc. or in terms of money (for example, in the form of supplementary income to weaker sections of the society). The government can know the relative cost of these policies, their effects on consumption pattern and welfare level of the weaker sections of the society, etc., with the aid of indifference curve analysis.

Food Subsidy versus Supplementary Income Policy: The government often provides subsidies to help low income group people to meet their requirements of food and reach a certain minimum level of nutrition. In India, the government has been giving such a relief or subsidy to the poor in the case of wheat. The resultant loss to the government is ultimately passed on to the consumers.

The effect of food subsidy and supplementary income policy of the government is illustrated in Fig. 9.26. Consider the case of food subsidy. Suppose that under food-subsidy programme, the needed families are enabled to purchase food at half the market price, the other half being paid by the government as subsidy. The effect of this subsidy on consumer's welfare is shown in Fig. 9.26, where the quantity of food is measured along the X-axis and money on the Y-axis.

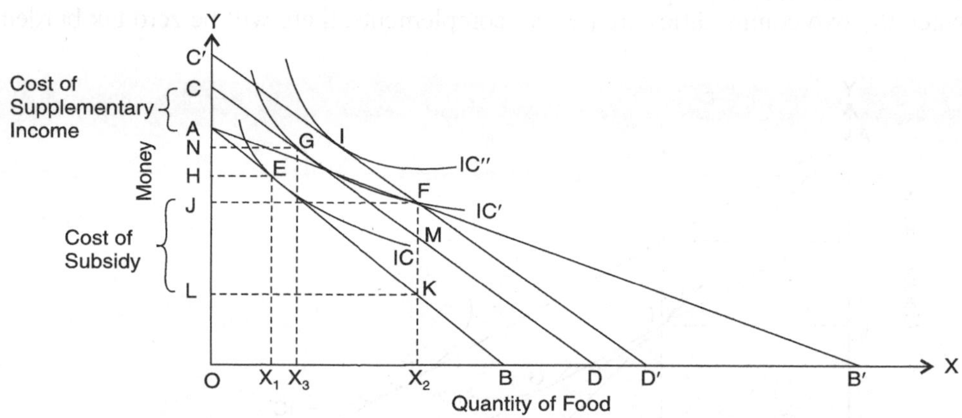

Fig. 9.26. Food subsidy versus supplementary income.

The total money income of the consumer is assumed to be OA. If the whole income is spent on the purchase of food, the consumer can buy OB quantity of food, given the market price of food. The budget line is, therefore, AB. The consumer is in equilibrium at point 'E', where the indifference curve IC touches this budget line. The consumer consumes OX_1 quantity of food at this point paying HC of his income and having OH income left over to spend on other commodities.

Since, it is assumed that the subsidy paid by the government is equal to half the market price of food, the consumer is enabled to purchase double the quantity of food. Thus, with subsidy, the consumer will face a new budget line AB' such that OB′ = 2 OB. With this budget line, the consumer is in equilibrium at point 'F' on it. At this point, a higher indifference curve IC′ touches new budget line AB′. By purchasing OX_2 quantity of food, the consumer is spending JC amount of money.

In the absence of food subsidy the relevant budget line is AB. If no food subsidy was given, the consumer would have spent LA amount of money (which is also the market price of food) for OX_2 quantity of the commodity. After food subsidy, the consumer pays only JA money. Therefore, LA – JA = LJ or KF (the vertical distance between the budget lines AB and AB′ at OX_2 quantity of food) amount is paid by the government as food subsidy to the food producers. In other words, the government subsidizes the consumer by an amount equal to KF or LJ, which is also the cost of subsidization to the government.

Following are the implications of the food subsidy policy adopted by the government:

1. The welfare of the consumer rises from IC to IC' in the Fig. 9.26.
2. The market price of food (LA) remains unaffected by this policy, though the effective price to the consumer is reduced (a subsidy per unit of consumption equal to OB′/OB)
3. The government contributes LJ portion of the market price. Hence, the cost of the subsidization policy to the government is equal to LJ or KF.
4. The food subsidization programme of the government benefits not only the consumers, but also the producers of food stuff, since more food is consumed (an increase from OX_1 to OX). More consumption by the consumers is particularly useful in providing minimum nutritional requirements of the population especially, when there is surplus food.
5. The assistance to the consumers via the food subsidy imposes a certain pattern of consumption, a definite choice of spending their income.

Now, we are in a position to find out the money value of this food subsidy (KF), *i.e.*, to know as to how much money will make the consumer as well off as the food subsidy does. For this purpose, the government has to grant a *supplementary income* to the consumer so that he reaches the same higher indifference curve IC′. The required amount of money or cash subsidy (given original price conditions) can be found out by drawing a budget line CD parallel to the initial budget line and touching the indifference curve IC′ at point 'G'. In this situation, the consumer consumes OX_3 quantity of food by paying NC amount of money like food subsidy, the cash subsidy also benefits consumers as well as producers, since more food is consumed as a result of subsidy. Cash subsidy or grant required to bring the consumer to the indifference curve is AC. This is the cost of the supplementary income policy to the government. However, the cost of food subsidy is KF, which is greater than the cost of supplementary income by MF_3. Thus, the consumer reaches the same level of welfare with less cash relief (AC) as he does with more food subsidy (KF). But, the quantity of consumption of subsidized food is relatively smaller in the former situation (supplementary income policy). The market price of the subsidized food again remains unaffected.

We observe that from the point of view of economic efficiency, cash subsidy is preferable to a food subsidy, since money equivalent of the subsidy is less than the cost of subsidy to the government. So long as the indifference curves remain convex and smooth, the cost of food subsidy always exceeds that of cash subsidy irrespective of the magnitude of the subsidy and preferences of the consumers. In the words of *Watson* and Getz "The cost of giving subsidies to consumers is always greater than the money equivalent of the subjective gain to the consumers". Further, as a special case of general principle, one can make a man happier by giving him cash instead of a commodity, which he really wants. Relief payments in cash are preferable to a subsidy, since these are economically more efficient, providing either a greater gain at the same cost to the government or the same gain at a lower cost.

Though food subsidy may not be justified on the ground of economic efficiency, but it induces the consumers to consume more food. In times of surpluses in the economy, the government in its value judgement has priority for the amount of commodity demanded. Therefore, the policy of food subsidy is pursued which also helps in attaining production—balance in the economy. Use of food subsidy to dispose of the food surpluses to the needy people would be an ideal measure to improve their health and efficiency by increasing the consumption of food grains in such a situation.

Comparing the two alternative policies, it is concluded that both the policies achieve the government's role of enabling the consumer to reach a higher welfare level implied by a higher indifference curve IC′ in Fig. 9.26. Though the cost of food subsidy programme is higher for the government, it ensures more consumption of food. The choice of policy depends upon the goals of the government and the indirect effect of the policy. A more costly food subsidization policy may be adopted for eliminating the food surplus in the country. On the contrary, supplementary income policy though less costly, may result in inflationary tendencies in the economy on account of increased income of some needy groups. This will ultimately decrease the welfare of the consumers. However, the food subsidy policy leaves prices unaffected. At times, when the government is severely constrained by the shortages of resources, it may prefer to adopt supplementary income policy (lump-sum income transfer) to help the weaker sections of the society. In this manner, we see that indifference curve technique helps in efficient policy formulation by giving insight into the implications of alternative government policies.

Equal Sized Cash Grant—If instead of compensating lump-sum subsidy to the consumer the government provides a cash grant of equal size the price ratio will remain constant at the initial level as given by the slope initial budget line AB. The new budget line C′D′ passes through point F and is parallel to initial budget line AB. The cash grant KF equals AC or BD′. Now, the consumer attains equilibrium at point F on the indifference curve IC″. Since this indifference curve lies above the indifference curve IC′, equal sized cash grant ensures more welfare to the consumer than the compensating cash subsidy. The consumption in any case is greater than that in the pre-subsidy/grant situation. Therefore, cash grant lump-sum subsidy should be preferred to excise subsidy from the welfare point of view.

Education Subsidy: In the case of food subsidy, the government pays a part of the price which reduces the effective price of the food to the consumer. However, governments often provide subsidy by making available a certain quantity of the good or service free of cost or at a considerably lower price. The aim of the government is not to provide free or very cheap education to all sections of the society, but only to the poorer sections. Free or highly subsidized education in government institutions is an important example. People requiring larger or different types of educational facilities have to pay higher price for these services in the private institutions. The effect of such fixed quantity subsidy on the consumer welfare is illustrated.

The budget line before the subsidy is AB. Let us suppose, the consumer is in equilibrium at point 'E' on this line by demanding OX_1 quantity of educational services. The consumer retains OY_1 amount of money to be spent on other commodities. Assume that the government introduces free education service in government schools equal to OX_2 in quantity. Now, the relevant budget line of the consumer is ACDB. AC part of the budget line parallel to the X-axis indicates, consumer can avail OX_2 quantity of the schooling absolutely free, thereby saving the entire money income for other commodities. If the consumer desires to consume more than the subsidized quantity OX_2, he will have to bear the entire cost of education himself in some private school along the DB portion of the budget line. With the ACDB budget line, the consumer can choose to consume at point 'C' on this line. This brings him to a higher indifference curve IC. Therefore, the point 'C' in the post-subsidy situation should be preferred to point 'E' in the pre-subsidy situation. At this point, the consumer consumes OX_2 educational service, which is less than the earlier service consumed by $X_1 X_2$. The money income of $A Y_2$ which was earlier used to avail educational service is now available for other uses.

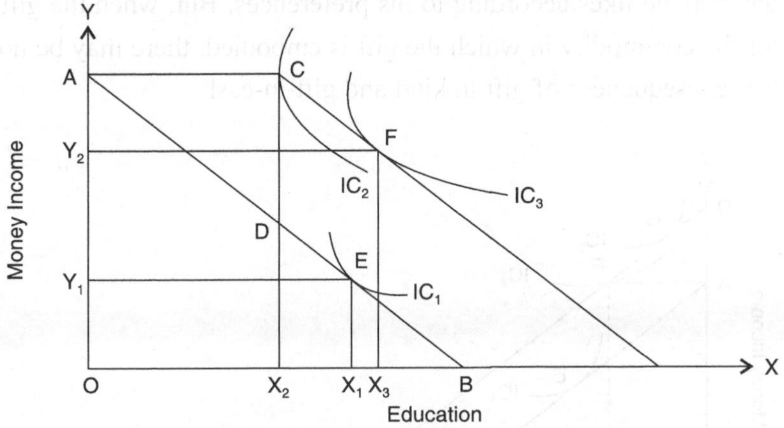

Fig. 9.27. Subsidizing education.

In under-developed countries marked by poor families, the demand fot educational services may rise, when education is subsidized. The demand for educational services in such case in the pre-subsidy situation will be less than OX_2 and the poor family chooses a point along the AD portion of the budget line in Fig. 9.27. Further, when educational services are not made absolutely free, the AC portion of the budget line in Fig. 9.27 will have a negative slope. This generally happens in the case of higher education, professional and technical services, where education is partly subsidized.

There is another way to subsidize education, wherein the families are enabled to educate their children in whatever school they like and also reach a higher level of satisfaction (point 'F' on indifference curve IC in Fig. 9.27). The family is in a position to provide OX units of educational services in some private school by making an effective payment of $A Y_2$. If the family continues to send its child to the government school, it will remain at point 'C'. On account of resource consideration, this scheme is followed only in the developed countries. The private sector in the developing countries may also pursue this scheme, which coexists along with the normal education subsidization programme of the government.

Economics of Gift

A gift may be given in cash or in kind. The cost of providing gift to a donor will remain the same in both the situations. However, for a recipient of the gift, the gift in cash on one hand and in kind on the other hand will make a lot of difference.

Suppose, you plan to give OQ quantity as gift to your friend on his birthday. The initial budget line AB is tangent to indifference curve IC_1. At point 'E' a gift equal to OQ or AF extends this budget line to AFC. The gift receiver maximizes his satisfaction at point 'F' of the budget set AFC. A gift-in-kind raises the welfare of the recipient from IC_1 to IC_2. When instead of this gift in kind, its money equivalent is given, the gift receiver may become better off by remaining on indifference curve IC_2 and the new budget line DC. This new budget line is parallel to the initial budget line AB and passes through point 'F'. The gift receiver becomes better off with gift-in-cash, because he can spend the cash in any way he likes according to his preferences. But, when the gift receiver has a strong preference for the commodity in which the gift is embodied, there may be no (or not much) differences in welfare consequences of gift in kind and gift-in-cash.

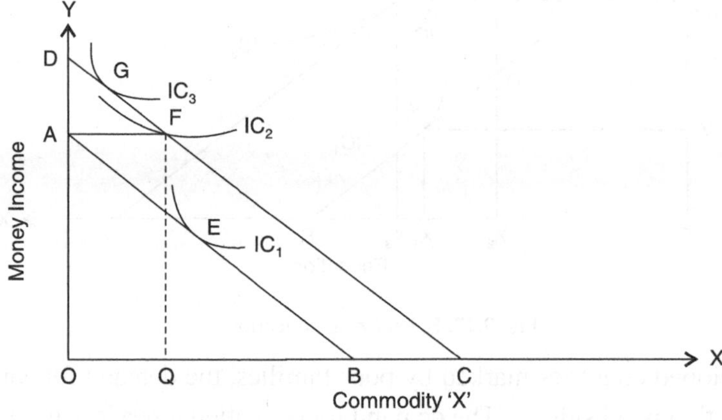

Fig. 9.28. Welfare consequences of gift in kind and gift-in-cash.

Rationing

During the periods of war or famine, when there is acute shortage of goods, price control is implemented to check prices from rising and rationing is introduced. The mechanism of rationing involves the distribution of goods in short supply among the consumers in an equitable manner. Every consumer is issued a ration card indicating the quantity of different goods, say, wheat and rice, which he can buy every month or fortnightly. The rationing mechanism operates through the budget constraint on one hand and a ration constraint (similar to a budget line) on the other hand.

The budget constraint is on account of the limited income of the consumer, given the prices of goods and services. The ration constraint limits the quantity of a commodity (or more than one commodity) that can be bought. The ration constraint is super imposed with the budget constraint so as to obtain the effective budget set.

Indifference curve analysis can be used to explain under what conditions rationing of goods by the government may act as a potentially binding constraint or an actually binding constraint for a consumer and further how it affects his welfare.

Suppose a consumer consumes two commodities 'X' and 'Y'. Given the income of the consumer and the prices of these commodities, the budget constraint of the consumer can be shown by the budget line AB in Fig. 9.29. The consumer can purchase the maximum quantity OA of commodity 'Y' and the maximum quantity OB of commodity 'X'. The budget set or the market opportunity set of the consumer is given by the area of triangle OAB, from which the consumer can make a choice of the two commodities. In the absence of rationing, the most preferred combination of the two commodities is represented by point 'E', where the budget line is tangent to indifference curve IC.

When the government imposes a ration limit or ration quota of OX_1 for commodity 'X', the ration constraint (shown by a vertical line parallel to Y-axis in Fig. 9.29) proves to be ineffective in restricting the consumption of commodity 'X'. In this case, the ration limit is so large that it is neither an actually binding constraint nor a potentially binding constraint, since point X_1 lies to the right of point 'B'. As the utility maximizing choice of the consumer remains unaffected, the rationing has no effect on the consumer's welfare.

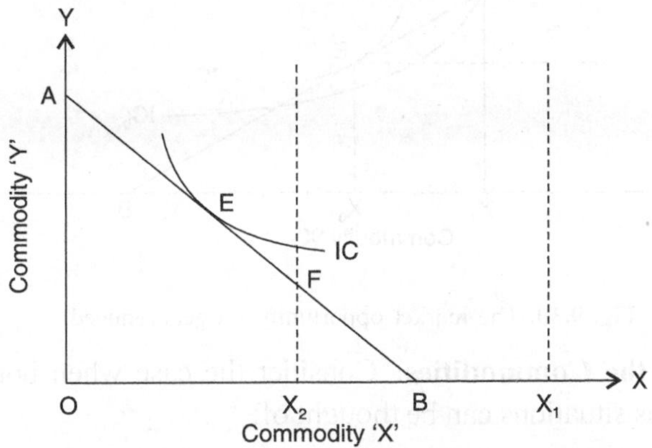

Fig. 9.29. The budget constraint of the consumer.

Now, assume that the ration limit decreases to OX_2 such that point X_2 is to the left of point B in Fig. 9.29. This ration limit reduces the feasible consumption set (set of attainable combinations of two commodities) of the consumer from OAB to $OAFX_2$. However, this ration quota is only a potentially binding constraint, since the ration quota makes any set of two commodities lying in the region X_2 FB outside the reach of the consumer. This quota is not effective in restraining the consumption of the consumer. The consumer can continue to consume the same combination of the two commodities indicated by point 'E'. Though the consumer can purchase the ration amount, but, he is not willing to consume commodity 'X' as much as the ration limit permits him. At equilibrium point 'E', the consumer consumes quantity of commodity 'X', which is smaller than the ration amount OX_2. Here, the consumer's welfare remains undisturbed, when such rationing is introduced by the government. This can be interpreted to be the case of a poor consumer whose optimum consumption basket of the two commodities is small on account of his low income and remains unaffected when ration limits are fixed at a higher level.

Now, consider a more relevant case of rationing, where the ration limit is not only a potentially binding constraint (the market opportunity set gets reduced to OA FX_1 in Fig. 9.30), but, it is also an actually binding constraint. In this case, the ration limit fixed is OX_1, which lies to the left of the equilibrium point 'E'. The consumer is forced to consume only OX_1 of commodity 'X' and not OX_0 as he was consuming before the ration limit was imposed. When ration limit is an actually binding constraint; the truncated budget line of the consumer becomes AFX_1 with link at point 'F'. On AFX_1, both budget constraint and ration constraint are satisfied. This new equilibrium point lies at lower indifference curve IC_0. Thus, the ration quota makes the consumer to buy less of rationed commodity 'X' and more of non-rationed commodity 'Y' (than what he otherwise preferred). In this manner, the welfare of the consumer is reduced from IC_0 to IC_1, when ration quota becomes an actually binding constraint.

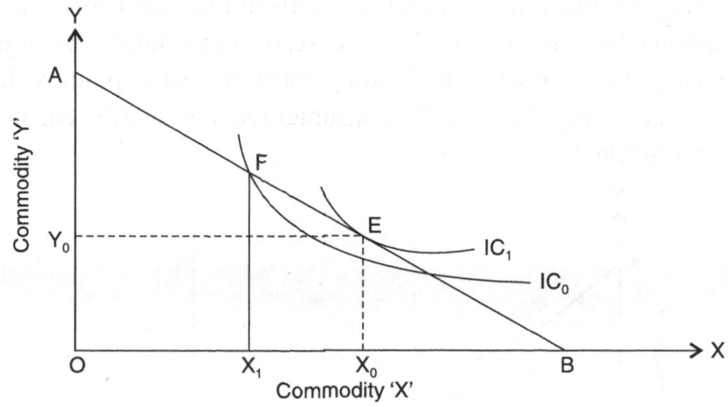

Fig. 9.30. The market opportunity set gets reduced.

Rationing of Both the Commodities: Consider the case when both the commodities are subject to rationing. Various situations can be thought of:

1. Ration limits on both the commodities are neither potentially nor actually binding. Such rationing has no affect on the market opportunity set or the welfare level of the consumer, since the ration limit is very large and beyond the two extremes of the budget line AB [Fig. 9.31(*a*)].
2. Ration limits on both the commodities are not actually binding, but potentially binding. In Fig. 9.31(*b*), the consumer is in equilibrium at point 'E' buying OX_0 of commodity 'X' and OY_0 of commodity 'Y'. Now, suppose ration limits for the two commodities are fixed at OX_1 and OY_1 respectively, indicating the maximum quantities of the two commodities that can be bought. It is clear from the figure that the ration quantities OX_1 and OY_1 are greater than OX_0 and OY_0 of the two commodities that the consumer was purchasing with his given price in come situation. The ration limits don't restrict the consumption of the two commodities. Hence, these are not actually binding. These limits merely narrow down the market opportunity set at both ends on X and Y-axis. This can be interpreted to be the case of a poor consumer,

whose optimum consumption basket of the two commodities is small on account of his low income and remains unaffected when ration limits are fixed at higher levels. If the income of the consumer rises to such an extent that the budget line lies outside the ration limits, the ration quota will become both potentially binding as well as actually binding. This case is discussed in the next point.

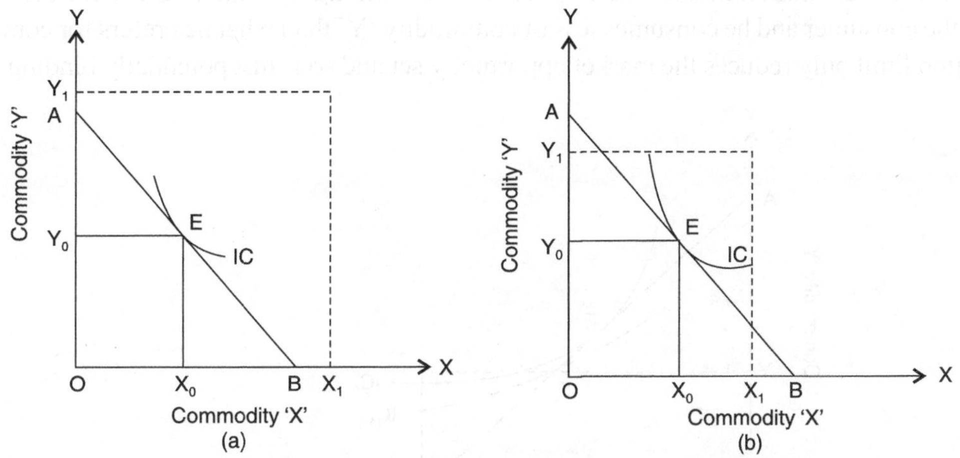

Fig. 9.31. Ration limits do not restrict the consumption of commodities.

Ration limits on both the commodities are potentially as well as actually binding. In Fig 9.32, the consumer is in equilibrium at point 'E' in the absence of rationing of the two commodities. He decides to consume OX_0 quantity of commodity 'X' and OY_0 of commodity 'Y' at this point. Introduction of ration limits, on the two commodities respectively forces the consumer to consume less quantities of both the commodities (OX_1 and OY_1 respectively at point 'F' in Fig. 9.32) than he would do without the restrain of rationing. Therefore, the rationing in this case is potentially as well as actually binding on him and reduces his welfare from IC_0 to IC_1 at the prevailing market prices. Therefore, it is an ineffective method of distribution of the commodities.

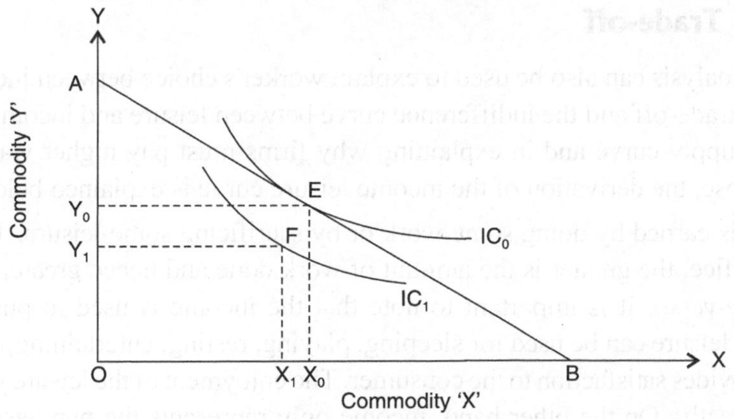

Fig. 9.32. Ration is binding for both the commodities.

Ration limit is binding on one of the two commodities. In Fig. 9.33, the consumer is in equilibrium position at point 'E' on the budget line AB and indifference curve IC_0. It is clear from this figure that the ration limit OX for commodity 'X' is greater than his equilibrium consumption of this commodity, while it is not so for commodity 'Y'. The ration limit of OY, for commodity 'Y' is fixed at a lower level and is potentially as well as actually binding on the consumer. It forces the consumer to shift to point 'F' on a lower indifference curve IC_1. Therefore, binding by rationing lowers the level of welfare of the consumer and he consumes less of commodity 'Y' than what he prefers for commodity 'X', the ration limit only reduces the market opportunity set and so is just potentially binding.

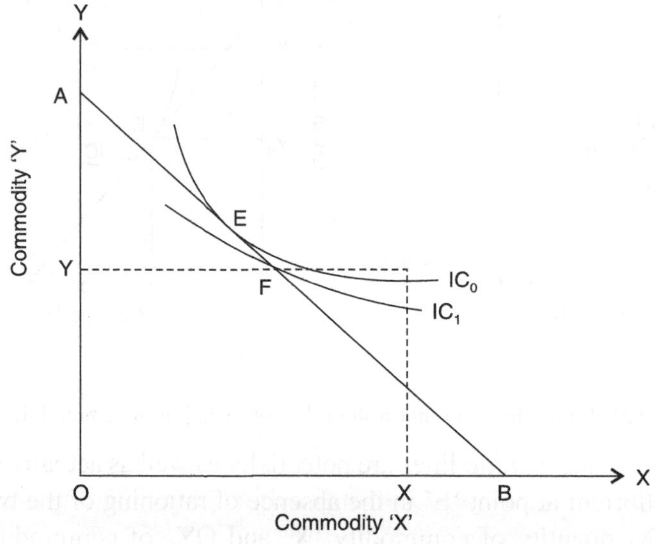

Fig. 9.33. Ration is binding for only commodity 'Y'.

If ration limit on commodity 'X' is potentially as well as actually binding, while it is only potentially binding for commodity 'Y', similar explanation and diagram can be given.

Leisure Income Trade-off

Indifference curve analysis can also be used to explain worker's choice between income and leisure. The income leisure trade-off and the indifference curve between leisure and income can be used for deriving worker's supply curve and in explaining why firms must pay higher wages for overtime work. For this purpose, the derivation of the income leisure curve is explained below.

The income is earned by doing some work or by sacrificing some leisure. The greater is the amount of this sacrifice, the greater is the amount of work done and hence greater is the income of the worker and *vice-versa*. It is important to note that the income is used to purchase goods for consumption, while leisure can be used for sleeping, playing, resting, entertaining, etc. Both income as well as leisure provides satisfaction to the consumer. The enjoyment of the leisure yields satisfaction to the consumer directly. On the other hand, income only represents the purchasing power which can be used for the satisfaction of various wants through the purchase of goods and services. Now, it is possible to draw indifference curves between income and leisure.

Fig. 9.34 shows income leisure trade-off through indifference curves representing different combinations of income (earned by working) and leisure time providing equal satisfaction to the worker. The further away indifference curve is from the origin, the higher the level of satisfaction it means for a worker. These indifference curves have usual properties (downward sloping, convex to the origin and never cut each other).

These indifference curves between income and leisure are also called trade-off curves, since they show the trade-off between income and leisure. The trade-off is given by the slope of the indifference curve measuring marginal rate of substitution between income and leisure. This trade-off means how much income the worker is willing to accept for, say one hour sacrifice of leisure time. The trade-off between income and leisure varies at different income-leisure levels.

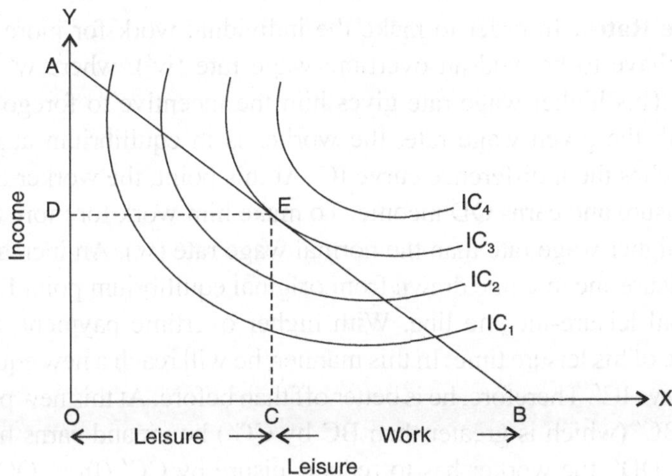

Fig. 9.34. Income leisure equilibrium.

Income-leisure constraint (line) is superimposed to know the market rate of exchange between income and leisure. In Fig. 9.34, income is measured along the vertical axis and leisure time along the horizontal axis. It is further assumed that the maximum time available for either leisure or work is OB hours a day. The worker can either use all the OB hours for leisure, in which case he earns zero income. He can also choose to work all the OB hours (leisure equal to zero) and earn a maximum income OA. Alternatively, he may use part of the OB hours for leisure and the remaining hours for work, in which case he would earn some income. The line AB is called income leisure constraint.

Income-leisure constraint shows the various combinations of income and leisure among which the worker has to make a choice. It tells how much time of leisure a worker must give up so as to earn a certain level of income. The slope of the income-leisure line AB in Fig. 9.34 is equal to OA + OB. But, OA is the total income earned for working OB hours and OB indicates the total hours worked to obtain OA income. Therefore, OA + OB is equal to wage rate per hour of work. In brief, slope of the income-leisure line is equal to the market wage rate. In other words, to increase leisure by one hour, a worker has to forego the opportunity of earning income (equal to wage per hour) which he can earn by doing work for an hour. The steeper is the income-leisure constraint, the higher is the wage rate per hour.

Income-Leisure Equilibrium: Income-leisure constraint along with the indifference map between income and leisure would determine the actual choice of income and for leisure to the worker in his equilibrium position. This will also automatically show the amount of work (in terms of hours worked) done by him in this optimal situation. This equilibrium analysis assumes that the worker is free to work as many hours per day as he likes and the wage rate is assumed to remain same irrespective of the number of hours he chooses to work.

Fig. 9.34 depicts the worker's equilibrium at point (E) of tangency of his income-leisure constraint with the highest possible trade-off curve IC_3. Given the wage rate (w), the worker maximizes his satisfaction by working for BC (or OB – OC) hours, earning income OD and using the remaining time OC for leisure. Wage rate per hour (w) is equal OD/OC, which is same as the slope of income-leisure line AB.

Overtime Wage Rates: In order to make the individual work for more hours (or sacrifice his leisure), he would have to be paid an overtime wage rate (w′), where w′ is greater than the normal wage rate (w). This higher wage rate gives him the incentive to forego more leisure time. Consider Fig. 9.35 with the given wage rate, the worker is in equilibrium at point E, where the income-leisure line touches the indifference curve IC. At this point, the worker chooses to work for BC hours, enjoy OC leisure and earns OD income. To make him work for more than BC hours, it is required to pay him a higher wage rate than the normal wage rate (w). An increase in the wage rate is depicted by a new leisure-income line drawn from original equilibrium point E to its left, which is steeper than the original leisure-income line. With higher overtime payment, the worker will be induced to give up some of his leisure time. In this manner, he will reach a new equilibrium point F on a higher indifference curve IC′. Therefore, he is better off than before. At this new point of equilibrium, the worker works for BC′ (which is greater than BC by CC′) hours and earns higher income OD′. To increase income by DD′, the worker has to reduce leisure by CC′ (from OC to OC′).

The new income-leisure line BEF is linked at point 'E'. Since no rational employer will pay higher wage rate than w for working less than (or equal to) BC hours, the new equilibrium point 'F' of the worker occurs to the left of point 'E'. The new wage rate (w′) is given by the slope of EF line. Clearly w′ (new wage rate) is higher than the 'w' (original wage rate).

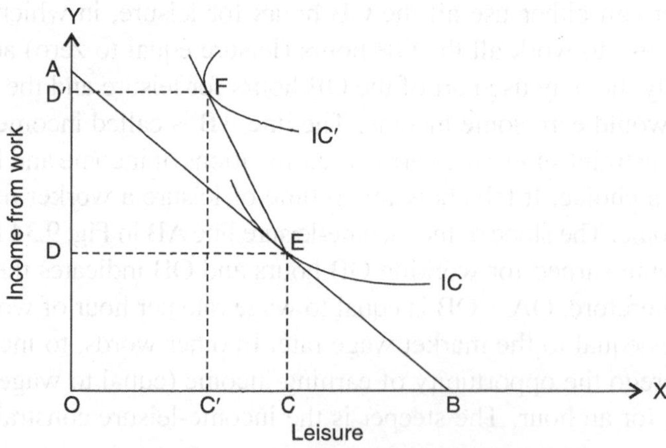

Fig. 9.35. Normal wage rate vs. overtime wage rate.

Wage Offer Curve and Labour Supply Curve: Indifference curve technique gives an insight into the individual's choice of the amount of labour time he is willing to offer and supply at various wage rates. This is depicted in Fig. 9.36, where X-axis shows leisure and Y-axis shows the income from work.

It is assumed that the worker has OB hours at his disposal to be divided between leisure and work. The original income-leisure line is AB, given the wage rate (w_1) the worker is in equilibrium at point E″ where the income-leisure line touches the indifference curve IC. In equilibrium, the worker works for BC hours and obtains OD income. Suppose the wage rate rises to W_2 (= OA_2/OB). The new income-leisure line J\B touches a higher indifference curve IC_2 at point E_2. The higher wage rate induces the worker to reduce his leisure time from OC_1 hours to OC_2 hours. As a result, the working hours increase to BC_2 and income increases to OD with further increase in the wage rate to W (= OA/OB), the worker chooses point E on still higher indifference curve IC and income-leisure line BA. He has even less leisure time OC hours and supplies BC work hours. Now, he earns a further high income OD. A still higher wage rate W_4 (= OA/OB) will make the worker so much better-off that he is induced to cut down the working time to BC_4, but, he still earns a higher income OD_4'. Worker's equilibrium point E_4 corresponding to this situation lies to the right of previous equilibrium point implying that his leisure time has increased. However, he is on yet higher indifference curve IC_4 and income-leisure line BA_4'. The curve obtained by joining points E_1, E_2, E_3 and E_4 is called *wage offer curve* (See Fig. 9.36).

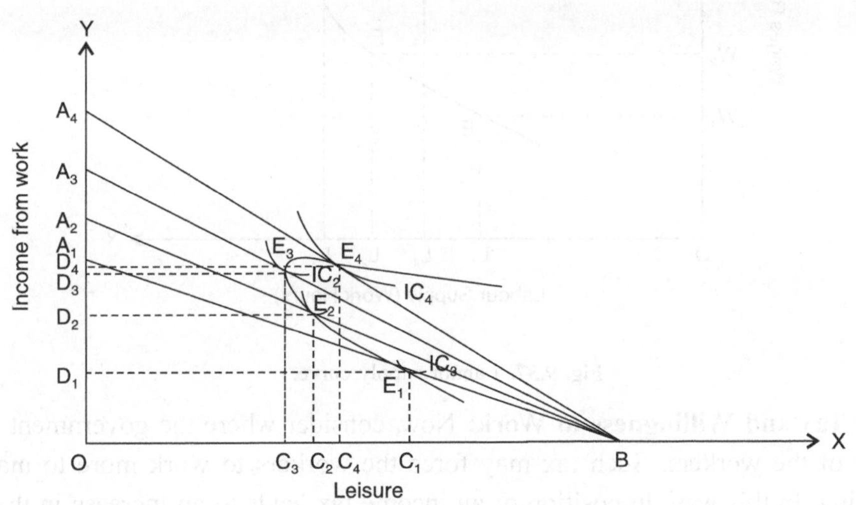

Fig. 9.36. Wage offer curve.

Wage offer curve shown in Fig. 9.36 can be used to derive the labour supply curve. Labour supply curve is depicted in Fig. 9.37, where work hours (labour supply) are shown along the X-axis, while wage rate is shown on the Y-axis. At wage rate of W_1, the work hours supplied are BC. This is plotted as point 'E' where labour supply OL, is equal to work hours BC. in terms of Fig. 9.37.

When wage rate rises to W_1' the labour supply increases from OL_1 to OL_2 (equal to BC_2 in terms of Fig. 9.36) plotted as point 'F' in the figure. A further rise in the wage rate to W_1 raises the labour supply to OL_3 (equal to BC_3 in terms of Fig. 9.36). A still higher wage rate of W_4 reduces the labour supply to OL_4 (equal to BC_4 in terms of Fig. 9.37 plotted as point H in the figure). Labour supply curve is obtained by joining points E, F, G and H

The labour supply curve shown in Fig. 9.37 traces out the supply of labour (work hours) at different wage rates. This curve is upward sloping up to point 'G'. Beyond this point, it bends backward. The reason for this is that the total effect of a change in wage rate on labour supply is the result of income effect and substitution effect. The income effect of a wage rate rise induces the worker to increase leisure and decrease the work hours. On the other hand, the higher cost of leisure per hour induces the worker to substitute income for leisure by working for more hours. When wage rate increases from W_1 to W_2 and W_3, the substitution effect outweighs the income effect. Consequently, the work hours (labour supply) increase. However, further increase in the wage rate leads to a curtailment in labour supply. This happens, because, at higher wage levels, the requirements of the worker are almost met and the worker decides to opt for more leisure.

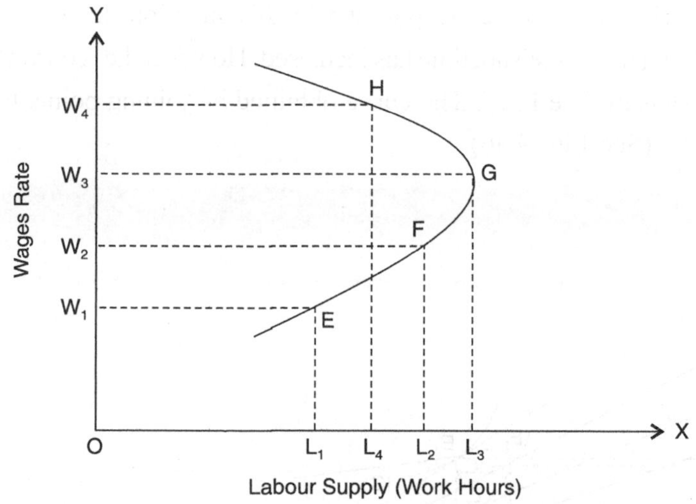

Fig. 9.37. Labour supply curve.

Income Tax and Willingness to Work: Now, consider where the government levies a tax on the income of the workers. Such tax may force the workers to work more to maintain their standard of living. In this way, imposition of an income tax leads to an increase in the volume of output and national income through more work on the part of the workers. However, many economists are of the opinion that the imposition of a tax on income may work as disincentive to work leading to a fall in the volume of output and national income. Which of the two effects will actually work in the economy, depends on the income elasticity of demand of the workers. The effect of income tax on the willingness to work and thus on the side of national income under the two cases is considered in

Fig. 9.38 (*a*) and (*b*). In this figure, the total time available with the worker has been taken as OB, which is shown along X-axis. The income is depicted on the Y-axis and the income leisure line is AB. Given the preference for leisure and work (represented by indifference curves), the worker is initially in equilibrium at point 'E' where the income-leisure line touches the indifference curve IC. Here, he works for BC hours to earn OD income and enjoys OC leisure time.

Case I (Inelastic Income Demand): Consider that the government imposes a tax on the income of the workers with low level of income. A certain minimum level of income, say OG amount is assumed to be exempted from tax. In order to earn OG income, the worker has to work for BH hours. If he works for more than BH hours, he has to pay tax to the government. As a result his earnings from work will be reduced by the amount of tax paid. So, the income-leisure line will take the shape of BJA (the portion JA′ is below JA). The worker will now, obviously be on a lower indifference curve IC′ and his new equilibrium position will be at point 'F'. He now works for more hours (BC′ instead of be) to partly compensate for the reduction in his income due to tax. Despite this, his income falls from OD to OD′. Thus, inelastic income demand stimulates workers to work for longer hours and to sacrifice a part of their leisure. We can expect that the output will rise leading in turn, to a higher level of national income.

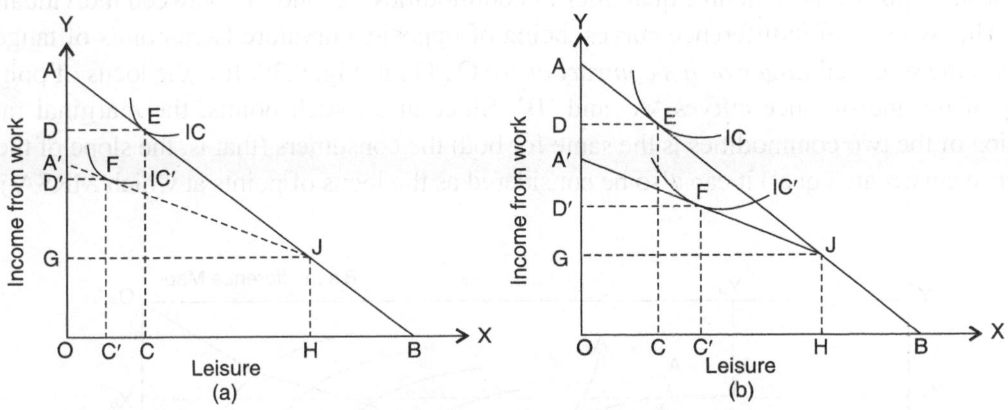

Fig. 9.38. Income vs. leisure.

Case II (Elastic Income Demand): Now, consider the case, where workers enjoy a good standard of living and they have a preference for leisure also. Under this condition, a tax on income will adversely affect the incentive to work. As a result of taxation, the new income-leisure line is BJA. The new equilibrium position 'F' is on a lower indifference curve IC′ and is to the right of original equilibrium point 'E'. At this new equilibrium, the worker reduces his working time by CC′ and increases leisure time *from* OC to OC′. In this situation, the worker works *for* BC′ hours and earns OD′ income which is much less than his pre-tax income. Therefore, in case of a worker with income elastic demand, a tax acts more as a disincentive than as an incentive. A tax on income reduces the *hours* of work, thereby reducing the output and national income.

Theory of Exchange

Indifference curve technique can be used to explain as to why individuals (groups of individuals or countries, regions and so on) exchange commodities with each other. We can show that under certain conditions, exchange of commodities may lead to an increase in the welfare of at least one individual without any reduction in the welfare of the other, such that the overall welfare which can be enjoyed from a given bundle of commodities can be increased. For this purpose, we make use of an *Edgeworth* box, named after the British economist F. Y. *Edgeworth,* who first used this construction.

Suppose, there are two individuals 'A' and 'B', and two commodities 'X' and 'Y', whose total quantities are given, measured along the sides of the *Edgeworth* box as shown in Fig. 9.39. The tastes of the two individuals are assumed to remain unchanged. The indifference map depicting reference pattern of consumer 'A' is represented by indifference curves A_1 '—' A_3, etc. from origin OA (bottom left comer of the *Edgeworth* box) and of consumer B by indifference curves B_1, B_2, B_3, etc., from origin O_A (top right comer of the *Edgeworth* box). The indifference curves are convex to their respective points of origin and have other usual properties of the indifferene curves. The further up an indifference curve of 'A' or the *further* down an indifference curve of 'B' lies, the greater is the satisfaction level of the two consumers respectively. Any point of the *Edgeworth* box represents a certain distribution of the available quantities of commodities 'X' and 'Y' between individuals 'A' and 'B'. The two sets of indifference curves, being of opposite curvature have points of tangency, which form the so called *Edgeworth's contract curve* O_A O_B in Fig. 9.39. It is the locus of points of tangency of the indifference curves 'A' and 'B'. Since at all such points, the marginal rate of substitution of the two commodities is the same for both the consumers (that is, the slope of the two indifference curves are equal) it can also be considered as the locus of points at which MRSA y, x = MRSBy,x'.

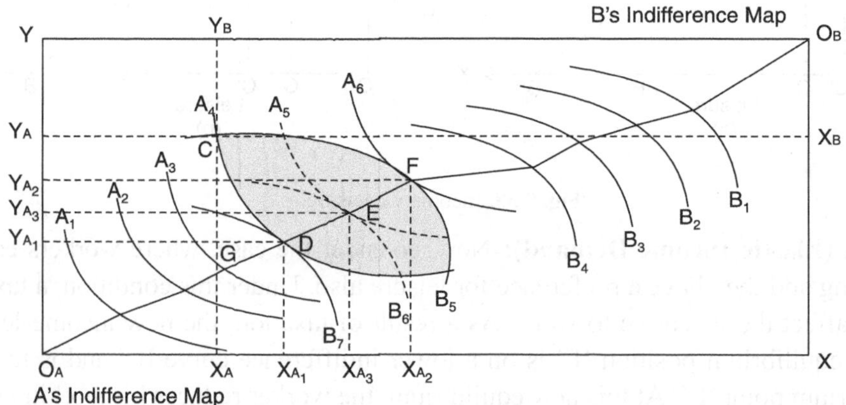

Fig. 9.39. The edgeworth box.

Only the points lying on the contract curve represent optimal distribution of the available quantities of commodity 'X' and commodity 'Y' between the two consumers. Any point other than on the contract curve would mean a lower level of satisfaction for at least one individual. Consider point 'C' of the contract curve. At this point, consumer 'A' has OX_A of commodity 'X' and OY_A of commodity 'Y', while consumer 'B' has OX_B (equal to remaining quantity X_AX) of commodity 'X' and OY_B (equal to remaining quantity Y_AY) of commodity 'Y'. With this distribution of the two commodities, consumer 'A' is on indifference curve A_4, while consumer 'B' is on indifference Curve B_5. If 'A' and 'B' exchange some of the quantities of the two commodities, at least one of them will be better off (without the other being worse off) by moving to any point on the section DF of the contract curve.

Suppose, the consumers exchange the two commodities such that they arrive at point 'D'. Here, the consumer 'A' gives away $Y_AY_{A_1}$ of commodity 'Y' in exchange for $X_A X_{A_1}$ of commodity 'X'. Consumer 'A' will retain his initial level of satisfaction, since points 'C' and 'D' lie on the same indifference curve A_4 (he is no worse off than before). On the other hand, consumer B will reach a higher welfare situation (moving from indifference curve B_5 to the higher one B_7). The opposite situation will be obtained, when the consumers arrive at the distribution denoted by point 'F' (another boundary point) through exchange of the two commodities. In this case, consumer 'A' will attain a higher indifference curve A_6, while consumer 'B' will retain his initial level of satisfaction since points 'C' and 'E' lie on the same indifference curve B_5'. Finally, if the consumers reach at any other distribution of the two commodities between points 'D' and 'F' (say, point 'E'), both the consumers 'A' and 'B' will be better off, reaching higher indifference curves (A_5 and B_6 respectively) as compared to their initial positions. Thus, it is to the mutual advantage of the individuals to move from a point off the contract curve to the point on the contract curve.

All points on the contract curve are known as *Pareto optimal*. They indicate the situation *of* maximum social welfare, where no individual can be made better *off* without making the other worse off. The distribution cannot be improved from the point *of* view *of* economic efficiency. The movement *off* the contract curve can make one individual better *off* only at the expense of the other. The points *off* the contract curve are called as *Pareto sub optimal*, where there is possibility of making all individuals better *off* or some better *off* without making an other worse-off. The equilibrium exchange of commodities (trading) between the two individuals takes place only on the contract curve.

All points on the contract curve are not equally advantageous to both the individuals. As one moves from point 'D' to 'F' in Fig. 9.39, individual 'A' will be moving to this higher indifference curve, but, individual 'B' will be going towards his lower indifference curves. While trading, individual 'A' would like to move near point 'F', while individual B would like to go towards point 'D'. The final distribution or the rate of exchange of the two commodities and gains from their exchange will depend on the relative bargaining strengths of the two individuals. If individual 'A' is more powerful, the exchange (trading point) will be settled near point 'F'. On the other hand, if individual 'B' is more powerful, the exchange will be settled near point 'D'. Thus, the actual exchange will settle within the limits of points 'D' and 'F' on the contract curve. Since, movement along the contract curve implies increase in the satisfaction (or welfare) of one individual and reduction in the satisfaction of the other, contract curve is sometimes called as conflict curve.

Sometimes, the actual choice among the different efficiency points is made on the basis of some other considerations like equity or fairness. At times, considerations of equity may require choosing an inefficient point in place of the efficient one. This happens, when the government decides to benefit the poor at the expense of the rich. However, it's always better to select an efficient point on the contract curve rather than the point of inefficient allocation (say, point 'G' rather than point 'C' in Fig. 9.36), so that the objectives of equity as well as efficiency are met simultaneously.

Self-Assessment Questions

1. Direct taxes are better than indirect taxes. Explain with the help of indifference curve analysis.
2. The extent of excess burden under indirect tax depends on the curvature of the indifference curve. Discuss particularly in the light of perfect substitutes and perfect complementary commodities.
3. If you compare a specific tax with a lump-sum tax of an equal yield, which one should be preferred by an individual tax payer?
4. Compare a lump-sum tax and an equal yield general tax on all commodities imposed at the same rate. Will the result change, if an equal yield general tax is imposed on income. Also compare a general tax on income and equal yield general tax on all commodities.
5. Explain the implications of the food subsidy policy adopted by the government with the help of indifference curve technique.
6. "The cost of giving subsidies to the consumers is always greater than the money equivalent of the subjective gain to the consumers". Explain with the help of indifference curves.
7. "Cash subsidy programmers are not necessarily more beneficial than food subsidy programmes", Do you agree? Explain with the help of indifference curve technique.
8. Explain the implications of subsidizing education using indifference curve analysis.
9. Explain the economics of gift with the help of indifference curve technique.
10. Is rationing a better method of distributing a commodity in short supply than the market from the point of view of welfare of the consumers?
11. Explain the income-leisure trade-off. Why must firms pay higher wages for overtime work? Explain the derivation of worker's labour supply curve from the wage offer curve.
12. Examine whether taxation is disincentive to work when there is (*a*) inelastic income demand, (*b*) elastic income demand.
13. How does exchange increase economic welfare? Use *Edgeworth's* box diagram.
14. Define Pareto optimum. Illustrate it with the help of *Edgeworth's* contract curve.
15. Define the concept of price consumption curve (PCC). Where does it start from and why? What will be its elasticity of demand for its various possible shapes? Use diagrams.
16. What is price effect? How does a change in the price of a commodity affect the equilibrium of the consumer?
17. What is the difference between a price consumption curve and a conventional demand curve? Derive demand curve with the help of price consumption curve.
18. What is a Giffen good? Derive the demand curve from the price consumption curve in case of a Giffen good.
19. Show how the equilibrium of the consumer is affected when there is a rise or a fall in the income of the consumer.

20. What is an income consumption curve? Draw an *Engel* curve with the help of an income consumption curve for a luxury commodity. How is it related to the demand curve?

21. What is the difference between a normal commodity and an inferior commodity? Derive an *Engel* curve for an inferior commodity.

22. Distinguish between an *Engel* curve and an *Engel* expenditure curve.

23. Explain the possible shapes of price consumption curve and income consumption curve. How will it look like, when the two commodities are (*i*) perfect substitutes, (*ii*) perfect complements of each other?

24. Show that price effect is the sum of substitution effect and income effect, using *Hicksian* and *Slutsky* approaches. Under what conditions will the law of demand not apply. Draw diagrams.

25. How do the income and substitution effects of a rise in the price of a commodity explain shifts in a consumer's equilibrium?

26. Distinguish between compensating variation and equivalent variation to explain the decomposition of price effect.

27. (*a*) Distinguish between an inferior commodity and a Giffen commodity. Which is an exception to the law of demand?

    (*b*) What will be the shape of the demand curve, when the mathematical sign of income effect is positive and is larger than the substitution effect?

    (*c*) While all Giffen goods are inferior, all inferior goods are not Giffen goods. Explain.

28. If the mathematical sign of the income effect is negative, will the consumer buy less of it when the price of the commodity falls?

29. Is positive income elasticity of demand the only condition for an inverse relationship between the price of a commodity and quantity demanded?

30. Suppose, the price of a commodity rises. Does it follow that the income and substitution effects of the price change always work in the same direction if the income elasticity of demand is negative? Will the demand curve be downward sloping?

31. Explain Giffen paradox. Does it result from income effect or substitution effect or both?

32. Discuss graphically the procedure of breaking up of price effect into substitution effect and income effect in the case of (*i*) perfect substitutes, and (*ii*) perfect complements.

33. Why is substitution effect always negative? Why does *Slutsky's* substitution effect exceed the Hicksian substitution effect?

34. What is substitution effect? How is *Slutsky* substitution effect different from *Hicksian* substitution effect? Which one is better?

35. Why is substitution effect always negative? Draw compensatory demand curve for a normal and a Giffen commodity and comment upon its shape.

Practical Questions

1. A family income is ₹ 300 per month. It buys 50 units of commodity A at a price of ₹ 2. It per unit and units of commodity 'B' at a price of ₹ 4 per unit. The price of commodity 'A' rises to ₹ 5 per unit and the price of commodity B falls to ₹ 2 per unit.

(*a*) Why don't the families buy the same quantities of the two commodities as before?

(*b*) Why will the satisfaction level of the family be lowered? Give reasons for your answer in each case.

2. A consumer purchases 100 units of good 'X' and 75 units of good 'Y' at given money prices and given money income. Suppose the price of 'X' rose by ₹ 3 and that of 'Y' fell by ₹ 4. Analyze the typical consumer's response to the change in prices if his money income is held constant.

Objective Type Questions

I. Fill in the blanks with the appropriate words:

(*i*) A fall in the price of a commodity, ceteris paribus, will lead to more of it being sold as a result of two effects: .... and ....

(*ii*) The substitution effect of a price fall always leaves the amount demanded either the same or .... than before.

(*iii*) The income effect of a price, if positive, will result in a .... quantity demanded.

(*iv*) For a good to have an upward-sloping demand curve, the income effect must be both .... and .... than the substitution effect.

II. Choose the Correct Answer:

(*i*) The price consumption curve shows

(*a*) The changes in price of both the commodities, money income remaining the same

(*b*) Changes in the price of one of the commodities, holding the consumer's income and price of the other commodity constant

(*c*) The change in the tastes of a consumer, money income and prices of both the commodities remaining the same

(*d*) Change in the income of a consumer, holding constant the relative prices of the both commodities.

(*ii*) The demand curve for a good may be derived with the help of

(*a*) Constitution curve

(*b*) Income consumption curve

(*c*) Price consumption curve

(*d*) Budget line.

(*iii*) Income consumption curve shows

(*a*) How the consumption of two goods is affected by change in income?

(*b*) How the consumption of one commodity is affected by change in income?

(*c*) None of the above

(*d*) All the above.

(*iv*) If income consumption curve of a consumer first rises and then falls as one moves towards right along the X-axis and is convex from above, it implies

(*a*) Commodity 'Y' is inferior

(*b*) Commodity 'X' is inferior

(*c*) Both 'X' and 'Y' are inferior

(*d*) Both are normal commodities.

(*v*) Negative income effect refers to the situation

(*a*) When income and demand for a commodity move in opposite directions

(*b*) When income and demand for a commodity move in same directions

(*c*) When income moves in positive direction and demand moves in negative direction

(*d*) All the above directions.

(*vi*) Normal goods have

(*a*) Positive income effect

(*b*) Negative income effect

(*c*) Sometime positive and sometime negative income effect

(*d*) None of the above.

(*vii*) Other things remaining the same, the proportion of income spent on food diminishes as income increases. This statement is known as

(*a*) Hicks-Allen Effect

(*b*) Gossen's Law

(*c*) Greshem's Law

(*d*) Engel's Law.

Unit 10

CONSUMER SURPLUS

10.1 INTRODUCTION

The concept of consumer surplus occupies an important place in economic theory, particularly in consumer theory of demand, taxation policy of the government and welfare economics. Many welfare propositions can be derived by using a theoretical structure provided by consumer surplus. Marshall, his disciple A. C. Pigou and many other neo-classical economists did use it for deriving various welfare propositions and policy prescriptions in economics. The concept was originally developed by a French economist Arsene Jules Dupit in 1844, who sought to measure the consumer surplus that would accrue to the people consequent upon the construction of a bridge across a river. It was modified and made popular by Alfred Marshall. Recognising the importance of the concept in economic analysis, Hicks explained it with the help of indifference curves approach.

10.2 MARSHALL'S CONSUMER SURPLUS

Marshall introduced the concept of consumer surplus in his book '*Pure Theories of Domestic Values*' under the title '*Consumer's Rent*' in 1879. The concept was further elaborated in his magnum opus '*Principles of Economics*' with logical details.

Marshall's consumer surplus is based on the operation of law of diminishing marginal utility. Since according to this law, the marginal utility from a commodity falls with increase in its consumption, the consumer is willing to pay lesser and lesser price for each successive unit of the commodity. However, the consumer has to pay the same price for all the (similar or homogenous) units of the commodity. On the marginal unit of the commodity, the consumer gets the same amount of utility, which he derives from the money that he pays to purchase it. This shows that the consumer gets extra utilities over the price paid by him on all earlier units, but not on the marginal unit. The sum of all these extra utilities is known as the consumer surplus. It may also be referred as the benefit which a consumer derives by paying a lower price for a commodity for which he was prepared to pay a higher price, rather than go without it. In the words of Marshall "excess of the price which a consumer would be willing to pay rather than go without a thing over that which he actually does pay, is the economic measure of this surplus satisfaction and it may be called consumer's surplus".

Marshall's consumer surplus is based on those assumptions on which the Marshallian utility theory is based. The assumptions of cardinal utility, measurement of utility through measuring rod of money and constancy of the marginal utility of money are particularly more important. This consumer surplus is the excess of the price which a consumer is willing to pay for the commodity over and above, what he actually pays for it. It arises because the utility derived from the last unit of a commodity is equal to the price paid for it, while the utility derived from earlier units exceeds the price. Different consumers derive different amount of consumer surplus from a particular commodity, depending upon their tastes, preferences as well as social, political and economic factors.

10.3 MEASUREMENT OF CONSUMER SURPLUS

Consumer surplus may arise even in case of single unit purchase of a commodity. If a student is willing to pay ₹ 150 for this book, but he actually pays ₹ 120 only then ₹ 30 is the consumer surplus. However, in most of the situations, a consumer purchases more than one unit of a commodity. The consumer continues to purchase additional units of the commodity from the market, till the utility from an additional unit of the curiosity becomes equal to the disutility in terms of price paid for it. According to Alfred Marshall, consumer surplus can be measured in monetary units and is equal to the difference between the amount of money actually paid by the consumer for certain quantity of this commodity and the amount that he would be willing to pay for this quantity rather than do without it.

The consumer surplus can be estimated from the consumer's demand curve and the current market price of the commodity. The market price is assumed to be constant and remain unaffected by the purchases of this commodity by the consumer. Consumer surplus is graphically illustrated in Fig. 10.1. In this figure, the consumer demand curve for the commodity 'X' is AB and the current market price is OP. At this price, the consumer purchases OQ units of the commodity and pays an amount equal to OPBQ for it. However, the consumer would be willing to pay higher price for initial units of the commodity. For instance, he would be willing to pay OP price for OQ. Quantity, OP_2 price for OQ_2 quantity, OP_3 price for OQ_3 quantity and so on. The fact that the actual price in the market is lower than the price he would be willing to pay for the initial units of the commodity 'X' implies that his actual expenditure is less than he would be willing to spend to acquire these units of commodity 'X'. *The difference between the actual price and the price which the consumer is willing to pay is called the Consumer surplus.*

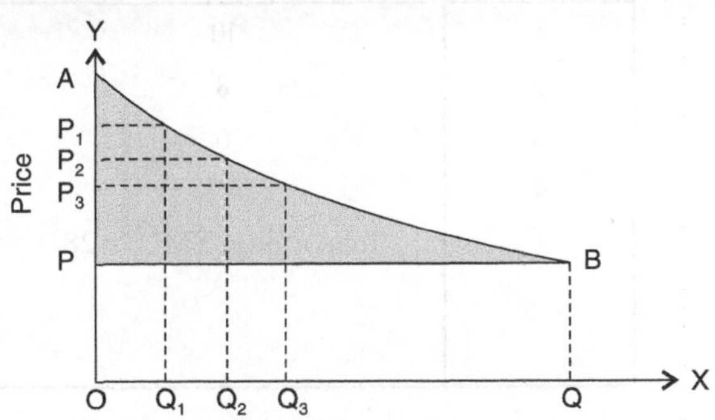

Fig. 10.1. Consumer demand curve.

Now, we may write consumer surplus as under:

Consumer Surplus = Aggregate Willingness Price – Total Actual Price

= Area under the Demand Curve (up to OQ quantity) – Price × Quantity

= Area OABQ – Area OPBQ

= Area PAB

The shaded area PAB indicates the net gain to the consumer by consuming OQ units of commodity 'X'.

Consumer Surplus in Utility Terms

The amount of money which a consumer is prepared to pay for a commodity shows the amount of utility he derives from that commodity. The greater the amount of money he is willing to pay, the greater is the utility he will derive from it. It is the marginal utility of a unit of a commodity that determines the price a consumer will be prepared to pay for that unit. Therefore, the consumer surplus as a measure of surplus utility can also be obtained through marginal utility curve. For this purpose, consider Table 10.1 showing diminishing marginal utility (from 10 to 4) with the consumption of each successive unit of the commodity. The consumer is in equilibrium when he purchases four units of the commodity, making its marginal utility equal to the given price of the commodity (₹ 4).

Table 10.1. Diminishing marginal utility vs. consumer surplus.

Units	*Marginal utility*	*Consumer surplus (Market Price ₹4)*
1	10	10 – 4 = 6
2	8	8 – 4 = 4
3	6	6 – 4 = 2
4	4	4 – 4 – 0
	Total utility (ΣMU) = 28	Total consumer surplus = 28 – 16 = 12 (or 6 + 4 + 2 + 0) = 12

It is clear from the Table 10.1 that the consumer purchases four units of the commodity for which marginal utility is equal to price. At this margin, what a consumer is willing to pay (marginal utility) is equal to price. Hence, there is no surplus utility for the fourth unit of the commodity. However, for the earlier three units, the marginal utility of the consumer is greater than the price actually paid by the consumer. The first, second and third units of the commodity give excess utility (marginal utility—market price) or consumer surplus of 6, 4 and 2 respectively. Therefore, the total consumer's surplus is equal to 6 + 4 + 2 = 12. The total consumer surplus can also be obtained by the difference of total utility (what consumer is willing to pay) and total price (what he actually pays). Here, the total utility (the sum of marginal utilities of the units of the commodity purchased) is equal to 10 + 8 + 6 + 4 = 28, whereas, the total price (price per unit multiplied by the number of units purchased) is equal to 4 × 4 = 16. Hence, the total consumer surplus by this alternative method is also the same, *i.e.,* 28 – 16 = 12. Now, we may write:

Consumer Surplus = Σ Total Utility – Total Price = U – Price × Number of Units Purchased

Assuming commodities to be indivisible, consumer surplus can be shown by the shaded area as depicted in Fig. 10.2(*a*). Horizontal straight line 'L' indicates the market price and is based on the assumption that the market price is the same for all the units of the commodity. The consumer will not purchase more than four units of the commodity, as beyond four units, the marginal utility the consumer will get becomes less than the price he has to pay.

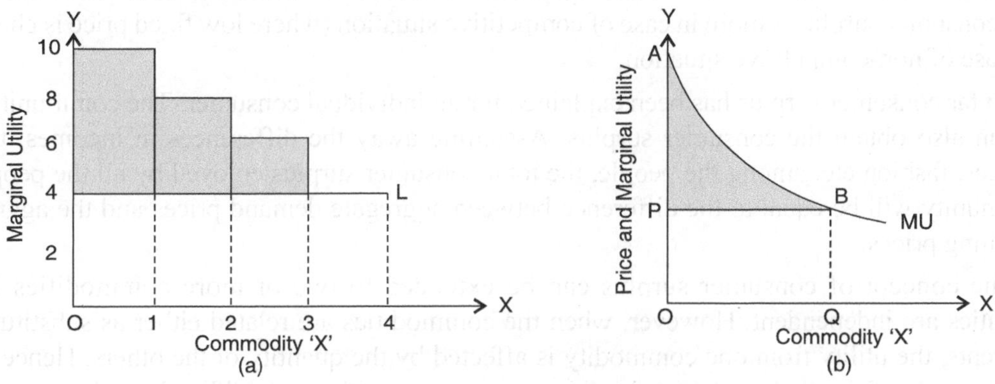

Fig. 10.2. Price and marginal utility for commodity X.

When the commodity under consideration happens to be a divisible commodity such as water, milk, oil, etc. or the commodity is assumed to be divisible, the marginal utility curve slopes downward. This curve indicates that as the consumer consumes more units of the commodity, its marginal utility falls. Since marginal utility shows the price, which a person will be willing to pay for the various units, marginal utility as well as price are represented on the Y-axis in Fig. 10.2(*b*). X-axis shows the number of units of commodity 'X'. At OP price, the consumer will be in equilibrium by purchasing OQ units of the commodity, as for OQ units of the commodity, marginal utility is equal to the given price. This last unit does not yield any consumer surplus. For the intra marginal units, *i.e.,* units prior to marginal unit, marginal utility is greater than the price. Thus, these units provide surplus to the consumer.

The total utility (sum of the marginal utilities) for OQ units of the commodity is equal to area OABQ, *i.e.,* the area under the marginal utility curve up to the point 'Q'. In other words, the consumer would be prepared to pay OABQ price for OQ units of the commodity 'X'. But, the consumer actually pays the sum equal to OPBQ for OQ units of this commodity. This leaves the surplus shown by the shaded area PAB in Fig. 10.2(*b*), which is equal to area OABQ – area OPBQ in this figure. The consumer surplus is the area under the marginal utility curve above the rectangle OPBQ as shown in Fig. 10.2(*b*).

If, however, the market price of the commodity rises above OP, the consumer will buy less than OQ units of the commodity 'X'. This will reduce consumer surplus. On the contrary, if the market price falls below OP, the consumer surplus will increase on account of purchase of more units of this commodity in new equilibrium. Therefore, given the marginal utility curve of the consumer, the greater is the price, the smaller is the consumer surplus and *vice versa*. It is also important to note that if instead of charging the same price for the various units of the commodity the producer of the commodity fixes different prices for the different units of the commodity, then, the consumer surplus will be smaller. No consumer surplus will accrue to the consumer, if each consumer is charged a price equal to what he will be prepared to pay.

The consumer surplus will be more if the marginal utility curve (or demand curve) starts at a higher initial price. It so happens in case of necessities (having low elasticity of demand) like salt and food items for which the consumer is ready to pay very high price rather than go without the commodity. That is why, the government taxes luxuries and not necessities to avoid exploitation of the poor. Further, consumer surplus is more in case of competitive situation (where low fixed price is charged) than in case of non-competitive situation.

So far consumer surplus has been explained for an individual consumer. The community as a whole can also obtain the consumer surplus. Assuming away the differences in incomes, tastes, preferences, fashion etc. among the people, the total consumer surplus enjoyed by all the people of the community will be equal to the difference between aggregate demand prices and the aggregate actual selling prices.

The concept of consumer surplus can be extended to two or more commodities if the commodities are independent. However, when the commodities are related either as substitutes or compliments, the utility from one commodity is affected by the quantity of the others. Hence, total consumer surplus from the purchase of two or more commodities may differ from the sum of the consumer's surplus from the two or more commodities.

10.4 CRITICISMS OF MARSHALL'S CONSUMER SURPLUS

The concept of consumer surplus has been severely criticized ever since it was propounded and developed by Alfred Marshall in' '*Principles of Economics*'. Most of the critics have not denied the theoretical validity of the concept of consumer's surplus. However, a number of economists like Gobi Nicholson, Cannon, Patten, Davenport, Tausig, Samuelson and others have criticized the concept of surplus on several grounds. Critics have described it as quite imaginary, hypothetical, unreal and useless. Some critics have even challenged the validity of the concept itself and argue that it has no practical value. Marshall's concept of consumer surplus has also been criticized on the ground of its being based upon unrealistic, questionable and obscure assumptions. Most of the criticism of the concept has been levelled against its possible measurement as the area under the demand or marginal utility curve. The important criticisms of the concept have been explained as follows.

1. Concept is Hypothetical

A contemporary of Marshall, Nicholson described the concept of consumer's surplus as hypothetical, illusionary and unreal. According to him, it would give absolutely erroneous result, when applied to real problems. He says, 'of what avail is it to say that the utility of an income of (say) £100 a year is worth (say) £1000 a year. Nicholson and other critics argue that it is difficult to say and know how much price a consumer would be willing to pay rather than go without it. The consumer has just to pay and accept the price that prevails in the market. Even the measuring rod of money does not indicate the amount of money which the consumer would be prepared to part with in return for the commodity he purchases. Thus, it is difficult to measure consumer surplus. However, the fact that a consumer gets extra psychic utility from a commodity than the price he pays for it, cannot be denied.

2. Unrealistic Assumptions

The presupposition of the cardinal measurement of utility is one of the biggest deficiencies of the concept of consumer surplus. Critics have contended that utility is a subjective phenomenon and is not measurable in quantitative cardinal terms. Therefore, it is not possible to measure consumer surplus.

Marshall also assumes that the marginal utility of money is constant, which does not change with in crease or decrease in the money stocks with the consumer. By assuming constant marginal utility of money, Marshall ignores the income effect of a price change. The income effect of a price change may be negligible in case of most of the commodities. However, for commodities like food grains, the income effect of the price change cannot be ignored. To overcome this problem, the consumer surplus must be measured on an (income) compensated demand curve.

3. Ignorance of Interdependence

The concept of consumer's surplus has been criticized on the ground that it ignores interdependence between the commodities. One cannot regard the utility from commodity as independent of the other for the purpose of measuring consumer surplus. In case of most of the commodities, the amount that a consumer is prepared to pay as a price depends on the availability of their substitutes and complements. One finds it hard to assume that the related commodities have no effect on the surplus utility derived by the consumer. Consumer receives different surplus utilities from the same commodity under different circumstances. The consumer can properly appreciate the utility from fountain pen, when it is accompanied by ink.

Further, it is difficult to ascertain utility obtained by a consumer from different units of a commodity having several substitutes. In the absence of the existence of substitutes of a commodity, the consumer is prepared to pay higher price for the commodity, as he has no choice in this situation. On the other hand, a small rise in the price of the commodity induces the consumer to abandon it in favour of its substitutes, when these are available. Therefore, the magnitude of the consumer surplus will be greater in the former case. Since the degree of substitutability is different for different commodities, the concept of consumer surplus becomes imprecise, vague and ambiguous. To overcome this difficulty, Marshall suggested that the substitutes be grouped together under a common demand schedule. But, this suggestion is impractical.

4. Different Consumers with Different Economic Positions

It is reasonable to hold that different people have different marginal utilities of money, which are not comparable. In an economy characterized by inequalities of income and wealth, the marginal utility of money is low for rich people. They will be ready to give up more money to obtain additional units of a certain commodity as against relatively poor people. As a result, the consumer surplus will differ from person to person. Further, with change in economic position of a consumer, consumer surplus for a commodity will also change.

In view of the above, there is no justification for sharing Marshall's statement that the differences in people's income, tastes and preferences can be safely ignored while measuring their consumer surplus. For the same commodity, some consumers would be willing to pay more, while others would be willing to pay less or even nothing, depending upon their tastes, habits, likings and sensibilities. A rupee worth of satisfaction to a poor man is a much greater thing than a rupee worth of satisfaction to a rich man. In this connection Trussing has rightly remarked. "A rich man will pay for hot house fruits or vegetables a sum quite out of question for a person of modest means. The latter might secure at a season of greater plenty precisely, the same things for a price much lower. The rich man probably gets no greater enjoyment from his expensive purchases or if so by no means in proportion to the higher price he pays".

5. Complete Demand Schedule not Available

Measurement of consumer surplus requires a complete demand schedule of a commodity. Critics argue that a complete and reliable list of demand and prices is never available to the consumer. Consumer surplus based on a hypothetical demand schedule can be highly conjectural except at ruling prices.

6. Unascertainable in Case of Necessities

Many critics point out that consumer's surplus from necessities and prestige goods is indefinite and not ascertainable. Patten's distinction between pain and pleasure economy is relevant here. Pain economy refers to those commodities necessary for existence. Their consumption does not yield any positive satisfaction. However, when a person is not able to satisfy his want for a necessary commodity, he experiences pain and is prepared to give up even a large fortune to secure it. For example, a thirsty rich man stranded in a forest may be willing to pay a very high price to acquire a glass of water. Further, under terrible famine conditions, even a destitute may be prepared to get food for next to anything, so as to overcome intense pain. Utility of necessities to consumers is very high, while their market prices are generally very low on account of their relative abundance. Consumer surplus, if calculated for such commodities will be fantastically high. Therefore, calculation of consumer surplus for necessities is highly unrealistic. Similarly, the utility of prestige goods depends upon the prevalence of high prices. If prices were low, utility of these goods will diminish and so the consumer surplus. Economists like Tausig have pointed out that it is not possible to measure consumer surplus of prestige goods like diamonds.

10.5 CONSUMER SURPLUS IN TERMS OF INDIFFERENCE CURVES

The concept of consumer surplus has been under constant attack, since the publication of the 'Principles of Economics' in 1890. Economists like Walrus, Pareto, Nicholson and Cannon criticized the concept vehemently. Among the neo-classical, Knight and Robbins challenged the validity of the concept. Even Cambridge began to lose faith. Gradually, the concept disappeared from the text books. However, recent developments in the late thirties, popularized and rehabilitated this concept afresh with attempts made by Hicks, Allen and Henderson.

Hicks demonstrated the consumer surplus by means of indifference curves in his '*Value and Capital*' (later on he modified the concept in his 'Revision of Theory of Demand'). He made it a useful economic concept by giving up the assumption of cardinal utility measurement and constancy of marginal utility of money. Hick's measurement of consumer surplus through ordinal utility concept went a long way in proving the validity of the consumer surplus concept. Initially, the consumer surplus using indifference curves has been explained, assuming constancy of marginal utility of money.

Measurement of consumer surplus with the help of indifference curves technique (with constant marginal utility of money) is illustrated in Fig. 10.3. In this figure, the quantity of commodity 'X' is measured along the X-axis, while money income is taken along the Y-axis. Suppose, a consumer has OA amount of money income which he can spend on commodity 'X' or other commodities. The consumer is indifferent among various points on the indifference curve IC, through point 'A'. This indifference curve shows the amount of money the consumer is willing to pay for commodity 'X' at its different quantity levels. Since the scale of preferences of the consumer represented by his indifference curves depend on his tastes and not on his income or market price of the commodities, the budget line is not relevant here. Now, if the consumer selects point E on the indifference curve IC" he is willing to give up AD amount of money income to get OC quantity of commodity 'X' rather than do without it. In other words, OD amount of money and OC quantity of commodity 'X' give same satisfaction to the consumer as OA amount of money, as both 'A' and 'E' combinations lie on the same indifference curve IC.

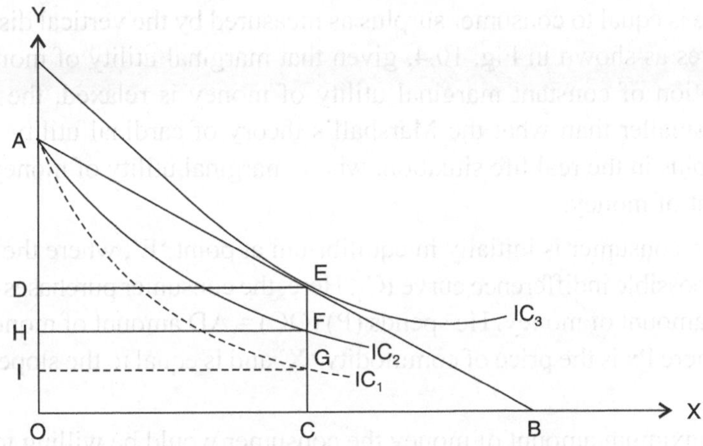

Fig. 10.3. Measurement of consumer surplus.

Suppose that the market price of commodity 'X' is such that we get AB budget line. Price of commodity 'X' is given by slope of this line, *i.e.,* OA/OB. Given this price of commodity 'X', the consumer is in equilibrium at point 'F', where the budget line AB is tangent to indifference curve IC_2. Since point 'F' is on a higher indifference curve, the combination of money income (OG) and quantity of commodity 'X' (OC) at this point represents a higher level of satisfaction as compared to any point of ICI indifference curve. Here, the consumer gives up AG amount of money to acquire OC quantity of commodity 'X'. Therefore, the consumer pays EF (or DG) less amount of money than what he is prepared to pay (AD) for OC quantity of commodity 'X'. Thus, AD – AG = DG (or EF) is the amount of consumer surplus from purchasing OC quantity of commodity 'X'. This shows that consumer surplus is equal to the vertical distance between indifference curves.

Marshall's consumer surplus measured so far by using indifference curves assumes constant marginal utility of money. So, the indifference curves IC_1 and IC_2 will be parallel to each other and have the same slope at any given quantity of commodity 'X'. This implies that income effect of the price change on the quantity demanded is zero, so that the amount of money that the consumer is prepared to pay for a commodity rather than go without it does not change as the money income is given up to obtain the larger quantity of the commodity. Assuming marginal utility of money income equal to one, it can be shown that the slope of indifference curve IC_1 is same as the slope of indifference curve IC_2 for OQ quantity of commodity 'X'.

Slope of IC_1 for OQ quantity of commodity 'X'

= MRSx, M = MUx / Mum = MUx /1 = MUx

= Slope of IC_2 for OQ quantity of commodity 'X'

10.6 CONSUMER SURPLUS WITH DECLINING MARGINAL UTILITY OF MONEY

The magnitude of Marshall's consumer surplus as measured by the area under the demand curve (or marginal utility) curve is equal to consumer surplus as measured by the vertical distance between the two indifference curves as shown in Fig. 10.4, given that marginal utility of money is constant. If, however, the assumption of constant marginal utility of money is relaxed, the size of consumer surplus will become smaller than what the Marshall's theory of cardinal utility implies. Fig. 10.4 depicts consumer surplus in the real life situation, where marginal utility of money declines with an increase in the amount of money.

In Fig. 10.4, the consumer is initially in equilibrium at point 'E', where the budget line AB is tangent to the highest possible indifference curve IC_3. Here, the consumer purchases OC of commodity 'X' by giving up AD amount of money. He spends (P) (OC) = AD amount of money on OC quantity of commodity 'X', where Px is the price of commodity 'X' and is equal to the slope of the budget line AB.

To know the maximum amount of money the consumer would be willing to pay for the same quantity OC of commodity 'X' rather than do without it, an indifference curve IC_2 is drawn through point A (where he does without commodity 'X'. This indifference curve IC_2 is flatter (having smaller slope) than indifference curve IC), for any given quantity of commodity OX showing that the marginal utility of money changes inversely with the amount of money income (declining marginal utility of money). The consumer would be indifferent between point 'A' and point 'F', where he buys none of commodity 'X' (on one hand) and OC of commodity 'X' (on the other hand). Hence, AH is the amount, the consumer is willing to pay for OC quantity of commodity 'X' than do without it. Since, for OC quantity of this commodity, the consumer actually pays AD amount of money, the difference AH – AD = DH (or EF) is the consumer surplus enjoyed by him.

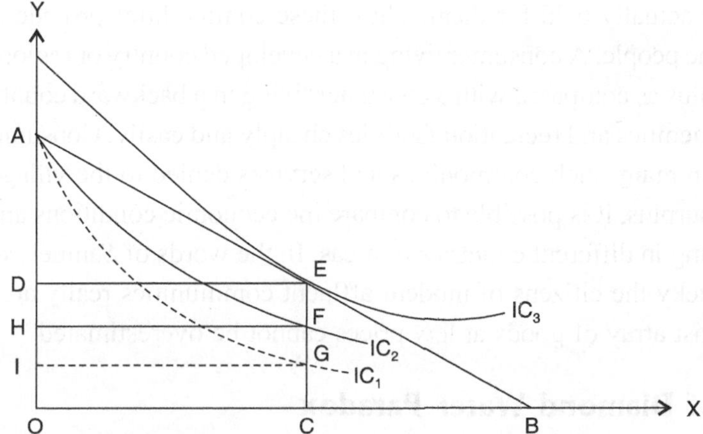

Fig. 10.4. Consumer surplus measured by the vertical distance between the two indifference curves.

To compare this consumer surplus with the Marshall's measure, another indifference curve IC, through point 'A' is drawn, which is vertically parallel to indifference curve IC, implying constant marginal utility of money. In other words, this indifference curve has the same slope as that of indifference curve IC. In Fig. 10.4, on indifference curve ICI, to obtain OC quantity of commodity 'X', the consumer is willing to give up AI amount of money. Thus, Marshall measure of consumer surplus is DI or EG, which is larger than consumer surplus DH or EF obtained under the assumption of declining marginal utility of money. This is also clear from the slope of IC, which is equal to the slope of IC_1 and is greater than that of the slope of IC_2.

10.7 IMPORTANCE OF CONSUMER SURPLUS

The concept of consumer surplus has an important role to play both in economic theory as well as economic policies of the government as well as the producers of the commodities, especially monopolists. Marshall and Pigou have attempted to show the practical utility of the doctrine in welfare economic analysis. Theoretical and practical importance of the concept of consumer surplus is explained below.

1. Distinction between Value-in-Use and Value-in-Exchange

Adam Smith visualized the distinction between value-in-use and value-in-exchange and pointed out that for a commodity, the former is greater than the latter. Value-in-use of a commodity indicates the utility or satisfaction derived by the consumer (demand price), while value-in-exchange signifies the price paid by the consumer (market price). The difference between the two is the amount of consumer surplus enjoyed by the consumer from the consumption of the commodity. This consumer surplus clearly brings out that the price, which a consumer pays for a commodity does not exactly measure the utility derived by him. Utility is often much more than the price paid by him.

The value-in-use of several commodities like common salt, match box, newspaper is far greater than the price actually paid for them. Thus, these commodities provide a great amount of consumer surplus to the people. A consumer living in a developed country or region derives relatively greater consumer surplus as compared with a consumer living in a backward country or region, since he is able to get the amenities and recreation facilities cheaply and easily. Consumers in towns enjoy consumer surplus from many such commodities and services denied to the villagers. Therefore, by looking at consumer surplus, it is possible to compare the economic conditions and the standards of living of people residing in different countries or areas. In the words of Samuelsson "The important thing is to see how lucky the citizens of modem affluent communities really are. The privilege of being able to buy a vast array of goods at low prices cannot be overestimated."

2. Explanation of Diamond Water Paradox

The famous puzzle of diamond-water paradox in economic theory can also be explained in terms of consumer surplus. Water is very useful and necessary for survival. But, diamonds are more expensive than water, which are less useful and satisfy less important needs than water. This is explained below.

The marginal utility of water is very low on account of its abundant supply, while that of diamonds is very high due to its small supply. If had only few litres of water were available, marginal utility of water would have been much greater than that of diamonds. It is important to note that the total utility (given by area under marginal utility curve) has a role in determining the demand for a commodity. The price (the value in exchange) is determined by the marginal utility and the marginal cost. There would be no demand for a commodity if its price is higher than the marginal utility for the potential buyers. Thus, if the price of water is fixed higher than its marginal utility, then only a very small quantity will be sold. As a result, the price of water will show a tendency to decline and will ultimately be equal to its marginal utility to the consumers. Similarly, the price of diamonds will also be equal to their marginal utility to the potential users. Therefore, low marginal utility of water ensures its low price, while high marginal utility of diamonds is responsible for their high price. This is illustrated in Fig. 10.5 with the help of two linear marginal utility curves.

In Fig. 10.5, MU_W depicts the marginal utility curve for water, while MU_D represents the marginal utility curve for diamonds. X-axis shows the quantity of water and diamonds, while Y-axis shows the marginal utilities of the two commodities. As the total use-value (total utility or benefit) of water is large, its marginal utility curve for different units of water is at a high level. On the other hand, the marginal utility curve for diamonds for its different quantities is at a low level on account of their small total use-value. Consumers are prepared to pay far greater amount of money for the initial units of water than those of diamonds.

For OQ_W quantity of water, the marginal utility is equal to EQ_W. Hence the price determined is OP_W. Likewise, for OQ_D quantity of diamonds, the marginal utility equals FQ_D. Therefore, its price is determined at OP_D which is much higher than that of water. In other words the supply of water at a low price is very large, while the supply of diamonds even at very high price is quite small and non-existent at a low price. The consumer's surplus is measured by the difference of total value-in use and total value-in-exchange.

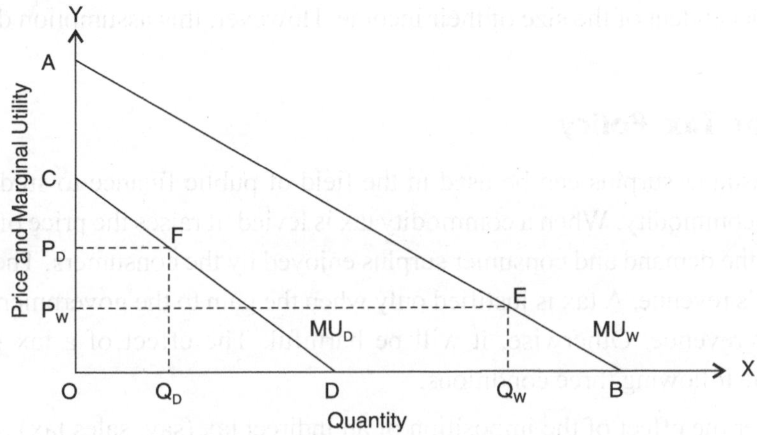

Fig. 10.5. Linear marginal utility curves.

Consumer surplus for water is given by P_wAE ($OAEQ_w - OP_wEQ_w$) which is much higher than that of diamonds, *i.e.,* area P_DCF ($OCFQ_D - OP_DFQ_D$). Further, the total utility from water (area $OAEQ_w$) exceeds the area $OCFQ_D$ (total utility from diamonds).

3. Importance to a Monopolist

The concept of consumer surplus is very important in fixation of price under monopoly so as to maximize profits. If the consumers stop getting consumer surplus from a commodity, the increase in price by the monopolist will not be profitable for him. Prices of those commodities can be increased easily on which consumers enjoy a high amount of surplus. Further, while fixing prices under price discrimination, a monopolist has to see the amount of consumer surplus which buyers derive. He may charge prices such that some or no consumer surplus is left with the consumers. If the monopolist is not afraid of any competition and is not interested in keeping his customers satisfied, he can fix such high price for his product that leaves no consumer surplus with the customers. Pigou calls it price discrimination of first degree. In the second degree price discrimination, a monopolist allows a certain amount of consumer surplus to exist.

4. Importance in Cost-Benefit Analysis

The cost-benefit analysis has become very popular these days to judge the desirability of investment in various projects. Here, the costs and benefits do not merely mean money costs and money benefits. These also include real costs and real benefits in terms of satisfaction and resources. The amount of consumer surplus expected from certain investment projects like flyover, road, park, dam, etc. can be considered as important benefits flowing from these projects.

The use of the concept of consumer surplus for formulation of policies on projects requires the summation of consumer surpluses derived from a project by different consumers belonging to various income groups. The validity of such summation rests on the assumption that one rupee worth of consumer surplus means the same thing for all consumers. This requires constancy of marginal utility of money independent of the size of their income. However, this assumption does not seem to be scientific.

5. Evaluation of Tax Policy

The concept of consumer surplus can be used in the field of public finance to study the economic effects of a tax on a commodity. When a commodity tax is levied, it raises the price of the commodity and hence, reduces the demand and consumer surplus enjoyed by the consumers. The tax also brings gain in government's revenue. A tax is justified only when the gain to the government is greater than the increase in tax revenue. Otherwise, it will be harmful. The effect of a tax revenue can be considered under the following three conditions.

First, consider the effect of the imposition of an indirect tax (say, sales tax) on the consumer surplus for an industry operating under constant costs or constant returns. In Fig. 13.6, DD is the demand curve and PS is the supply curve of the commodity before the imposition of the tax. E is the point of equilibrium, where demand and supply curves intersect each other. At this point, the equilibrium price is OP and the equilibrium quantity is OQ. This is the position of maximum welfare in the absence of any government intervention. Here, consumers derive consumer surplus given by the area of the triangle PDE. This is net benefit to the consumers from the consumption of OQ units of the commodity.

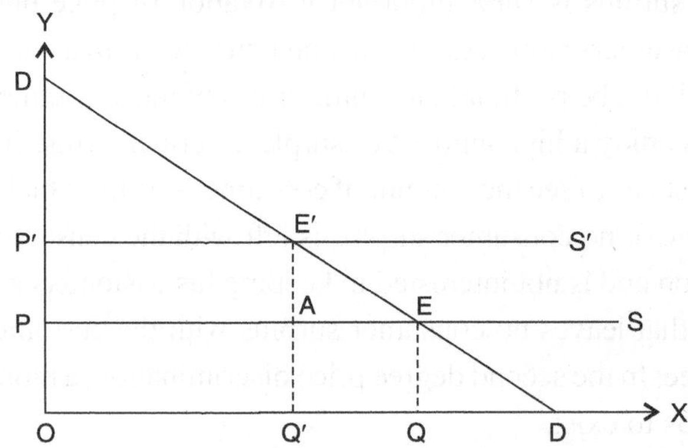

Fig. 10.6. Consumer surplus loss from tax under constant returns (Units Tax).

6. Economic Effects of a Subsidy

Marshall applied the concept of consumer's surplus for prescribing a suitable fiscal policy by the government, which will maximize the social welfare of the community. According to him, the total welfare of the community can be increased by imposing taxes only on the products of the increasing cost industry. The proceeds so obtained should be spent on providing subsidies on the products of the decreasing cost industry.

Grant of a subsidy on a commodity by the government causes a fall in the price of the commodity by the amount of subsidy and hence, rises in the quantity and consumer surplus. A subsidy on one hand, implies a financial loss to the government. On the other hand, it means gains to the consumers in terms of increase in consumer surplus. A subsidy is justified, if the gain to the consumers (additional net satisfaction) conferred through it outweighs the loss to the government. The concept of consumer surplus is of considerable importance in determining the desirability of giving subsidy on a particular commodity. The economic effects of a subsidy are evaluated below in relation to conditions of increasing returns, constant returns and diminishing returns in an industry. It also shows the case of *decreasing costs or increasing returns in an industry* (declining supply curve). In the absence of subsidy, demand curve DD and supply curve SS cut each other at point 'E' At this equilibrium point, equilibrium price is OP and equilibrium quantity is OQ. This gives a consumer surplus equal to the triangular area PDE. Now, suppose the government grants a subsidy equal to SS' per unit of the commodity. This will shift the supply curve below to the position S'S'. The new equilibrium price falls to OP′ and the equilibrium quantity rises to OQ′. The new consumer surplus is equal to the triangular area P′DE′. As a result of the subsidy, the increase in consumer surplus is equal to the area P′PEE′. However, the burden of subsidy on the government is P′BAE′, which is less than gain in consumer surplus. Therefore, under conditions of decreasing cost in an industry or increasing returns, subsidy is justified, as it brings more gain to the people than the financial burden imposed on the government. Further, if the tax proceeds collected by laying the tax on the product of increasing cost in an industry are used for granting subsidy on the product of decreasing cost in an industry, there will be net addition to the total welfare of the community, since the loss suffered in consumer surplus as a result of taxation on the product of the increasing cost in an industry will be more than compensated by the gain in consumer's surplus consequent to the grant of subsidy on the product of the decreasing cost in an industry.

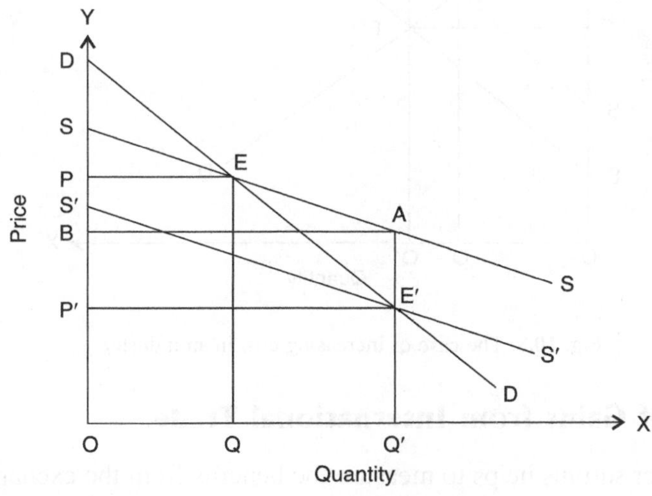

Fig. 10.7. The case of constant returns in an industry.

Now, consider the case of constant cost or constant returns in an industry. The initial supply curve PS intersects the demand curve DD at point 'E'. At the equilibrium point, the equilibrium price and equilibrium quantity are OP and OQ respectively. Suppose that the subsidy equal to PP′ per unit of the commodity is granted by the government. As a result the supply curve will shift below to the position P′S′. The price will fall to OP′ and the quantity will rise to OQ′. The new consumer's surplus is equal to P'DE'. The government will pay total subsidy equal to P′ PAE′ *i.e.,* (PP′). (OQ′) or (AE′). (P′E′), which is greater than the gain in consumer surplus by (P′ DE′ – PDE′ P′ PE E′) by the area of triangle AEAE′. Since the burden of subsidy is greater than the gains to the consumer, it is not conducive to provide subsidy on the product of such an industry.

Finally, Fig. 10.8 represents the case of increasing cost in an industry. In the absence of any subsidy, equilibrium price is OP and equilibrium quantity is OQ, when initial supply curve SS and demand curve DD intersect at equilibrium point 'E'. The consumer surplus is equal to area PDE. Now, suppose, the government grants a subsidy SS' per unit of the commodity, which pushes down the supply curve to the position S' S' The new equilibrium price and equilibrium quantity are OP′ and OQ′ respectively, corresponding to new equilibrium point E′ (where new supply curve S′S′ and demand curve DD cut each other). The new consumer's surplus is given by the triangular area P′ DE′. The gain in consumer surplus as a result of subsidy is given by the area P′ PEE′ (*i.e.,* P′DE′ – PDE) is evidently smaller than total subsidy provided by the government, *i.e.,* (SS). (OQ) = (AE'). (P′E′) = P′ B AE′. Therefore, this is also not a fit case for it being granted subsidy as it will not increase the social welfare.

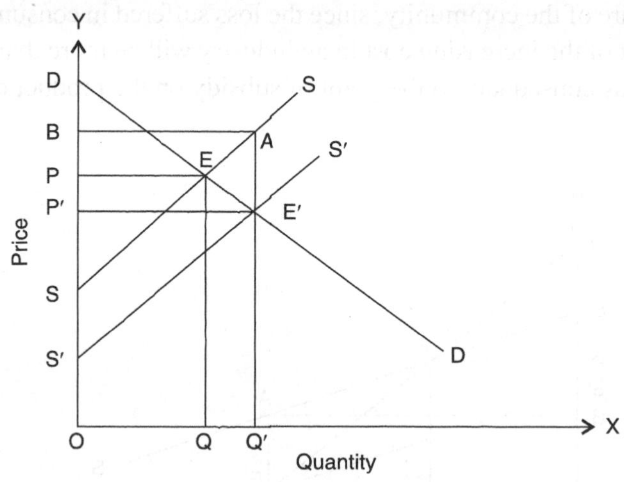

Fig. 10.8. The case of increasing cost in an industry.

7. Measurement of Gains from International Trade

The concept of consumer surplus helps to measure the benefits from the exchange of commodities, particularly from international trade. The fact that the buyer gets more satisfaction from the commodity than the price he pays for it implies that he will get net benefit from such exchange. No exchange is expected to take place, when utility of a person from a commodity is equal to the price paid for it. Further, through international trade, a country gets commodities at lower prices than what it is prepared to pay for them. Consumer surplus measures the benefits in terms of satisfaction, which the people of different countries will get through international trade. It also enables to compare the relative gains from the international trade of different countries.

Self-Assessment Questions

1. Explain the concept of consumer surplus. How far is it possible to measure it?
2. Critically examine Marshall's consumer surplus. Explain how Hicks has solved this problem?
3. Explain how the consumer surplus is measured with the help of indifference curves, when (*i*) marginal utility of money remains constant, and (*ii*) marginal utility of money is declining?
4. Bring out the practical importance of the concept of consumer surplus.
5. Explain the role of consumer surplus in explaining diamond-water paradox.
6. Discuss the importance of the consumer's surplus in the evaluation of fiscal policy of the government.

Unit 11 REVEALED PREFERENCE THEORY

11.1 INTRODUCTION

The theory of demand given by *Marshall* (Marshall's utility analysis) as well as by Hicks-Allen (indifference curve analysis) provides psychological explanation of the consumer's behaviour by applying introspective method. Both the theories are based on introspection and subjectivity. They derive laws about consumer's demand from how he would react psychologically to certain hypothetical changes in price and income. These theories require a lot of information from the consumer, which a consumer is generally incapable of providing. For example, the construction of indifference map under indifference curve approach requires that a consumer must be able to state his indifference as well as his preferences among all possible combinations of commodities precisely and rationally. As preferences cannot be observed, the indifference technique remains non-operational. In the absence of knowledge of indifference curves, the preference indifference approach cannot be used to analyze a consumer's choice problem.

The indifference curve technique is considered to be superior to Marshall's approach, as it gives at least the same result with smaller number of restrictive assumptions. However, the revealed preference hypothesis developed by Samuelson (a Nobel Prize Winner) provided a scientific explanation of a consumer's behaviour without relying on the restrictive assumptions and limitations of the marginal utility analysis and indifference curve approach. It seeks to explain the law of demand from the observed (actual) consumer's behaviour as revealed in the market. It also allows us to separate the price effect into income effect and substitution effect in a manner different from that used under indifference curve technique.

The term 'revealed preference' was introduced by Samuelson in 1938–39. The alternative approach to consumer behaviour made a major break-through in the theory of demand by making use of hypothesis suggested by Samuelson. This theory of Samuelson revealed that preference does not require the consumer to supply any information about himself. It is based on his behaviour that is revealed through his purchases in the market at different prices. This approach seems to be nearer to reality. The revealed preference theory is behavioural in the sense that we seek to know people's preferences by studying their market demand. Here, we move from behaviour to preferences. Since this theory is based on the observed market behaviour of the consumers, it has been used in econometric research. Even John Hicks admits that one major advantage of revealed preference theory is that it is explicitly designed to allow econometricians to make use of it.

11.2 ASSUMPTIONS OF REVEALED PREFERENCE THEORY

The revealed preference theory is based on the following assumptions:

1. **Rationality:** The consumer is assumed to behave rationally in the sense that he prefers a bundle of goods that contain more quantities of the commodities. This assumption of rationality underlies all logical explanations of a consumer's behaviour.
2. **Consistency:** The revealed preference theory rests upon this basic assumption, which has been called as *consistency postulate*. It can thus be stated, "no two observations of choice behaviour are made which provide conflicting evidence to the individual's preference". In other words, if an individual chooses a combination (or bundle) 'A' in one situation (given by his budget constraint) in which bundle 'B' was also available to him, he will not choose combination 'B' in any other situation (given by his new budget constraint) in which combination 'A' is also available. If he chooses 'A' rather than 'B' in one particular situation and chooses 'B' rather than 'A' in another, when 'A' and 'B' are present in both the situations, then he is not behaving consistently. Symbolically, if A>B, that is, if combination 'A' is revealed to be preferred to 'B' (not expensive than A) by any individual, then 'B' cannot be revealed to be preferred to 'A' by him at any other time, when 'A' and 'B' are present in both the cases.

The postulate explained above is the exact logical equivalent of Hicks formulation of consistent behavior in his *Revision of Demand Theory*. He calls it the 'two term consistency', since comparison here is between two situations. This is explained with the help of Fig. 11.1. In this figure, two combinations (bundles) of two commodities 'X' and 'Y' are shown on X-axis and Y-axis respectively. Z_1 and Z_2 are represented on two different budget lines AB and CD respectively. Five different cases are considered with different relative positions of Z_1 and Z_2.

A consumer chooses bundle Z on budget constraint AB when bundle Z_2 is affordable (Z_2 lies on budget constraint CD, inside the budget constraint AB). When bundle Z_2 (lying on budget constraint CD having different price income situation) is chosen, bundle Z_1 is not affordable. Hence, the choice of bundle Z_1 in one situation and bundle Z_2 in another situation is consistent.

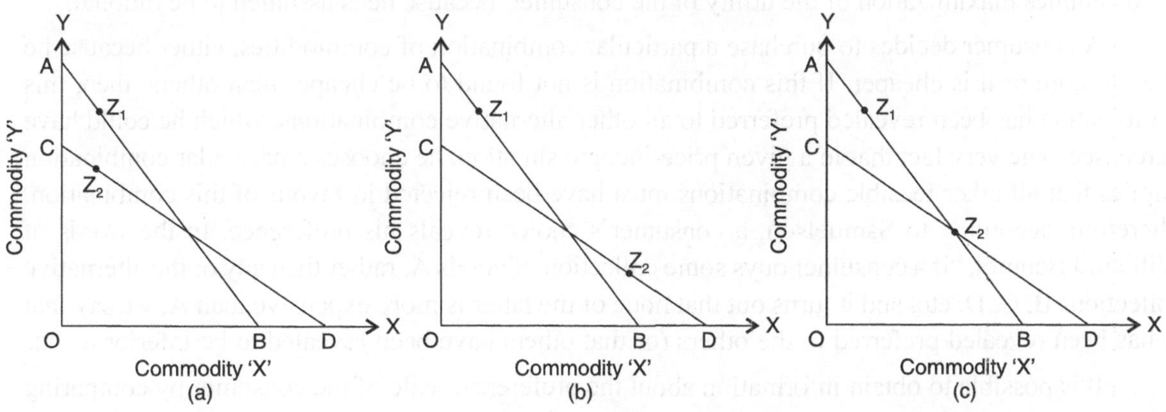

Fig. 11.1. Combinations of two commodities.

When the individual chooses Z_1, Z_2 is not affordable and *vice-versa*. Thus, the choice of Z_1 in one situation and Z_2 in another situation is consistent.

The choice of the individual is Z_1 on budget constraint AB and the choice is Z_2 on CD budget constraint. He chooses Z_2, when Z_1 is affordable and he chooses Z_2 on CD, when Z_1 is not affordable. Hence, the individual behaviour is consistent.

The individual chooses Z_1, when Z_2, is not affordable and chooses Z_2, when Z_1 is still affordable. Thus, the individual behaviour is consistent.

When the consumer's behaviour is inconsistent, it implies choice of Z_1 on AB, when Z_2 is affordable and the choice of Z_2 on CD, when Z_1 is affordable.

The theory like the earlier ones assumes that the consumer is consistent in making a choice. In other words, the amount of each commodity is a single valued function of all prices and income. With the same set of prices and income the consumer will always choose the same set of commodities.

3. **Transitivity:** The assumption of transitivity is an application of the logical theory of ordering. Suppose, in a particular situation, three bundles Z_1, Z_2 and Z_3 of two commodities are available to a customer. If he prefers Z_1 to Z_2 and Z_2 to Z_3, then, he must prefer Z_1 to Z_3 symbolically.

If $A > B$ and $B > C$, then $A > C$, thus the ordering has always to be unit directional and never circular.

11.3 REVEALED PREFERENCE AXIOM

Samuelson's revealed preference theory has preference hypothesis as a basis of his theory of demand. The consumer has the option of choosing from the set of bundles belonging to the feasible consumption set. The consumer by choosing a bundle of goods over others reveals his preference for that particular bundle, given his budget constraint (determined by his income and prices). The choice of a bundle by a consumer reveals his clear and definite preference for that over all other alternative bundles available under that budget constraint. The revealed preference for a particular combination of goods implies maximization of the utility of the consumer, because he is assumed to be rational.

A consumer decides to purchase a particular combination of commodities, either because he likes it more or it is cheaper. If this combination is not found to be cheaper than others, then, this combination has been revealed preferred to all other alternative combinations, which he could have purchased. The very fact that in a given price-income situation, he chooses a particular combination implies that all other feasible combinations must have been rejected in favour of this combination. Therefore, according to Samuelson, a consumer's choice reveals his preference. In the words of William J Baumol, "if a consumer buys some collection of goods A, rather than any of the alternative collections B, C, D, etc. and it turns out that none of the latter is more expensive than A, we say that A has been revealed preferred to the others (or that others have been revealed to be inferior to A).

It is possible to obtain information about the preference scale of the consumer by comparing his preference revealed in different price situations. Before that, it is necessary to find the complete set of combinations which are revealed inferior to one particular combination 'A'. According to

Samuelson, when a consumer prefers to have bundle 'A' rather than bundle 'B', either he gets more satisfaction from this bundle than another, or, he cannot afford to purchase another bundle, while he can purchase bundle 'A'. To quote his lines, "Through any observed equilibrium point 'A', draw the budget equation straight line with arithmetical slope given by the observed price ratios. Then all combinations of the goods on or within the budget line could have been bought in preference to what was actually bought. But, they were not. Hence, they are all 'revealed' to be inferior to A".

Suppose that AB is the budget line with the given income and prices of the two commodities 'X' and 'Y'. Given the price-income situation as represented by this budget line, the consumer can choose any combination of the two commodities lying within or on the triangle GAB (the area of consumer choice). In other words, all combinations lying on this budget line AB such as 'C', 'D', 'E' and those lying below this line such as 'F', 'G', 'H' and 'I' are alternative combinations open to him, from among which he has to choose. If the consumer chooses a combination indicated by point 'E' (lying on budget line AB) out of all options open to him, 'E' is said to be revealed preferred to one indicated by equally expensive points C or D (also lying on budget line AB). Point 'E' is also revealed preferred to every point, such as 'F', 'G', 'H' and 'I' lying below the budget line, as these points represent smaller amounts of both the commodities than point 'E' (points 'F' and 'G') or than do some other points on the budget lines (points 'H' and 'I' in comparison to points 'C' and 'D' respectively on budget line AB). Thus, such lower points 'F', 'G', 'H' and 'I' are cheaper than point 'E'.

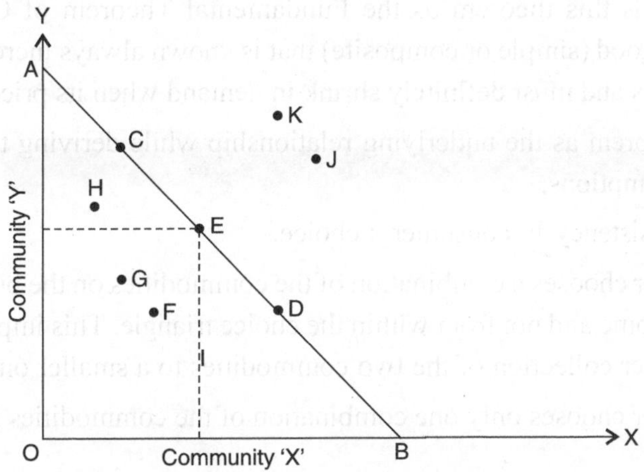

Fig. 11.2. Community X vs. community Y.

Point E is the equilibrium point representing the actual choice of the consumer. Every point on or below the budget line AB is revealed inferior to point 'A', since the consumer purchases combination 'A' rather than any of these other no more expensive combinations ('C', 'D', 'F', 'G' 'H' and 'I'). The consumer's choice, thus, reveals his preference for combination 'A' by rejecting other combinations.

The points above the budget line, such as 'J' and 'K' are more expensive than point 'E'. These are beyond the reach of the consumer with the present price-income situation. None of such point can be revealed inferior to point 'E'. Thus, the chosen bundle is revealed to be preferred to all other alternative bundles available to him under the given budget constraint.

It is clear from the above discussion that Samuelson's revealed preference theory is based upon the strong form of preference hypothesis, *i.e.*, strong ordering. Under strong ordering, relation of indifference between various alternative combinations is ruled out. It is different from weak ordering, where the consumer is indifferent between various combinations of the commodities (under indifference curves analysis).

The revealed preference axiom can be translated into index number form. If in two situations, Z_1 and Z_2 are the combinations of the commodities, P_1 and P_2 are their respective price vectors, then, the statement that the consumer chooses Z_1 over Z_2 can be expressed by the formula that L P_1 Z_1 ;:: L P_1 Z_2. Here, L P_1 Z_1 implies the total expenditure on the Z_1 combination of commodities and L P_1 Z_2 implies total expenditure on the Z_2 combination of the commodities. The condition indicated by the above formula shows that the consumer could have bought affordable combination Z_2 when he actually bought Z_1 by spending his income on Z_2 instead of on Z. This index number of formulation is convenient, but it does not convey any additional economic sense.

11.4 DERIVATION OF DEMAND THEOREM

Revealed preference hypothesis can be used to derive the Marshall's law of demand or demand theorem. Samuelson calls this theorem as the Fundamental Theorem of Consumption Theory. According to him "Any good (simple or composite) that is known always increases in demand when money income alone rises and must definitely shrink in demand when its price alone rises".

He keeps this theorem as the underlying relationship while deriving the demand curve and makes the following assumptions:

(*i*) There is consistency in consumer's choice.

(*ii*) The consumer chooses a combination of the commodities on the budget line by spending his entire income and not from within the choice triangle. This implies that the consumer prefers a larger collection of the two commodities to a smaller one.

(*iii*) The consumer chooses only one combination of the commodities in every price-income situation.

(*iv*) Income elasticity of demand is positive. On logical deduction, it will imply negative price elasticity of demand.

The geometrical proof of the fundamental theorem is illustrated. Here, the consumer is shown to have his budget line AB representing the price-income situation confronting the consumer. The income of the consumer in term of commodities 'X' (shown along the X-axis) is OB and in term of commodities 'Y' (shown along the Y-axis) is OA. By choosing the combination of these two commodities indicated by point 'E' on the budget line AB, he reveals his preference for this combination of the commodities to all other combinations that lie within or on the triangle OAB, the combination indicated by point 'E' provides maximum satisfaction to the consumer.

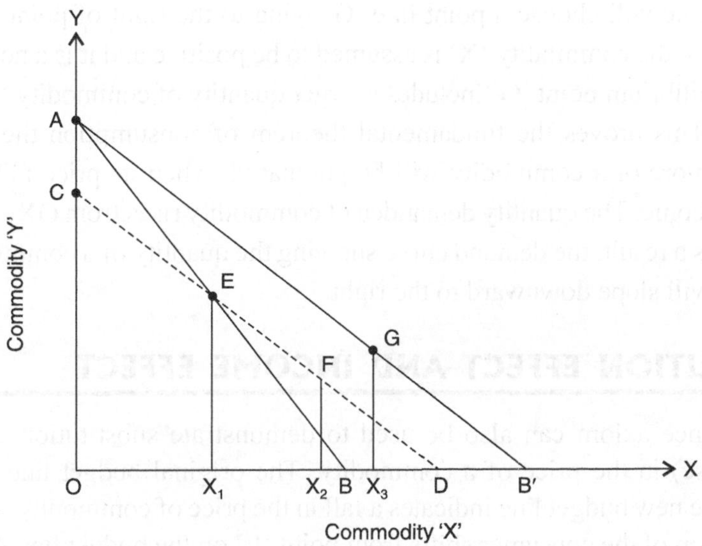

Fig. 11.3. Derivation of the fundamental theory.

Suppose the price of commodities 'X' falls, so that the budget line shifts to new position AB. What we need to prove now is that at the reduced price of commodities 'X', the consumer purchases a larger quantity of commodities 'X' than what was purchased at its original price. Since fall in the price of commodities 'X' raise the real income of the consumer, a cost difference variation (compensating variation) in the income of the consumer is to be made. To take the real income constant an imaginary budget line CD is drawn passing through the original point of revealed preference, 'E' and parallel to the new budget line AB′. The budget line CD represents lower price of commodities 'X' (as given by new budget line AB′). The budget line CD represents lower price of commodities 'X' (as given by new budget line AB′). The consequent reduction in income by drawing budget line CD is just sufficient to cancel out the increase in real income caused by the fall in the price of commodities 'X'. The cost difference variation in income equal to AA′ leaves the consumer with enough real income to enable him to continue purchasing combination 'E', if he so wishes, it is shown by the parallel shift of the new budget line AB′ to the 'compensated' budget line CD.

The combination 'E' is still available to the consumer on budget line CD. He will not choose any combination to the left of 'E' (on the segment CE), since combination 'E' was chosen in preference to all other points within or on the triangle OAB. All the points of segment CE lie within the triangle OAB. Choice of the point on the segment CE would violate the assumption of consistency. The consumer will either continue to buy the same combination 'E' (in which case the quasi-substitution effect is zero) or will choose a point such as 'F' on the segment ED of the imaginary budget line CD. This means a larger quantity of the commodity 'X' and smaller quantity of commodity 'Y' than in the original price-income situation. The substitution effect can never cause a reduction in purchase of the commodity, whose price has decreased.

Now, if we remove the fictitious reduction, in income and allow the consumer to move on the new budget line AB′, he will choose a point like ‘G’ lying to the right of point ‘F’ (since income elasticity of demand for the commodity ‘X’ is assumed to be positive and it is a normal commodity). The new revealed equilibrium point ‘G’ includes a larger quantity of commodity ‘X’, resulting from the fall in its price. This proves the fundamental theorem of consumption theory, as started by Samuelson. That is, more of a commodity will be purchased, when its price falls, whose demand varies directly with income. The quantity demanded of commodity rises from OX_1 to OX_3 on account of a fall in its price. As a result, the demand curve showing the quantity of a commodity demanded at its alternative prices will slope downward to the right.

11.5 SUBSTITUTION EFFECT AND INCOME EFFECT

The revealed preference axiom can also be used to demonstrate substitution effect and income effect of a fall (or rise) in the price of a commodity. The original budget line AB shifts to AB. Relative flatness of the new budget line indicates a fall in the price of commodity ‘X’. Consequently, the equilibrium position of the consumer shifts from point ‘E’ on the budget line AB to point ‘G’ on the budget line AB. The movement from point ‘E’ to point ‘G’ (due to change in relative prices) is the price effect. We can use Slutsky method to decompose this price effect into substitution effect and income effect.

To neutralize the income effect, the money income of the consumer is reduced by CA to hold purchasing power constant (so that combination ‘E’ still remains affordable). Geometrically, this is done by drawing compensatory budget line CD parallel to new budget line AB and passing through point ‘E’. Thus, this imaginary budget line reflects the new fallen price. When combination E is bought at the lower price of combination ‘G’, there is a reduction cost, which is the ‘cost difference’.

The old combination ‘E’, now on imaginary budget line CD is still affordable to the consumer. All combinations to the left of point ‘E’ on the segment CE were available to him in the initial situation (as these all fall within triangle OAB) and were rejected in favour of combination ‘E’. The assumption of consistency requires that the consumer will either choose combination ‘E’ or what is more likely, he will choose a combination on segment ED.

If the consumer chooses combination ‘F’, the movement from point ‘E’ to point ‘F’ indicates the substitution effect. The consumer always substitutes relatively cheaper commodity ‘X’ for the “expensive one (commodity ‘Y’). It can never be negative. So, point ‘F’ cannot lie to the left of point ‘E’. When points E and F happen to coincide, the substitution effect will be equal to zero. In such situation, the whole of the price effect will be equal to income effect.

When the income equal to cost difference variation is restored back to the consumer he buys more of commodity ‘X’ (given a positive income elasticity of demand, which means with an increase in income, quantity demanded will increase). Now, the new equilibrium ‘G’ lies vertically to the right of point ‘F’. The movement from point ‘F’ to point ‘G’ represents income effect. The income effect, given the positive income elasticity of demand will reinforce the substitution effect. In quantity terms, price effect, substitution effect and income effect are shown as increase in the demand for commodity ‘X’ from OX_1 to OX_3, from OX_1 to OX_2 and from OX_2 to OX_3 respectively.

∴ Price Effect = Substitution Effect + Income Effect

or $$X_1 X_3 = X_1 X_2 + X_2 X_3$$

The mathematical sign of all the three effects is negative. Thus, when the price of a commodity falls, the quantity demanded rises. This makes the demand curve for a commodity downward sloping. Hence, the law of demand is established. A negative income effect or a positive income elasticity of demand for a commodity is a necessary condition for the validity of the law of demand and a negative substitution effect is sufficient to make demand curve of a commodity downward sloping.

11.6 DERIVATION OF INDIFFERENCE CURVES

The revealed preference assumptions permit us to derive indifference map of the consumer on the basis of enough observations on his market behaviour. Unlike the indifference curve approach, Samuelson's revealed preference theory does not require the consumer to rank his preferences rationally and consistently for all possible combinations of commodities. Nor he is required to provide any other information about his tastes. The only assumptions required about the consumer are that (*a*) his choice is consistent, (*b*) his tastes are independent of his choice over time and does not change, (*c*) that the consumer is rational in the Pareto sense that is, and he prefers more goods at less price.

The initial budget line of the consumer is AB and he reveals his preference for combination represented by point 'E' on this budget line. All other points on this line and below it denote combinations revealed inferior to 'E'. Now, we draw lines EC and ED through point 'E' and parallel to X-axis and Y-axis respectively. All combinations of the two commodities on these lines and lying in the region defined by them to the right and above of point 'E' are preferred to this point, as these contain more quantity of at least one commodity and no less of either commodity (see shaded area in the figure). Combinations of commodities in the remaining area in two parts (below CED and above the budget line AB) are still not ranked and fall in the ignorance zone.

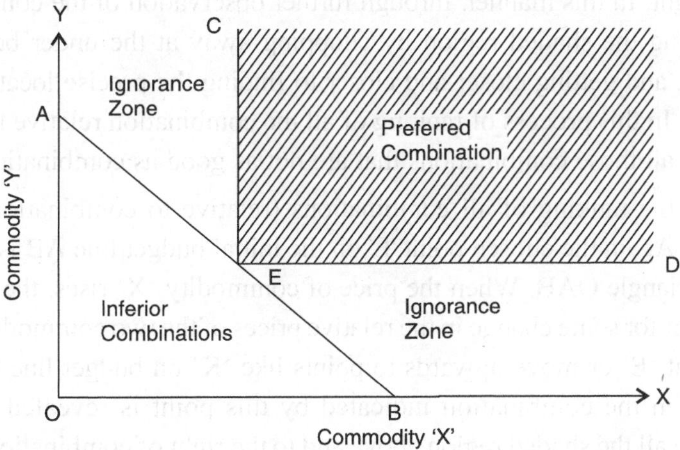

Fig. 11.4. Determination of inferior combinations preferred combinations and ignorance zones under revealed preference hypothesis.

We may rank the combinations in the ignorance zone by adopting the procedure represented. In this figure, the new budget line FG as a result of a fall in the price of commodity 'X' passes through point 'R' lying below point 'E'. The consumer will choose either combination indicated by point 'R' or a point to the right of point 'R' on new budget line FG, since points on FR violate the assumption of consistent choice, being below the original budget line and hence revealed to be inferior to point 'R'. Suppose, the consumer chooses the combination indicated by point 'H'. In other words, we can find some budget line FG, which will lead the consumer to buy a combination indicated by point 'H'.

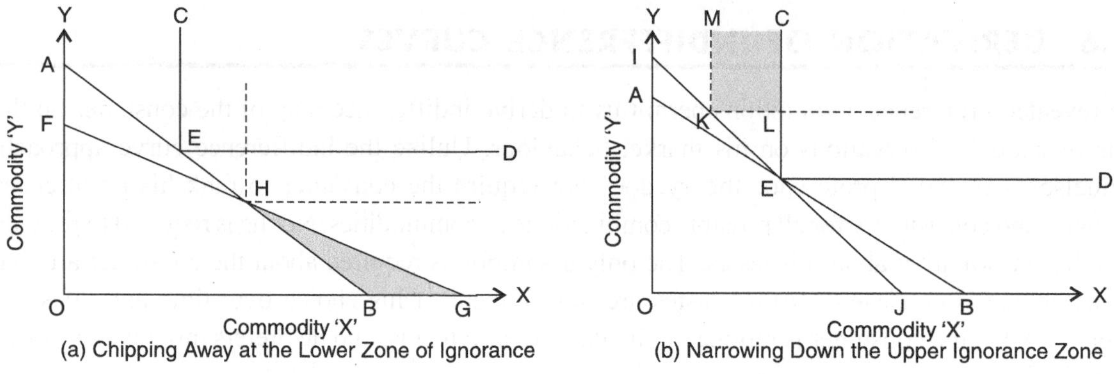

Fig. 11.5. Transitivity assumption and revealed preference theory.

Any point on or below line FG is revealed inferior to point 'H' (since the choice of the consumer reveals preference in favour of combination indicated by point 'H'). This point has in turn, been revealed inferior to point 'E' in the original situation. Hence, by the transitivity assumption, every point on or below line FG is revealed inferior to point 'E', this also implies that the triangle BHG shown by shaded area in Fig. 11.5(*a*) is revealed inferior to point 'B'. It can, therefore be chopped off from the lower zone of ignorance. We can repeat this procedure by considering other points in the lower zone of ignorance, drawing corresponding budget lines, according to which such combinations are bought. In this manner, through further observation of the consumer's behaviour, we can go on extending the shaded region by chopping away at the under belly of the zone of ignorance indefinitely, and getting closer and closer to finding the precise location of indifference curve through point E. In this process of ranking of all the combination relative to combination 'E', we keep on excluding all those combinations that are not as good as combination 'E'.

Now, consider the ranking of all combinations (relative to combination 'E') lying in the upper ignorance zone. Again the chosen point 'E' on the initial budget line AB is revealed preferred to all other points in triangle OAB. When the price of commodity 'X' rises, the new budget line IJ passes through point 'E' for some change in the relative prices of the two commodities. The consumer will either stay at point 'E' or move upwards to points like 'K' on budget line IJ. If the consumer chooses point 'K', then the combination indicated by this point is revealed to be preferred to combination 'E'. Since all the shaded region above and to the right of combination 'K' is revealed to be preferred to the one indicated by the point 'K', so, by transitivity assumption, this shaded region is also revealed to be preferred to combination 'E'.

The above procedure can be repeated with other budget lines passing through point 'E', each of which yield a point in the segment IE, that is revealed to be preferred to point 'E'. Thus, the upper ignorance zone gradually narrows down and the indifference curve through point 'E' can be located within as narrow a range as possible.

Convexity of Indifference Curves

The revealed preference axiom helps us to construct the indifference curve of the consumer just by observing this behaviour (actual choice) in various market situations (prices). It is possible to establish the convexity of the indifference curve through point 'E' by proving that it cannot have any other shape. The mathematical proof that the upper and lower chopping away sequences converge and exactly narrow the zone of ignorance down to a single indifference curve involves more advanced theorems in differential equation and is beyond the scope of this book.

The indifference curve through point 'E' cannot be the straight line AB, as the choice of point 'E' shows that all the other point on line AB are inferior to point 'E'. The consumer cannot be at the same time indifferent between them. It cannot be a line or curve (like NP) cutting line AB at point 'E', as this would imply that the points below the line AB mean indifference to the consumer, while he has already revealed his preference for point 'E' on this line. Further, the indifference curve can also not be concave through point 'E', because, all such points have already been ranked as inferior to point 'E'. Therefore, the indifference curve through point E must lie below shaded area CED and above budget line AB. This proves that the indifference curve must have a negative slope (otherwise it would enter the shaded area of preferred combinations) and it must be convex to the origin.

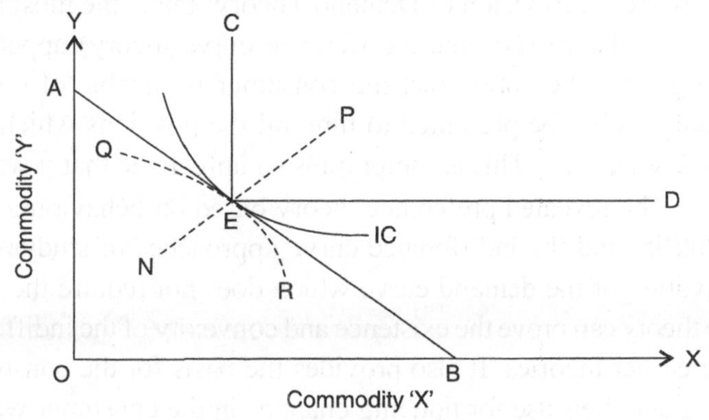

Fig. 11.6. Convexity of the indifference curve.

11.7 APPRAISAL OF REVEALED PREFERENCE THEORY

The course of development of the pure 'theory of demand would describe, revealed preference theory as a move from psychological to behaviouristic explanation a consumer's behaviour in market. The utility theory' was purely subjective. It sought to explain observed, consumer behaviour in terms of motivation and psychological valuation. The indifference curve analyses released the theory of consumer choice from psychological implication—to some extent, but, it did not explain the observed behaviour of the consumer. The indifference curves continued to remain a sort of psychological postulate.

The revealed preference theory as the third root of the logical theory of demand emunciated the demand theory from observed consumer behaviour. It was the first attempt to formalize a consumer's behaviour from market observations alone. This theory has gained some advantages over the two alternative formulations. It frees the consumer theory of the vestiges of psychological and introspective analysis. It also drops 'utility maximization' and 'continuity' assumptions making rationalization of consumer behaviour less difficult than in the other two models. Commenting on the earlier two theories of demand, Samuelson remarks, "For just as we do not claim to know by introspection the behaviour of utility, many will argue we cannot know the behaviour of ratios of marginal utilities or of indifference directions." Further, "The introduction and meaning of the marginal rate of substitution as an entity independent of any psychological, introspective implications would be, to say the least, ambiguous, and would seem an artificial convention in the explanation of price behaviour". The propagator of the indifference curve analysis, J.R.Hicks himself admitted in his later work, 'A Revision of Demand Theory' that, "the most awkward of the assumptions into which the older theory (*i.e.*, the indifference curve theory) appeared to be impelled by its geometrical analogy was the notion that the consumer is capable of ordering all conceivable alternatives that might possibly be presented to him, all the positions which might be represented by points on his indifference map. This assumption is so unrealistic that it was bound to be the stumbling block".

The revealed preference theory based on behavioural approach is no doubt an advance over the utility and the indifference curve approaches of studying demand. It gives a direct way to the derivation of the demand curve which does not require the use of the subjective concept of utility. The theory can prove the existence and convexity of the indifference curves under weaker assumptions than earlier theories. It also provides the basis for the construction of index numbers of the cost of living and their use for noticing changes in the consumer welfare, when prices change.

Though Samuelson provides a ethologically superior approach in the sense that it is based on actual data, yet it is not free from flaws. It has been subjected to scathing criticisms by a number of economists:

(*i*) According to critics, the observed market behaviour of the consumer can at best be termed as that of revealed choice and not that of *revealed preference*. The consumers often face situations involving uncertainty and risk. Their choice at a particular point may be a part of game theory strategy and not the revelation of his preference. Only under conditions of perfect competition, choice of a bundle by a consumer may reveal his preference for it.

(*ii*) Though Tapes Maunder accepts that behaviourism has great advantages in the sense that it treads only on observed ground and so it cannot go wrong. However, when a sufficiently large number of observations are taken, a definite preference between two situations might not emerge. Such situations of indifference are, however, made methodologically inadmissible by Samuelson in his theory. But, if the existence of indifference even between a few combinations in the vicinity of the combination actually chosen by the consumer is admitted, it would not be possible to prove demand theorem with the help of revealed preference.

(*iii*) Samuelson proves the demand theorem by assuming positive income elasticity of demand. When, however, the income elasticity of demand is negative, Samuelson's revealed preference theory is unable to establish the demand theorem. Given negative income elasticity of demand, it is not possible to know on the basis of revealed preference, the direction of change in demand as a result of change in price. Therefore, the revealed preference theory fails to enunciate the demand theorem when: (*a*) income elasticity of demand is negative and the positive income effect is smaller than the substitution effect, and (*b*) the income elasticity of demand is negative and the positive income effect is stronger than the substitution effect. Therefore, Samuelson's theory fails to explain the case of inferior goods and account for the Giffen's paradox, in which case income elasticity of demand has to be negative.

(*iv*) Samuelson's theory says nothing about the market demand curve.

Self-Assessment Questions

1. Explain the concept of revealed preference. Is this concept a refinement over the utility theory or indifference curve theory?
2. Distinguish between weak ordering and strong ordering.
3. State the assumptions of revealed preference theory and explain how the law of demand (Fundamental Theorem of Consumption) is derived from these assumptions?
4. Explain how the revealed preference theory can be used to derive an indifference curve? Prove that it is convex to the origin.
5. Give a critical appraisal of the revealed preference theory.

Unit 12 SCALE OF PRODUCTION

12.1 INTRODUCTION

The scale of production has an important bearing on the cost of production. It is the manufacturers' common experience that larger the scale of production, the lower generally is the average cost of production. That is why the entrepreneur is tempted to enlarge the scale of production so that he may benefit from the resulting economies of scale. These economies are broadly speaking of two types: Internal economies and external economies, which we shall presently consider in some detail. But before we do that, we shall dwell on the economies and diseconomies of large-scale production.

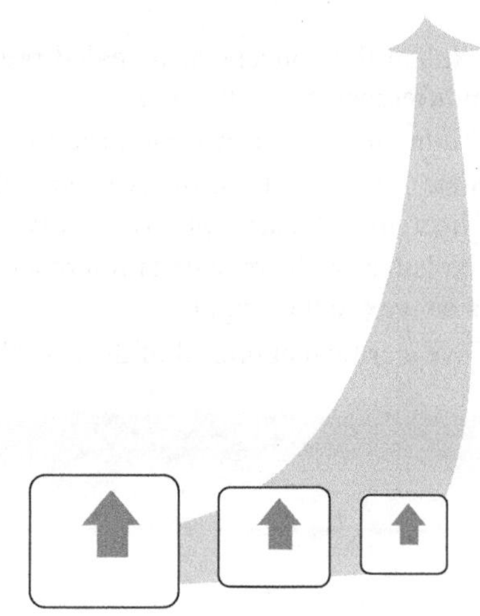

Fig. 12.1. Increase in a company's productivity.

12.2 ECONOMIES OF LARGE-SCALE PRODUCTION

The modem factory system, with its extensive use of machinery and division of labour, is responsible for large-scale production. The following are its chief advantages:

Efficient Use of Capital Equipment

There is a large scope for the use of machinery which results in lower costs. A large producer can install up-to-date and expensive machinery. He can also have his own repairing unit. Specialized machinery can be employed for each job. The result is that production is very economical. A small producer, with a small market, cannot keep the machinery continuously working. Keeping it idle is uneconomical. A large producer can utilize the machinery continuously and reap the resulting economies.

Economy of Specialized Labour

In a big concern, there is ample scope for division of labour. Specialized labour produces a larger output and of better quality. It is only in a large business that every person can be put on the job that he can best perform. The large-scale producer thus gets the best out of every person he employs.

Better Utilization and Greater Specialization in Management

A capable manager is obviously under-utilized in a small concern. Therefore, when the scale of production is enlarged, there is optimal use of the manager's time and ability. Also, he is able to delegate some of his less important functions to his assistants and increasingly specialize in the jobs where his ability is most fruitful.

Economies of Buying and Selling

While purchasing raw material and other accessories, a big business can secure specially favourable terms. While selling its goods it can attract customers by offering a greater variety and by ensuring prompt execution of the orders placed with it. A lower rate of profit results in larger sales and higher net profits in a large-scale business.

Economies of the Overhead Charges

The expenses of administration and distribution per unit of output in a big business are much less. Interest, the pay bill, and other overhead charges are the same whether production is on a large or a small-scale. Thus, the same amount of expenditure being distributed over a larger output, results in a lower cost per unit.

Economy in Rent

A large-scale producer makes a saving in rent too. If the same factory is made to produce a large quantity of goods, the same amount of rent is divided over a large output. This means a smaller addition to the cost per unit in the form of rent.

Experiments and Research

A large concern can afford to spend liberally on research and experiments. It is well known that, in the long-run, these expenses are more than repaid. Successful research may lead to the discovery of a cheaper process. This may bring a large profit. Only a large-scale business can incur such expenditure.

Advertisement and Salesmanship

A big concern can afford to spend large amounts of money on advertisement and salesmanship. Ultimately they do bear fruit. Also, the amount of money spent on advertisement per unit comes to a low figure when production is on a large-scale. The salesmen can make a careful study of individual markets and thus acquire a hold on new markets or strengthen it in the old ones. Thus, a large-scale producer has a greater competitive strength.

Utilization of Byproducts

A big business will not have to throw away any of its byproducts or waste products. It will be able to make an economical use of them. A small sugar factory, for instance, has to throw away the molasses, whereas a big concern can turn it into alcohol. By utilizing byproducts, it can lower the cost of production.

Meeting Adversity

A big business can show better resistance in times of adversity. It has much larger resources. Losses can be easily borne. A small concern will simply collapse under such a strain.

Cheap Credit

A large business can secure credit facilities at cheap rates. Its credit in the money market is high and the banks are only too willing to give advances. Low costs of credit reduce cost of production.

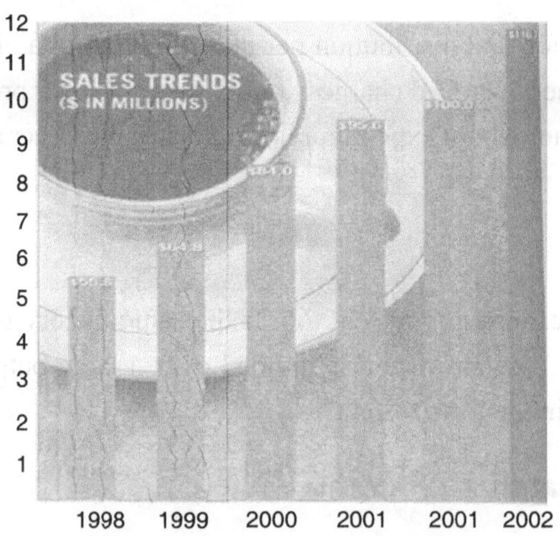

Fig. 12.2. Increasing sales in a business.

These are some of the advantages that a large-scale business has over a small-scale business. But let us see the other side.

12.3 DISECONOMIES OF SCALE

Large-scale production is not without its disadvantages. Some of these disadvantages are:

Over-worked Management

A large-scale producer cannot pay full attention to every detail. Costs often rise on account of the dishonesty of the employees or waste of materials by them. This is due to the lack of supervision. Owing to laxity of control, costs of production go up. The management is overworked.

Individual Tastes Ignored

Large-scale production is a mass production or standardized production. Goods of uniform quality are turned out irrespective of the preferences of individual customers. Individual tastes are not, therefore, satisfied.

No Personal Element

A large-scale business is generally managed by paid employees. The owner is usually absent. The sympathy and personal touch, which ought to exist between the master and the men, are missing. Frequent misunderstandings lead to strikes and lock-outs. This is positively harmful to the business.

Possibility of Depression

Large-scale production may result in over-production. Production may exceed demand and cause depression and unemployment. It is not always easy or profitable to dispose of a large output.

Dependence on Foreign Markets

A large-scale producer has generally to depend on foreign markets. The foreign markets may be cut-off by war or some other political upheaval. This makes the business risky.

Fig. 12.3. Machinery and equipments are indivisible.

Cut-throat Competition

Large-scale producers must fight for the markets. There is wasteful competition which does no good to society. Many promising businesses are ruined by senseless competition. There is also competition and bidding for resources and inputs.

International Complications and War

When the large-scale producers operate on an international scale, their interests clash either on the score of markets or of materials. These complications sometimes lead to armed conflicts. Many modern wars arose on account of the scramble for materials and markets.

Lack of Adaptability

A large-scale producing unit finds it very difficult to switch on from one business to another. In a depression, small firms are able to move away from declining trades to flourishing ones easily. In this way, they are able to avoid losses. This adaptability is lacking in a big business.

Fig. 12.4. Easy finance is a part of economies of scale.

Conclusion

Inspite of these drawbacks, large-scale production offers several economies. The tendency in manufacturing and transport industries is to increase the scale. The advantages outweigh the disadvantages. The scale of production is enlarged till the firm has reached the optimum size. At this scale of production, the total profits are the maximum or the average cost per unit is the minimum. At this stage, marginal cost equals price (*i.e.,* marginal revenue). The producer goes on producing more, so long as the price exceeds marginal cost. He will stop when marginal cost has overtaken price or marginal revenue, and the two have been equalized. "Differences in efficiency between firms will show themselves not in differences in marginal costs but in differences in output. The more efficient firms will have a larger output."

12.4 CONCEPT OF INDIVISIBILITY

A very important source of economy in a big concern arises from the use of an indivisible factor of production. This concept of indivisibility requires careful understanding. Just think of a hostel kitchen. It must have a minimum equipment of utensils and servants, *e.g.,* it must have at least one cook and one boy servant. This is the indivisible factor. Now if this equipment can satisfactorily serve fifteen students, it will be obviously uneconomical to have only ten students to serve. Charges per head will be unnecessarily higher and the cook and the servant will remain idle for some time. A large group of students will keep them fully employed and get the utmost out of them.

Similarly, a professor is indivisible. Suppose he can effectively impart instruction to a class of fifty students. In a small college, where the number in a class may be smaller, the authorities will not be making full use of him.

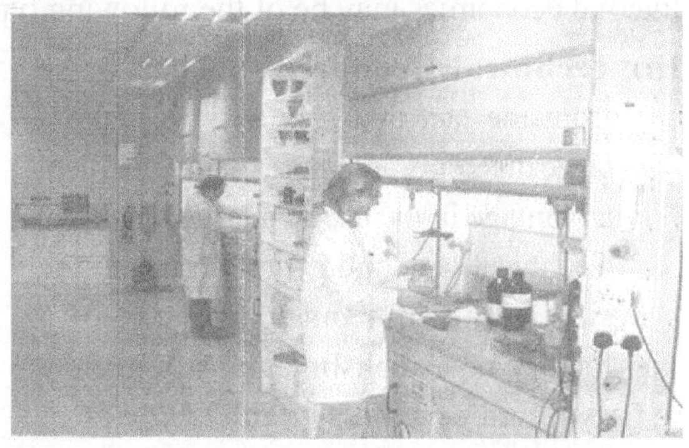

Fig. 12.5. Research and development.

The same is the case with a factory. Take the case of a sugar factory. It must have a minimum equipment of building, plant, clerical staff and other miscellaneous establishments. Even a worker is indivisible. One operator may be required for each machine irrespective of its capacity. Similarly, a manager is indivisible whether the factory works below capacity or at full capacity. In case the factory is working below capacity, this equipment will not be fully used, a part of it will be wasted. Hence, the scale of production must be such as to use the indivisible equipment fully, otherwise it will be uneconomical.

Several of our industries, notably iron and steel and the jute industries, are generally working below capacity, which is obviously wasteful. The indivisible equipment is not being fully employed. The point, therefore, is that when production is carried on a large-scale, equipment will not remain idle, and the indivisible factors will be fully employed. It will mean more economical production.

Stigler has mentioned several types of indivisibilities: (*i*) Indivisibility of machinery, (*ii*) Marketing indivisibilities—these relate to the employment of salesmen, maintenance of purchasing department and advertisement. The larger the scale the smaller will be the cost per unit, (*iii*) Financial indivisibilities—these relate to the managing costs of loans. Securities issued in large quantities can be listed on the stock exchange, (*iv*) Research indivisibilities—once certain costs have been incurred in investments, the larger the scale, the more economical it is.

12.5 INTERNAL AND EXTERNAL ECONOMIES

As we have said already, economies of large-scale production can be grouped under two headings: internal economies and external economies. We shall first discuss internal economies.

Internal Economies

Internal economies are those economies in production, those reductions in production costs, which accrue to the firm itself when it expands its output or enlarges its scale of production. The internal economies arise within a firm as a result of its own expansion independent of the size and expansion of the industry.

The internal economies are simply due to the increase in the scale of production. They arise from the use of the methods which small firms do not find it worthwhile to employ.

Internal economies may be of the following types:

(*a*) **Technical Economies:** They arise from the fact that it is easy to make a large machine, and there is a mechanical advantage in the use of a large machine. Technical economies pertain not to the size of the firm but to the size of a factory or establishment. A firm may own and operate several factories or establishments. The size of the establishment depends on the nature of the industry. For instance, in agriculture and dairy, large plants can be duplicated in several small establishments. In such industries, the size of the typical establishment is small. In other industries, *e.g.,* mining, technical economies are available only in large establishments; hence the typical unit is large.

Fig. 12.6. Better management.

There are four different ways in which technical economies can arise: (*i*) Large size—economies arise only when large machines are used, *e.g.,* a bigger boiler or a bigger furnace. It has a bigger productive capacity but uses proportionately less energy. A bigger machine does not require more staff to operate it. The cost of construction is also relatively smaller.

(*ii*) Linking process—a dairy may have its own fodder farm or a sugar factory its own cane farm: The integration of the two is more economical. Similarly, paper-making and pulp-making can be combined with great advantage, (*iii*) Superior technique—Some machines represent superior techniques. The bigger works can use them with greater advantage. For instance, only a big newspaper can use a rotary press. Similarly, only large establishments can use power-driven machinery economically, (*iv*) Increased specialization—scope for specialization is also available in a large plant. Specialization and division of labour are highly advantageous. For instance, only in a big school, we can have specialist teachers.

(*b*) **Managerial Economies:** These economies arise from the creation of special departments or from functional specialization. They also result from the delegation of routine and detailed matters to subordinates. The managerial expenses can be reduced by increasing the size of an establishment or by grouping a number of establishments under one management. In a small factory, a manager is a worker, foreman and a manager all rolled in one. Much of his time is wasted on things having little economic significance. In a big concern, such jobs can be delegated to junior employees and the manager confines himself to jobs which bring more profits. This is vertical division of labour. But there are possibilities of horizontal division too when each department is placed under an expert. The job is done more efficiently and more economically. All this is possible when production is carried on a large-scale.

(*c*) **Commercial Economies:** They arise from the purchase of materials and scale of goods. Large businesses have bargaining advantages and are accorded a preferential treatment by the firms they deal with. They are able to secure freight concessions from railways and road transport, cheap credit from the banks, prompt delivery, careful attention, and considerate treatment from all dealers. This means more profits. A large firm can employ experts and carry on research and experiments. It can use material testing and grading machinery. It can buy and sell when the market trends are more favourable. In selling, it can cut down selling costs and in purchasing, it can have a wider choice.

(*d*) **Financial Economies:** These economies arise from the fact that a big firm has better credit and can borrow on more favourable terms. Its shares enjoy a wider market, which encourages a prospective investor. This only shows superior bargaining strength and does not necessarily indicate greater efficiency.

(*e*) **Risk-bearing Economies:** A big firm can spread risks and can often eliminate them. This it does by diversifying output. Diversification imparts a big firm strength and stability and makes it less vulnerable to changes in commercial fortunes. There is also diversification of markets, of sources of supply and of processes of manufacture.

Real and Pecuniary Economies

Internal economies can be classified as real economies and pecuniary economies. Real economies arise from reduction in the physical quantity of inputs.

These may be economies in (*i*) production, (*ii*) marketing or salesmanship, (*iii*) managerial due to specialization, decentralization in decision-making and mechanization *e.g.*, computerization, and (*iv*) transport and storage economies. Pecuniary economies arise from lower prices for inputs, lower interest rates, and lower rates for advertising and lower transport costs paid by bigger firms.

Internal Economies (Its effect)

On *y*-axis is the cost and *x*-axis is the quantity of output. Due to the internal economies of scale the cost of production per unit will go on decreasing up to a minimum point *viz.*, M that is 'ON' cost is the minimum possible cost. Hence, the firm will be beneficial to produce 'OQ' quantity of output.

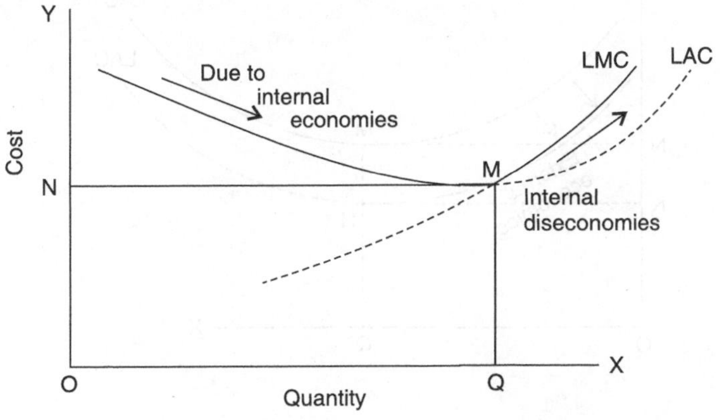

Fig. 12.7. Internal economies vs. diseconomies.

On the other hand the 'LAC' may start increasing due to internal diseconomies of scale that is on the right hand side of 'NM' cost.

External Economies

External economies are those economies which accrue to each member firm as a result of the expansion of the industry as a whole. Expansion of an industry may lead to the availability of new and cheaper raw materials, tools and machinery, and to the discovery and diffusion of a superior technical knowledge. Some raw materials and tools may be made available at reduced prices, because as the industry grows, subsidiary and correlated firms may spring up in the vicinity of the industry to provide it with raw materials and tools at reduced prices.

Further, as an industry expands, trade journals may appear which help in the discovery and diffusion of the technical knowledge. Moreover, with the expansion of an industry, certain specialized firms may come into existence which work on its "waste products". The industry can then sell them at a good price.

Thus, the entry of new firms enlarging the size of an industry may enable all firms to produce at lower cost. The large-scale firm reaps internal economies. The large-scale industry brings to the firms external economies. There is every possibility of external economies to be reaped when a young industry grows in a new territory. Various types of external economies are given below:

(*a*) **Economies of Concentration:** These economies relate to advantages arising from the availability of skilled workers, the provision of better transport and credit facilities, stimulation of improvements, benefits from subsidiaries, and so on. Scattered firms cannot enjoy such economies. These are the advantages of a localized industry. Every firm in the industry shares the common stock of knowledge and experience. Concentration of firms enables the transport system to cut down costs. Such economies are of special importance in a country like India which has not yet been fully industrialized.

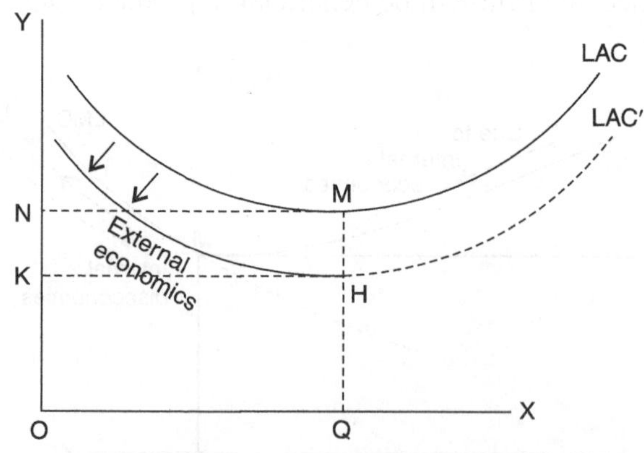

Fig. 12.8. External economies LAC to shift down at each level of output.

(*b*) **Economies of Information:** These economies refer to the benefits which all firms engaged in an industry derive from the publication of trade and technical journals and from central research institutions. In a localized industry, research and experiments are centralized. Each individual firm need not incur expenditure on research. It can draw such benefits from the common pool. Such schemes are beyond the capacity of individual firms. Firms in a scattered industry cannot have such facilities.

(*c*) **Economies of Disintegration:** When an industry grows, it becomes possible to split up some of the processes which are taken over by specialist firms. For example, a number of cotton mills located in a particular locality may have the benefit of a separate calendaring plant.

Due to external economies the cost of production per unit may be reduced. It also may help in the shift of the LAC (Long-run average cost curve) downward to LAC′. It depends on how powerful the external economies are. Before the external economies the firm may be producing at 'ON' amount of cost and 'OQ' amount of quantity but now it may be producing the same quantity *viz.* 'OQ' at a lower cost 'OK'.

12.6 RELATION BETWEEN INTERNAL AND EXTERNAL ECONOMIES

No hard and fast line can be drawn between internal and external economies. Whether particular economies are internal or external depends upon what operations it is profitable to combine. Internal economies are the result of expansion of individual firms, whereas external economies are the result of expansion or development of the entire industry of which the individual firms are members.

It is worth noting that as commercial and technical education spreads, and other such developments take place, the field of internal economies is being narrowed and that of external economies is being widened. This is the result of progress in different fields.

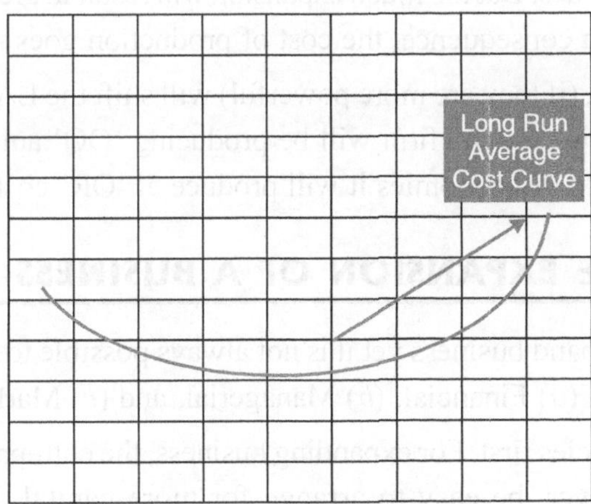

Fig. 12.9. Diseconomies occur when output goes beyond the minimum point of the long-run average cost curve.

12.7 INTERNAL AND EXTERNAL DISECONOMIES

We should also take note of diseconomies, both internal and external. It is possible that the expansion of a firm's output may lead to rise in costs and thus result in diseconomies instead of economies. This may be due to the fact that inferior or less efficient factors may have been brought into use. When a firm expands beyond proper limits, it is beyond the capacity of the manager to manage it efficiently. This also is an example of an internal diseconomy.

In the same manner, the expansion of an industry may result in diseconomies which may be called external diseconomies. The result is that the individual firms in the industry are faced with diseconomies instead of economies.

It is common experience that, when an industry in an industrial centre expands, there is a keener competition among the firms for the factors of production and the raw materials. As a consequence, the prices of raw materials and of the factors of production go up. All firms have now to pay higher wages, higher rents and higher rates of interest besides higher prices for the raw materials. Suitable labour ceases to be available; and capital also becomes scarce. The result is that, with the expansion of an industry the costs of production go up instead of falling.

The main point is that the additional factors of production, the employment of which becomes now necessary, are less efficient and they are obtained at a higher cost. It is in this manner that diseconomies result as an industry expands.

Thus, as the scale of production of an individual increases, there are internal economies as well as internal diseconomies. But, the internal economies generally outweigh internal diseconomies. That is why, as the scale of production increases, average cost of production falls. But if the scale is increased beyond a proper limit, the internal diseconomies will swallow up the internal economies and the cost of production will rise instead of falling. In the same manner, when an industry expands, the firms enjoy external economies. But too much expansion will result in greater external diseconomies than external economies. As a consequence, the cost of production goes up instead of falling.

External diseconomies, (if they are more powerful) will shift the LAC (Long-run average cost curve) upward to LAC′. In this case the firm will be producing 'OQ' amount of quantity earlier at 'ON' cost, now due to external diseconomies it will produce at 'OR' cost.

12.8 LIMITS TO THE EXPANSION OF A BUSINESS

Although it is profitable to expand business yet it is not always possible to do so. The main obstacles in the growth of business are: (*a*) Financial, (*b*) Managerial, and (*c*) Market obstacles.

We take financial obstacles first. For expanding business, the entrepreneur needs fresh supplies of capital. It may not, however, be easy to arrange for more capital. Still the difficulty is not insurmountable. Successful businessmen, who have a reputation for honesty and efficiency, will find ample capital forthcoming. Finance, it is said, is a mere camp follower.

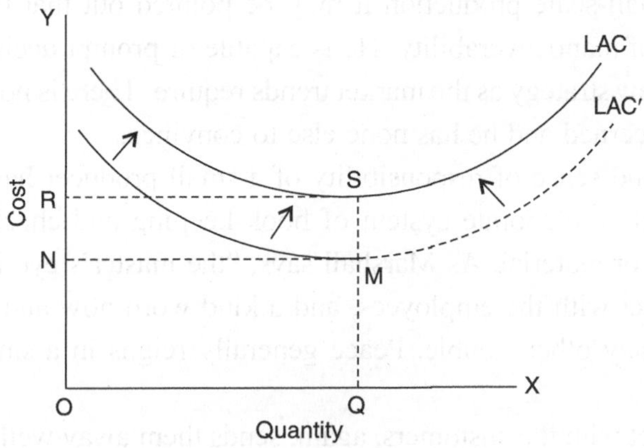

LAC shift up due to external diseconomies.

Fig. 12.10. Long-run average cost curves.

A high hurdle is the managerial obstacles. An entrepreneur, however capable, cannot satisfactorily tackle problems beyond a certain range and complexity. That is why a business cannot be expanded indefinitely. A point will be reached when the entrepreneur will find that his business has become unmanageable. Supervision will then become ineffective. Safeguards against fraud will add to the cost. Internal economies will gradually disappear.

But there are other difficulties too. As business is expanded, prices of the factors of production will rise; more may have to be paid in the form of rent, wages and interest to attract additional supplies of the inputs. The cost will, therefore, rise. On the other hand, the additional output may depress the price in the market. Hence, the cost will sooner or later overtake the revenue.

The firm will go on expanding till the marginal revenue (additional income from the additional output) exceeds the marginal costs (additional costs incurred on producing the additional output). The limit of expansion will be reached when the marginal revenue is equal to marginal costs. At that point, the firm will be maximizing its profits and, therefore, it will have no incentive to expand its output any further.

Conclusion

These are some of the factors which govern the expansion of a business and limit its growth. No wonder that business stops growing beyond a certain stage. The main reason relates to the emerging diseconomies.

Advantages of Small-scale Production

We have studied the advantages of large-scale production. But small-scale production also has economies of its own:

(*i*) In favour of small-scale production it may be pointed out that the small manufacturer possesses greater degree of manoeuverability. He is capable of prompt decision-making and quick execution. He can adopt new strategy as the market trends require. There is no divided responsibility. He is the only person concerned and he has none else to convince.

(*ii*) The initiative and sense of responsibility of a small producer have not been sapped by routine. He does not need an elaborate system of book-keeping and checks to prevent fraud or eliminate waste of labour or material. As Marshall says, "the master's eye is everywhere".

(*iii*) Personal contact with the employees, and a kind word now and then, will rule out the possibility of a strike or any other trouble. Peace generally reigns in a small concern and peace means prosperity.

(*iv*) Personal contact with the customers, again, sends them away well satisfied and produces good results. Custom is stable and demand is steady. This means absence of risk.

(*v*) The small-scale producer's advantage is the greatest where the demand is limited and fluctuating. A large-scale business is not suited to cater for such a demand and is therefore seriously handicapped.

(*vi*) The small businessman is usually the sole proprietor. Self-interest is a strong spur to his activity. He works long and late. Hard work is bound to make a success of a business.

Conclusion

With the wide dissemination of technical knowledge, the number of external economies is increasing while that of internal economies is decreasing. This helps the small producer. Also, where business cannot be reduced to a routine, a small producer has an advantage over a big producer. All these factors explain the advantages of small businesses.

Disadvantages

The small-scale producer cannot reap those economies which are available to a big concern. His drawbacks can be enumerated thus:

(*i*) There is less scope for the use of modern machinery and labour-saving devices. Hence cost per unit is high.

(*ii*) There is little scope for division of labour. The advantages of division of labour are, therefore, lost to him. Hence production is uneconomic.

(*iii*) The small-scale producer is at a disadvantage in the purchase of raw materials and other accessories. This pushes up the cost.

(*iv*) He cannot afford to spend large sums of money on research and experiments. Hence, he cannot make innovations and thus reduce costs.

(*v*) Cost of rent, interest, advertisement, etc., per unit of output is higher. That is, he has higher overhead charges.

(*vi*) With his limited resources he cannot meet bad times. This means instability.

(*vii*) He cannot secure cheap credit. This means higher costs.
(*viii*) Byproducts have to be thrown away.

Fig. 12.11. Small businesses.

12.9 SURVIVAL OF SMALL BUSINESSES

The advantages enjoyed by small-scale business enable it to compete successfully against big business. There are, besides, other circumstances which help a small business and in which large-scale production is not economical. When, for instance, the demand for a commodity is small, expansion of business is inadvisable. There are several factors which help the small producers to survive:

Geographical Factors

The demand for the product may be strictly local. Small firms can meet local needs more economically. If the raw materials are bulky and scattered, production will have to be decentralized and carried on in small units, where they can draw on the local supplies. Similarly, in scarcely populated regions, it is more economical to carry on production in small and scattered units.

And, where markets and sources of supply overlap and the producers and consumers are in close contact with one another, *e.g.*, in milk supply, smaller firms are found to be more economical. Expansion of firms is checked by market resistance, especially if transport costs are high.

Psychological Factors

The small producer is also helped by psychological factors. Consumers have their own preferences based on superiority, real or imaginary, of the goods they use. Thus, it is not only the distance which breaks a market but also prejudices, taste and habits of the consumers. This gives each a protected clientele. To overcome this resistance very expensive publicity may be necessary.

The geographical obstacles can be overcome by setting up branches and the psychological obstacles by widening the range of production. But these devices are often neither feasible nor economical, because they 'crop up' against the managerial obstacle to expansion.

Some Modern Developments

A small producer in modern times has been helped to hold his own against a big producer by developments like electricity, co-operative movement, and dissemination of scientific and technical knowledge through technical journals. Such knowledge is no longer the monopoly of the big business.

Entrepreneur's Attitude

The entrepreneur's own inclination, too, is responsible for the existence of small firms. "From a mixture of motives—from a love of independence and uncertainty, from pride or ambition, or the urge to create—men may prefer to run a small business of their own rather than act as subordinates at a higher rate of pay."

Conclusion

These are some of the reasons why a small-scale producer is able to hold his own against a big producer. That also explains why small-scale businesses exist side by side with the large-scale business.

12.10 SMALL-SCALE INDUSTRIES (SSIs)

Small-scale industries definition has undergone many changes from time to time since 1950s. Today the definition of SSIs is on the basis of investment. In February 1997 the investment limit in SSIs and ancillary industries were raised to ₹ 3 corer and that of tiny units to ₹ 25 lakh. In 1999 the investment limit of SSIs was brought down to ₹ 1 crore.

SSIs play a vital role in economic development specially in a developing country like India. The following are the main arguments of SSIs.

- *Production argument:* SSIs give immediate production. In our country the population is more and due to this the demand for goods are more. Small-scale industries help to meet this demand.
- *Employment argument*: The SSIs are labour-intensive, they provide employment to many people. The problem of unemployment may be reduced to a certain extent.
- *Less capital argument:* In large-scale industries we require huge amount of investment, but in SSIs we can start the units with smaller amount of capital.
- *Less skill argument:* Labour can be employed with lesser amount of training.
- *Latent-resources argument:* SSIs can help in tapping the unexploited resources and using them.

- *Decentralization argument:* SSIs helps a in small town's development. They can spread to different parts of the country. In case of large-scale industries concentration is in big cities only. This can stop the migration of labour from small towns to big cities.
- *Equity argument:* SSIs help in encouraging small entrepreneurs to enter into the business. This may be vital, so as to reduce the gap between the rich and poor.
- *Import and export promotion argument:* As local resources are used in many SSIs, there is less burden on import bill. SSIs are very beneficial as far as exports are concerned. In India its share in exports is increasing. In 2000–2001 (estimated 13. 13 billion $ worth of exports were accounted from SSIs.
- *Less-industrial disputes argument:* In SSIs there are very less number of industrial disputes, as the number of workers in SSIs are very less compare to large-scale industries.
- *Support to large-scale industries argument:* Many large-scale industries output is consumed as an input in SSIs. Hence, SSIs and large-scale industries are interdependent.

There are many other benefits from SSIs, that does not mean that there are no problems. SSIs suffer from many problems. In different countries of the world SSIs have played a vital role in their economies. After the liberalization and globalization the role of SSIs and its definition is changing in many parts of the world.

Role of Small-Scale Industry in Under-developed Countries

The small-scale industry has a special role to play in an under-developed country. Considering the resource position of the under-developed countries, the small-scale industries fit in excellently in their development plans for several reasons: (*i*) they have a vast employment potential; (*ii*) They offer limitless opportunities for self-employment; (*iii*) They require less capital and capital is what such countries lack; (*iv*) They promote capital formation; (*v*) They require fewer skill; (*vi*) They reduce the country's import bill; (*vii*) They provide quick yields so that inflationary pressures are contained; (*viii*) They promote decentralization of industries; (*ix*) The decentralized industries can bring about even distribution of income and wealth; (*x*) They can lend valuable support to large-scale industries; (*xi*) By diverting surplus labour from land they can reduce pressure on land.

Self-Assessment Questions

1. Carefully distinguish between internal and external economies. In what principal ways does the firm enjoy internal economies? How do they affect firm's average cost curve over different ranges of output?
2. Explain the external and internal economies in Production. Discuss the part played by them in bringing about Increasing Returns.
3. Discuss the relative merits of large and small-scale production.
4. What are the factors limiting the size of a firm? What part do "Indivisibilities: and "Economies of Scale" play in determining the size of the firm?
5. Discuss the role of small-scale industries in a developing economy.

Unit 13 PRODUCTION POSSIBILITY CURVE AND PRODUCTION FUNCTION

13.1 INTRODUCTION

In this chapter, we propose to deal with two fundamentals of the theory of production, *viz.,* production possibility curve and production function.

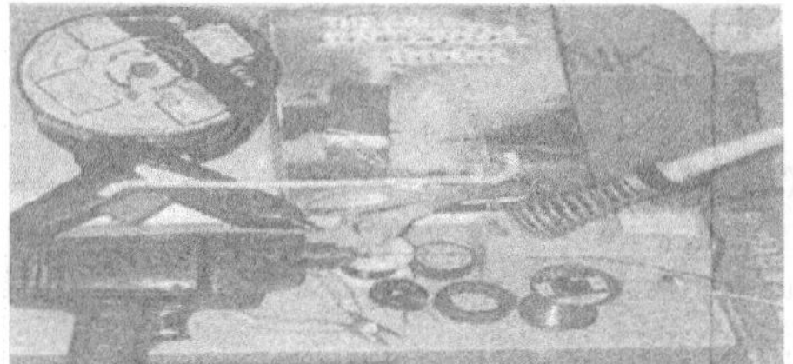

Fig. 13.1. Material resources.

Fig. 13.2. Resources are used for production of goods in the economy.

13.2 PRODUCTION POSSIBILITY CURVE

We know that the resources, both human and material, at the disposal of the community are strictly limited and they are capable of alternative uses, whereas we want to produce innumerable commodities, *i.e.,* the ends are unlimited. We have, therefore, to choose the most desirable assortment of goods that we can produce with the resources that we command and with a given state of technical knowledge. Had the resources at our disposal been unlimited, there would have been no problem, and we would have produced more of everything to satisfy our wants. If some resources were lying idle, then also it would have been possible to increase the production of all goods. But, in an economy characterized by full employment, some good can be produced only by foregoing the production of some other good. This is in keeping with the opportunity cost principle.

An economy has a certain population and some millions of workers of various grades; it has mastered certain techniques of production; it has certain resources in the form of land, water and other natural resources. That is, it has a certain number of factors or inputs. The society has really to decide how these resources can be utilized to produce the various possible commodities. In other words, it has to discover its production possibility curves.

The production possibility curve shows the maximum output of any one commodity that the economy can produce together with the prescribed quantities of other commodities produced and the resources utilized. In short, the production possibility curve tells us what assortment of goods and services the economy can produce with the resources and techniques at its disposal. The assortment on the curve is regarded as technologically efficient and below it as inefficient, for the simple reason that the economy is capable of producing a bigger assortment at least in respect of one commodity without decreasing any other. Any assortment which is beyond the frontier is really beyond the economy's power and is unattainable. The production possibility curve depicts the society's menu of choices.

We shall illustrate the concept of the production possibility curve by means of a table and a diagram. We take only two commodities, although in the real world, the commodities that can be produced are numberless. We take only two, because a larger number cannot be represented on a two dimensional diagram. But the principle will be clear and can be applied to any number of commodities.

Let us take two commodities X and Y that a firm can produce. If it decides to devote more of its resources to the production of X, it must sacrifice to that extent production of some limits of Y as shown in Table 13.1.

Table 13.1. Alternative production possibilities.

Production Possibilities	*X (Thousands)*	*Y (Thousands)*
A	0	15
B	1	14
C	2	12
D	3	9
E	4	5
F	5	0

As in the case of indifference curves, we first suppose that all the resources at the disposal of the economy are devoted to the production of good X. In that case 5,000 X-products is the maximum that it can produce. Now let all the productive resources available be devoted to the production of Y with the result that 15,000 Y will be produced but no X. These are the two extreme limits, *viz.*, 5,000 X but no Y and 15,000, Y but no X. In between these two extreme limits, there are numerous combinations of X and Y that can be produced.

The production possibility curve can be depicted by means of diagram given below.

In this diagram (Fig. 13.1), A represents the extreme limit at which all Y's are produced. Now, if we want to produce some X, some Y will have to be sacrificed. For instance, in order to produce 1,000 X we shall have to be content with 14,000 Y instead of 15,000. That is, we have transformed, as it were, one thousand Y into 1,000 X, and so on in the Table 13.1. Thus, production possibility schedule is the same thing as production transformation schedule and the curve in the diagram (Fig. 13.3) is called the Production Transformation Curve.

In the diagram, the curve marks the production possibility frontier and all points on the curve represent production possibility, the points inside the curve are attainable combinations and those outside such as *s*, *t* are unattainable combinations. Any point inside the curve represents an under utilization of resources or under-employment. A fuller utilization will shift the curve outwards.

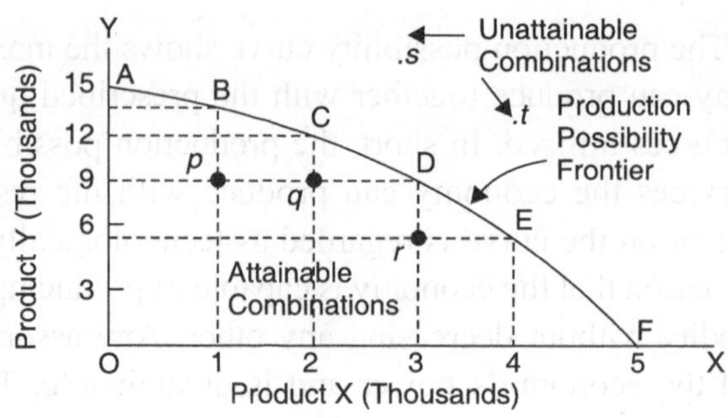

Fig. 13.3. Production possibility curve.

Increase in the resources at the disposal of the firm will take it to a higher production possibility curve.

Marginal Rate of Transformation

We have seen above that, in order to produce more X, we must sacrifice some Y, *i.e.,* Y's can be transformed into X's. The rate at which one product is transformed into another is called marginal rate of transformation. For instance, marginal rate of transformation between good X and good Y is the amount of Y which has to be sacrificed for the production of X. We can also see from the Table 13.1 that for the production of additional units of X, increasing quantities of Y have to be sacrificed. Hence, the marginal rate of transformation increases as more of X and and less of Y is produced. This makes the production possibility curve concave to the origin. The marginal rate of transformation (MRT) at any point on the production possibility curve is given by the slope of the curve at that point.

Iso-Revenue Lines

We have seen that the production possibility curve shows the various combinations of the two goods which can be produced with given resources. The question remains as to which of these various combinations the firm will decide to produce. Which is considered the most desirable? Surely, the firm will have to decide which combination out of the so many available will be most profitable. In order to hit on the most desirable combination, we shall introduce the price factor or the revenue factor (price paid by the purchaser is revenue for the seller). The producer must maximize his revenue. We shall, therefore, draw the iso-revenue

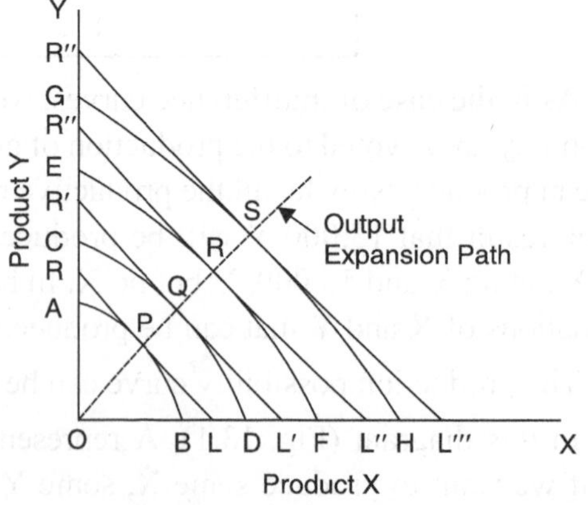

Fig. 13.4. Iso-revenue lines.

line yielding the same revenue output expansion path. In Fig. 13.4 RL, R′L′, R″L″ and R″ ‘L‴ are the iso-revenue lines, each showing that every point on the line represents the same revenue from the sale of the products X and Y. AB is our production possibility curve at which RL is the tangent touching it at P. Similarly, R′ L′ touches CD at higher production possibility curve at Q and R′ ‘L’ touches EF at a still higher curve at R and R” ‘L’, iso-revenue line touches GH, the higher curve, at S. Joining P, Q, R and S, we get output expansion path. The iso-revenue lines are parallel to one another since the prices of the products are taken as fixed. The slope of the iso-revenue line represents the ratio of the price of X to the price of Y.

Output expansion path shows the revenue maximizing locus of different combinations of two products as resources of the firm change keeping prices of products constant. If the resources at the disposal of the firm are represented by the production possibility curve AB, then it will choose for production the combination of X and Y represented by the point P. At this point, its revenue will be maximum. Here the marginal rate of transformation MRTxy on the given production possibility curve will be equal to the price ratio of the two products, *i.e.*, Py/Py similarly, as regards the points Q, R and S, P, Q, R, S expansion path is the locus of all the revenue maximizing product combinations with the varying amount of resources that the firm commands.

Uses of Production Possibility Curve

The production possibility curve can be put to a number of practical uses. Besides helping in the solution of the basic problems of production, viz., what and how, *i.e.*, what is to be produced and how and with what combinations of resources it is to be produced, the concept of the production possibility curve can be put to the following uses:

(*i*) The planning authority of a developing country may decide after a certain stage to divert its resources from the production of necessities to luxuries and from producer goods to consumer goods.

(*ii*) A democratic country may decide to devote its resources less to the production of privately manufactured goods purchased by price and more by public sector enterprises supplied free but financed by taxes such as public utilities, free education, free medical services, etc.

(*iii*) The production possibility curve can also help in guiding the diversion of resources from current consumption goods to capital goods like machines and increases productive resources to attain higher levels of production. Many more alternatives can be imagined.

13.3 EFFICIENT ALLOCATION OF RESOURCES

We have been examining the problem of resource allocation from the point of view of an individual firm. Let us widen the horizon and try to see how the resources of the entire economy can be most efficiently utilized. What, in other words, is the criterion for the optimum utilization of the country's resources? The resources will be most efficiently allocated from the consumers' point of view if the highest possible level of satisfaction has been attained. From the point of view of national income, resource allocations will be regarded as efficiently employed if they make the maximum possible contribution to the national income. There will be misallocation, if the net national output is less than what it can be.

In a free enterprise economy, this important function is performed by the resource prices. For attaining maximum efficiency of resource allocation, there is constant shifting and reallocation of resources between different uses in response to changes in the tastes and preferences of people, changes in the category and the quantities of available resources and changes in techniques of production. Resource prices furnish the mechanism for rectifying misallocations of the resources in the economic system.

Criterion of Maximum Efficiency

Thus, the criterion for a correct or efficient utilization of resources is that the net national product has been maximized, *i.e.*, at the existing technology it has attained a peak level. Conversely, the resources will not be correctly allocated if the net national product is below its maximum potential. However, in case of misallocation, automatically such forces will be set in motion as it will bring about a reallocation of the resources so as to maximize the national product.

The Principle

The question now is as to how the optimum allocation of resources can be achieved. Or, if there is a misallocation of resources among the various uses, how it is to be rectified. The law of substitution or equimarginal returns solves the problem. A community can allocate its resources in the most efficient manner by acting on this principle. This means that the resources should be so allocated among their various uses that the value of the marginal product in each use is the same. If it is not the same, then it has to be equalized by the application of the Law of Substitution, *i.e.*, by transferring resources from one use to another.

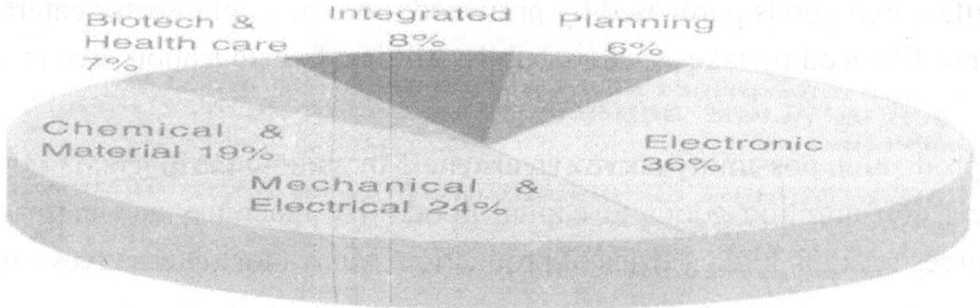

Fig. 13.5. An example of allocation of resources into various areas.

For instance, if the value of the marginal product of resources in one use is greater than it is in other uses, it is obvious that they will be more valuable to the society if they are used where the value of the marginal product is higher. Some units of the resource, therefore, must be transferred from the lower value to the uses with higher value of marginal product. That would increase the total value of the economy's output.

Since some price has to be paid for a factor, no factor will be used to such an extent as to reduce its marginal productivity to zero. Each scarce factor will be allocated among the various industries or uses in such a manner as to equalize the value of its marginal *product in every industry* where it is employed. If the value of the marginal product of labour, say, in the iron and steel industry, is greater than that in the sugar industry, labour will be shifted from the latter to the former, till the marginal productivities of labour in the two industries are equalized. In the same manner, if land is devoted to sugarcane cultivation it yields more than that if it is devoted to growing cotton, it will obviously pay to withdraw some land which cultivates cotton and divert it to sugarcane. This diversion will continue till the value of the marginal product in the two alternative uses of land has been equalized.

Thus, the factors of production will be optimally allocated among the various alternative uses when there is no inducement for diverting them from any one use to another. This will be the case only if the marginal return in each use is equal. So long as it is not equal, reshuffling will go on.

Thus, "the best allocation of the factors of production is when the value of the marginal production of a factor is the same in every line in which it is employed, or the equilibrium situation with regard to allocation of factors is that in which the community places the same value upon marginal product of the factor in every industry" (Benham).

The reshuffling of the resources between different uses takes places through the mechanism of resource prices. When the value of the marginal product of a given resource is lower in some industries, it is clear that the firms will not be willing to pay for it more than the value of its marginal product. On the other hand, where the value of its marginal product is higher, the firms will be keen to use more of it and they will offer to pay a higher price which is above the value of its marginal product in the former case. The owner of the resources who is keen to maximize his income will transfer the resources from the less remunerative, to the more remunerative uses. This transfer will continue till the value of the marginal product is equalized in all uses. When equality between the values of the marginal product has been attained, the resources will be making the maximum contribution to the net national product.

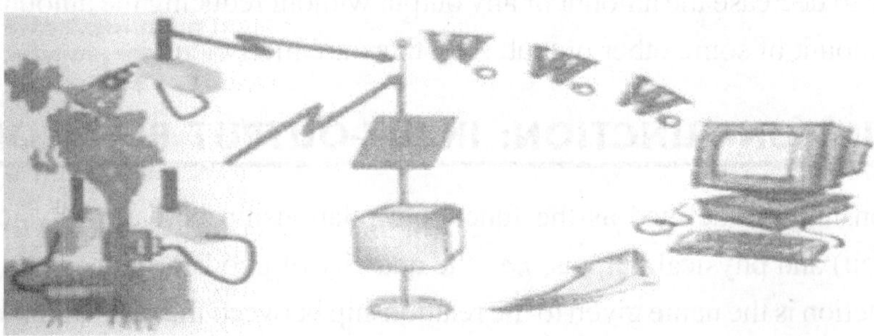

Fig. 13.6. Input and output.

An illustration will make it clear. Let us take firms in two industries using resource A and producing two products X and Y. In accordance with the principle enunciated above, the resources will be correctly allocated among firms of the two industries when the value of marginal product of A in firms of the industry producing X (V of MPax) is equal to the value of marginal product of A in firms of the industry producing y = Y (v of MPay). Thus,

V of MPax = V of MPay = Pa

or MPPax × Px = MPPay × Py = Pa

V of MP means value of marginal product. Pa is the price per unit of resource A.

Px is the price of product X.

Py is the price of product Y.

Now if demand for the commodity X in the market increases, the price of X will rise, with the result that V of M Pax increases. This means that it has become more valuable for the community to utilize resource A more in the production of X than in the production of Y. The firms producing X will feel that at price Pa, the resource A is in short supply. Hence, they will raise its price to induce the owners of A resource to transfer its units to an industry producing X from that producing Y. As a consequence of larger quantities of A resource being used in X-producing industry, MP Pax will decrease. As the output of X expands, its price declines. Thus V of M Pax goes down. On the other hand, reduced use of A resource in Y-producing industry will result in the increase of MP Pay. Since output of Y decreases, its price Py will rise. As a result of increase in MP Pay and in Py, V of M Pay increases. Such transfer of resources from Y-producing industry to X-producing industry will continue till V of MPax becomes equal to V MPay. Since the value of the marginal product of A resource is now higher in both industries, the new price per unit of A will be higher. This resource will again be making its maximum contribution to the net national product.

Conclusion

The following statement clinches the issues underlying an efficient utilization of the resources: "Efficient transformations are those in which ceteris paribus: (1) it is not possible to increase the amount of any output without increasing the amount of some input or decreasing the amount of some other output; (2) it is not possible to decrease the amount of any output without reducing the amount of some input or increasing the amount of some other output. All others are inefficient.

13.4 PRODUCTION FUNCTION: INPUT-OUTPUT RELATIONSHIP

Production function may be defined as the functional relationship between physical inputs (*i.e.*, factors of production) and physical outputs, *i.e.*, the quantity of goods produced. As Stigler puts it, "the production function is the name given to the relationship between the rates of input of productive services and the rate of output of product. It is the economist's summary of technological knowledge."

Thus, the production function expresses the relationship between quantity of output and the quantities of various inputs used in production. The physical relationship between a firm's physical input and output depends on a given state of technological knowledge.

Like demand, production function refers to a period of time. Accordingly, it refers to a flow of inputs resulting in a flow of outputs over a period of time, leaving prices aside. It shows the maximum amount of output that can be produced from a given set of inputs in the existing state of technology. The output will change when the quantity of any input is changed or the minimum quantities of various inputs required to produce a given quantity are changed.

In real life, a manufacturer wants to know how much of the various factors or inputs, viz., land (*i.e.,* natural resources), labour and capital will be required to produce a unit or given quantity of a commodity during a given period of time. It is necessary for him to know this so that he may be able not only to assess his requirements of productive services but also roughly to estimate the probable cost. It will thus indicate the varieties of the productive resources and their possible combinations used for the purposes of production.

Production function of course depends, inter alia, on (*a*) quantities of resources used, (*b*) state of technical knowledge, (*c*) possible processes, (*d*) size of the firms, (*e*) nature of organization, (*f*) relative prices of the factors of production and the manner in which the factors of production are combined. As these things change, production function will change too. For instance, output can be increased by increasing the quantity of factors of production or of some of them. It can also be increased by varying the proportion in which the factors are combined. Adoption of more efficient techniques of production, too, will add to the output. The less efficient the techniques the smaller will be the output.

Production changes with period of time. In the very long period, it changes altogether because the same inputs produce different outputs. In the long-run, the production function depicts the whole set of choices available to the producer, *i.e.,* what inputs will produce what output. In the short-run, the choices available to the producer are restricted because some of the factors are fixed and cannot be changed in the short period and only some can be varied. In this situation, the producer tries to find out the relation between the variable inputs and the outputs.

Since production function is concerned with physical aspects of production, it is more a concern of an engineer or a technician than of an economist. Only a technician can say what specific quantity of a good can be produced by the use of the various productive resources and their combinations.

Production function can be expressed as under: $x = f(a, b, c, d, \ldots\ldots)$

Here X is the output of a commodity per unit of time and $a, b, c, d, \ldots.$ are the various productive resources which go into the making of the quantity of the commodity; f is function, *i.e.,* which varies.

Every management has to make a choice of the production function depending not only on industrial knowledge and the prices of the various factors of production but also on its own capacity to manage. It has also to select the various factors and knit them together in economical combinations. These two choices are interlinked. The over-riding consideration is to seek a combination, which gives the minimum average cost and maximum aggregate profit.

For understanding the nature of production function the following points may be emphasized:

(*i*) The production function represents a purely technical relationship in physical quantities between the inputs of factors and the output of the products, it has no reference to money price. The price factor is left out altogether.

(*ii*) The output is the result of a joint use of the factors of production. It is obvious that the physical productivity of one factor can be measured only in the context of this factor being used in conjunction with other factors.

(*iii*) The nature or the quantity of the various factors and the manner in which they are combined will depend on the state of technical knowledge. For instance, labour productivity will depend on the quality of labour as determined by their education and training. Similarly, the productivity of machines will be determined by the technical advances embodied in them. Again, it is on the basis of technical knowledge at the time that labour, machines and other factors will be combined in the processes of production. Thus, the state of technical knowledge is treated as given (*i.e.,* as a parameter) for specifying a production function A change in technology will mean a shift to another production function. It will alter the cost condition, improvement in technology will result in a larger output from a given combination of the factors of production.

(*iv*) In specifying the production function of a firm, we have to take into account the variability of the factors of production and also whether they are divisible or indivisible: These features of the factors of production will determine their productivities and hence, the nature of the production function.

Types

Production function may take several forms: Broadly speaking (*a*) it can be a fixed proportions production function, or (*b*) it can be a variable proportions production function. In the case of fixed-proportions production function, the factors of production are used in a fixed proportion. For instance, a fixed number of workers may be required to produce a unit/units of the product and this proportion cannot be varied by substituting one factor for the other factors. In the case of variable proportions production function, the technical coefficient of production is variable. In other words, the quantity of a factor of production required to produce a given unit of product can be varied by substituting some other factor/factors in its place. This means that in this case a given quantity of a product can be turned out by several alternative combinations of factors of production as is shown in an iso-quant map.

Suppose we require 40 workers to produce 200 units of a product. The technical coefficient of production in this case is 1/5. In case the technical coefficient of production is fixed then in a case like this one-fifth of labour must be employed for the production of a unit of the commodity in question and there is no scope for varying its proportion through substitution of some other factor. This is the case of fixed proportions production function in which the factors of production *e.g.,* labour and capital must be used in fixed proportions in the production of a certain level of output.

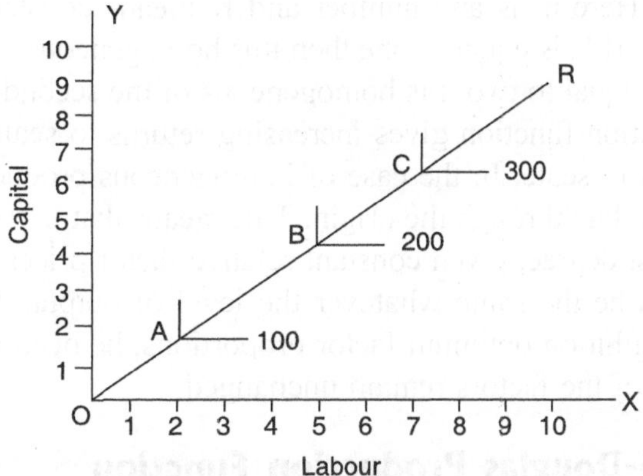

Fig. 13.7. The fixed proportion production function.

The fixed proportion production function can be illustrated by the following diagram:

In this diagram, OR represents the fixed labour capital ratio. This ratio must be maintained whatever the level of output. Since this ratio is fixed, the isoquants relating to such a production function are shown as right-angles. Suppose the ratio is 2 : 3 *i.e.*, 2 units of capital and 3 units of labour, when 100 units of the product are to be produced; then for producing 200 units 4 units of capital and 6 units of labour will be required, and so on. It may be noticed that along each iso-quant, the marginal product of a factor is zero. For instance, at B an iso-quant of 200, if the amount of capital used is fixed the use of extra labour makes no addition to the total product, *i.e.*, the marginal product of labour is zero. However, doubling both factors will result in doubling the output, and so on.

In this case, as already mentioned, the ratio in which the factors of production are used is not fixed but it is variable. That is, a given quantity of the product can be produced by several alternative combinations of factors. In the iso-quant map various equal product curves are drawn to show how different combinations of factors of production can be used to produce a given level of output.

Linear Homogeneous Production Function

The linear homogeneous production function implies that if all the factors of production are increased in same proportion, the output also increases in the same proportion. That is, the doubling of all inputs will double the output and trebling them will result in the trebling of the output, and so on. This represents a case of constant returns to scale. This type of production function is called by the economists as a well behaved production function because it can be easily handled and used in empirical studies. It can be used by computers in calculations. That is why it is widely used in linear programming and input-output analysis. It is also extensively used in model analysis of production, distribution and economic growth.

This is a production function, which is homogeneous of the first degree. That is, it shows that the increase in output in the same proportion follows a given change in the factors of production. This has been put mathematically as:

$$mP = f(mX, mY)$$

Here m is any number and K means constant. This function is homogeneous of the Kth degree. If K is equal to one then this homogeneous function is homogeneous of the first degree and if K is equal to two it is homogeneous of the second degree, and so on. If K is greater than one the production function gives increasing returns to scale and if it is less than one it gives decreasing returns to scale. In the case of homogeneous production function, the expansion path is always a straight line through the origin. This means that in the case of homogeneous production function of the first degree, given constant relative factor prices, the proportions between the factors used will always be the same whatever the level of output. This makes the task of the entrepreneur easy. Having hit on optimum factor proportions, he need not change the decision so long as the relative prices of the factors remain unchanged.

Cobb-Douglas Production Function

A well known empirical production function is the Cobb-Douglas production function. It takes two inputs, labour and capital, and is expressed by the following equation:

$$Q = Kla\ C(I - a)$$

Here Q is the quantity of output, L is the labour employed, K and a are positive constants ($a < 1$) and C is the quantity of capital used.

Self-Assessment Questions

1. Explain a linear homogeneous production function.
2. What is 'production function'? How does it help in understanding a producer's equilibrium?
3. Explain with the help of production possibility curve how economics is concerned with the problem of employment and allocation and growth of a community's resources.
4. Explain the following problems in economics with the help of production possibility curve: (*i*) Choice between the production of consumer goods and producer goods in an economy; (*ii*) The problem of unemployed resources; (*iii*) The problem of economic growth.

Unit **14**

LAWS OF RETURN

14.1 INTRODUCTION

We shall first study the laws of return, which are different aspects of one law, viz., the law of variable proportions, and then returns to scale and in the next chapter equal product curves.

There are three laws of returns known to economists, the laws of diminishing, increasing and constant return. "There is said to be increasing, decreasing or constant returns accordingly as the marginal returns rise, fall or remain unchanged" as the quantity of a factor of production is increased. In terms of cost, an industry is subject to increasing, decreasing or constant returns accordingly as the marginal cost of production falls, rises or remains the same, respectively, with the expansion of an industry.

14.2 LAW OF DIMINISHING RETURNS

Statement of the Law

In the absence of the law of diminishing returns, "the science of political economy", says Cairnes, "would be as completely revolutionized as if human nature itself were altered". Such is the importance of the law of diminishing returns in economic theory.

The law of diminishing returns was supposed to have a special application to agriculture. It is the practical experience of every farmer that "successive applications of labour and capital to a given area of land must ultimately, other things remaining the same, yield a less than proportionate increase in produce." If by doubling labour and capital he could double the yield of his land and so on, it can be easily seen that one acre of land could be made to produce as much wheat as could suffice for the entire population of the world. This cannot be done but simply due to the operation of the law of diminishing returns. If investment is increased, the total yield will no doubt increase, but at a diminishing rate.

Marshall stated the law thus: "An increase in capital and labour applied in the cultivation of land causes in general less than proportionate increase in the amount of produce raised, unless it happens to coincide with an improvement in the art of agriculture." The phrase 'in general' in this statement is important. It means that there may be cases where the law does not hold good. It refers to limitations of the law.

Table 14.1. Three aspects of the law of diminishing returns.

No. of workers	*Total return*	*Marginal return*	*Average return*
(1)	(2)	(3)	(4)
1	80	80	80
2	170	90	85
3	270	100	90
		—	
4	368	98	92
			—
5	430	62	86
6	480	50	80
7	504	24	72
8	504	0	63
9	495	– 9	55
10	440	– 55	44

From the Table 14.1, it appears that there are three different aspects of the law of diminishing returns:

(1) Law of Total Diminishing Returns (Column 2): In this sense, the returns begin to diminish from the 9th worker. Every successive worker employed does make some addition to the total output. But the 8th adds nothing and the 9th and 10th are a positive nuisance. As workers cannot be productive, no prudent farmer will employ more than seven workers in the conditions represented by Table 14.1.

(2) Law of Diminishing Marginal Returns (Column 3): Marginal returns go on increasing up to the 3rd worker. This is so because the proportion of workers to land was at first insufficient and the land was not being properly tilled. This phase of cultivation is unstable and will not be found in practice. When the farmer knows that he can get more than proportionate return by employing an extra hand, he will certainly do so. The marginal, *i.e.,* the additional, return goes on falling from the 3rd man onwards till it drops down to zero at the 8th, the 9th and 10th men are merely a cause of obstruction to the others and are responsible in making the marginal return negative. The point at which the addition made to the total output by each successive unit of the variable factor starts diminishing is known as the point of diminishing marginal returns.

It can be seen that the total output is at its maximum when marginal output is zero. It should be remembered that the marginal return is not what can be attributed to the last unit whose employment is considered just worthwhile, as all men are supposed to be alike. The marginal return is simply the addition that the marginal unit makes to the total return.

(3) Law of Diminishing Average Returns (Column 4): The average return reaches the maximum at the 4th worker, *i.e.,* one step later than the marginal return reaches the maximum. Then the marginal return falls more sharply. The two equalize somewhere between the 4th and 5th, *i.e.,* when the 5th worker works part-time. But we do not employ men in fractions in real life. Therefore, it is not always possible to equalize the marginal and the average returns. It is also clear that it is possible for the average output to increase while the marginal output falls.

Diagrammatic Representation. The law can be diagrammatically represented as in Fig. 14.1.

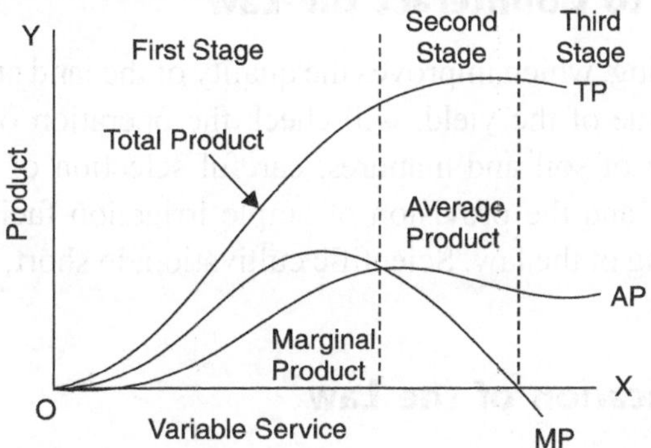

Fig. 14.1. Stages of the law of diminishing returns.

The total production (*i.e.,* return) goes on increasing till it reaches the maximum where the third stage starts. The marginal return reaches the maximum at the earliest and starts diminishing at the first stage. The average return starts diminishing next, *i.e.,* where the second stage begins.

This is in keeping with the above table. Obviously, no sensible entrepreneur will operate in the third stage where the marginal product is zero, unless, ofcourse, the variable factor is free. Economically, the second stage is the significant region where the average product is greater than the marginal product, which is still positive. It can be seen that the total output *curve is* the *steepest where* the *marginal output is the* largest. The law of diminishing returns is also called the law of diminishing physical productivity.

Limitations of the Law of Diminishing Returns

The law of diminishing returns does not apply to all situations. There are several exceptions to the law as it applies in agriculture:

(*i*) **Improved methods of cultivation:** Man's ingenuity is ever striving to counteract the operation of this law by improving the technique of cultivation. Scientific rotation of crops, improved seeds, modern implements, artificial manures and better irrigation facilities, etc. is bound to give increasing return. But science cannot keep pace with the increasing demand for food. The niggardliness of nature must ultimately assert itself and the law must operate sooner or later.

(*ii*) **New soil:** When a virgin soil is brought under cultivation, the additional return for each successive dose of labour and capital may increase for a time. But after a point, the tendency of diminishing returns will set in. Hence, in the case of a new soil, the law of diminishing returns does not apply in the beginning.

(*iii*) **Insufficient capital:** If capital applied hitherto has not been insufficient, increased application will, at first, yield more than proportionate return. Later, however, the marginal return will decrease. The early stage is an exception to the law of diminishing return.

How to Counteract the Law

Anything, which improves the quality of the land and makes it yield more, or anything, which adds to the value of the yield, will check the operation of the law. Use of modern implements, judicious mixing of soil and manures, careful selection of the seed and proper sowing, deeper and deeper tillage, and the provision of ample irrigation facilities, etc. can enable a farmer to counteract the working of the law. Scientific cultivation, in short, can check the operation of the law of diminishing returns.

Application of the Law

Besides agriculture, the law also applies to extractive industries like mining, fisheries and also to building industry. The law operates when mining operations are extended to inferior, distant or deeper mines, when fishing operations are concentrated in one place and when more and more storeys are raised on a building.

Why the Law Specially Applies to Agriculture

We have seen that the law of diminishing returns has a wide application. But it specially applies to agriculture and other extractive industries. One thing that is common to all these industries is the supremacy of nature. It is, therefore, often remarked that the part that nature plays in production corresponds to diminishing returns and the part which man plays conforms to the law of increasing returns. The inference is that agriculture, where nature is supreme, is subject to diminishing returns, while industry, where man is supreme, is subject to increasing returns.

There are several reasons why agriculture is subject to the law of diminishing returns:

(*i*) The agricultural operations are spread out over a wide area, and consequently supervision cannot be very effective.

(*ii*) Scope for the use of specialized machinery is also very limited. Therefore, economies of large-scale production cannot be reaped.

(*iii*) There are further limitations arising from the seasonal nature of the industry. Agricultural operations are likely to be interrupted by rain and other climatic changes. Man is not a complete master of nature, and it is no wonder that the law of diminishing returns operates in agriculture.

Similarly, it is understandable that manufacturing industries should be subject to the law of increasing return. Here man's ingenuity has the fullest scope to show itself. By the introduction of division of labour and the use of the most modern appliances, production can be greatly increased. Concentration of workers under one roof renders supervision easy and effective. Nature's malignant influences are thus held constantly at bay. Man is free to plan, undertake and execute. He can realize all the possible economies, internal and external.

But it is wrong to say that agriculture is always subject to diminishing returns and manufacturing always to increasing returns. The law of diminishing returns applies everywhere. To borrow Wicksteed's words. "This law is as universal as the law of life itself." Its application is not confined to agriculture only; it applies to manufacturing industries too. If the industry is expanded too much and becomes unwieldy, supervision will become lax. The law of diminishing returns will, therefore, set in both in agriculture and industry earlier. The only difference is that in agriculture it sets and in industry much later.

Thus, both laws apply in all types of industrial extractive as well as manufacturing. As a matter of fact, they are two aspects of the same law, which also known as the Law of Variable Proportions.

Law of Diminishing Returns in a Firm

The discussion of the law of diminishing returns in relation to land, since the times of the English classical economists, has obscured its real significance. There is nothing peculiar about agriculture for the law to be exclusively associated with it. As a matter of fact, in agriculture, the law has been held in check by scientific cultivation in progressive countries. This is evident from the fact that whereas consumption of food has increased on account of higher standards of living, the number of people engaged in the production of food has actually gone down.

The fact is that the law of diminishing returns does not apply to agriculture alone. It has got a general application and can, therefore, be put in a general form. The law of diminishing returns simply refers to a principle of combination of the factors. In a general way, it can be stated that if a variable factor is combined with some constant factors, the average and the marginal return for that variable factor will diminish. Benham states the law thus: "As the proportion of one factor in a combination of factors is increased after a point the average and marginal product of that factor will diminish."

Why the Law of Diminishing Returns Operates

The operation of the law of diminishing returns can be attributed to several causes:

(*i*) **Wrong Combination:** In the initial stages, the fixed factor is not fully used since the units of variable factor are too few. Hence, increase in the variable factor in the initial stages proves productive on account of fuller utilization of the fixed factor and of better co-operation and greater specialization in the variable factor units. We are moving towards the optimum combination. But after a stage, increase in the variable factor brings down the marginal return. Thus, the law of diminishing returns operates because the combination of the factors of production ceases to represent a correct proportion. It ceases to be an optimum combination. There is too much of one factor in relation to the others. The fixed factor has reached its maximum capacity and there is no further possibility of specialization of the variable factor. This explains the operation of the law of diminishing returns. When proper balance is restored the law of diminishing returns will no longer operate.

But the law of diminishing returns is a misnomer. We saw that in the beginning the marginal return increases. It is only ultimately that the law operates. This is why Bounding calls it "the law of eventually diminishing marginal physical productivity."

(*ii*) **Scarcity of Factors:** The law of diminishing returns operates due to the scarcity of the factors of production. In the words of Chapman, "The expansion of an industry, provided that additional supplies of some agent in production, which is essential cannot be obtained, is invariably accompanied at once or eventually by decreasing returns, other things being equal."

(*iii*) **Imperfect Substitutes:** A little reflection will show that the law of diminishing returns operates because the factors of production are imperfect substitutes for one another. As Robinson says, "What the law of diminishing returns really states is that there is a limit to the extent to which one factor of production can be substituted for another, or, in other words, that the elasticity of substitution between factors is not infinite. If this were not true it would be possible when one factor of production is fixed in amount and the rest are in perfectly elastic supply, to produce part of the output with the aid of the fixed factor, and then, when optimum proportion between this factor and other factors was attained, to substitute some other factor for it and to increase output at constant cost. Thus, the law of diminishing returns entails that the various elements required for the production of any commodity should be divided into groups, each group being a factor of production, in such a way that the elasticity of substitution between one factor and another is less than infinite.

Importance of the Law of Diminishing Returns

We have quoted Cairns when he says that in the absence of the law of diminishing returns, "The science of political economy would be as completely revolutionized as if human nature itself were altered." Such is the great importance of the law of diminishing returns. The law of diminishing returns has a very wide, almost universal application. Uptill Marshall, it was thought that the law of diminishing returns applied to agriculture whereas the laws of increasing or constant returns applied to manufacture. But it is now held that the law of diminishing returns applies in all fields of production, whether agriculture, mining or manufacture. Whenever we find that some factors of production are fixed and cannot be varied and other factors are varied, then techniques of production remaining the same, diminishing returns are bound to follow, sooner or later. There is no escape.

The validity of the law of diminishing returns is not merely based on theoretical reasoning but it has been supported by extensive empirical evidence. It has been remarked that if the diminishing return did not occur we could grow sufficient food grains in a flower pot merely by increasing the dozes of labour and capital. It is obvious that if the successive applications of dozes of labour and capital resulted in obtaining constant returns, the whole population of the world could be fed by growing crops on a tiny piece of land. As population increased, we could use more labour and capital on a piece of land to get proportionate increase in agricultural output and there would be no fear of famine and starvation. As Professor Lipsey remarks, "Indeed, where hypothesis of diminishing returns is incorrect, there would be no fear that the present population explosion will bring with it a food crisis. If the marginal product of additional worker applied to a fixed quantity of land were constant, then the world's food production would be expanded in proportion to the increase in population merely by keeping the same proportion of the population on farms. As it is, diminishing returns means an inexorable decline in the marginal product of each additional labourer as an expanding population is applied, with static techniques, to a fixed world supply of agriculture. But let there be no misunderstanding. We need not arrive at the dismal conclusion that since the law of diminishing returns is universally true, the average and marginal returns must eventually decline and humanity is doomed. There is no such fear. Experience of both developed technology may be able to keep the law of diminishing returns in abeyance. We see from the Indian experience that improved technology has ushered in what is known as the 'green revolution' and, in a short span of time, we have not only been able to ban hunger and starvation from the land, but we have also now a comfortable surplus. The ghost of law of diminishing returns seems to have been laid.

At the same time, we must point out that this happy experience is no contradiction of the law of diminishing returns. The law clearly states that if there is no charge in technical knowledge, capital equipment, and other aids to production, the law of diminishing returns is kept in check for the time being. But who can say that the improvement in technology and addition to capital equipment will keep pace with a galloping population. We have only suspended the operation of the law of diminishing returns by improving techniques of production through the application of science and technology, but if we fail to keep up the technical progress in a sufficient measure, the law of diminishing returns may assert it self. As Lipsey observes, "Unless there is a continual and rapidly accelerating improvement in techniques of production, the population explosion must bring with it decline in living standards over much of the world and eventual widespread famine."

The law of diminishing returns has formed the basis of a number of economic doctrines propounded by the English classical economists, especially Malthus and Ricardo. It was represented as an inexorable law of nature. It accounted for a lot of pessimistic thinking in economics and earned for it the title of a 'dismal science' The Malthusian theory of population, which says that population increases faster than the food supply, is obviously based on the fact that the production of food is subject to the law of diminishing returns.

Ricardian Theory of Rent: The Ricardian theory of rent explains the determination of rent on the assumption that inferior lands have to be cultivated on account of the operation of the law of diminishing returns. The margin of cultivation descends, and rent rises. The optimum size of business is explained again by the working of this law.

Theory of Distribution: The marginal productivity theory, which determines the share of a factor of production in the national dividend, is also based on the operation of this important law.

Conclusion

The law of diminishing returns, therefore, occupies a very important place in the realm of economic thought.

14.3 THE LAW OF VARIABLE PROPORTIONS

The law of variable proportions (of which the law of diminishing returns is one aspect) shows the efficiency of factor combination. Incidentally, the three stages of the law of diminishing returns showed above throw light on how efficiently have the factors (land and labour) been combined in the process of production. The average return shows the amount of the product obtained per unit of labour for the various land-labour ratios and the total product column (Column 2) shows the total output obtained from that unit of land for the various land-labour ratios.

In stage I, as more and more labour is used, the average product of labour increases, which reflects the increasing efficiency of labour. In this stage, the total product increases also for this unit of land, which shows that the efficiency of land too is increasing. Hence, this stage shows that both land and labour are being efficiently utilized.

The second stage shows decreasing average product and marginal product of labour. But since the total output goes on increasing the marginal product is positive. This stage shows the decreasing efficiency of labour. But the efficiency of land continues to increase because the total return continues to increase. In the third stage, the average product (of labour) decreases still further. Also, the marginal product becomes negative and the total product is decreasing. Hence, in this stage, both labour and land have been used inefficiently.

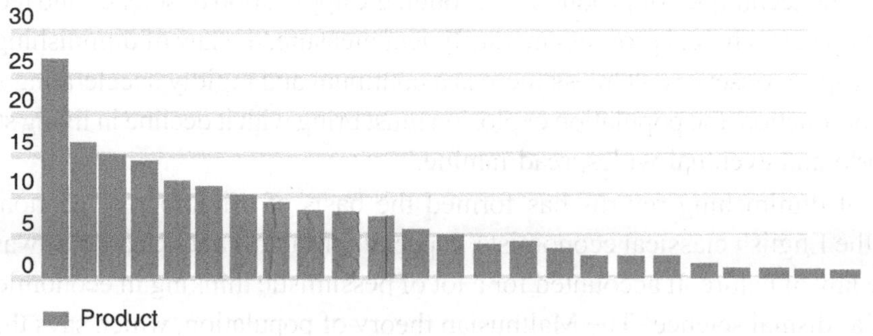

Fig. 14.2. Diminishing returns.

Thus, the combination of land and labour attained maximum efficiency of labour at the boundary line between stage I and II and maximum efficiency of land at the boundary line between stage II and stage III. Stage II represents higher efficiency of land-labour ratio than that of the other two stages.

The productive resources of land and labour both command a price in the market and have to be paid for. Since, in stage I, product per unit of both land and labour increases, the firm will keep expanding and move to the boundary between stage I and stage II. But when it enters the second stage, it finds that the return per unit expenditure on labour decreases while that of land increases. The proportions in which land and labour will be used will depend on their relative prices or costs per unit. If the price of land is low relative to the price of labour, the firm will operate more in the beginning of stage II, and, conversely, less the price of labour relative to the price of land, it will operate towards the end of the stage II. Stages III and I are ruled out. Stage I is ruled out because throughout this stage average product of both land and labour are still increasing and stage III is ruled out because the average product of both factors is decreasing.

It will be seen that the name of the law "law of diminishing returns" is a misnomer. This law is also called the law of proportionality. This law tells us how the total output or marginal output is affected by a change in the proportion of the factors used. Since the return to the variable factor does not change at the same rate in all stages, it is also called the law of non-proportional returns.

When, after a stage, the marginal return begins to diminish, it is not due to the fact that either the prices of the factors of production have gone up or the price of the output has gone down. It is rather due to the technological facts underlying the production of the product in question. Every industry has its own peculiar set of technical facts; for example, agriculture is dominated by the nature of land and manufacturing industry by capital. In agriculture, the marginal return starts diminishing early, whereas in a manufacturing industry, it starts diminishing very late, which a wise entrepreneur can altogether avoid. In some industries, the return may remain constant. This is all due to the technological peculiarities of each industry.

In agriculture, marginal return increases in the beginning but then decreases later, whereas in industry it continues increasing but may decrease if the industry is expanded too much. It is thus wrong to say that one law applies in one industry and another in another industry. The fact is that there is only one law, which applies everywhere, and which is properly called the Law of Variable Proportions. This law operates in all industries, although its different stages are to be found in different industries or its different stages are larger or shorter in different industries. In some industries, the stage of increasing marginal return finishes earlier and diminishing marginal return starts as in agriculture and, in some other industries, the stage of increasing marginal return is so long that the marginal return starts diminishing only when the scale of production is unduly enlarged as in the case of almost all manufacturing industries.

Fig. 14.3. Labour and capital.

The law of variable proportion occupies a very important place in economic theory. It describes the production function with one variable factor while the quantities of other factors of production are fixed. That is, it describes the input-output relation in a situation when the output is increased by increasing the quantity of one input, keeping the other inputs constant. When the quantity of one factor is increased and the quantities of the other factors of production are kept constant, naturally the proportion between the variable factors and the fixed factor is altered. That is, the ratio of the variable factor to that of the fixed factor goes on increasing as a quantity of the variable factor is increased. It is because in this law we study the effect on output of variations in factor proportion, this law is called the law of variable proportions. In fact, the law of variable proportions is the new name for the well-known law of diminishing returns.

Marshall, thought that there were three separate laws of production, *viz.*, the laws of diminishing, increasing and constant returns. The modern economists are of the view that these three laws are not three separate laws but are only three phases of one general law of variable proportions.

The law of variable proportions has been variously stated by the economists. In the words of Stigler, "As equal increments of one input are added, the inputs of other productive services being held constant, beyond a certain point the result in increment of product will decrease, *i.e.,* the marginal product will diminish." Professor Samuelson states the law thus, "An increase in some inputs relative to other fixed inputs will, in a given state of technology, cause output, to increase; but after a point the extra output resulting from the same additions of extra inputs will become less and less." Professor Benham also states the law almost in similar words, "As the proportion of one factor in a combination of factors is increased, after a point, first the marginal and then the average product of that factor will diminish."

It will be seen that these statements are really statements of the law of diminishing returns, which should be considered as an old name for the new law of variable proportions. Prof. Bounding considers that the expression 'diminishing returns' is a loose one, He, therefore, called it the law of Eventually Diminishing Marginal Physical Productivity. He defines the law thus, "As we increase the quantity of any one input which is combined with a fixed quantity of other inputs the marginal physical productivity of the variable input must actually decline."

Thus, we find from the statements of the law of variable proportions given above that this law relates to the behaviour of output as on the quantity of one factor is varied by keeping the quantities of the other factors constant. It states further that the marginal product and the average product of the factor kept constant will eventually diminish.

Assumptions of the Law of Variable Proportions

The law of variable proportions, as stated above holds true under certain conditions. The following are its main assumptions:

(*a*) It is assumed that the state of technology remains unaltered. It is obvious that improvements in technology are bound to raise the marginal and average product and they will not diminish as the law says.

(*b*) It is also assumed that of the various inputs employed in production at least some must be kept constant. This is so because only in this way we can change the factor proportions and find out its effects on the output. Hence, this law does not apply where all factors of production are proportionately varied. Behaviour of output when all inputs are varied comes under, 'returns to scale' which we shall discuss later.

(*c*) The law of variable proportions is clearly based upon the possibility of varying proportions in which the various factors are combined in production. It does not apply to cases where the factors have to be used in fixed proportions to yield fixed products. In cases where the various factors are to be used in rigidly fixed proportions, the increase in one factor would not lead to any increase in input, that is, the marginal product of the factor will be zero and not diminishing. But such cases are very uncommon and hence the law of variable proportions has almost a universal application.

14.4 AVERAGE-MARGINAL RELATIONS

When we study trends in marginal and average returns (or outputs) we can discover certain unique relationship between them:

(1) So long as the marginal return exceeds the average return (see columns 3 and 4 of Table 14.1), each new average return will be larger than the previous one, *i.e.,* the average output continues to increase. Conversely, if average output is rising, it can be safely concluded that the marginal output is larger than the output.

(2) When the marginal return goes below the average return, average output begins to decline. This is so, because the new marginal return, which is lower, brings down the average. That is, when the average product is decreasing, the marginal product is less than the average product.

(3) The average output remains constant when the marginal and average returns are equal. Conversely, if the average output remains constant, it can be inferred that the marginal output is also constant and the two are equal. Also, when the average product is maximum, marginal product equals average product. In such cases, the average and marginal curves coincide and they are horizontal, parallel to the X-axis.

14.5 LAW OF INCREASING RETURNS

Another aspect of the universal law of variable proportions is the law of increasing returns. An industry is subject to the law of increasing returns if extra investment in the industry is followed by more than proportionate returns, *i.e,* if the marginal product increases. In terms of cost, the law of increasing returns means the lowering of the marginal costs as industry is expanded. As marginal cost indicates price, we can say that the law of increasing returns operates in an industry if, with every expansion of its output, the price of the product falls.

These two laws of increasing and diminishing returns can also be explained in terms of the optimum business unit. We shall have increasing returns when we are moving towards the optimum and diminishing returns when we move beyond the optimum.

Why the Law of Increasing Returns Operates

We have already seen what economies can be reaped if the scale of production is increased. Advantages of specialization of labour and machinery and other commercial and miscellaneous economies make' it possible to lower the cost of production, and we have increasing returns.

Economies among the economies of mass production which contribute to greater productivity at less cost may be mentioned.

(*i*) Use of non-human and non-animal power resources (water and wind power, steam, electricity, atomic energy);

(*ii*) Automatic self-adjusting mechanism;

(*iii*) Use of standardized, interchangeable parts;

(*iv*) Breakdown of complex processes into simple repetitive operations;

(*v*) Specialization of functions and division of labour; and

(*vi*) Many other technological factors.

No Scarcity of Factors: The law of diminishing returns operates when there is dearth of an essential factor. But if there is no dearth, the law of increasing returns will operate. The expansion of an industry, provided that there is no dearth of suitable agents of production, tends to be accompanied, other things being equal, by increasing returns.

Right Combination: The law of diminishing returns operates when the factors have been combined in wrong proportions. Now when we try to correct the combination, increasing returns will follow till the balance is completely restored.

Full Use of Indivisible Factors: The concept of indivisibility, too, has a close bearing on the law of increasing returns. A manufacturer sets up a plant to cope with a peak demand, but in actual practice it may be producing below capacity. In that case, if an addition is made to some other factor or factors, the indivisible factor will be more fully employed, and increasing returns will follow.

14.6 LAW OF CONSTANT RETURNS

There can be a situation when neither the law of diminishing returns nor the law of increasing returns operates, but there is instead constant return. An industry is subject to the law of constant returns when, whatever the output or scale of production, the cost per unit remains unaltered, or increased investment of labour and capital results in a proportionate increase in the output.

Marshall pointed out that the part played by nature corresponded to diminishing returns and the part played by man to increasing returns. That is why in agriculture, where nature is said to be supreme, there is diminishing return. In manufacturing industries, where man's ingenuity has the fullest play in effecting all sorts of economies unhampered by external forces, there operates the law of increasing returns. It is conceivable that some industry may lie midway between the two, where neither there is diminishing return nor increasing return, but there is constant return.

Think of an industry where the raw materials, representing nature's part, account for the same proportion of the total cost as the manufacturing cost which is man's part. In such a case, the law of constant return will operate.

In every industry, the two opposite tendencies are at work. When it is expanded some costs rise and the others fall. It is possible that there may be an industry where these two tendencies just neutralize each other, and we have constant return. The example of an industry making blankets out of pure natural wool is sometimes given in this connection. It is said that the raw material (wool) is subject to diminishing returns, but this tendency is just counter-balanced by the economies in the manufacturing costs, and there is a constant return.

The concept of the optimum can help us to understand the operation of the laws of returns. We have said that movement towards the optimum means increasing returns, and the movement beyond it the diminishing returns. But, if we keep to the optimum, for however short a period it may be, we shall have constant returns.

14.7 RETURNS TO SCALE

Distinction between Laws of Returns and Returns to Scale

The laws of returns are often confused with 'returns to scale'. The two may be clearly distinguished. By "returns to scale" is meant the behaviour of production or returns when all the productive factors are increased or decreased simultaneously in the same ratio. In other words, in returns to scale, we analyze the effect of doubling, trebling, and quadrupling and so on of all the inputs of productive resources on the output of the product.

The returns to scale may clearly be distinguished from the Law of Variable Proportions. In the law of variable proportions, while some co-operating factors of production may be increased (or decreased), at least one factor (*e.g.,* land in agriculture or entrepreneur in industry) remains constant or cannot be increased, so that the proportion among the factors of production changes and we see how returns or output is affected by such changes in the supply of the productive resources. In returns to scale, on the other hand, all the necessary factors of production are increased/decreased to the same extent so that whatever the scale of production, the proportion among the factors remains the same.

Three Phases of Returns to Scale

A layman, uninitiated into the techniques of economic analysis, would perhaps expect that, with the doubling of all productive factors, the output would also double and with trebling of all factors of production, production would also be trebled, and so on. But actually this is not so. In other words, actually the output or returns do not increase/decrease strictly according to the change in the scale.

We know that in the case of the law of variable proportions, as we increase some of the co-operating factors, the marginal product or return increases at first, then stays constant and ultimately it starts diminishing. Similarly, when we increase the scale, *i.e.,* increase all the factors of production together to the same extent, the marginal product or return increases at first, *i.e.,* up to a point, then constant for some further increases in the scale of production is increased still further.

Table 14.2. Returns of scale.

S. No.	*Scale product*	*Total or returns (in quintals)*	*Marginal product (in quintals)*	
1	1 W + 3 A	2	2	Stage I: Increasing Returns
2	2 W + 6 A	5	3	
3	3 W + 9	9	4	
4	4 W + 12 A	14	5	
5	5 W + 15 A	19	5	Stage II: Constant Returns
6	6 W + 18 A	24	5	
7	7 W + 21 A	28	4	Stage III: Decreasing Returns
8	8 W + 24 A	31	3	
9	9 W + 27 A	33	2	

Note. 'W' stands for workers and 'A' stands for acres of land.

In other words, there are three distinct phases of, or stages in, the behaviour of the marginal product. Let us take a numerical example to explain the behaviour of the returns to scale.

In the Table 14.2 we see that, at the outset, when we employ one worker on 3 acres of land, the total product is 2 quintals. Now to increase output, we double the scale, but the total product increases to more than double (to 5 instead of 4 quintals) and when the scale is trebled, the total product increases from 5 quintals to 9 quintals—the increase this time being 4 quintals as against 3 in the previous case. In other words, the returns to scale have been increasing. If the scale of production is further increased, the marginal product remains constant up to a certain point and, beyond it, it (the marginal product) starts diminishing. In the table at Serial No.9, the marginal product or return falls to only 2 quintals.

Explanation

Now, we may try to explain why we get the above-mentioned three phases or stages, *i.e.,* what makes the returns to scale behave in the manner they do. The chief reason of this kind of behaviour is that when in the beginning, the scale of production is increased, increased division of labour becomes possible and is adopted and, as a result thereof, output increases rather rapidly. In the Table 14.2, when there is only one worker working on three acres of land, there is no scope for division of labour. When there are two workers instead and six acres of land, *i.e.,* the factors of production are doubled, there will be increased scope for division of labour and output not only doubles but increases still more and the returns to scale increase.

In this way, up to a certain point, the returns to scale will go on increasing until there is no further scope for division of labour. Beyond this point, the marginal product or the returns to scale will cease to increase and will remain constant for certain further increases in scale (*e.g.,* in the Table 14.2 when 5 workers and 15 acres of land are used instead of 4 workers and 12 acres of land, the marginal product remains 5 quintals as before; similarly for Serial No. 5 to Serial No .6).

But when scale is increased beyond Serial No. 6, the scope for division of labour is reduced with the result that the marginal return or product begins to decline. In short, the main underlying cause of the changing returns to scale is the possibility or otherwise of the division of labour or specialization.

However, it is very important to state here, that, in actual life, the scale of production cannot be increased beyond a certain limit. To increase the scale of production means that all factors being used in production can be increased at will and indefinitely. But it is not so in practice. While land, labour and capital can be increased at will, organization or enterprise does not increase, since the entrepreneur or organizer remains the same. In other words, there is at least one factor of production which cannot be varied at will, and, hence when more output is desired, the proportion among the factors of production used must change.

Hence, the returns to scale are more of theoretical interest than being relevant to actual life. In practice, it is the law of variable proportions, which is of universal application.

Returns to scale can also be explained with the help of iso product or equal product curves. This is explained in the next chapter.

Causes of Diminishing Returns to Scale

Diseconomies, both internal and external, account for the diminishing returns to scale.

(We have discussed these diseconomies in the previous chapter).

Self-Assessment Questions

1. State and explain the law of diminishing returns and indicate its significance in economic theory and policy.
2. 'The part played by nature conforms to diminishing returns while the part which man plays conforms to increasing returns". Critically examine this statement.
3. State the law of diminishing marginal returns and in this context explain the significance of indivisibility of factors.
4. Discuss the view that diminishing returns arise out of defective factor proportions.
5. What do you understand by optimum factor combination? Explain fully with the aid of indifference curves.
6. State clearly the law of variable proportions. Illustrate diagrammatically. How does it affect the supply curve?

   Or

   The laws of diminishing returns and increasing returns are two phases of the law of variable proportions. Discuss.
7. Explain the law of increasing returns. Do increasing returns necessarily lead to monopoly?

   Or

   How far are increasing returns compatible with competition?
8. Enunciate the law of constant returns and indicate the cases where it operates.
9. Explain the reasons for the operation of (*a*) the law of diminishing returns, and (*b*) diminishing returns to scale.
10. What is the difference between law of returns and returns to scale? Enumerate the factors that cause decreasing returns to scale.

Unit 15 ISOQUANTS OR EQUAL PRODUCT CURVES

15.1 INTRODUCTION

In recent years, a new technique has been developed to study the theory of production and to show the equilibrium of a producer regarding a combination of factors. This technique is of iso-product curves which are parallel concepts to the indifference curves in the theory of consumption.

Just as an indifference curve represents various combinations of two goods which give a consumer equal amount of satisfaction, similarly an iso-product curve also shows all possible combinations of the two inputs physically capable of producing a given level of output.

15.2 MEANING OF EQUAL PRODUCT CURVES

Since an iso-product curve represents those combinations which will allow the production of an equal quantity of output, the producer would be indifferent between them. Iso-product curves are, therefore, called product-indifference curves. They are also known as iso-quants or equal-product curves. Any point on the iso-quant is a recipe for the same output as any other point on the same curve.

The concept of equal-product curves can be easily understood from the Table 15.1. In this Table 15.1 assumed that two factors X and Y are being used to produce a given product.

Table 15.1. Equal product combinations.

Combinations	*Factor X*	*Factor Y*
A	1	12
B	2	8
C	3	5
D	4	3
E	5	2

To begin with, combination A, representing 1 unit of factor X and 12 units of factor Y, produces a given quantity (say, 40 units) of a product. All other combinations in the table are assumed to yield the same amount, *i.e.,* 40 units of the product. Thus, combination C representing 3X + 5Y, combination D representing 4X + 3Y and combination E having 5X + 2Y will all produce 40 units of the product. If we now plot all these combinations on a graph paper and join them, we shall get a continuous and smooth curve called iso-product curve on which are represented the various combinations A, B, C, D and E of Table 15.1. IP represents all those combinations with which 40 units of the product can be produced. The shape of the isoquants shows the degree of substitution between the two factors used in production. Indifference curves and iso-product curves can be distinguished. Though iso-product curves are similar to the indifference curves of the theory of demand, one important difference between them is worth noting. While an indifference curve shows all those combinations of two goods which provide equal satisfaction to a consumer, it does not tell us exactly how much satisfaction is derived by the consumer from those combinations. This is because utility or satisfaction being a mental phenomenon cannot be measured in absolute terms. Thus, there are no physical units in which satisfaction can be measured. That is why we label indifference curves as I, II, III, etc. showing that higher indifference curves provide greater level of satisfaction, but we cannot say how much greater the level of satisfaction is. On *the other hand we can* label iso-product curves in the physical units of the output produced without any difficulty. Production of a good being a physical phenomenon lends itself to absolute measurement in physical units.

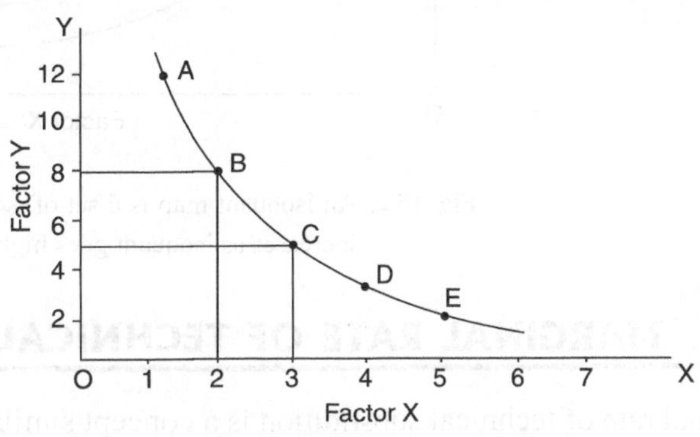

Fig. 15.1. An isoquant.

Moreover, if we draw an iso-product map showing various iso-product curves, it is possible to say by how much production is greater or less on one iso-product curve than on another.

We have drawn an iso-product map in Fig. 15.2 showing equal product curves IP, IP′, IP″ and IP‴, which represent 40 units, 60 units, 80 units, 100 units, of output respectively. Thus, iso-product curve IP′ represents an output 20 units greater than on iso product curve IP and iso-product curve IP‴ yields output 60 units greater than on IP. It is, therefore, possible not only to lable iso-product curves by physical units but also to judge how much greater or less is the size of the output on one iso-product curve than on another. This is an advantage.

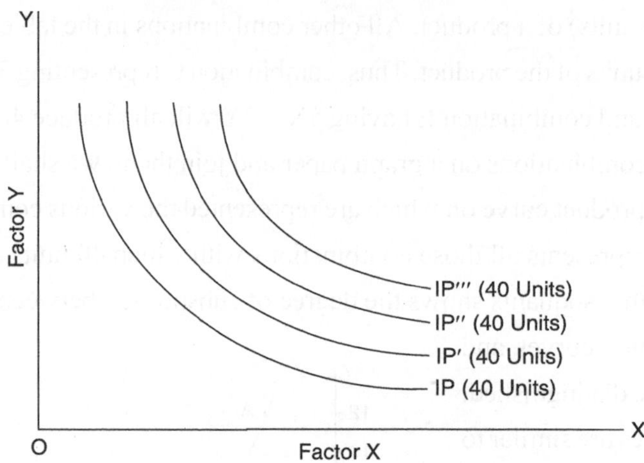

Fig. 15.2. An isoquant map is a set of isoquants. The output level increases as isoquant goes higher to the right.

15.3 MARGINAL RATE OF TECHNICAL SUBSTITUTION

Marginal rate of technical substitution is a concept similar to the marginal rate of substitution in the theory of demand. Marginal rate of technical substitution of X for Y is the number of units of factor Y which can be replaced by one unit of factor X, quantity of the output remaining unchanged. The concept of marginal rate of technical substitution can be easily understood from the Table 15.1. We reproduce below the same table to find out the marginal rate of technical substitution.

As mentioned earlier, in this table various combinations of factors X and Y yield output equal to 40 units of the product. From the comparison of combinations A and B, it will become clear that here 4 units of factor Y can be replaced by 1 unit of factor X without any change in output. Therefore, 4 : 1 is the marginal rate of technical substitution (MRTS) at this stage.

Table 15.2. Marginal rate of technical substitution.

Combination	*Factor X*	*Factor Y*	*MRTS of X for Y*
A	1	12	
B	2	8	4 : 1
C	3	5	3 : 1
D	4	3	2 : 1
E	5	2	1 : 1

Now by comparing combinations B and C, it will be found that 3 units of factor Y can be replaced by 1 unit of factor X without any loss of output. Therefore, here the marginal rate of technical substitution is 3 : 1. Similarly, the marginal rate of technical substitution between C and D is 2 : 1 and between D and E is 1 : 1. Algebraically, it can be stated that:

$$\text{MRTS} = \frac{X}{Y}$$

But $\frac{x}{y}$ shows the slope of a curve. Therefore, MRTS is the slope of the iso-product curve at a given point and can, therefore, be found out by tangent of the angle. The marginal rate of technical substitution at point R will be equal to the slope of the tangent DE. Slope of the tangent DE is equal to OD/DE. Hence, the marginal rate of technical substitution at point R will be equal to OD/DE. Likewise, marginal rate of technical substitution at point S of the iso-product curve will be OG/OH.

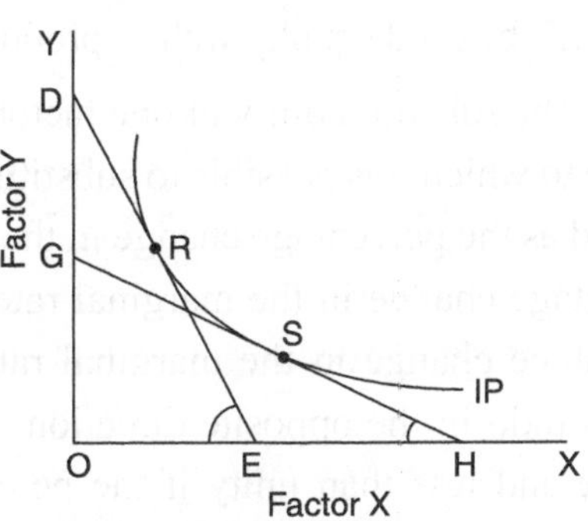

Fig. 15.3. Marginal rate of technical substitution.

Law of Diminishing Marginal Rate of Technical Substitution

An important feature of the marginal rate of technical substitution is worth noting. Marginal rate of substitution of X for Y will generally diminish as the quantity of X is increased relative to the quantity of Y. In other words, as the quantity of factor X is increased relative to the quantity of Y, the number of units of Y that will be required to be placed by one unit of factor X will diminish, quantity of the output remaining unchanged. This is known as the law of diminishing marginal rate of technical substitution which is only an extension of the law of diminishing returns to the relationship between the productivity of two factors.

As the quantity of factor X is increased, and the quantity of factor Y is decreased, the marginal productivity of X will diminish and marginal productivity of Y will increase and, therefore, less of Y will be required to be replaced by one unit of X to maintain the same level of output as more of X and less of Y is used.

Elasticity of Substitution between Factors

In the theory of demand, we explained the concept of elasticity of substitution between goods in the scheme of consumption of a consumer. That is, we explained to what extent one good could be substituted by a consumer for another good. In the theory of production, on the other hand, we are concerned with the factors of production instead of the commodities for consumption. Here we discuss to what extent a factor of production, say labour, can be substituted for another factor, say capital. That is, we are concerned with what may be called elasticity of technical substitution. Just as the marginal rate of substitution of commodity X for commodity Y falls as X is substituted for Y along an indifference curve, similarly the marginal rate of technical substitution (MRTS) of factor X for factor Y declines as factor X is substituted for factor Y along an iso-quant or equal product curve.

"The relative change in the factor-proportions (or input ratios) as a consequence of relative change in the marginal rate of technical substitution is known as elasticity of substitution between factors".

The rate at which the marginal rate of technical substitution falls is a measure of the extent to which the two factors can be substituted for each other. If they are perfect substitutes, that is, if either factor can be used equally well to produce the product, the marginal rate of substitution will not fall.

The substitutability of one factor for another depends on the elasticity of substitution, *i.e.,* the degree to which it is possible to substitute one factor for another. The elasticity of substitution can be defined as the percentage change in the rates of the factors used, say X and Y, in response to a given percentage change in the marginal rate of technical substitution. This elasticity is unity if a given percentage change in the marginal rate of technical substitution induces an equal change in the factors ratio in the opposite direction; it will be greater than unity if it induces greater percentage change and less than unity if the percentage change induced in the factors ratio is less than the percentage change in the MRTS. Thus,

$$\text{Elasticity of Substitution} = \frac{\text{I(X/Y)} \times \text{MRTS}}{\text{(I/IRTS) (X/Y)}}$$

A high elasticity of substitution means that the factors can be substituted freely for one another, while in the case of low elasticity they can be used only in definite proportions.

We can refer to the shape of isoquants or equal product curves to determine the magnitude of elasticity of substitution between factors. The measure of elasticity depends on the curvature of the isoquants. The greater the convexity of isoquant the less will be the substitution elasticity, and vice versa. In case the two factors are perfect substitutes of each other and the isoquants between them are straight lines, substitution elasticity between them is infinite. On the other hand, when the two factors are perfect complements and their isoquants are right angled, the substitution elasticity between them is zero. Besides, since there is an inverse relationship between the marginal rate of substitution and factor-ratio (*i.e.,* as the factor-ratio increases, the marginal rate of technical substitution falls), elasticity of substitution between factors is always negative.

The concept of elasticity of substitution also occupies an important place in the theory of distribution. It affects the distributive shares of the factors of production. For example, the relative shares of labour and capital will largely depend on the elasticity of substitution between them. If capital can be freely substituted for labour, the share of labour relative to the share of capital is bound to decline.

15.4 APPLICATION OF EQUAL PRODUCT CURVES

The iso-quant technique is applicable to agriculture and to all lines of manufacture. The marginal rate of technical substitution guides in the substitution of some units of one input for some units of another input, in some cases, increased use of labour can help in making a reduction in the use of raw materials, because spoilage and wastage of material may be cut to the minimum. Similarly, by adding to the supervisory staff, labour may be economized or the introduction of machinery may cut down the use of labour. In this way, the businessman tries various permutations and combinations and the iso-quant technique helps him in reaching the most economical combination.

Properties of Equal Product Curves

Properties of iso-product curves are the same as those of indifference curves. Their properties can also be proved in the same manner as in the case of indifference curves. The following are the important properties of iso product curves:

(*i*) **Sloping Downwards:** Iso-product curves slope downwards from left to right. This is so because if the quantity of a factor X is increased, the quantity of factor Y must be decreased so as to maintain the same level of output.

In Fig. 15.4 on *y*-axis K (capital) and *x*-axis 'L' (Labour) iso-quant are negative sloping that means as the increase in one more unit-of' L′ than we have to decrease certain amount of capital (K). Due to this the iso-quant curve slopes downward from left to right. In other words, it has a negative slope.

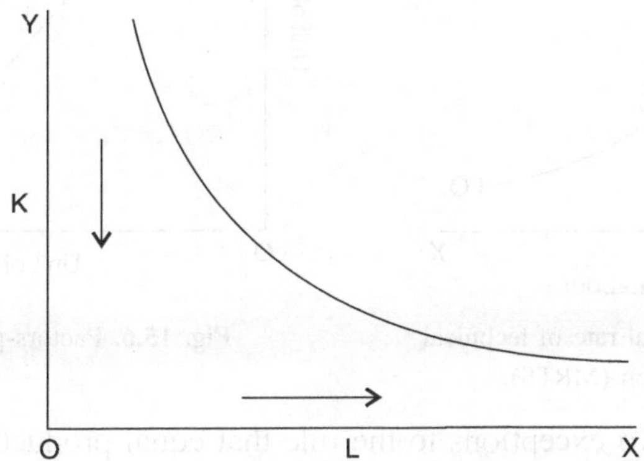

Fig. 15.4. Downward sloping isoquant.

Table 15.3. Marginal rate of technical substitution for labour and capital.

	Labour	—	*Capital*	*Marginal rate of technical substitution*
A	1	—	12	
B	2	—	8	1 : 4
C	3	—	5	1 : 3
D	4	—	3	1 : 2
E	5	—	2	1 : 1

(*ii*) **Convexity:** Iso-product curves are convex to the origin. This is due to the fact that marginal rate of technical substitution falls as more and more of X is substituted for Y. Iso-product curves being concave would mean that the marginal rate of technical substitution of X for Y increases as more and more of X is substituted for Y. But increasing marginal rate of technical substitution is not realistic. As explained above owing to the operation of the law of diminishing returns, the marginal rate of technical substitution falls as more and more substitution takes place.

MRTS = Marginal Rate of Technical Substitution

$$MRTS = \frac{\Delta K}{\Delta L}$$

ΔK = Change in Capital

ΔL = Change in Labour.

In the diagram it is clear that with the increase in unit of labour we have to reduce the unit of capital. Initially more and more capital and than less and less capital is substituted for each unit of labour. This gives us a 'convex' iso-quant curve.

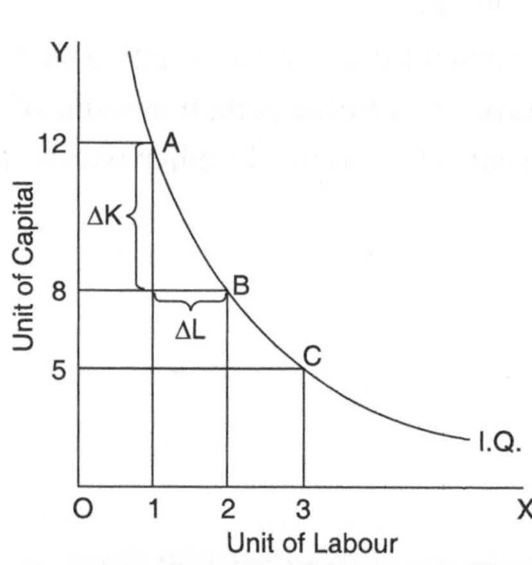

Fig. 15.5. Marginal rate of technical substitution (MRTS).

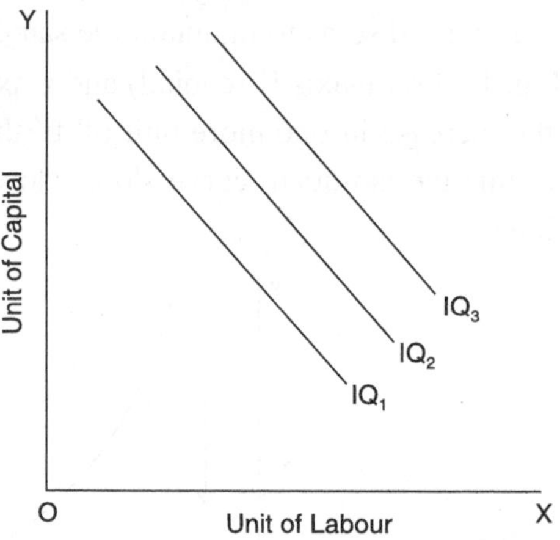

Fig. 15.6. Factors-perfectly substitute.

However, there are two exceptions to the rule that equal product curves are convex to the origin: In the curves there would be a common combination of factors which will lie on both these curves such as combination C in Fig. 15.7. It would then mean that the same combination C which yields 40 units of output according to one iso-product curve, can produce 60 units according to another iso-product curve. This is absurd. How can the same combination produce two different levels of output.

(*iii*) **The Iso-quant is an Oval-sloped Curve:** As we take the combination of an abundant factor say capital (K) with relatively less factor labour 'L', this indicates that the marginal productivity of the abundant factor say K is zero and the *vice versa.*

K_1, K_2, K_3 are tangent to Iso-quant IQ_1' IQ_2 and IQ_3' which shows that above this point the productivity of capital is zero. In the same way L_1' L_2' and L_3 are tangent to IQ_1' IQ_2 and IQ_3 which indicate beyond this point productivity of labour is zero. When we join K_1' K_2' K_3 and L_1' L_2' L_3 we get the ridge lines.

The 'Ridge Lines' are the loans of locus of points of iso-quant where marginal productivity of the concerned factor is zero. The ridge line indicates that the region outside the ridge lines are useless or uneconomic to the producer.

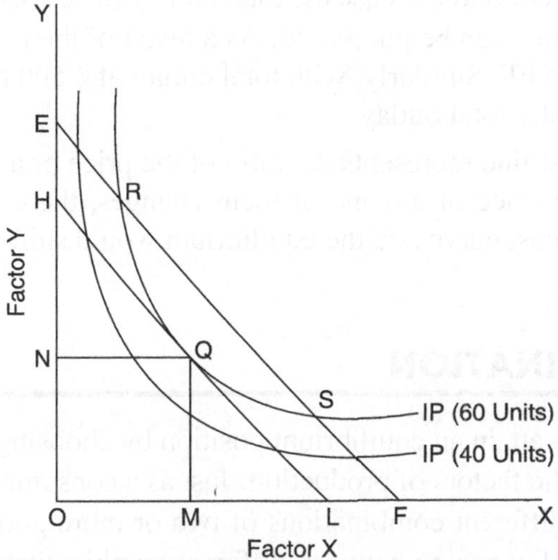

Fig. 15.7. Tangency between isoquant and lowest possible isocost line such as the point Q gives optimum combination of factors to minimum cost of production given the level of output.

15.5 ISO-COST LINE

The combination of factors with which a firm produces the product also depends on the prices of the factor and the amount of money which a firm wants to spend. Iso-cost line represents these two things—the prices of productive factors and the total amount of money which a firm wants to spend. Each iso-cost line will show various combinations of two factors which can be purchased with a given amount of total money.

Suppose a producer wants to spend ₹ 300 on factors X and Y. If the price of the factor Y is ₹ 3 per unit and if he spends the whole sum of ₹ 300 on it, then he can purchase 100 units of Y. Let OH in Fig. 15.8 represent 100 units of Y.

Now, if the price of X is ₹ 5 per unit and the whole sum of ₹ 300 is spent on it, 60 units of X can be purchased. Let OL in Fig. 15.8 represent 60 units of X.

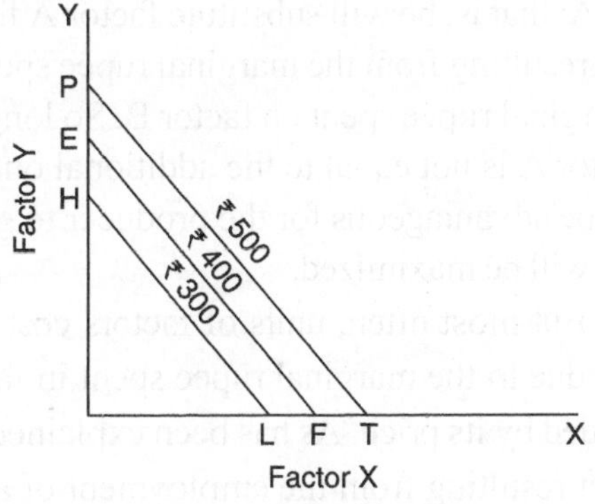

Fig. 15.8. Iso-cost lines.

If we now join together the points H and L, we shall get the iso-cost line HL on which will lie all those combinations of factors X and Y which can be purchased with ₹ 300. This line is called iso-cost line since the total cost or total money spent remains the same. Whatever the combination, which lies on it, is purchased. The iso-cost line is also known as price line or outlay line.

Now, if the producer decides to increase the total money to be spent on the productive factors to ₹ 400, more of both the factors can be purchased. As a result of the increase in the total outlay to ₹ 400, iso-cost line will shift to EF. Similarly, with total outlay of ₹ 500 the iso-cost line will be PT. Higher iso-cost will show greater total outlay.

The slope of the iso-cost line represents the ratio of the price of a unit input X to the price of a unit of input Y. In case the price of anyone of them changes, there would be a corresponding change in the slope of the iso-cost curve and the equilibrium would shift too producer's equilibrium optimum.

15.6 FACTOR COMBINATION

The producer will try to attain an equilibrium position by choosing at the most economical or the least cost combination of the factors of production. Just as a consumer is faced with the problem of making a choice between different combinations of two or more goods, similarly a producer is confronted with the problem of choosing between different combinations of two or more factors of production.

A rational entrepreneur would try to maximize his money profits from the production and sale of commodities, just as a consumer tries to obtain maximum satisfaction from the consumption of commodities. To produce a given output various combinations of factors of production are possible. But a rational producer or a firm would seek to produce that output with the 'optimum' or 'least-cost' combination of factors of production. (In Economics factors of production are also called 'inputs'.) The producing firm will use its productive resources in such proportions or such ratios that whatever the output produced, the cost outlay should be as small as possible for that output. Or, we can say that the firm should use that combination of resources which produces the maximum output for given cost outlay.

In arriving at an optimum or least cost combination, the producer is guided by the principle of substitution or that of equal marginal returns. If a rupee spent on factor A results in a greater output than a rupee spent on factor B, it would pay the producer to divert expenditure from factor B to factor A; that is, he will substitute factor A for factor B. He will be in equilibrium when the additional output resulting from the marginal rupee spent on factor A equals the additional output resulting from the marginal rupee spent on factor B. So long as the additional output due to the marginal rupee spent on factor A is not equal to the additional output resulting from the marginal rupee spent on factor B, it will be advantageous for the producer to go on substituting one factor for the other. In this way the output will be maximized.

But most often, units of factors cost much more than ₹ 1 each. In such cases, the additional output due to the marginal rupee spent in factor A would be equal to the marginal product of factor A divided by its price. As has been explained earlier, the marginal product of a factor is the additional product resulting from the employment of an additional unit of the factor. It, therefore, follows that the marginal product of a factor divided by the price of the factor is the additional product resulting from a rupee spent on the factor. Suppose the marginal product of a factor is 120 units of output and the price of the factor is ₹ 10 then, $120 \div 10 = 12$ *i.e.,* 12 is the additional output resulting from the marginal rupee spent on that factor.

The condition for the least – cost combination may, then, be put in the following form:

MPa / Pa = MPb / Pb = MPa / Pa

where MPa is the marginal product of factor A and Pa is the price of A, and so on. If

MPa / Pa is greater than MPb / Pb it will be to the advantage of the entrepreneur to employ more of factor A and less of factor B. He will employ more of one factor and less of the other till the above 'proportionality rule' is satisfied.

It is in this manner, that the firm is able to discover the least cost combination which means producing the maximum output with a given cost.

It will have been clearly understood that it is not the marginal products of the various factors that are sought to be equalized by the producer for maximizing output. What he seeks to equalize are the marginal products of the various factors divided by their respective prices. Of course, when the prices of all factors are equal, in that case alone will he seek to equalize the marginal products of the various factors? In that case, the denominators Pa' Pb Pn will all be equal to each other, so that all that the producer does is to attempt to equalize the numerators, *i.e.*, the marginal products of the various factors (MPa′ MPb . . . . . MPm)′. But seldom are the prices of the various factors equal to each other. We can use the iso-product curve technique also for this purpose.

15.7 PRODUCER'S EQUILIBRIUM WITH EQUAL PRODUCT CURVES

Iso-product curves show the various possible combinations with which a given level of output can be produced. Thus, iso-product curve shows the technical conditions of production. On the other hand, iso-cost lines represent total amount of outlay to be spent and the ratio of the prices of the two factors. Now the question arises: which combination of factors a producer will choose to produce a given level of output? In other words, at what point on the iso-product map the producer will be in equilibrium regarding the factors combination, given the level of output to be produced. This can be illustrated as shown in Fig. 15.9.

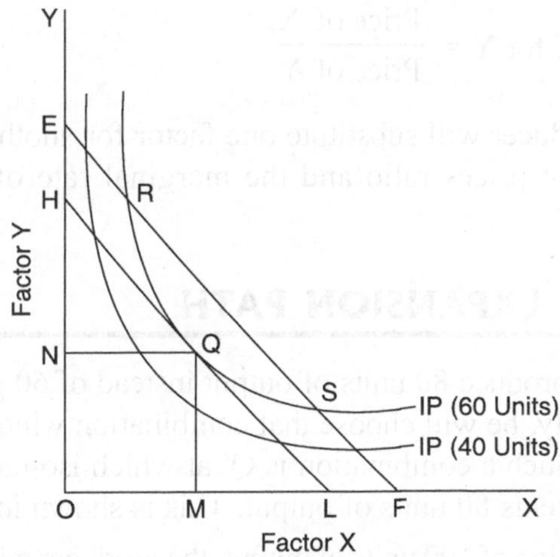

Fig. 15.9. Tangency between isoquant and lowest possible iso-cost line such as the point Q, gives optimum combination of factors to minimum cost of production given the land of output.

We assume that the producer wants to produce a given level of output as cheaply as possible, because in doing so his profits will be maximized. In other words, the producer will try to strike least cost combination of factors to produce a given level of output

Suppose a producer has decided to produce 60 units of a product. 60 units of the product can be produced by any of the combinations such as R, S, Q, which lie on the iso-product curve IP in Fig. 15.9. He will choose that combination on the iso-product curve IP which gives him the lowest cost of production for the production of 60 units of the product.

It will be clear that the producer will choose combination Q at which iso-cost line HL is tangent to the iso-product curve IP. Combination Q will cost the producer least for producing 60 units of output. The producer will not choose any other combination on iso-product curve IP' such as R, S, because all these lie on the higher iso-cost line (EF) than Iso-cost line HL and will, therefore, mean greater total outlay for producing 60 units of output. The producer will not go the left of Q, for he will not be able to produce 60 units of output by any combination which lies to the left of Q on IP′ .

Hence, we conclude that the producer will be in equilibrium by choosing the factor combination Q to produce 60 units of the output. Factor combination Q is an optimum factor combination for him to produce 60 units of output. This is so because factor combination Q will give him the lowest cost of production.

15.8 COINCIDENCE OF MRTS AND PRICE RATIO

It will be evident from Fig. 15.9 that at point Q marginal rate of technical substitution will be equal to the ratio of prices of the factors. Marginal rate of technical substitution is given by the slope of the iso-product curve and the price ratio of the factors is given by the slope of the iso-cost line. The slope of the iso-product curve IP′ and the iso-cost line HL are equal at the point of tangency Q, and the marginal rate of technical substitution (MRTS) will be equal to the price-ratio of factors X and Y at point Q.

Thus, at the point of equilibrium:

$$\text{MRTS of X for Y} = \frac{\text{Price of X}}{\text{Price of Y}}$$

This means that the producer will substitute one factor for another in search of the cheapest method of production until the prices ratio and the marginal rate of technical substitution are approximately equal.

15.9 SCALE LINE OR EXPANSION PATH

If now the producer wishes to produce 80 units of output instead of 60 units, which combination of factors will he select? Obviously, he will choose that combination which will cost him the least for producing 80 units of output. Such a combination is Q′ at which iso-cost line is tangent to the iso-product curve IP″ which represents 80 units of output. This is shown in Fig. 15.10.

Similarly, for the production of 100 units of output, the producer will choose factor combination Q″ and for 120 units of output his equilibrium will lie at Q‴. If points like Q, Q′, Q″, Q‴ are joined together, we get what is called scale line or expansion path.

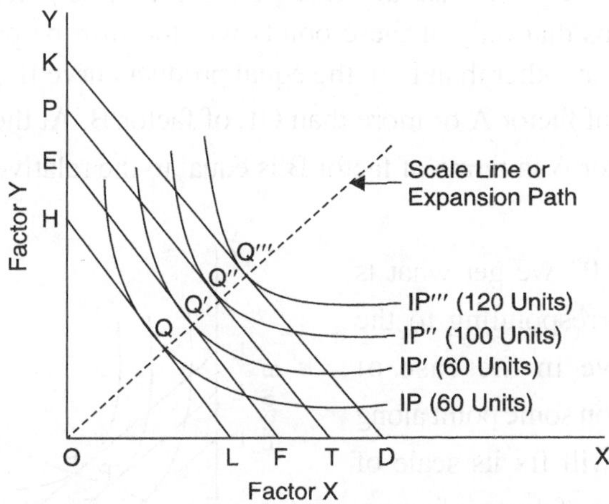

Fig. 15.10. Expansion path is the locus of various optimum combinations of factors given the factor prices.

This line is known as a scale line because it shows the way in which the producer will adjust the scale of his operations as he changes the scale of his output. This is also called expansion path as along this line he will expand his output, if relative factor prices remain the same. Given the prices of factors X and Y, a producer, who is able to vary the amounts of both these factors, will always fix his scale of output at some point along the scale line such as Q, Q′, Q″, Q‴. Producing on the scale line shows the cheapest way of producing each level of output, given relative factor prices.

An iso-quant or the equal product curve represents different input combinations, or input ratios which can produce a specified level of output, whereas the scale line shows different levels of output with input ratio remaining the same.

It must be noted that slope of the scale line will depend on the relative prices of the factors and the shape of the iso-product curves. One cannot know at which point on a scale line the producer will be in equilibrium until one knows that output he wishes to produce. How a producer will decide about the level of output to be produced by him will depend upon the conditions in the product market.

Application of Equal Product Curves to Returns to Scale

The equal product curves can be used to show how returns to factors of production will vary as the scale of production is varied. In Fig. 15.11, IP_0' IP_1' and IP_2 are the three equal product curves.

They constitute the firm's equal product map like an indifference map. Along the X-axis, we indicate factor A and along the Y-axis the factor B. We take here the returns with two variable factors. LM, L′ M′ and L″M″ are the price lines or outlay lines tangential to the respective equal product curves. In this situation, according to the proportionality rule

$$\frac{\text{Price of factor } a = OL = OL' = OL''}{\text{Price of factor } b = OM = OM' = OM''}$$

As in the case of indifference curves indicating the consumer's equilibrium, in this case also the producer will be in equilibrium position at the points P, P′ and P″ respectively on the equal product curves IP_0' IP_1' and IP_2' because at these points the price lines are tangential to their respective curves. This means that only at these points will the firm be producing in the cheapest manner. At any other point (say other than P on the equal product curve $IP_0)'$ the producer will have to use either more than OM of factor A or more than OL of factor B. At the points P, P′ and P″, the marginal productivity of factor A in terms of factor B is equal to the relative money prices of factors A and B.

By joining P, P′ and P″ we get what is known as the scale line corresponding to the income consumption curve in the case of indifference curves map. It is on some point along the scale line that the firm will fix its scale of output given the relative prices of the two factors. The scale line shows how a producer varies his scale of operations. It indicates the most economical combination of the factors of production or the cheapest way of producing each output. The shape of the equal product curves and the relative prices of the factors used will determine the shape of the scale line. Thus, the scale line shows the varying combinations of the factors of production as the scale of output is varied. A change in the relative prices of the factors will change the course of the scale line.

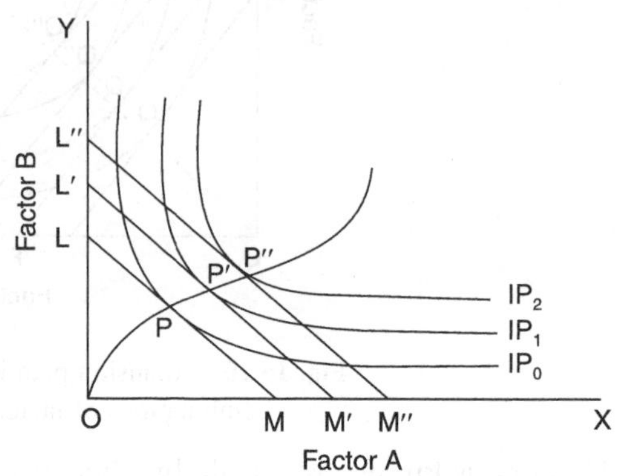

Fig. 15.11. Iso product curves and return to scale.

The equal product map like the one given above shows (*a*) whether the returns to scale will increase, decrease or remain constant as the scale of production is varied, and (*b*) whether the proportion between the factors of production employed will vary or remain constant as we move along the scale line.

Shape of the Scale Line

The following diagram (Fig. 15.12) shows how variations in the amounts of the factors used and in the output obtained determine the shape of the scale line. Suppose the return is constant so that doubling the amount of each factor results in doubling of the output, that is, a certain proportionate change in the amount of each factor used leads to the change in the output exactly in the same proportion.

In a situation like this, the scale lines will be straight through the origin. P′ Q′ R′ S′, PQRS and P″ Q″R″ S″ are the three straight scales lines. The returns to scale along each scale line on the equal product map are constant. This is shown by the fact that the distance between the three equal product curves along each scale line is the same, *i.e.*, OP = PQ = QR = RS and OP′ = P′ Q′ = R′ S′ and so on.

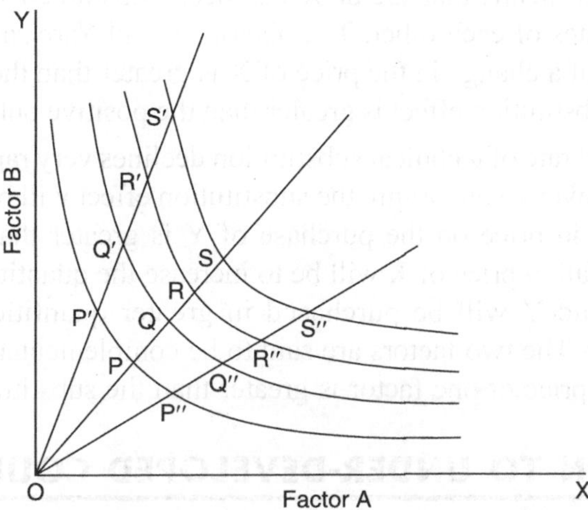

Fig. 15.12. Shape of the scale line.

In a diagram like this, given relative factor prices, *i.e.,* with a constant price slope, not only are the returns to scale constant but the returns to outlay are also constant. Similarly, the returns to scale and returns to outlay are interchangeable and the same.

But, if there is an equal product map where the relative prices are not constant and where the returns are not constant, the returns to scale and returns to outlay will not be the same. When as the output changes, the proportion between factors also changes, it will be necessary to speak of returns to outlay instead of returns to scale. However, here for the sake of convenience, we assume that proportion between the factors remains constant, whatever the scale of production.

15.10 EFFECT OF CHANGE IN INPUT PRICE ON INPUT USE

This effect is similar to what we discussed in the case of indifference curves and it can be illustrated diagrammatically in the same manner as price effect on consumer's equilibrium by indifference curves. The total effect on the use of the input of a change in its price is made up of two components: the substitution effect and the output effect. The substitution effect is the effect on the use of the input due exclusively to the change in the relative price of the inputs, the output remaining the same. This effect is invariably negative, because a rise in the price of an input must lead to a reduction in its use and a fall in price to its greater use. The output effect indicates the effect on input use due to change in the level of output, the input price remaining unchanged. This effect, too, is always negative, because increase in cost reduces both the output, and *vice versa.*

15.11 SUBSTITUTE AND COMPLEMENTARY FACTORS

Just as some goods are substitutes and complementary goods for others, similarly substitute and complementary relationship can be found to exist among factors of production. We have said above that if a factor X becomes cheaper relatively to factor Y, there will be a tendency to buy more of X and less of Y. This in effect means that factor X has been substituted for factor Y. In this case factors X and Y are substitutes of each other. Two factors X and Yare said to be substitutes when the substitution effect on Y of a change in the price of X is greater than the output effect on it. This is so because the negative substitution effect is greater than the positive output (or expansion) effect.

But when the marginal rate of technical substitution declines very rapidly (*i.e.*, when the equal product curves are highly convex to the origin, the substitution effect will be very small. In this case, the output effect of the fall in price on the purchase of Y is greater than the substitution effect. Hence, the net effect of the fall in price of X will be to increase the quantity purchased of Y also. In this case, both factors X and Y will be purchased in greater quantities. This means they are complements of one another. The two factors are said to be complementary to each other when the output effect of a fall in the price of one factor is greater than the substitution effect.

15.12 APPLICATION TO UNDER-DEVELOPED COUNTRIES

The theory of production is not a dry and abstract theory having little relevance to practical problems. It has a special significance for the under-developed countries which are faced, like others, with factor proportions problem. These countries have excessive rural population dependant on agriculture where their marginal productivity is practically nill. That is, if a sizeable proportion of them is withdrawn, it would not significantly affect output. Such countries are characterized by 'structural disequilibrium at the factor level' as Kind learner puts it. There is obviously a need for the adoption of more labour-intensive methods than capital-intensive methods. The factor combinations should embody high labour capital ratios. As economic development proceeds, the composition of demanded goods will change, calling for a change in factor proportions in the processes of production.

Self-Assessment Questions

1. What are iso-product curves? Explain their characteristics.
2. What is the significance of tangency between an Isoquant and an iso-cost line?
3. Show with the help of curves that different combinations of two factors of production give the same output (iso-product). Explain the characteristics of the curves drawn.
4. Given the iso-product curve of a firm and the prices of the two inputs it uses, find the condition that the firm must fulfil to produce (*i*) a given output at the least possible cost, and (*ii*) the largest output at a given total cost.

Unit **16**

COST AND COST CURVES

16.1 INTRODUCTION

The cost of production of an individual firm operating in a market has an important influence on the market supply of a commodity. It is very necessary to have a clear idea about the concept of cost of production and then proceed to study the cost curves.

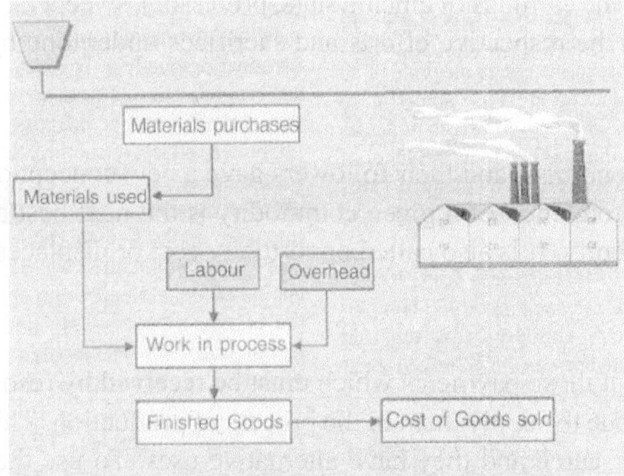

Fig. 16.1. Costs arise in the production process.

16.2 NOMINAL AND REAL COST

Money Cost

The cost may be nominal cost or real cost. Nominal cost is the money cost of production. It is also called expenses of production. These expenses are important from the point of view of the producer. He must make sure that the price of the product, in the long-run, covers these expenses including normal profit; otherwise he cannot afford to carry on the business.

Real Cost

Attempts have been made to "pierce the monetary veil" and to establish cost on a real basis. The real cost of production has been variously interpreted. Adam Smith regarded pains and sacrifices of labour as real cost. Marshall includes under it "real cost of efforts of various qualities" and "real cost of waiting." This is called the social cost by Marshall.

From the point of view of the community, as a whole, the money costs do not tell the whole story. It is the real cost which is more important.

Money Cost and the Real Cost do not Coincide

It is very seldom that the real cost of a commodity may be equal to the money cost. As Marshall puts it, "If the purchasing power of money in terms of effort remained about constant, and if the rate of remuneration for waiting has remained about constant, then the money measure of costs corresponds to real costs; but such a correspondence is never to be assumed lightly."

Thus, there is very little connection between money costs and real costs. The two can never be equal in a world of change, as our world is, whether we consider the long period or the short period. The value of land depends on scarcity. The question of cost in terms of effort and sacrifice in this case does not arise. The earnings of cinema stars, professors, sweepers, peasants, businessmen; etc. seldom correspond to the respective efforts and sacrifices undergone by each class.

Opportunity Cost

The Austrian school of economists and their followers gave a new concept of real costs. According to them, the real cost of production of a given commodity is the next best alternative sacrificed in order to obtain that commodity. It is also called opportunity cost or displacement cost.

Economic Costs

By economic costs is meant those payments which must be received by resource owners in order to ensure that they will continue to supply them in the process of production. This definition is based on the fact that resources are scarce and they have alternative uses. To use them in one process is to deny their use in other processes. Economic cost includes normal profit.

Implicit and Explicit Costs

Costs of production have also been classified as explicit and implicit costs. Implicit costs are costs of self-owned and self-employed resources such as salary of the proprietor or return on the entrepreneur's own investment. These costs are frequently ignored in calculating the expenses of production.

Explicit costs are the paid-out costs, *i.e.,* payments made for productive resources purchased or hired by the firm. They consist of the salaries and wages paid to the employees, prices of raw and semi-finished materials, overhead costs and payments into depreciation and sinking fund accounts. These are a firm's accounting expenses.

If we add to the money expenses two items, viz. alternative or opportunity costs and normal profits, we get the full costs of a firm as distinguished from business costs which are synonymous with a firm's total money expenses as computed by ordinary accounting methods. The entrepreneur must be sure of normal profit if he is to continue in business. In this sense normal profit too is a cost.

16.3 ALTERNATIVE, OPPORTUNITY OR TRANSFER COSTS

In modern economic analysis, the term real cost is interpreted in the sense of opportunity cost or transfer cost. The American economist Davenport explains this concept as follows: "Suppose, for example, that a child has been given both a pear and a peach, that some predatory boy tries to seize them and that the only method of saving either is to drop one, say the pear, in the wayside weeds, and to run for shelter with the peach while the aggressor is picking up the pear. What has the peach cost? True, the peach was a gift. In a certain sense, therefore, it costs nothing. Nevertheless it is retained only on terms of foregoing the pear. The term cost seems not quite satisfactory to cover the case. Perhaps displacement would be preferable. Or, if one offers you choice between a ride and an evening at the theatre, it is awkward to say that the acceptance of one is at the cost of the other. Yet the resistance of taking one is the letting go of the other. Or, if with a dollar which you have earned you have a choice between buying a book, or a pocket knife, and finally buy the book, the resistance overcome is best expressed, not by the labour devoted to the earning of the dollar, and not by the dollar itself, but by the alternative application of the dollar. The highest cost of the book—the best test or measure of its worth to you was in the significance of its strongest competitor, the knife."

Since productive resources are limited, the production of one commodity can only be at the expense of another. The commodity that is sacrificed is the real cost of the commodity that is produced. In the words of Henderson, "Real cost of anything is the curtailment of the supply of other useful things, which the production of that particular thing entails. Economists define costs of production of a particular product as the value of the foregone alternative products that resources used in its production could have produced. The costs of resources to a firm are their values in their best alternative uses."

Suppose with a sum of ₹ 1000 a manufacturer can produce two radio sets or a small refrigerator. Suppose further that he decides to produce the refrigerator rather than the radio sets. In this case, the real cost of the refrigerator is equal to the cost of two radio sets, *i.e.*, the alternative foregone. Conceived on these lines, cost of production means not the effort and sacrifices undergone, but the most attractive alternative foregone or the next best choice sacrificed. Real costs are thus not entities, ultimate and independent of utility, but they are sacrifices of competing demands.

In a money economy, it is "the amount of money necessary to induce the factors of production to be devoted to this particular task rather than to seek employment elsewhere."

Significance of Opportunity Costs

There are competing demands (depending upon the marginal utility of the consumers) for the same resources. Since the resources are scarce, certain demands are satisfied only by the sacrifice of other demands. The resources tend to move from those uses in which their demand price (marginal utility to the consumers in the aggregate) is lower to those in which it is higher until they tend to be distributed in various uses (for the production of various commodities and services) in such a way as to equalize their marginal utilities in the various uses.

It is thus the demand price or marginal utility which determines how much of a particular factor of production will be utilized for the production of a particular commodity. The supply of a commodity, therefore, ultimately depends upon the attraction offered by the demand price (or marginal utility) to the relevant factors of production. If this demand price is not high enough, these factors will be used for the production of commodities the demand price for which is high enough to attract them.

Thus, the cost of production of a commodity is fundamentally the sum-total of retention prices that have to be paid to the productive services for retaining them in a particular industry, and this must at least be equal to what they can command elsewhere.

Application of Opportunity Cost Doctrine

The opportunity cost doctrine has a wide application in the field of economic theory. It applies to the determination of values both internally and internationally. It also applies to income distribution.

Limitations: There are, however, some limitations in its application:

(*i*) *Specific:* It does not apply to productive services which are specific. A specific factor has no alternative use. Its transfer cost or opportunity cost is, therefore, zero. Hence, the payment made to this factor is of the nature of rent (preferably called non-cost outlays).

(*ii*) *Inertia:* Further, the doctrine of opportunity cost does not take into consideration the element 01 inertia. The factors may be reluctant to leave an occupation. In a case like this, where a factor's preference may have to be overcome, a payment exceeding the purely transfer cost will have to be made to induce it to an alternative occupation.

(*iii*) *Non-pecuniary considerations:* In view of these non-pecuniary considerations, the notion of objective costs must be given up. The theory of opportunity costs can be re-stated thus: "The cost of productive service X in making A is equal to the amount B that X could produce plus (or minus) the non-pecuniary returns (or cost) attached to producing B. It has been suggested that non-pecuniary returns should be converted into pecuniary returns to restore objectivity to the theory. But it is not always possible to find a common monetary denominator for the purpose.

(*iv*) *Factors not homogeneous:* Besides, it should be remembered that units of productive service are rarely homogeneous. This obstructs their transfer.

(*v*) *Wrong assumption:* Moreover, the theory is based on perfect competition which seldom exists.

(*vi*) *Individual and social costs:* Another discrepancy may arise on account of their difference in individual and social costs. A product may cost the factory owner ₹ 10 but to the society it will cost something in the form of ill-health due to the smoke that his factory emits.

Conclusion

Inspite of all these limitations and complications, the theory of cost, viz., theory of opportunity or alternative costs, is the most acceptable one at present. Certain features of this theory are worth noting:

(*i*) Cost of production of a commodity depends on demand prices of other commodities to the production of which the same productive service can contribute.

(*ii*) This cost analysis is not vitiated by the fact that a commodity is produced by the combination of several factors because marginal product of each factor can be ascertained.

16.4 SOCIAL COST

It is the amount of cost the society bears due to industrialization. Industrialization has certain economic and social merits, but along with the merits, they bring about certain demerits also. They are like, development of slums, air-pollution, noise pollution, land pollution, social inequalities, and so on. The amount of cost the society bears due to industrialization is referred as social cost. Bhopal gas tragedy is one of the major examples of social cost. People suffer from certain diseases for which the government has to incur heavy expenditure on health care and research.

16.5 ENTREPRENEUR'S COST

In what follows, we shall use the term 'cost of production' in the sense of money cost or expenses of production. This is entrepreneur's cost.

The entrepreneur's cost of production includes the following elements: (*i*) wages of labour; (*ii*) interest on capital; (*iii*) rent or royalties paid to the owners of land or other property used; (*iv*) cost of raw materials; (*v*) replacement and repairing charges of machinery; (*vi*) depreciation of capital goods; and (*vii*) profits of the manufacturer sufficient to induce him to carry on the production of the commodity.

Entrepreneur's costs may be classified as—(*i*) production costs, including material costs, wage costs, interest costs, etc., both direct and indirect costs; (*ii*) selling costs, including costs of advertising and salesmanship; (*iii*) managerial costs; and (*iv*) other costs, including insurance charges, rates, taxes, etc.

16.6 SHORT-RUN AND LONG-RUN COST CURVES

After discussing the concept of cost as used in economics, we are now in a position to study the nature of cost curves, both in the Short-Run and the Long-Run. The shape of the cost curve shows how a change in output affects the costs. There will be a shift in the cost curve, if factors, other than a change in output, have affected the costs.

Meaning of Short-Run and Long-Run

Short-Run is a period of time within which the firm shows its output by varying only the amount of variable factors, such as labour and raw materials. In the Short-Run, fixed factors, such as capital equipment, top management personnel, etc., cannot be varied. In other words, in the Short-Run, the firm cannot build a new plant or abandon an old one. If the firm wants to increase production in the Short-Run, it can do so only by overworking the existing plant, by hiring more workers and buying more raw materials. It cannot increase its output in the Short-Run by enlarging the size of its existing plant or building a new plant of a larger size. The Short-Run is a period of time in which only variable factors can be varied, while fixed factors remain the same.

On the other hand, Long-Run is a period of time during which the quantities of all factors, variable as well as fixed, can be adjusted. Thus, in the Long-Run output can be increased by increasing capital equipment or by increasing the size of the existing plant or by building a new plant of a greater productive capacity.

Fig. 16.2. Social cost due to air pollution.

Short-Run Fixed and Variable Costs

The cost of production for the entrepreneur may be analyzed from another point of view. Some costs vary more or less proportionately with the output, while others are fixed and do not vary with the output in the same way. The former are known as prime costs and the latter as supplementary costs of production or overhead costs.

The supplementary or fixed costs must be paid even though production has been stopped temporarily. They include rent of the factory building, interest on capital invested in machinery, and salaries of the permanently employed staff.

The prime costs, on the other hand, are variable costs. They vary with output. These costs include the cost of raw materials used in the making of the commodity as well as the costs of casual or daily labour employed. They are incurred only when the factory is operating.

The distinction between variable and fixed costs applies only to a short period. Nothing can remain fixed for a long time. In the long-run, the staff would change, amount of capital invested would be different, the dimensions of the factory, too, may change, and so on.
Hence, in the very long run, all costs are variable.

Total Fixed Cost: Total cost is the sum of:

Table 16.1. Cost of production of a firm.

Units of output	*Total fixed cost*	*Total variable cost*	*Total cost (2) + (3)*	*Average fixed cost (2) ÷ (3)*	*Average variable cost (3) ÷ (1)*	*Average cost (5) + (6)*	*Morginal cost*
(1)	(2)	(3)	(4)	(5)	(6)	(7)	(8)
0	30	0	30	—	—	—	—
1	30	10	40	30	10	40	10
2	30	18	48	15	9	24	8
3	30	24	54	10	8	18	6
4	30	32	62	7.5	8	15.5	8
5	30	50	80	6	10	16	18
6	30	72	102	5	12	17	22

Fixed cost (factory land, building and machinery…..)

Plus the total variable cost (raw material charges, electricity…)

$$TC = TFC + TVC$$

Total fixed cost = Total fixed cost + Total variable cost

$$AFC = \frac{TFC}{Q}$$

$$\text{Average fixed cost} = \frac{\text{Total fixed cost}}{\text{Quantity}}$$

$$AVC = \frac{TFC}{Q}$$

$$\text{Average variable cost} = \frac{\text{Total variable cost}}{\text{Quantity}}$$

$$\text{Average cost} = \frac{\text{Total cost}}{\text{Quantity}} = \frac{TC}{Q}$$

Or

Average cost = Average fixed cost + Average variable cost

$$AC = AFC + AVC$$

$$\text{Marginal cost} = \frac{\text{Change in total cost}}{\text{Change in quantity}}$$

$$MC = \frac{C}{Q}$$

The total cost function is:

$$C = 15x - 6x^{-2} + x^3$$

whereas 'x' is output and 'c' is total cost

1. Find out the following:

(*a*) Average cost function

$$\text{Average cost} = \frac{\text{Total cost}}{\text{Quantity}}$$

$$AC = \frac{TC}{x}$$

$$AC = \frac{15x - 6x^2 + x^3}{x} = 15 - 6x + x^2$$

(*b*) Minimum 'AC' or when is AC (Average cost) is minimum.

2. (*i*) For the 'AC' to be minimum, first derivation should be equal to zero, that means:

$$\frac{d}{dx}(AC) = 0$$

$$\frac{d}{dx}(15 - 6x - x^2) = 0$$

$$-6 + 2x = 0$$

$$2x = 6$$

$$x = 3$$

(*ii*) The second derivation of 'AC' should be greater than zero

$$\frac{d}{dx}(f) = -6 + 2x > 0 + 2 > 0$$

Hence, the condition is satisfied, where $x = 3$ 'AC' is minimum

(*c*) What is minimum 'AC'

substitute in 'AC' $= 15 - 6x + x^2$, the value of $x = 3$

$15 - 6 \times 3 + (3)^2$

$15 - 18 + 9$

$24 - 18 = 6$

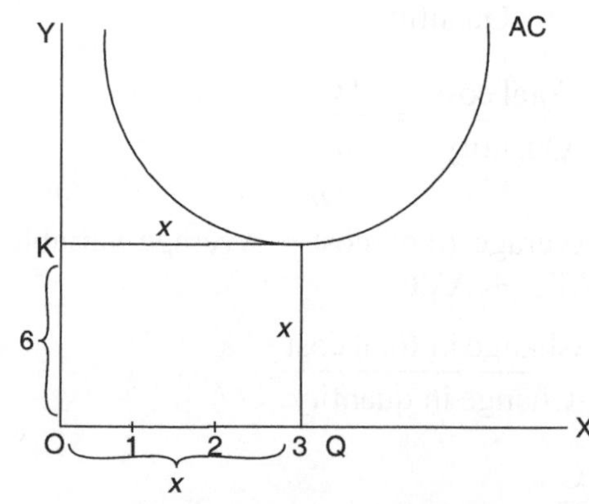

Fig. 16.3. Average cost is the cost per unit of output the AC is a 'U' shaped curve.

(*d*) Marginal cost function

Marginal cost function is obtained by taking the derivation of the total cost function.

$$TC = 15x - 6x^2 + x^3$$

$$\frac{d}{dx}(TC) = 15x - 6x^2 + x^3$$

$$MC = 15 - 12x + 3x^2$$

(*e*) When is the marginal cost the minimum? for 'MC' to be minimum the first derivation of 'MC' should be equal to zero.

(*i*) $$\frac{d}{dx}(MC) = 15 - 12x + 3x^2$$

$$-12 + 6x = 0$$

$$6x = 12$$

$$x = 2$$

(*ii*) The second derivation of 'MC' should be greater than zero.

$$= -12 + 6x$$

$$\frac{d}{dx}(MC)\, f'' = -12 + 6x + 6 > 0$$

Thus the condition is satisfied.

(*iii*) How much is marginal cost?

$$15 - 12x + 3x^2$$

When $x = 2$, marginal cost is minimum

$$15 - 12x + 3x^2$$

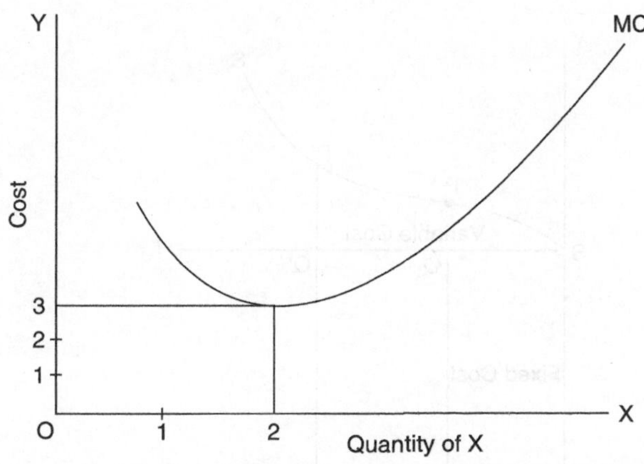

Fig. 16.4. Marginal cost curve is also U shaped.

It depicts the slope (1st derivative) of total cost curve.

Substitute $x = 2$

$$15 - 12 \times 2 + 3 \times (2)^2$$
$$15 - 24 + 12$$
$$\therefore \quad 27 - 24 = 3$$

where $x = 2$, Marginal cost = 3, that is, the 'MC' is minimum.

(*f*) When are average cost and marginal cost equal? At the point of minimum 'AC' 'MC' cuts 'AC' and that is the point when AC = MC.

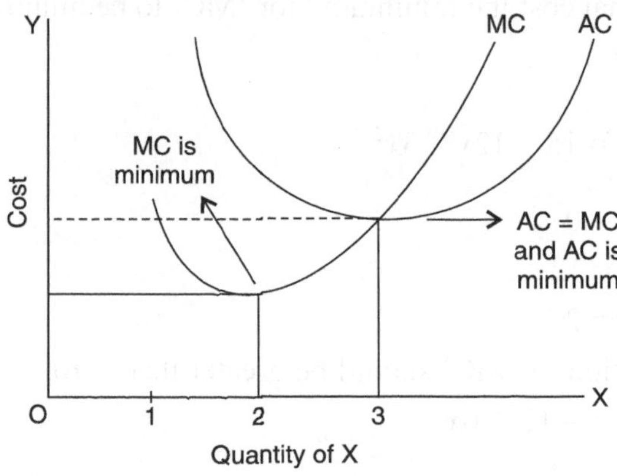

Fig. 16.5. Average and marginal cost.

When $x = 3$, AC is minimum, at the same point 'MC' is cutting 'AC', thus AC = MC when $x = 3$.

Short-run: Total, Average and Marginal Costs

Total cost of a given output is the sum of total fixed cost and total variable cost. As far as the total fixed cost is concerned, it remains constant for all units of output, but we have to incur more variable

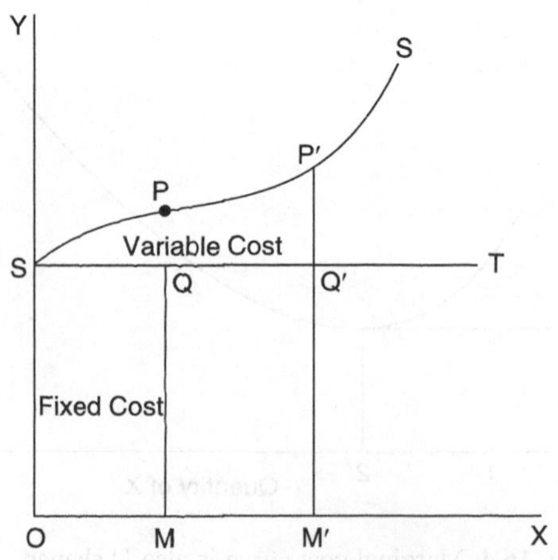

Fig. 16.6. Total cost: fixed and variable in the short seen.

costs when output increases. Total variable cost is zero, when output is zero and it increases with an increase in output, though the rate of increase is not constant. At first it increases rapidly but, then, due to economies of larger production, it does not increase as fast as before, thought it jumps up rapidly at a later stage (when output increases from 4 units to 5 units) due to diseconomies that set in.

In Fig. 16.6 SS is the total cost curve. It includes the total fixed cost (the distance between the curve ST and X-axis) and the total variable cost (represented by the distances between the curves SS and ST).

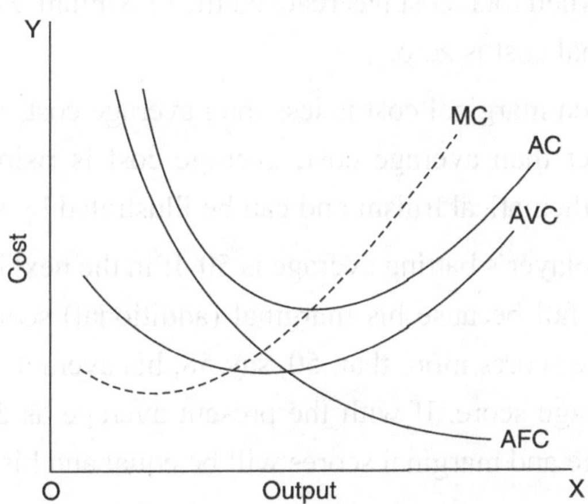

Fig. 16.7. Average and marginal cost in the short seen.

Average cost per unit is the total cost divided by the number of units produced. It is the sum of average fixed cost and the average variable cost. In Fig. 16.7, we have drawn both the average fixed cost curve and the average variable cost curve. The total fixed cost being fixed for all units of output, average fixed cost is a falling curve in the shape of a rectangular hyperbola. Average variable cost curve (AVC) at first falls and then rises, as there emerge the diseconomies of large production.

By adding the two costs, average fixed and average variable, we get the average cost (AC) per unit of output. At first, the average cost is high due to large\fixed cost and small output. As output increases, the fixed cost is thinly spread over the larger number of units produced, and the average cost accordingly falls. This is due to the various internal economies and the fuller use of indivisible factors. But when diminishing returns set in due to difficulties of management and limitations of plants and space, the variable costs, and therefore, the average costs, start increasing. The lower end of the curve turns up and gives it a V-shape. That is why average cost curves are *y*-shaped.

Marginal cost is the addition to total cost caused by a small increment in output. Marginal cost may be defined as the change in total cost resulting from the unit change in the quantity produced. Thus, it can be expressed by the formula:

$$\text{MC} = \frac{\text{Change in Q}}{\text{Change in TC}}$$

Marginal cost curve (MC) in Fig. 16.7 also falls at first due to more efficient use of variable factors as output increases and then it slopes upward as further additions to the output interfere with the most efficient use of the variable factors.

Relation between Marginal and Average Costs: It can be seen that average variable cost continues to decline so long as the marginal cost is below it but it starts rising at the point where MC crosses AVC. The marginal cost will always rise more sharply than the average variable cost. Similar relation holds between marginal cost and average cost.

Total Marginal Cost Relationship: When total cost is increasing at an increasing rate, its corresponding marginal cost is rising; when total cost is increasing at a decreasing rate, its corresponding marginal cost is falling; and when total cost has reached the maximum, *i.e.,* it is increasing at a zero rate, its corresponding marginal cost is zero.

It will be seen that when marginal cost is less than average cost, average cost is falling, and when marginal cost is greater than average cost, average cost is rising. This marginal-average relationship is a matter of mathematical truism and can be illustrated by a simple example.

Suppose that a cricket player's batting average is 50. If in the next innings, he scores less than 50, say 44. His average will fall because his marginal (additional) score is less than his average score; if in the next innings he scores more than 50, say 58, his average will rise because marginal score is greater than his average score. If with the present average as 50, in the next innings, he scores just 50, then his average and marginal scores will be equal and his average score will neither rise nor fall.

In the same way, let us suppose that the average cost of a producer is ₹ 15. If by producing another unit. his average cost falls, the additional (marginal) unit must have cost him less than ₹ 15. If the production of the additional unit raises his average cost, the marginal unit must have cost him more than ₹15. And, finally, if his average cost remains unchanged, the marginal unit must have cost him exactly ₹ 15. In other words, in the third case, his marginal and average costs are equal.

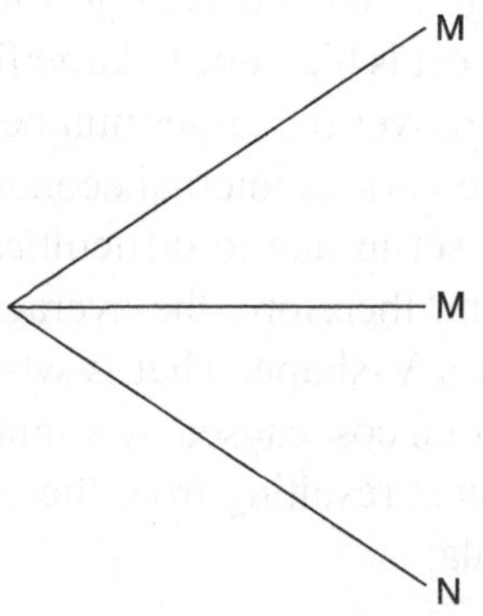

Fig. 16.8. Average and marginal relationship.

In Fig. 16.8, a represents average cost and M represents marginal cost. It is clear from this figure that when marginal cost is above (greater than) average cost, average cost rises. It is as if marginal cost were pulling average cost up towards itself. Similarly, when marginal cost is below the average cost, average cost falls as if the marginal cost were pulling the average cost downwards. When marginal cost is the same as the average cost, average cost remains constant as if marginal cost were pulling average cost along horizontally.

We can see in Fig. 16.8 that so long as marginal cost curve lies below the average cost curve, the latter is falling, and where marginal cost curve lies above the average cost curve, the average cost curve is rising. Therefore, at the point of intersection, where marginal cost equals average cost, average cost curve has just ceased to fall but has not yet begun to rise. This, by definition, is the minimum point on the average cost curve.

It must be carefully understood that we cannot deduce about the direction in which marginal cost is moving from the way average cost is changing, that is, we cannot make any generalization about whether marginal cost will be rising or falling when average cost is rising or falling. If average cost curve is falling, marginal cost must be below it but it (MC curve) may itself be rising or falling. If average cost curve is rising, marginal cost curve must be above it, but it (MC curve) may itself be rising or falling. This can also be easily understood with the example of batting average.

Suppose that a player's batting average is 60. In his next innings he scores 54, his average score will fall to 57. But his present marginal score of 54 may well be greater than his previous marginal score. He might, for instance, have had a 'duck' in his previous innings so that his marginal score has risen considerably. But as long as average score is falling, marginal score whether rising or falling will be less than average score.

Deriving Marginal and Average Cost Curves from total Cost Curve: In Fig. 16.9, SS is the total cost curve. To get the average and marginal cost for a given point P on the total cost curve, we proceed as follows:

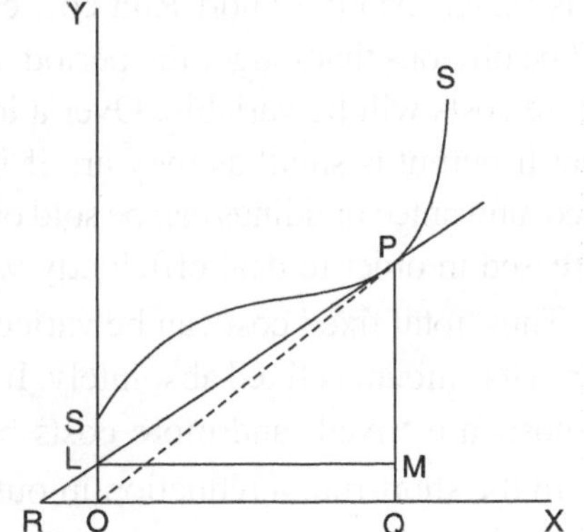

Fig. 16.9. Derivation of AC and MC curves from the total cost curves.

Draw a straight line from P to the origin O. Then average cost at the point P equals the value of tangent of the angle (POX) that the straight line makes with the X-axis. In this figure, it is equal to PQ/OQ. Similarly, we can know the corresponding average costs at different points of the total cost curve. By joining all these points we get a V-shaped average cost curve (AC in Fig. 16.10).

To know the marginal cost at the point P, we draw a tangent to the curve SS at the point P:

Then the marginal cost corresponding to the total cost at P is given by the value of the tangent of the angle that RP makes with the X-axis. In this case, it is equal to the value of the tangent of angle PRQ and this equals PQIRQ or which is the same thing as PM/LM.

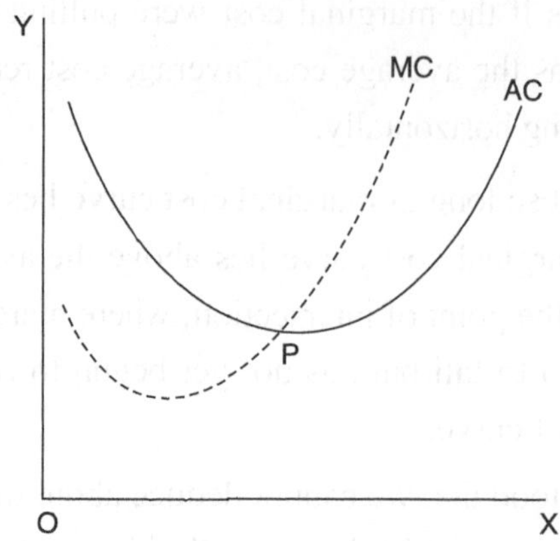

Fig. 16.10. MC and AC curves.

Similarly, we can know the marginal cost at different points of the total cost curve and by joining them, we get the marginal cost curve (MC in Fig. 16.10).

Long-Run Average Cost Curves

The Long-Run average cost curves will normally be V-shaped just as Short-Run cost curves are, but they will always be flatter than the Short-Run ones. The longer the period to which the curve relates, the less pronounced will be the V-shape of the cost curves. By the long period, we mean the period during which the size and organization of the firm can be altered to meet changed conditions.

Why LAC Curves are Flatter: The simple explanation of why the Long-Run average cost curve is flatter than the Short-Run cost curve may be given in terms of fixed and variable costs. It should be obvious that longer the period at the disposal of the producer, the fewer costs will be fixed and more costs will be variable. Over a long period of time, there are very few costs which are just as great if output is small as they are if it is large. Over a long period, the size of the plant can be changed, unwanted buildings can be sold or let, and administrative and marketing staff can be decreased or increased in order to deal efficiently with smaller or larger outputs and sales.

Thus, total fixed cost can be varied to a considerable extent over long periods, whereas in the short-run its amount is fixed absolutely. In other words, the longer the period under consideration, the fewer costs are 'fixed' and more costs become 'variable'.

In the short-run, a reduction in output will raise average costs because fixed costs will work out at a higher amount per unit of output. In the long period, however, the fixed costs can be reduced somewhat if output continues at a low level. Average fixed cost will, therefore, be lower in the long than in the short-run.

Variable costs will not rise as sharply in the long-run as they do in the short-run. In the long-run, the size of the firm can be increased to deal with an increased output more satisfactorily and the management can better tackle the various problems of larger output.

Thus, in the long-run, average costs will be lower and the variable costs will not rise as sharply as in the short period. Hence, LAC cost curves are flatter than the short-run ones.

A more adequate explanation of the flatter long-run average cost curves may be given in terms of greater divisibility of the factors of production in the long-run. In the long-run, the indivisible factors of production (like the plant, building, elaborate marketing organization) can be used more economically because in the long-run, they are, in fact, to some extend divisible. In the short-run, the shape of the cost curve of the firm depends on the action of the law of variable proportions, with capital and management as fixed (indivisible) factors. In the long-run, the cost curve of the firm depends on what are called the "returns to scale". In the long-run, the amount of capital can be altered and the management can be arranged differently, if necessary. They are no longer completely indivisible.

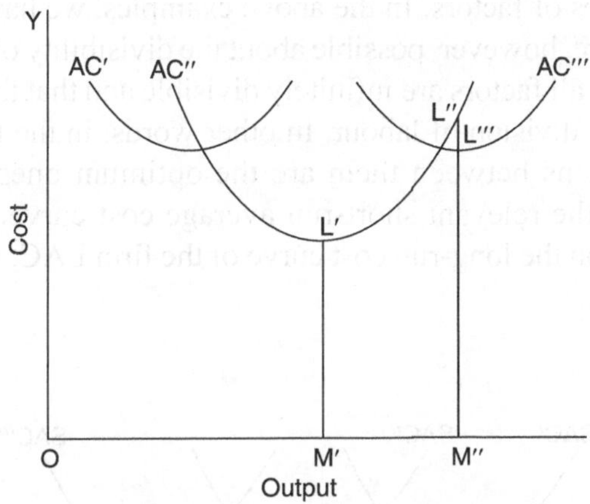

Fig. 16.11. Change the scale of operation.

If all the factors of production can be used in varying proportions, it means that the scale of operations of the firm can be changed. Each time the scale of operations is changed, a new short-run cost curve will have to be drawn for the firm. The accompanying figure will bring this out. To begin with, let us suppose that the firm has the short-run cost curve AC″. In that case, the optimum output will be OM′ at the lowest average cost M′ L′. Now if output is desired to be increased to OM″, in the short-run, it can be obtained at the average cost M″ L″ along the short turn cost curve AC″, because in the short-run the 'scale' of operations is fixed. But, in the long-run, a new and bigger plant can be built on which OM″ is the optimum output. That is, the firm now has the short-run average cost curve AC‴, and that by increasing the scale of its operations, the firm can produce the output OM″ at a cost of M″ L‴ instead of M″ L″.

Thus, it will have been seen that, at any given scale of operations, the firm will encounter regions of rising and falling costs, while in the long-run the firm can produce on a completely different cost curve to the left or the right of the original one. For each different scale, there will be an output where average cost is at a minimum.

At this output, the firm is said to be producing at its technical 'optimum', given its scale of operations. Output is 'optimum' in the sense that average cost is at a minimum. Therefore, in the long-run, the firm will be able to adjust its scale of operations so that it produces any given output at the lowest cost.

Look at the diagram. If the firm in question wishes to produce output OM′ it will find it best to produce at that scale which has the average cost curve SAC′. If OM″ quantity is desired, it will be best to produce on the curve SAC″, and for output OM‴ on the curve SAC‴. In each case, it will be producing the desired output at the lowest possible cost. It should, of course, be clearly understood that only in the long run can the scale of operations be altered; in the short-run it will be fixed, and the average cost of output above or below the optimum level will necessarily rise along the short-run curve in question, whether it be SAC′ or SAC″ or SAC‴. A long-run average cost curve can, therefore, be drawn and it will show what the long-run cost of producing each output would be.

The shape of the long-run average cost curve will depend on the assumptions made. One assumption relates to the prices of factors. In the above examples, we have assumed constant factor prices. Various assumptions are, however, possible about the divisibility of factors of production. The simplest case is to assume that all factors are infinitely divisible and that there are no economies to be reaped from, for example, the division of labour. In other words, in the long run, all factors can be adjusted so that the proportions between them are the optimum ones and production can take place at the lowest point on the relevant short-run average cost curve. As will be seen from the (Fig. 16.12), on this assumption the long-run cost curve of the firm LAC, is a horizontal straight line.

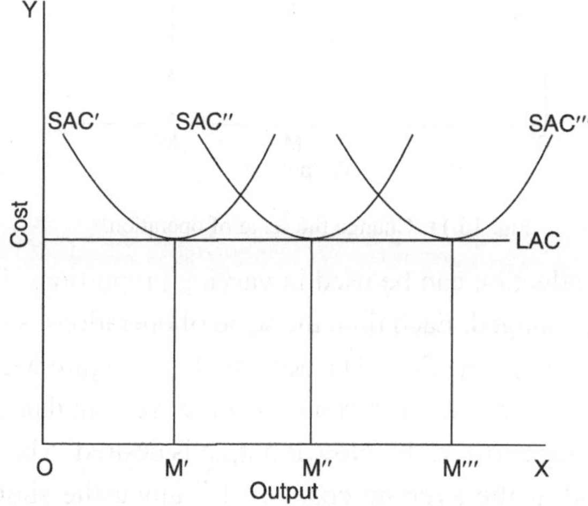

Fig. 16.12. Horizontal LAC curve with constant factor prices and divisible factors.

But this is not a realistic assumption. It is very unlikely that all factors are infinitely divisible even in the long-run. And as output is increased, the firm may reasonably expect to reap some economies from the division of labour that will become more and more practicable as the scale of operations becomes larger.

It is a common observation that some factors of production are indivisible. In particular, management is likely to be incompletely divisible. It is mere commonsense that an entrepreneur will be unlikely to produce twice a given output as efficiently as he produces a given output. It is, therefore, reasonable to expect that, even in the long-run, firms will produce more cheaply at some scales of output than at others, if for no other reason, at least because, beyond a certain point, management becomes more difficult and less efficient. Certain combinations of factors will thus produce at lower costs per unit than others. This means that, in the more probable conditions, the short-run average cost curves of the firm will have different minimum points.

In the figure given below, it will be seen that the short-run average cost curve SAC_2 has a lower minimum point than either the curves SAC. The optimum output of the firm is obtained at point M. The long-run average cost curve, which is a tangent to all the short-run curves, will be the curve LAC. It will, therefore, be U-shaped itself. But, as will be obvious from Fig. 16.13, it will be flatter than the short-run cost curves, the U-shape will be less pronounced.

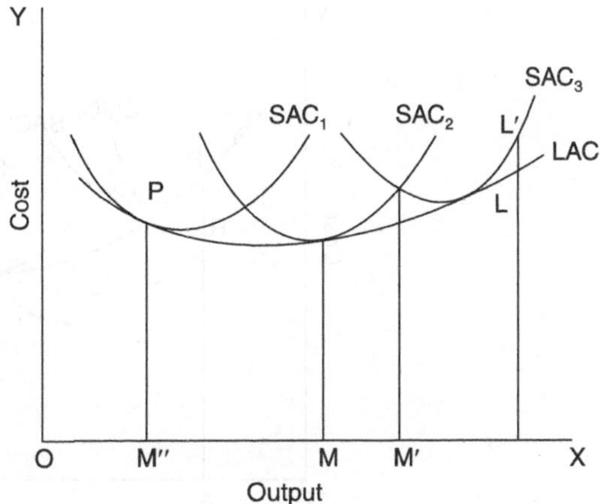

Fig. 16.13. LAC curve: An envelope of SAC's.

Economists generally call this curve as 'envelope', since it envelops all the short-run curves. It is also called the "planning curve" of a firm.

From the LAC curve it should be clear that for any given output, average cost cannot be higher in the long-run than in the short-run. After all, any adjustment in production which may be expected to cut costs, and which may be possible to make in the short-run, must also be feasible in the long-run. On the other hand, in the short-run, it is not always possible to produce a" given output in the cheapest possible way. If a different output is to be produced, it is impossible to change the amounts used of all factors of production in the short-run. While in the long-run all possible adjustments can be made.

The conclusion, therefore, follows that at no point can the long-run average cost curve lie above a short-run average cost curve or the long-run average cost curve can never cut a short-run average cost curve, though they may be tangential to each other.

Long-Run Marginal Cost Curve

In the diagram, we have drawn long-run marginal cost curve LMC from short-run average cost and marginal cost curves and long-run average cost curve. Just as every point of the continuous long-run average cost curve corresponds to some point of a short-run average cost curve, similarly every point of the continuous long-run marginal cost curve corresponds to some point on a short-run marginal cost curve.

If the output to be produced is OA, then in the long-run it must be produced on point P on the short run average cost curve SAC, and the long-run average cost curve LAC, because only point P minimizes the cost for output SAC,. OA. Corresponding to point P on SAC, and LAC, there is a point R on the short-run marginal cost curve SMC. Then AR is the relevant short-run marginal cost for output OA in the long-run. Therefore, the point R must lie on the long-run marginal cost curve corresponding to output OA.

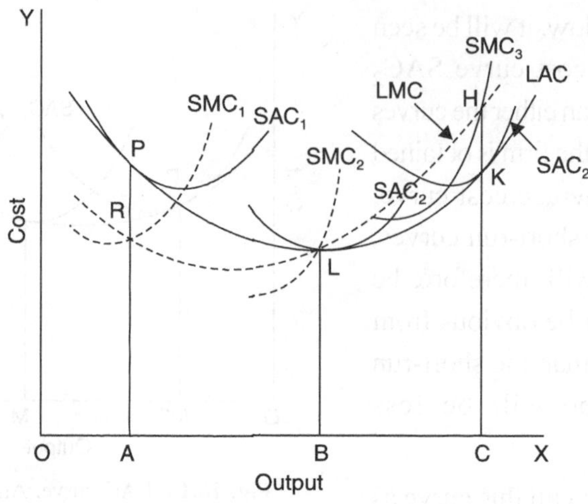

Fig. 16.14. Derivation of long-run marginal cost curve.

If the output OB is to be produced, then in the long-run it will be. produced on point L on the short run average cost curve SAC_2 and long-run average cost curve LAC, L is also the point on the short-run marginal cost curve SMC_2 corresponding to output OB. Therefore, point L must also lie on the long-run marginal cost curve corresponding to output OB.

Similarly, if output OC is to be produced, then in the long-run it must be produced on point K of the short-run average cost curve SAC_3. Corresponding to K on SAC_3, the relevant point on the SMC_3 is H. Therefore, H must also lie on the long-run marginal cost curve corresponding to output OC.

By joining points such as R, L and H, we get long-run marginal cost curve LMC. The long-run marginal cost curve, like the long-run average cost curve, is U-shaped.

It is clear from Fig. 16.14 that the long-run marginal cost curve is flatter than the short-run marginal cost curves. This is what one would expect, because the U-shape of the long-run average cost curve is less pronounced than that of the short-run average cost curves. The relationship between the long-run marginal cost curve and long-run average cost curve is the same as that between short-run marginal cost curve and short-run average cost curve. That is, when the long-run marginal cost curve lies below long-run average cost curve, the latter is falling and when the LMC curve lies above LAC curve, the latter is rising. The long-run marginal cost curve cuts the long-run average cost at the latter's lowest point. This is so because long-run marginal cost is equal to the long-run average cost when the latter is neither rising nor falling.

Why LAC Curve First Falls and then Rises? That the LAC curve slopes downwards as the scale of production is enlarged is due to the various economies of scale, *e.g.,* (*i*) larger scope of specialization of labour, (*ii*) increasing use of specialized machinery, (*iii*) other technological improvements. The LAC curve rises after a point because of the various diseconomies of scale, *e,g.,* rising cost of the inputs and the difficulty of management, etc.

Optimum Plant: The plant is said to be of the optimum size which is operated at the point of its minimum average cost of production. It is the minimum point of whose short-run average cost curve coincides with the minimum point of the long-run average cost curve. In Fig. 16.4, plant SAC_2 is operated at its minimum cost of production for producing OB output. It is being used to its full capacity to turn over an optimum output. Any size of the plant which is either bigger or smaller than SAC_2 will be producing at higher average cost.

Optimum Output: In Fig. 16.14, OB is the optimum output. It is optimum because it is the least cost output. If the output is smaller (*e.g.*, OA) or larger (*e.g.*, OC), it will be obtained at a higher cost of production as compared with OB output.

Optimum Firm: The firm which produces optimum output (*i.e.*, the least cost output) with the optimum plant is called the Optimum Firm. The firm producing OB output by operating SAC_2 plant is said to have achieved the optimum size. Since the minimum cost point of SAC_2 coincides with the minimum point of the long-run average cost curve, the optimum firm can also be defined as the firm which produces at the minimum point of the long-run average cost curve (LAC). The size of the optimum firm is different in different industries. For instance, it is smaller in agriculture and other industries like mining, whereas it is bigger in manufacturing industries like automobile industry.

L-Shaped Long-Run Average Cost Curve

We have said that the long-run average cost curves are V-shaped. But empirical studies have shown that the LAC curves are L-shaped, rather than V-shaped. It is found that there is a rather rapid downward slope in the early part of the curve, *i.e.*, in the initial stages of production.

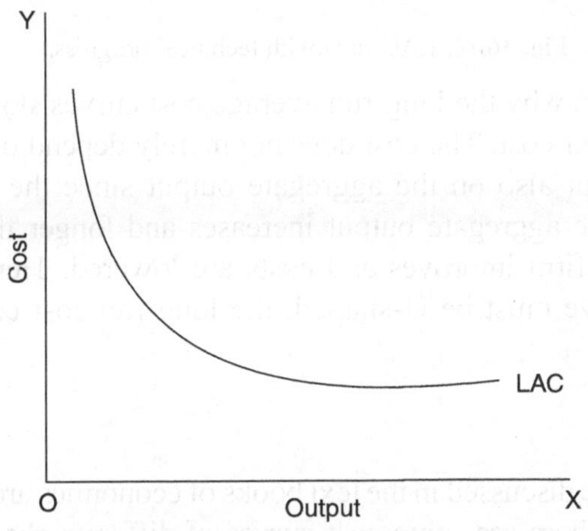

Fig. 16.15. 'L' shaped LAC.

The following reasons are given in support of this view:

(*a*) Rapid technical progress brings about a sharp decline in unit cost. At first, the unit cost is high and remains quite high for an initial scale of production. But then the unit cost takes a downward course and remains constant so that the LAC curve is flat at the right, making the curve L-shaped. This is due to technical progress.

The figure explains that, in the absence of technical progress, the long-run average cost curve is V-shaped, technical progress would convert it into an L-shaped curve. Initially, in the figure given in Fig. 16.15, the output is OMI and the unit cost is OC and the relevant long-run average cost curve is LAC_1 but when the output is expanded in response to increased demand to M_2, the cost of production per unit is OC_1 on the curve LAC_1, which is quite high. But if technical progress is going apace, it may be possible to produce the same output at a unit cost of OC_2 on the curve LAC_2; this cost is much lower since a more modern plant has been installed due to technical progress. With further expansion of the output to OM_3 and technical progress gathering momentum, the unit cost drops further to OC_3 on the long run average cost curve LAC_3. It is thus that the long-run average cost curve LAC takes L-shape.

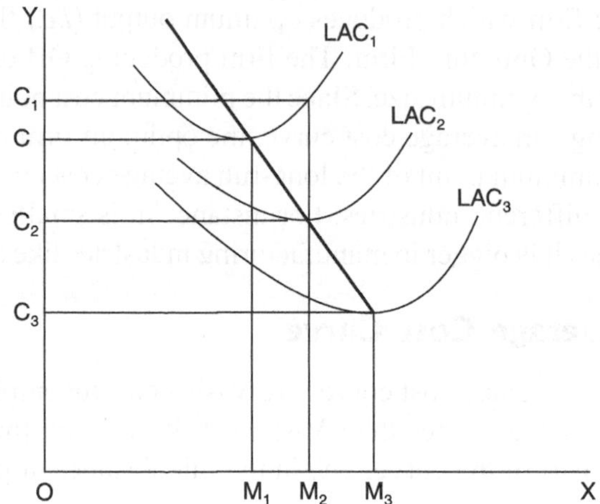

Fig. 16.16. LAC falls with technical progress.

(*b*) The second reason why the long-run average cost curves slope downwards is 'learning' to produce at lower cost. The cost does not merely depend on how much is produced in a given period but also on the aggregate output since the time the firm commenced operations. As the aggregate output increases and longer the period that has elapsed, efficiency of the firm improves and costs are lowered. Hence, although the short-run average cost curve must be U-shaped, the long-run cost curves may be U-shaped or L-shaped.

Empirical Cost Curves

Most of the cost curves that are discussed in the text books of economics are theoretical or conventional and they are U-shaped. But there are some cost curves of different shapes which are found in the real world. They are called empirical cost curves.

Dish-Shaped Curve

An attempt has been made to reconcile the theoretical and empirical approaches. The U-shaped cost curves apply to cases where the plant is indivisible but can be used with changing quantities of variable factors. In such cases, change in output results through a change in variable factors when the returns are non-proportionate giving rise to U-shaped cost curves. But in the case of a fairly divisible and flexible plant, the cost curves may be horizontal over a range of output. When a plant is divisible it is possible to maintain the factor proportion so that all the factors have to be increased in the same proportion as the increase in the output. The result is that the costs are constant. Under these circumstances the cost curves will be dish-shaped. You will notice that at first both AC and MC fall, and then *they* remain constant for a wide range of output and then rise forming a sort of dish.

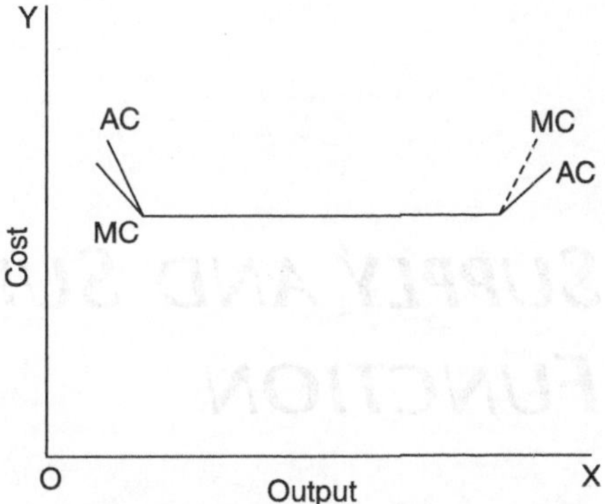

Fig. 16.17. Dish shaped AC and MC.

The U-shaped curve of the traditional theory was questioned by economists both on theoretical and empirical grounds. For instance, George Stigler suggested that the short-run average variable cost curve has a flat stretch over a range of output so that the long-run cost curve is L-shaped rather than U-shaped. It has been argued that managerial diseconomies can be avoided by improved methods of modern management.

Inverse J Cost Curves

More recently, the economists have questioned even the L-shaped cost curve. It has been said that there are economies of scale at all levels of output, although their magnitude becomes small beyond a certain scale of output. Hence, we get cost curves of the shape of an inverse J as shown in Fig. 16.18.

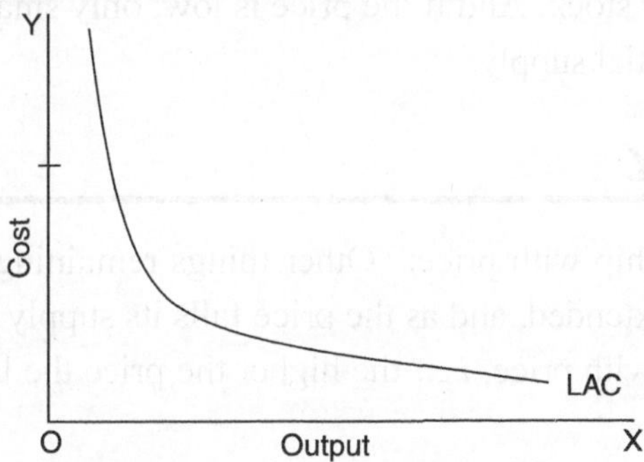

Fig. 16.18. Inverse 'J' cost curve.

Self-Assessment Questions

1. What is meant by the equilibrium of a firm and of the industry? Indicate the conditions of equilibrium of both under perfect competition.
2. Distinguish between AC and MC and discuss the significance of this distinction in the analysis of firm's equilibrium.

Unit **17**

SUPPLY AND SUPPLY FUNCTION

17.1 INTRODUCTION

Supply means the amount offered for sale at a given price. "We may define supply as a schedule of the amount of goods that would be offered for sale at all possible prices at anyone instant of time, or during anyone period of time, for example, a day, a week and so on, in which the conditions of supply remain the same." **(Meyers)**

Supply should be carefully distinguished from stock. Stock is the total volume of a commodity which can be brought into the market for sale at a short notice and supply means the quantity which is actually brought in the market. For perishable commodities, like fish and fruits, supply and stock are the same because whatever is in stock must be disposed. The commodities, which are not perishable, can be held back, if prices are not favourable. If the price is high, larger quantities are offered by the sellers from their stock. And if the price is low, only small quantities are brought out for sale. In short, stock is potential supply.

17.2 LAW OF SUPPLY

Supply has functional relationship with price: "Other things remaining the same, as the price of a commodity rises its supply is extended, and as the price falls its supply is contracted." The quantity offered for sale varies directly with price, *i.e.,* the higher the price the larger is the supply, and *vice versa.*

Corresponding to the demand schedule already explained, we can construct an individual's supply schedule. Also, depending on the amount supplied at various prices by all the sellers in a market, we can obtain the supply schedule of the market. Supply schedule represents the relation between prices and the quantities that people are willing to produce and sell.

It will be seen that when price is as high as ₹ 7 per dozen as many as 43 dozen apples are offered for sale. As the price falls, the amount supplied decreases. When the price is as low as ₹ 1 a dozen, only 10 dozen apples are offered for sale. This means that as price falls supply is contracted, and as price rises supply is extended. This is the Law of Supply.

Suppose the following is the (market) supply schedule of apples:

Price per dozen (₹)	*Quantity supplied (in dozens)*
7	43
6	40
5	36
4	31
3	25
2	18
1	10

The supply schedule given above can be represented in the form of a Supply Curve (Fig. 17.1 given below):

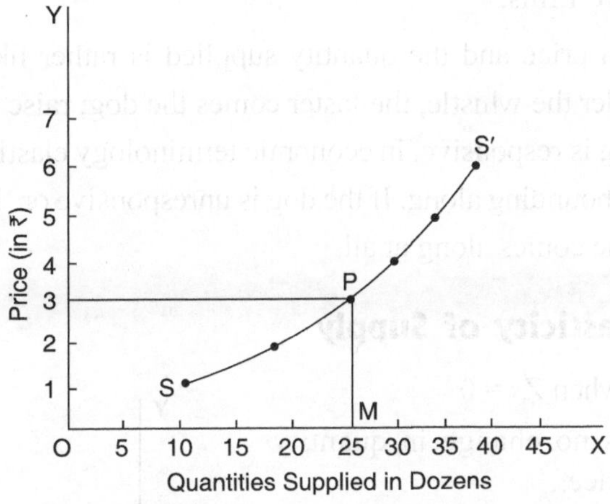

Fig. 17.1. Supply curve shows positive relationship between price of the commodity and quantity supplied.

In this diagram, quantities supplied are measured along OX, and prices along OY, SS′ is the supply curve. If from any point P on the supply curve, PM is drawn perpendicular to OX and PO′ to OY, then at PM (= O′ O) price, PO′ (= OM) quantity will be supplied.

It should be noted that the supply curve slopes downwards from right to left, as contrasted with the demand curve, which slopes from left to right. The reason is that as price falls demand is extended, but supply is contracted; and, conversely, as price rises demand is contracted, but supply is extended.

If the price falls too much, supply may dry up altogether. The price below which the seller will refuse to sell is called the reserve price. At this price, the seller buys his own stock, as it were.

17.3 ELASTICITY OF SUPPLY

When a small fall in price leads to great contraction in supply, the supply is comparatively elastic. But when a big fall in price leads to a very small contraction in supply, the supply is said to be comparatively inelastic. Conversely, a small rise in price leading to a big extension in supply shows elastic supply, and a big rise in price leading to a small extension in supply indicates inelastic supply.

The elasticity of supply is really the measure of the ease with which an industry can be expanded and of the behaviour of the marginal costs. If a slight increase in price is followed by the entry of many new firms having minimum average cost equal to price and the cost does not rise, the supply is said to be perfectly elastic. In case, however, the increased output can be obtained only by an infinite increase in price and no new firm is attracted to the industry, the supply will be inelastic. In between these two extremes, there will be different degrees of elasticity. The degree of elasticity will depend, in a particular case, on the slope of the marginal cost curve and the shape of the average cost curves of the successive firms.

The relation between price and the quantity supplied is rather like the relation between a whistle and a dog—the louder the whistle, the faster comes the dog; raise the price and the quantity supplied increases. If the dog is responsive, in economic terminology elastic, quite a small crescendo in the whistle will send him bounding along. If the dog is unresponsive or 'inelastic', we may have to whistle very loudly before he comes along at all.

Different Types of Elasticity of Supply

Elasticity of supply when $Zs = 0$

This means there is no change in quantity supplied due to change in price.

$$\Sigma s = \frac{\Delta S}{\Delta P}$$

$$= \frac{O}{PP_1}$$

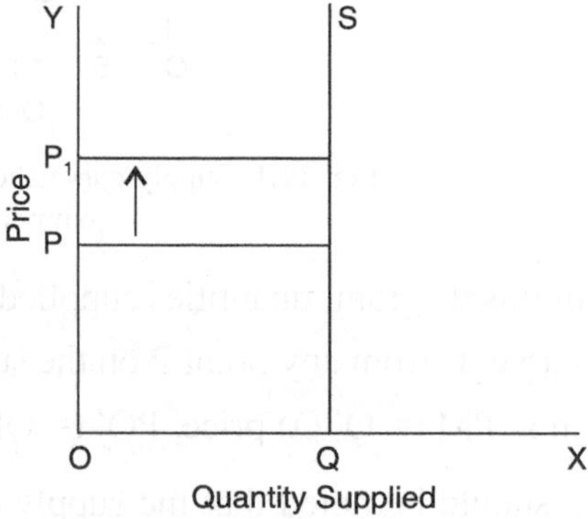

Fig. 17.2. Vertical supply curve imphes zero elasticity.

This is when quantity supplied remains same even after price increases or decreases, then it is said to be perfect inelasticity of supply.

In the above diagram price increased from 'OP' to 'OP_1' but the quality remained unchanged.

(*i*) When elasticity of supply is infinite or $\Sigma s = \infty$.

$$\Sigma s = \frac{\Delta S}{\Delta P}$$

$$= \frac{QQ_1}{O}$$

(Numerator is changing and denominator is zero it is equal to ∞)

$$\Sigma s = \infty$$

In other words there is no change in price but there is change in quantity supplied. This is known as '*perfectly elastic supply*'.

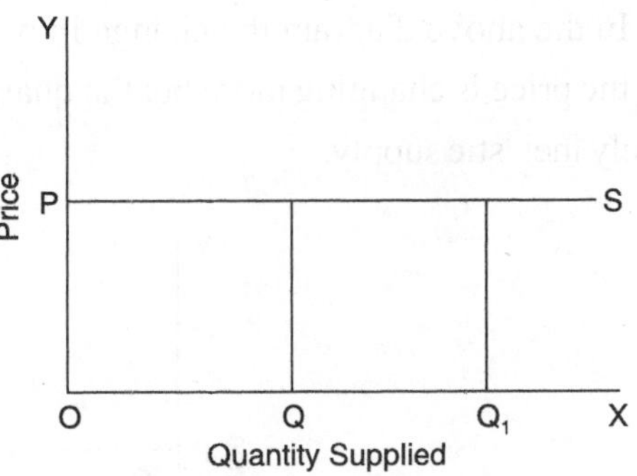

Fig. 17.3. Perfectly elastic supply.

(*ii*) Elasticity of supply when $\Sigma s = 1$.

$$\Sigma s = \frac{\Delta S}{\Delta P}$$

$$= \frac{QQ_1}{PP_1}$$

where $PP_1 = QQ_1$, this means, the amount of change in price is equal to the amount of change in quantity supplied. This is known as "*Unit elastic supply*".

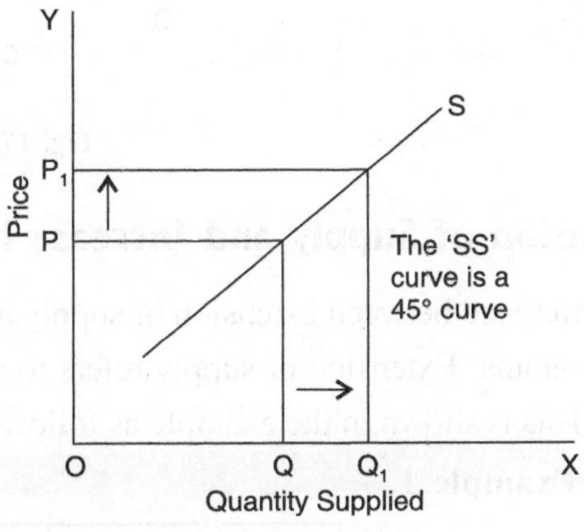

Fig. 17.4. Unitary elastic supply.

(*iii*) Relatively inelastic supply $\Sigma s < 1$

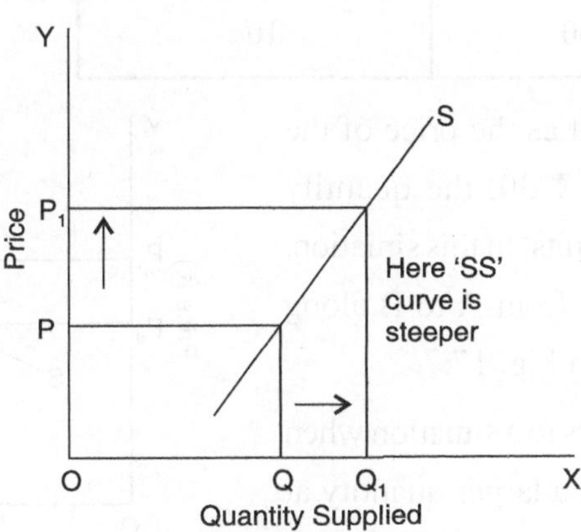

Fig. 17.5. Inelastic supply.

$$\Sigma s = \frac{\Delta S}{\Delta P} = \frac{QQ_1}{PP_1}, \text{ where } PP_1 > QQ_1$$

In the above diagram the change in price is greater than the change in quantity supplied, that means the price is changing more but the quantity supplied is relatively less. Hence, this is referred as relatively inelastic supply.

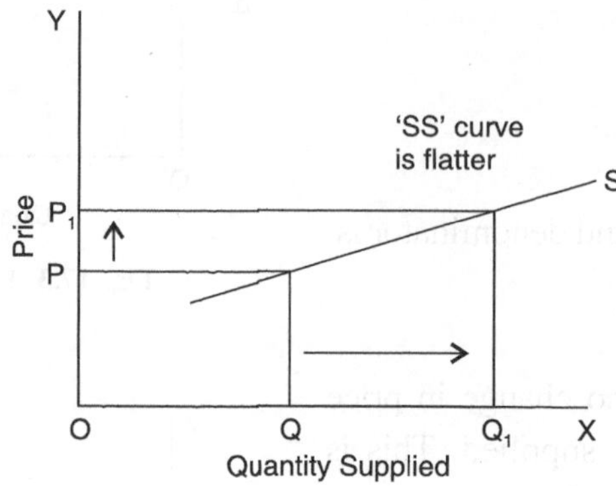

Fig. 17.6. Elastic supply.

Extension of Supply and Increase in Supply

The difference between extension of supply and increase in supply can be shown through examples and diagrams. Extension of supply refers to a situation when more quantity is supplied at a higher price. This is shown in the example as follows:

Example 1.

Price (₹)	*Quantity (Units)*
20	4
30	10

It would be seen here that as the price of the commodity rises from ₹ 20 to ₹ 30, the quantity supplied rises from 4 units to 10 units. In this situation, there will be upward movement from A to B along the supply curve SS, as shown in Fig. 17.7.

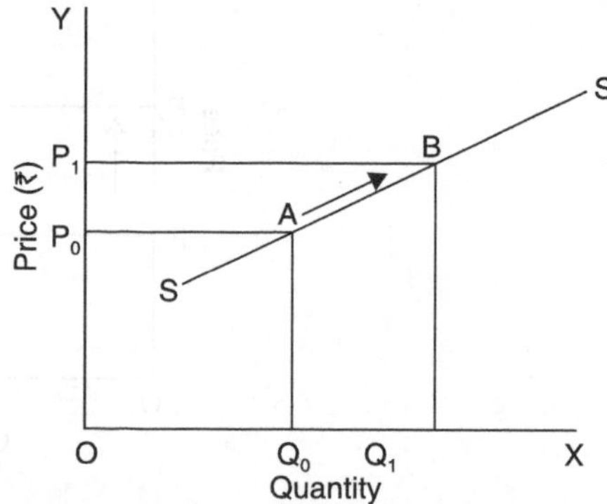

Fig. 17.7. Extension of supply.

An increase in supply refers to a situation when the producer is willing to supply a larger quantity at the same price because of change in factors other than the price of the commodity. In this situation, there will be rightward shift in the supply curve.

Example 2.

Price (₹)	*Quantity (Units)*
20	4
20	6

It would be seen here that at a price of ₹ 20, 4 units of the commodity are supplied initially. But as a result of change in factors other than the price of the commodity, 6 units of the commodity are supplied at the same price of ₹ 20. This is illustrated in Fig. 17.8 by movement from A on S to B on S_1. This rightward shift of supply curve from S to S_1 shows increases in supply.

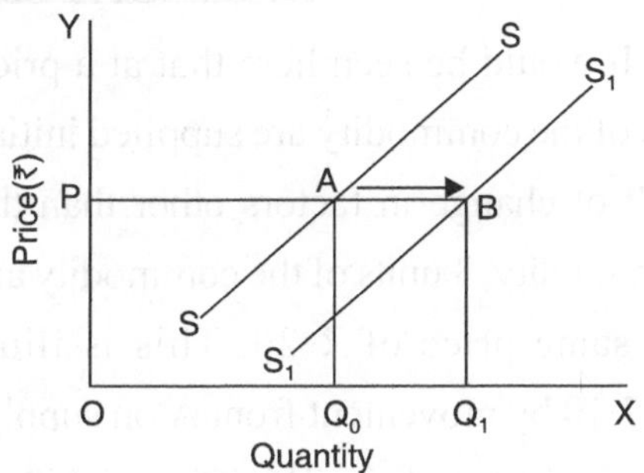

Fig. 17.8. Increase in supply.

Contraction of Supply and Decrease in Supply

The difference between contraction of supply and decrease in supply can also be illustrated through example, and diagrams. Contraction of supply refers to a situation when a smaller quantity is supplied at a lower price. This is shown in example 3 and Fig. 17.9 as follows:

Example 3.

Price (₹)	*Quantity (Units)*
20	4
10	2

It would be seen here that as the price of the commodity falls from ₹ 20 to ₹ 10, the quantity supplied falls from 4 units to 2 units. In this situation, there will be downward movement from A to B along the supply curve SS as shown in Fig. 17.9.

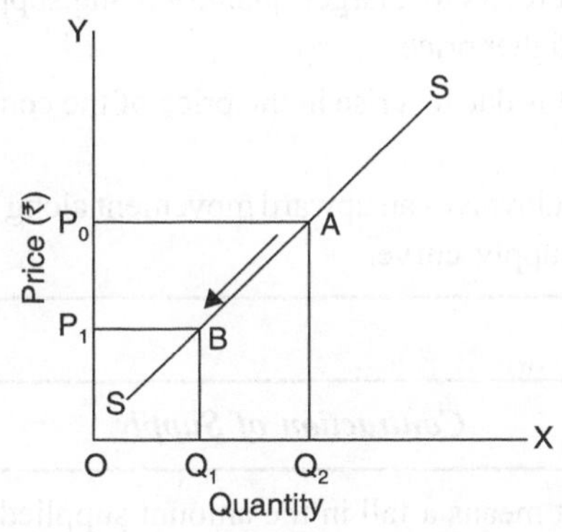

Fig. 17.9. Contraction of supply.

A decrease in supply refers to a situation when the producer is willing to supply a smaller quantity at the same price because of change in factors other than the own price of the commodity. In this situation, there will be leftward shift in the supply curve. This is explained in example 4 and Fig. 17.10.

Example 4.

Price (₹)	*Quantity* (*Units*)
20	4
20	3

It would be seen here that at a price of ₹ 20, 4 units of the commodity are supplied initially. But as a result of change in factors other than the price of the commodity, 3 units of the commodity are supplied at the same price of ₹ 20. This is illustrated in Fig. 17.10 by movement from A on supply curve SS to B on supply curve S_1S_1. This leftward shift from supply curve S to supply curve S_1 shows decrease in supply.

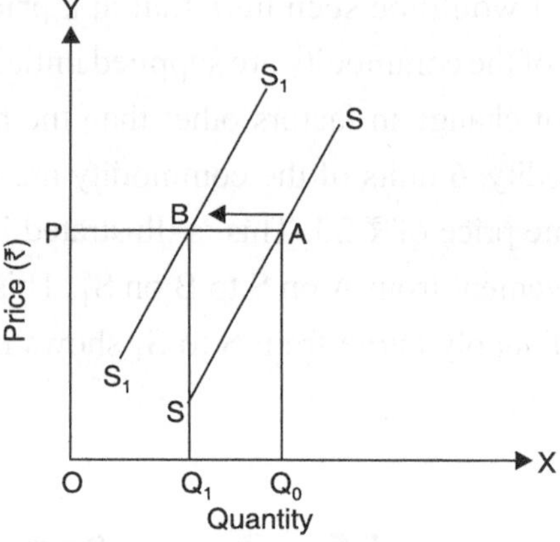

Fig. 17.10. Decrease in supply.

We may sum up the distinction between change in quantity supplied and change in supply as follows:

Extension of Supply	*Increase in Supply*
1. It refers to a larger quantity being supplied at a higher price. 2. It is due to a rise in the price of the commodity. 3. It involves an upward movement along the same supply curve.	1. It refers to a larger amount being supplied at the same price. 2. It results from changes in factors other than the price of the commodity. 3. It leads to a rightward shift of the supply curve.

Contraction of Supply	*Decrease in Supply*
1. It means a fall in the amount supplied due to a fall in the price of the commodity. 2. It is due to a fall in the price of the commodity. 3. It involves a downward movement along the same supply curve.	1. It means a smaller amount being supplied at the same price. 2. It results from changes in factors other than the price of the commodity. 3. It leads to a leftward shift of the supply curve.

Causes of Change in Supply

The increase and decrease in supply may take place on account of a number of factors:

(*i*) Cost of production of a commodity may rise due to increase in the costs of the various factors of production (or resource prices) like raw materials and intermediate products, used in its production. This will result in a decrease in supply. Conversely, a fall in the prices of such factors will lead to greater production and consequently an increase in supply.

(*ii*) As regards agricultural commodities, better rainfall, improvement in irrigation, bigger doses of fertilizers, improved seeds and better methods of production naturally would increase supply. On the contrary, failure of rains, floods, fires, dust-stones, pests earthquakes, etc., will decrease the supply. Food supply recently increased in India owing to larger production brought about by the 'Green Revolution' and larger supply of agricultural inputs like fertilizers, water supply, pesticides, credit, etc.

(*iii*) Improvement in technique lowers cost of production and increases supply. On the other hand, higher taxation imposed on the output of a commodity or on the factors required for its production will decrease the supply.

(*iv*) Improvement in the means of communication and transport may increase the supply of a particular commodity if imports from foreign countries are encouraged. It may, however, reduce the supply if exports are facilitated.

(*v*) Political disturbances or a war may disorganize or divert channels of trade and thus create scarcity of certain kinds of goods.

(*vi*) Supply may be consciously decreased by agreement among the producers, *e.g.*, agreement among the oil producing countries to cut back production. Also, a part of the supply may be destroyed in order to raise prices. During the Great Depression the production of rubber, tea and some other commodities was restricted through international agreements among the producers. Coffee was thrown into the sea in Brazil.

Fig. 17.11. Imigation increases agricultural production and supply.

(*vii*) The supply of goods is also determined by the goals set by the producing firms for themselves. They can decide to produce more or less of a commodity or stop the production of one and undertake that of another.

(*viii*) The supply of a commodity also depends on the price of that commodity and the prices of other commodities. Higher the price, greater is the supply that will come forth. If the prices of other goods are more attractive, then the production of these commodities will be stimulated relatively to a particular commodity.

(*ix*) The supply also depends on the number of sellers. Entry of more sellers will increase the supply and their exit will decrease the supply.

(*x*) Sellers price expectations. If the sellers fear that the prices will fall in the future, they will hasten to unload the supply now and the supply will increase. On the other hand, expectation of rise in future will induce them to withhold supply and the supply will contract.

(*xi*) Taxation of output, sales, imports, etc., also affects the supply. By levying high import duties, a government may restrict the supply of a foreign commodity to encourage its production at home; Government may also restrict production of certain articles for reasons of health (*e.g.*, opium in India).

Conclusion

Thus, changes in prices, supply of inputs, production techniques, monopoly control, and taxation are some of the factors which bring about changes in supply.

17.4 SUPPLY FUNCTION

So far we have discussed the changes in supply in response to certain factors in simple, non-technical terms. We give below practically the same thing in technical terms.

The behaviour of the suppliers of goods follows a general and consistent pattern as they react to some identifiable set of functional supply determinants. Thus, the supply function identifies the immediate determinants of supply for all goods. In other words, they explain variations in the quantity of goods supplied. This supply function can be put as under:

$$Qx = F\ (Px,\ Py,\ Pi,\ T,\ MT)$$

The supply function is merely a mathematical notation which reads as follows: The quantity supplied of any good Qx varies with the prices of that good Px, the price of their goods Py, the price of factor inputs Pi, technology T and time periods MT. We analyze below these separate functional relationships.

Supply as a Function of Price

This functional relationship can be put in the form of an equation Q*x* = F (P*x*). This means that the quantity supplied of good X varies directly with its price. That is if the price of X goes up, its supply would increase, and *vice versa*. In other words the quantity supplied changes in the same direction as the price of the good concerned. That is, there is a direct functional relationship between a change in the price of a good and change in its quantity supplied. It leads to the law of upward sloping supply. However, direct relationship between price and quantity supplied is consistent but it is not irrefutable since there is some exception. Some factors other than mere change in price may determine the supply of a commodity *e.g.*, change in tastes, weather, fashion, etc.

Supply as a Function of Price of other Goods

Albert O. Hirschman discusses in his book it economic interdependence as it governs the supply of goods. According to him interdependent relationship in supply can be of two types: horizontal and vertical. There is horizontal relationship between goods when they are used at the same stage of production *e.g.,* at the consumption or factor input level. In this case, the two goods compete with each other for the purchaser's choice. Consequently, there will be a unique, pecuniary linkage relationship between the two that is essentially a demand cross elasticity relationship.

Fig. 17.12. Supply of goods.

But in the case of vertical relationship one good is an input for the production of another. A good has a forward linkage relationship when it is used as a factor input for another, but the good produced has a backward linkage relationship. Whatever the case may be, there is an important functional relationship between the price of one good and the supply of another.

When the relationship is horizontal, it is almost always an inverse relationship. That is, if the price of one good rises, the demand for the other good will increase. The coefficient of cross elasticity is negative. On the other hand, when the resource transferability is low as between production of say wheat and cars, coefficient of cross elasticity is low or zero.

In the case of forward vertical relationship, an increase in the price of the final product will induce a rise in the price of the factor input. The coefficient of cross elasticity will then be positive. The strength of relationship and the size of the coefficient will depend upon the extent to which one good is uniquely an input for another.

Supply as a Function of the Price of Inputs

The functional relationship between the supply of a good and the price of its factor inputs is a backward vertical relationship that is always negative. This means that as the price of factor inputs increases, the cost of production must go up which results in decrease in supply reflecting increased relative scarcity of the good. The size of the coefficient of cross elasticity for each of the several factor inputs will depend on their relative importance in the production of goods.

Supply as a Function of Technology

It is obvious that technology is the most important determinant of the supply of goods. Applied technology reflects the entrepreneur's talent to make use of scientific discovery, invention and engineering advances in the production process. Technological advancement results in the production of new goods, new efficiency levels in production, the development of the new industries and better resource distribution within industries.

Self-Assessment Questions

1. Explain the law of supply. What are its limitations?
2. With the help of diagrams explain the elasticity of supply. How it can be measured at various points on a supply curve?
3. Explain increase and decrease in supply. Give the causes of change in supply.
4. What is supply function? Explain the determinants of supply.

Unit **18**

MARKET AND MARKET STRUCTURES

18.1 INTRODUCTION

The father of economics Adam Smith in his book 'The Theory of Moral Sentiments' (1759), wrote about the main characteristics of human beings. According to him a human being is very selfish or posseses self-love as well as there exists an invisible hand. The concept of self-love in human being is one of the most important factor in "the value theory" as well as in the development of market.

A human being weighs between what he pays and what he receives "in return". This is one of the basic characteristic of a human being. Generally a human being carries out economic activities till a point where he thinks that what I am paying is equal to what I am receiving. A human being willingly trades or carries out an exchange till he feels that what I am giving is less and what I am receiving is more, once he realizes that what I am giving is equal to what I am receiving, he stops further trade.

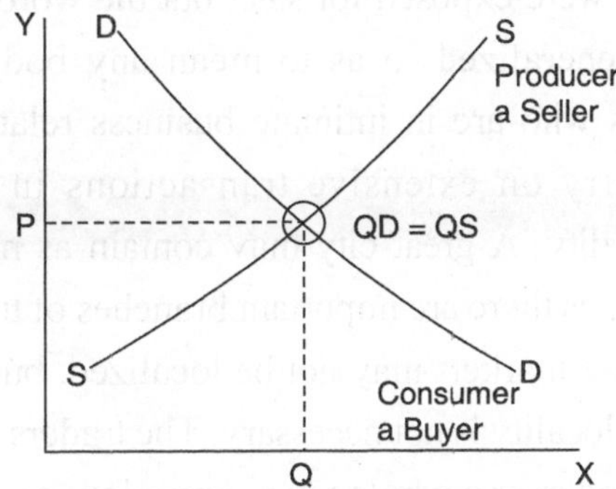

Fig. 18.1. Buyer and seller create market.

This is one of the basic philosophy of consumers, and the same thing in Marshallian words can be referred as consumer's surplus. On the other hand producer can be referred as producer surplus. Both the concepts are based on the selfish motives of maximizing returns in terms of their efforts (or money).

'DD' demand curve is derived from the consumer's behaviour in relation to price. A consumer (demand curve) is interested in paying least and wants more in return at the point of price he feels that what he is giving. Buyer and seller create marketing is equal to what he is receiving. On the other hand a seller or producer (supply curve) is interested in getting the maximum price by giving less and less, at point 'P' he feels that what I am giving is equal to what I am receiving. Price is determined at a place where 'DD' and 'SS' are equal. This is the concept referred as 'market'. On the basis of this 'market' the whole free enterprise or capitalistic economy is based. Market plays a very important role in determining the shape, size and extent of the economy of a country. In value theory the,

(*a*) Classical value theory is based an supply side concept (cost of production of a good).

(*b*) Neo-classical, is based on demand side concept (utility of a good) and

(*c*) Modern-economic theorists take into account both the supply side and demand side economics that is nothing but the concept of market. (In other words demand and supply determines price).

18.2 MARKET

Meaning of Market

"Originally", says Jevons, "a market was a public place in a town where provisions and other objects were exposed for sale; but the word has been generalized so as to mean any body of persons who are in intimate business relations and carry on extensive transactions in any commodity. A great city may contain as many markets as there are important branches of trade, and these markets may not be localized, but the idea of locality is not necessary. The traders may be spread over a whole town, or region, or a country and yet form a market if they are, by means of fairs, meetings, published price lists, the post-office or otherwise, in close communication with each other."

Fig. 18.2. A marketplace.

In the words of Cornet, a French economist, "Economists understand by the term market not any particular marketplace in which things are bought and sold but the whole of any region in which buyers and sellers are in such free intercourse with one another that the price of the same goods tends to equality easily and quickly."

Thus, the essentials of a market are: (*a*) a commodity which is dealt with; (*b*) the existence of buyers and sellers; (*c*) a place, be it a certain region, a country or the entire world; and (*d*) such intercourse between buyers and sellers that only one price should prevail, for the same commodity at the same time.

Classification of Markets

Markets may be classified:

(*a*) On the basis of area as local, national and world markets;

(*b*) On the basis of time, as market price on any particular day or moment, short-period price, long-period price, or secular markets covering a generation; and

(*c*) On the basis of nature of competition obtaining there in as perfect markets and imperfect markets.

Size of the Market

In the case of some commodities, the market is very wide covering the whole country or even the whole world, whereas in certain other cases, the size of the market is very limited covering a small village. The size of the market depends upon several factors:

Character of the Commodity: In order to have a wide market, a commodity must be (*i*) portable; (*ii*) durable; (*iii*) suitable for sampling, grading and exact description; and (*iv*) such as its supply can be increased. Such commodities are wheat, gold, government securities, etc. Bulky articles like bricks and perishable articles like fresh fruit and vegetables have a narrow market.

Nature of demand: Commodity, which is in universal demand (*e.g.,* gold and silver), will have a wide market. Similarly, commodity of general consumption has a wide market.

Means of communication and transport: The size of the market depends upon the extent to which means of communication and transport have been developed. A properly developed transport and communication system has enabled commodities to be carried long distances and establish wide contacts. This has widened the markets.

Peace and security: Obviously, goods cannot be marketed in distant places unless peace and order prevail. In war-time, due to insecurity in war zones, markets get restricted. Thus, the extent of the market depends on the peace prevailing in the region.

Currency and credit system: If the currency and credit system of the country are well-developed, marketing can be conveniently and profitably carried on over extensive areas. The extent of the market very largely depends on the state of the currency and the confidence it inspires.

Policy of the state: Markets may be restricted by the policy of the State. Prohibitive duties and quotas restrict the market. The zoning system (*e.g.,* wheat zones) which allows free movement of goods only within a certain zone has the same effect. Thus, the Government policy can also affect the extent of the market.

Degree of division of labour: We know that division of labour is limited by the extent of the market. The converse of this is also true. That is, the extent of the market also, in turn, depends upon the degree of division of labour. The greater the division of labour the cheaper the articles and wider the market.

Perfect and Imperfect Markets

A distinction is made between perfect market and imperfect market. "A market is said to be perfect when all the potential sellers and buyers are promptly aware of the prices at which transactions take place and all the offers made by other sellers and buyers, and when any buyer can purchase from any seller and conversely. Under such a condition, the price or a commodity will tend to be the same (after allowing for cost of transport including import duties) all over the market." Thus the prevalence of the same price for the same commodity at the same time is the essential characteristic of a perfect market.

On the other hand, a market is said to be imperfect when some buyers or sellers or both are not aware of the offers being made by others. Naturally, therefore, different prices come to prevail for the same commodity at the same time in an imperfect market. In a perfect market, on the other hand, the same price rules throughout the market.

Conditions of a Perfect Market: For a market to be perfect the following conditions are essential:

(*i*) *Free and perfect competition:* In a perfect market, there are no restrictions either on the buyers or on the sellers. They should be absolutely free to buy from or sell to anybody they like. In other words there should be no monopolies.

(*ii*) *Cheap and efficient transport and communication:* Same price for the commodity will not rule if the information about changes in prices cannot be quickly transmitted or if the commodity cannot be cheaply and speedily transported. Hence, efficient transport and communication system is essential for a perfect market.

(*iii*) *Wide extent:* A perfect market is sometimes considered synonymous with a wide market. We have already discussed above the extent on which the extent of the market depends. In order to have a wide market, a commodity should be portable, durable, and gradable and should have a wide demand.

Fig. 18.3. Transport and communication.

Let us now examine some cases and find out whether the markets are perfect or imperfect.

Market for invested capital (stocks and shares) is the nearest approach to a perfect market, since the stock exchange market is highly organized.

Market for precious metals, first-class bills of exchange, foreign currencies and important raw materials are also efficiently organized and may be regarded as perfect.

Markets for consumers' goods, which are retail markets, are less perfect. Retail prices differ appreciably in different localities.

Producers' goods are, as a rule, purchased wholesale; the markets for such goods are more perfect.

Labour market is mostly imperfect. This is due to the comparative immobility of labour, their weak bargaining power and the ignorance that generally prevails in labour circles.

The market for real estate is relatively perfect. Owing to big amounts involved the buyers' take a lot of trouble before they make a purchase.

In the money market, the rate of interest varies according to the risk of default and the period of the loan. Hence, money market may be regarded as imperfect. It is especially so in India.

18.3 MARKET FORMS OR MARKET STRUCTURES

The type of market depends on the degree of competition prevailing in the market. Broadly speaking, there are two types of competition prevailing in the markets: (*i*) Perfect competition, and (*ii*) Imperfect competition.

Perfect competition and pure competition: Modern economists draw a distinction between perfect competition and pure competition. Perfect competition is a wider concept. In order that there should be perfect competition, the market should satisfy not only the conditions of pure competition but also a few more.

Imperfect competition may also take several forms, *e.g.*, monopolistic competition, oligopoly, duopoly or monopoly.

Thus, at one extreme stands perfect competition and at the other monopoly: In between these two extremes, there are all degrees of competition or lack of competition.

The following Table 18.1 shows at a glance different types of market forms on the basis of the nature of competition.

Table 18.1. Different types of market forms.

Use of the market	*No. of firms*	*Nature of the commodity*
	A. Perfect Competition	
Perfect or pure competition	Infinite	Homogeneous
	B. Imperfect Competition	
(*a*) Monopolistic Competition	Many	Differentiated
(*b*) Perfect Oligopoly	A few	Homogeneous
(*c*) Imperfect Oligopoly	A few	Differentiated
	C. Pure or Absolute Monopoly	
Pure or Absolute Monopoly	One	Homogeneous

Now we shall study these forms in some detail. We take first pure and perfect competition.

Pure Competition

Pure competition is said to exist when the following conditions are fulfilled:

(*i*) *Large number of buyers and sellers:* One condition of pure competition is that there should be operating in the market a large number of buyers and sellers. If that is so, no single seller or purchaser will be able to influence the market price, because the output of any single firm is only a small proportion of the total output and of the total demand. Hence, market price has to be taken as given and unalterable by every purchaser and seller. Thus, no individual purchaser can influence the market price by varying his own demand and no single firm is in a position to affect the market price by varying its own output. "Thus the market price is a parameter to be reacted to rather than a variable to be determined."

(*ii*) *Homogeneous product:* The second condition is that the commodity produced by all firms should be standardized or identical. In case all firms produce Kalyan-S wheat.

It is immaterial for the purchaser as to who has produced it. He can buy it as well from the other. This condition ensures that the same price rules in the market for the same commodity. The product of each firm is a perfect substitute for the products of all other firms in the industry.

It is the purchaser's opinion which will determine whether the products are identical or not. Even if the products are really identical, the purchaser may have a prejudice against the output of a particular firm and may consider it different. Hence, under pure competition, the consumers do not differentiate between the products of different firms.

When the quality is the same, the commodities are perfect substitutes for one another and their cross elasticity is infinity. In these circumstances, if a firm raises its price, it will lose all the customers. It can sell as much as it likes at the prevailing price. Why should it then think of lowering its price? Hence, a firm cannot raise its price nor need to lower it. That is why the prevailing market price is accepted and acted upon by all the dealers.

If the above two conditions, viz., homogeneous product and large number of buyers and sellers, are found in a market, it is said to be under pure competition.

Shape of Demand Curve in Pure Competition: When there is pure competition, the average revenue curve (AR) or demand curve of a firm is a horizontal straight line which means that any firm can sell any quantity at the prevailing price. Since the number of firms is very large, no individual firm has the power to vary the market price. Also, since the products are identical from the consumer's point of view, the price paid by them cannot be different. This is represented by the following Fig. 18.4.

OX and OY are the two axes. Along OX is represented the output and along OY the Price/Revenue. At OP price, a seller can sell as much as he likes. He cannot charge more and he will not charge less. If he raises the price, he will lose all his customers and if he charges less, he will be unnecessarily losing.

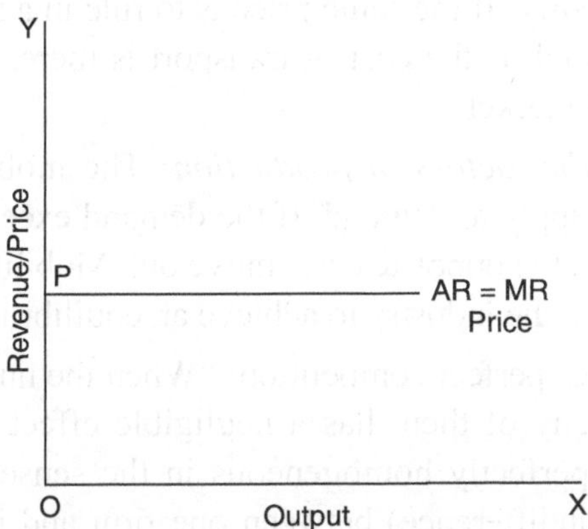

Fig. 18.4. Average revenue curve or sales curve of a firm under perfect competition.

Examples of pure competition are to be found in the case of farm products, *e.g.,* wheat, cotton, rice, etc. In this case, there is a large number of producers, each producing an insignificant portion of the total market supply. In other fields, we seldom come across' pure competition.

Perfect Competition: Conditions

There is said to be perfect competition when every purchaser and seller is so small relative to the entire market that he cannot influence the market price by increasing or decreasing his purchases or his output.

Perfect competition is a wider term than pure competition. Besides, the two conditions of pure competition mentioned above, viz., the homogeneity of the product and the existence of a large number of dealers, several other conditions must also be fulfilled to make it a perfect competition.

Thus, the conditions of perfect competition are :

(*i*) Large number of buyers and sellers.

(*ii*) Homogeneous product.

(*iii*) *Free entry or exit:* There should be no restrictions, legal or otherwise, on the firms' entry into, or exit from, the industry. In this situation all the firms will be making just normal profit. If the profit is more than normal, new firms will enter and extra profit will be competed away; and if, on the other hand, profit is less than normal, some firms will quit, raising the profits for the remaining firms. But if there are restrictions on the entry of new firms, the existing firms may continue to enjoy supernormal profit. Only when there are no restrictions on entry or exit, the firms will earn normal profit.

(*iv*) *Perfect knowledge:* Another assumption of perfect competition is that the purchasers and sellers should be fully aware of the prices that are being offered and accepted. In case there is ignorance among the dealers, the same price cannot rule in the market for the same commodity. When the producers and the customers have full knowledge of the prevailing price, nobody will offer more and none will accept less, and the same price will rule throughout the market. The producers can sell at that price as much as they like and the buyers also can buy as much as they like.

(*v*) *Absence of transport costs:* If the same price is to rule in a market, it is necessary that no cost of transport has to be incurred. If the cost of transport is there, the prices must differ to that extent in different sectors of the market.

(*vi*) *Perfect mobility of the factors of production:* The mobility is essential in order to enable the firms to adjust their supply to demand. If the demand exceeds supply, additional factors will move into the industry and in the opposite case, move out. Mobility of the factors of production is essential to enable the firms and the industry to achieve an equilibrium position.

Mrs. Robinson thus defines perfect competition: "When the number of firms being large, so that a change in the output of any of them has a negligible effect upon the total output of the commodity, the commodity is perfectly homogeneous in the sense that the buyers are alike in respect of their preferences (or indifference) between one firm and its rivals, then competition is perfect, and the elasticity of demand for the individual firm is infinite."

Here is a comprehensive definition: "Perfect competition is the name given to an industry or to a market characterized by a large number of buyers and sellers all engaged in the purchase and sale of a homogeneous commodity, with perfect knowledge, of market prices and quantities, no discrimination and perfect mobility of resources."

Chamberlain thus brings the distinction between pure competition and perfect competitions: "Purity requires only the absence of monopoly, which is realized when there are many buyers and sellers of the same (perfectly standardized) product. Perfection is concerned with other matters as well: mobility of resources, perfect knowledge, etc. Perfection is a different thing from its purity, meaning by the latter its freedom from monopoly elements."

Imperfect Competition

Imperfect competition takes three main forms :

(*a*) Monopolistic competition,

(*b*) Oligopoly, and

(*c*) Monopoly.

We shall briefly describe below these forms of imperfect competition.

Monopolistic Competition: The main features of monopolistic competition are as under:

(*i*) Under monopolistic competition, the number of dealers is not large; at any rate not so large as under perfect competition.

(*ii*) The products are not homogeneous; they are, on the other hand, differentiated, inter alia, by means of different labels attached to them such as different brands of toilet requisites.

(*iii*) Either in ignorance or on account of transport costs or lack of mobility of the factors of production, same price does not rule in the market throughout. Rather different prices are charged by different producers for products which are really similar, but are made to appear different through advertisement, high pressure salesmanship and labeling and branding. The result is that each producer comes to have a hold on a clientele from whom he can charge higher prices.

(*iv*) Under monopolistic competition, the demand curve or sales curve or what is also called average revenue (AR) curve, is not a horizontal straight line. It is, on the other hand, a downward sloping curve. This means that the seller can sell more by reducing price, whereas under perfect competition, he need not reduce the price for he can sell any amount at prevailing price. Under monopolistic competition, the producer can charge higher prices, because his customers are attached to him.

The seller can thus have a price policy of his own, whereas a seller under perfect competition has no price policy; he has merely to accept the market price.

(*v*) Thus, under monopolistic competition, the demand for the product is not perfectly elastic; it is responsive to changes in price.

This form of market is a blend of the monopoly and competition and has been called monopolistic competition or 'competing monopolists' by Chamberlain, an American economist. In the real world, we have neither absolute monopoly (*i.e.,* absence of competition) nor perfect competition, but monopolistic competition, *i.e.,* partly monopoly and partly competition. The products are not complete substitutes for one another but they are close substitutes.

As mentioned already, monopolistic competition is only one form of imperfect competition where there is a fairly large number of sellers but products are differentiated. Other forms of imperfect competition are oligopoly and ordinary monopoly.

Oligopoly: When in a market, there are only a few sellers of a product, it is called oligopoly. The basic characteristic of an oligopolistic situation is the fact that every seller can exercise an important influence on the price output policies of his rivals. This is due to the fact that the number of sellers is not very large and each seller controls a substantial portion of the supply. Every seller, therefore, is so influential that his rivals cannot ignore the likely adverse effect on them of a given change in the price-output policy of any single manufacturer. This rival consciousness, or the recognition on the part of the seller of the fact of interdependence, is the most important feature of oligopolistic situations.

Oligopoly differs from monopoly and monopolistic competition in the sense that, in monopoly, there is a single seller; in monopolistic competition, there is quite a large number of them; but in oligopoly, there is only a small number of sellers.

Oligopoly without product differentiation: Under oligopoly, the pricing theory is fundamentally the same as in other forms of competition with this difference that the larger the number of firms the greater will be differences in marginal costs and more remote will be the possibility of collusion or agreement whether tacit or explicit. When they all deal in a standardized product and each is producing a considerable portion of the total output, the price and output policy of each producer is likely to affect the others appreciably, but none can predict precisely how. The price which will be fixed in oligopoly without product differentiation is thus indeterminate.

Oligopoly with product differentiation: In case there is product differentiation, monopoly agreements are even less likely. Since products are not similar, any producer in oligopoly can raise or lower his price without any fear of losing customers or immediate reactions from his rivals. Cut throat competition is unlikely. However, keen rivalry among them may create conditions of monopolistic competition. The price, in the long run, may settle at a level between the monopoly price and that in cut-throat competition.

Monopoly: When there is monopoly, a single producer or seller controls the entire market. There are no substitutes for his product. He controls the entire supply and he can fix the price. He is the firm and he also constitutes the industry. It is a one-firm industry. Thus, under monopoly, the distinction between the firm and industry disappears. The average revenue (AR) curve (or the demand curve) always slopes downwards to the right as in monopoly competition, but it is less elastic in monopoly than in monopolistic competition. In monopoly, there is no need to differentiate products because no close substitutes are available. It is one product, homogeneous and completely under the control of the monopolist.

Market Classifications and Cross Elasticity of Demand

Some economists (*e.g.,* Tiffin) have used the concept of cross elasticity of demand for measuring the extent of competition among the firms. In this way, on the basis of the cross elasticity of demand an attempt has been made to classify the market structures. In other words, we can distinguish between the various types of market situations on the basis of cross elasticity of demand. Stonier and Hague observe in this connection, "In perfect competition, the cross elasticity of demand for the product of a single firm with respect to a change in the price of the rest of industry will be infinite. That is to say, the proportionate fall in the demand for the product of a single firm will be infinitely large compared with any given proportionate fall in the price of the product of the whole industry. Similarly, in monopolistic competition, the cross elasticity of demand for the product of a single firm with respect to a change in the price of the other products made in the monopolistic 'group' will be very high. The cross elasticity of demand for the product of a monopolist with respect to a fall in the price of other products in the economy will be very low." In other words, when the cross elasticity of demand is infinite, it is a case of perfect competition; when it is very high it is a case of monopolistic competition and when it is very low, it is a case of monopoly.

But cross elasticity of demand is a very unsatisfactory measure of the extent of competition prevailing in the market. It has been pointed out by some economists (*e.g.,* Chamberlain) that cross elasticity of demand of any perfectly competitive firm is zero (and not infinity). As mentioned above, under monopoly also cross elasticity of demand is zero. Hence, on the basis of cross elasticity, the two market situations of pure competition and pure monopoly are lumped together whereas they are two opposite extreme cases. In a perfectly competitive situation, cross elasticity of demand is zero because a firm is producing a product that has so many identical substitutes produced by other firms. Hence if a purely competitive firm tries to raise its price, its product will be ousted by the homogeneous products of other firms.

Cross elasticity as a criterion for classification of markets is also criticized on the ground that it ignores "the two basic determinants of market structure: the degree of closeness or remoteness of substitution among products and the number of firms in the relevant group or industry."

Thus, we may conclude that cross elasticity of demand, as a criterion of market classification, is not satisfactory. The best way to classify markets is, therefore, on the basis of number of firms in the industry and the nature of the product (that is, closeness or remoteness of substitutability).

18.4 CRITERIA FOR CLASSIFICATION OF MARKET

We have already given the classification of markets. The following criteria for the classification of markets have been suggested:

1. Substitutability of Products

This criterion refers to the existence and closeness of substitutes *i.e.,* the extent and form of competition among the firms in the industry. This criterion may be measured by the conventional price cross-elasticity (*ep*) for the products of any two firms (*i* & *j*)

$$ep.ji = \frac{dqj.pi}{dpi.qj}$$

This formula measures the degree to which the sales of the firm are affected by the price charged by the firm in the industry. If the elasticity is high, the products of the two firms will be close substitutes. In the case of perfect substitutes (*i.e.* homogeneous products), the price cross-elasticity between every pair of producers approaches infinity. On the other hand, if the products are differentiated, but can be substituted for one another, the price cross-elasticity will be finite and positive. If products are not substitutes, their price cross-elasticity will tend to zero.

2. Inter-Dependence

This refers to the extent to which firms in the industry take into account the reactions of competitors. This criterion is related to the number of firms in the industry and the degree of differentiation of the products. If the number of firms is large, no firm will take into account the actions of the rivals and each firm will act accordingly. But if there are only a few firms in the industry, they will all be alert as to what rivals may be doing and mould their own policy accordingly.

The degree of interdependence of the firms will be measured by an unconventional quantity, cross-elasticity for the products of any two firms, thus will be:

$$\text{E}q.ji = \frac{dpi.qi}{\text{D}qj.pj}$$

This formula measures the proportionate change in the price of *j*th firm resulting from an infinitesimally small change in the quantity produced by the *i*th firm. The higher the value of this elasticity the stronger the interdependence of the firms. In case the number of the firms in the industry is large, each firm will tend to ignore the reactions of the competitors whether the products are close substitutes or not. In a case like this, the quantity cross-elasticity between each pair of the producers will tend to be zero. But if the number of firms in the market is small *e.g.*, oligopoly, there will be marked interdependence even when the products are differentiated. The quantity cross-elasticity in this case will be finite.

In the case of a monopolist both elasticities will be zero, because there is only one firm in the industry and there are no close substitutes.

There is the third criterion viz the condition of entry *i.e.,* whether new firms are free to gain entry into the industry without hindrance or not.

The 'condition of entry' has been defined by the expression:

$$E = \frac{Pa - Pc}{Pc}$$

Here E is the condition of entry, Pc is the price under pure competition and Pa is the price actually charged.

Self-Assessment Questions

1. Explain the concept of market. Give criteria for classification of market.
2. Explain the concept of equilibrium price.
3. Discuss the main features of following firms in short.

   (*i*) Perfect competition (*ii*) Monopoly

   (*iii*) Monopolistic competition (*iv*) Oligopoly.

Unit **19**

REVENUE AND REVENUE CURVES

19.1 INTRODUCTION

Average revenue is the revenue per unit of the commodity sold. It is found by dividing total revenue by the number of units sold. But since different units of a commodity are sold at the same price, in the market, average revenue equals price at which the commodity is sold. Thus, average revenue means price. Since the consumer's demand curve is a graphic relation between price and the amount demanded, it also represents the average revenue or price at which the various amounts of a commodity are sold, because the price offered by the buyer is the revenue from the seller's point of view. Therefore, average revenue (AR) curve of the firm is really the same thing as demand curve of the consumer.

On the other hand, marginal revenue at any level of a firm's output is the net revenue earned by selling another (additional) unit of the product. Algebraically, it is the addition to the total revenue earned by selling '*n*' units of product instead of $n - 1$, where *n* is any given number. The word net in this definition is important. If the price of a product falls when more of it is offered for sale then that would involve a loss on the previous units which were sold at a higher price before and will now be sold at the reduced price along with the additional one. This loss in the previous units must be deducted from the revenue earned by the additional unit.

Suppose a firm is selling 7 units of the output at the price of ₹ 16 per unit. Now, if it wants to sell 8 units instead of and thereby the price of the product falls to ₹ 15 per unit, then the marginal revenue will not be equal to ₹ 15 at which the eighth unit is sold. Seven units, which were sold at the price of ₹ 16 before, will now all have to be sold at the reduced price of ₹ 15 and that will mean the loss of one rupee on each of the previous 7 units. The total loss on the previous units would be equal to ₹ 7. Therefore, this loss of ₹ 7 should be deducted from the price of ₹ 15 of the eighth unit while reckoning the marginal revenue. The marginal revenue in this case, therefore, will be ₹ 15 – ₹ 7 = ₹ 8 and not ₹ 15 which is the average revenue.

The marginal revenue can also be directly found by taking out the difference between the total revenues before and after selling the additional unit as follows:

Total revenue when 7 units are sold at the price of

₹ 16 = 7 × 16 = ₹ 112

Total revenue when 8 units are sold at the price of

₹ 15 = 8 × 15 = ₹ 120

Therefore, Marginal Revenue or the net revenue earned by the 8th unit = 120 – 112 = ₹ 8

Thus, Marginal Revenue of the *n*th unit.

= difference in total revenue in increasing the sale from $n - 1$ to n units.

Or

= Price of *n*th unit minus loss in revenue on previous units resulting from price reduction.

Generally speaking, marginal revenue is less than price as indicated by the above formula. But in perfect competition, when a firm can sell any amount at the ruling market price, marginal revenue is equal to average revenue or price since there is no loss incurred on the previous units.

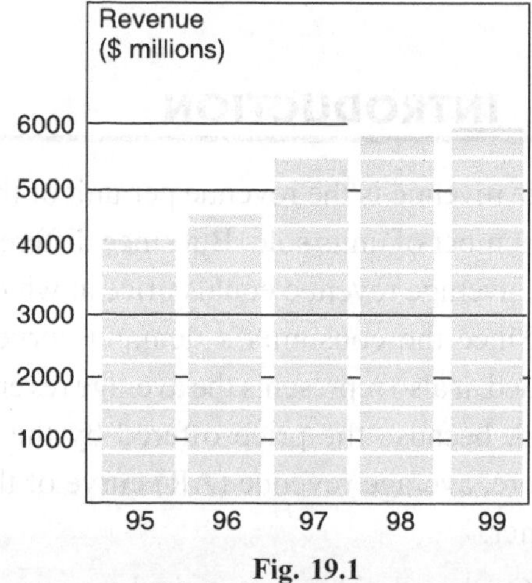

Fig. 19.1

19.2 RELATIONSHIP BETWEEN AVERAGE REVENUE AND MARGINAL REVENUE

Let us consider the relationship between marginal, average and total revenue at previous levels of output more fully with the help of a table given below. This table represents a situation of a hypothetical firm.

Table 19.1. Total average and marginal revenue schedules.

Number of unis sold	*Price or average revenue*	*Total revenue AR × (addition quantity sold)*	*Marginal revenue made to total revenue*
(1)	(2)	(3)	(4)
1	22	22	22
2	21	42	20
3	20	60	18

4	19	76	16
5	18	90	14
6	17	102	12
7	16	112	10
8	15	120	8
9	14	126	6
10	13	130	4

In the above table, Column 2 shows the average revenue, while Column 4 shows the marginal revenue. Marginal revenue has been derived from the total revenue column of the table. Thus, in going from two to three units the marginal revenue is 18 and this is found out by subtracting 42 from 60, and so on. The table further indicates that when average revenue is falling, marginal revenue is less than average revenue.

(*i*) Total Revenue = Price × Quantity

$$TR = P \times Q$$

(*ii*) Average Revenue = $\frac{\text{Total revenue}}{\text{Quantity}}$

$$AR = \frac{TR}{Q}$$

(*iii*) Marginal Revenue = $\frac{\text{Change in total revenue}}{\text{Change in quantity}}$

$$MR = \frac{\Delta TR}{\Delta Q}$$

Example. If the demand curve is given as

$P = 10 - 4\,Q$ then find (*i*) The total revenue TR, and

(*ii*) The marginal revenue MR

$$TR = P \times Q$$

$$= (10 \times 4Q) \times Q$$

$$TR = 10Q - 4Q^2 \quad ...(i)$$

Marginal revenue = Derivation of total revenue

$$\frac{D}{DX}(TR) = MR = 10Q - 4Q^2$$

$$MR = 10 - 8Q = 0$$

$$8Q = 10$$

$$Q = \frac{10}{8} = \frac{5}{4}$$

Under Perfect Competition

When competition is perfect, as already seen, the average revenue curve of the firm is a horizontal straight line. This is so because an individual firm under perfect competition, by its own action, cannot influence the price. The seller under perfect competition can sell any amount of the commodity at the ruling market price. In this case:

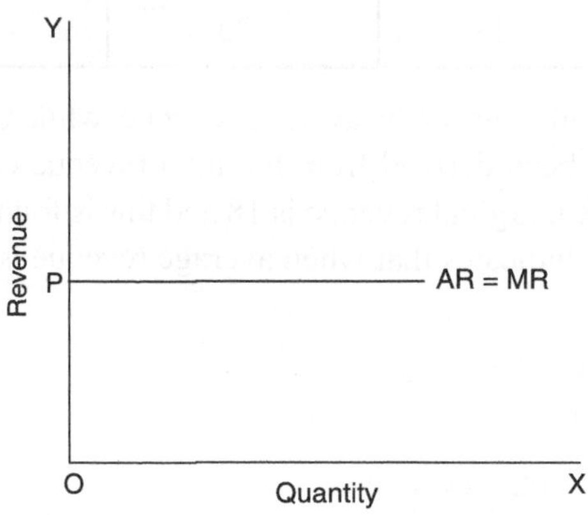

Fig. 19.2. AR and MR curves under perfect competition.

When average revenue curve is the horizontal line the marginal revenue curve coincides with the average revenue curve. This is so because additional units are sold at the same price as before and no loss is incurred on the previous units which would have resulted—if the sale of additional units would have forced the price down.

The average revenue and marginal revenue curves of a firm under perfect competition are shown in Fig. 19.2.

Under Imperfect Competition

By converting the schedules of Average Revenue given in table along side into curves, we get two downward sloping curves and find that marginal revenue curve is below average revenue curve. This is shown in Fig. 19.3 AR is the average revenue curve and MR, the dotted curve, is the marginal revenue curve. As we shall see in a later chapter, the divergence between the average revenue and marginal revenue as shown in the figure here is actually found when a firm is working under conditions of monopoly or imperfect competition. It is quite obvious that when price is falling as indicated

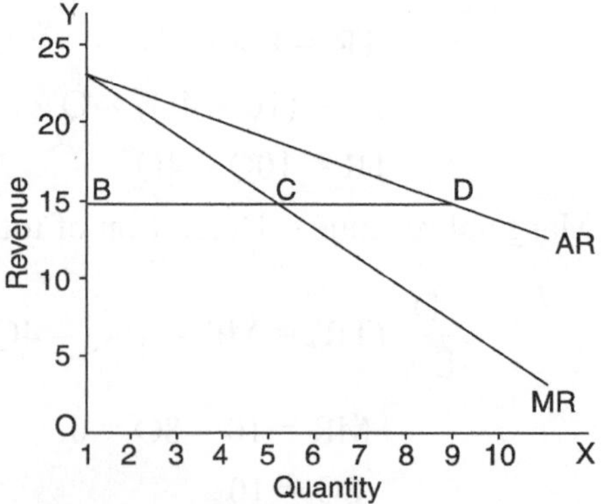

Fig. 19.3. AR and MR curves under imperfect competition.

by the declining AR curve, the marginal revenue must always be less than average revenue, because a falling price must mean some loss on the sale of additional supply. That is why MR curve lies below AR curve.

How much is MR below AR? We have seen above that when average revenue curve falls downward, the marginal revenue curve lies below it (or to the left of it). Now the question arises how far to the left (or below) will it lie? This will depend on the shape of the AR and MR curves: (*a*) They may be straight downward sloping lines or (*b*) they may be convex to the origin; or (*c*) they may be concave to the origin.

(*a*) When both the marginal revenue curve and average revenue curve are straight lines and sloping downwards, as shown in Fig. 19.3, the marginal revenue curve will cut in the middle of any line perpendicular to the Y-axis. That is, if from D, any point on the average revenue curve, we draw DB a perpendicular to the Y-axis, then marginal revenue curve MR must pass through the middle of this perpendicular, *i.e.,* through C, where DC = BC.

(*b*) However, if the average revenue curve is convex to the origin, as in Fig. 19.3, the marginal revenue curve MR cuts any line perpendicular to the Y-axis more than half-way from the average revenue curve, *i.e.,* DC > BC.

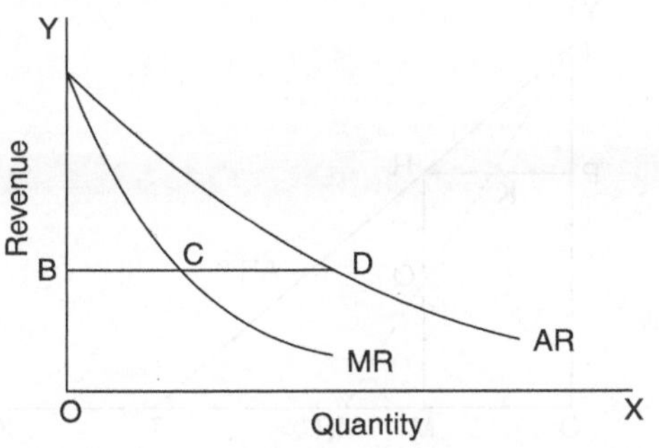

Fig. 19.4. Convex AR and MR.

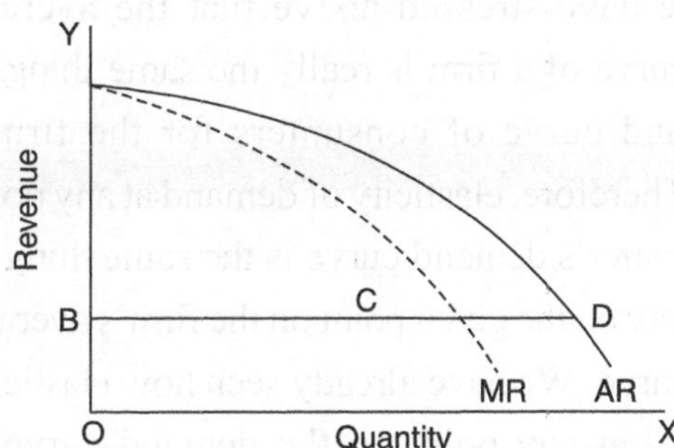

Fig. 19.5. Concave AR and MR.

(*c*) Again, where the average revenue curve is concave to the origin (Fig. 19.5), the marginal revenue curve cuts any perpendicular line to the Y-axis less than half-way from the average revenue curve, *i.e.,* DC < BC.

Revenue Curve in Oligopoly Market

In oligopoly market the demand curve is of a kinky nature. It is referred as kinky demand curve.

In the above diagram. X-axis is quantity and Y-axis is price. 'DD' is total market demand curve, whereas 'd_1d_1' is the individual firm demand curve, but this firm is a leader which is selling maximum output. Hence in the oligopoly the demand curve takes the slope of 'd_1 ED'. It is having a bend kink at point E.

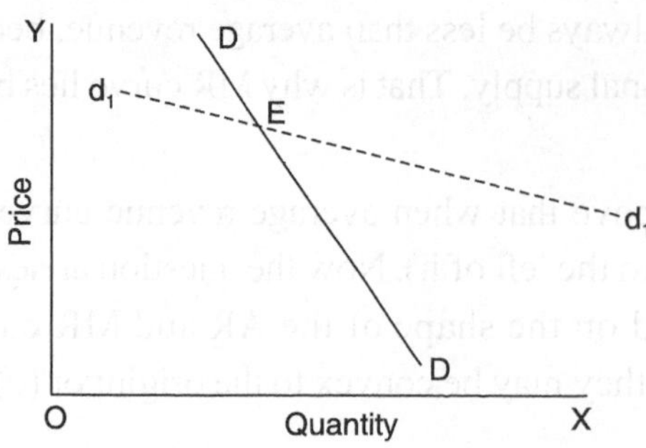

Fig. 19.6. Demand under oligopoly.

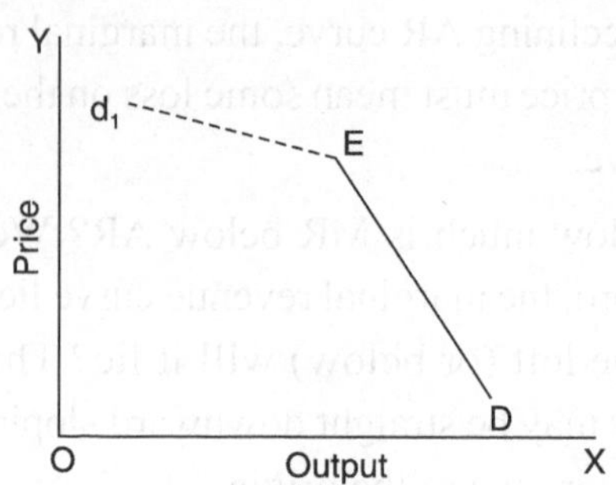

Fig. 19.7. Kinky demand curve.

The above diagram shows the 'kinky demand curve' concept of oligopoly market.

Elasticity of Demand, Average Revenue and Marginal Revenue

There is a very useful relationship between elasticity of demand, average revenue and marginal revenue at any level of output. We shall make use of this relation extensively when we come to the study of price determination under different market conditions. Let us study briefly what this relation is:

We have stressed above that the average revenue curve of a firm is really the same thing as the demand curve of consumers for the firm's product. Therefore, elasticity of demand at any point on a consumer's demand curve is the same thing as the elasticity on the given point on the firm's average revenue curve. We have already seen how elasticity of demand at any point on the demand curve is measured. With this measure of point elasticity of demand, we can study the relationship between average revenue, marginal revenue and elasticity of demand at any level of output.

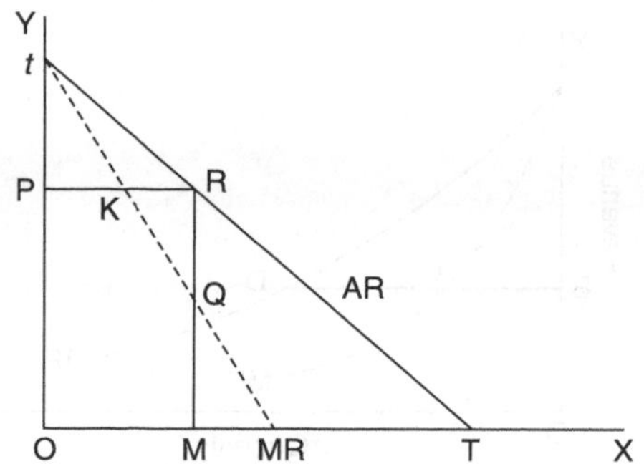

Fig. 19.8. AR, MR and price elasticity of demand.

In Fig. 19.8, AR and MR respectively are the average and the marginal revenue curves. Elasticity of demand at point R on the average revenue curve

$$= \frac{RT}{Rt}$$

Now, in triangles PtR and MRT

$\angle t$PR = $\angle$RMT (right angles)

$\angle t$RR = $\angle$RTM (corresponding angles)

$\angle$PtR = $\angle$MRT (being the third angle)

Therefore, triangles PtR and MRT are equiangular,

Hence, $$\frac{RT}{Rt} = \frac{RM}{tP} \qquad ...(i)$$

In the triangle PtK and KRQ

$$PK = RK$$

$$\angle PKt = \angle RKQ \qquad \text{(vertically opposite)}$$

$$\angle tPK = \angle KRQ \qquad \text{(right angles)}$$

Therefore, triangles PtK and RQK are congruent (*i.e.,* equal in all respects).

Hence, $$Pt = RQ \qquad ...(ii)$$

From (*i*) and (*ii*) we get

$$\text{Elasticity at} \quad R = \frac{RT}{Rt} = \frac{RM}{tP} = \frac{RM}{RQ}$$

Now, it is obvious from Fig. 19.8 that

$$\frac{RM}{RQ} = \frac{RM}{RM - QM}$$

$$\text{Hence, elasticity at R} = \frac{RM}{RM - QM}$$

It will also be clear from the figure that RM is average revenue and QM is the marginal revenue at the output OM which corresponds to the point R on the average revenue curve. Therefore,

$$\text{Elasticity at R} = \frac{\text{Average revenue}}{\text{Average revenue} - \text{Marginal revenue}}$$

If, A stands for Average Revenue

M stands for Marginal Revenue

e stands for Point Elasticity on the Average Revenue Curve

Then $$e = \frac{A}{A - M}$$

It follows from this that

$$eA - eM = A$$

$$\therefore \quad eA - A = eM$$

$$\therefore \quad A(e - 1) = eM$$

$$\therefore \quad A = \frac{eM}{e - 1}$$

Hence, $$A = M\left(\frac{e}{e-1}\right)$$

And also, $$M = A\left(\frac{e-1}{e}\right)$$

The general rule therefore is: At any output,

$$\text{Average Revenue} = \text{Marginal Revenue} \times \frac{e-1}{e} \text{ and Marginal Revenue}$$
$$= \text{Average Revenue} \times \frac{e-1}{e},$$

where e stands for Point Elasticity of Demand on the Average Revenue Curve.

With the help of these formulae, we can find marginal revenue at any output from average revenue at the same output, provided we know the point elasticity of demand on the average revenue curve. If the demand elasticity of a firm's average revenue curve is equal to one, marginal revenue equals zero, because:

$$M = A\left(\frac{e-1}{e}\right) = A\left(\frac{1-1}{1}\right)$$
$$= A \times 0 = 0.$$

Similarly, when demand elasticity on a firm's average revenue curve is 2, the marginal revenue equals half the average revenue. This is because:

$$M = A\left(\frac{e-1}{e}\right) = A\left(\frac{2-1}{1}\right)$$
$$= A\left(\frac{1}{2}\right) = \frac{1}{2}A.$$

By applying the formula for various elasticities of demand at different points (or at different levels of output) on the average revenue curve, it will be found that marginal revenue is always positive at any point or output where the elasticity of the average revenue curve is greater than one, and marginal revenue is always negative where the elasticity of the average revenue curve is less than one.

19.3 RELATIONSHIP BETWEEN AR, MR, TR AND ELASTICITY OF DEMAND

By making use of the formula given above $MR = AR\frac{e-1}{e}$, where MR is marginal revenue, AR is average revenue and e is elasticity of demand, we can find out the relationship between AR, MR and TR on the one hand and elasticity of demand on the other.

If the elasticity of demand e is equal to one then:

$$MR = AR\left(\frac{e-1}{e}\right)$$

$$= AR \times \frac{0}{1} = 0$$

$$= AR \times \left(\frac{1-1}{1}\right)$$

Similarly, it can be shown that if $e > 1$, MR is positive and if $e < 1$, MR is negative.

The relationship can be illustrated by the following diagram (Fig. 19.9).

In this diagram DD is a straight line demand curve or AR curve, MR is the marginal revenue curve and OD is the total revenue curve. At the middle point C of AR curve elasticity is one ($e = 1$). On its lower half it is less than one-one ($e > 1$). Referring to the formula.

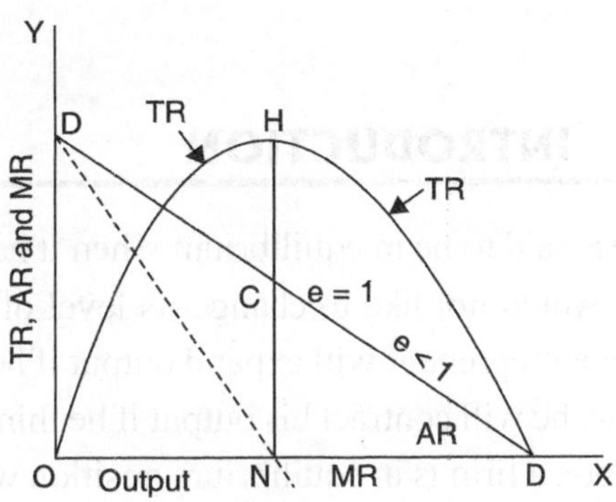

Fig. 19.9. AR, MR and TR.

Self-Assessment Questions

1. Explain the relationship between average revenue and marginal revenue with the help of the concept of elasticity of demand.
2. Distinguish between total tevenue, average revenue and marginal revenue. Explain their relationship.
3. Show low average and marginal revenue curve can be derived from total product curve.
4. Why do average and marginal revenue curves of a firm all under in perfect competition?
5. Explain the average revenue curve of a firm under perfect competition. Is it identical with its marginal revenue curve? Give reasons. What is the shape of this curve?
6. What is the importance of average and marginal revenue curves in determining producer Equilibrium?
7. Explain "marginal revenue curve of a firm cannot be above its average revenue curve."
8. Show that the equality between a firm's marginal revenue and marginal cost is a necessary, but not sufficient, condition for profit maximization.
9. Explain the meaning of average revenue and marginal revenue of a firm. Explain and illustrate the nature of their respective curves in perfectly competitive and monopoly markets.
10. Establish the relationship between the marginal revenue, the average revenue and the elasticity of demand. Can the elasticity of demand be less than unity at the equilibrium price of a commodity (*a*) under perfect competition, and (*b*) under monopoly?

Unit 20 EQUILIBRIUM OF THE FIRM AND INDUSTRY

20.1 INTRODUCTION

A firm is said to be in equilibrium when it has no incentive either to expand or to contract its output. A firm would not like to change its level of output only when its total profits are the maximum. A rational entrepreneur will expand output if he thinks he can increase his total profits by doing so, and likewise, he will contract his output if he thinks he can avoid losses and thus increase his total profits. Therefore, a firm is in equilibrium position when it is earning maximum money profits.

Having studied marginal revenue and average revenue in the previous chapter, we are now in a position to discuss the conditions of equilibrium of the firm. Here, we shall attempt only an analysis of the conditions of a firm's equilibrium in general and not with reference to any particular market forms. The firm's equilibrium conditions with particular reference to different market forms, *i.e.,* under perfect competition, monopoly and imperfect competition, will be discussed in later chapters.

Fig. 20.1. Conditions of firm's equilibrium.

Before explaining a firm's equilibrium, we assume that the entrepreneur, *i.e.,* the owner of the firm, is rational. The rationality on the part of the entrepreneur implies that he tries to maximize his money profits. This is a fundamental assumption in the theory of production and without this; the equilibrium of the firm cannot be easily explained. A corollary from the assumption of rationality is that whatever output the firm produces, it produces as cheaply as possible given the existing production techniques. We further assume, for the sake of simplicity, that the firm produces only one product. Our analysis would, however, remain valid also in case of multiple product firm. But when a firm produces two goods or more, certain other complications arise which we wish to avoid at this stage.

The equilibrium of the firm can be explained in two ways:

(*i*) With the help of total revenue and total cost curves, and

(*ii*) With the aid of marginal revenue and marginal cost curves.

20.2 EQUILIBRIUM OF FIRM: BY CURVES OF TOTAL REVENUE AND TOTAL COST

A rational entrepreneur will expand output if he thinks he can increase his profits by doing so and he will likewise contract output if thereby he can avoid losses and thus increase profits. He will be in equilibrium position at the level of output where his money profits are the maximum. In other words, he will then have no inducement either to expand or contract his output when he is earning maximum money profits. Now, profits are the difference between total revenue and total cost. Hence, the point where this difference is the maximum will represent the position of maximum profits and, therefore, of equilibrium.

A cost-revenue situation of a hypothetical firm is depicted in Fig. 20.2, where TC represents total cost curve and TR represents the total revenue curve. It will be noted that total cost curve TC starts not at the origin but at the height OF. This is so because it is assumed that even if the firm produces nothing (or shut down), it has to bear certain costs of production due to fixed factors. These are the fixed costs.

Break-even Point

From the Fig. 20.2, it is clear that at any output smaller than OL, total cost exceeds total revenue and the firm is having losses. At the output OL total cost equals total revenue and the firm is having neither losses nor profits. This point L is called 'Break-even point'. At the outputs larger than ON, the total revenue is less than total cost so that the firm is having losses. Point N is again a break-even point. Between OL and ON will lie the optimum point of maximum profits.

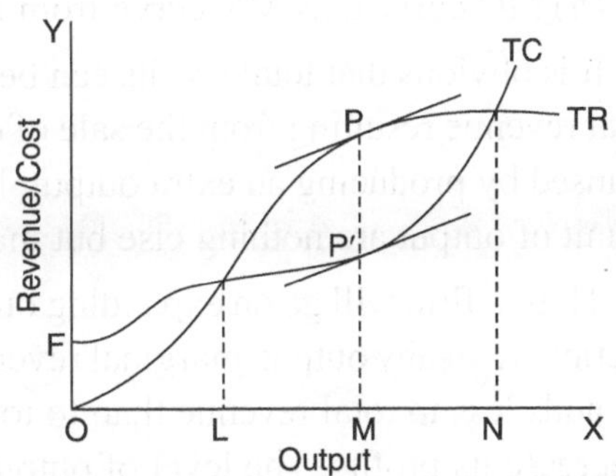

Fig. 20.2. Equilibrium of firm: total revenue and total cost.

The maximum-profit will lie revenue-cost spread is the largest or in other words where the vertical distance between the total revenue and total cost curves is the greatest. The maximum profit point in our diagram is M where PP′ is the longest vertical distance between the two curves. Hence, at this point, the firm is in equilibrium position and is earning maximum profits PP′ by producing OM output. The maximum profit point will in fact be at that output where the slopes of the two curves are the same, that is to say, where the tangents to the total cost and total revenue curves respectively are parallel as is shown in Fig. 20.2.

Limitations

This way of finding out of point of maximum profits by total revenue and total cost curves is reasonable and is also often used by businessmen but it has some limitations:

First, maximum vertical distance between the total revenue and total cost curve is difficult to see at a glance. Many tangents have to be drawn before one reaches the appropriate one corresponding to the maximum profit point. Secondly, in this method, it is not possible to discover price per unit at various outputs at first sight. Total revenue has to be divided by total number of units produced in order to get the price per unit. For example, at the equilibrium output OM the price can be found by dividing MP by OM.

Owing to these limitations, complicated problems of equilibrium analysis cannot be discussed easily and clearly in this way of representing equilibrium of the firm. Modern economists, therefore, adopt a method which shows marginal quantities, *i.e.,* marginal cost and marginal revenue at first sight.

Now, we turn to this second way of representing equilibrium of the firm.

20.3 EQUILIBRIUM OF FIRM: BY CURVES OF MARGINAL REVENUE AND MARGINAL COST

We know that a firm will be in equilibrium when it is earning maximum profits. We shall see presently that for a firm, to make maximum profits, two conditions are essential:

(*i*) Marginal Revenue (MR) = Marginal Cost (MC), and

(*ii*) MC curve cuts MR curve from below at the equilibrium point.

It is obvious that total profits can be increased by expanding output as long as the addition to the total revenue resulting from the sale of extra unit of output is greater than the addition to the total cost caused by producing an extra output. Now the addition to total revenue and total cost due to an extra unit of output are nothing else but marginal revenue and marginal cost respectively.

Thus, a firm will go on expanding output as long as marginal revenue exceeds marginal cost of production. If, at any output, marginal revenue falls short of marginal cost, *i.e.,* if an additional unit of output adds less to total revenue than to total cost, the firm will contract output to avoid losses and thus increase its profits. The level of output where marginal revenue and marginal cost are equal is the point of maximum profit.

Before this point of equality of marginal revenue with marginal cost is reached, the firm will be increasing its total profits by producing more as it is adding more to the total revenue than to the total cost. But if production is carried beyond this point of equality, the profits will start decreasing as the extra revenue will be smaller than the extra cost of production of a unit of output.

The whole argument can be explained with the help of Fig. 20.3 where MC is the marginal cost curve and MR the marginal revenue curve. AC and AR are the average cost and average revenue curves respectively. At the output OM, marginal cost equals marginal revenue (MR and MC curves intersect at E above this point). This represents the point of maximum profits and hence of equilibrium.

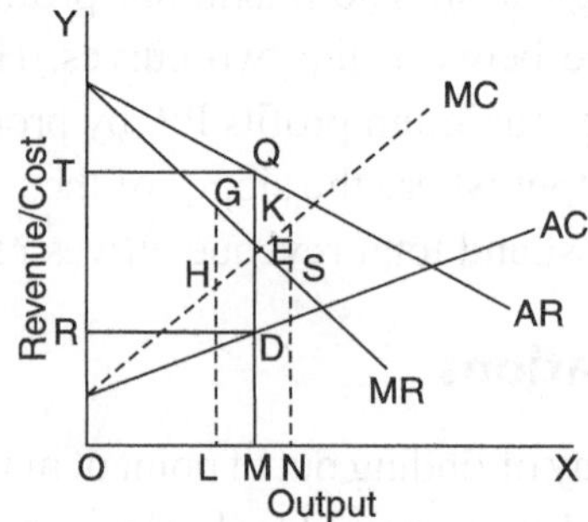

Fig. 20.3. Equilibrium of the firm: MR and MC.

At outputs smaller than OM, marginal revenue exceeds marginal cost and hence, there is scope for increasing profits by increasing output. For example, at output OL, marginal revenue is LG and the marginal cost is LH, and LG is greater than LH. It means that by producing the Lth unit, the firm is adding more to revenue than to its cost and, therefore, it will be profitable for it to produce the Lth unit.

Similarly, for every other unit till the Mth one, the marginal revenue exceeds marginal cost, and, therefore, the firm can increase its total profits by producing up to OM output. If the firm stops producing at OL, the units of output which could have added more money to the firm's revenue than to its cost would not have been produced and profits would have been smaller by the area GHE than they could have been. Thus, a firm has an incentive to produce up to OM level of output.

But if the output is increased beyond OM, marginal cost would exceed marginal revenue and the production of each additional unit beyond OM output would add more to total cost than to total revenue. For example, at ON output, the marginal cost is KN whereas the marginal revenue is SN and KN is greater than SN. Thus, production of more units than OM would involve losses, and reduce the total profits. Therefore, the firm would not like to produce beyond OM.

Hence, we conclude that firm's profits at OM output are the maximum and the firm is in equilibrium when:

Marginal Cost = Marginal Revenue.

This is one condition which is necessary but which is not sufficient for equilibrium.

In Fig. 20.3, the total profits earned by the firm in the equilibrium position can be easily found. At output OM, the average cost is DM while the average revenue is QM. Therefore, the profit per unit will be equal to QD and the total profits will be equal to the rectangle QDRT.

At an equilibrium position, the marginal cost curve must cut the marginal revenue curve from below. The condition that for a firm to be in equilibrium marginal cost must equal marginal revenue is no doubt a necessary condition but not a sufficient condition of equilibrium. For attaining equilibrium, a second condition must also be satisfied, viz., that the marginal cost (MC) curve must cut the marginal revenue (MR) curve from below at the point of equilibrium. This means that, beyond the equilibrium output, marginal cost must be greater than marginal revenue. If this condition is not met, a firm will not be earning maximum profits and hence will not be in equilibrium, as we shall see in the Fig. 20.4.

In Fig. 20.3, the point E (*i.e.,* output OM) satisfies these second conditions also, as the MC curve cuts the MR curve from below at E and MC is greater than MR beyond E. It will be clearly not profitable, therefore, to expand output beyond OM. But there can be such a cost-revenue situation, which satisfies the first condition of MC being equal to MR but the second condition of MC cutting MR curve from below is not met.

In Fig. 20.4, MR is the straight line marginal revenue curve (as we have already seen, a straight line marginal curve is actually faced by a firm under perfect competition). MC is the marginal cost of the firm. At point T where MC and MR intersect, the marginal cost equals marginal revenue but from the figure it is clear that at T marginal cost curve MC is cutting marginal revenue curve MR from above and, therefore, marginal cost is less than the marginal revenue beyond the point T. Obviously, T cannot be a position of equilibrium since after T, marginal cost is less than marginal revenue and it will be profitable for the firm to expand output. At T or output ON, the firm instead of making maximum profit is making maximum losses. At point P in the same figure, however, marginal cost curve is cutting marginal revenue curve from below and marginal cost beyond the point P is greater than marginal revenue. Hence, if the firm expands output beyond P (*i.e.*, OM output), it will be adding more to cost than to revenue clearly an unprofitable move. Thus, we conclude that in this figure, the point P, and not point T is the profit maximizing point. In this equilibrium position, the firm is producing equilibrium output OM.

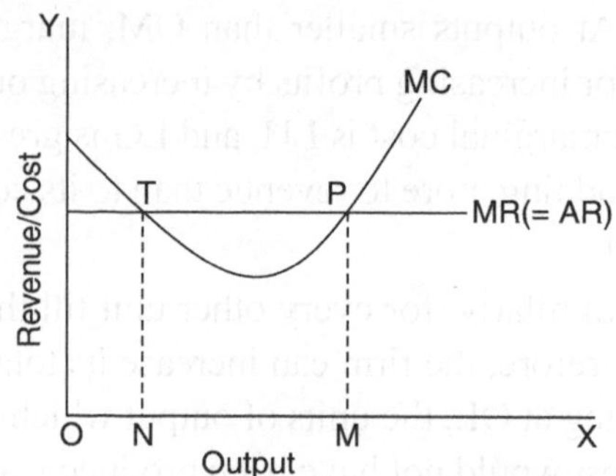

Fig. 20.4. MC cutting MR from below.

Similarly, point E in the Fig. 20.5 cannot be a position of equilibrium though MC equals MR at this point. This is because at E marginal cost curve is cutting the marginal revenue curve from E, both MC and MR curves are falling downwards, yet MC is falling more steeply than MR. Therefore, beyond E, MR is greater than MC. Hence, it will be profitable for the firm to expand output. Hence, E cannot be the position of the firm's equilibrium. For the firm to be in equilibrium, in Fig. 20.5(*a*) MC beyond E must rise upwards to cut the MR curve from below. If it does not rise upwards beyond E, then there can be no definite position of equilibrium in cost-revenue situation presented in Fig. 20.5(*a*).

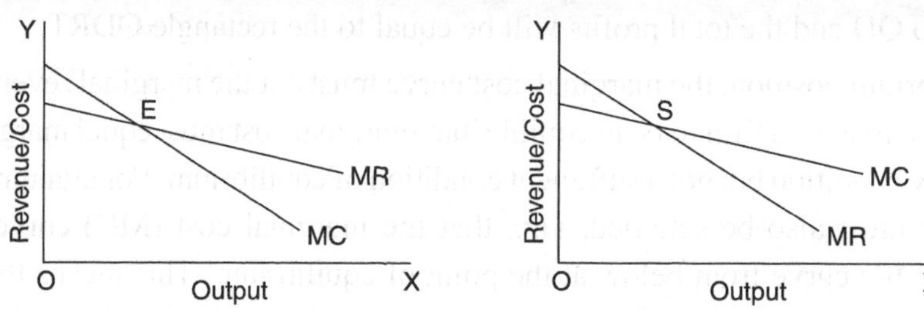

Fig. 20.5. Equilibrium when both MC and MR are falling.

It should be carefully noted that point S in Fig. 20.5(*b*) is really a position of equilibrium under the given cost-revenue situation. At S, MC equals MR and also MC curve is cutting MR curve from below. Although at S both MC and MR are falling downwards, yet MC is falling less rapidly than MR and, therefore, beyond S, MC is greater than MR. It will be unprofitable to expand output beyond S; nor will the firm move to the left of S, since it can increase its total profits by producing until S.

Two Conditions

Thus, we repeat that for a firm to be in equilibrium position, two conditions must be satisfied;

(*i*) MC = MR; and

(*ii*) MC curve must cut MR curve from below at the equilibrium output.

These two conditions of equilibrium hold good both in the short-run as well as in the long- run. Whether the period is short or long, a firm aims at maximization of profits and the profits are maximized only when the above two conditions are satisfied. But there is one difference. In the short-run, it the short-run marginal cost curve and in the long-run, it is the long-run marginal cost curve which is relevant for comparing with the marginal revenue curve.

Again, these two fundamental conditions, viz., marginal cost being equal to marginal revenue and MC curve cutting MR curve from below, are valid whether a firm is working under perfect competition, monopoly or imperfect competition. The difference lies only in the shape of the marginal revenue and marginal cost curves. Under perfect competition, MR and AR curves are horizontal straight lines and they coincide, but under imperfect competition MR and AR curves are downward sloping.

20.4 EQUILIBRIUM OF INDUSTRY

An industry is said to be in equilibrium when there is no tendency for it to increase or decrease its output. Now, it will have no tendency to expand or contract its output only when the demand for and supply of its product are in equilibrium. If, for instance, the demand for its product exceeds the supply, the output is bound to increase. On the other hand, if the supply is greater than the demand for its product, the supply will have to be contracted to restore the equilibrium between demand and supply. Hence, equality between demand and supply for the product of industry is very essential if the industry is to be in equilibrium.

We know that the equilibrium of the firm does not determine the price under perfect competition. A firm operating under perfect competition has to accept the price prevailing in the market. But it is the equilibrium of the industry as a whole that determines the price under perfect, competition. This means that there must be equilibrium between demand for the product of the industry and the supply of that product by the industry. Hence, we may say that industry is in equilibrium at the level of output at which the quantity demanded and the quantity supplied of its product are equal.

20.5 CONDITIONS OF EQUILIBRIUM

We have said above that an industry is said to be in equilibrium when there is no tendency for its output to increase or decrease. Now the output of the industry can vary (*a*) by the expansion or contraction of output by the individual firms and (*b*) by the entry or exit of the firms. Thus, an industry would not be in equilibrium when the individual firms have incentive to change their output nor is there any tendency for the new firms to enter or the existing firms to leave it.

Thus, besides equality between demand and supply of industry's products, two conditions must be satisfied if there is to be the equilibrium of the industry.

(*a*) Each and every firm should be in equilibrium. This will happen, as already explained, at the output where marginal cost is equal to marginal revenue and marginal cost curve cuts the marginal revenue curve from below at the equilibrium point.

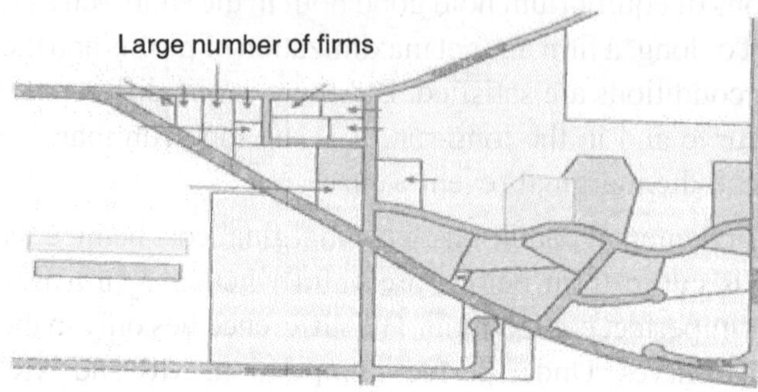

Fig. 20.6. Competitive industry.

(*b*) Industry as a whole should be in equilibrium, *i.e.,* there should be no tendency for the firms either to move into or out of the industry. This will happen when all the entrepreneurs, *i.e.,* owners of the firms in the industry, are earning only 'normal profits', that is, profits which are just sufficient to induce them to stay in the industry, and when no entrepreneur outside the industry thinks that he could earn at least normal profits if he were to enter it.

Thus, the concept of normal profits is important in defining and describing equilibrium of the industry. If we assume that all the entrepreneurs in a certain industry have the same transfer earnings, there would be a fixed amount of normal profits for the whole industry. Every entrepreneur must earn at least this fixed amount of normal profits, if he is to stay in the industry.

If firms in the industry are earning profits above the normal, there will be incentive for the firms outside the industry to enter it. This is so because there is every reason for the entrepreneurs outside the industry to expect that they would be able to earn at least normal profits if they entered this industry. Thus, there will be a tendency for the number of firms in that industry to increase.

If, on the other hand, some of the firms in the industry are earning profits below normal (or when they are having losses), they will leave the industry and search for normal profits elsewhere. Thus, the number of firms in that industry will tend to diminish.

Thus, equilibrium of the industry or full equilibrium, as it is sometimes called, would be attained when industry as a whole is in equilibrium (*i.e.,* there is no movement into or out of the industry) and also all the individual firms in it are in equilibrium, *i.e.,* they are equating marginal cost with marginal revenue, and their MC curves cut MR curves.

Short-run and Long-run Equilibrium

We might distinguish between the short-run and the long-run equilibrium of an industry. We have said that the industry is in equilibrium when all the firms comprising the industry: are making normal profits. But this is a long-run view. In the short-run, it may be that the firms are making supernormal profits. In that case, new firms will enter the industry to take advantage of this favourable situation. On the other hand, it may be that the circumstances are so unfavourable that the firms in the industry are incurring losses. In that case, some firms will tend to leave the industry. In both these cases, the industry cannot be said to be in equilibrium. Since in the short-run, by definition, the entry or exit of the firms is ruled out, the condition of making only normal profits by the existing firms in the case of short-run equilibrium is not required. Hence, we can say that the industry is in short-term equilibrium (*a*) when the short-run demand for and the supply of the industry's product are equal and (*b*) when all the firms in it are in equilibrium, even though they may be making supernormal profits or having losses depending upon the demand conditions of the industry's product.

In the long-run, exit or entry of the new firms is possible. Hence, only normal profits will be made by the firms. Super-normal profits will be competed away by the entry of the new firms and, if there are losses, they would be eliminated by the exit of some of the existing firms. Thus, an industry will be in equilibrium in the long-run if the following two conditions are satisfied beside the equality between the long-run supply and the demand for the industry's product: (*a*) all the firms in the industry should be in equilibrium and (*b*) there should be no incentive to entry into the industry by the new firms or compulsion for the existing firms to leave it. In other words, the number of firms should be in equilibrium.

20.6 INCORPORATING NORMAL PROFIT INTO AVERAGE COST CURVE

A firm's decision to stay or leave the industry will depend not only on whether it is covering average total cost as it is generally defined but also on whether it is earning at least normal profits. It is, therefore, useful to include normal profits in average cost. This inclusion of normal profits in average cost helps us to judge easily whether firms have a tendency to stay or leave the industry. If we do not include normal profits in the average cost, we shall have to compare the current level of earnings with normal profits which is an unnecessary complication.

If price is equal to average cost including normal profit of all the firms, it means that all the firms are making just normal profits besides covering average cost of production. We can then easily conclude that industry is in equilibrium as in this situation the firms would have no tendency either to enter or leave the industry.

If the price is greater than average cost including normal profits, it means that existing firms are making super-normal profits. This will induce new firms to move into the industry. This movement will continue until the super-normal profits are competed away.

On the other hand, if the price is less than the average cost including normal profits, it follows that firms are making sub-normal profits, *i.e.*, having losses; therefore, some firms will be forced to quit the industry until the existing firms are at least covering average cost including normal profits.

In Fig. 20.7, we have drawn a curve ACP which represents average cost of production and

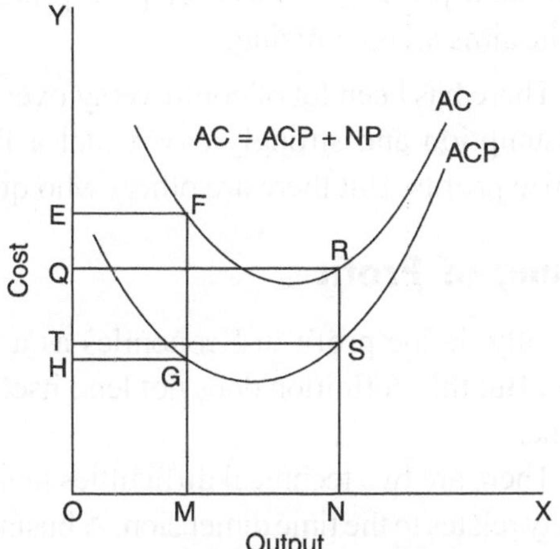

Fig. 20.7. Incorporating normal profits into AC.

does not include normal profits. If in ACP we add normal profits, we get AC curve which is the summation of the average cost of production and normal profits calculated per unit. The normal profits per unit will fall progressively as output increases. This is because a fixed sum of total normal profits will be spread over a progressively large number of units of output. Consequently, the vertical distance between ACP and AC = (ACP + NP) curve will steadily fall but the two curves will never meet. For instance, at the output level OM, the normal profit per unit is FG and at output ON, the normal profit per unit is RS. It should be carefully noted that rectangles showing normal profits such as EFGH and QRST would be of equal areas as we are assuming that normal profits represent a fixed sum of money.

As already pointed out, it is reasonable to assume that there will be a fixed amount of normal profits in an industry. This normal profit is a fixed amount, (*i.e.* independent of the level of output) which the firms must earn if they are to remain in the industry. As the normal profits represent a fixed sum of money, it means that as output increases normal profits calculated per unit of output will fall as a fixed sum will be spread over a large number of units of output. This will be an additional reason for the average cost curve to slope downward over the low ranges of output.

20.7 VALIDITY OF PROFIT MAXIMIZING DOCTRINE

We have seen in the analysis of a firm's equilibrium, that a producer is not interested in reducing either his average cost or total cost to the minimum or in maximizing his revenue. What he is interested really is in the difference between his total cost including normal profit and total revenue which is his profit. It is said that he wants to make this difference as big as possible. In other words, a firm seeks to maximize it profits. But is this assumption valid?

But let us be clear as to what we mean by profit maximization. The normal profits are minimum income which the entrepreneur must get if he is to stay in business. The normal profits are included in that cost and, therefore, do not come under the profit maximizing principle. Therefore, it is the super-normal profits, *i.e.,* true or pure profits, which is the residual income of the entrepreneur, which he aims at maximizing.

There has been lot of controversy over this issue. There are economists who doggedly stick to this assumption and strongly assert that a firm exists and operates for no other purpose than to maximize profits. But there are others who question the validity of maximizing doctrine.

Meaning of Profit

We usually define profit in Economics as a reward for enterprise or for risk-taking or uncertainty bearing. But this definition does not lend itself to any quantitative interpretation to enable us to settle the issue.

There are two technical difficulties in interpreting the concept of profit maximization: The first difficulty relates to the time dimension. A businessman is said to maximize his profit for each accounting period, say a year. But this is not a good assumption, when dealing with a continuing business. Because a business can certainly increase its profits in a particular year by utterly neglecting the figure, *e.g.,* clearing all the stock of finished goods at the end of the period.

The economist, therefore, as distinguished from the businessman, lays emphasis on the future in the concept of profits. According to this interpretation, profits may be defined as the maximum dividend that a company can pay without impairing its ability to pay same dividend in subsequent years.

The second difficulty about the concept of profits relates to the criterion for evaluating risk for which profit is a reward.

Leaving aside the dispute regarding the interpretation of the term 'profits', let us try to see whether the doctrine of profit maximization is a mere theory to be found only in textbooks on Economics or whether the firms do actually try to maximize profits.

Arguments

The following arguments are put forward to show that the assumption of profit maximization is amply borne out by business behaviour:

(*i*) The businessmen sometimes assert that it is their business to look after social welfare, rather than personal gain.

Thus, the actual behaviour of businessmen is in accordance with profit maximization doctrine.

(*ii*) The postulate of profit maximization certainly applies to industries and it is the behaviour of the industry, rather than of an individual firm which determines the flow of products and the demand for inputs.

Arguments Against

Those who question the validity of the profit maximization postulate put forward the following arguments:

(*i*) Enlightened businessmen vehemently deny that their object is to maximize profits. Service of society rather than personal profit is said to be their aim.

(*ii*) The profit-maximization doctrine would be the rule, if business decisions were taken by those who are to get the profits. Most business decisions are taken by business executives or salaried managers, rather than by owners of firms.

(*iii*) The objective of profit maximization is difficult. If a businessman is to maximize his profits, he must fix a price, so as to equalize marginal revenue and marginal cost. This means that he must be able to estimate demand at all prices and marginal cost at all outputs. This is a fantastically difficult task and is seldom attempted in practice.

(*iv*) Besides being difficult to calculate precisely, profit maximization is also regarded as immoral. "Profit maximization requires the businessman to use every trick he can think of to keep wages and fringe benefits down, to extract the last possible dollar from the consumer, to sell as low quality merchandise as he can legally hoodwink the customer into buying, to use income solely for the benefits of the stock holder, to disclaim any responsibility to the community, to wrangle the lowest possible price from his vendors regardless of its effect on them, and so on."

(v) The business policies and practices actually pursued by businessmen are not consistent with the profit maximization doctrine. The calculus of maximization does not fit the notions which actually sway businessmen. They are guided by a sense of fairness, adequacy, etc. They are satisfied with a satisfactory rate of profit instead of pursuing maximum profits.

Conclusion

Thus, profit maximization is unrealistic since it is difficult to calculate and not very ethical to pursue. Marginal analysis as a tool of profit maximization is a valid technique for selecting the most efficient technique out of the various alternatives available, where the alternatives can be clearly specified and where it is possible to estimate costs and revenue reasonably well. But this is not always possible.

We may conclude in the words of Robert Dorfman thus: "On balance, the maximization hypothesis is not as firmly grounded in the facts of life as a fundamental scientific hypothesis should be. But substantial and prolonged divergences from the behaviour it implies are rare particularly in industries with many participants. It, therefore, can still be entertained as a sound working hypothesis."

Full Cost Pricing Principle

For many years, Chamberlain's and Joan Robinson's price theory of monopolistic competition had come to be generally accepted. According to this theory, the firms were able to act automatically on the principle of profit maximization without fear of rivals' reactions. They fixed prices so as to maximize their profits and this they did by equating marginal cost to marginal revenue (MC = MR). But empirical studies made by Oxford economists under the leadership of professors Hall and Hitch (Price Theory and Business Behaviour) showed that the firms did not use the marginality rule (MC = MR) and that oligopoly was the main market structure in the business world. According to Hall and Hitch, the firms did not act automatically or irrespective of what their rival firms did. Rather they were continuously watching the reactions of the rival firms: The traditional theory could not adequately explain the oligopolistic interdependence.

In such a situation, the firms do not attempt to maximize short-run profits by acting on the marginality rule (MC = MR) but aim at maximizing long-run profit by acting on the average-cost principle. That is, the firms do not set their price and output at the intersection of MC and MR curves but they set them at a level which covers the average variable cost, (AVC) and average fixed cost (AFC) and normal profit margin in the business in question. Thus P = AVC + AFC + Normal Profit. Firms do not seek abnormal profits for fear of losing business to rivals, actual or potential. Hall and Hitch found that the firms are ignorant not only of their demand curves but also of their marginal cost, especially in multi-product firms. Rather they follow the full cost principle which gives them a 'fair profit' and covers the full cost of production. Hall and Hitch found that the firms' main concern is with price and not output as the traditional history implies.

Profit Maximization and Single Owner Entrepreneur

We have examined above one assumption underlying the traditional theory of the equilibrium of the firm, viz. profit maximization through the marginality principle (*i.e.,* equating marginal cost with marginal revenue). We have shown that, according to Hall and Hitch, it is the fall cost principle rather than the marginal principle which is found to operate in the business world. The traditional theory also assumes that the firm on which profit is sought to be maximized is owned by a single owner-entrepreneur whose sole concern is to maximize profit. In modern business world, however single entrepreneur is an exception rather than the rule. It is the professional manager who actually controls the business because the dominating form of business organization today is a joint stock company. There is thus a divorce between ownership and management. The single owner-entrepreneur was supposed to act with 'global rationality' and there were no time information or other constraints resting upon him from pursuing the single aim of profit maximization.

Obviously this assumption is unrealistic, because actually it is the manager who has the decision-making power. He may as well pursue goals other than profit maximization, *e.g.,* social welfare, employees' welfare, stability and growth. The salaried also lack the motivation that a single ownerentrepreneur has for maximizing profit.

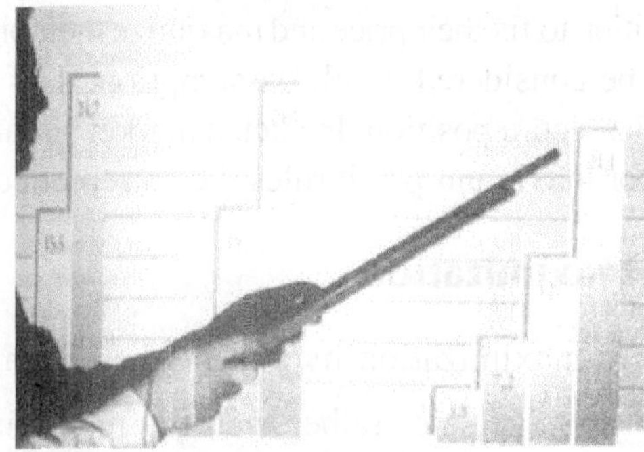

Fig. 20.8. Sales maximization.

Conclusion

The fact is that given the uncertainty in and complexity of the modern business world, lack of full and accurate information, the limited time and limited activity of the manager/entrepreneur and other constraints, the firms do not seek the maximization of profits, sales, growth or anything else. They at best try to exhibit satisfactory behaviour satisfactory profit, satisfactory sales, satisfactory growth etc. This is known as 'behaviourism'.

20.8 GOALS OTHER THAN PROFIT MAXIMIZATION

We have discussed above the profit maximization principle. It gives the impression that every businessman aims at maximizing his profits regardless of all other considerations. This, however, is not so. On the other hand, in the world of reality, businessmen pursue several other goals. Among these we may mention security motive, sales maximization motive or utility maximization motive; we shall say a word about each.

Security Motive

It is said that when an entrepreneur fixes the price for his product, his aim is not to get maximum possible profit, but to satisfy his sense of security. In other words, he aims at getting a good income for many years to come so that he does not suffer from any sense of insecurity. This means that the entrepreneur's objective is to secure a steady flow of profit for a long time. Professor K.W. Rothschild observes in this connection. "Profit maximization has up till now served as the wonderful master-key that opened all the doors leading to an understanding of the entrepreneur behaviour. But there is another motive which cannot be lightly dismissed and which is probably of a similar order of magnitude as the desire for maximum profits; the desire for secure profits.

If we take the market structure into consideration, we might say that so far as imperfect competition and monopolistic competition with a large number of firms or absolute monopoly are concerned profit maximization seems to be a valid assumption. In the case of perfect competition, a firm has to accept the prevailing price and has no option, therefore, the question of profit maximization does not arise. In the case of monopolistic competition and absolute monopoly, the entrepreneurs are in a position to fix their price and maximize their profits. But in the case of oligopoly, profit maximization cannot be considered a valid assumption. The oligopolies have both the desire and the power to achieve a secure position. In such a market situation, therefore, the desire for security rather than the desire for maximum profit rules the entrepreneur's mind.

Sales Maximization

The sales maximization hypothesis has been put forward by Professor Baumol. In his view, maximization of sales rather than the maximization of profits is the ultimate objective that the entrepreneur pursues. He says that sales have become an end in themselves and not merely as a means to further other objectives like operational efficiency and profits. Baumol, therefore, regards sales maximization as the most valid assumption governing, the behaviour of a firm. By sales is meant the revenue earned by selling the product. Therefore, it is also called Revenue Maximization Hypothesis.

However, Prof. Baumol concedes that while promoting sales businessmen do not ignore altogether the goal of profits. He, therefore, modifies his position by saying that the entrepreneur promotes sales subject to the limitation that cost incurred are covered and a usual rate of return on investment is secured. Hence, according to Prof. Baumol, the objective is the sales maximization subject to minimum profit constraint. He says "So long as profits are high enough to keep stock holders satisfied and contribute adequately to the financing of company's growth, management will bend its efforts to the augmentation of sales revenue rather than to further increase in profits.

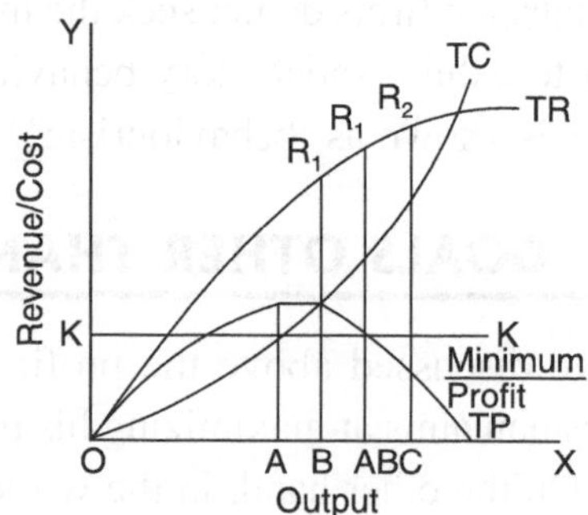

Fig. 20.9. Maximizing sales.

The diagram (Fig. 20.9) illustrates how, a firm aims at maximum revenue or sales consistent with earning minimum profit. This model is a compromise between total sales and profits. But it is also understood that after MR = MC, increase in sales can only be at the expense of profits. This puts a limit to sales increase because minimum profits must be made.

Here TR is total revenue, TC is total cost and TP curve represents total profit. At the output OA, profits are maximum. But if the firm aims at only sales maximization, output will be OC which corresponds to R_2 at the top of TR giving maximum total revenue. But actually this firm will produce and sell OB corresponding to R, total revenue because it gives minimum profit.

Utility Maximization

There are economists like Benjamin Higgins, Melvin Redder and Tibor Scitovsky who say that maximization of satisfaction or utility is the over-riding consideration which governs a businessman's behaviour. This goal is also called Preference Function Maximization. These economists point out that profit maximization does not necessarily result in maximization of satisfaction. In their view, we should not only consider the satisfaction that an entrepreneur gets from his material possessions which he may get from his profits, but also the satisfaction which he may get from the leisure that he is able to enjoy. The entrepreneur's attitude towards work and leisure is a very important consideration if the entrepreneur is to maximize his utility or satisfaction. According to this view, an entrepreneur would try to reach the highest possible indifference curve in order to derive the maximum possible satisfaction and this will happen where his net profits curve is tangent to indifference curve.

We may, however, add that to assume an entrepreneur's willingness to work as independent of his income seems to be an unrealistic assumption. Generally, it is the income motive which is a more powerful motive that sways the businessman's behaviour. But as Scitovsky has pointed out "The assumption that the entrepreneur's willingness to work is independent of his income need not imply that he is not interested in the materials rewards of his work. It may also mean that he is so keen on making money that his ambition cannot be damped by a rise in income. This is likely to be the case partly because the desire for success is more insatiable than the demand for the material goods and partly because it is not a high but a rising income that an entrepreneur tries to maximize his satisfaction or what he calls utility index rather than profits. He says that profit maximization is a condition of survival in perfect competition. But profit maximization motive is much weaker under the conditions of imperfect competition. There are three types of desires which in Higgins' opinion lead to non-profit maximization: (*a*) Desires and forces which lead the entrepreneur to produce at a point below the profit maximization motive, *e.g.,* desire for leisure; (*b*) forces which lead the entrepreneur to produce at a point above the profit maximization output, *e.g.,* desire to wield more power and enjoy greater prestige; and (*c*) forces which makes the entrepreneur stay where he is irrespective of the profit maximizing output. This may be due to his reluctance to make experiments.

Conclusion

We may, therefore, conclude by saying that there is not only one goal which the businessmen pursue, but there are several goals which they keep before them while running their business. Much depends upon the psychology of the businessman and the market environment in which he operates.

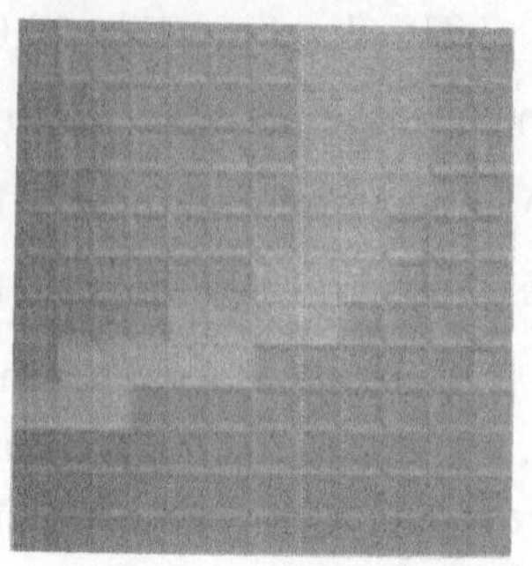

Fig. 20.10. Utility maximization.

Self-Assessment Questions

1. Explain the necessary and sufficient condition for the equilibrium of a firm.
2. "A firm is in equilibrium where its marginal revenue is equal to its marginal cost." Explain.
3. Examine the significance of the equality between marginal revenue and marginal cost in the theory of firm under different types of market conditions.
4. "All firms do not always aim at profit maximization". Explain.
5. Compare with the help of diagrams the equilibrium of the firm under perfect competition and under imperfect competition from the point of view of the most efficient utilization of resources.
6. "While under perfect competition, the individual firm can attain equilibrium only under increasing cost conditions, under monopoly it can be in equilibrium, whatever the cost condition." Discuss.

Unit 21 NATIONAL INCOME AND CIRCULAR FLOW OF INCOME

21.1 INTRODUCTION

Macro economics deals with the broad national aggregates like national income, national product, employment, consumption, investment, money supply, government budget, balance of payment etc. Of all these macro aggregates, national income and national product are the most significant aggregates. National income is considered as the most comprehensive measure of level of economic activity and index of economic growth of an economy. An understanding of the concept and measurement of national income is, therefore, essential in the study of macro-economics. This is what we propose to do in this and the following chapters. We begin this chapter by explaining the concept of national income in general. Secondly, we take up the circular flow of income to show how different sectors of the economic system are interrelated.

21.2 WHAT IS NATIONAL INCOME ?

National income is defined as the value of all final goods and services produced by the normal residence of the country or outside, in a year. National income is, a monetary expression of the current achievements of the people of a country expressed through their production activities. According to Dornbusch and Fischer, national income is the value of final goods and services produced by domestically owned factors of production within a given period.

There are several points worth noting in this definition of national income.

Monetary Expression

In the first place, national income is expressed in monetary terms. It adds together the value of all final goods and services produced in a country during a year. Since a vast number of diverse goods and services are produced in the economy, it is necessary when adding them to use some kind of common denominator. We cannot add together unlike items, such as apples and oranges, or hairpins and aeroplanes, or services of barbers and doctors since they are expressed in different units like kilograms and metres. Thus, in order to aggregate all goods and services it is essential to express them in money terms, such as rupees, dollar etc. Which is the common denominator? We can assign monetary value in terms of market prices or in terms of factor costs. As we shall explain later, national income is expressed both at market prices and at factor costs. However, at the general level here, we are expressing national income in terms of the market prices of goods and services. The output of different goods and services is valued at market prices, and the values are added together to give national income.

Final Goods and Services

The second point to be noted about national income is that it reflects the values of final goods and services. To understand this point clearly, let us differentiate between two types of products, viz. final products and intermediate products.

Final products are those goods and services which are sold to the final users during the year. These goods and services are purchased for final consumption by consumers and for investment by producers, and not for resale. All consumer goods and services like food items, refrigerators we buy for the consumption of our family are final goods. Purchases of capital goods like machines, buildings are also final goods. Producers buy these capital goods for their own use (as investment) and not for resale. Thus, final goods are meant for final use by consumers and producers. They are finished goods for final consumption and investment.

Intermediate products are those goods and services which are used by the producers as inputs into a further stage of production. These goods move from one stage of production to another in the production of a final product. These are the products which are purchased by producers from other producers and are resold after converting them into final goods. For example, seed, fertilizers, etc. purchased by farmers are intermediates products. Farmers grow wheat, rise and other crops by using these intermediate products. When the farmers sell wheat, rice etc., they recover the cost incurred on these intermediate products. It is tantamount to selling of these intermediate products.

To measure national income accurately, all goods and services produced during a year must be counted once, but not more than once. Most products go through a series of production stages before reaching the market. As a result, components of more products go are bought and sold many times. For example, flour mills sell flour to bakeries, and bakeries use this flour in making bread which is sold to households. How should we treat such intermediate products in computing national income? The answer is that national income includes only the value of final goods and services. Intermediate products are excluded from national income because their value is already included in the final products in which they are used. For instance, since flour is used in making bread, the total values of bread includes the values of flour also. If we add the value of flour to the value of bread, the value of flour would be included twice. To add intermediate goods to the final goods would be double counting—that is, the flour would be counted more than once. National income includes the value of bread and not of flour used in making bread. Hence, national income is the total value of final goods and services produced.

Flow

National income is a flow concept. It is the flow of goods and services. A flow is quantity which is measured over a period of time. Nationa income is a very important flow variable in economics. It tells us how many rupees worth of goods and services are flowing in the economy per unit of time.

Conventionally, national income is expressed over one year. It is in this sense we say that national income of India in 2001 to 2002 was ₹ 12,58,800 corers.

Current Output

Another point to be noted about national income is that it measures the value of currently produced goods and services. It excluded pure exchange transactions such as sale and purchase of second-hand goods or used goods, purchase and sale of securities and transfer payment. These transactions are excluded from national income because nothing new is produced in the current year.

The reason for excluding second-hand sales *i.e.* sale of used goods, from national income is fairly obvious. Such sales do not reflect any current production whereas national income relates to current production only. For example, if I sell my second-hand car, this transaction would not be included in national income because no current production is evolved. When this car (as a new car) was originally produced and it was purchased by me, its value was included in that year's national income. On the same token, we count the construction of new houses as part of national income, but we do not add the sale of existing (old) houses. However, the value of the services of the commission agents involved in the second-hand sales are included in the national income of the current year as these services are rendered in the current year itself. These commission agents or brokers provide current services in bringing buyers and sellers together, and these services are rightly a part of current output.

Sale and purchase of financial assets (both old and new) like bonds and shares are also excluded from national income because these transactions do not directly involve current production. They are not payments for goods and services. They represent transfer of purchasing power and the ownerships rights from one person to another. Thus, if you purchase shares of a company, you get ownership rights over a part of company's resources. However, the services of the share brokers are included in national income as these services are rendered in the current year.

The reasoning applies to transfer payments, such as social security payments (pensions etc.) donations and gifts. Transfer payments are received by households, enterprises and others without making any corresponding contribution to the production process in the current period. They are unilateral payments for which no productive services are rendered in the current period. The recipients of these transfer payments do not make any contribution to current production of goods and services. They only bring about a transfer in the purchasing power. For instance, old-age pensions from government to its employees transfer money from government to its employees without any output being produced in the current year.

Residents and Domestic Territory

National income is defined as the value of final goods and services produced by the normal residents of a country. Normal residents are those persons who ordinarily reside in a country in which they live and whose economic interest lies in that country. They may or may not be the citizens of that country, *i.e.,* normal residents include national, as well as foreign nationals. These normal residents of a country produce goods and services by selling their factor services to production units located within and outside the domestic territory of a county. Domestic territory refers to the geographical or political boundary of a country excluding foreign embassies of this country located outside its geographical territory. The money value of final goods and services produced by the production units located within the domestic territory of a country is called domestic product.

National income is the money value of final goods and services produced by the normal residents of a country operating within and outside the domestic territory of a country during a particular year. It is the value of final goods and services produced by all production units located within the domestic territory of a country plus net factor income received from abroad. This will become clear later when we explain various national income aggregates and different methods of measuring national income.

Finally, it is necessary to guard against confusing national income with the sum total of individual personal incomes. National income is not the sum total of personal incomes. Personal incomes include transfer incomes also, and transfer incomes are excluded from national income. Furthermore, not all of the national income accrues to individuals as their personal incomes due to undistributed profits, savings of the governments, etc.

21.3 ECONOMIC MODELS

In order to explain economic events and functioning of the economy, economists use models. An economic model is an explanation of how the economy works. Economic models are simplification of the real world. A model is based on a set of assumptions to simplify the economic events and problems that economists want to explain.

There is an old joke on how economists sometimes use assumptions to oversimplify the problems they face. The joke goes like this:

A chemist, a physicist and an economist were trapped on a desert island, trying to find out how to open a can of food. Let us heat the can over a fire until it bursts said the chemist.

No, no, said the physicist. Let us throw the can on the rocks from the top of a high tree.

I have no idea, said the economist, let us assume we have a can opener.

However, good economists do not build models on the basis of unrealistic assumptions. A good model is based on a set of assumptions that are reasonable and somewhat realistic. Moreover, a good model is simplification of reality, but while doing this it concentrates on the most important phenomena and omits details that are relatively unimportant. Such a model is useful because is explains reality reasonably well. Just as an architect constructs a model of a building which is a simplification of the actual building, so too an economist constructs a model of the economy to illustrate particular features of the economy.

We have used such a model in this chapter to explain the circular flow of income so that we can understand the interactions among different sectors of the economy in a simplified way.

21.4 CIRCULAR FLOW OF INCOME

We have explained earlier that the basic concept of micro economics is the individual market. However, the basic concept in macro economics is the circular flow of income. In an economy, people are engaged in carrying out various economic activities like production, exchange and consumption. While carrying out these activities, they are involved in making various transactions with each other. This gives rise to inter-dependence between them. This interaction and inter-dependence is called the circular flow of income.

Meaning of Circular Flow of Income

As we know, national income is a flow concept. Every year a large number of goods and services are produced which give rise to national income. These goods and services are produced in the production units by combining different factors of production. Producers purchase the factor services to produce goods and services. The national income or output generated is distribution as factor income to the owners of factors of production in the form of wages, rent, interest and profits. Those who receive this income spent it on goods and services produced by production units. The income earned or generated are spent on purchase of goods from these production units. As such, production gives rise to income, income gives rise to expenditure and expenditure gives rise to income again. Thus, in the economy, goods services and factor services are being constantly exchanged between different individuals like producers and households. This flow of goods and services and factor services among producers, households and other individuals in the economy is known as circular flow of income. Thus, circular flow of income is defined as the flow of payments and receipts for goods and services and factor services between different sectors of the economy.

This flow of national income is circular is nature. There is a constant flow of income and expenditure among different sectors of the economy. Incomes are created in the production units in the process of production. Income flows for production units in the form of factor payments to households and then from households to production units. In this way, income flows in circular way among different sectors of the economy. Goods and services flow in one direction and money payments to acquire these flow in the opposite direction, thereby leading to a circular flow. It is called circular because it goes on continuously and indefinitely in a circular way ; it has neither any beginning nor any end.

Economic transactions like sale and purchase of goods and factor services generates two kinds of flows, viz. flow of goods and services and money flow. Accordingly, circular flow of income can be viewed from two different angles ; real flows and money flows.

Real flows: Real flow of income consists of flow of factor services from the owner of factor services to the producers and flow of goods and services from the producers to the buyers of these goods and services. Thus, real flow consists of flow of factor services and flow of goods and services among different sectors of an economy.

Money flows: In the modern monetized economies, economic transactions involve the use of money. Flow of factor services generates factor income in the form of money. Buyers of goods and services pay in cash for goods and services purchased. Money flows comprise of these flows of money payments. Thus, money flow consist of flow of money incomes for factor services, such as money wages, rent, interest etc. and money expenditure incurred on the purchase of goods and services.

In fact, real flows and money flows are two sides of the same coin. Real flow of goods and services is matched by an equal but reverse money flow. For instance, if a labourer sells his labour service to a producer and thereby earns a wage income of ₹ 5,000 a month, there will be a money flow of ₹ 5,000 in the form of factor income from the producer to the labourer, and at the same time the flow of labour service of the same value from the labourer to the producer. The same is true for the entire economy. National income is both a flow of goods and services and flow of money incomes. The circular flow of income involves the basic principle that expenditure of the buyer creates income for the seller by the same amount. Accordingly, flow of goods and factor of services (*i.e.,* real flows) from the seller to the buyer creates the income or money flow from the buyer to the seller.

Economic Sectors of an Economy

To illustrate and explain the circular flow of income in an economy in a convenient way, the economy is divided into four sectors : (*i*) household sector, (*ii*) business sector *i.e.,* the firms, (*iii*) government sector, and (*iv*) foreign sector.

Household sector: Households are the main owners of factors of production - land, labour and capital. They sell the services of these factors of producers and in return receive their income. They spend a large part of their income in purchasing goods and services from the producers. However, they save a part of their income and at the same time they pay taxes to the government out of their income.

Business sector or firms: In economics we use the terms business sector, producers and firms interchangeably. Firms hire services of factors of production from households to produce commodities that they sell to households, to other firms, to government or to other countries. Firms are the principal buyers of factors of production and main producers of commodities. Business sector comprises of both private and government enterprises.

Government: Government is taken in the sense of general government so as to exclude government enterprises. General government gets its income largely from taxes imposed on households and business sector in the form of direct and indirect taxes. It buys goods and services from the producers and factor services from the households. It uses these commodities and factor services in providing free services, such as police, education, medical facilities, sanitation facilities, judicial services etc. to the people so as to satisfy their collective wants.

Rest of the world: Different sectors of the economy have transactions not only with each other, but also with foreign countries, *i.e.,* rest of the world. A country exports goods and services to other countries and similarly it imports goods and services from other countries. In the same way, factor services move across the border of a country and the firms of this country may purchase the factor services from other countries.

In order to study circular flow of income in a simplified way, we combine the above-mentioned four sectors to make the following three models of circular flow :

(*i*) Two-sector model consisting of the household and the business sectors.

(*ii*) Three-sector model comprising the households, business and government sectors, known as closed economy model and

(*iii*) Four-sector model consisting of households, business and government sectors and the rest of the world, and known as open economy model.

These three models of circular flow of income are studied here in detail.

Two-Sector Model Without Saving

To understand the basic essence of circular flow of income, we begin with a simplified two sector model consisting only of households and firms (production units). Thus, we are imagining a hypothetical economy where there is no government and which has no relation with rest of the world. In such an economy the household sector owns all the factors of production. This sector sells the factor services to the firms and receives income from them in the form of wages, rent, interest and profits. The money payments made by firms to households are cost-expenditures for the firms and factor incomes for the households. Firms or the production units use the factor inputs to produce goods and services which are sold to the households. The household sector pays for these goods in the form of money and thereby firms receive money payments from the household. The interaction of firms and households takes place in two sets of markets—factor markets and product markets. Factor markets are those markets where factor services are bought and sold. Product markets and goods markets are the markets where goods and services are bought and sold.

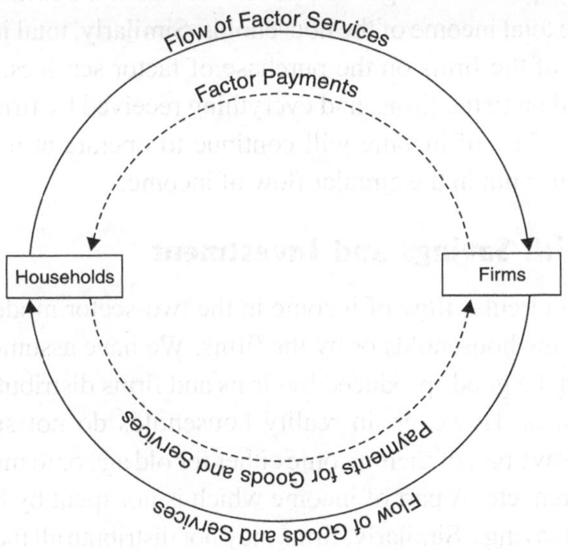

Fig. 21.1. Two sector models without saving.

The circular flow is better understood by referring to Fig. 21.1 showing the money and real flows in a two-sector economy. In the upper loop, the factor service flow from the households to the firm is indicated by the arrow mark. This is the real flow, in return, money flow from firms to households as factor incomes (is indicated by a dashed arrow). This is the money flow. Flow of factor services from households to firms gives rise to a reverse money flow from firms to households. Factor services are sold by households through factor markets. This leads to a flow of money income from firm to households. In the lower loops, goods and services produced by the firms flow from the firms to households as indicated by the arrow mark. This is the real flow. The households pay for these goods and services in money which creates money flow, indicated by a dashed arrow. Note that flow of goods and services from firms to households gives rise to money flow in the opposite direction from households to firms. Goods and services are sold by firms through product markets. This leads to flow of payments from households to firms.

The outer circle represents the real flows (indicated by solid line) and the inner circle represents money flows (indicated by dashed line). Real flow consists of flow of factor services from households to firms and flow of goods and services from firms to households. Money flows comprise of flow of factor incomes from firms to households and flow of money expenditure on goods and services from households to firms. By combining both types of money flows we find a circularity in the money flows. The money payments go around in a circular manner (as shown by the continuous dashed arrows). In the same way we get the circular flow of goods (real flow) by combining both types of real flows.

In the two sector model, if households spend all their incomes on buying consumer goods produced by firms, and firms distribute all the money collected from the sale of their products to households as factor income, then the circular flow of income will remain constant. As the households spend all their income on the purchase of goods and services from the firms, total money receipts of the firms will be equal to the total income of the households. Similarly, total income of the households is equal to the expenditure of the firms on the purchase of factor services. Everything received by households would be passed on to the firms, and everything received by firms would be passed back to households. The circular flow of income will continue to operate at unchanged level. In other words, there would be equilibrium in the circular flow of income.

Two-Sector Model with Savings and Investment

In the foregoing analysis of circular flow of income in the two-sector model we have assumed that there is no saving either by the households or by the firms. We have assumed that household sector spends the entire income on the goods produced by firms and firms distribute all their receipts to the households as factor incomes. However, in reality households do not spend all the income on consumption. Instead, they save part of their income either for old age or to meet expected expenditure like marriage of their children, etc. A part of income which is not spent by households on consumer goods and services, is called savings. Similarly, firms may not distribute all their receipts to households as factor income, rather they may save a part of their receipts in the form of depreciation provisions and undistributed profits which may be used for undertaking investment. How do we illustrate savings and investment in our model of circular flow of income?

To keep our analysis simple, we assume that all savings are made by the households. The act of saving by the households reduces the consumption expenditure and thus the circular flow of income. Households receive income from firms and pass back only a part of it through consumption expenditure since part of the income is saved. Saving thus represents a sort of withdrawal or leakage of expenditure from the circular flow of income between households and firms. Withdrawal or leakage is the amount of money which is withdrawn from the flow of income. It reduces the flow of income in the country.

However, savings may be used for undertaking investment expenditure. Investment refers to expenditure on goods which help in producing other goods in the production process. Expenditure on plant, machinery, etc. are example of expenditure. These capital goods are not purchased by the consumers, rather they are purchased by the firm only. In an economy, both consumer goods and capital goods are produced. In our simplified model, we have assumed so far the production of consumers goods only. Now we expand our model to incorporate capital goods. Firms produce two types of goods now. The first types of goods are consumer goods, which are sold by the firms to the households. The second type of goods are capital goods (or investment goods), which are sold by the firms that produce them to the other firms that use them.

Now consider the effect of investment. Investment expenditure creates income for the firms that produce capital goods and for the factors used in production of these goods. This income does not arise from the expenditure of the households, rather it is over and above the income that arises from the households expenditure. Investment expenditure thus results in an addition to the circular flow of income, and as a result the level of income rises. Thus, investment expenditure is an injection into the circular flow of income. An injection is the amount of money which is added to the flow of income. It increases the flow of income in an economy.

How do the firms obtain the required funds for undertaking investment? The firms may use part of their profits (*i.e.,* undistributed profits) for undertaking investment. To simplify our analysis we assume that firms do not retain anything as undistributed profit since the entire income is distributed among households as factor incomes. This implies that investment undertaken by firms is financed through savings of the households. To some extent the firm may borrow directly from households. However, households and firms interact with each other through financial institutions (capital market) like banks, insurance companies, mutual funds, etc. Financial institutions intermediate between saver and investors or lenders and borrowers. In our simplified model, we assume that whatever is saved by the households is deposited with the financial institutions (capital market) and the firms take loan from these financial institutions to undertake investment. Households are the net lenders as they save part of their income. Firms are net borrowers since they borrow funds to undertake investment. Thus, savings of the household sector flow to the firms in the form of investment through the medium of capital market.

Circular flows of income in a two-sector model incorporating saving and investment is illustrated in Fig. 21.2.

In Fig. 21.2 a new sector known as capital market has been added. Now a part of income of the households flows to firms in the form of consumption expenditure and a part of the income flows to capital market in the form of savings as indicated by the dashed line labelled S. These savings flow to the firms through the capital market to finance investment by firms. The investment flow is shown by the dashed arrow labelled I.

It is important to note that there would be equilibrium in the circular flow of income if the investment expenditure by the firms is equal to the savings of the household sector. As explained above, saving is a leakage from the circular flow of income as a result of which circular flow of income falls. Investment, on the other hand, leads to increase in the circular flow of income. Equality between savings and investment (S = I) means that concretionary effect of saving on the level of income is just equal to expansionary effect of investment on the level of income. Thus, equilibrium condition of circular flow of income is:

$$S = I$$

However, investment is undertaken by the firms, while savings are done largely by households. Therefore, savings and investment in an economy need not necessarily be equal. Whenever savings exceed investment (S > I), the income flow declines. Excess of saving over investment implies that whatever income leaks out from the circular flow in the form of savings is not neutralized by an equivalent injection if the form of investment exceeds savings (I > S), the income flow increases. Excess of investment over savings implies that whatever income leaks out from the circular flow of income in the form of savings is more than neutralized by an injection in the form of investment. This pushes up the level of income in the economy.

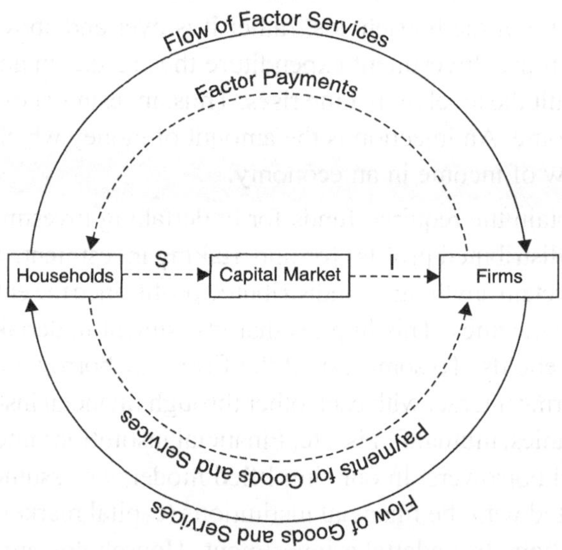

Fig. 21.2. Two sector model with saving.

Three-Sector Model of Circular Flow of Income : Model with the Government Sector

We have explained the nature of circular flow of income by looking into the primary flow of income between households and firms. Now we expand our model of circular flow of income by adding the government sector to the two-sector model. A three-sector model comprising of households, firms and government is a more realistic model because government performs a wide variety of economic functions in a modern economy. Therefore, there is a need of including the activities of the government in the circular flow of income. To keep our analysis simple, we will include three major activities of the government in the circular flows, viz. (*i*) taxes, (*ii*) government spending on commodities and factor services, and (*iii*) transfer payments.

The government imposes taxes both on households and firms. It levied taxes on households in the form of personal taxes and commodity taxes. Income tax on individuals and indirect taxes like sale taxes, excise duties on consumer goods are some of the important taxes levied on households. Thus, a part of the households income flows to the government in the form of taxes. The government imposes taxes on the firms as well. Corporation tax is the most important tax falling in this category. Therefore, a part of the firms earning is taxed away in the form of corporate tax. This gives rise to income flow from firms to the government. Thus, income flows from households and firms to the government in the form of taxes.

The government spends the money collected through taxes to discharge various functions in the economy, such as administration, law and order, etc. The government spends a part of its tax revenue in purchasing factor services from households and making payments to them in the form of wages and salaries. The government incurs expenditure in buying a whole range of goods and services from the firms and make payments in turn. Thus, the government buys factor services from households and goods and services from the firms. Accordingly, income flows from the government to households and firms in the form of government expenditure on factor services and commodities.

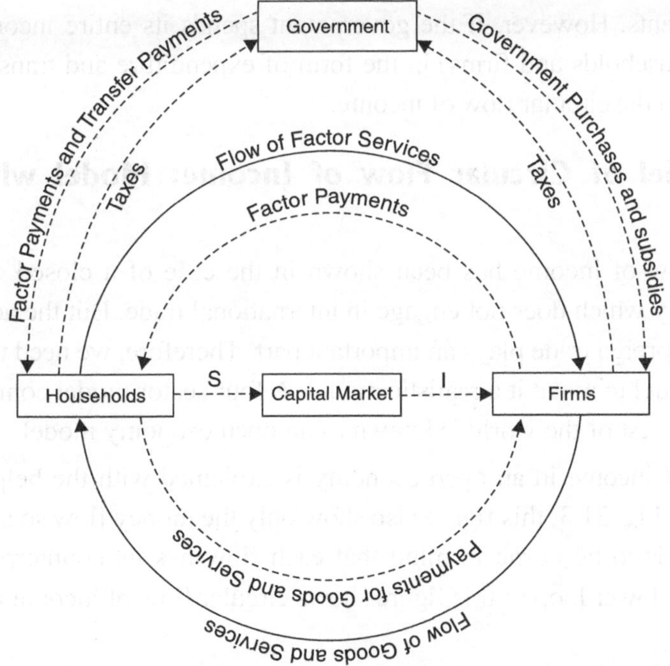

Fig. 21.3. Three sector model.

The government incurs expenditure in the form of transfer payments as well. The government undertakes various social securities and welfare schemes in every economy. Expenditure incurred on these schemes are called transfer payments. Old-age pension, unemployment allowance, scholarships are examples of transfer payments received mainly by the households. Similarly, government gives subsidies and makes transfer payments to firms in order to encourage production. Fertilizer subsidies and food subsidies are such transfer payments. Transfer payments are unilateral payments for which no real services are rendered in return for them. Accordingly, in case of these transfer payments, there is a flow of money payments from government to household and firms, but there is no reverse real flow.

The circular flow of incomes and expenditures in a three-sector model is shown in Fig. 21.3. This figure shows the primary money flows and real flows between households and firms. However, the figure presents only the money flow between the government and households as well as between government and firms. The corresponding real flows from and to the government have not been shown to avoid overcrowding in the diagrams.

Taxes constitute leakages from the flows because they reduce the income and, therefore expenditure of the households and firms. On the other hand, the government expenditure is injection in the flows because it adds to the aggregate demand in the form of government purchases of factor services from the households and goods and services from the business sector. Similarly, the transfer payments by the government are injection in the circular flows. Thus, the government may affect the level of circular flow of income through its activities of imposing taxes, incurring expenditure and making transfer payments. However, if the government spends its entire income (received in the form of taxes from households and firms) in the form of expenditure and transfer payments, there would be equilibrium in the circular flow of income.

Four Sector Model of Circular Flow of Income: Model with the Foreign Sector

So far the circular flow of income has been shown in the case of a closed economy. A closed economy is an economy which does not engage in international trade. But the actual economy is an open economy where foreign trade plays an important part. Therefore, we need to include the rest of world sector in our model to make it a realistic model. A four sector model comprising households, firms, government and rest of the world is known as an open economy model.

Circular flow of income in an open economy is explained with the help of a flow chart as shown in Fig. 21.4 like Fig. 21.3, this figure also show only the money flow so as to avoid crowding in the diagram. It needs to be borne in mind that each flow has its counterpart real flow in the opposite direction. The lower loop of this figure shows circular flow of income in respect of foreign trade.

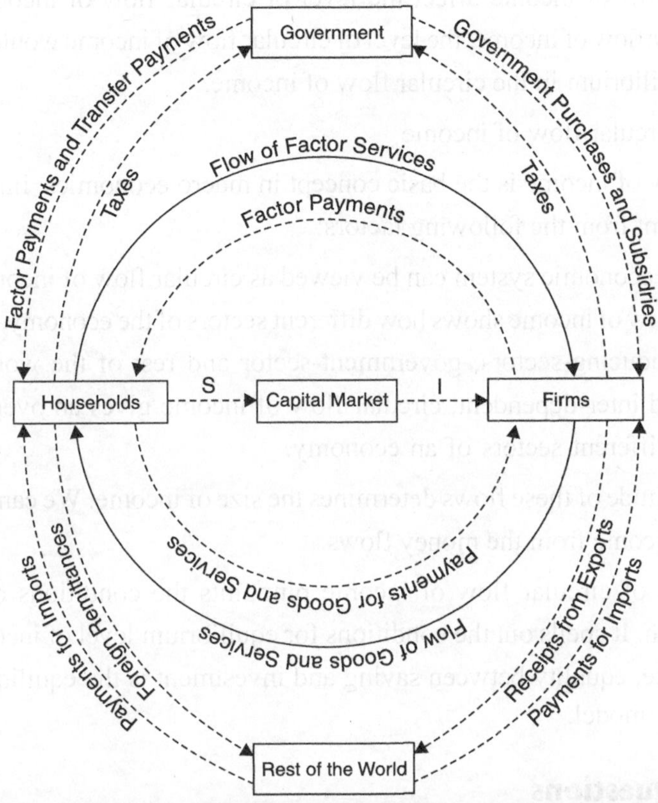

Fig. 21.4. Four sector model.

Interaction between the domestic economy and rest of the world takes place through flow of goods and services (international trade) and flow of factor services. The household sector buys goods imported from abroad and makes payment to the foreign sector. On the other hand, the households sector receives foreign remittances in foreign exchange by selling some of the factor services abroad. For example, some of the Indian people may be working abroad and they may remit income to their families in India. Thus, there is outflow of expenditure from households to the foreign sector to pay for the imported goods and inflow of income for the services rendered by them in foreign countries.

The business sector exports goods and services (like shipping, insurance, banking etc.) to foreign countries and receive payment in the form of receipts from exports. On the other hand, the business sector makes payments to the foreign sector for import of goods and services. This is the flow of expenditure out of the economy. Like the business sector, modern governments also export and import goods and services from foreign countries. However, for the sake of simple analysis, we have not illustrated it in the diagram. Similarly, there is inflow and outflow of capital services which are not shown in the diagram for simplified analysis.

Inflow and outflow of income affect the level of circular flow of income. If the inflow of income is equal to the outflow of income, the level of circular flow of income would remain unaffected, *i.e.,* there would be equilibrium in the circular flow of income.

Importance of circular flow of income

The circular flow of income is the basic concept in macro economics. Importance of circular flow of income is evident from the following factors:

1. The entire economic system can be viewed as circular flow of income and expenditure. Circular flow of income shows how different sectors of the economy, namely, household-sector, producing-sectors, government-sector and rest of the world-sector are inter-related and inter-dependent, circular flow of income gives an overview of interaction between different sectors of an economy.
2. The magnitude of these flows determines the size of income. We can, therefore, measure national income from the money flows.
3. The study of circular flow of income pinpoints the conditions of macro economic equilibrium. It spells out the conditions for equilibrium level of income in an economy, for instance, equality between saving and investment is the equilibrium condition in a two-sector model.

Self-Assessment Questions

1. Distinguish between:
   (*i*) "Gross Domestic Product" at market prices and "Net Domestic Product" at factor cost.
   (*ii*) "Gross National Product" at market prices and "Net National Product" at factor cost.
   (*iii*) "Net National Product" at market prices and "Net Domestic Product"at market prices.
   (*iv*) Factor income and transfer payments.
2. Differentiate between:
   "National Disposable Income" and "Personal Disposable Income"
   "Private Income" and "Personal Income".
3. Distinguish between national income at current prices and national income at constant prices.
4. Show the relationship between the following:
   "Net National Product" at market prices and "Gross Domestic Product" at factor cost.
   "Gross Domestic Product" at market prices and "Gross National product" at factor cost.
5. Show how "Personal Income" and "Personal Disposable Income" are interrelated?
6. What are transfer payments? How do they differ from factor payments? How are they treated in the estimates of national income?

7. Define "Gross Domestic Product" at market prices and "Net National Product" at factor cost. Bring out their relationship.
8. Define "Private Income" and "Personal Disposable Income". How are the two related?
9. Explain any three national income aggregates. How are they related to each other?
10. Complete the following equations:
    - (*i*) GNP = NNP + ...
    - (*ii*) NNP = NDP + ...
    - (*iii*) $GDP_{MP} = GDP_{FC}$ + ...
    - (*iv*) GDP = NDP + ...
    - (*v*) National Income at Factor Cost = National Income at Market Price
    - (*vi*) DPI = PI – ....
11. Complete the following equations:
    - (*i*) Net factor income from abroad = GNP_{FC} ....
    - (*ii*) Net indirect tax = Indirect taxes – ....
    - (*iii*) $NDP_{MP} = GDP_{MP}$ + ...
    - (*iv*) $GNP_{MP} = GNP_{MP}$ – ....
    - (*v*) Personal Income = Personal Disposable Income + ...

Unit 22

NATURE OF GOODS AND SERVICES PRODUCED

22.1 INTRODUCTION

In an economy producers produce a large variety of goods and services for the satisfaction of human wants. The goods and services produced are so varied that it is desirable to classify them into some convenient groups so that they are easily understood. We explain here the nature of goods and services produced by grouping them into various categories in terms of their end-use.

Goods may be classified into economic goods and non-economic goods. Economic goods are those goods which are produced by scarce resources and are capable of satisfying human wants. Economic goods have definite economic value or price. For a goods to be an economic goods, that is, to have an economic value or price, two conditions must be fulfilled:

1. The goods must be wanted by consumers or by producers as they satisfy human wants.
2. The production of the goods must require use of scarce resources.

Thus, economic goods possess economic value because of their scarcity and because they satisfy human wants. These goods have to be produced with resources which involve cost. Since resources are scarce, economic goods produced from these scarce resources are also scarce. Scarcity is the underlying characteristic of economic goods. They are available in limited quantity in relation to their demand. Therefore, they command a price. Generally, economic goods are man-made and not a free gift of nature. Food, cloth, cars, T.V., houses, tools, machinery etc. are all economic goods. Non-economic goods on the other hand, are those goods which, though satisfying human wants, do not possess economic value or price because they are available in unlimited quantity. Non-economic goods are a gift of nature which are freely available. That is why they are also called free goods. For example, air, sunshine, water in the river, sand in the desert are all non-economic goods or free goods. We can see that air satisfies condition (1) but not condition (2) mentioned above. They have great utility, but they are available in unlimited quantity in relation to their demand. We need air in order to live, yet air is available to us in unlimited quantity. We can obtain as much air as we want; it is not scarce and hence we do not pay for it.

We have seen that over the years, as population and production increased, many free goods have become economic goods, such as land for mining, water for human use in cities. However, in economics we are not concerned with free goods.

22.2 MATERIAL GOODS AND NON-MATERIAL GOODS

Economic goods are divided into material and non-material goods. Material goods are those economic goods which have some shape, which can be seen and touched and can be transported. They are tangible, shirts, pencils, cars, television, etc. are material goods.

Non-material goods, on the other hand, do not have physical characteristics. They cannot be seen, touched or transported. They are intangible. We can utilize these goods without ever being conscious of their physical existence. Non-material goods are better known as services. Examples of services are services of doctors, lawyers, teachers, engineers, retailers, wholesalers, domestic servants etc. Some services are designed to meet the final demand of consumers, while others are sold to producers. For instance, a barber provides the haircut service to the consumer, while an engineer working in the company or in a government department sells his services to the producer as his services are used in the production of goods.

The significant thing about services is that there is no time gap between the production and consumption of services. Production and consumption both take place simultaneously. Services are used in the very instance of their performance. For instance, a doctor attending his patient is providing medical services which are being produced by the doctor and consumed by the patient instantaneously. Material goods, on the other hand, have to be produced first and consumed afterwards. Production of goods takes time, often a very long time, and consumption of these goods comes afterwards. Therefore, production and consumption of goods forms a process. It should be noted that material goods can be stored, while non-material goods cannot be stored.

22.3 INTERMEDIATE GOODS AND FINAL GOODS

Intermediate goods are those goods which are further processed before they are used or are sold to consumers. Such goods are mostly converted into final goods. They are used by the producers as inputs into a further stage of production. They are purchased by producers from some other producers and are resold after converting them into final goods. That is why demand for intermediate goods is derived demand (from final goods). Flour used in making bread; bricks, cement and iron used in making houses and factories are all intermediate goods. Similarly, goods lying with traders for resale in the same year are intermediate goods.

Final goods are those goods which are sold to the final users during the years. These goods are purchased for final consumption by consumers and for investment by producers, and not for resale. These goods are meant either for consumption or for investment. Final goods are not further processed before being sold to consumers and producers.

These are the goods which a economy finally wants. Cars, television sets, cloth, food, machinery, equipments etc. are final goods.

It should be noted that the distinction between intermediate and final goods is not on the basis of product itself but on the basis of the use made of it. For example, flour bought by a baker is an intermediate good, but if purchased by the household, it is a final good. Similarly, coal used in factories is an intermediate good, but if used in the domestic kitchen, it is a final good. The general rule for treating a good as an intermediate good or a final good is that if the good is sold by the one business unit to another for resale or for further processing, it is an intermediate good; but if it is not sold for resale or for further production but for personal consumption or for investment, it is a final product.

The distinction between intermediate goods and final goods is very important in national accounting. The value of final goods is added in the calculation of national income. But the value of intermediate goods is not included in national income as their value is already included in final goods.

22.4 CONSUMER GOODS AND PRODUCER GOODS

Consumer goods are those goods which satisfy the wants of the consumers directly. These goods are available for final consumption to the consumers. The consumers may be households or general government. For example, food stuff, shirts, pens, television, services of hairdressers, defense and government administrative services are all consumers' goods. The aim of the production is to provide consumers with those goods which give them satisfaction. Therefore, consumer's goods is the end of the whole production process.

Producer goods are those goods which do not satisfy the wants of the consumers directly, but help in the production of more goods. These goods are produced for use in future production process. Unlike consumer goods, producer goods are not desire for their own sake, but only because they assist in the production of other goods. The demand for producer goods is indirect or derived from the demand for other goods which they help to produce. These goods are stages on the road towards the end of the whole production process. Machinery, equipments, plants, buildings, stock of raw materials are all producers' goods.

However, there is not a hard-and-fast line of demarcation between consumer goods and producer goods. Goods may be consumer goods in some circumstances and producer goods in others. The same goods can be consumer goods and also producer goods. It depends on its use. Cotton thread used by a housewife would clearly be considered to a consumer goods. But if purchased by a tailor it might be a producer goods. Similarly, a car might be a producer goods to a sales representative who uses it for business purposes, but to a person who uses his car solely for the use of his family it would be a consumer goods.

22.5 SINGLE USE AND DURABLE USE GOODS

Goods can be classified into single-use and durable-use according to the duration over which they satisfy a particular want. Single-use goods are those goods which are used up in a single act of consumption (in case of consumer's goods) or production (in case of producer's goods). They loose their identity in one act of consumption or production. They cannot be used more than once. For instance, each piece of bread is used up as soon as you eat it. Milk, bread, matches, food grains are examples of single-use consumer goods; and oil, electricity, iron and steel, coal are some of the single-use producers goods. From this point of view, services (like services of doctors, hair-dresser, etc.) are similar in character to single use goods because they are used in a single act of consumption.

Durable use goods, on the other hand, are those goods which can be used again and again in consumption or production over a considerable period of time. The fact that they have been used on one day does not prevent them from being used again on the next day. They do not lose their identity in their first use, but they continue to provide their utility over a long period of time. For instance, a television set is a durable-use consumer goods; it can be used for a number of years by its owner. Furniture, television sets, clothes, shoes are some of the durable-use consumers' goods, while factories, tools, machinery, tractors are some of the durable-use producers' goods.

22.6 NATIONAL INCOME AGGREGATES

It is defined as the value of all final goods and services produced by the normal residents of a country in a year. However, there are a number of aggregates related to national income. These are interrelated aggregates. They explain national income from different angles and points of view. In this chapter, we examine these national income aggregates.

Scientists, economists and detectives have many things in common. They all want to know what is happening in the world around them. To know this they depend on theories and observations. They build theories to explain what is happening around them. To develop these theories, to explain how the economy works and to test the validity of these theories, economists use data or economic statistics. The government in every country collects data about various facets of the economy like national income, unemployment, rate of inflation, etc. this chapter concentrates on one type of such macro economic variable, *i.e.* national income aggregates, national income is often considered as the best measure of how well the economy is performing, Jane Austen has aptly said, "A large income is the best recipe for happiness I ever heard of,"

Some important relations relating to national income aggregates:

Before studying the different aggregates of national income, it would be useful to note the following relations relating to these aggregates.

1. Domestic Product and National Product

A distinction is made between national and domestic product according to whether we measure the output produced by nationals of a country or whether we measure what is produced within the domestic territory of a country. *Domestic product (or domestic income) is defined as the value of all final goods and services produced by all the enterprises located within the domestic territory of a country during a year*. These goods and services are produced domestically, both by the nationals or citizens of the country as well as foreign nationals working in this country. National product (or income), on the other hand, refers to the amount of final goods and services produced by the normal residents of a country whether operating within the domestic territory of the country or outside. It is the income earned by the nationals of a country. Thus, while the concept of domestic product is geographical in character, the concept of national product relates to nationals or citizens of a country.

The distinction between domestic product and national product arises because of the fact that modern economies are open economies, having transactions with rest of the world in the form of exports and imports, flows of factor incomes, etc. Thus, domestic product of India is the value of output produced by all enterprises located within the Indian territory. However, a part of the domestic product may accrue to foreigners because this part of the domestic product is produced by enterprises owned by foreigners. This gives rise to income received by foreigners from enterprises located in the domestic territory or India. For instance, Maruti Udyog in India produces Maruti cars, which is a part of domestic product (income) of India. However, part of this product accrues to Suzuki company of Japan in the form of profits earned by it from its production activity in India. These profits are part of Japan's national product (income) because they are the income of Japanese-owned capital in India. On the other hand, Indian nationals may own some enterprises located abroad and hence a part of the output originating in those enterprises accrue to them. Similarly, some Indian nationals may work abroad and earn income I thereby. This gives rise to factor income received by Indian nationals from abroad. *The difference between the factor income received from rest of the world and the factor income accruing to rest of the world is the net factor income from abroad.* Hence, the difference between national product and domestic product is equal to the net factor income from abroad.

Thus, National Product = Domestic Product + Net Factor Income from Abroad

2. National Product at Market Prices and National Product at Factor Cost

A distinction is drawn between the national product at market prices and national product at factor cost. *National product (income) at market prices is the value of final goods and services produced by normal residents of a country calculated at their market prices. On the other hand, national income or national product at factor cost expresses national product as the sum of all factor payments (wages, interest, rent, profits).* In every economy, production is the result of the cooperation of factors of production, viz., land, labour, capital and enterprise. The payment made to these factors for their contribution to the production process is called factor cost and the resultant product is called product at factor cost.

The difference between national product (income) at factor cost and national product at market prices arises because the prices that the consumers pay for goods are different from the price that the firms receive. Market prices of goods are inclusive of indirect taxes, such as excise duty, sales tax, etc. The effect of these indirect taxes is to make the market prices which consumers pay for goods higher than the prices that the firms receive. These taxes are not a part of factor earnings. These indirect taxes must be subtracted from national product at market prices to get national income at factor costs. Subsidies, on the other hand, makes the market prices lower than the factor cost. For instance, the cost of providing 1 kg of wheat to the consumers at the factor cost may be ₹ 10. However, the government may like to provide wheat to the consumers at a lower price, say ₹ 7 per kg. For this purpose, the government grants a subsidy of ₹ 3 per kg. This will lower the market price of wheat to ₹ 7 per kg. In this situation, national product at market would be lower than the national product at factor costs.

Indirect taxes minus subsidy are known as net indirect taxes. Market value of goods and services differs from the earnings of factors of production to the extent of net indirect taxes. Therefore, national product at market prices differs from national product at factor cost to the extent of net indirect taxes.

Thus,

National Product at Factor Cost = National Product at Market Prices – Indirect Taxes + Subsidies

Or

National Product at Factor Cost = National Product at Market Prices – Net Indirect Taxes

3. Gross Domestic Product and Net Domestic Product

Domestic product or domestic income can be measured either on a gross basis or on a net basis. There is a distinction between gross and net national product according to whether investment is taken in gross or net terms, *i.e.,* whether depreciation is included or not. In the process of production of commodities, some amount of economy's stock of plants and equipments is used up or wears out during the year. This consumption of fixed capital in the process of production is known as depreciation. Thus, the loss of value of fixed capital assets during the production process due to normal wear and tear is called depreciation. It is general practice with producers to provide for depreciation allowance to meet the consumption of fixed capital. If we deduct depreciation from gross investment, we get net investment (capital formation).

Gross product does not make allowance of depreciation in the estimation of domestic product. But the net domestic product makes allowance of depreciation.

Thus,

National Domestic Product = Gross Domestic Product – Depreciation

It is obvious from above that we may distinguish between 'domestic' and 'national' product. Similarly, we may distinguish between 'gross' and 'net'. In view of this, economists identify four aggregates relating to production in an economy, viz.,

1. Gross Domestic Product (GDP),
2. Gross National Product (GNP),
3. Net Domestic Product (NDP),
4. Net National Product (NNP).

Again, each of these aggregates can be calculated either at market prices or factor cost. Thus, we have the following eight possible national income aggregates.

1. Gross Domestic Product at Market Prices (GDP_{MP})
2. Gross National Product at Market Prices (GNP_{MP})
3. Net Domestic Product at Market Prices (NDP_{MP})
4. Net National Product at Market Prices (NNP_{MP})
5. Gross Domestic Product at Factor Cost (GDP_{FC})
6. Gross National Product at Factor Cost (GNP_{FC})
7. Net Domestic Product at Factor Cost (NDP_{FC})
8. Net National Product at Factor Cost (NNP_{FC})

We explain below these national income aggregates and the relationship in them in detail.

1. Gross Domestic Product at Market Prices (GDP_{MP})

   Gross domestic *product at market prices* is *the value of all 'final goods and services at prices prevailing in the market produced in the domestic territory of a country during a given year.* Being gross, it is inclusive of depreciation, *i.e.,* consumption of fixed capital in the process of production has not been excluded. That is why it does not reveal complete flow of goods and services among various sectors in the economy. GDP_{MP} simply shows what is produced within the domestic territory of a country by normal residents of a country, national as well as non-nationals. It measures contribution of both nationals and non-nationals in total production. GDP at market prices measures the value of final goods and services at their market price. Market value of the final goods and services is calculated by multiplying the physical quantities of these goods and services by their market prices.

2. Gross National Product at Market Prices (GNP_{MP})

   Gross national product at market prices is the most important and commonly used measure of national income. It is *defined* as *the aggregate market value of all final goods and services produced by normal residents of a country during a year.* It differs from GDP_{MP} to the extent of net factor incomes earned from abroad. To get GNP_{MP} from GDP_{MP} we have to add to GDP_{MP} the income earned from abroad by the normal residents of a country in the form of wages dividends, interests, profits. Clearly, this is a pair of factor income earned by nationals of a country, but it is not part of the domestic production. By the same token, some part of the domestic product may have been generated by non-nationals operating in this country. Income earned by non-nationals must be deducted from GDP_{MP}. GNP_{MP} therefore, is the total value of final goods and services produced in the domestic territory of a country plus net factor income from abroad.

Thus, $GNP_{MP} = GDP_{MP}$ + Net Factor Income from Abroad

Net factor income from abroad may be positive or negative. If net factor income from abroad is positive, GNP_{MP} would be greater than GDP_{MP}. On the other hand, if net factor income from abroad is negative, GNP_{MP} would be less than the GDP_{MP}.

Thus, GNP_{MP} differs from GDP_{MP} in two ways. First, while GDP_{MP} includes entire production within the domestic territory of a country both by nationals and non-nationals; GNP_{MP} measures the income (product) generated by nationals of a country both within and outside the country. Secondly, the concept of gross national product is a wider concept than the gross domestic product. In addition to gross domestic product, it also includes net factor income from abroad.

GNP_{MP} is one of the most useful tools for analyzing the performance of an economy. It can be used to measure the performance of the economy over time by comparing the production of goods and services during one period with the that of other period. But it does not exclude depreciation and hence it does not reveal true or actual flow of goods and services produced in the economy.

3. Net Domestic Product at Market Prices (NDP_{MP})
   Net domestic product at market prices is the market value of all final goods and services at prices prevailing in the market produced in the domestic territory of a country during a given year after making allowance for depreciation. In view of wear and tear of capital goods in the process of production, there is the need for deducting depreciation from the gross product to get the net increase in availability of goods in the economy. Net domestic product at market prices is the difference between gross domestic product at market prices and depreciation.

Thus, $NDP_{MP} = GDP_{MP} - \text{Depreciation}$

NDP_{MP} is the measure of net availability of final products. It is the measure of national income which is available for consumption and investment in the economy.

4. Net National Product at Market Prices (NNP_{MP}). Net national product at market prices is similar to NDP_{MP}. It shows the *market value of all final goods and services produced by normal residents of a country during a year after making allowance for depreciation.* It differs from GNP_{MP} in that the depreciation of capital is subtracted.

Thus, $NNP_{MP} = GNP_{MP} - \text{Depreciation}$

NNP_{MP} is considered to be a more accurate measure of the true output of the economy than GNP_{MP}. It reflects how much is produced over and above that amount which is required to keep the nation's stock of capital intact. It clearly gives a better indication of long run economic growth than GNP_{MP} does.

5. Gross Domestic Product at Factor Cost (GDP_{FC})
   Gross domestic product at factor cost is the estimate of gross domestic product in terms of earnings of factors of production. *It is the sum total of earnings received by various factors of production in terms of wages, interest, rent, profits, etc. within the domestic territory of a country in a year.* It measures factor income generated within the domestic territory irrespective of whether generated by residents or non-residents. Being gross, it makes no provision for the depreciation.

As explained above, market value of goods and services differs from the earnings of factors of production because of net indirect taxes. Therefore, if we deduct net indirect taxes from gross domestic product at market prices, we get gross domestic product at factor cost.

Thus, $GNP_{FC} = GNP_{MP} - \text{Net Indirect Taxes}$

6. Gross National Product at Factor Cost (GNP_{FC})
   Gross national product at factor cost estimates the gross national product in terms of earnings of factors of production. *It is the sum total of earnings received by various factors of production in terms of wages, rent, interest, etc. by normal residents of a country in a year.* It differs from GNP_{MP} to the extent of net indirect taxes.

Thus, $GNP_{FC} = GNP_{MP} - \text{Net Indirect Taxes}$

7. Net Domestic Product at Factor Cost (NDP_{FC})

   Net domestic product at factor cost is the estimate of the domestic product in terms of earnings of factors of production within the domestic territory of a country in a year. It is the sum total of factor incomes earned within the domestic territory of a country net of depreciation during a year. It is also known as domestic factor income as it shows the income generated within the domestic territory of the country by all the producers in a year. It measures factor incomes generated within the territory of a country both by the residents and non-residents. It differs from gross domestic product at factor cost to the extent of depreciation.

Thus, $NDP_{FC} = GDP_{FC} - \text{Depreciation}$

Net domestic product at factor cost includes the following:

(*a*) *Compensation of Employees:* Compensation of employees is defined as all payments made by producers to their employees in the form of wages and salaries and other payments made in cash and kind in return for labour service.

(*b*) *Operating Surplus*: It is the sum total of property income and income from entrepreneurship. In other words, it is the sum total of interest, rent, profits and other similar incomes.

(*c*) *Mixed Income:* It is composite of labour .income and property income in case of those producers where it is difficult to differentiate between labour element and capital element in the services of a factor of production. It covers total income of own—account workers like doctors, street hawkers, etc. and income of unincorporated enterprises like farmers, small-scale handicraft producers. Here the income is in the nature of partly labour income and partly property income.

Thus, net domestic product at factor cost or net domestic income is the sum total of compensation of employees, operating surplus and mixed income earned by the factors of production in the domestic territory of a country in a year.

8. Net National Product at Factor Cost (NNP_{FC}) or National Income.

   When we calculate the value of all final goods and services produced by the normal residents of a country, whether operating within the domestic territory of a country or outside it, at their factor cost, it is called net national product at factor cost or national income. *National income can be defined as factor income accruing to the normal residents of a country during a year.* It is the sum total of domestic factor income and net factor income earned from abroad.

Thus, NNP_{FC} (or National Income) = Domestic Factor Income + Net Factor Income earned from abroad

It may be noted that factor income from abroad can be negative as well as positive. National income will be less than domestic factor income if net factor income from abroad is negative. But, if net income from abroad is positive, national income will be larger than domestic income.

National income can also be found out by deducting depreciation) % from gross national product at factor cost.

Thus, NNP_{FC} or National Income GNP_{FC} – Depreciation

National income is the sum of compensation of employees, operating surplus and mixed income accruing to the normal residents of a country. Therefore, it is clear that national income relates to factor incomes created in producing an economy's final goods and services. The factor payments to the factors of production are the factor cost of production. National income in this sense is also called national income at factor cost or NNP_{FC} Technically national income is taken in the sense of net national product at factor cost (NNP_{FC}).

National income is a particularly good measure of net production because it is not affected by changes in indirect taxes. When indirect taxes are increased, GNP_{MP} rises even though there is no increase in actual production. But national income is not affected by the taxes. National income is the best indicator for making international comparisons of relative income levels.

Interrelations between Various National Income Aggregates

We have explained above various concepts of national product and domestic product in gross and net terms and at market prices and factor cost. We have also explained that each one of them is interrelated to others. We can arrive at one particular aggregate from another aggregate by making certain adjustments. The way the eight national income aggregates are interrelated is shown diagrammatically in Fig. 22.1

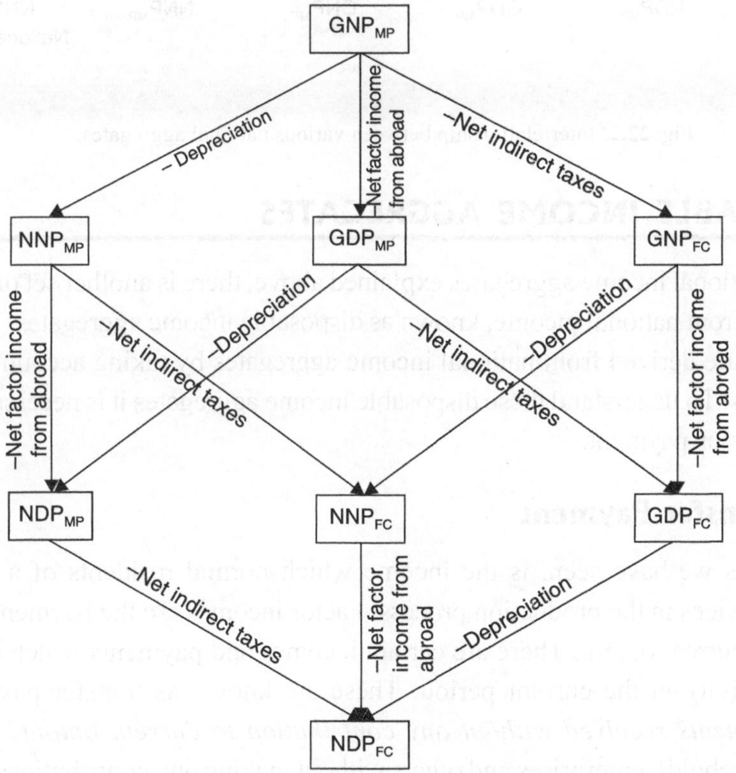

Fig. 22.1. Interrelationship between various national income aggregates.

Fig. 22.2 summarizes the interrelationship between some of these national income aggregates.

			Net Factor Income from Abroad (6)		
		Net Indirect Taxes (5)	Net Indirect Taxes (5)	Net Factor Income from Abroad (6)	
	Net Indirect Taxes (5)	Depreciation (4)	Depreciation (4)	Net Indirect Taxes (5)	Net Factor Income from Abroad (6)
Mixed Income (3)	Mixed Income (3)	Mixed Income (3)	Mixed Income (3)	Mixed Income (3)	Mixed Income (3)
Operating Surplus (2)	Operating Surplus (2)	Operating Surplus (2)	Operating Surplus (2)	Operating Surplus (2)	Operating Surplus (2)
Compensation of the Employees (1)	Compensation of the Employees (1)	Compensation of the Employees (1)	Compensation of the Employees (1)	Compensation of the Employees (1)	Compensation of the Employees (1)
NDP_{FC} or Domestic Factor Income	NDP_{MP}	GDP_{MP}	GNP_{MP}	NNP_{MP}	NNP_{FC} or National Income

Fig. 22.2. Interrelationship between various national aggregates.

22.7 DISPOSABLE INCOME AGGREGATES

In addition to the national income aggregates explained above, there is another set of national income aggregates derived from national income, known as disposable income aggregates. These disposable income aggregates are derived from national income aggregates by taking account of certain types of transfer payments. To understand these disposable income aggregates it is necessary to understand the concept of transfer payment.

Concept of Transfer Payment

National income, as we have seen, is the income which normal residents of a country earn by rendering factor services in the production process. Factor incomes are the payments made in return for contribution to current output. There are certain incomes and payments which are not related to any production activity in the current period. These are known as transfer payments. *Transfer payments are payments received without any contribution to current output*. These payments are received by households, enterprises and others without making any contribution to the production process in the current period. Old-age pensions, unemployment relief, welfare payments, gifts, donations, fines, taxes are all transfer payments. They are unilateral payments (one-sided payments) for which no productive services are rendered in the current period. The recipients of these transfer payments do not make any contribution to current production in return for them. Therefore, transfer payments do not reflect any production of goods and services. They only bring about a transfer of the purchasing power, *i.e.,* transfer of power to purchase output from those who provide money to those who receive it. For instance, pensions from government to its employees transfer money from government to its employees without any output being produced in the current period.

Transfer payments are of two types, viz. current transfers and capital transfers. A current transfer is one which is made out of the current income of the payers and adds to the current income of the receivers. A capital transfer, on the other hand, is one which is paid out of the capital or wealth of the payer and adds to capital or wealth of the receiver. We are nearly concerned with current transfers only.

A person may receive income not only in the form of factor income, but also in the form of transfer payments (transfer incomes). For example, the person may receive pensions, gifts or donations. Similarly, a person may use part of his factor income in making transfer payments to others like having gifts, donations, fines, taxes, etc. *Income inclusive of all current Transfers is called disposable income.* Disposable income is the income received from all sources available to the people.

Thus, Disposable Income = Income + Net Current Transfers

Disposable income can be higher or lower than income depending upon whether net current transfers (*i.e.,* the difference between current transfer receipts and current transfer payments) are positive or negative. There are various variants of disposable income. We may refer to national disposable income or disposable income of the private sector. We take up here both national disposable income and disposable income of the private sector.

National Disposable Income

National disposable income is defined as the sum total of national income at market price and current transfers received from rest of the world. It is the income received by the residents of a country from all the sources for spending as well as for saving during the year. A country may receive current transfers from other countries in the form of gifts and donations. Similarly, a country may make current transfers to other countries by sending gifts, donations, etc. to these countries. The difference between the current transfers received from the rest of the world and current transfers paid to the rest of the world is known as net current transfers received from the rest of the world. It is these current transfers from and to other countries that affect national disposable income. However, current transfers from one sector to another sector within a county do not affect national disposable income of a country. Such intra-country transfers from one sector to another sector merely increase the disposable income of the recipient sector and reduce the disposable income of the payer sector by the same amount.

While estimating national disposable income, we take national product at market prices as the relevant national income aggregate. Accordingly, we use two concepts of national disposable income, viz., Gross National Disposable Income (GNDI) and Net National Disposable Income (NNDI).

Gross national disposable income is the sum total of gross national product at market prices and net current transfers received from the rest of the world.

Thus, GNDI = GNP_{MP} + Net current transfers received from rest of the world

Similarly,

NNDI = NNP_{MP} + Net current transfer from rest of the world

Disposable Income aggregates of the private sector

There are various types of disposable income aggregates belonging to the private sector. However, the main disposable income aggregates of the private sector are:

(1) Private income,

(2) Personal income,

(3) Personal disposable income.

These are discussed below.

1. **Private Income:** Private income refers to the current income received from all sources of private sector consisting of private enterprises and factor owners. It is the total of factor income (including retained profits of the corporations) from all sources and current transfers from the government and rest of the world accruing to the private sector.

It can be obtained from national income (or NNP_{FC}) by making various adjustments, *i.e.,* additions and deductions.

The following types of incomes are deducted from national income:

(*i*) Income from property and entrepreneurship accruing to the government commercial enterprises and administrative departments.

(*ii*) Savings of non-departmental enterprises of the government.

Thus, private income does not include the income accruing to the government sector because this part of national income is not available for distribution and hence, does not form a part of the income of the private sector.

The following incomes are added to national income:

(*i*) Interest that the government pays on national debt. The government sometimes borrows funds from the public to meet its consumption expenditure. It has to pay interest on public debt. Since public debt is traditionally used by the government for consumption purposes, the interest paid on national debt is conventionally treated as transfer payment, and it forms part of private income.

(*ii*) Net current transfers received from the government administrative departments. These transfers are in the form of old-age pension payments, unemployment allowances, medical allowances, scholarships, gifts etc.

(*iii*) Net current transfers like gifts and grants received from other countries. For instance, the Indian Government may give food articles, clothes, medicines, etc. as gift to other countries to help them during the periods of natural calamities like floods, earthquakes, etc. Similarly, the Indian Government may receive similar types of gifts, relief etc. to fight the natural calamities, The difference between the transfer payments received from abroad and payments made to rest of the world is known as the net current transfers from abroad.

Private sector gets some such transfer incomes which are part of private income but not of national income.

Thus, Private Income = National Income – Income from property and entrepreneurship accruing to the government. Commercial entrepreneurship accruing to the government, commercial enterprises and administrative departments – Saving of non-departmental enterprises of the government + interest on national debt + net current transfer from government + net current transfer from abroad.

The concept of private income explains the division of national income between the private sector and the government sector of the economy.

Private income is the pre-tax income of the private sector. Government can decide about tax burden on the private sector on the basis of the magnitude of private income.

2.**Personal Income:** Personal income is defined as the sum total of all current incomes received by persons or households from all sources. *It is the income actually received by persons from all sources in the form of factor incomes and current transfer payments during a year.*

The income which the households actually receive is different from what they have earned during the year. A certain part of the income which people have earned may not be actually received by them. Some part of the income earned by the firms or corporations is not distributed among the shareholders. A part of it is retained by the firms for further investment in the firms. These are called 'undistributed profits' or 'retained earnings'. These incomes accrue to firms. A part of the income of the firms is used to pay corporate tax on the profits earned. It is called 'corporate profit tax'. Corporate profit tax accrues to the government. Similarly retained earnings of foreign companies in India are part of the private income, but are excluded from personal income. Accordingly, personal income can be obtained from private income as:

Personal Income = Private income – undistributed profits – corporate profits tax

– retained earning of foreign companies

The concept of personal income is useful in finding out the amount of purchasing power that is actually in the hands of the people. It is a rough indicator of consumers' economic welfare. Personal income is the basic magnitude for studies of distribution of individual income as well as of individual tax burden of personal taxes.

3.**Personal Disposable Income:** *Personal disposable income is that part of personal income which is available to the individuals to be used the way they like.* In other words, it is the income available to the households which they can spend on consumption or can save as they desire.

Disposable income is always less than personal income. Households cannot use the entire personal income. A part of the personal income is taken away by the government by way of personal taxes like income tax, wealth tax, etc. In addition, there are miscellaneous receipts of the government administrative departments in the form of fee, fines, etc. paid by households. Only that part of individual income which remains after payment of personal taxes and miscellaneous payments to the government is the actual amount available for spending by the households.

Thus, Personal disposable income = personal income – personal taxes – miscellaneous receipts of the government administrative departments. Households can use personal disposable on consumption and saving personal disposable income is a useful measure of potential demand for goods and services in the economy. The businessmen can plan their production activities on the basis of this information.

Thus, Personal disposable income = consumption expenditure of households + households savings.

Interrelationship Among Disposable Income Aggregates and the Private Sector

In Fig. 22.3 we summarize the inter-relationship among national income and three disposable income aggregates of the private sector, *i.e.,* private income, personal income and disposable income.

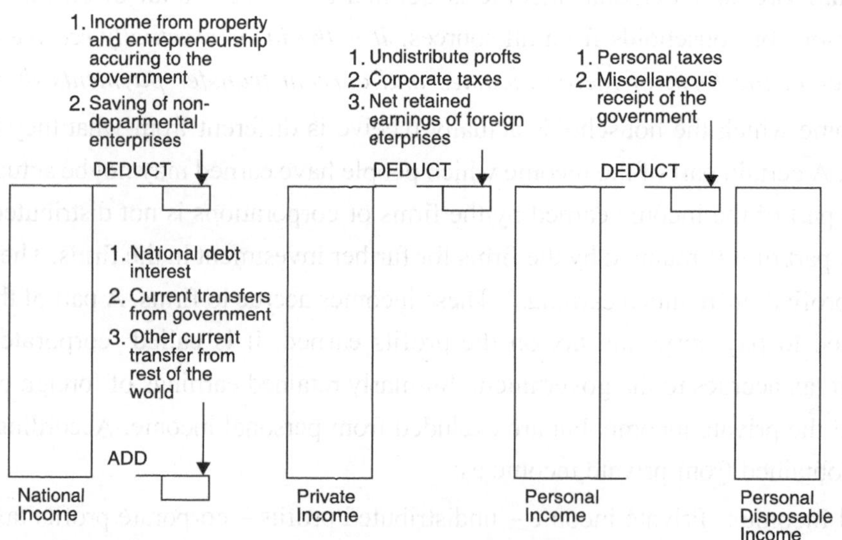

Fig. 22.3. Interrelationship among disposable income aggregates and the private sector.

Interrelationship Among National Income Aggregates

The interrelationship among some of the national income aggregates explained in this chapter can be illustrated in the following way:

Domestic Product and Related Aggregates

1. **Gross Domestic Product at Market Prices (GDP_{MP})**

   = Value of all final goods and services produced within the domestic territory of a country

2. **Net Domestic Product at Market Prices (NDP_{MP})**

   = GDP_{MP} – Depreciation

3. **Net Domestic Product at Factor Cost (NDP_{FC})**

   = NDP_{MP} – Net Indirect Taxes (*i.e.,* – Indirect Taxes + Subsidies)

4. **Net National Product at Factor Cost (NNP_{FC}) or National Income**

   = NDP_{FC} + Net Factor Income from Abroad

5. **Private Income**

   = NNP_{FC}
   – Income from property and entrepreneurship accuring to the government
   – Savings of non-departmental enterprises
   + National debt interest
   + Current transfers from the government
   + Other current transfers from rest of the world.

6. **Personal Income**

   = Private income – Undistributed profit – Corporation taxes

It is useful to have a brief idea of two other concepts of national income. viz. (*i*) Per Capita Income, and (*ii*) National income at current prices and national income at constant prices.

Per capita income is average income of the normal residents of a country in a particular year. It is income per head of population. It is obtained by dividing national income of a country by its population. Symbolically, Per capita income = National income – Population

For instance, if national income of a country is ₹ 15,00,000 crores and the population is 100 crores, in this case the per capita income will be 15,00,000 corers (1500000 crores) ÷ (100 crores)

Per capita income is calculated both at current prices as well as at constant prices. While estimating per capita income at current prices, we take national income. At current prices is the numerator in the above formula. Similarly, for the purpose of arriving at real per capita income (per capita income at constant prices), real national income (national income at constant prices) is taken as the numerator.

Per capita real income is traditionally taken as an index or measure of economic welfare and economic development. It enables us to know the average income and the standard of living of the people on average. An increase in per capita real income leads to an improvement in the living standard of the people as well as economic development. However, per capita prices is not a perfect index of economic development and welfare.

National Income at Current Prices and at Constant Prices

National income can be calculated at current prices and at constant prices accordingly, we refer to *national income at current prices and national income at constant prices.*

National income at current prices is the money value of all final goods and services produced in a country during a particular year, expressed at market prices prevailing in that year. In other words for national income at current year, we use same year's output and same year' market prices. For example, if we measure national income of India for the year 2005–2006 at 2005–2006 prices, it is national income at current prices.

National income at constant prices, on the other hand, measures 'final goods and services constituting the national income at the market prices prevailing in a particular year, which becomes the base year. Goods and services are included in national income of each year valued at the prices of the base year. For instance, if we take 1990–91 as base year prices and express national income of 2002–03 at 1990–91, the national income so estimated is known as national income at constant prices.

National income at current prices can change partly because of a change in the physical quantities of final goods and services produced and partly because of change of the market prices at which these goods and services are valued. Therefore, national income at current prices does not reflect in the real national output (*i.e.*, goods and services produced). But national income at constant prices is affected by changes in physical units of final goods and services only. Consequently, an increase in national income at constant prices indicates a real increase in the physical entities of goods and services. That is why national income at constant price as is known as real national income. Thus, national income at constant prices reflect real growth of an economy.

National income at current prices is converted into national income at constant prices by eliminating the effect of price changes on national income with the help of a suitable price index. Price index is that number which measures the changes in prices between different years. The price index base year is invariably taken as 100. The price index of the current year is obtained by multiplying the ratio of current prices to the prices of the current year by 100.

National income at current prices is converted into national income at constant prices with the help of the following formula:

$$= \text{National income at current prices} - \text{Prices index of current year} \times 100$$

Self-Assessment Questions

1. Briefly bring out the end-use classification of goods and services.
2. Differentiate between intermediate and final goods. What is the significance of the distinction from the view point of national income accounting?
3. What are the commodities included in the computation of national income?
4. (*a*) Distinguish between economic goods and free goods.
   (*b*) Differentiate between material goods and services.
   (*c*) Distinguish between consumer goods and producer goods.
   (*d*) Differentiate between single-use and durable-use goods.
5. Distinguish between
   (*a*) Final goods and intermediate goods.
   (*b*) Real flows and money flows.
   (*c*) A closed economy and an open economy.
6. What will happen to the level of circular flow of income in each of the following situations:
   (*a*) $S = I$
   (*b*) $S > I$
   (*c*) $I > S$.

Unit **23**

MEASUREMENT OF NATIONAL INCOME

23.1 INTRODUCTION

National income is often considered as the most comprehensive measure of how well the economy is performing. It is necessary and important, therefore, to measure national income of a country so as to have an idea of the performance of the economy. Measuring national income is an extremely complicated and gigantic task. However, economists have devised various ways of estimating national income. In fact, national income estimates are made in every country these days. In India, the task estimating national income is entrusted with the Central Statistic Organization (C.S.O.), a department of Ministry of Planning and Programme implementation. In this chapter, we examine how economists measure a country's national income that is generated from production. *While measuring national income it is important to keep in mind that national income is taken in the sense of 'net national product at factor cost* (NNP_{FC}). However, while estimating NNP_{FC} we would first be required to estimate the gross domestic product (GDP).

Just as doctors take a patient's temperature to find out how sick the patient is, economists use national income statistics to get a quantitative measure of the economy's performance. It is important to know how economists measure a country's national product and national income that is generated from this. However, measurement of national income has always posed problems. It goes to the credit of Simon Kuznets that he has solved many of these measurement problems. In acknowledgment of this contribution, one of the first Nobel Prizes in economics was given to Simon Kuznets.

23.2 THREE WAYS TO MEASURE NATIONAL INCOME: AN OVERVIEW

We know, in the production process in an economy goods and services are produced by the combination of factors of production. Goods and services produced are distributed as factor incomes to the owners of factors of production. The income earned or generated is spent on the consumer and capital goods. Thus, production gives rise to income, income gives rise to expenditure and expenditure gives rise to income again. Put in terms of circular flow of income, we can distinguish three successive stages or phases of the circular flow:

(*i*) Production of goods and services by producers with the use of productive resources,
(*ii*) Distribution of incomes to the owners of productive resources, and
(*iii*) Expenditure of incomes on the purchase of final consumer and capital goods.

These three phases of production, income and expenditure are shown in Fig. 23.1

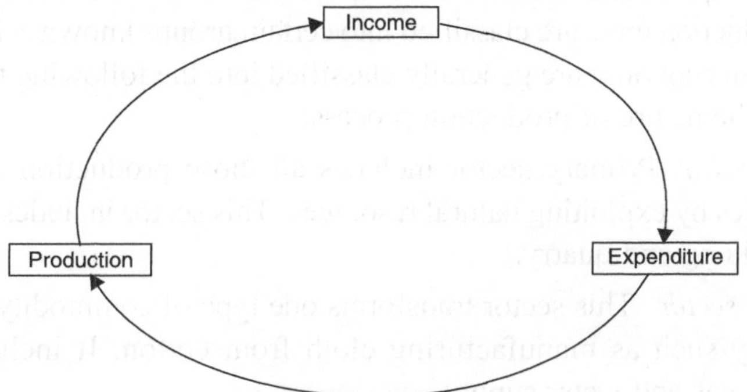

Fig. 23.1. Phases of circular flow.

Corresponding to these three phases of circular flow of income—production, income and expenditure—national income of a country can be viewed in three ways: as a flow of goods and services produced, as a flow of income generated and as a flow of expenditure on goods and services. Accordingly, there are three different ways or methods of measuring national income:

1. Net Product Method or Value Added Method
2. Income Method
3. Expenditure Method.

These three different ways of measuring national income are three different points at which the flow of income round the whole circuit of circular flow of income is measured. All the three methods give the same measure of national income but they refer to conceptually different activities in the economy and provide different ways to look at national income. Therefore, each method is important in its own way.

These three methods of measuring national income are now explained in detail.

23.3 NET PRODUCT OR VALUE ADDED METHOD

The net product or value added method measures national income as the sum total of net final output produced or net value added by all the producing units in an economy during a year.

Value added method involves the following steps:

1. Identifying production units and classifying them into industrial sectors
2. Estimating the net final output or net value added by production units
3. Estimating net domestic output
4. Estimating net factor income from abroad so as to arrive at net national product at factor cost or national income.

We discuss these steps in detail.

Step 1: Classification of Production Units

The net output method requires that national product should be measured industrywise. Therefore, as the first step, the production units are classified into certain groups knownas industrial sectors. All the production units in an economy are generally classified into the following three broad industrial sectors on the basis of the nature of production process:

(*i*) *Primary sector*: Primary sector includes all those production units which produce commodities by exploiting natural resources. This sector includes agriculture, forestry, fishing, mining and quarry.

(*ii*) *Secondary sector:* This sector transforms one type of commodity into another type of commodity such as manufacturing cloth from cotton. It includes manufacturing, electricity, gas and water supply.

(*iii*) *Tertiary sector or service sector:* This sector provides various types of non-tangible goods, *i.e.,* services, as compared to the primary and secondary sectors, which produce tangible goods. This sector includes trade, transport and communication, banking, insurance, government and professional services.

These three broad sectors in an economy are further divided into sub-sectors. For example, primary sector is divided into agriculture, forestry, mining, etc. The classification of industrial sectors varies from country to country. However, in India, CSO has distinguished 15 sectors for the measurement of national income.

Step 2: Estimation of Net Value Added by Each Enterprise

The second step in the value added method is estimation of net value added at factor cost by each of the enterprises. National income is the value of final goods and services produced. Therefore, we need to calculate the value of final goods and services produced by each enterprise. We insist on final goods and services so as not to include intermediate products (the value of which is already included in final goods and services) and thereby avoid double-counting. In practice double-counting is avoided by taking the *value added* by each enterprise. *Value added is the value of a firm's output minus the value of intermediate products.* Intermediate products are all goods and services used as inputs into a further stage of production. Value added by a firm is the value the firm adds to the intermediate inputs to get the final output. Thus, Maruti Udyog buys steel, tyres and other inputs and adds value to these inputs by producing a car. When we measure national income by net product method, we count only the value added at each stage of production. Value added by *Maruti Udyog* is the value of cars produced by it less the value of the intermediate goods like steel and tyres used in producing cars.

The estimation of net value added at factor cost by each enterprise involves the following steps:

(*i*) The estimation of value of gross output by each enterprise is made by multiplying its product by appropriate market prices. This can also be calculated by adding the sales and change in stocks. The value so computed is called 'gross' because it contains many duplicate items in the form of intermediate goods, such as raw materials, fuel, coal, electricity and semi-finished goods. Cost of intermediate goods and services is included in the value of gross output. It is called gross also because it is estimated without deducting depreciation.

(*ii*) Gross value added by an enterprise is calculated by deducting the value of intermediate consumption from the value of gross output. Use of intermediate products for the production of goods and services is called intermediate consumption. We need to deduct intermediate consumption from the value of gross output to avoid double-counting.

(*iii*) Net value added at market price by each enterprise is estimated by deducting the value of depreciation from the gross value added by an enterprise estimated in step (2) above.

(*iv*) From the net value added at market price deduct net indirect taxes (or deduct indirect taxes and add subsidies) so as to arrive at net value added at factor cost by an enterprise.

Thus, Net Value Added at Factor Cost =

Value of Gross Output – Intermediate Consumption – Depreciation – Net Indirect Taxes

Step 3: Estimating Net Domestic Output

By adding the net value added at factor cost by all the producing enterprises in a sector, we get the net value added at factor cost of that industrial sector. The sum total of net value added at factor cost of all the industrial enterprises in the domestic territory of a country gives us the net domestic product at factor cost.

Step 4: Estimating of Net Factor Income from Abroad

The fourth and the final step is to estimate net factor income from abroad. Net National Product at factor cost, *i.e.,* National income is obtained by adding net factor income from abroad to the net domestic product at factor cost.

Thus, National Income = Net Value Added at Factor Cost of Primary Sector

+ Secondary Sector + Tertiary Sector

+ Net Factor Income from Abroad

Precautions in Estimation

While estimating national income by value' added method, the following precautions should be taken:

- *Value of the goods produced for self-consumption,* such as food grains produced by farmers for the consumption by their families, should be included. They are not sold in the market and therefore do not have market price. Their value is to be estimated or imputed.
- *Own account production of fixed assets*, such as residential buildings by households and factory-buildings by entrepreneurs, should be included.
- We should include the *imputed rent of owner occupied houses.* Many people live in their own houses. They do not pay any rent; they are enjoying housing services similar to the

people who are staying in rented houses. To take account of the housing services enjoyed by house owners, value of these housing services is estimated from the market rent of similar accommodation. Such an estimated rent is called imputed rent.

- *Services of housewives, such as cooking meals, looking* after *the* children, are excluded from national income because there is no way of evaluating these services. These services are produced and consumed at home and never enter the market place. For example, meals cooked at home by housewives are similar to meals cooked at restaurants, yet the value added in meals cooked at home is excluded from national income. Similarly, while the value of commercial day care services is included in national income, but taking care of your own child is excluded from national income. In these cases, an imputation is called for in principle, but it is not done in actual practice to keep the things simple.
- National income measures the value of currently produced goods and services. *Sale and purchase of existing commodities or second-hand goods and services* such as old cars, existing houses, old paintings are not included because these transactions have not contributed anything to the flow of goods and services in the current year. We do, however, count the commission of brokers in the sale of these commodities since these services are performed in the current year.
- Sale and purchase of bonds and share are excluded from national income since they only reflect the transfer of an asset, not an addition to the national income. However, services provided by the brokers are included as explained above.

Difficulties in Estimation

Measurement of national income by value added method involves many difficulties. The main difficulties are:

1. Unsold amount of goods add to inventories. Increase in inventories of goods is included in national income because these goods reflect current production of goods and services. However, there is the problem of *valuation of inventories* in view of the changes in prices.
2. Estimation of depreciation also poses a problem, whether it is to be valued at historical cost basis (*i.e.*, the cost price when capital goods were purchased) or replacement cost basis.
3. National income accountants are not very clear whether certain products like education, transport expenses are *final products or intermediate products.*
4. In many cases, it is not possible to draw a clear-cut line of demarcation between intermediate goods and the final goods. Whether a product is a final product or an intermediate product depends on its use. Flour is a final good for a household but an intermediate product for a baker.
5. Finally, *lack of adequate and reliable data*, particularly in the case of subsistence and unincorporated sectors, is a serious problem in the measurement of national income in underdeveloped countries.

The value added method of estimating national income gives us useful information about national income by industrial origin, *i.e.*, share of different sectors in national income. For example, what is the contribution of the agricultural sector in national income can be known with the help of value added method.

23.4 INCOME METHOD

Goods and services are produced with the help of various factors of production, viz., land, labour, capital, enterprise, etc. Therefore, it is natural that output produced is shared among these factors of production. Factors of production get this share in the form of factor incomes. Factor income is the reward that the factors of production get for their factor services.

The income method measures national income at the phase of factor payments made to primary factors for the use of their factor services. Under this method, national income is calculated by adding up all the incomes generated in the course of producing the national product. National income is taken as the sum total of all the incomes accruing to the primary factors of production used in producing the national product. This method of calculating national income involves the following steps:

1. In the first stage, producer enterprises which employ factor services are identified. These enterprises are classified into various industrial groups, such as agriculture, mining, forestry, manufacturing, electricity, trade, transport and communication, banking, insurance, government and professional services.
2. In the second stage, the factor incomes are grouped under different categories. Factors of production are traditionally classified into four categories, viz., land, labour, capital and enterprise or organization. Accordingly, factor payments comprise rent, wages, interest and profits. However, in national income accounting, factors of production are classified into two primary factors, viz., labour and capital. In some production activities however, labour and capital are provided by the same persons. Accordingly, factor income is classified into the following three broad categories:

(*i*) Labour income or compensation of employees

(*ii*) Capital or property income or operating surplus

(*iii*) Mixed incomes.

Labour Income or Compensation of Employees

Labour income, also known as compensation of employees, is income from work for others. It is the payment to the workers for their labour. It is the payments made by producers to their employees in the form of wages and salaries and other payments made in cash and kind and social security benefits. Labour income includes:

(*a*) *Wages and salaries in cash*, including bonus, commission, dearness allowance, house rent allowance, travelling allowance to travel to and from the workplace, leave travel concession (LTC), sick leave allowance, etc.

(*b*) *Supplementary labour income* in the form of employers' contribution (not of employees) towards social security schemes for employees, such as provision for pension, provident fund, group insurance, gratuity, etc. It is important to note here that the contributions made by the employees themselves towards social security schemes are not included in the social security contributions while estimation compensations of employees are paid out of wages and salaries.

(*c*) *Payment to employees in kind* like rent free accommodation, free medical, free educational facilities, free or subsidized food, uniforms, free transportation, recreation and holidaying facilities, crèches for children of employees, free provision of goods and services produced by the employees, imputed interest on interest free loans etc.

Thus,

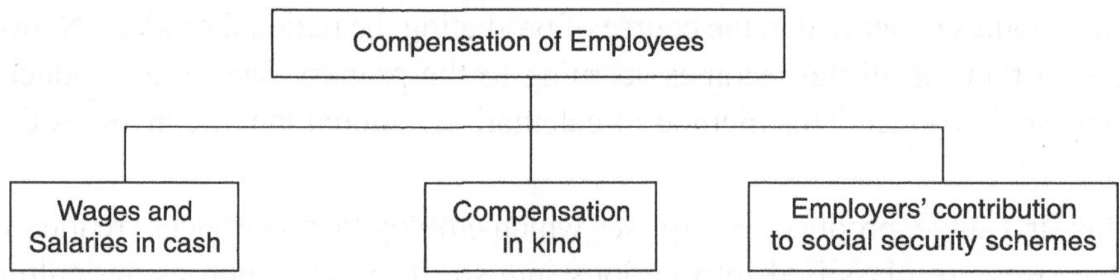

Fig. 23.2. Components of compensation of employees.

Operating Surplus

It is the income earned from the ownership and control of capital. It is also known as income from property and entrepreneurship. Capital income includes rent, interest, royalties, dividends, undistributed profits of corporations before corporation taxes. and profits of the government enterprises. *Rental payments* are incomes to people who own land and buildings and rent them out. The rents they receive from their tenants are rental payments. The income from rent includes rent on land as well as rent on buildings. It may be noted that rent of self-occupied houses in the form of imputed rent is also part of rental income. *Royalty income* consists of income received for granting the rights of mining to others and royalties earned from patents and copyrights. *Interest payments* are incomes received from lending to others. It includes interest received from lending to business firms, interest on government bonds (but not on war bonds and consumer credit), net interest paid by commercial banks, imputed interest on life insurance policies.

Income earned by entrepreneurs from entrepreneurship in the form of profits is known as income from entrepreneurship. It includes dividends and undistributed profits. *Dividend* is that part of profit which is distributed to the shareholders of the companies. Large companies do not distribute their entire income to the shareholders in the form of dividends. They keep some part of the income with them in the form of '*undistributed profits*'. These undistributed profits are utilized in paying corporate profit tax and are partly kept in the form of corporate saving.

Mixed Income

Mixed income is composed of labour income and capital income of those people who provide both labour and capital services in the production process. Such income is partly labour income and partly capital income. It is mixture of income from work and income from property and entrepreneurship. Mixed income includes the income of own-account workers and income of unincorporated enterprises. Such incomes include earning from agriculture, trading, transport, sole proprietorship, various professions like legal and medical professions and incomes of own account workers like plumbers, carpenters, etc.

3. In the third stage the domestic factor income is estimated. Income paid out by each producer enterprise is estimated by adding together three kinds of incomes, viz., compensation of employees, operating surplus and mixed incomes. Incomes paid out to all the factors of production in a particular industrial sector, such as agriculture, manufacturing, etc. is found out by adding the incomes paid out by each enterprise in that sector. Then we add the incomes paid by all the industrial sectors to get the domestic factor income. Thus, the sum total of compensation of employees, capital incomes and mixed incomes by all the production units in the domestic territory of the economy during the accounting year gives the measure of domestic factor income.
4. In the last stage, net factor income earned from abroad is added to domestic factor income to arrive at national income. Net factor income from abroad, as noted earlier, is the difference between the factor income received from abroad for providing factor services and the income paid for the factor services provided by non-residents in the territory of a country. It is the difference between factor incomes arising out of factor services rendered by the normal resident of a country to the rest of the world less factor incomes arising from factor services rendered to them by the rest of the world. The components of net factor income from abroad are:
   (*a*) Net compensation of employees
   (*b*) Net income from property and entrepreneurship, *i.e.,* net income from interest, rent, ividends and profits; and
   (*c*) Net retained earnings of resident companies abroad.

Thus,

National Income = Compensation of employees + Capital incomes or operating surplus + Mixed incomes + Net factor income from abroad

Precaution in Estimation

- While calculating national income by income method, we should include the following two items since they constitute income in kind:
  (*i*) Value of production for self-consumption, such as agricultural products used by the farmers for the consumption by their families.
  (*ii*) Imputed rent of the self-occupied houses by the owners of these houses.

- Imputed value of the services provided by the owners of production units in production process should also be included the following items should not be included in the income for diverse reasons:

All *transfer incomes* (payments) like old age pensions, unemployment relief, scholarships to the students, assistance given by government and other agencies to meet exigencies like flood, drought, etc. should be excluded from national income because they have been received without rendering any productive services in exchange in the current year. Such payments lead only to transfer of income from one pocket to another. These transfer incomes do not reflect any production of foods and services in the current year.

Illegal incomes like income of smugglers, illegal drug traders, gamblers and illegal arm dealers are excluded from national income as they are the result of illegal activities and are unaccountable.

Interest on national debt is excluded from national income since it is treated as transfer income on the assumption that the government borrowings are used for consumption purposes. This is the national income convention as public debt in the past was used for unproductive purposes.

Money income received from the sale of second-hand goods, boundaries, etc. are excluded from national income because they do not can tribute anything to the current flow of goods and services. These as actions reflect only changes in the ownership of pre-existing input. However, the commission charged by brokers on such as actions should be included in the national income.

Private transfer payments, such as pocket money given by parents to their children, money given to elders by their children, etc., are excluded as they are merely transfer of money from one individual to another.

- Windfall gains, such as income from lotteries, should not be included as they do not contribute to current flows of goods and services.
- In calculating national income, we include profits before deduction of corporation tax. Therefore, corporation tax should not be included separately.
- Wealth tax, gift tax, etc., are paid out of current out of past savings. Hence, they should not be regarded as part of national income.

Difficulties in Estimation

Estimates of national income by income method poses various difficulties, the major difficulties are:

1. Firstly, it is difficult to estimate mixed incomes. Mixed incomes are earned by the unincorporated sector, and it is difficult to get reliable information from such an unorganized sector.
2. Interest on national debt is not included in national income as per the national income convention on the assumption that government borrowings are used for consumption (unproductive) purpose. However, some economists object to this since a part of the government borrowing is used for productive purposes.

3. Incomes received are generally calculated from income-tax returns. Therefore, income method is of limited use in underdeveloped countries because a very small part of the income earners are tax payers in these countries.

Income method of estimating national income is useful because it provides information about distribution of national income among various factor categories like share of wages and profits, etc. in national income.

23.5 EXPENDITURE METHOD

The third method of calculating national income is the expenditure method; *It measures national income at the disposition stage, i.e., the disposition of final products.* It estimates national income by measuring the final expenditure on gross domestic product. In other words, it measures national income by estimating expenditure on final products. The final products are those which are purchased for consumption and investment. As such expenditure on consumption and investment constitutes the value of the final products. Expenditure is done by private individuals like households and government. Accordingly, consumption expenditure is classified into private and government final consumption expenditure. Expenditure on investment is done by producers and government within the economy. In an open economy, there is foreign component of expenditure in the form of net exports.

Having understood the basic framework of expenditure, let us explain the expenditure method. Estimation of national income by expenditure method involves the following steps:

1. All the economic units which incur expenditure on final products are divided into four groups:
   (*i*) Households,
   (*ii*) Business sector,
   (*iii*) Government sector,
   (*iv*) Rest of the world.
2. Final expenditure on final goods and services in the economy is divided into four broad categories:
   (*i*) Consumption expenditure,
   (*ii*) Investment expenditure,
   (*iii*) Government expenditure,
   (*iv*) Net exports.

   These four categories of expenditure correspond closely to the four sectors into which the economy is divided as explained in step 1 above.
3. The third step involves the *measurement of the components of final expenditure*. Different components of final expenditure are measured as follows:

Estimation of Private Final Consumption Expenditure

Private final consumption expenditure comprises of expenditure on the purchase of consumer goods and services (except houses) by households and private non-profit institutions serving households like schools, clubs, charitable hospitals, etc. It is divided into three major sub-categories:

(*i*) Expenditure on non-durable goods, such as food, beverages, etc., which are used immediately or within a short span of time.

(*ii*) Expenditure on durable goods like TVs, cars, etc., which could be used for a longer period of time.

(*iii*) Expenditure on services like transport services, medical services etc.

We calculate the final consumption expenditure by the households and private non-profit institutions serving the households on the domestically produced consumer goods and services by multiplying the volume of sale of these goods and services in the market with the retail prices.

While calculating consumption expenditure, several points should be noted. First, expenditure on purchase of new houses is excluded from consumption expenditure since it is taken as investment expenditure. Second, only currently produced goods and services are included. Expenditure on purchase of old goods like old cars should be excluded because these goods do not represent current output.

Third, production for self-consumption by producers should he included. Production for self-consumption is a part of production and income, and since this part of production is used for consumption by the producers, it is also a part of final consumption expenditure.

Lastly, imputed rent on the self-occupied houses is also included in the final consumption expenditure. By living in their own houses, the owners are consuming or using the housing services.

Estimation of Investment Expenditure

Investment means addition to the physical stock of capital goods, such as machinery, factories, residential houses and addition to a firm's inventories of goods during a given period. Investment consists of investment goods bought for future use. Investment expenditure is the expenditure on investment or capital goods. Capital goods are produced by firms and they may be bought by firms, by households (purchase of residential houses) or by governments.

Investment expenditure is divided into three sub-categories:

(*i*) Expenditure on business fixed investment, *i.e.,* expenditure on the purchase of new plants, machinery, equipments, factories, transport equipments, construction works (like irrigation, dams, telephone lines, etc.) and breeding stock.

(*ii*) Inventory investment, *i.e.,* change in inventories of the firm which are in the warehouses, goods on store shelves, on showroom floors, which have not yet been sold or converted into a final good.

(*iii*) Expenditure on residential investment, *i.e.,* expenditure on the purchase of new houses by households and landlords.

- *Expenditure on machinery, equipment* (business fixed investment) can be estimated by taking the value of final sales at market prices. Own account production of machinery and equipment by the producers has to be added to get the final expenditure on machinery and equipment.
- *Inventory investment, i.e.,* increase in stock of goods—final goods awaiting sale, semi-finished goods, raw materials, etc., with producers and retailers, is calculated at market

price. Net increase in stock of consumer goods with households is excluded from inventory investment on the assumption that goods with the consumers are consumed the moment they are purchased. We include inventory investment as an investment item because it represents goods produced but not used for current consumption. Inventory investment in an economy is calculated by taking the difference between the opening stock and the closing stock.

- *Expenditure on residential houses* can be found out by estimating the total money spent on construction of new houses. Total expenditure on new housing is equal to the expenditure on the material inputs like cement, steel, bricks, wood, etc. and factor payments to labour and capital in the form of wages, salaries, rent, interest and profits. Own-account production of houses, expenditure on major repairs and renovations are to be included in the expenditure on residential houses. Housing construction is counted as investment because it provides utility slowly over a long time. However, investment in housing is different from investment in capital goods in that houses are purchased by households while capital goods are purchased by firms.

Thus, expenditure on machinery and equipment, changes in inventories and expenditure on residential housing give us total investment expenditure or gross investment. However, a part of this expenditure is incurred to replace the worn-out capital. *The amount necessary for replacement is called depreciation*. By deducting depreciation from gross investment, we get *nil investment,*

Thus,

Net Domestic Investment = Gross Fixed Business Investment + Inventory Investment + Gross Residential Investment – Depreciation

Estimation of Government Expenditure

The third category of spending is government expenditure. The government expenditures are of two types:

(*i*) Current expenditure on goods and services, *i.e.,* Government final consumption expenditure.

(*ii*) Capital expenditure, *i.e.,* Public investment.

Capital expenditure of the government is generally taken along with private investment expenditure. Therefore, we take here *general government final expenditure.* The final expenditure of the general government is also known as government final consumption expenditure. It consists of expenditure on administration, defense expenditure, expenditure on maintenance of law and order, expenditure on social welfare services, education, sanitation, etc. The government incurs expenditure in providing these services to the public to satisfy their collective wants. That is why this expenditure is regarded as government final consumption expenditure. Very often government expenditure does not produce marketable products. These government services have no market price. Therefore, there arises the problem of how to value the government services. Government final consumption expenditure is valued in terms of cost to the government since the government services have no market price. The cost of these services to the government is the sum total of compensation of employees and the cost of the goods and services purchased by the government to provide these services. For example, cost of defense services comprises wages and salaries paid to military personnel and cost of military equipments.

Though the government does not sell these services in the market, yet sometimes it charges a very nominal amount as fees from those individuals who get these services. For instance, government hospitals take nominal charges from the patients and government educational institutions charge nominal fees from the students. Such receipts by the government should be deducted from the total cost of these services to arrive at the net expenditure on these services.

It is important to note that a large part of the government expenditure is on transfer payments like social security schemes, unemployment compensation and welfare payments. These transfer payments redistribute existing income and are not made for goods and services produced in the current period. They are therefore excluded from national income as they do not generate any output in the current period.

Estimation of Net Exports

The final spending item is *net exports. Net exports are the difference between the value of goods and services exported to other countries and the value of goods and services imported from other countries.* In an open economy a country has transactions with rest of the world through, among other things, international trade, *i.e.,* exports and imports of goods and services.

A country exports some of its' goods to other countries. For example, India exports tea, coffee, jute and cotton fabrics, cars and bicycles to other countries. A country also exports various types of services, such as shipping, insurance, banking, transport and tourist services. For instance, when foreigners use Indian ships to transport goods and passengers India exports shipping services. There are also exports of goods and services in the form of direct purchases made in the domestic market by non-resident households and others. For example, when tourists come to India from abroad, they make direct purchases in India in the form of purchases of food, handicrafts, transport and accommodation. On the same token, a country imports various types of goods and services from other countries.

Why are net exports added when computing national income through expenditure approach? There are two reasons. First, exports represent foreign spending on domestic goods. When foreigners purchase goods and services we produce, their spending adds to the demand for domestically produced goods and services. Goods and services exported to other countries are produced by producers operating within the domestic territory of a country. Hence, exports of goods and services is a part of domestic product. For instance, when goods which India exports are produced in India, they are not counted in consumption or investment or government purchases in India. Thus, exports need to be added to get a measure of production. The second reason is that expenditure on imports of goods and services is part of the aggregate spending by the residents of a country, though it is a part of the domestic product of other countries. For example, if an Indian household imports a *Toyota car* from

Japan, it is included in consumption expenditure even though it is not produced in India. To measure what is produced in India, the expenditure on *Toyota car* must be deducted. Imports must be subtracted to find out what is total production in the economy. Thus, net exports account for domestic spending on foreign goods and foreign spending on domestic goods. Since net exports are exports minus imports, adding net exports to spending is the same as adding exports and subtracting all imports.

The sum total of four items—consumption, investment (net), government spending and net exports is the total final expenditure which gives us net domestic product at market prices. By deducting net indirect taxes, we get net domestic product at factor cost.

In the last stage, net factor income earned from abroad is added to net domestic product at factor cost to arrive at Net National Product at factor cost or National Income.

Thus,

y represents national income,
C stands for consumption expenditure,
In represents net investment,
G stands for government expenditure,
(X – M) represents net exports,
NIT stands for net indirect taxes,
NYA represents net income from abroad.

Precautions in the Estimation

While estimating national income by expenditure method, we need to take the following precautions:

1. All final products should be included irrespective of whether expenditure is incurred on them or not. Many final products are not purchased from the markets and hence no expenditure is incurred on them, but these must be included in the national income. Goods meant for self-consumption, such as farmers consuming part of the food grains produced by them, must be assigned some value based on market prices of the similar products. Similarly imputed value to the owner occupied houses must be assigned because the owners of these houses are consuming the housing services.
2. Expenditure on intermediate products is excluded. The reason is that the value of intermediate goods is already included as part of the market price of final goods in which they are used. To add the expenditure on intermediate goods to the expenditure incurred on the final goods would be double-counting.
3. All expenditures on second-hand goods should be excluded. National income measures the value of currently produced goods. Expenditure on second-hand goods reflects only the transfer in the ownership of these goods; it does not lead to any addition to the economy's output.
4. Expenditure on financial assets like shares and bonds is excluded because it reflects only the transfer in the ownership of these assets.
5. Government expenditure on *transfer payments* is not included in expenditure and therefore national income. Transfer payments are payments which are made without

any factor services rendered in return in the current period. Although these payments play an important part in achieving certain social objectives, they do not create current production. Transfer payments are not, therefore, a part of expenditure on final output.

Expenditure method involves the same types of difficulties which arise in the case of value developing countries about expenditure.

The expenditure method provides information about the level of consumption and investment in the economy. It also shows the relative share of private sector and public sector in the total expenditure of an economy.

The main components of national income at the output, income and expenditure stages of calculation of national income are summarized in Table 23.1 and Fig. 23.3 for easy and quick reference.

Table 23.1. Components of net national product at factor cost in all of its three phases.

Output Method	*Income Method*	*Expenditure Method*
1. Gross Value added at Market Prices in : (*a*) Primary sector (*b*) Secondary sector (*c*) Service sector	1. Domestic Factor Income : (*a*) Compensation of Employees (*i*) Wages and Salaries (*ii*) Supplementary labour incomes	1. Final Expenditure on Gross Domestic Product (*a*) Private Final Consumption Expenditure (*b*) Government Final
2. Depreciation	(*iii*) Compensation in kind	Consumption Expenditrue (*c*) Gross Domestic
3. Net Indirect Taxes	(*b*) Operating Surplus (*i*) Net Interest (*ii*) Net Rent (*iii*) Dividends (*iv*) Undistributed corporate profits (*v*) Profits of Govt. Companies (*c*) Mixed Incomes	Capital Formation (*d*) Net Exports of Goods and Services
4. Net Factor Income Earned from Abroad	2. Net Factor Income Earned from Abroad	2. Depreciation 3. Net Indirect Taxes 4. Net Factor Income Earned from Abroad
Net National Product at Factor Cost **= 1 – 2 – 3 + 4**	**Net National Product at Factor Cost** **= 1 + 2**	**Net National Product at Factor Cost** **= 1 – 2 – 3 + 4**

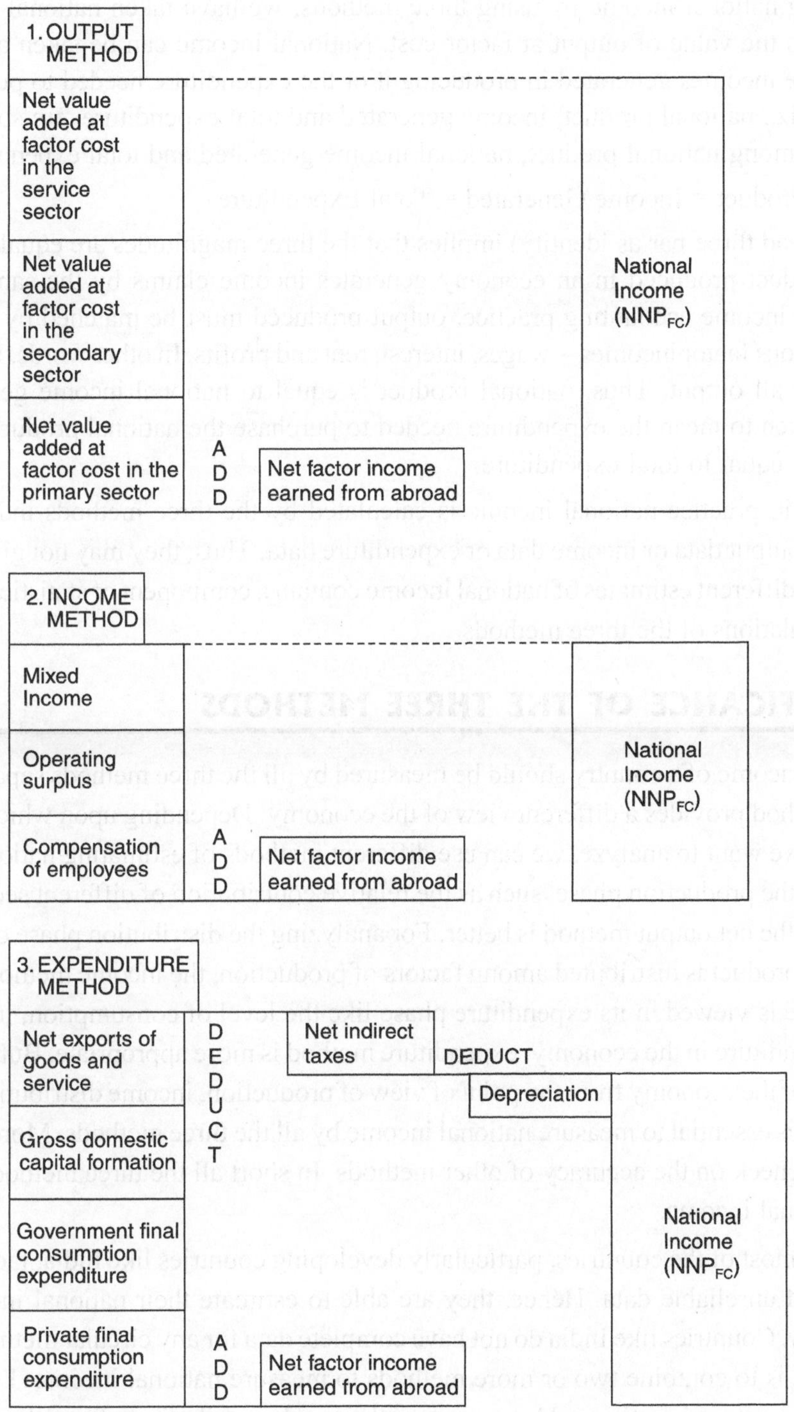

Fig. 23.3. Summary of measurement of national income.

23.6 THE IDENTITY OF OUTPUT, INCOME AND EXPENDITURE

While calculating national income by using three methods, we have taken national income in the technical sense as the value of output at factor cost. National income can be taken as the value of final output or the incomes generated in producing it or the expenditure needed to purchase it. The three concepts, viz., national product, income generated and total expenditure, are so defined so as to give identity among national product, national income generated and total expenditure. That is,

National Product ≡ Income Generated ≡ Total Expenditure

Here, ≡ (read three-bar as identity) implies that the three magnitudes are equal by definition. The national product produced in an economy generates income claims by the same amount. In terms of national income accounting practice, output produced must be matched by the claims on that output of various factor incomes—wages, interest, rent and profits. In other words, factor incomes must account for all output. Thus, national product is equal to national income generated. Total expenditure is taken to mean the expenditure needed to purchase the national product. That is why national output is equal to total expenditure.

However, in practice national income is calculated by the three methods independently of each other using output data or income data or expenditure data. Thus, they may not give an identical total. That is why different estimates of national income contain a component of statistical discrepancy to reconcile calculations of the three methods.

23.7 SIGNIFICANCE OF THE THREE METHODS

Ideally, national income of a country should be measured by all the three methods separately. This is because each method provides a different view of the economy. Depending upon which phase of the national income we want to analyze, we can use different methods of estimating national income. If it is viewed from the production phase, such as the relative contribution of different sectors in the net output produced, the net output method is better. For analyzing the distribution phase of income, like how the national product is distributed among factors of production, the income method is used. And if national income is viewed in its expenditure phase like the level of consumption, investment and government expenditure in the economy, expenditure method is more appropriate. But, order to have a complete view of the economy from the point of view of production, income distribution and pattern of expenditure, it is essential to measure national income by all the three methods. Moreover, method provides a cross-check on the accuracy of other methods. In short all the three methods should give us the same national income.

However, most of the countries, particularly developing countries like India, face the problem of inadequate and unreliable data. Hence, they are able to estimate their national income by each method separately. Countries like India do not have complete data for any circular method. Therefore, the usual practice is to combine two or more methods to measure national income. For instance, in India contribution culture is estimated by output method and contribution of small-scale registered manufacturing units is estimated by income method.

23.8 DIFFICULTIES IN MEASUREMENT OF NATIONAL INCOME

National income is quite a complicated task. It is beset with difficulties of various kinds. These difficulties can be broadly classified into two categories:

(*i*) Conceptual difficulties

(*ii*) Practical difficulties.

While conceptual problems are of general nature and appear in almost all the countries, practical difficulties have particular relevance to underdeveloped countries.

Conceptual Difficulties

Conceptual difficulties relate to the definitions of the concepts of National Income. Some of the important conceptual difficulties are:

1. **Inclusion of services:** There is the basic problem of what should be included in output and, therefore, national income. The problem is associated with the inclusion of services in national income. There is difference of opinion as to whether services should or should not be included in the national income. Marxian economists believe that services should be excluded from national income, while others say that services should be included in national income. Both views prevail in actual practice. For example, in socialist countries all services are excluded from the computation of national income. In the capitalist countries and other countries including India, services are included in national income.
2. **Identifying intermediate goods:** As we know, national income comprises final goods and services only; intermediate goods are excluded from national income. However, in actual practice, it is difficult to draw a clear-cut distinction between intermediate goods and final goods. Many goods can be intermediate as well as final goods depending upon their use. For example, flour used by a bakery is an intermediate good, while flour used by a household is a final good, similarly, transport expenditure incurred by a person to reach his office is intermediate cost; but if this expenditure is incurred by him to take his family on holidays, it is expenditure on final goods. It is difficult to decide what part of the expenditure on transportation is intermediate cost and how much of this expenditure is of the nature of final expenditure. Any mistake in identifying cost may lead to overestimation or underestimation of national income.
3. **Identifying factor incomes:** There is also the problem of separating factor incomes from non-factor incomes. National income comprises only factor incomes, *i.e.,* incomes paid in exchange for factor services like wages, rent, interest, etc. Non-factor incomes, *i.e.,* payments received which look like factor incomes but are not actual factor payments, are not included in national income. For example, interest payments on loans taken for consumption, payments received by selling old houses, old cars, sale of shares, etc., are such non-factor incomes. Individuals and businesses mix the two types of incomes and it is difficult in practice to separate the two.

4. **Services of housewives and other similar services:** National income largely includes those goods and services for which payment in money form is made. There are many services for which no payment is made in money form. One of these is services of housewives in their own homes, such as cooking, looking after the household, taking care of children. Similarly, men do many services for themselves and for the family members, such as shaving, are gardening one's own garden, teaching one's own children. No payment is made for these services and, therefore, they are not included in national income. It is difficult to impute the value of these services because there is no statistically sound method of estimating their value and also because these services are performed out of love, affection and regard, which makes their valuation impossible. Therefore, national income convention has followed an easy way out by excluding these services from national income. This method of overcoming this difficulty has led to some anomalies. All these services can be performed by the paid hands, such as maid servant, gardener, tutor, etc. If they are performed by hired persons, national income will increase, though actual output is the same. By the same token, national income of underdeveloped countries is underestimated because these unpaid services are relatively more important in these countries.
5. **Imputing unpaid services:** There are some services rendered without involving any payment. For example, government provides various free services to the people, such as general administration, police, etc. However, there is no record of such free services. Moreover, there is no standard method of imputing the value of these services. In practice, some ad hoc method is used for imputing their value.
6. **Income of the foreign companies:** It is a matter of controversy, whether the income of foreign firms should be included in national income or not. One viewpoint is that the income which the foreign firms retain in the country should be included in national income, and the income which is repatriated abroad should not be included. This is the convention which is normally followed, in case of such incomes.
7. **Valuation of inventory changes:** Inventory valuation is a very difficult and cumbersome job. The problem of inventory valuation is how to take the valuation of stock of goods, whether the valuation should be done at the original cost or at current prices. The practice, however, is to carry out valuation at current prices.
8. **Estimation of depreciation:** Estimation of depreciation is also a very difficult task. Depreciation of a piece of capital can be estimated at its original cost or at its replacement cost. However, the usual practice on the part of the firms is to estimate the depreciation provisions on the basis of the original cost of their assets.

Practical Difficulties

Practical difficulties relate partly to difficulties associated with under-developed stage of the country and partly to non-availability of reliable statistical data. Some of the important practical difficulties are as follows:

1. **Lack of occupational specialization:** For national income calculation it is necessary that producers be classified into various specific occupations. But in developing countries like India, occupational classification of producers into distinct groups is almost impossible, particularly in the agricultural sector. A substantial proportion of working population undertakes more than one activity during a year. This makes the estimation of national income difficult. For example, a small agriculturist may work in the agricultural sector during the cultivation period, in cottage and household industry during the off season, and he may go to the urban area and may work as a casual worker or as a rickshaw puller. In such a case, it is very difficult to assign any particular occupation to him and allocate his income to that particular occupation.
2. **Non-monetized sector:** The large, unorganized non-monetized sector of a developing economy like India serves as the biggest bogey for national income calculation. *Non-monetized sector refers to that part of the economy where goods and services are exchanged through barter without the use of money.* In a developing economy, agriculture is carried on a subsistence basis. A very large part of production does not come to the market for sale. It is partly kept by producers for their personal consumption and is partly exchanged for other goods. Such goods and services which do not enter the market need to be included in national income. At present there is no objective method of estimating the value of such goods and services. The absence of data about such goods and services makes the imputation all the more difficult. Therefore, estimates of national income have the stamp of guess-work and arbitrary imputation.
3. **Inadequate information regarding income and output:** Another difficulty that arises particularly in underdeveloped countries is that a very large number of producers are not sure of the exact quantity and the value of output they produce. A very large part of production activity in these countries is unorganized, consisting of small farmers, small shopkeepers and small independent artisans. Most of the small producers do not keep account of their production and income. Under these circumstances, the estimates of output and income are simply guess-work.
4. **Unreported illegal income:** Sometimes people distort facts and provide false information about their income to evade income-tax and wealth tax. This leads to generation of black money, *i.e.,* income which is evaded from income-tax, etc. For example, a significant part of the Indian economy operates as the parallel or hidden economy and the income generated there goes as unreported income. Obviously, national income estimates to that extent have an, element of underestimation.
5. **Non-availability of reliable statistical data:** The most important difficulty in the estimation of national income in a developing country like India is the non-availability of reliable data. There are a number of gaps here, which are:

(*i*) There is a dearth of agencies and statistical organizations collecting national income data.

(*ii*) A large number of enumerators entrusted with the task of collecting data at the village level are semi-illiterate and untrained, in the collection of data. They do not possess requisite knowledge of collecting, classifying and analyzing data.

(*iii*) Thirdly, there are also major gaps of data in respect of agricultural byproducts like fruits, vegetables, timber and fire woods. Price on several products like livestock, poultry products are inadequate. Moreover, data in respect of consumption, savings and investment expenditures are incomplete.

The data in many cases are incomplete, full of deficiencies and in some cases non-existent. National income estimates based upon inadequate inaccurate and incomplete data need not be dependable.

Self-Assessment Questions

1. How would you treat the following items in estimating a country's national product
   (*i*) Sale of an old car
   (*ii*) Purchase of shares in the stock market
   (*iii*) Services of housewives.
2. How would the domestic product be affected by the following transactions? Give reasons for your answers.
   (*i*) Sale of an old car by its owner and purchase of a new scooter with the money.
   (*ii*) Sale of an old house through brokers who are paid a commission.
3. How are the following treated in national income calculations?
   (*i*) Intermediate goods,
   (*ii*) Pocket allowance of children,
   (*iii*) Owner-occupied houses,
   (*iv*) Pensions,
   (*v*) Income from smuggling.
4. Why are the services of housewives not included in national income? Should they be included?
5. Explain various components of income in the income method of estimation of national income.
6. Why should the following not be included in national income? Give reasons.
   (*i*) Intermediate on national dept,
   (*ii*) Income from the sale of an old TV set,
   (*iii*) Payment of pension by the government to its employees,
   (*iv*) Income of a smuggler.
7. Explain briefly the net output (production) method or value added method of estimating national income.
8. Explain clearly the income method of estimating national income of a country.

9. Explain clearly the expenditure method of estimating national income.
10. Explain various categories in which the final expenditures are divided.
11. Explain briefly different methods of estimation of national income.
12. Discuss the difficulties which arise in the esitmation of national income, particularly in the context of a developing country.
13. Explain any four major difficulties in estimation of national income.
14. Define net income earned from abroad and describe its various components.
15. Explain briefly the basis of classification of production units into primary, secondary and territory sectors.
16. What precautions are necessary while estimating national income by value added method and income method?

Numerical Problems

1. From the data given below, estimate the compensation of employees:

	(₹ in thousand)
(*a*) Wages and salaries received by the staff in cash	528
(*b*) Value of free housing facilities	162
(*c*) Subsidy on lunch/dinner to the staff	32
(*d*) Employer's contribution to social security	28
(*e*) Compensation received by an injured worker from the insurance company	10

(**Ans.** ₹ 750 thousand)

2. From the following data relating to a firm, estimate the compensation of employees:

(*a*) Wages and salaries	45
(*b*) Commission paid to sales staff	15
(*c*) Value of free medical facilities	5
(*d*) Value of subsidized food (element of subsidy)	10
(*e*) Travel allowance (towards actual expenses)	25

(**Ans.** ₹ 75 thousand)

3. From the following data about a firm estimate the compensation of employees:

	(₹ in 000)
(*a*) Commission paid to sales staff	12
(*b*) Travelling allowance paid to staff toward actual expenses	18
(*c*) Employers contribution to social security	15
(*d*) Wages and salaries paid to staff	155
(*e*) Interest-free loan given to staff	20

(**Ans.** ₹ 182 thousand)

4. Calculate compensation of employees from the following data:

	(₹ in Lakhs)
(*a*) Wages and salaries	350
(*b*) Employers' contribution to social security schemes	40
(*c*) Value of free medical facilities to employers	60
(*d*) Bonus	35
(*e*) Employees' subscription to provident fund	30

(Ans. ₹ 485 lakhs)

5. Calculate emoluments of employees:

	(₹ in crores)
(*a*) Dearness allowance	10
(*b*) Social security contribution by employees	5
(*c*) Travel expenses on business tour reimbursed by employees	20
(*d*) Wages and salaries in cash	460
(*e*) Free food to employees during lunch	20

(Ans. ₹ 490 crores)

6. Calculate compensation of employees from the following data:

(*a*) Wages and salaries in cash	20,000
(*b*) Free accommodation by employers to employees	4,000
(*c*) LIC premium paid by employees	500
(*d*) Employers' contribution to P.F.	2,000
(*e*) Income tax paid by employees	5,000

(Ans. ₹ 26,000)

7. Calculate operating surplus from the following data:

(*a*) Royalty	5
(*b*) Rent	75
(*c*) Interest	30
(*d*) Gross domestic Product at factor cost	400
(*e*) Profit	45

(Ans. ₹ 155 crores)

8. Find operating surplus from the following data:

	(₹ in lakhs)
(*a*) Rent	60
(*b*) Interest	40
(*c*) Mixed income	200
(*d*) Undistributed profit before tax	90
(*e*) Dividends	60
(*f*) Subsidies	20

(Ans. ₹ 250 crores)

9. Estimate operating surplus from the following data:

	(₹ in crores)
(*a*) Rent	170
(*b*) Interest	180
(*c*) Undistributed Profit before Tax	300
(*d*) Mixed income	400
(*e*) Dividends	200
(*f*) Net indirect taxes	210
(*g*) Corporate tax	80

(Ans. ₹ 850 crores)

10. Find out compensation of employees from the following data:

	(₹ in crores)
(*a*) Rent	15
(*b*) Interest	10
(*c*) Profit	5
(*d*) Gross domestic product at factor cost	175
(*e*) Consumption of fixed capital	15

(Ans. ₹ 130 crores)

Unit **24**

INFLATION, DEFLATION, REFLATION INFLATION

24.1 INTRODUCTION

Inflation is a global phenomenon in present day times. There is hardly any country in the world today which is not afflicted by the specter of inflation. It is on account of this that the phenomenon of inflation has widely attracted the attention of the economists the world over, but despite that there is no generally accepted definition of the term 'inflation' as it is a highly controversial term which has undergone modifications. Different economists have offered different definitions of inflation. In fact, there is a plethora of definitions on the subject. The layman, however, understands by the term 'inflation' a sizeable and a rapid increase in the general price level. Inflation in the popular mind is generally associated with rapidly rising prices which cause a decline in the purchasing power of money.

24.2 DEFINITIONS OF INFLATION

Prof. Crowthers has defined inflation "as a state in which the value of money is falling, *i.e.,* prices are rising. But this definition of Prof. Crowthers is defective and does not offer a complete picture of the phenomenon of inflation. This definition has been criticized on two grounds:

(*i*) According to Crowthers, every increase in the price level is inflationary and has harmful consequences for the economy. This, however, is contrary to experience. An increase in the price level in the midst of depression is inflation and has no harmful effects on the economy. On the contrary, it serves as a stimulant for the revival of the economy.

(*ii*) Prof. Crowthers's definition emphasizes the symptoms rather than the cause of the disease. The rise in the price level is a symptom rather than the cause of inflation. This definition fails to explain why the price level increases from time to time.

Prof. Hawtrey defines inflation as the "issue of too much currency." This definition is also defective like Crowthers's. It is vague insofar as it does not explain as to what is meant by over issue of currency. The definition does not offer a clear criterion of the term "over issue of currency". As such, it is unsatisfactory.

Prof. Kemmerer has defined inflation "as too much currency in relation to the physical volume of business being done. Even this definition is not satisfactory. Obviously, this definition involves a comparison between the two quantities—the volume of currency on the one side and the volume of physical goods and services on the other side. The difficulty with this definition is that it suffers from vagueness. It is not possible to determine accurately the demand for money. There is no dependable technique whereby the physical volume of goods and services can be accurately converted into the demand for money. As such, Kemmerer's definition cannot be looked upon as a satisfactory definition.

Prof. Coeburn has also emphasized the same point as has been done by Prof. Kemmerer in the above definition. He says, "*Inflation is too much money chasing too few goods*." Coeburn's definition also involves a comparison between the quantity of money on the one side and the supply of goods and services on the other side. This definition is subject to the same limitations as Kemmerer's definition.

Prof. Golden Weiser offers a similar definition which reads as follows: "*Inflation occurs when the volume of money actively bidding for goods and services increases faster than the available supply of goods.* This definition also emphasizes the same point, namely, that the value of money increases at a faster rate than the supply of goods and services.

Modern economists do not agree that money supply alone is the cause of inflation. As pointed out by Hicks, "Our present troubles are not of a monetary character." Johnson defines inflation as a sustained rise.

Broman defines inflation "as a continuing increase in the general price level." Shapiro also defines inflation "as a persistent and appreciable rise in the general level of prices."

The above definitions given by Kemmerer, Coeburn, Golden Weiser belong to the same category. They seek to establish cause and affect relationship between supply of money and the price level. According to these definitions, the rise in the price level is caused by an increase in the supply of money. The increase in the supply of money is the cause; the rise in the price level is the effect.

But the above cause and effect relationship between supply of money and the price level was reversed in Germany after the First World War. The rise in the price level, instead of being the result, was actually the cause of the expansion of money supply in Germany in the post-war period. In other words, the hyperinflation which took place in Germany in the post-war period could not be explained by the normal cause and effect relationship between supply of money and the price level as pointed out in the above definitions. It was the rise in prices which caused the expansion of money supply in Germany. It is in this context that Prof. Paul Enzi has drawn a distinction between 'money inflation' and 'price inflation'. According to him money inflation is the first stage of inflation in which the excess of money supply over business requirements pushes up the price level. Price inflation is the second stage of inflation when the rising price level necessitates a rapid expansion of the supply of money. During the price inflation, the prices rise so rapidly that even the money supply cannot keep pace. This stage of inflation is referred to as hyperinflation. To our mind, Prof. Paul Enzi's definition of inflation quoted in the beginning of this chapter fully explains the phenomenon of inflation. In the words of Prof. Enzi, "Inflation is that state of disequilibrium in which an expansion of purchasing power tends to cause or is the effect of an increase of the price level." An analysis of this definition reveals the fact that the rise in the price level is not only the result but also the cause of the money supply.

The definition discussed above looks upon inflation as a purely monetary phenomenon. But recently the Cambridge economists, including Pious and Keynes, have analyzed inflation as a phenomenon of full employment. Prof. Keynes has linked up the concept of inflation with the phenomenon of full employment. According to Keynes, an inflationary rise in the price level cannot take place before the point of full employment. An expansion of money supply will not lead to a rise in the price level so long as there are unemployed resources in the economy. The price level will rise only after the point of full employment has been reached. An expansion of money supply before the point of full employment will increase output and employment, not the price level. The price level will increase only if the expansion of money supply is continued even beyond the point of full employment. According to Keynes, the rise in the price level after the point of full employment is true inflation. It is possible for the price level to rise even before the point of full employment if there arise certain bottlenecks in the expansion of output in the economy. But this rise in the price level cannot be termed as true inflation. Prof. Keynes has referred to this pre-full employment inflation as semi-inflation.

24.3 APPROACHES TO THE THEORY OF INFLATION

There are two main approaches to the theory of inflation:

(1) The Quantity Theory of Money Approach,

(2) The Excess Demand Approach.

The Quantity Theory of Money Approach

This approach to inflation is based on the quantity theory of money. According to this approach, it is the increase in the quantity of money which causes an inflationary rise in the price level. The definitions of inflation are offered by Hawtrey. This approach looks upon inflation as a purely monetary phenomenon. It has been subjected to criticism in recent years:

(*i*) This approach does not adequately explain the phenomenon of hyperinflation which took place in Germany in the post-war period. As pointed out above, it was the rise in the price level which caused an increase in the supply of money there. In other words, the rise in the price level was the cause and the increase in the money supply was the result.

(*ii*) This approach is not applicable to an economy which suffers from depression and unemployment. An expansion of money supply in such an economy may not necessarily result in an inflationary rise in the price level. An expansion of money supply in such an economy instead of raising the price level will increase output and employment. Inflation may not result consequent upon any expansion of money supply in an economy suffering from depression and unemployment.

The Excess Demand Approach

This approach has been developed in recent years by the Cambridge economists, particularly Prof. Keynes. According to them, "Just as the price of any good is determined by the demand for it and the supply of it, so also the general price level is determined by the total demand for and total supply of the group of goods concerned." Thus, according to this approach, inflation is that situation in which the total demand for goods exceeds the total supply of goods at current prices. The sole cause of inflation, according to this approach, is the existence of a persistent excess demand in the economy.

The phenomenon of excess demand can arise in a number of situations:

(1) War Period: During war-time the government expenditure invariably goes up and results in a substantial increase in the demand for various goods and services. It is on account of this that price level shows a rising trend during war-time.

(2) Planning Period: The phenomenon of excess demand can also arise during a period of developmental planning. The demand for investment goods invariably goes up under the impact of developmental planning. This results in an increase in the general price level in the economy.

(3) Period of Rapid Technological Improvement: The excess demand for goods and services may also rise during a period of rapid technological developments in the economy. The reason being that technological developments necessitate fresh investments in the various sectors of the economy. This naturally increases the demand for investment goods of various types.

A situation of excess demand can also arise when the total supply of goods and services declines for certain reasons without a corresponding fall in their demand. Such a situation will also result in the emergence of excess demand leading to an inflationary rise in the price level.

We have outlined above the two approaches to the theory of inflation. There is, however, a fundamental difference between these two approaches. The excess demand can become effective only through an increased supply of money. The increased supply of money is, thus, the causal factor of inflation. Ultimately, there is no basic difference between the quantity theory of money approach and the excess demand approach. The excess demand approach is, however, more popular than the quantity theory of money approach. It is, therefore, to the excess demand approach that we now turn for a detailed analysis.

Causes of Inflation

The above explanation of the excess demand approach highlights the various factors that cause the emergence of excess demand in the economy. The emergence of excess demand in the economy can be attributed to two main factors: (*i*) increase in the demand for goods and services, and (*ii*) decrease in the supply of goods and services.

Factors Causing an Increase in Demand: *Both Keynesians and monetarists believe that inflation is caused by increase in demand.* Following are the factors which cause an increase in the size of demand:

(*i*) *Increase in public expenditure:* An increase in the public expenditure consequent upon the outbreak of war or developmental planning invariably causes an increase in the demand for goods and services in the economy. In fact, this is an important cause giving rise to the emergence of excess demand in the country.

(*ii*) *Increase inprivate expenditure:* An increase in private expenditure, consumption expenditure as well as investment expenditure is an important cause of the emergence of excess demand in the economy. When business conditions are good, private entrepreneurs start investing more and more funds in new business enterprises, giving rise to an increase in the demand for the services of factors of production. This results in an increase in factor prices. When factor incomes increase, there is more and more of expenditure on consumption goods. The ultimate effect of an increase in private expenditure is to push up the demand for commodities as well as factors of production.

(*iii*) *Increase in exports:* An increase in the foreign demand for the country's products reduces the stock of commodities available for home consumption. It is evident that when more and more of commodities are exported to foreign countries, less and less of them are available for domestic consumption. This naturally creates a situation of shortages in the economy, giving rise to inflationary pressures.

(*iv*) *Reduction in taxation:* The reduction in taxation offered by the government can also be an important cause for the emergence of excess demand in the economy. When the government reduces taxes, it results in an increase in the purchasing power in the hands of the public. With increased purchasing power, the people are in a position to buy more and more of goods and services for private consumption.

(*v*) *Repayment of past internal debts*: When the government repays its past debts to the public it results in an increase of purchasing power which the latter uses for buying goods and services for consumption purposes. This naturally leads to an increase in aggregate demand in the economy.

(*vi*) *Rapid growth of population*: A rapidly growing population has the effect of raising the level of aggregate effective demand for goods and services in a country. This acts as an inflationary force and tends to raise the prices to higher levels.

(*vii*) *Black money*: The existence of huge amount of black money in the economy is also responsible for increase in demand. People spend such unearned or easy money extravagantly on buildings, marriages, luxurious items etc.; thereby creating demand for commodities.

(*viii*) *Deficit financing:* In order to meet its mounting expenses, the government resorts to deficit financing by borrowing from the public and printing notes in huge quantity. This raises aggregate demand in relation to aggregate supply.

(*ix*) *Cheap money-policy:* Cheap money policy or the policy of credit expansion also leads to increase in the supply of money which raises the demand of goods and services.

(*x*) *Increase in consumer spending*: The demand of goods and services increases when the consumer spending increases. It may be due to easy availability of credit etc. It increases the demand of goods and services.

Factors Causing a Decrease in Supply: Following are the factors which result in a reduction in the supply of goods and services:

(*i*) *Shortage of supplies of factors of production*: Occasionally, the economy of a country may be confronted with shortages of such factors as labour, capital equipment, raw materials, etc. These shortages are bound to reduce the production of goods and services for consumption purposes. In fact, the shortage of productive factors is a serious obstacle to any effort to increase production in the country.

(*ii*) *Industrial disputes*: In countries where trade unions are strong, they help in curtailing inflation. Trade unions resort to strikes and if they happen to be unreasonable from employers' point of view and are unreasonably prolonged, they force the employers to declare lock-outs. In both causes industrial production falls, thereby reducing supply of goods.

(*iii*) *Natural calamities*: Natural calamities like floods, droughts etc. adversely affect the supplies of agricultural products. The latter, in turn, create shortage of food products and raw materials, thereby helping inflationary pressures.

(*iv*) *Operation of law of diminishing returns:* In most of in the country which is using old and obsolete machines and outdated methods of production, the law of diminishing returns operates. This raises cost per unit of production, thereby raising the prices of products, leading to inflation.

(*v*) *Lop-sided production*: If the stress is placed on the production of comfort and luxury goods, thereby neglecting essential and consumer goods in the country, it creates shortage of goods in the market and hence causes inflation.

(*vi*) *Hoarding by traders:* At a time of shortages and rising prices, there is a tendency on the part of traders and merchants to hoard essential commodities for profitable purposes. The stocks of essential goods often go underground during a period of inflation and rising prices, causing further scarcity of these goods in the market.

(*vii*) *Hoarding by consumers:* It is not only the traders and the merchants who resort to hoarding at a time of inflation. The individual consumers also hoard essential commodities to avoid payment of higher prices in future. They also hoard essential commodities to ensure their uninterrupted availability for private consumption.

24.4 TYPES OF INFLATION : DEMAND INFLATION AND COST INFLATION

Broadly speaking there are two main causes of inflation: (*i*) an increase in effective demand, and (*ii*) an increase in production costs. The former gives rise to demand pull inflation, while the latter leads to cost push inflation.

Demand Pull Inflation or Demand Inflation

Demand inflation is caused by an increase in the aggregate effective demand for goods and services in the economy. It is the direct result of an excess of aggregate effective demand over the aggregate supply of goods and services. The process of the initiation of demand inflation is somewhat like this. To start with, there is an increase in the supply of money. This increase in the supply of money is soon followed by a fall in the rate of interest. The fall in the rate of interest leads to an increase in investment in the economy. The increase in investment is followed by an increase in the money incomes of the factors of production. With increased money incomes, there is an inevitable increase in the expenditure on consumption goods. It is natural on the part of the factors of production to spend additional amounts on consumption goods when their money incomes register an increase consequent upon an increase in the demand for their services. Increased consumption expenditure inevitably necessitates a further increase in investment expenditure. Since the economy was already operating at the point of full employment, an increase in investment expenditure will naturally result in demand inflation. This demand inflation will be marked by a considerable rise in commodity and factor prices in the economy. General shortages (of goods and services), lengthening queues, increasing imports, rising wage earning, increasing employment and rising profit are some of the indicators of the presence of demand inflation in an economy.

This type of demand inflation generally arises in the post-war period, when people rush up to increase demand for goods and services. During the war period, the people generally keep postponing their purchases on account of the all-round shortages of commodities in the economy. As soon as the war is over and the availability of consumption goods shows some improvement, the people rush to the markets to satisfy their long standing demand for goods. The demand inflation can be tackled by the government by curtailing unnecessary demand through the adoption of monetary and fiscal measures.

Cost Inflation or Cost Push Inflation

It is also known as supply inflation. Cost inflation is not due to excessive aggregate demand but is caused by an increase in production costs. The factors of production may deliberately raise the prices of their services through various types of collusive activities. Cost inflation is generally caused by three factors: (*i*) an increase in wages, (*ii*) an increase in the profit margins, and (*iii*) imposition of heavy commodity taxes. The increase in wages may be caused by a monopolistic lab our union through pressure tactics. As is well known, the labour day is well-organized into powerful trade unions. These unions, taking advantage of their organized strength, invariably dictate their own terms to the employers. This attempt on the part of the trade unions to push up the wages invariably causes cost inflation in the economy.

Cost inflation may also be caused by an organized attempt on the part of the industrialists to push up their profit margins. When such attempts are made, the prices cannot remain at their old levels. The rise in the prices caused by the raising of profit margins has its own repercussions on the working of the economy. But the profit-push elements are not so important in causing inflation as the wage-push elements are. There are two reasons for this. Firstly, profit constitutes rather a small part of the total price of the commodity. Even if the profit margin is raised a little, it may not have any significant effect on the price of the commodity. Secondly, the industrialists generally do not like to raise the profit margin beyond a certain limit for fear of alienating their customers. The wage-push elements are, therefore, a more important cause of cost inflation. Powerful trade unions get the wages pushed up even without an equivalent increase in the productivity of the workers. Under these circumstances, the increase in wages cannot but result in an increase in prices. The industrialists, on their part, shall never be prepared to absorb the increase in wages by lowering down their own profit margins. So any increase in the wages of the workers cannot but result in an increase in the price level and hence in cost inflation. It should, however, be remembered that cost inflation, when it takes place, does not remain confined to one particular sector or one particular industry. When cost inflation arises in one particular industry, it soon spreads to the other sectors of the economy as well. This reason being that the various sectors of the economy are linked with each other.

The output of one industry may serve as the input of another industry. So, if the prices of output in one industry rise, it raises the production cost in another industry as well.

The cost inflation starting in one industry now becomes an all around phenomenon for the economy.

Again, the government may impose heavy levels taxes on different commodities and in sellers' market the producers can easily shift the tax burden on to the shoulders of the consumers so long along with a margin of their own. These invariably causes cost inflation in the economy.

It should however be remembered that demand inflation and cost inflation are not mutually exclusive concepts. Demand inflation, when it starts, may soon land the economy into cost inflation. An increase in the prices of consumption goods is invariably accompanied by the demand for higher wages on the part of the workers. The prices of raw materials may also register a rise under the impact of demand inflation. An increase in wages and the prices of materials will naturally lead to the emergence of cost inflation in the economy. It is, thus, difficult to demarcate the line between demand inflation and cost inflation. Increasing commodity taxation, rising wages, falling profit margins, frequent devaluations of national. The currency (to push up exports) are important indicators of the presence of cost-push inflation and in the economy.

Of the two types of inflations, cost inflation is much more difficult to control than demand inflation. Demand infl ation can be tackled by adopting various types of monetary and fiscal measures to mop up surplus purchasing power from the hands of the public, but cost inflation be easily controlled through monetary and fiscal measures. The reason is obvious. Any a attempt to cut down wages by the authorities will be met by stiff resistance on the part of the workers.

The theory of inflation would be complete only if the two sides, namely, the demand side and supply side are integrated to provide a viable explanation of the phenomenon of rising prices.

24.5 KEYNESIAN CONCEPT OF INFLATIONARY GAP

Keynes' views on inflation have already been referred to in the preceding pages. As pointed out there; an expansion of money supply, under conditions of unemployment, does not lead to an inflationary rise in the price level. It leads rather to an increase in output, though in the later stages of expansion, even the price level may increase due to certain bottlenecks. But this rise in prices before full employment is not real inflation. Real inflation comes into being only if monetary expansion continues beyond the point of full employment. Then every additional expansion of money supply shall exert its full effect on prices, raising them to higher and higher levels. Thus, according to Keynes, expansion of money supply need not frighten us so long as there are unemployed human and material resources in the economy. Keynes does not deny that prices may rise even before the point of full employment is reached, but that, would not be real inflation. It shall only be "bottleneck inflation" as he puts it.

Keynes tried to explain the phenomenon of inflation in terms of his well known concept of inflationary gap in his famous pamphlet entitled. How to Pay for the War? The Keynesian concept of inflationary gap represents the technique of statistically measuring the pressure of inflation in the economy. The inflationary gap for the economy as a whole may be defined in the words of Prof. Koriyama, "as an excess of anticipated expenditure over available output at base prices. The anticipated total expenditure referred to in the above definition depends upon the net disposable income of the community. The net disposable income of the community, in its own turn, is arrived at by subtracting taxation and saving out of the total money income.

Net disposable income = Total money income – Taxation – Saving.

Anticipated total expenditure of the community is determined by the aggregate consumption, investment and government outlays. Thus,

Total anticipated expenditure = C + I + G, where, C represents consumption expenditure, I denotes investment expenditure, and G shows government outlay on goods and services.

The real output, on the other hand, is determined by the conditions of employment plus the technological basis of the economy. The inflationary gap is a situation where the anticipated expenditure (*i.e.,* the demand for output) exceeds the available output at pre-inflation prices. It is measured by the difference between the net disposable incomes on the one hand and the available output on the other.

The inflationary gap may develop in the economy like this. To start with, there is an increase either in private investment or government outlays. This has the result of raising the money income of the community to higher levels, but the real output of goods and a service does not increase because the economy is already operating at the point of full employment. The failure of the economy to raise its output in response to the increase in money incomes results in the emergence of the inflationary gap. The inflationary gap is, thus, the result of excess demand in the economy. In other words, the inflationary gap is equal to net disposable income minus real output of goods and services.

"To illustrate the concept of inflationary gap, we can take the example of a wartime economy which is generally a full-employment economy. The value of gross national product in an economy (whether wartime economy or peacetime economy) is determined by the aggregate consumption. Expenditure (C) plus private net investment (1) plus government outlay (G) on goods and services. Let us suppose that the value of gross national product is ₹ 270 crores at preinflation prices. Actually, this represents the total output of the economy at preinflation prices. Now, if out of this total output of ₹ 270 crores the government takes away output equivalent to ₹ 90 crores for war purposes, then only ₹ 180 crores worth of output is available for civilian consumption. In this way, ₹ 180 crores represents the supply side of the economy. It is the value of the available supply of goods for civilian consumption. Now let us take the demand side into consideration. If the price level in the economy is not to rise, then the incomes paid out to the factors of production should be in proportion to the value of goods at pre-inflation prices. In other words, the money income paid to the factors of production must also be equal to ₹ 180 crores. In that case, there shall be no inflationary gap and hence no rise in the price level. Let us now suppose that the money income paid to the factors of production is ₹ 300 crores. If out of this total money income the government takes away ₹ 50 crores by way of taxes, then the total disposable income left with the community would be ₹ 250 crores. Assuming that the community pays another sum of ₹ 50 crores by way of saving, then the net disposable income would be ₹ 200 crores. This is the actual amount of money income which is available to the community for spending purposes. But, as pointed out above, the civilian consumption goods available amount to ₹ 180 crores at the pre-inflation prices. When the net disposable income of ₹ 200 crores is allowed to compete with the available output of ₹ 180 crores, there arises an inflationary gap equivalent to ₹ 20 crores.

The above process has been summarized in Table 24.1.

Table 24.1. Demand side vs. supply side.

Demand Side		*Supply Side*	
Total money income	300	Gross national product (at pre-inflation prices)	270
Minus taxes	50	*Minus* war expenditure	90
Total disposable income	250	Available output for civilian consumption (at pre-inflation prices)	180
Minus Saving	50		
Net disposable income	200		

Hence, Inflation Gap = 200 – 180 = ₹ 20 crores.

From this Table, it is clear that there is an inflationary gap of ₹ 20 crores in the economy. So long as this Inflationary gap continues to exist the price level shall go upward. But If some how this inflationary gap of ₹ 20 corers is wiped out, there shall be no inflation at all. The government can reduce a part of the inflationary gap by cutting down disposable income through taxes. But the whole of the gap cannot be wiped out through taxation because in that case there is bound to be tax resistance and popular unrest. So it is advisable to remove the inflationary gap through taxes as well as induced saving. Yet another way to reduce or narrow down the inflationary gap is to increase the supply of consumption goods. But in war-time the scope for increasing the supply of consumption goods for civilians is rather limited. So the only methods available for narrowing down the inflationary gap during war-time are taxes, and public borrowing. It should, however, be remembered that the inflationary gap cannot be compatibly wiped out during war-time. Hence, the possibility of inflation is always there in a war-time economy.

We have seen above that the inflationary gap arises in a war-time economy. But, it is quite possible for the inflationary gap to emerge in a planned economy as well. Under developmental planning, the public expenditure considerably increases, giving rise to an increase in the money income of the community. But the supply of consumption goods does not increase in the same proportion on account of the existence of bottlenecks in the economy. This naturally results in the emergence of an inflationary gap which inevitably results in an increase in the price level. The basic point to remember is that there shall be no rise in the price level if the amount of disposable income in the community and the volume of output available are the same. But in case the amount of disposable income exceeds the volume of output available, an inflationary gap is bound to rise in the economy. If, on the contrary, the volume of output exceeds the disposable money income, then a deflationary gap is bound to emerge, giving rise to a falling price level in the economy. If the danger of inflation is to be avoided in a developing economy, it is important to wipe out the inflationary gap as much as possible. The task, however, is not easy. The nature of investment in a developing economy is such that there is a prolonged gestation period between investment and the ultimate production of goods and services, giving rise to inflationary pressures during the intervening period.

The concept of inflationary gap can be illustrated by means of a diagram as shown in Fig. 24.1.

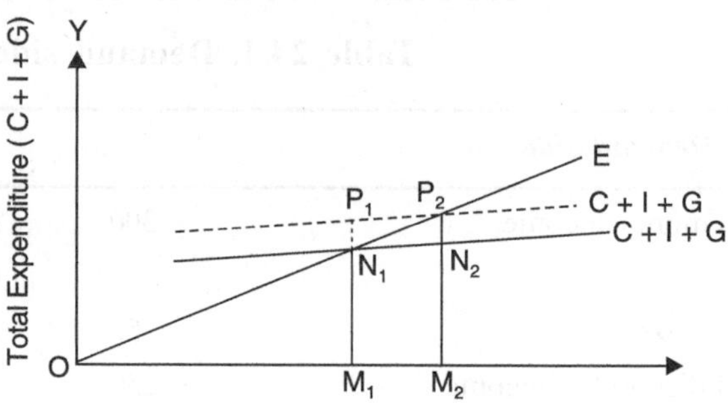

Fig. 24.1. Gross national product.

In this diagram, the X-axis represents the gross national product or the real income of the community. The Y-axis shows the total anticipated expenditure (C + I + G). C indicates consumption expenditure, I denotes private investment expenditure, and G represents government expenditure. The total anticipated expenditure of the economy is indicated by the C + I + G function. The line OE is the equilibrium line indicating that the economy is in equilibrium when the output of goods and services (as represented by the GNP) equals the demand for them (as represented by the total expenditure). The C + I + G curve intersect the line OE at the point N_1. This gives us the equilibrium income indicated by OM_1. This OM_1 represents the full employment income at the pre-inflation prices. The aggregate monetary demand here is shown by the C + I + G curve, which is equal to N_1M_1.

M_1 is equivalent to the total output of goods and services amounting to OM_1. Since the total money income is equal to the total available output, there is no question of any excess demand; hence, there is no possibility of the emergence of an inflationary gap in the economy.

Now let us suppose that for some reasons the government increases its expenditure by a certain amount, say P_1N_1 as shown in the above diagram. This raises the total government expenditure from the earlier level of G to G′. Thus, the new expenditure function in the economy is C + I + G′. Since OM_1 is the real income of the economy at the full employment level, it does not increase with the increased government expenditure (G′) amounting to P_1N_1. Now P_1N_1 represents the excess of monetary demand over the available output of goods (*i.e.*, OM_1). Thus, P_1N_1 represents the inflationary gap in the economy. It naturally raises the price level to higher and higher levels. Since the economy is already operating at the point of full employment, the supply of money income increases more rapidly than the output of goods and services in the economy. With the expenditure increasing faster than the output of goods and services in the economy, the prices will naturally rise to equate the increased expenditure with the money value of output at a higher price level. The inflationary gap may, therefore, be defined as the amount by which the monetary demand exceeds the value of current output at existing prices. In order to keep prices constant, the output should be increased by an amount that is sufficient to absorb the excess demand caused by the increased government expenditure. In the context of the above diagram, the price level can remain constant only if the output of goods and services increases from OM_1 to OM_2. In other words, the output of goods an services is the economy must increase by M_1M_2. This amount of output is equal to the excess demand P_1N_1 caused by the increased government expenditure. The inflationary gap of P_1N_1 in the above diagram can be wiped out only if the output of goods and services increases by M_1M_2'.

The concept of inflationary gap is a very useful concept in economic analysis. It is of great practical significance. The inflationary gap not only measures statically the pressure of inflation in the economy; it also highlights the nature and the extent of ant-inflationary measures, both fiscal and monetary, which the government can adopt to cure the economy of the malady of inflation. In the words of Prof. Koriyama, "An analysis of the inflationary gap in terms of such aggregates as national income, investment outlays and consumption expenditures clearly reveals what determines public policy with respect to taxes, public expenditure, saving campaigns, credit control, wage adjustments—in short, all the conceivable anti-inflation measures affecting the propensities to consume, to save and invest which together determine the general price level."

An Analysis of Inflationary Pressures in the Economy

It is easy to explain inflationary pressures in an economy in terms of the inflationary gap both from the demand side and the supply side. By demand is meant the income demand or the demand for money income for commodities and services, while supply here indicates the available output of goods and services on which money income can be spent by the community. On the demand side, the main inflationary factors are: (*i*) the supply of money, (*ii*) disposable income, (*iii*) consumer expenditures and business outlays, and (*iv*) foreign demand. During war-time, the supply of money increases due to increased demand deposits (consequent upon increased governmental spending) and expansion of bank credit, exerting upward pressure upon the price level. The volume of disposable income also records a rise due to a large increase in national income. No doubt, a part of the disposable income is saved, but a major portion is spent on consumption goods, thus, tending to raise prices still further. Business outlays also increase during an inflationary boom, raising total spending to still greater heights. And finally, an increased demand for domestic goods and services, on the part of foreign countries, exerts strong inflationary pressure on prices.

In contrast to a sharp rise in monetary demand (at a time of war) the supply of goods and services tends to increase at a slow rate, widening the inflationary gap still further. Why does the output of goods and services increase at a slow rate? The main reason is that during an inflationary boom the human and material resources are already fully employed and as such any attempt to increase output is accompanied by several bottlenecks and shortages of labour, raw materials and equipment. The situation is rendered still more difficult by the wage-price spiral. Demands for wage increases often lead to price rise. In addition, expectations also play an important role in the speed-up of inflation. The expectations of higher prices in future lead to hoarding both on the part of the consumers as well as businessmen. Expectations of wage increases often induce some businessmen to increase the prices of their products even before the upward wage adjustments have actually been made.

24.6 TYPES OF INFLATION

There are several types of inflation observable in an economy. These can be classified as under:

Creeping, Walking, Running and Galloping Inflations

This classification is made on the basis of the 'speed' with which the prices increase in the economy.

(1) **Creeping Inflation:** When the price rise is very slow like the pace of a snail or creeper, it is called creeping inflation. It is the mildest type of inflation. The government has sometimes to resort to creeping inflation to make the economy dynamic. This type of inflation serves as a tonic for a backward and underdeveloped economy. Under this, the prices rise slowly; industry and trade receive stimulus and the country slowly and gradually develops economically. It is on account of its stimulating effect that some economists welcome it for the economic development of a backward economy. In fact, there are some economists who support creeping inflation in the form of a slow and gradual rise in prices to keep the economy away from stagnation. But there are also some economists who look upon creeping inflation as potentially dangerous. Their view is that if proper control is not exercised over creeping inflation, it may assume alarming proportions with the lapse of time. They, therefore, suggest that creeping inflation must be controlled effectively in time before it is too late. It has been pointed out that the price level rises approximately by 2% annually under creeping inflation. As such, creeping inflation may not be considered to be too dangerous for the smooth functioning of the economy.

(2) **Walking or Trotting Inflation:** When prices rise moderately and the annual inflation is a single digit, it is called walking or trotting inflation. The rate of the increase of the price level acquires greater speed under walking inflation. Rouges speaking, the price level under walking inflation rises approximately by 5% annually. If proper control is not exercised over walking inflation in time, it can easily assume the form of running inflation.

(3) **Running Inflation:** When the prices rise rapidly like the naming of a horse at a rate of speed 10 to 20 per cent per annum, it is called manning inflation. The rate of the increase of price level gets further accelerated under running inflation. The price level under this type of inflation rises approximately by 10% every year. In case, the government fails to curb running inflation in time, it may easily develop into galloping inflation.

(4) **Galloping Inflation or Hyperinflation:** *When prices rise very fast at double or triple digit rates from more than 20 to 100% per annum or even more, it is called hyper or galloping inflation.* In fact, this is the most dangerous type of inflation. Under this type of inflation, the prices rise every minute, and there is no upward limit to which the price level may rise in course of time. Lord Keynes has referred to this type of inflation as the time inflation. This type of inflation invariably occurs after the point of full employment. Under this, the price level rises approximately by 16% every year.

There are two classic examples of galloping inflation in recent history, (*i*) the Great Inflation of Germany after the First World War, and (*ii*) the Great Chinese Inflation after the Second World War. In both of these countries, the inflationary forces had assumed highly alarming proportions. The above classification, as already pointed out, has been made on the basis of the 'speed' with which the price level rises in the economy. Under creeping inflation, the prices rise up by 50% in 25 years but under walking, running and galloping inflations this rise of 50% in the price level takes place in 10, 5 and 3 years respectively.

In fact, these stages of inflation are similar to the stages of the physical development of a child. Just as a child first learns to cramel and then in course of time learns to walk, run, and finally gallop, creeping inflation can also develop into walking, running and then galloping inflations in due course of time.

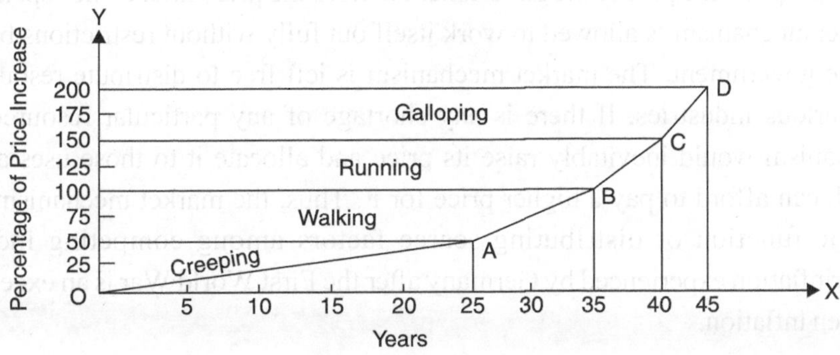

Fig. 24.2. Types of Inflation.

The above explanation of inflation can also be represented by means of a diagram. In the above diagram, the 'years' have been represented on the X-axis and the percentage increase in the price level on the fifth Y-axis. In the list period of 25 years, the prices of the commodities have gone up by 50%. The OA line, represents creeping inflation. In the second period of 10 years, the, rises have gone up by 50%. The AB line in the above diagram denotes walking inflation. In the period of 5 years, the prices again shoot up by 50%, and the BC line shows running inflation. In the same manner, the prices rise by 50% in the fourth period comprising three years in duration. The line CD represents galloping inflation. Thus, in a total period of 43 years, all *i.e.,* four types of inflation take place in succession and the price level rises by 200% during the entire period.

Comprehensive and Sporadic Inflation

The former type of inflation occurs when the prices of all commodities register a rise in the economy. It is comprehensive inflation. Normally speaking, inflation, when it takes place is comprehensive inflation. The prices of almost all the commodities show an upward trend during a period of inflationary spiral.

Sporadic inflation, on the other hand, is sectoral inflation. Under this type of inflation, the prices of all the commodities do not register a rise. Only the prices of a few commodities show an upward trend. The prices of a few commodities may rise upwards on account of central physical bottlenecks which may impede any attempt to increase their production. For example, the prices of food grains may show an upward rise on account of the failure of crops, consequent upon the failure of rains. Hence, sporadic inflation is of a sectoral nature. It can be dealt with effectively if the government resorts to the imposition of direct price control on the sale of the affected commodities.

Open and Repressed Inflation

Inflation can also be classified into open and repressed inflation according to the government's reaction to the presence of inflationary pressures in the economy.

(1) **Open Inflation:** Inflation is said to be open when the government takes no steps to check the rise in the price level. Open inflation is allowed to continue unchecked without any attempt on the part of the government to hold the price line. Under open inflation, the market mechanism is allowed to work itself out fully without restrictions being imposed by the government. The market mechanism is left free to distribute resources amongst the various industries. If there is any shortage of any particular resource, the market mechanism would inevitably raise its price and allocate it to those uses and industries which can afford to pay a higher price for it. Thus, the market mechanism performs its classic function of distributing scarce factors among competing industries. The hyperinflation experienced by Germany after the First World War is an excellent example of open inflation.

(2) **Repressed Inflation:** Inflation may be said to be repressed inflation when the government actively intervenes to check the rise in the price level. The government may check the rising trend in the price level by resorting to price control and rationing of scarce items in the economy. During the Second World War, the inflationary forces were kept under check through the imposition of war-time controls in almost all the countries of the world. As soon as the war is over and the war-time controls are withdrawn, repressed inflation inevitably bursts out into open inflation. The war-time controls, however, check the rising prices and distribute the scarce commodities through a system of price control and rationing. Thus, the administration of controls on prices and rationing of scarce goods is an inseparable feature of repressed inflation. It is on account of this that repressed inflation invariably results in such evils as profiteering, black-marketing, hoarding and corruption on a large scale. This may also "lead to the diversion of economic resources from the more essential to the less essential industries, the reason being that the price mechanism under repressed inflation is not allowed to function freely: The prices of essential goods are statutorily fixed, while those of non-essential goods are left free and uncontrolled. The margin of profit being higher in non-essential goods, the economic resources are bound to be diverted to the production of such goods to the detriment of the community.

Full Inflation and Partial Inflation

Prof. Pigous has classified inflation into (*i*) full inflation, and (*ii*) partial inflation. According to Prof. Pigous, the price level consequent upon the expansion of money supply in the pre-full employment state is referred to as partial inflation. There is only a slight increase in the price level under partial inflation. The increase in the supply of money goes to mobilize the idle resources in the economy. This results in an increase in the volume of employment in the economy. Thus, the increase in the supply of money before the point of full employment goes to increase the volume of output and employment rather than the price level.

But the increase in the supply of money after the point of full employment does not increase output and employment (because there already exists full employment of resources in the economy), but leads to a sharp uninterrupted rise in the price level. Such a situation is referred to as the situation of full inflation.

Peace-time, War-time and Post-war Inflation

(*i*) **Peace-time inflation:** This classification of inflation has been done on the basis of 'time'. By peace-time inflation, we mean the rise in the price level during peace-time. This type of inflation is very often the result of increased governmental expenditure on ambitious developmental projects in the economy. Such inflation very often occurs during a period of planned economic development in backward and underdeveloped economies.

(*ii*) **War-time inflation, on the contrary, arises during a period of war:** Modern wars, as is well known, are total wars, necessitating huge governmental expenditure on their successful prosecution. During war-time, the increase in the output of goods and services does not keep pace with the expansion of money supply. An inflationary gap inevitably emerges which results in a rising price level.

(*iii*) **Post-war inflation:** This generally takes place immediately when the pent-up demand finds open expression on the relaxation of price and physical controls by the government. The rise in the price level under post-war inflation may even be more rapid than during war-time inflation.

Other Types of Inflations

Inflation may also be classified on the basis of the 'factors' which cause this-Phenomenon. Under this head, we shall consider not only currency and credit inflations but also profit-induced, deficit-induced, wage-induced and scarcity-induced inflation.

(*a*) **Currency Inflation:** This is the classic type of inflation marked by an excess supply of money in relation to the available output of goods and services. Since the excessive supply of money is confronted with a limited supply of goods and services, it inevitably results in an inflationary rise in the price level. This type of inflation generally occurs at a time of war.

(*b*) **Credit Inflation:** Sometimes the government encourages an expansion of credit without expanding the supply of money in circulation. This is known as credit inflation. The main objectives of credit inflation are: (*i*) to lighten the burden of indebtedness of the farmers, (*ii*) to expand production, and (*iii*) to mobilize financial resources for development plans.

(*c*) **Profit-induced Inflation:** Sometimes the production costs start declining, and consequently, the prices also show a declining trend. But the government does not allow the prices to fall by resorting to artificial means. In such a situation, the prices do not go up but at the same time they are not allowed tc fall down. This situation results in an increase in the profit margins of the producers. Prof. Keynes refers to this type of inflation as profit-induced inflation. Under profit-induced inflation, the prices continue to stay at the old levels.

(*d*) **Deficit-induced Inflation:** Very often, it happens that the government fails to set up its income to meet the increased expenditure consequent upon the outbreak of the war. This results in a deficit in the budget of the government. The government is not able to cover this deficit by resorting to new taxes and public borrowings. Under these circumstances, the government is forced to cover the deficit by resorting to the printing press. This is known as deficit-induced inflation. The government of a backward, underdeveloped country may also be forced to resort to deficit financing to finance its developmental plans. This may result in a rising price level. Since the deficit in the budget is covered by resorting to the printing press, this type of inflation is known as deficit-induced inflation.

(*e*) **Wage-induced Inflation:** When the workers organize themselves into powerful trade unions and force the employers to increase their wages, this inevitably pushes up production costs. Consequently, the prices of goods and services rise upward. This may be referred to as wage-induced inflation.

(*f*) **Scarcity-induced Inflation:** When the supply of money does not increase but the supply of goods decreases on account of natural calamities, the prices show an upward trend. This may be called scarcity-induced inflation or production inflation

Besides the above, there are other types of inflations as well, namely:

(*g*) **Mark-up Inflation:** This term is quite current in the USA. This type of inflation is attributed to the peculiar method of pricing (of goods and services) adopted by the gigantic business organizations operating in that country. According to this method, the big business organizations calculate their production costs first and then add to these costs a certain mark-up to yield the targeted rate of profit on their capital investment. The mark-up is invariably on the high side and constitutes not an insignificant cause of inflationary pressure in USA. The mark-up method is being abused by the monopoly business organizations to inflate their profits. The higher the demand, the greater is the size of the mark-up.

(*h*) **Ratchet Inflation:** A ratchet, when it takes hold of a mechanism, holds it in a fixed position. Under ratchet inflation, the prices in certain sectors are not allowed to fall (or, are held in a fixed position) even though there are strong reasons for the prices to decline. Sometimes, it happens that the aggregate demand in the economy is not high, but it is not properly distributed among the various sectors. In certain sectors, the aggregate demand is excessive, while in others it is quite low. In the former sectors, the prices would register a rise, while in latter sectors, the prices should decline. But the prices are not allowed to fall in accordance with the low aggregate demand in the latter sectors due to resistance from the industrialists and trade unions. Thus, while the prices in the excess-demand sectors rise, they are not allowed to fall in the deficient-demand sectors. The net result is a rise in the general price level. This is known as 'ratchet inflation'.

(*i*) **Stagflation:** A new type of inflation had come into vogue in the post-war period particularly since the sixties. This is known as stagflation. It is not inflation in the strict Keynesian sense. Inflation in the Keynesian sense is accompanied by overfull employment. All the remedies suggested by J. M. Keynes were intended to tackle this type of inflation. But the present day inflation is quite different from the traditional inflation which the world had to bare prior to the sixties. The present-day inflation is accompanied, not by full employment but by increasing unemployment. The term "stagflation" appropriately depicts the present day inflationary situation in the world. It is inflation accompanied by stagnation on the development front. High prices and high unemployment go hand-in-hand. "Stagflation" is a global phenomenon today. No country, whether developed or developing, is free from its clutches. The whole western world, particularly Great Britain, Italy, USA are in the grip of "stagflation" today. The developing countries, including India, have also fallen prey to this most vicious type of inflation. Apart from its debilitating effects, it is the most difficult type of inflation to deal with. The well known Keynesian remedies, such as, budget surpluses, higher taxes and spending cuts have not only arrested inflation, but have also aggravated the unemployment situation in various countries of the world. Any step taken to ease the unemployment situation through increased capital investment adds to the inflationary fire while any policy adopted to deal with inflation through cuts in public expenditure, increases the number of unemployed. The world stands today between the devil (of inflation) and the deep sea (of unemployment).

(*j*) **Sectoral Inflation:** Sometimes the rise in prices may not be general, but restricted to a particular sector of the economy. This type of inflation is referred to as sectoral inflation. If timely steps are not taken, the inflation in a particular sector may soon spread to other sectors of the economy. It may, then, cease to be sectoral inflation. For example, agricultural production suffered a serious setback in India during 1979–80 due to drought conditions. Agricultural prices shot up. This inflation, however, did not remain confined to the agricultural sector for long. The manufacturers also pushed up the prices of their products due to the higher cost of raw materials and increased wages.

(*k*) **Imported Inflation:** It refers to that type of inflation which is caused in a country due to the operation of external inflationary pressures which are transmitted to the country concerned through foreign trade. For example, if a country depends to a very large extent on imported goods and services, any inflationary pressure is bound to have its repercussions on its domestic economy. Several successive hikes in the prices of petroleum and petroleum products by the oil exporting countries after 1973 have had their impact on the price situation in India.

24.7 STAGES OF INFLATION

It is often said that like tuberculosis, inflation passes through three stages. In the first stage, the rise in prices is slow and gradual. In this stage, it is comparatively easier to check the inflationary rise in the prices of goods and services. But if inflation is not effectively checked in the first stage then like tuberculosis it enters into the second stage. Inflation, in the second stage, becomes a serious headache for the government. The prices of goods and services now start rising much more rapidly than before. The government finds it difficult to keep the rising price level under check. In the second stage, it is not possible to eliminate inflation completely, but if the government takes effective steps, it may be possible to prevent a further rise in the price level. In the third stage, inflation assumes alarming proportions. In this stage, inflation degenerates into hyperinflation or runaway inflation. The prices of goods and services now start rising almost every minute and it becomes impossible for the government to check them. The entire economy of the country is seriously disrupted. Finally, the government is compelled to resort to demonetization of the currency.

The above three stages of inflation can be illustrated with the help of an example. In the first stage, the prices do not rise in the same proportion in which the supply of money increases. In other words, the prices rise in a proportion less than that of the increase in the supply of money. For example, if the supply of money increases by 10%, the prices rise by 5% or even less than that. In the second stage, the prices rise exactly in the same proportion in which the supply of money increases. In other words, if the supply of money increases by 10%, the price level also goes up exactly by 10%. In the third stage, the prices rise in a much greater proportion than the increase in the supply of money. In other words, if the supply of money increases by 10%, the price level may rise by 15% or even more. Now, we shall describe the above three stages one-by-one.

1. Pre-full Employment Stage

As said above, the rise in the price level in the fullest stage is less than proportionate to the increase in the supply of money. Let us suppose that the supply of money increases by 10%. As a result, there will be an immediate rise in the price level. Consequently, the production of goods and services will receive stimulus. As a result of the increase in the output of goods and services, the price level will come down. But if the supply of money is again increased by 10%, the price level will rise up, giving encouragement to the production of goods and services in the economy. In this way, if there is a continuous increase in the supply of money, a stage will come when the output of goods and services may not increase in the same proportion in which the supply of money increases. The reason being that with the expansion of production, the supply of the factors of production, goes on declining. The hitherto unutilized resources are now already fully mobilized for production. With the lapse of time, there arises scarcity of productive resources in the economy. Consequently, the rate of increase of production slows down.

2. Full Employment Stage

If the supply of money continues to increase without any interruption, then after some time production will cease to increase, or in other words, production will become stagnant. The reason being that the productive resources are already fully employed. In other words, there is already full employment of productive resources in the economy. Extra resources are not available for a further expansion of production. Hence, the further expansion of production comes to an end. Since production becomes constant, the price level now starts increasing in the same proportion in which the supply of money increases.

3. Post-full Employment Stage

If the supply of money continues to increase even after the point of full employment, then for some time the price level will increase in the same proportion in which the supply of money increases. But after that the supply of money increases so much that the public loses confidence in it and the increase in the price level is much more than the increase in the supply of money. For example, if the supply of money increases by 10%, then the price level increases by 20%, 30% or even 40%. In such a situation, it becomes difficult, if not impossible, to check the rise in the price level. This is the final stage of inflation. In this stage, the prices rise so high that money exchange comes to be replaced by commodity exchange in due course of time. Finally, the entire economy collapses with dangerous economic and political consequences for the country.

24.8 EFFECTS OF INFLATION

A period of prolonged, persistent and continuous inflation results in the economic, political, social and moral disruption of society. The effects of inflation can be discussed under two sub-heads: (*i*) effects on production, and (*ii*) effects on distribution.

(*i*) Effects on Production

The phenomenon of inflation produces a very deep impact on the production of wealth in the economy. Inflation may not always be detrimental to productive activities in the economy. Mild inflation (which may more appropriately be called creeping inflation) may actually be good for the economy, particularly when there are unemployed productive resources in the country. An expansion of money supply in an underemployed economy will result in a slow and gradual rise in the prices. The production costs in such an economy do not increase in the same proportion as the prices with the result that the profit margins of the businessmen continue to increase, creating optimistic conditions in the economy. Encouraged by these rosy conditions, the businessmen increase their investments in productive activities, generating more income and employment in the economy. This process of increased investments and increasing employment continues till the point of full employment is reached. But after the point of full employment of productive resources any expansion of money supply is bound to result in hyperinflation. Thus an expansion of money supply up to the point of full employment may not be harmful for the economy. In fact mild inflation may serve as a tonic for the economy of the country. But any expansion of money supply after the point of full employment will degenerate into runaway or hyperinflation. And hyperinflation as already pointed out above is very harmful for the economy. It creates business uncertainty which is inimical to production.

It is this hyperinflation which has harmful consequences for the economy. In fact, hyperinflation disrupts the smooth functioning of the economy. This type of inflation has the following adverse effects on the productive activities of the country:

(1) Since hyper inflation results in a serious depreciation of the value of money, it discourages savings on the part of the public with reduced savings, the process of capital accumulation suffers a serious setback.

(2) If the value of money undergoes considerable depreciation, this may even drive out the foreign capital already invested in the country.

(3) With reduced capital accumulation the investment will suffer a serious setback which may have an adverse effect on the volume of production in the country.

(4) The volume of production will not only decline on account of the slowing down of capital accumulation, it may also decline on account of business uncertainty which may discourage entrepreneurs and businessmen from taking business risk in production.

(5) The pattern of production in the economy may also undergo changes under the impact of runaway inflation. This type of inflation may result in the diversion of productive resources from the essential goods industries to the luxury goods industries, creating further shortages of consumer goods for the common man.

(6) Since runaway inflation results in a seller's market, it may lead to a serious deterioration in the quality of goods produced in the economy.

(7) Inflation also leads to hoarding of essential goods both by the trader's as well as consumers. The traders hoard stocks of essential commodities with a view to making higher profits or with a view to selling scarce items in the black market. The consumers also resort to hoarding of essential goods for fear of paying higher prices in the future. They may also hoard essential goods with a view to ensuring their continuous and uninterrupted supply for themselves.

(8) The worst part of inflation is that it gives stimulus to speculative activities on account of the uncertainty generated by a continually rising price level. Instead of earning increased profits out of increased production, the businessmen find it easier to increase their profits through speculative activities.

(9) The most serious effect of inflation is that it disrupts the smooth working of the price mechanism thereby creating an all-round confusion in the economy.

(10) The economic system loses its flexibility under the impact of inflationary forces which have the knack of reducing the motilities of productive resources in the economy.

(11) The worst effect of hyperinflation is that in due course of time it results in a flight from domestic currency on account of its constantly diminishing value. In an advanced stage of hyperinflation, the people lose confidence in their home currency and rush to buy foreign currencies of stabler value to safeguard their assets. In fact, there is a scramble on the part of the people to exchange home currency for foreign currency in the foreign

exchange market. Nevertheless, as pointed out above, a mild dose of inflation serves as a stimulant by energizing and activating idle resources in the economy. It induces movement of real resources to the expanding sectors of the economy. It encourages entrepreneurs to make investments in new enterprises which lead to an increase in productive capacity and, ultimately, in the volume of production: price stability need not be treated as price rigidity. Economic stability, in fact, is consistent with an annual increase of 3 to 4 per cent in the general price level. This produces salutary effect on the economy as a whole.

(*ii*) Effects on Distribution

Inflation produces a deep impact on the distribution of income and wealth in society. A prolonged period of persistent inflation results in redistribution of income and wealth in favour of the already richer and more affluent classes of society. The distributive share accruing to the business classes increases much more than that of wage-earning or rentier classes. Businessmen, traders, merchants, and speculators reap rich harvests on account of windfall profits accruing to them as a result of the inflationary rise in prices. Prices under the pressure of inflation rise much more than the production costs. There is always a time lag between the rise in production costs and the rise in the price level. This time lag brings rich profits to the business classes. Moreover, the stocks and inventories of businessmen invariably go up in value because of the constantly rising price level "under the impact of inflation. The business classes, thus, make all-round gains during a period of inflation. The fact of the matter is that the flexible income groups, such as, businessmen, merchants and traders are always the gainers in a period of inflation while the fixed-income groups, such as, workers, salaried employees, teachers, pensioners, etc., are always the losers on account of the inflationary rise in prices. Inflation is always unjust. It is like a steeply regressive tax. Inflation throws the economic burden on the shoulders of those sections of the community who are the least able to bear it.

Effects of Inflation on Various Groups

The concrete effects of inflation on various groups of society are as follows:

1. **Debtors and Creditors:** During inflation, debtors are generally the gainers while the creditors are the losers. The reason is that the debtors had borrowed when the purchasing power of money was high and now return the loans when the purchasing power of currency is low due to rising prices. In other words, the debtors while reaping their debts return less purchasing power to the creditors than what they had actually borrowed. Since the creditors receive less in real teams, they are the losers during inflation.

2. **Wage and Salary Earners:** Wage and salary earners mostly suffer during inflation because wages and salaries generally do not rise in the same proportion in which the cost of living rises. Then there is the time lag between the rise in the cost of living/and the rise in wages and salaries. If the workers and salary earners are well-organized into powerful trade unions, they may not suffer much during inflation, but if they are unorganized or ill-organized, as they generally are, they may suffer much as their wages and salaries may not increase at all or may not increase in the proportion in which the cost of living increases.

3. **Fixed-income Groups:** The fixed-income groups are the hardest hit during inflation because their incomes, being fixed, do not bear any relationship with the rising cost of living. Persons who live on past savings, pensioners, interest and rent receivers suffer most during inflation as their incomes remain fixed while the prices soar high. Inflation, it is said, is also a killer of older, retired people who, with the advent of winter, find their pensions inadequate to buy fuels with their existing fixed pensions.
4. **Entrepreneurs:** Inflation is a boon to the entrepreneurs whether they be manufacturers, traders, merchants or businessmen, because it serves as a tonic for business enterprise. They experience windfall gains as the prices of their inventories (stocks) suddenly go up. They also gain because their costs do not go up as rapidly as the prices of their products. The costs of labour, raw materials and equipments, etc., do not catch up with the rise in prices of products. Inflation converts the entrepreneurs into 'profiteers' who put the community to ransom through their profiteering and hoarding activities.
5. **Investors:** Investors are generally of two types: (*i*) investors in equities (shares), and (*ii*) investors in fixed interest—yielding bonds and debentures. Inflation bestows favours on the former and is rather harsh on the latter. Dividends on equities increase with the increase in prices and corporate earnings and as such, the investors in equities are favourably affected. Incomes from bonds and debentures, however, remain fixed and as such, investors in them are adversely affected. The small middle-class investors generally invest in fixed interest yielding bonds and securities and therefore, have much to lose during inflation. Frequently, they find their savings' largely, if not completely, wiped out as a result of the depreciation in the value of money. The rich-class investors, on the other hand, invest in equities on which the dividends go up during inflation and are thus beneficially affected.
6. **Farmers:** Farmers are generally the gainers during inflation. The price of farm products go up while the costs incurred by them (the farmers) do not go up to the same extent.

Further, there is generally a time lag between the rise in prices and the increase in costs. Moreover, the farmers are generally debtors and can repay their debts during inflation in terms of less purchasing power. It should, however, be remembered that small farmers do not gain as much from high prices as the big farmers do, because the former do not have a considerable surplus to dispose of in the market.

Thus, inflation redistributes wealth and income in such a manner as to injure the interests of consumers, creditors, salary and wage earners, fixed-income groups, small investors, and to favour businessmen, merchants, traders and farmers. Socially, inflation is unjust. It transfers wealth to those sections who have already too much of it.

24.9 NON-ECONOMIC CONSEQUENCES OF INFLATION

It needs hardly to be said that inflation has far-reaching social and political consequences for society. As already pointed out above, inflation is socially unjust and inequitable for society, because it redistributes income and wealth in favour of those classes and sections who are already affluent and well-off. This creates a sense of grievance and heart-burning in those sections of society which are adversely affected by inflation. This naturally leads to social conflict in society which can have very serious political consequences for the country in question. Besides creating political instability, inflation also deals a serious blow to business morality and ethics. The lure of quick profits results in a serious deterioration in the quality of products, besides tempting the businessmen to resort to adulteration and other anti-social tactics to boost up their profits. The general morality of the people in the country also suffers a serious decline with the resulting all-round corruption in the country. This leads to general discontentment in the public which may result in loss of faith in the integrity and honesty of the government. This discontentment very often creates an explosive political situation, preparing the ground for the establishment of a fascist regime in the country. It is pointed out that Hitler's rise to power in Germany was the direct outcome of the post-war inflation of the 'twenties'. Inflation, thus, not only disrupts the smooth functioning of the economy but it also prepares the ground for social and political upheavals.

Apart from these general evils, inflation poses a serious danger to underdeveloped countries. As is well known, an underdeveloped country needs huge capital resources for its speedy economic development. But inflation, by discouraging savings, slows down the process of capital accumulation in the economy. Inflation not only reduces domestic capital accumulation, it also discourages the inflow of foreign capital into the country. With reduced capital resources, an underdeveloped country finds it difficult to step up its economic development. Inflation also discourages production by tempting the businessmen to resort to speculation, because speculative activities bring them rich dividends than productive activities.

24.10 NEED FOR ACTION

The above study of inflation and its harmful consequences serves to emphasize the need for adopting a prompt and effective anti-inflationary policy on the part of the government. As pointed out by Prof. Koriyama, the consequences of following a policy of *laissez-faire* with respect to persistent inflation would be dangerous indeed. Every inflationary boom, left unchecked, has within itself the seeds of a pending depression. An uncontrolled inflation soon sets in motion certain forces which, if unchecked, would land the economy into a serious slump with all the consequences flowing from it. Let us now analyse those deflationary forces which inevitably accompany an inflationary boom at its height.

1. Fall in Consumer Demand

An uncontrolled inflationary boom invariably results in a decline in aggregate consumer demand for two reasons. Firstly, under the impact of inflation, the distribution of income and wealth undergoes a change in favour of the rich and against the poor. This shift in money income from the poor (with a high propensity to consume) to the rich (with a low propensity to consume) adversely affects consumer demand. Secondly, the adverse psychological effect of reduced real income also serves to depress the demand of the consumers. A serious reduction of real income automatically induces a cautions attitude on the part of consumers who now curtail their demand for consumption goods to the minimum, consistent, of course, with the maintenance of health and working efficiency. The demand for durable consumer goods receives a sharp setback and adversely affects not only the consumer goods industries concerned directly, but also the connected capital goods industries. As a consequence, the consumer demand may fall too low to permit the absorption of the entire output. This may usher in the much-dreaded slump.

2. Fall in Investment Demand

An uncontrolled inflationary boom invariably results in a decline in investment demand. Firstly, during inflation owing to the rosy conditions prevailing in business circles, more investment might take place than is warranted by the needs of the situation. This overinvestment coupled with a reduction in consumer spending soon sets in motion certain forces which increase business uncertainty and diminish profitable investment opportunities in the future. As a consequence, anticipatory purchases of inventories (stocks) receive a setback. Secondly, the price-wage spiral accompanied by a short decline in consumer spending breeds additional uncertainty and spreads pessimism. Yet businessmen refuse to reduce prices in response to falling consumer demand or to accept lower profit margins with the result that markets weaken, giving rise to a recession in income, output and employment.

3. Fall in Foreign Demand

An uncontrolled inflationary boom will also invariably lead to a decline in the demand for the goods of the country in foreign lands. This decline in foreign demand may be due to the too high prices of exported goods owing to domestic price inflation. The decline in foreign demand unless offset by a corresponding increase in domestic demand, will have the effect of reducing output and employment in export industries, with a spreading impact on the entire economy of the country concerned. A decline in foreign demand will contribute to a depression of domestic business activity via the reverse operation of the foreign trade multiplier.

The above discussion, thus, highlights the necessity of quick, prompt and effective action on the part of the government to check and control the inflationary boom before it is too late, failing which it shall soon degenerate into a slump accompanied by mass unemployment and economic distress.

24.11 ANTI INFLATION POLICY

Our above discussion of inflation suggests three lines of action to check and control an inflationary boom, namely (1) monetary measures, (2) fiscal measures, and (3) other measures. We shall discuss the monetary measures first.

1. Monetary Measures

These measures are adopted by the central bank of the country and include such steps as an increase in rediscount rates, sale of government securities in the open market, an increase in reserve ratios and adjustments in selective controls to arrest an inflationary credit boom. Each of these steps has its own limitations, though it can be said that monetary measures are more effective in checking an inflation than in curbing a depression.

(*a*) **Increased Rediscount Rates:** To curb inflation, the central bank generally increases the rediscount rates. An increase in rediscount rates increases the cost of borrowing funds for business and consumer spending and thus, discourages excessive activity based on borrowed funds. The whole thing happens in this manner. An increase in rediscount rates leads to an increase in bank rates (*i.e.*, the interest rates charged by the commercial banks), because there is a definite relationship between the two. An increase in bank rates tends to discourage borrowings by businessmen and consumers from banks resulting in a fall in the intensity of inflationary pressures in the economy. But the increase in rediscount rates as a weapon to check an inflationary boom has its limitations too. Firstly, if the bank rates (*i.e.*, interest rates on loans charged by commercial banks) do not rise in the same proportion with the rise in rediscount rates, there will be no decline in the business and consumer borrowing, and hence, the inflationary pressures will continue even though the rediscount rates have been raised. Secondly, the effectiveness of higher rediscount rates as an anti-inflationary weapon shall be considerably undermined if the commercial banks have an easy access to additional reserves. For example, the commercial banks which are in possession of large amounts of short-term government securities can increase their reserves by selling some of those securities to the central bank or by converting the maturing securities into cash. Instead of borrowing from the central bank after rediscount rates, it might prefer to sell low-yield securities during inflation. Thirdly, an increase of rediscount rates will fail to check inflation if non-bank holders (*e.g.*, insurance companies, etc.) of government securities were to convert their holdings into cash. This conversion of non-bank holdings into cash would have the effect of increasing the velocity of money consequent upon increased cash balances. At a time of rising prices and falling value of money, there is a strong temptation on the part of holders of fixed income yielding assets to convert them into cash.

(*b*) **Sale of Government Securities in the Open Market:** Another method to check the inflationary boom is to resort to sales of government securities to the public by central bank. As the 'public purchases and pays for those government securities, the commercial banks' reserves with the central bank are correspondingly reduced and they are obliged to adopt a restrictions credit policy in relation to business requirements. This process helps in creating tight money conditions in the market, and thus arresting the further growth of the inflationary boom.

But the sale of the government securities as an anti-inflationary weapon is also subject to limitations. Firstly, this policy may be rendered ineffective if the commercial banks are able to increase their reserves by selling their stocks of government securities to the central bank. Further, the non-bank holders of government securities may also, in the absence of other buyers, sell them to the central bank and deposit the proceeds with the commercial banks. 'The deposits and reserves of the commercial banks are thus increased, neutralizing the effect of sale of government securities by the central bank.

Secondly, this policy may also be offset by increased borrowings from or by increased sales of treasury bills to the central bank by the commercial banks. Thirdly, the import of gold may also offset the anti-inflationary effect of this policy to a certain extent.

(*c*) **Higher Reserve Requirements:** An increase in reserve requirements of the member-banks also serves as an anti-inflationary weapon during inflation. It absorbs the excess reserves of the banking system and thus prevents them from forming a basis for further credit expansion. If, for example, the central bank raises the legal reserve requirements from 20 to 25 per cent of the demand deposits, the member-banks shall now be required to keep larger reserves with the central bank and, to that extent, their power to create credit shall become limited.

Higher reserve requirements as an anti-inflationary weapon are also subject to limitations. Firstly, if the commercial banks happen to have very large excess reserves, even the raising of reserve requirements may not significantly curtail their power to create credit. Secondly, the ability of commercial banks to increase or replenish their reserves through sale of government securities may render higher reserve requirements ineffective to check credit expansion. Thirdly, a large inflow of gold on account of the existence of an export surplus will also, by increasing the member-banks' reserves, offset the anti-inflationary effect of higher reserve requirements.

(*d*) **Consumer Credit Control:** This is a device which is generally introduced during inflation to curb excessive spending on the part of consumers. As is well known, in advanced countries installment purchasing plays an important role in consumer spend. Most of the durable consumer goods, such as, radios, television sets, washing machines, etc., are purchased by the consumers on installments credit. During an inflationary boom, facilities for installment buying are reduced to the minimum to curtail exclusive spending on the part of consumers. This is done (*i*) by raising the minimum initial payment on specified goods, (*ii*) by extending the application of consumer credit control to a large number of goods, and (*iii*) by decreasing the length of the payment period, etc.

(*e*) **Higher Margin Requirements:** Like the consumer credit control, this is also a method of selective credit control. The central bank in its pursuance of an anti-inflation policy may raise the margin requirements to higher levels. As is well known, every commercial bank before granting a loan to a businessman against collateral security keeps a certain specified margin say, 20 per cent or 30 per cent. For example, if the value of security offered by the businessman is ₹ 10,000 and the bank keeps a margin of 20 per cent, then it means that it will advance more than ₹ 8,000 to the businessman. This margin is necessitated by the possibility of a fall in the value of the security. Now, in order to discourage excessive credit on the part of member banks, the central bank may direct them to keep higher margins, say 50 per cent instead of 20 per cent. In that case, the member bank shall not be able to lend more than ₹ 5,000 against security of the value of ₹ 10,000. The higher the margin requirement, the lower the amount of the loan that the borrower can obtain from the bank. Thus, higher margin requirements have the effect of checking undue monetary expansion.

2. Fiscal Measures

Fiscal policy is now recognized as an important instrument to tackle an inflationary situation. The major anti-inflationary scale measures are the following:

(*a*) **Government Expenditure:** During inflation, as is well known, effective demand increases far too much due to unregulated private spending. The increased private expenditure presses heavily against the limited supply of goods and services available in the market. To counteract increased private spending, the government should, at such a time, reduce its own expenditure to the minimum extent possible to help limit the aggregate demand. As against this, it may, however, be said that it is not so easy to reduce government expenditure particularly in the war period when any decrease in military expenditure is simply unthinkable. Secondly, any drastic cut in government expenditure to cure inflation may actually land the economy in a slump. Thirdly, this policy of a cut in government spending may actually come into clash with a long-range public investment programme. So, a policy of reduced government spending, howsoever important, has its limitations in actual practice. And yet this policy appears to be dispensable to curb inflationary boom.

(*b*) **Taxation:** Taxation acquires increased importance as an anti-inflationary weapon during an inflationary boom. The problem during inflation is to reduce the size of disposable income in the hands of the general public in view of the limited supply of goods and services in the market. It is, therefore, necessary to take away the excess purchasing power from the public in the form of taxes. The rates of existing taxes should be steeply increased while new taxes should be imposed on commodities and services so as to leave less money supply with the public to spend. Perhaps the best anti-inflation tax is personal income tax with steep rates and high surcharges. This would reduce the spendable income in the hands of the public, and thus, help to curb inflationary pressures. In general, anti-inflation measures must aim at reducing current incomes in the hands of those sections which, if not taxed, would contribute to raising the price level.

While taxes, direct as well as indirect, should be raised to the maximum limits possible to reduce spendable incomes, tariffs (*i.e.,* customs duties) on imports should be lowered down as much as possible to encourage increased imports to step up the supply of goods at home to absorb the increased money supply in the economic system. The tariffs on necessities of life and other items in short supply should be particularly reduced so as to contain inflationary pressures in the economic system by increasing the supply of goods and services. Care should, however, be taken that while increasing taxation to curb inflationary pressures, money incomes are not so much deflated as to provoke a recession in the economy.

(*c*) **Public Borrowing:** Public borrowing is another anti-inflation weapon which is often utilized to contain inflationary pressures in the economy. The object of public borrowing is to take away from the public excess purchasing power which, if left free, would surely exert an upward pressure on the price level in view of the limited supplies of goods and services in the economy. Public borrowing may be voluntary or compulsory. Ordinarily, public borrowing is voluntary, left to the free will of the individuals. But voluntary borrowing has one disadvantage, and that is, it does not bring to the government sufficient amounts to have really effective impact on the inflationary pressures. It, thus, becomes essential in due course of time to resort to compulsory saving from the public (also known as defected pay). According to this plan, a certain percentage of the wages or a salary is compulsorily deducted in exchange for savings bonds which become redeemable after a few years. This has the effect of blocking purchasing power for a definite period so as to relieve pressures on the limited supplies of goods and services. It has also the added advantage of releasing blocked purchasing power at the first symptom of a recession in business activity. Compulsory borrowing was resorted to in Great Britain during the Second World War at the instance of Keynes to fight inflation. It was adopted by India also in 1963 to check inflation, though under mounting public pressure it had to be withdrawn by the Government of India. Compulsory borrowing suffers from two limitations. Firstly, it involves the use of compulsion which is generally unpalatable to the public. Secondly, it results in discontent if applied to those sections of the community which are not in a position to contribute to this scheme in view of their limited pay packets. As such, the government needs to exercise a good deal of caution in implementing compulsory borrowing schemes.

(*d*) **Debt Management:** The existing public debt should be managed in such a manner as to reduce the existing money supply and prevent further credit expansion. Anti-inflation debt management usually requires the retirement or repayment of bank held debt out of a budgetary surplus. The idea is that the government securities held by commercial banks should be retired by the government out of a budgetary surplus. This would check the power of commercial banks to increase their securities and add to their reserves for the purpose of credit expansion. There is, however, one snag here. At a time of inflation, despite its best efforts, the government may not succeed in having a budgetary surplus. Due to the excessive increase in expenditure, the government may actually be faced with a deficit budget. In that case, the government can adopt another method to retire bank held debt. It can retire this debt by sale of bank-ineligible bonds to non-blank investors like insurance companies, savings banks, individuals, etc. This will have the effect of taking away spendable money from the public and, thus, contribute to a lessening of pressure on the limited stock of goods and services available in the market. But this method is also subject to limitations. It would be rendered ineffective if the non-blank investors were unwilling to give up spend able money in exchange for government bonds. It would also prove futile if the non-blank investors utilized, for purchasing government bonds, idle funds which would not have been spent at all.

(*e*) **Overvaluation:** An overvaluation of domestic currency in terms of foreign currencies will also serve as an anti-inflationary measure in three ways. Firstly, it will discourage exports and thereby result in an increased availability of goods and services in the domestic market. Secondly, by encouraging imports from abroad, it will add to the domestic stock of goods and services and, thus, absorb the excessive purchasing power in the economy. Thirdly, by reducing the prices of those foreign materials which enter domestic production, it will help in checking an upward cost-price spiral. Overvaluation as an anti-inflationary weapon also suffers from limitations. For example, if other countries are also suffering from inflation, then the country concerned shall have to overvalue its currency considerably to neutralize the inflationary effect of the rising cost of imports. But a good deal of caution needs to be exercised if overvaluation is to be used as an anti-inflationary weapon, because it's deflationary imitations for the balance of payments may be serious.

3. Other Measures

Among the other anti-inflationary measures may be included such things as, (*a*) an expansion of output, (*b*) wage policy, and (*c*) price control and rationing. They can be used to supplement the monetary fiscal measures undertaken to contain inflationary pressures.

(*a*) **Expansion of Output:** Increased production is the best antidote to inflation because, as pointed out above, the inflationary gap arises partly due to the inadequacy of output. But it becomes rather difficult to increase output at a time of inflation because of the full utilization of resources. The productive resources are already fully employed. How to get additional productive resources to increase output? It is suggested that if it is not possible to increase output as a whole, steps should be taken to increase the output of those goods which seem to be extremely sensitive to inflationary pressures by shifting productive resources from the less inflation-sensitive goods. In other words, a reallocation of productive resources is suggested to step up the output of inflation-sensitive goods, such as, food, clothing, housing and other essential consumer goods. If the prices of these essential consumer goods are kept down through expansion of output, it will greatly help the authorities to curb inflationary pressures in the economy. Again, during an inflationary boom, factor prices (*i.e.,* prices of raw materials and labour) may rise up with an increase in output, thus, adding more fuel to the inflationary fire. Efforts should, therefore, be made by the authorities to keep the factor prices in check. Some selective controls may have to be devised to prevent a rise in monopoly factor prices. It is also suggested by certain quarters that output should be increased by making the workers work for longer hours in factories. Trade unions are, however, sure to resist this unless and until it is accompanied by "overtime allowances". Even if output is increased through payment of overtime allowances, that would be no solution because the overtime allowances paid to workers would add to the money income stream of the community unless, of course, the overtime allowances are either taxed away or taken in the form of loans by the government. A more feasible suggestion would be to increase output through encouraging technical innovations in industry. It is also essential at a time of inflation to maintain industrial peace in the country by reducing strikes and lockouts to the minimum. It may not be so easy to ensure perfect industrial peace, because during an inflationary boom the workers are generally discontented and their grievances mount with the rising cost of living. Attempts should, however, be made to devise some labour management machinery which may help to keep industrial strife to the minimum. Labour grievances should be attended to soon and in time to avoid work stoppages which are bound to inhibit production at a critical time. Lastly, it is also suggested that during inflation the government may adopt a liberal import policy to offset the domestic shortage of goods. As a matter of policy, the government should import inflation. Sensitive and essential goods in exchange for export of non-essential and inflation-insensitive goods. If the balance of payments position of the country does not permit liberal imports, the government may even have to agree to short-term credits from international agencies, like the IMF for this purpose.

(*b*) **Wage Policy:** During an inflationary boom, wages cannot be left free to chase prices upward. They have to be controlled so as to contain inflationary pressures in the economy. Wage increases may be allowed to workers only if their productivity, *i.e.,* output per worker, increases. If this principle is observed, higher wages shall not lead to higher unit costs, and hence, to higher unit prices. But if the wages in a particular industry are already sub-standard, they may be get raised without increasing the prices of goods produced, *i.e.,* by reducing the profit margins of the producers. It is important for the government at such a time to keep down the cost of living through its anti-inflation programme, for if it fails to do so, the workers' unions would be perfectly justified in asking for higher wages from their employers, and the government should let them do so. Even then the government can deduct tax or borrow a part of money wages as a part of its anti-inflation program me. But one' thing is, however, clear. Complete wage freeze is rather difficult to achieve using peacetime inflation, because trade unionism is a powerful force now in advanced economies. This is rendered still more difficult by the fact that wages are not only costs to employers but also incomes to the workers, and any step taken in the direction of a wage freeze may give rise to uncontrollable deflationary movements in future.

(*c*) **Price Control and Rationing:** Price control of essential consumer goods was resorted to on a fairly wide scale in various countries of the world to fight .inflation during and after the Second World War. The object of price control is to lay down the upper limit beyond which the price of a particular commodity would not be allowed to rise. Anyone selling the concerned commodity above the legally fixed price runs the risk of being prosecuted by the State. To ensure the successful functioning of price control, two conditions shall have to be satisfied. Firstly, the government should have under its control adequate stock of the commodity concerned. Fixing the price without having adequate stock of its own will surely result in failure. *Secondly*, the demand for the concerned commodity should be controlled through rationing, failing which, taking advantage of the fixed price, the richer sections shall be able to buy a major portion of the available stocks.

Keynes was not favourably inclined to price control on the ground that it failed to bring about equilibrium between purchasing power and the available output. It increases the pressure of consumption and results in shortages. He, therefore, wanted to deal with the situation by reducing the volume of purchasing power in, the hands of the public via taxation and forced savings, and then to allow the public to exercise a free choice in the purchase of consumer goods. Price control, in his opinion, led to loss of consumer's freed.

Despite this, price control and rationing seem inevitable as weapons to contain inflationary pressures in the economy. They seem to be indispensable to control and check the prices of at least essential goods during inflation, But there cannot be adopted a general policy of price control and rations view of the tremendous administrative difficulties in carrying it out in actual practice.

24.12 RELATIONSHIP BETWEEN INFLATION AND PHILLIPS' CURVE

The Phillips' curve acquires considerable significance in the context unemployment our of an inflationary situation. The curve pinpoints the need of having a high percentage of unemployment in an economy if a non-inflationary price stability is to be achieved. Actually, the Phillips' curve traces the relationship between the rate of money wage increase and the rate of unemployment in the economy. This curve is named after AW Phillips who made a pioneering study of the relationship between the percentage of money wage increase and the percentage of unemployment in the economy. His study related to the UK, and was published in 1958. The curve has been shown in Fig. 24.3.

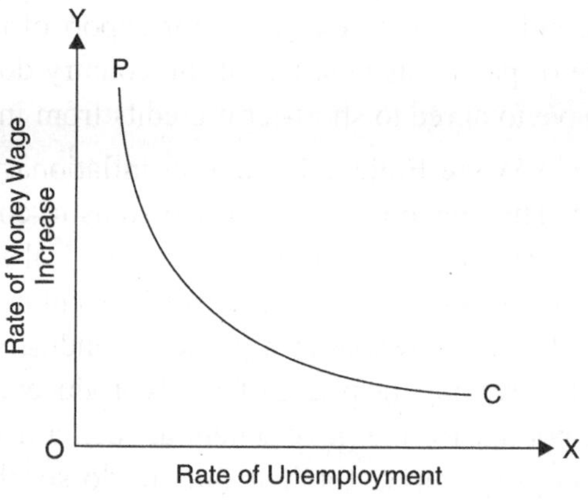

Fig. 24.3. Phillips' curve.

The curve slopes downwards from left to the right, indicating that there is an inverse relationship between the rate of money wage increase and the rate of unemployment. It implies that if the wage-push inflation (or, the rate of money wage increase) is to be avoided and non-inflationary price stability is to be achieved, then a high rate of unemployment has to be accepted in the economy. The conclusion is clear. If the wage-push inflation is to be avoided, then the society must be prepared to accept a high rate of unemployment. With unemployment in the economy, the trade unions are more anxious to get employment for their members rather than agitate for higher wages.

Hence, the existence of a high rate of unemployment is the symptom for the avoidance of wage-push inflation in a capitalist society in the Phillips' curve. It should, however, be noted that every increase in the rate of money wages is not inflationary in character. If an increase in money wages is accompanied by an equivalent increase in labour productivity it will not stoke the fire of inflation.

The economic situation in the USA during the period 1950–60 was almost a perfect fulfilment of the Phillips' curve. For every reduction of one percentage point in the unemployment rate, there was a 3/4 point increase in the rate of growth of money wages.

But the Phillips' curve ceased to apply to the US situation during the 1970s. The relationship between money wages and unemployment underwent a dramatic change. The Phillips' curve, as an economic law, ceased to operate. The reason, of course, was the onset of stagflation, an unprecedented situation, marked both by high inflation and a high rate of unemployment. The rate of money wages increased, but the rate of unemployment, instead of declining, actually went up during this period. The Phillips' curve stood falsified. Keynesian theories proved inadequate to explain the global phenomenon of stagflation.

24.13 INFLATION IN AN UNDERDEVELOPED ECONOMY

We have seen above the character of inflation in a developed economy. Let us now examine the nature of inflation in an underdeveloped country. Inflation in an underdeveloped country is slightly different from inflation in an advanced country. As we have seen above, inflation in an advanced economy generally sets in only after the point of full employment is reached. (According to Keynes, inflation may sometimes set in before the point of full employment even in an advanced economy due to increases in money wages, shortages of raw materials and equipment, and the operation of the law of diminishing returns. But, generally speaking, inflation sets in, in an advanced economy, only after title point of full employment is reached. Keynes calls it as true inflation). But in an underdeveloped economy, inflation generally sets in earlier than the point of full employment. In an advanced economy, increases in money supply result in the mobilization of idle resources instead of leading to a rise in the price level. But in an underdeveloped economy, due to the limited and inelastic supply of resources, increases in the money supply invariably result in a rise in the price level. Keynes calls it as bottleneck inflation, which sets in even before the point of full employment is reached.

There are certain additional causes for the early setting in of inflation in an underdeveloped country. As is well known, an underdeveloped country generally incurs huge public expenditure to quicken up its planned economic development. In its developmental projects, the emphasis is generally laid on social overheads and basic, heavy industries rather than on the development and expansion of consumer goods industries. Since the production of consumer goods does not keep pace with the expansion of money income, it invariably results in an inflationary rise in the price level.

Besides, the marginal propensity to consume of the people in underdeveloped countries is generally high with the result that the farmers in these countries do not bring the entire agricultural surpluses in the market for sale. The high demand for consumer goods naturally pushes up the prices of these goods. Further, the underdeveloped countries are generally primary producing countries. A good part of these primary products is exported to foreign countries, creating additional shortages of these goods in the country.

An important peculiarity of these underdeveloped countries is the large magnitude of disguised unemployment that prevails there. Unfortunately, this disguised unemployment and underemployment is not so readily responsive to an expansion of money supply or increased effective demand. Despite the increase in the supply of money, the output of goods and services does not increase so readily on account of the existence of disguised unemployment and underemployment. In developed countries, on the contrary, the existence of unemployed manpower actually helps in increasing the output of goods and services consequent upon an expansion in the supply of money. The immobility of productive factors, the rigidity of social structure and the ignorance of market conditions are other factors which act as obstacles in increasing production.

In view of the underdeveloped character of the banking and credit institutions, it is more difficult to deal with inflation in an underdeveloped than in a developed economy. The physical and credit controls in an underdeveloped economy are not as efficacious as they are in an advanced economy so far as the curbing of inflation is concerned.

From the above discussion, it is apparent that an underdeveloped economy is placed in a difficult position. In fact, it is confronted with a dilemma. If it remains as it is, it means economic stagnation, poverty, low incomes and low living standards. If on the other hand it launches upon rapid economic growth through deficit financing or expansion of bank credit, it results in the emergence of inflation, inflicting untold misery on the poor people. The choice, therefore, is between economic stagnation and inflation. Inflation, however, is the lesser evil. An underdeveloped country should go in for rapid growth, even though it may bring some inflation its wake. Inflation is perhaps the price which underdeveloped counties have to pay to attain rapid economic growth. This does not, however, imply that inflation is an inevitable consequence of the process of economic growth. It can be forestalled through the adoption of a well conceived and well-executed anti-inflation policy by the government of an underdeveloped country.

24.14 INFLATION AND ECONOMIC DEVELOPMENT

There is a great controversy among economists as to whether inflation promotes economic development. There is a group of economists, including Keynes, which are of the view that inflation promotes the economic development of a country. The following arguments are advanced by these economists in the support of their contention.

(1) The first argument adduced by these economists is that inflation redistributes income and wealth in favour of the entrepreneurial classes who have a high propensity to save or low propensity to consume. With the redistribution of income and wealth in favour of these classes, the rate of savings is automatically stepped up, leading to a higher level of capital accumulation in the economy. These classes utilize their increased savings for further investments in productive enterprises, thereby increasing the aggregate income, output and the volume of employment in the economy.

(2) Inflation invariably creates optimistic conditions in the economy and affords fresh opportunities for businessmen and the entrepreneurs in new productive enterprises. Since the costs do not rise as rapidly as prices, the profit margins of the businessmen go up, tempting them to make more and more investments in new industrial enterprises.

(3) An underdeveloped economy, as is well known, is generally short of financial resources which act as an obstacle to its economic development. There is little scope for additional taxation in such an economy on account of the low income of the people. Nor is there much scope for public borrowings as the level of savings in such an economy is rather low. This poverty of financial resources in an underdeveloped economy can be made good to some extent by resorting to deficit financing to cover the deficit in the government budget. Deficit financing can provide adequate funds to the government of an underdeveloped country for launching development projects for quick economic development. There may be no harm in resorting to deficit financing for economic development, because inflation initiated by this type of deficit financing is self-terminating on account of the expansion in output which accompanies deficit financing for development purposes. This deficit financing may not be harmful to an underdeveloped country from another point of view as well. There is, generally, a tendency on the part of the people in such a country to hoard money underground. Deficit financing will result at least in the initial stages in offsetting or neutralizing this hoarding tendency of the public in an underdeveloped country. There shall, therefore, be no rise in the price level at least in the initial stages of deficit financing, which has an important place in the economy of an underdeveloped country.

(4) There is no doubt that there will be some inflationary rise in prices at least in the initial stages consequent upon deficit financing in a developing economy. The reason being that the supply of consumer goods in such an economy does not increase as rapidly as the supply of money in the initial stages of deficit financing. Thus, inflation becomes somewhat inevitable in the process of economic growth. In fact, economic growth and inflation generally go together. Inflation leads to economic growth, and economic growth, in its turn results in inflation.

There is another group of economists headed by Prof. Milton Friedman which believes that inflation in no way promotes the economic development of a country. The following arguments have been put forward by these economists in support of their contention.

(1) Inflation, it is pointed out, distorts the saving habits of the people and slows down the rate of capital accumulation in the economy. Inflation may even drive out the foreign capital already invested in the economy. There is, of course, no possibility of foreign capital coming into an economy which is suffering from persistent and prolonged inflation. It goes without saying that the process of economic development is bound to suffer a serious setback with a slowing down of the capital accumulation in the economy.

(2) Inflation, as is well known, by leading to a continuously rising price level, puts a premium on speculative activities. The businessmen find it more profitable to speculate in certain scarce commodities rather than to increase their existing production. With the businessmen resorting more and more to speculative activities, the production of goods and services in the country suffers a serious setback.

(3) Inflation, by leading to a rising price level, invariably reduces the volume of exports from an economy. Not only that, it also increases the volume of imports into the country. The reduction in exports and the increase in imports invariably reduce the volume of domestic output and employment thereby slowing down the economic development of the country in question.

It is, thus, the considered opinion of these economists that inflation in no way promotes the economic development of a country. The question, as we have seen above, is rather controversial. But, in our opinion, inflation by increasing the national income, output and employment may, on the whole, be said to be a factor which directly and indirectly promotes the process of economic development in the country.

24.15 REFLATION

Meaning of Reflation: Inflation and reflection resemble each other in certain respects. In the words of Prof. Cole, "Reflection may be deemed as inflation deliberately undertaken to relieve a depression." In other words, reflection is type of controlled inflation. When deflation reaches to an extreme limit and the prices of goods and services fall to extremely low levels, then the government may resort to reflection to protect the economy of the country from serious consequences. The government then expands the money supply with a view to pushing up the prices to the normal level.

Difference between Indention and Reflection: As pointed out above, inflation and reflection resemble each other in certain respects. The supply of money is increased, both under inflation as well as reflection. Both lead to a rise in the existing price level. Even then there are some notable differences between inflation and reflection, which are as follows:

(1) Inflation, besides being optional, can also be due to natural causes. But reflection is always optional and is adopted by the government according to a preconceived plan. Inflation can also be adopted according to a preconceived plan but sometimes it may be due to natural causes. For example, if the volume of agricultural production declines due to certain natural calamities, it may easily result in inflation, but reflection cannot take place like that. It is always adopted according to a preconceived and deliberate plan.

(2) Inflation invariably occurs in the boom stage of the trade cycle, but reflection takes place only in the recovery stage of the trade cycle. What this means is that reflection occurs before the point of full employment, whereas inflation takes place only after the point of full employment.

(3) The prices of goods and services rise very rapidly under inflation, whereas they rise slowly and gradually under reflection.

(4) If proper check is not exercised on inflation it may easily ruin the economy of the country. Reflation, on the other hand, brings about decided improvements in the already shattered economy of the country.

24.16 DEFLATION AND DISINFLATION

Deflation is the opposite of inflation. In the words of Prof. Crowthers, "*Deflation is that state of the economy, where the value of money is rising or the prices are falling.*" This definition is not free from defects. From this definition, it appears that every fall in the price level is deflation but actually this may not be so. Sometimes the price level starts falling down without any contraction in the supply of commodities. Now such a fall in the price level cannot be called deflation.

There is still another definition of deflation. According to this definition, deflation may refer to that state of the economy where the supply of money at a particular time is less than its demand. In other words, the supply of money in the economy is not sufficient to meet business requirements of the economy. Deflation is bound to result in such a state of the economy. The prices of goods and services will fall and the value of the money will start rising. This definition has one important defect in so far as it does not tell us how to make an accurate estimate of the money requirements of the economy.

According to Prof. Pious, "*Deflation is that state of falling prices which occurs at that time when the output of goods and services increases more rapidly than the volume of money income in the economy.*" Thus, according to Pious, every fall in the price level is not deflation. Deflation occurs at that time when the output of goods and services increases at a faster rate than the money income. A fall of prices in the following situations may be termed deflationary according to Pigou: (*a*) If the money income diminishes but the output remains constant, (*b*) If the money income and the output both diminish, but the money income diminishes much more rapidly than the output, (*c*) If the volume of output increases but the money income remains constant, (*d*) If the volume of output and money income both increase, but the output increases faster than the money income, (*e*) If the volume of output increases but the volume of money income diminishes. In each of these cases, the fall in prices will be deflationary.

From the above definitions, the reader might perhaps get the impression that a contraction in the supply of money causes a fall in the price level, or the fall in the money supply leads to a fall in the price level. This may, however, be not wholly true. The fall in the price level is not only the result of the fall in money supply; it can also be the cause of the contraction in the supply of money. If the prices continuously go on falling, the economy may not need as much money supply as before. Thus, the falling price level is both the result as well as the cause of the fall in the supply of money. From this point of view, Prof. Paul Enzi's definition appears to be the best definition of deflation. Deflation, according to Einzi "is a state of disequilibrium in which a contraction of purchasing power tends to cause, or is the effect of, a decline of the price level."

Meaning of Disinflation

Disinflation is different from deflation. Disinflation may be defined as the process of reversing inflation without creating unemployment or reducing the output in the economy. In fact, disinflation is an attempt to counter a highly inflationary situation in the same manner as reflection is an attempt to cure a highly deflationary situation. Whenever there is excessive expansion in the supply of money and the prices start rising to higher and higher levels, then the government may resort to a policy of disinflation to bring the prices down to the normal level. After the Second World War, the prices in almost all the countries had gone up very high on account of persistent inflationary pressures operating in the economy. The governments in these countries had to resort to a policy of disinflation to bring down the prices. In this way, when inflation assumes serious proportions and the prices rise to extremely high levels, then it is a policy of disinflation which brings the prices down to their normal levels.

Difference between Deflation and Disinflation

At first sight, there appears to be close resemblance between deflation and disinflation. The supply of money undergoes contraction both under deflation as well as disinflation. Both of them lead to a fall in the price level. But despite this resemblance, there are certain important differences between deflation and disinflation.

(1) Deflation can be optional. It may be the result of a deliberate government policy. It can also be due to certain natural causes. But disinflation is always optional and the result of a deliberate government policy. Disinflation can never be due to natural causes, whereas deflation may sometimes be the result of certain natural factors. For example, if on account of adequate and timely rains there are bumper crops; it may easily lead to a situation of deflation in the economy. But this deflation is the outcome of natural causes. Deflation can also be the result of a preconceived and deliberate governmental policy. But disinflation is always the result of a pre-planned and deliberate governmental policy.

(2) The prices can be brought down to the normal level with the help of disinflation. But deflation may bring the prices down—even below the normal level. In other words, there is no limit below which the prices cannot fall as a result of deflation.

(3) The policy of disinflation is generally adopted at a time when inflation assumes highly dangerous proportions. In fact, disinflation is adopted to keep inflation under control. Deflation, on the contrary, may be the direct result of certain natural factors.

(4) Deflation by leading to a fall in production may create mass unemployment in the economy, but there is no such difficulty under a policy of disinflation, the reason being that the government while adopting a policy of disinflation sees to it that there is no unemployment in the economy as a consequence of this policy.

Deflationary Gap

The concept of deflationary gap is just the opposite of the Keynesian concept of inflationary gap. *The deflationary gap for the economy as a whole may be defined as a shortage of anticipated expenditure compared with the available output of goods and services at base prices*. The anticipated total expenditure referred to here is the net disposable income of the community. It is determined by deducting taxation and saving out of the total money income. The anticipated expenditure of the community is determined by the aggregate consumption, investment and government outlays. The real output, on the other hand, is determined by the conditions of employment plus the technological basis of the economy. *The deflationary gap is a situation where the anticipated expenditure (i.e., the demand for output) falls short of the available output at base prices.*

The deflationary gap may develop in the economy like this. To start with, there is a decline either in private investment or in government outlays. This has the result of reducing the money income to lower levels, but the real output of goods and a service does not decrease in the same proportion. The failure of the economy to reduce its real output in response to the decline in the money incomes results in the emergence of the deflationary gap. The deflationary gap is, thus, the result of the shortage of demand in relation to real output in the economy. Anticipated expenditure of the economy is indicated by the C + I + G function. The 45 degree line OE is the equilibrium line indicating that the economy is in equilibrium when the output of goods and services (as represented by the GNP) equals the demand for them (as represented by the total expenditure). The C + I + G curve intersects the line OE at the point P_1. This gives us the equilibrium income indicated by OM_1. This OM_1 represents the full employment income at the base prices. The aggregate monetary demand here is shown by C + I + G curve is equal to P_1M_1. This PM_1 is equivalent to the total output of goods and services amounts to OM_1. Since the total money income is equal to the total available output, there is no question of any shortage of demand arising in the economy; hence, there is no possibility of the emergence of a deflationary gap in the economy.

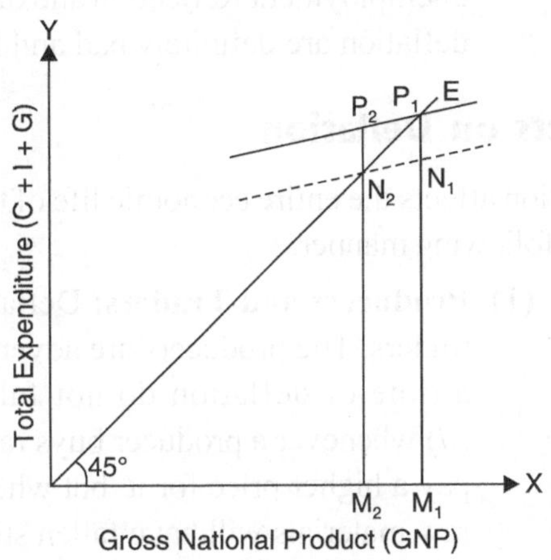

Fig. 24.4. Deflationary gap.

Let us suppose now that, for some reasons, the government reduces its expenditure by a certain amount, say, P_2N_2. This reduces total governmental expenditure from the earlier level of G to G′. Thus, the new expenditure function in the economy is C + I + G′. Since OM_1 is the real income of the economy at the full employment level, it does not decrease with the reduced government expenditure (G') amounting to P_2N_2. This P_2N_2 represents the deflationary gap in the economy. It naturally lowers down the price level. In the context of this diagram, the price level can remain constant only if the output of goods and services decreases from OM_1 to OM_2. In other words, the output of goods and services must be reduced by M_2M_1 the deflationary gap of P_2N_2 can be wiped out only if the output of goods and services decreases by M_2M_1. The position discussed in the preceding pages may be summed up as below:

(1) **Reflection:** It is a situation marked by rising prices and expansion of money supply. Reflection is deliberately undertaken by the government to relieve a depression. As a result of this policy, income, output and employment continue to increase till the economy reaches the point of full employment.

(2) **Inflation:** Inflation takes place when the expansion of money supply continues even beyond the point of full employment. It is accompanied by a constantly rising price level without any increase in output and employment.

(3) **Disinflation:** It occurs at a time when the prices start falling downwards upon the adoption of certain anti-inflationary measures by the government. Disinflation, it should be remembered, does not cause any decline in the existing level of income, output and employment.

(4) **Deflation:** It occurs at a time when the prices start falling consequent upon the contraction of money supply. Deflation is always accompanied by a decreasing level of income, output and employment. Deflation is bad because it results in an increasing degree of unemployment Reflection and disinflation are beneficial for the country, but inflation and deflation are definitely bad and harmful for the economy.

Effects on Deflation

Deflation affects the entire economic life of the country. The different sections of society are affected in the following manner:

(1) Producers and Traders: Deflation adversely affects both the producers as well as the traders. The producers are adversely affected on three counts, (*i*) the production costs at a time of deflation do not fall as rapidly as the prices of the finished products, (*ii*) whenever a producer buys raw materials etc. for the purpose of production, he has to pay a higher price for it, but when the finished product reaches the market, the prices of raw materials will have fallen still further and the producer will be compelled to sell his product at a reduced price, and (*iii*) the demand for commodities also goes down at a time of deflation. Consequently, the stocks of finished products pile up in the godown and the capital of the producer gets blocked in business. The traders are also adversely affected by deflation because the prices are high when they make the purchases, but by the time they are able to sell the goods, the prices undergo a further fall. Likewise, deflation also hits the farmers, particularly the smaller farmers, who do not have any reserves to fall back upon.

(2) Investors: Actually, there are two types of investors in a capitalist economy. Firstly, those investors whose income is fixed. Secondly, those investors whose income is variable. Deflation affects these two types of investors differently. The fixed-income investors actually gain by deflation, the reason being that their income is constant while the prices continue to fall as a result of deflation. Hence, with their fixed incomes, they are able to buy more goods and services than before. On the contrary, the variable income investors are adversely affected by deflation, the reason being that their income goes down consequent upon deflation. For example, the shareholders of a joint stock company get reduced dividends on their shares consequent upon the fall in prices.

(3) Salaried and Labour Classes: These classes are beneficially affected by deflation. The reason is that with the fall in prices, it is not easy to cut down the wages of the workers. Any attempt to reduce the wages is stoutly opposed. By the trade unions Likewise, it is not possible to cut down the salaries of the employees. Hence, both of these classes gain as a result of deflation. Their money income remains constant while the prices of goods and services decline. But these classes may suffer on account of deflation from another point of view. Due to falling profits, the smaller business establishments cut down their production. There is retrenchment of workers and employees who are now rendered unemployed and thrown on the streets. This creates serious discontentment in these classes. The trade unions oppose this retrenchment which leads to strikes and lockouts in course of time, giving rise to industrial unrest in the country.

(4) **Consumers:** The consumers are beneficially affected by deflation. Due to falling prices, the purchasing power of money rises up enabling the consumers to buy more goods and services than before. It should, however, be remembered that consumers are also of two types. Firstly, those consumers whose income remains fixed during deflation, such as, the salaried employees. Secondly, those consumers whose money income declines during deflation. The first category of consumers gain while the second category of consumers lose as a result of deflation.

(5) **Debtors and Creditors:** Creditors gain while debtors lose as a result of deflation. The creditors gain because whatever amount they receive in the form of interest, etc., carries now a higher purchasing power than before. The creditors also gain because at a time of deflation the demand for consumption loans goes up and the creditors can charge arbitrary rates of interest on them. But, as said above, the debtors are the losers at a time of deflation.

The farmers are the worst hit by deflation because the burden of indebtedness goes up as a result of falling prices.

Deflation affects the economic life of the country in other ways as well:

(1) *Increase in the Burden of Taxation:* The tax payers are adversely affected. by deflation because the real burden of taxation invariably goes up at such a time, the reason being that the value of money appreciates due to falling prices.

(2) *Increase in the Burden of Public Debt:* The burden of public debt invariably goes up at a time of deflation due to the rise in the value of money. The government now has to face an increase in the real burden of the public debt. To cover up the deficit in the budget, the government may have to borrow more funds from the public.

(3) *Increase in Unemployment:* At a time of deflation, the volume of output invariably goes down due to falling prices. Some business enterprises are even closed down, throwing the workers out of their jobs.

(4) *Adverse Effects on Banking:* At a time of deflation the number of borrowers goes down on account of the general recession in the economy. In fact, deflation creates a banking crisis in the economy.

(5) *Social and Moral Consequences:* At a time of deflation, there are increasing number of disputes between the employers and the employees. This creates industrial unrest in the country. The economic development suffers a setback and the economic, social and political life of the country gets upset.

Hence, deflation is extremely harmful for the economy of a country. Some economists are of the view that deflation is even more harmful than inflation. In fact, both inflation and deflation are bad because both of them adversely affect the economic growth of the country. In fact, economic growth cannot proceed in an uninterrupted and orderly manner in the face of violent fluctuations in the economy.

24.17 INFLATION VS. DEFLATION

Which is better, inflation or deflation? As we have already seen above, both inflation and deflation are harmful for society, but inflation may be considered to be the lesser of the two evils. In the words of Lord Keynes, "Inflation is unjust; deflation is inexpedient. Of the two, deflation is worse."

Actually, both inflation and deflation are bad from the social point of view, because both of them result not only in the redistribution of income and wealth but also cause serious distortions in the economic system.

Inflation may be considered to be unjust on the following grounds:

(1) It increases economic inequalities through its redistributive effects. By transferring purchasing power from the poorer to the richer sections, inflation widens the gulf between the richer and the poorer classes. The rich, under inflation, become richer while the poor become poorer. Inflation is, therefore, highly unjust and equitable.

(2) Inflation is also regressive in character. By raising the prices of essential goods, it imposes a heavier burden on the poorer sections of the community. Inflation especially hits the middle classes who are the worst sufferers from rising prices and increasing shortages.

(3) Inflation also results in an invisible taxation of the people. When the government resorts to deficit financing to cover up the deficit in its budget, the prices of goods and services invariably go up. The consumers are deprived of these goods and services and are not able to consume them to the extent desired. Inflation thus, diverts the goods and services meant for public consumption to the government, which is totally unjust and inequitable. Prof. C. N. Vakil has compared inflation with invisible robbery. According to him, "Inflation may be compared to a robber. Both deprive the victim of some possession with the difference that the robber is visible while inflation is invisible; the robber's victim may be one or a few at a time: the victims of inflation are the whole nation; the robber may be dragged to a court of law, inflation is legal."

(4) Inflation gives rise to a sort of artificial prosperity in the country. Inflation feeds inflation. The price level goes on rising and after some time it reaches its highest limit. This upsets the working of the economy and then the government is compelled to take certain steps which, return give rise to deflationary tendencies in the economy. The prices then start coming down, resulting in fall in profits and increasing unemployment. Every inflation may, thus, be said to contain the seeds of its own decay.

(5) Inflation is also highly demoralizing in character. It gives rise to a spirit of gambling among the people. It promotes speculative activities and diverts the businessmen from productive activities to speculation etc.

Deflation is Inexpedient

As already pointed out, inflation is unjust while deflation is inexpedient. Deflation is considered inexpedient on the following grounds:

(1) Deflation by reducing prices and production results in a marked decline in the national income of the country. With the decline in the national income the country becomes poorer than before.

(2) By leading to a fall in production, deflation causes a marked increase in unemployment. With the fall in prices and declining profit margins, the businessmen close down their establishments or cut down the volume of production giving rise to mass unemployment in society.

(3) By causing a downward movement in prices and production, deflation causes economic depression in the economy. The economy has to suffer all the evil consequences of depression. Business becomes dull; production is reduced, money income contracts and the volume of employment go down, creating highly pessimistic conditions in the economy.

(4) Deflation is also considered inexpedient because once it starts, it goes on together momentum and the crisis becomes deeper with the lapse of time.

(5) The social, economic, political and moral consequences of deflation are vicious. It may not be wrong to say that deflation ultimately results in a complete ruin of the economy.

It is thus clear that though inflation is unjust, it is better than deflation. That is why Lord Keynes looked upon inflation as the lesser of the two evils. It does not, however, imply that Lord. Keynes preferred inflation to price stability. Price stability is, of course, any day better than price inflation. In fact, price stability is an ideal situation which can promote the economic growth of the country without violent fluctuations. But if a choice is to be made between inflation and deflation, Lord Keynes would vote for the former, not the latter. He considered inflation better than deflation on the following grounds:

(1) Inflation redistributes income and wealth in favour of the richer sections. It does not result in curtailing the national income of the community. Deflation, on the other hand, has the undesirable effect of reducing the national income of the country.

(2) Besides reducing the national income, deflation also results in cutting down the volume of employment in the economy. Inflation, on the other hand, is a full-employment phenomenon. Hence, deflation cannot be considered desirable from the social point of view.

(3) Inflation, howsoever serious, can be controlled to some extent by the application of monetary and fiscal measures. Deflation, on the other hand, is rather difficult to check

despite the application of monetary and fiscal measures. Once deflation starts, it gathers momentum till the entire economy is enveloped in a severe depression. At such a stage, even monetary and fiscal polities become ineffective in checking the deepening depression. At a time of depression, the businessmen generally lose confidence in the future of their investments and no amount of monetary expansion is going to restore that confidence. Fiscal policy also fails to check the spreading depression in the economy.

(4) A moderate inflation may even be good for a depressed economy. A mild dose of monetary expansion can serve to stimulate the economic development of a depressed economy. Mild inflation is, therefore, any day better than deflation from the point of view of economic growth.

Self-Assessment Questions

1. What are the various types of inflation ?
2. Inflation is a phenomenon of full employment. Explain.
3. How did Keynes explain the phenomenon of inflation in terms of his concept of Inflationary Gap?

   Or

   Explain the Keynesian Theory of Inflationary Gap.
4. Outline a program of action to control and check an inflationary situation in an economy.
5. "Inflation is unjust; deflation is inexpedient. Of the two, deflation is worse." Explain.
6. Explain the causes of price inflation. Can inflation promote economic development?
7. Discuss the concept of deflation. How does it affect the level of economic activities? What measures would you suggest to control deflation?
8. What are the causes of inflation? What measures are needed to control inflation?
9. How does inflation affect the production structure and income distribution in an economy?
10. "Inflation in India is primarily a structural and not monetary phenomenon." Comment.
11. Distinguish between: (*i*) Inflation and Reflection, and (*ii*) Deflation and Disinflation.
12. "Monetary policy is far more effective for controlling inflation than fiscal policy." Discuss.

Index

A

B

C

D

K

L

M

N

O

P

R

S

T

U

V

W